GRAYSLAKE AREA PUBLIC LIBRARY

3 6109 004   W9-BUQ-146

Jordan

Jerash, Irbid & the Jordan Valley
p75

⭐ **Amman**
p42

Azraq & the Eastern Desert Highway
p227

Dead Sea Highway
p106

Madaba & the King's Highway
p121

Petra
p155

Aqaba, Wadi Rum & the Desert Highway
p193

NO LONGER OWNED BY
GRAYSLAKE PUBLIC LIBRARY

GRAYSLAKE AREA PUBLIC LIBRARY
100 Library Lane
Grayslake, IL 60030

THIS EDITION WRITTEN AND RESEARCHED BY

Jenny Walker, Paul Clammer

Contents

ON THE ROAD

BEDOUIN MAN AT WADI RUM P209

SIQ AL-BARID (LITTLE PETRA) P190

DEAD SEA P109

Contents

915.695
LON 2015
1.16 TS

3 6109 00494 3293

Welcome to Jordan

A safe haven in a region of conflict, Jordan has delighted visitors for centuries with its World Heritage sites, friendly towns and inspiring desert landscapes.

Ancient Hospitality

Jordan has a tradition of welcoming visitors: camel caravans plied the legendary King's Highway transporting frankincense in exchange for spices, and Nabataean traders, Roman legionnaires, Muslim armies and zealous Crusaders all passed through the land, leaving behind impressive monuments. These monuments, including Roman amphitheatres, crusader castles and Christian mosaics, have fascinated subsequent travellers in search of antiquity and the origins of faith. The tradition of hospitality to visitors remains to this day.

Petra: A World Wonder

Petra, the ancient Nabataean city locked in the heart of Jordan's sandstone escarpments, is the jewel in the crown of the country's many antiquities. Ever since Jean Louis Burckhardt brought news of the pink-hued necropolis back to Europe in the 19th century, the walk through the Siq to the Treasury (Petra's defining monument) has impressed even the most jaded of visitors. It is worth allowin g at least two days to make the most of a visit, particularly as the sites are far flung, best seen in early morning and late afternoon, and require a fair amount of walking.

Desert Landscapes

Take a ride through Wadi Rum at sunset and it's easy to see why TE Lawrence (Lawrence of Arabia) was so drawn to this land of weathered sandstone and reddened dunes. But Jordan's desert landscapes are not confined to the southeast: they encompass a salt sea at the lowest point on earth, canyons flowing with seasonal water, oases of palm trees and explosions of springtime flowers scattered across arid hills. Minimal planning and only a modest budget is required for an adventure.

Safe Haven

It takes tolerance to host endless waves of incomers and Jordan has displayed that virtue amply, absorbing in recent times thousands of refugees from Palestine, Iraq and, most recently, Syria. Despite contending with this and with ever-growing numbers of tourists who are often insensitive to conservative Jordanian values, rural life in particular has managed to keep continuity with the traditions of the past. While Jordan faces the challenges of modernisation and growing urbanisation, it remains one of the safest countries in which to gain an impression of the Middle East.

Why I Love Jordan

By Jenny Walker, Author

From the first *'ahlan wa sahlan'* said in welcome, I knew that Jordan was to become a lifelong friend. After going in search of TE Lawrence as a student, I have returned many times to the low-slung tents of the Howeitat, sipped tea with rug-makers and walked in the wake of shepherds. Beautiful though it is, and blessed with a disproportionate number of wonders, Jordan inspires this loyalty primarily because of its spirit of generous optimism – opening its arms to strangers and sharing its meagre wealth with neighbours in need.

For more about our authors, see page 352

For more about our authors, see page 352

Above: Wadi Rum, p209

Jordan

Jerash
The region's finest Roman ruins (p77)

Amman
Welcoming capital city (p42)

Wadi Jadid
Remote valley of ancient dolmens (p137)

Mt Nebo
View of Moses' Promised Land (p134)

Madaba
King's Highway town of mosaics (p123)

Mukawir
Haunting site of Salome's dance (p137)

Dead Sea
The lowest point on earth (p109)

Mujib Biosphere Reserve
Waterfalls in adventure-lover's paradise (p117)

Dana Biosphere Reserve
Terraced oasis in desert hills (p147)

Petra
Jordan's 'must see' ancient city (p155)

Red Sea
World-class coral gardens (p208)

Umm Qais
Atmospheric ruins laced with wildflowers (p96)

Azraq
Desert forts and pleasure domes (p232)

Karak
Crusader castle with a grisly past (p141)

Wadi Rum
Lawrence of Arabia's enigmatic desert (p209)

MEDITERRANEAN SEA

LEBANON

34°E   35°E

Quneitra

Sea of Galilee   Fiq

Umm Qais   Der'a   Suweida

Irbid   Ramtha   Bosra   Jebel Druze (1735m)

Jordan River   Jabir   Salkhad

Ajloun   Mafraq   Umm al-Jimal

WEST BANK   Jerash

Zarqa River   Zarqa   Qasr al-Hallabat

Suweileh   Qasr al-Azraq

Ramallah   Salt   AMMAN   Azr Wet Rese

Wadi Jadid   Qusayr Amra   Azraq

JERUSALEM   Suweimeh   Mt Nebo (820m)   Qasr

Madaba

Dead Sea   Machaerus (Mukawir)   The Badia

GAZA STRIP   Mujib Biosphere Reserve   Dhiban   Wadi Mujib

Lisan Peninsula   Ariha   Qatrana

ISRAEL & THE PALESTINIAN TERRITORIES   Karak   Mu'tah

Fifa   Safi   Wadi Hasa   Bayir

Tafila   Qasr al-Bint

Dana Biosphere Reserve   Qadsiyya

The Negev   Jebel Atatia (1641m)   Jebel al-Adhriyat (986m)

Shobak

Wadi Musa   Udruh   Al-Jafr

Jebel Haroun   Petra   Ma'an   Qa'al Jafr

EGYPT   Jebel al-'Unn (1022m)

Ras an-Naqb

Petra   Jebel 'Atrah (1382m)

Quweira

Eilat   Ar-Rashidiyyah   Jebel Rum   Wadi Rum   Diseh

Aqaba   Jebel Rum (1754m)

Ad-Durra   Al-Mudawwara

SINAI   Jebel Wmm Adani (1830m)

Gulf of Aqaba (Red Sea)   Haql

Nuweiba

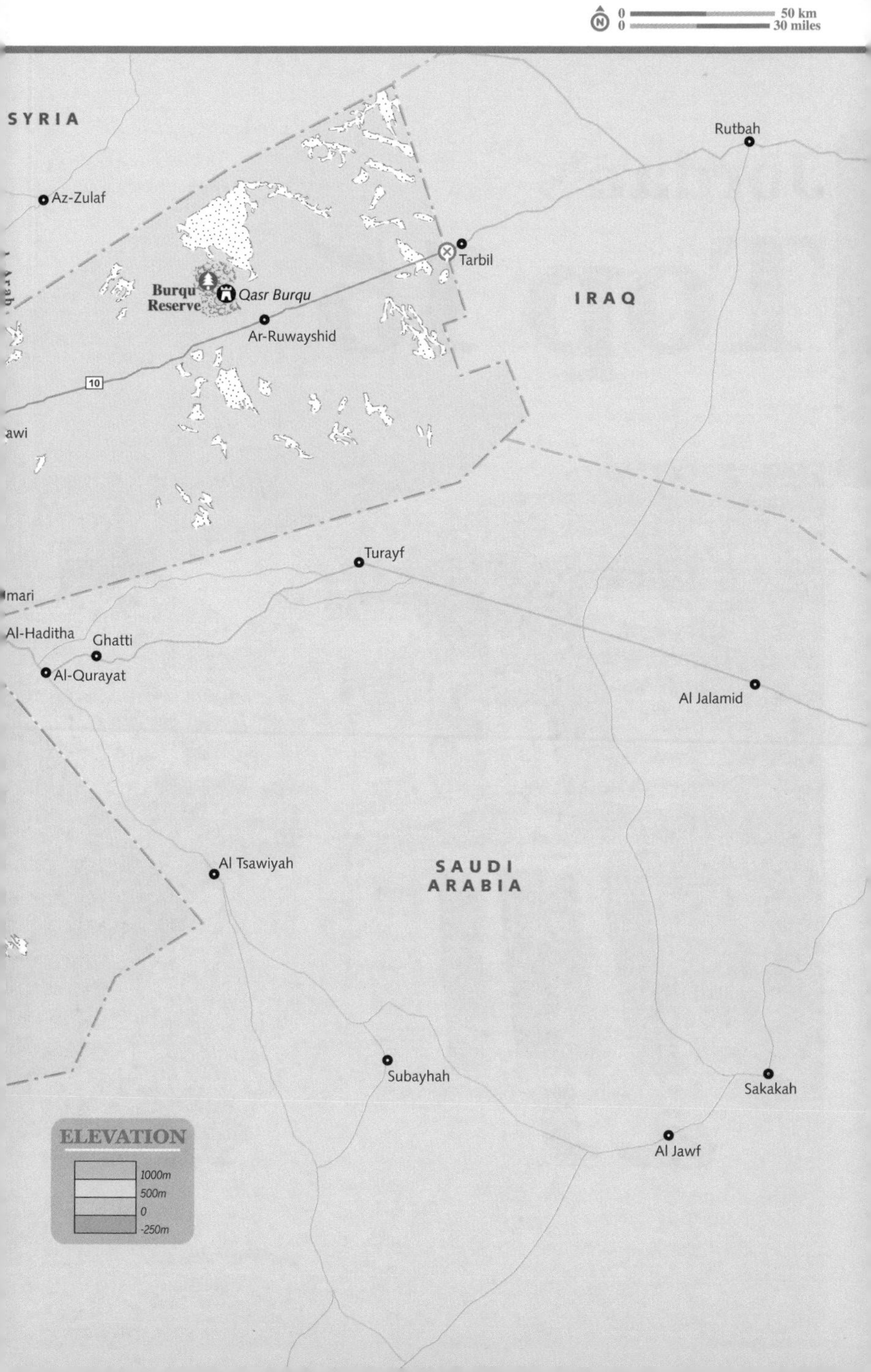

SYRIA

Rutbah

Az-Zulaf

Tarbil

IRAQ

Burqu
Reserve   Qasr Burqu

Ar-Ruwayshid

10

awi

Turayf

mari

Al-Haditha   Ghatti

Al-Qurayat

Al Jalamid

Al Tsawiyah

SAUDI
ARABIA

ELEVATION

1000m
500m
0
-250m

Subayhah

Sakakah

Al Jawf

Jordan's
Top 15

1

Petra

1 Ever since the Swiss explorer Jean Louis Burckhardt rediscovered this site in 1812, the ancient Nabataean city of Petra (p155) has been drawing the crowds – and with good reason. This is without doubt Jordan's most treasured attraction, and when the sun sets over the honeycombed landscape of tombs, carved facades, pillars and sandstone cliffs, its magic is abundantly evident. Allow a couple of days to do the site justice and visit the main monuments at optimum times of the day. Below left: Camel outside the Treasury (Al-Khazneh; p160)

Roman Ruins

2 For so small a country, Jordan punches well above its weight in world-class monuments, with some of the finest Roman ruins outside Rome. In addition to the Citadel and the well-preserved Roman Theatre in Amman, the black basalt ruins of Umm Qais and the extensive amphitheatres and colonnades at Jerash (p77) are highlights of the north. Visit Jerash's hippodrome during a chariot race when commentary from a red-plumed centurion will bring this ancient outpost of Rome to life. Below right: Roman ruins, Jerash (p77)

IMAGE IMAGE/ALAMY ©

Lawrence's Desert

3 It wasn't just the dramatic vistas of Wadi Rum (p209), with its burnished sandstone cliffs and vivid-coloured dunes, that impressed Lawrence of Arabia as he paced on camelback through the land of the Bedouin. He was also impressed by the stoicism of the people who endured the hardships of desert life. Today, it's possible to get a glimpse of that traditional way of life, with a few more creature comforts, by staying in one of the Bedouin camps scattered across this desert wilderness. Top left: Bedouin camp, Wadi Rum (p209)

The Dead Sea Experience

4 Floating in the Dead Sea (p109) is one of the country's great natural experiences. Floating is the right word for it: with an eye-stingingly high salt content, it is virtually impossible to swim in the viscous waters of this sea 415m below 'sea level' and equally impossible to sink. The experience is usually accompanied by a mud bath, a bake in the sun and a luxurious, health-giving spa treatment at one of the modern pleasure palaces lined up along the Dead Sea's shores.

Crusader Castles

5 As a frontier in the battle between Muslim and Christian forces for the soul, the Levant is dotted with castles. In Jordan, there are well-preserved examples at Ajloun and Shobak, but Karak Castle (p143), commanding the semi-arid hills above the King's Highway, is the most atmospheric. You don't need to be military-minded to be impressed by the enormous ramparts, but imagination helps to hear the dying howls of those pitched from the parapet by sadistic Renauld de Châtillon. Top right: Karak Castle (p143)

Madaba's Handmade History

6 For centuries, Madaba (p123), at the head of the ancient King's Highway, has been a crossroads for camel caravans transporting goods, legions of armies pushing the borders of various empires, and Christian pilgrims driven by faith in search of the Promised Land. To this day the town, with its churches, mosques, museums, markets and craft workshops, retains the marks of those cultural exchanges. Perhaps the best evidence of this rich past is Madaba's collection of mosaics, a heritage continued through the town's unique mosaic school.

DANITA DELIMONT/GETTY IMAGES ©

Diving with Damsels

7 It's no secret that the Red Sea is home to some of the most beautiful underwater seascapes in the world. Jordan's Red Sea shoreline along the Gulf of Aqaba is admittedly short, but this comparatively unexploited stretch of water encompasses pristine reefs, crumbling wrecks and kaleidoscopic coral gardens. Snorkelling and diving (p29) among damsel fish, turtles and seahorses is a memorable experience easily arranged through dive centres in and around the lively seaside city of Aqaba. Access is both from the beach and by short boat-ride. Bottom left: Coral reef, Red Sea

Soul Searching

8 For many people Jordan is more than just a traveller's destination: it's a place of pilgrimage. Sites resonating with spiritual significance abound in a country delineated by the Jordan Valley. This is where John is believed to have baptised Jesus at Bethany-Beyond-the-Jordan, and where, according to the Bible, the towns of Sodom and Gomorrah attracted the wrath of God. It is at Mt Nebo (p134), however, with its view of the Promised Land, that one most senses this is 'hallowed, holy ground'. Bottom right: Monolith of the 2000 Jubilee, by Vincenzo Bianchi, Mt Nebo (p134)

ANDRE SEALE/ALAMY ©

Walks on the Wild Side

9 In a region not commonly associated with hiking, Jordan has a surprising number of good walking paths. Trails thread through the northern forest reserves, adventurous routes lead above wadi waterfalls, and Bedouin guides help visitors negotiate myriad livestock trails in Petra and Wadi Rum. For inspiring walks on the wild side, a trip to Dana Biosphere Reserve (p147) is a must, with its turquoise lizards, secretive ibex, terraced orchards and eco-friendly lodges. Above top: Dana Biosphere Reserve (p147)

Exploring the Desert Castles

10 The plains of eastern Jordan are home to the 'desert castles', a collection of early Umayyad pleasure palaces, bathhouses and hunting lodges that appear strikingly incongruous in the barren surroundings. While visiting Jordan's eastern frontier requires planning, this region is full of surprises. Brooding Qasr Kharana (p239) tops the list, but other highlights include Qusayr Amra's saucy frescos and Lawrence's winter redoubt at Azraq. Above bottom: Calidarium interior (p238), Qusayr Amra

Wadi Mujib

11 Fresh water is in short supply in Jordan and it has become an issue of intense political importance in dialogue with neighbouring states. Various projects, such as the 'Red to Dead' Sea Canal and a pipeline from Wadi Rum's aquifers to Amman, are being explored with ever-greater urgency. That's one reason why the springs of the Mujib Biosphere Reserve (p117) are a highlight. The other reason is that the water flows through a spectacular wadi into a series of deep pools. Below top: Mujib Biosphere Reserve (p117)

Blooming Beautiful

12 Carpets of scarlet poppies strewn across the desert, ribbons of oleander in the wadis, the flutter of velvet petals on a black iris along the King's Highway: Jordan is home to beautiful wild-flower displays. For the best show, visit the Roman ruins of Umm Qais (Gadara; p96) in the far north of the country on a sunny afternoon in April: armfuls of knee-high daisies and thistles, yellow hollyhocks and pink mallow compete for a sliver of warmth between the fallen masonry. Below bottom: Umm Qais (Gadara; p96)

The King's Highway

13 It may not be a literal path of kings, but the King's Highway (p121) follows some pretty big footsteps. These include those of the Nabataeans (their fabled city of Petra lies at the south end of the King's Highway), the Romans (whose military outpost at Umm ar-Rasas is a Unesco World Heritage site) and the Crusaders (their Karak and Shobak castles are highlights in their own right). Smaller footsteps include those taken by Salome in her Dance of the Seven Veils at the desolate hilltop of Mukawir. Above left: Mukawir (Machaerus; p137)

Jordanian Hospitality

14 Despite its modest size, Jordan is home to diverse peoples who share a traditional sense of responsibility towards the visitor. It may sound unfashionably romantic to claim that Jordanians are more friendly than most, but it doesn't take long to realise that hospitality is an integral part of the local culture. Whether you're invited for mint tea by Palestinians, bread and salt by Bedouins or pomegranate salads by the Chechens in Amman (p42), your interaction with Jordanian people is sure to be a highlight of your visit.

Wadi Jadid

15 There's nothing new about Wadi Jadid ('New Valley' in Arabic; p137). Lying undisturbed, it typifies all that is constant in rural Jordanian life: grazing sheep, shepherds trotting through thistles astride pot-bellied donkeys, the smell of sage under hot summer sun. In fact the valley would be entirely unremarkable were it not for the clusters of ancient Bronze Age dolmen that dot the terraced hillsides. Heaved into place between 5000 and 3000 BC, these impressive stone monuments are worth the effort it takes to locate them. Below right: Dolmen, Wadi Jadid (p137)

Need to Know

For more information, see Survival Guide (p301)

Currency
Jordanian Dinar (JD)

Language
Arabic (English is widely spoken)

Visas
Visas, required by all visitors, are available on arrival (JD40 for most nationalities) at international airports and most of Jordan's land borders.

Money
ATMs are available throughout the country and credit cards are widely used.

Mobile Phones
Local SIM cards can be used for international calls and can be topped up with readily available prepaid cards. 3G is increasingly available.

Time
GMT/UTC plus two hours (plus three hours from April through September).

When to Go

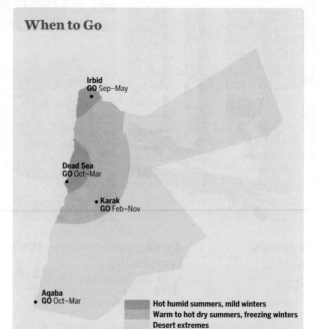

Irbid
GO Sep–May

Dead Sea
GO Oct–Mar

Karak
GO Feb–Nov

Aqaba
GO Oct–Mar

Hot humid summers, mild winters
Warm to hot dry summers, freezing winters
Desert extremes

High Season
(Mar–May)

➡ Perfect weather throughout Jordan with warm days and cool nights.

➡ Northern Jordan is blanketed in wildflowers in April.

➡ Reserve rooms in main tourist areas and expect higher rates.

Shoulder
(Sep–Feb)

➡ The best time to visit the Red Sea; prices in and around Aqaba rise accordingly.

➡ Bitter nights in the desert with rain or snow curtail many activities such as camping.

Low Season
(Jun–Aug)

➡ The desert in the middle of the summer is extreme. Temperatures throughout Jordan can be stifling.

➡ Prices are at their best but many places close in the low season.

Useful Websites

Jordan Jubilee (www.jordan-jubilee.com) Practical website about southern Jordan.

Jordan Tourism Board (www.visitjordan.com) Excellent official website.

Lonely Planet (www.lonely-planet.com/jordan) Destination information, hotel bookings, traveller forum.

RSCN (www.rscn.org.jo) Online booking for accommodation and eco-adventures in nature reserves.

Bible Places (www.bibleplaces.com) Biblical sights in Jordan.

Important Numbers

Country code	☑962
International access code	☑00
Ambulance	☑911
Fire	☑911
Police	☑911

Exchange Rates

Australia	A$1	JD0.654
Canada	C$1	JD0.652
Egypt	E£10	JD0.993
Europe	€1	JD0.966
Israel & Palestinian Territories	1NIS	JD0.203
Japan	¥100	JD0.695
New Zealand	NZ$1	JD0.605
UK	£1	JD1.193
US	US$1	JD0.709

For current exchange rates see www.xe.com.

Daily Costs

Budget:
Less than JD40

➡ Shared room in budget guesthouse: JD10–40

➡ Street fare and local markets: under JD5

➡ Public transport: JD5

➡ International Student Identity Card reduces cost of some tourist sites: JD5

Midrange:
JD40–120

➡ Double room in midrange hotel: JD40–90

➡ Eating in restaurants: JD5–10

➡ Car hire: JD25

➡ Entry costs/unguided activities: JD10

Top end:
Over JD120

➡ Double room in five-star hotel: over JD90

➡ Buffet meal: from JD10

➡ 4WD car hire: JD140

➡ Guided activities: JD50

Opening Hours

Opening times vary widely across the country. Many sights, government departments and banks close earlier in winter and during Ramadan. The following opening hours are therefore a rough guide only. Always remember that the official weekend in Jordan is Friday and Saturday, so expect curtailed hours on these days.

Banks 8am–3pm, Sunday to Thursday

Restaurants midday–midnight, daily

Cafes 9am–midnight, daily

Bars and Clubs 9pm to 1am, daily

Shops 9am–8pm, Saturday to Thursday; some close 2–4pm

Souqs 9am–8pm, daily

Arriving in Jordan

Queen Alia International Airport (p319) The Airport Express Bus (JD3) runs to Amman every 30 minutes (from 6am to 6pm); the night bus runs hourly (6pm to midnight). Taxis cost JD17 to downtown Amman (around 40 minutes). Car hire is available in the arrivals hall.

Passenger Terminal (p323) A taxi costs JD8 and takes 20 minutes from the ferry terminal and border to central Aqaba.

Wadi Araba (Yitzhak Rabin) Border (p323) A taxi from the border costs JD8 and takes 15 minutes to central Aqaba (JD50, two hours to Petra).

Getting Around

Public transport is limited to intercity buses and buses that serve the needs of local communities, making it hard to reach key destinations without time and patience.

Car Hiring a car is recommended, especially for visiting the Dead Sea, Eastern Desert and King's Highway. Driving is on the right.

Private Minibus Some hotels in Amman, Madaba, Petra and Aqaba organise minibus shuttle services and/or tours to key tourist destinations.

Taxi Many locals get around by shared taxi. Negotiating a half- or whole- day rate with a taxi driver is a useful alternative to car hire.

For much more on **getting around**, see p319

PLAN YOUR TRIP NEED TO KNOW

If You Like...

Roman Ruins

Pillars, pediments and pavements from ancient Rome are liberally strewn across Jordan, making the country one of the best in the world to see evidence of this once mighty empire.

Jerash Modern-day centurions clash swords in the hippodrome in the extensive ruins of Jerash. (p79)

Umm Qais With a view of the Golan Heights, these atmospheric ruins still command a strategic location. (p96)

Pella Little visited, these ruins are of one of the 10 cities of the ancient Decapolis. (p99)

The Citadel Perched above the modern capital, these ruins afford a vantage point of downtown's ancient amphitheatre. (p45)

Colonnaded Street, Petra The Roman presence at Petra is found in the detail – in a hero's tomb or fallen pillar. (p166)

Views of the Promised Land

On the east bank of the River Jordan, latter-day pilgrims can follow in the footsteps of former prophets. More than 100 sites in Jordan are mentioned in the Bible.

Bethany-Beyond-the-Jordan The most important biblical site in Jordan, this is the suggested location of Jesus's baptism. (p104)

Mt Nebo Moses supposedly finally saw the view of the Promised Land from here before dying. (p134)

Madaba Famed for the earliest map of the Holy Land, Madaba is notable for its Christian population. (p123)

Castle of Herod the Great, Mukawir Only a pillar remains atop the hill where Salome is said to have danced. (p138)

Lot's Cave She looked back, and for that Lot's wife allegedly turned into salt. (p119)

Jebel Haroun Revered equally by Muslims, this sacred site is thought to be Mt Hor of the Old Testament. (p175)

'Ain Musa Moses allegedly struck the rock either near Mt Nebo or in Wadi Musa near Petra. (p185)

Crusader Castles

Most people love a good castle and Jordan has plenty. Once guarding ancient trade routes or repelling religious adversaries, their crumbling battlements are a highlight of Jordan.

Karak Castle The king of castles, the Crusader stronghold of Karak is a highlight of Jordan. (p143)

Shobak Castle Built by Crusaders in the 12th century, this is the most picture-perfect of Jordan's castles. (p153)

Qala'at ar-Rabad (Ajloun Castle) Commanding the high ground, this castle was part of Saladin's defensive fortifications against the Crusaders. (p87)

Azraq Castle The winter home of Lawrence and Hussein in 1917, Azraq Castle protected an important oasis. (p234)

Mukawir Castle of Herod the Great, this is the haunting site of Salome's seductive dance. (p138)

Eastern Desert Castles Collectively misnamed as castles, these quirky Umayyad buildings invite exploration of the surrounding desolation. (p227)

Springs & Bathhouses

Jordan boasts dozens of thermal springs where the water averages 40°C and is rich in health-giving minerals. If you like your bath with bubbles, head to the Dead Sea spas.

Hammamat Ma'in Steam vents pepper the hillside at this spring near Madaba; it's suitable for single women. (p116)

Hammamat Burbita and Hammamat Afra West of the King's Highway near Tafila, these springs have pools and basic facilities. (p146)

Al-Pasha Turkish Bath Steam rooms, spa bath and obligatory scrubbing are available at this Amman favourite. (p55)

Petra Turkish Bath With separate baths for women, this is the place to unwind after hiking in Petra. (p179)

Dead Sea Spas Head to these spas for the ultimate in healthy bathing and luxurious pampering. (p111)

PLAN YOUR TRIP IF YOU LIKE...

Flora & Fauna

The desert may look deserted but it is home to the greatest survivors – both animal and vegetable. The desert comes alive in spring, from early April to late May.

Wildflowers In profusion across Jordan in mid-April, the best floral displays are around the northern hills. (p96)

Strawberry Oaks Ajloun Forest Reserve protects this rare woodland of red-barked trees. (p88)

Bird-watching Azraq Wetland Reserve hosts migrants and residents in the heart of the desert. (p236)

Black Iris Jordan's national flower blooms with deep purple petals along the King's Highway in April. (p121)

Ibex Perched on crags above the wadis of Dana Biosphere Reserve, this is one elusive goat! (p147)

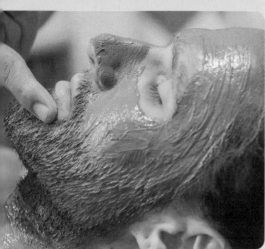

Top: Qasr al-Azraq (p234)
Bottom: Spa treatment (p112), Dead Sea

Fish The Red Sea is renowned the world over for its diversity of life underwater. (p29)

Royal Botanic Garden This newly opened garden is home to many of Jordan's native species. (p86)

Crafts with a Conscience

The revival of cottage industries is helping to sustain traditional ways of life in Jordan. Head to Madaba for souvenirs that leave behind more than you take away.

Hand-loomed rugs Goat-hair rugs are bringing life-changing opportunities to the women of Bani Hamida. (p138)

Palestinian embroidery The Haret Jdoudna Complex in Madaba provides an outlet for the once-dying art of cross-stitch. (p132)

Mosaics Associated with mosaic-making for centuries, Madaba is the place to buy a tree of life. (p132)

Painted ostrich eggs Ostriches once roamed the region; the art of egg painting has been preserved in Azraq. (p233)

Environmentally friendly products Wild Jordan in Amman sells eco-crafts from Jordan's nature reserves. (p66)

Lawrence of Arabia

Jordan is 'El Lawrence' country, the land the eccentric, camel-riding, dagger-wielding Englishman made his own during the Arab Revolt of 1917–19.

Wadi Rum Lawrence's ghost haunts 'Rumm the Magnificent', passing cliffs named 'Seven Pillars of Wisdom' in his honour. (p209)

Wadi Umran The words 'to Aqaba' float in the wind along this wadi – accessible still by camel. (p201)

Hejaz Railway The goods train rattles by on mended tracks once dynamited by Lawrence. (p54)

Rashidiyya Visit Wadi Rum in the season of re-enactments and watch the great Arab Revolt come alive. (p224)

Dana The 'chess-board houses of Dana' overlook Wadi Araba, 'fresh and green, thousands of feet below'. (p147)

Azraq Castle Lawrence was proud to ride between Aqaba and Azraq in three days; the journey now takes one. (p234)

The West Lawrence left Azraq 'riding into a glowing west, while...schools of cranes flew into the sunset'. (p236)

Bedouin Experiences

For centuries the Bedouin have inspired admiration for their reliance to the harshness of desert life. Nowadays many make their living sharing that life with visitors – an experience not to be missed.

Camping under goat hair With stars, tea and storytelling, Bedouin camps at Wadi Rum offer a night to remember. (p220)

Camel trek More driven than ridden nowadays, camels are still available for hire at Rum and Petra. (p217)

Sampling mensaf In Petra you can try *mensaf*, the Bedouin lamb, rice and pine nut speciality. (p186)

Amarin Bedouin Camp The museum in this camp outside Petra features the lives of the local Bedouin tribe. (p191)

Bedouin staples Camels' milk, dates and goats' cheese are staples of Bedouin food; learn how they are prepared at Feynan Ecolodge. (p152)

Walks on the Wild Side

Exciting hikes across sand dunes, through forests, and via the lush gorges of seasonally dry riverbeds (wadis) are possible mid-March to mid-October. See Taylor & Howard's *Jordan: Walks* for details.

Siq Trail This rewarding scramble (2km, three hours) leads through Wadi Mujib in knee-high water. (p117)

Wadi Dana Trail A classic Dana hike (16km, six hours), this steep trail descends through Bedouin grazing grounds. (p148)

Prophet's Trail Winding through Ajloun's orchards, this hike (8km, four hours) leads to the Prophet Elijah's alleged birthplace. (p90)

Makharas Canyon Hike This plod through soft sands (8km, 2½ hours) opens up the best of Wadi Rum. (p218)

Wadi Muthlim Enter Petra the Indiana Jones way (5km, 90 minutes) through this unnervingly narrow slot canyon. (p170)

Month by Month

TOP EVENTS

Jerash Festival, July

Hiking Season, March–April

Peak Wildflower Blooms, April

Dead Sea Ultra Marathon, April

Distant Heat, August

January

If you thought the desert was hot by default, think again! The desert is bitterly cold until March. But while most of Jordan shivers under chilly skies, those in the know head for Aqaba.

🏃 Red Sea Snorkelling & Diving

Aqaba, with its warm winter sunshine, hosts the annual holiday exodus of urbanites from the hills. The winter months, from December to March, are perfect for an underwater adventure, with clear skies and crystal-clear waters.

April

April is the most popular month to visit Jordan, with good reason. The weather is balmy and the semi-arid hills of Northern Jordan burst into magnificent, knee-high bloom.

🏃 Nature Walking

The spring, late March to mid-May, is the best time to visit Jordan's nature reserves. The elusive black iris (Jordan's national flower) blooms and nature lovers can hike through narrow wadis without fear of flash floods.

☆ Jordan Rally

The world's leading rally drivers participate in the 1008km Jordan Rally (www.jordanrally.com), attracting cheering crowds to the Dead Sea shore.

🏃 Dead Sea Ultra Marathon

Not just for a few crazed locals, the Dead Sea Ultra Marathon (www.deadsea-marathon.com) attracts athletes and amateurs – all heading below zero. The 50km race begins in Amman at 900m above sea level and ends 400m below the international tideline.

May

Still peak tourist season; the country heats up in May, leaving low-lying areas toasting. It's also peak season for flowering oleander, making the wadis pretty in pink.

🎆 Independence Day

On 25 May, Jordanians celebrate national day with bunting and flags and military parades in the capital. It's a good excuse for a chat, water pipe and mint tea with friends, and visitors are always made welcome.

🏃 Hiking & Camel Trekking

It may be heating up in Petra and Wadi Rum, but the desert is a quintessential experience in the heat. With sizzling days and breezy nights, you quickly slip into the rhythm of Bedouin life, rising early and napping after lunch.

June

Until 2018, the month of June is associated with high points in the Islamic year, the exact dates of which are based on the lunar calendar.

🍴 Ramadan

During the 30 days of Ramadan, Muslims must

refrain from eating, drinking and smoking between dawn and dusk. While there are some restrictions for visitors, Ramadan also brings special delicacies unavailable at other times.

✰✰ Eid al-Fitr

Marking the end of Ramadan, Eid al-Fitr is a time of festivity for Muslims. Disruptions to opening hours, and heavily booked transport and hotels are likely; on the upside, an invitation to join the party is an opportunity not to be missed.

July

The midsummer month of July brings hazy skies and suffocating heat, and few choose this time of year for a visit. Thankfully, it is cheered up by open-air cultural events.

✰✰ Jerash Festival

Hosted within world-class ruins, Jordan's best-loved cultural event brings ancient Jerash to life with plays, poetry recitals, opera and concerts. Held annually since 1981, the festival (www.jerashfestival.jo) runs for approximately two weeks either side of Ramadan.

✰ Traditional Concerts & Plays

In July and August traditional concerts and plays are held at the Odeon and Roman Theatre in Amman, as well as in Salt and Fuheis.

Top: Camel trekking (p217) around Wadi Rum
Bottom: Floating in the Dead Sea (p109)

August

Just when you think it can't get any hotter, August arrives with high temperatures radiating off the parched earth. Little wonder visitors are few.

Distant Heat

As you can't beat the heat, you may as well join it by building up a sweat at Jordan's annual dance in the desert. This all-nighter takes place in Wadi Rum and features top international electronic-dance-music artists.

September

Residents of Jordan sigh with relief in September as temperatures show signs of cooling and markets abound with figs, corn and fresh olive oil.

Eid al-Adha

Marking the end of hajj, the annual pilgrimage to Mecca, this Islamic holiday falls in late August or September until 2018. Shops close as owners join their families on these important days of celebration.

ISLAMIC HOLIDAYS

Ramadan, the month of fasting, and the two main Islamic holidays in the year, Eid al-Fitr and Eid al-Adha (marked by feasting and family festivities), are observed throughout Jordan. The dates are governed by the lunar calendar and therefore advance by roughly 10 days each year.

October

With the first signs of autumn showers, the scorched earth returns to life and everyone, including the farmers, makes hay while the sun shines.

Heritage Revival

From the end of September to the end of November you can board a steam train in Wadi Rum and ride alongside charging Bedouin on horseback – courtesy of the Jordan Heritage Revival Company (www.jhrc.jo).

November

Blustering with wind and heavy rains, November signals flash flood season as water chases through sun-dried wadis towards Wadi Araba. Not the best month for hiking, but good for sightseeing.

Jordan Running Adventure Race

Covered in a single stage, usually between Petra and Wadi Rum, this 160km ultra trail has become an established part of Jordan's sporting calendar. A shorter route attracts less masochistic participants.

Floating in the Dead Sea

With fewer tourists than in spring, you may find yourself bobbing alone in the Dead Sea if you visit Jordan in November. Early harvests of mangos and bananas from the Jordan Valley offer extra enticement!

Itineraries

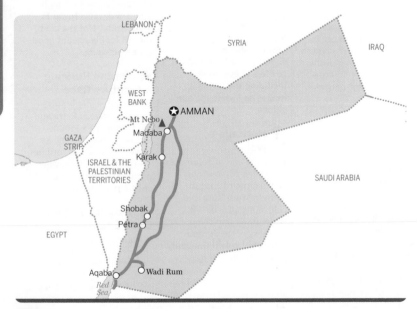

Amman to Aqaba Return

Thanks to its relatively compact size, Jordan rewards even the shortest of getaways, especially if you're prepared to hire a car. This route takes in most of Jordan's key sites in a journey along the King's Highway, the ancient backbone of the country.

On day one experience modern Jordan in the souqs of **Amman**. On day two, piece together a biblical history in the mosaic town of **Madaba** and, like Moses, survey the Promised Land from neighbouring **Mt Nebo**.

Spend day three following the caravans of history along the King's Highway, crossing mighty Wadi Mujib. Visit the Crusader castles in **Karak** and **Shobak** and listen for ghostly hooves against cobbles.

Rise early on day four to experience the Siq at **Petra** and climb to a High Place for lunch. On day five, slither through Wadi Muthlim and watch the sunset at Petra's iconic Monastery. Proceed to the seaside town of **Aqaba**, two hours away. On day six, wash off the desert dust in the spectacular Red Sea before returning to Amman (four hours via the Desert Highway) on day seven; with an early start, a desert lunch is possible at **Wadi Rum** en route.

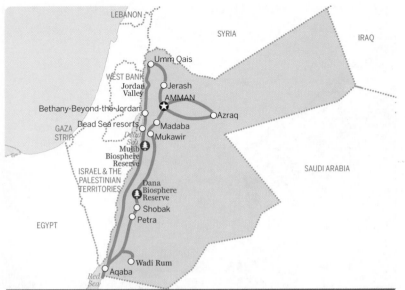

 Around Jordan

18 DAYS

With around 18 days you can unravel a path through Jordan's most famous sites, travelling in the footsteps of Roman legionnaires, Crusader craftsmen, Islamic warriors and Bedouin nomads. This route takes in Jordan's main highlights and throws in a few wild cards too.

Begin with two days in **Amman** and a third at the races – chariot races that is – at the spectacular Roman ruins of **Jerash**. For a springtime flower show, camp overnight at the oak woodlands of Ajloun Forest Reserve or spend day four wading knee-high among daisies at the ruins of **Umm Qais**. On day five descend to the subtropical Jordan Valley, pausing at the point where Jesus was allegedly baptised in **Bethany-Beyond-the-Jordan**.

Follow the River Jordan towards a night of luxury at the **Dead Sea resorts** followed by an early morning float on day six at the world's lowest point. Survey the West Bank from a higher vantage at the Dead Sea Panoramic Complex en route for **Mujib Biosphere Reserve**. Splash, swim and struggle through 'Petra with water' on the unguided Siq Trail. Dry out along the Dead Sea Highway to Lot's Cave and swap stories about the adventure over a vegetarian supper at candlelit Feynan Ecolodge.

Begin week two chilling in **Aqaba** for two days, sparing time for a dive or snorkel in the fabled Red Sea. With batteries recharged, tackle a hike in **Wadi Rum** on day 10 and stay overnight in a Bedouin camp. Spend the next three nights in Wadi Musa, joining Petra by Night for a magical introduction to the world wonder of **Petra**.

Head north from Petra via the ancient King's Highway on day 14, sparing time to pause at the imposing castle of **Shobak**. Break the journey at **Dana Biosphere Reserve** and relax on day 15, taking village walks or a longer hike with a guide.

Spend day 16 making the most of the King's Highway to Madaba, pausing at Karak and Herod's Castle in **Mukawir** en route. Allow two days for souvenir shopping in **Madaba**, the closest town to the international airport, or at craft shops in nearby Mt Nebo. If energy and extra time allows, end your visit with a day trip to **Azraq** and the Eastern desert castles.

BARNUTI DANIEL IOAN/SHUTTERSTOCK ©

Top: Roman Theatre
(p48), Amman

Bottom: Flat breads,
Ajloun (p87)

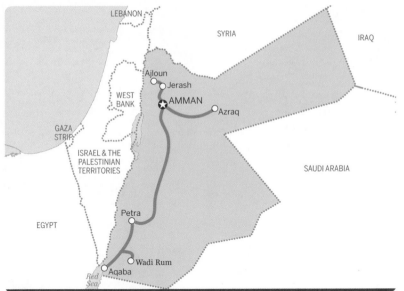

Border to Border

Jordan is plumb in the middle of a richly historic region, making it an essential part of a Middle East adventure. This 12-day route by public transport assumes entry by ferry from Egypt and exit by bus to Israel and the Palestinian Territories. Check the latest travel advisories before making this trip as the security situation in South Sinai (Egypt) is changeable.

Spend the first two days acclimatising to a new country in **Aqaba**: Jordan has a distinct character, immediately felt in the souqs and open-air restaurants of this seaside town. Spare time for a swim – Jordan's access to the Red Sea may be diminutive but the coral gardens are pristine and relatively unvisited. On day three take the morning bus and go in search of 'El Lawrence' in the magnificent desert of **Wadi Rum**. Hop astride a camel and head into the red sand dunes for an overnight camping experience with the Bedouin.

On day four rise at dawn with the locals, ready to catch the minibus to **Petra**. With two days in the pink city you can hike to the High Places, learn to cook Jordanian food at Petra Kitchen and watch the sunset from the Monastery and enjoy an evening in the famous Cave Bar.

On day six head north to **Amman** on one of the frequent Desert Highway buses via Ma'an. Spend a night sampling city nightlife, including an evening's stroll downtown through Amman's Roman ruins. Hike from the Citadel on day seven and reward the effort with the capital's best-loved Arabic street food at Hashem Restaurant.

Get off the beaten track on day eight by stopping over for two nights at **Azraq**. Azraq Fort was Lawrence's winter hideout and the nearby Azraq Wetland Reserve is a reminder of the fragility of life in the black Badia (stone desert). After crossing such barren lands, the shrunken waters of the oasis seem miraculous.

Head for the Roman ruins of **Jerash** on day 10. After visiting the extensive site on the morning of day 11, overnight in nearby **Ajloun**. With a crumbling castle and a nature reserve, Ajloun is a peaceful place to spend a last day in Jordan before heading to the border with Israel and the Palestinian Territories.

4 DAYS Gems in the North

With a long weekend, most visitors head straight for Petra on an overnighter from Amman. For a more rewarding use of time, leave the pink city for a longer visit and focus instead on Jordan's gems in the north. This trip bypasses the capital.

Hire a car or take a taxi from the airport in **Amman** and head to the Roman ruins of **Jerash**. On day two, amble down to the Jordan Valley via **Ajloun** and the Islamic castle of Qala'at ar-Rabad. Pause at the point where John allegedly baptised Jesus at **Bethany-Beyond-the-Jordan** and book in for some extreme R&R at the lowest place on earth. On day three, tear yourself away from the fluffy towels of the region's best spas (which come complete with a bob in the **Dead Sea** and therapeutic mud pack) and drive via the Dead Sea Panoramic Complex to steaming Hammamat Ma'in. From nearby **Mukawir**, where Salome reputedly danced for John's head on a platter, skirt the plateau ridge to the friendly mosaic town of **Madaba** and on day four visit Mt Nebo or the dolmens of Wadi Jadid. From Madaba, allow an hour to return to the airport.

6 DAYS Petra Plus

Travellers often ask: 'Is it worth making the effort to get to Petra with only limited time?' The answer is yes! While you can cover Petra in an exhausting day trip from the capital, this route takes you on a more rewarding route through the south if you're prepared to use taxis.

From Amman, take the bus along the Desert Highway to **Aqaba**. With plenty of accommodation, a lively ambience and excellent seafood, it'll be hard to leave town on day three. Take the early bus to Wadi Musa, the town closest to the Nabataean treasures of **Petra**. Amble through the Siq at midday, missing the morning tour groups. Watch the sunset turn the Royal Tombs pink, and return to the lively traveller scene in the town's Cave Bar.

Follow the ghosts of Crusaders along the King's Highway to **Shobak** on day four and stay overnight at **Dana Biosphere Reserve**. Hike down to **Feynan Ecolodge** on day five, prearranging transport along the Dead Sea Highway back to Aqaba (or north to Amman) on day six.

Plan Your Trip

Red Sea Diving & Snorkelling

Crystal-clear water, coral gardens and multicolour fish: these features have drawn expert divers to the Red Sea for years. But in Jordan you don't have to be certified to have fun – even the casual swimmer can easily and affordably don goggles and enjoy the spectacle.

Planning Your Dive or Snorkel

The Red Sea has a legendary reputation among underwater enthusiasts. Conglomerations of coral rise from the seabed, shallow reefs teem with brightly coloured fish, sheer drop-offs disappear into unplumbed depths and an eerie, ethereal blue pervades the cut-glass water.

While it is no secret that the Red Sea is one of the world's finest marine destinations, it's less known that Jordan has 27km of precious access to this underwater wonderland alongside the Gulf of Aqaba. This is good news for those divers and snorkellers who seek pristine reefs. It is also good news for those who favour an altogether low-key experience; indeed, the whole diving scene here is delightfully relaxed and unpretentious. In fact, even if you have no intention of diving and snorkelling, you may just find yourself lured into the water regardless by the friendly staff at the travellers' camps along the shore.

For a more structured experience in luxury surroundings, the Tala Bay complex offers a full range of underwater activities without the need to shuttle to and from Aqaba.

Best Water Activities

Best Dive
The Cedar Pride The coral-encrusted hulk of this sunken ship is Jordan's most famous dive site.

Best Snorkel
Japanese Garden Shore access and a gradual slope to a colourful reef make this the best place to hoist a snorkel.

Best Underground Garden
Gorgonian I Renowned for 16m fan coral and house-sized cabbage coral.

Gorgonian II Spectacular trimming of fire, stony and raspberry corals.

Best Turtle Encounter
Power Station Turtles regularly frequent this dive site. Don't be unnerved by the hammerheads – shark attacks are extremely rare.

Best Watering Holes
Royal Diving Club This is *the* place to dry your flippers while you wet your whistle.

Bedouin Garden Village Swapping fishy stories under a Bedouin tent is an 'après dive' highlight.

Clear Visibility

Surrounded by desert on three sides, the Red Sea was formed 40 million years ago when the Arabian Peninsula split from Africa, and it is the only tropical sea that is almost entirely enclosed by land. No river flows into it and the influx of water from the Indian Ocean is slight, resulting in minimal tides and high salinity. It is also windy – on average the sea is flat only 50 days a year. This unique combination of elements means that visibility underwater is usually unfailingly crystal-clear, contributing to the almost surreal sense of encounter with kaleidoscopic marine life.

High Accessibility

Enjoying the wonders of the deep is easy to organise, with many dive sites readily accessible to snorkellers. Dive centres offer accommodation close to the shore – handy for those who want to make diving and snorkelling the main focus of their visit to southern Jordan.

Those who prefer the buzz and amenities of Jordan's seaside city can easily find transport to and from Aqaba, making the dive sites accessible as a day trip from town. Tala Bay nearby offers midrange and top-end resort accommodation.

When, Where & How

When to Go

The water temperature is warm (an average 22.5°C in winter and 26°C in summer), making the in-water experience pleasant at any time of year. That said, it is important to bear in mind the high temperatures of summer which can make it uncomfortably hot on shore with a high risk of sunburn during the day.

Best Times

Late January–mid-May This is the best time to dive weather-wise. Bear in mind that late winter attracts holidaymakers from Amman, pushing up the price of accommodation in Aqaba. Spring is peak tourist season for international visitors and the busiest time for dive centres.

October–November The second most popular time to dive but prepare for the odd overcast or rainy day, which makes for comparatively disappointing viewing of marine life.

Worst Times

Mid-May–September The shore is usually miserably hot in the middle of the summer and the risk of burning is high both in and out of the water.

RESPONSIBLE DIVING & SNORKELLING

The Red Sea's natural wonders are just as magnificent as Jordan's historical and cultural splendours – and they need just as much protection. To help preserve the ecology and beauty of the reefs for posterity, please heed the following advice:

➡ Do not touch, remove or stand on coral, and avoid dragging equipment across the reef. Reefs are easily damaged by unthinking contact with feet and flippers.

➡ Minimise your disturbance of marine animals. In particular, do not ride on the backs of turtles or feed fish. Yes, sadly it happens!

➡ Avoid large surges of water or kicking up sand with your fins; this may smother the delicate organisms of the reef.

➡ Do not throw rubbish into the sea or leave it on the beach. Plastics in particular are a serious threat to marine life. Turtles often mistake plastic for jellyfish, their favourite food.

➡ Ensure boats are anchored to buoys, not attached to precious coral, and are not grounded on coral. If your captain is unmindful of this rule, report any misconduct to your dive centre on return to shore.

➡ Practise and maintain proper buoyancy control. Major damage can be done by divers descending too fast and colliding with the reef.

➡ Resist taking marine souvenirs, which depletes the beauty of a site and is illegal in Jordan. Remember too that shells are the 'castles of the hermit crabs'.

Late December–late January Although usually mild in Aqaba, freezing cold weather and occasional thunderstorms can sweep in from the desert at any time during winter. Wetsuits are a must and locals will wonder why you're bothering with the sea in chilly weather when you could be just enjoying a mint tea and chatting with friends.

Where to Go

Jordan's short coastline along the Gulf of Aqaba stretches between Israel and the Palestinian Territories and Saudi Arabia. Diving and snorkelling is focused between the port of Aqaba and the Saudi border. This stretch of coast is protected within the Aqaba Marine Park, part of the larger Red Sea Marine Peace Park, run in cooperation with Israel and the Palestinian Territories. Reefs here are in excellent condition, and the soft corals, especially those found on the *Cedar Pride,* are beautiful and varied.

There are about 15 sites worth visiting. The majority can be enjoyed by snorkellers as well as divers as they are easily accessible from either a jetty or the beach. Although you can enter the water at any spot along the coast, snorkellers tend to gravitate towards the private beach at the Royal Diving Club.

Sites are not signposted, nor are they remotely obvious from the road. If you want to dive or snorkel independently you'll have to ask for directions, or take your chances and search for 'obvious' offshore reefs. On the whole, to avoid wasting half a day trying to find an interesting stretch of water, it's better to take local advice.

How to Go

Dive Centres

Trips are easily organised through specialist operators in Aqaba or along the Red Sea coast and many hotels facilitate diving and snorkelling trips as well. There are a number of dive centres with a long-standing reputation for excellence.

Aqaba Adventure Divers Office (☑079 5843724; www.aqaba-diving.com) Operates dives in conjunction with Bedouin Garden Village.

Aqaba International Dive Centre Office (☑079 6949082; www.aqabadivingcenter.com) Popular, well-equipped and one of Aqaba's best.

International Arab Divers Village Office (☑03-2031808; www.aqabadive.com) Highly recommended year after year by Lonely Planet readers.

Diving & Snorkelling

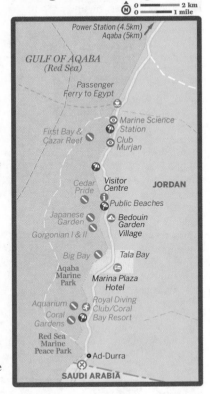

Dive Aqaba Office (☑03-2108883; www.diveaqaba.com) A highly professional training centre known for its high-quality teaching staff.

Red Sea Dive Centre Office (☑03-2022323; www.aqabascubadiving.com) One of the most established dive centres in Aqaba.

Royal Diving Club (☑03-2015555; www.coralbay.jo) Around 12km south of the city, the Royal Diving Club is one of Aqaba's most famous institutions. This is the place to come for the latest information on the condition of Jordan's key marine sites.

Choosing a Dive Centre

➡ Choose a reputable dive centre that makes safety a priority.

➡ If you have not dived for more than three months, take a refresher dive. The cost is usually applied towards later dives.

JOHN ELK III/GETTY IMAGES ©

Top: Diving the *Cedar Pride* wreck (p35)

Bottom: Reef snorkelling near Aqaba (195)

➡ Check hoses, mouthpieces and valves for cuts and leakage.

➡ Choose your wetsuit carefully: it may sound patronising but in the heat of summer they perish easily, leading to a chilly and unpleasant experience in winter months.

➡ Check that there is oxygen on the dive boat in case of accidents.

Costs

The satisfying part of diving and snorkelling in Jordan is that it doesn't have to cost an arm and a leg. In fact, for under JD10 per day you can bask above fan corals, swim with sardines, tread water among angels and float among clowns. The following table, based on prices offered at the Royal Diving Club, gives a rough idea of what costs to expect. With competitive rates for courses, Jordan is a good place to learn to dive or to enhance your skills at all levels.

DIVING ACTIVITIES	COST (JD)
Two dives from boat with tanks and weights	80
Full equipment rental per day	25
PADI scuba-diving course	280
Advanced open-water course	340
Emergency first-response course	115
Rescue-dive course/crew pack/certification	415

SNORKELLING ACTIVITIES	COST (JD)
Wetsuit hire per day	5
Full equipment rental	5
Whole-day trip by boat	45

The Underwater Experience

What to See Underwater

According to the **Royal Marine Conservation Society of Jordan** (☏06-5676173; www.jreds.org), the gulf has more than 110 species of hard coral and 120 species of soft coral forming spectacular reefs. These reefs are home to about 1000 species of fish, including colourful clownfish, parrotfish and angelfish, and a whole variety of life from dolphins to molluscs and sponges. Protected green turtles frequent the dive sites and harmless whale sharks pay a visit in summer.

Buy the plastic *Red Sea Fishwatchers Field Guide,* which can be taken underwater to identify species of fish and coral.

Internet Resources

Among the hundreds of internet references to help inform your underwater experience, the following are recommended.

Wind Finder (www.windfinder.com/forecast/aqaba) Check on current conditions to ensure you pick the best day for your dive.

H2O Magazine (www.h2o-mag.com) The website of the quarterly publication of the Red Sea Association for Diving and Watersports, with articles and updates on diving in the region.

Reef Check (www.reefcheck.org) A membership organisation working to save coral reefs in the Red Sea and elsewhere in the world.

Hazards of the Sea

It's worth familiarising yourself with the main marine hazards before snorkelling or diving – single-page colour guides to the Red Sea's common culprits can be bought in hotel bookshops around diving areas.

> **THE RED SEA – A SEVENTH WONDER**
>
> Ever wondered where the Mare Rostrum, or Red Sea, got its name? Some believe it was named after the red sandstone mountain ranges that surround the sea. Others insist it was named after the periodic blooms of algae that tinge the water reddish-brown. But whatever the etymology of the name, the Red Sea is now synonymous with underwater spectacles par excellence – and that's official! In 1989 a panel of scientists and conservationists selected the northern portion of this 1800km-long body of water as one of the Seven Underwater Wonders of the World.

Stonefish A poisonous fish with a nasty habit of lying half-submerged in the sand: wear something on your feet if you're wading out to a dive site. If stung by a stonefish, you should see a doctor immediately.

Lionfish These have poisonous spikes like stonefish. Calamine lotion, antihistamines and analgesics may reduce the reaction and relieve pain. Some swear by the application of urine!

Jellyfish Sometimes occurring in enormous groups, jellyfish can be something of a scourge of warm waters. Depending on the species, their sting can be very painful. The best remedy is to douse the rash with vinegar.

Sharks In this part of the Gulf of Aqaba, you're most likely to encounter white- or black-tipped reef sharks. Tiger sharks and the enormous, plankton-eating whale sharks are generally found only in deeper waters. Attacks from these apex predators are extremely rare in this area but obviously common sense applies if you have a bad cut or bleeding wound.

Coral The cuts from coral are notoriously slow to heal. Make sure you clean wounds thoroughly to avoid infection. Unlike the cold waters of northern seas, subtropical seawater is full of troublesome organisms that can cause serious infection.

Crown of Thorns Starfish Known as COTS, these invasive starfish feed on and kill local coral. Divers should notify their divemaster if they spot them.

Other Creatures to Avoid Moray eels, sea urchins, fire coral, blowfish, triggerfish and turkey-fish are better left alone.

Safety Advice

Any underwater adventure incurs some element of risk but with planning, knowledge and a bit of common sense, the risks can be minimised. Use the 'dive safe' checklist before you book your trip. If it's too late for that, the excellent Princess Haya Hospital (p206) in Aqaba is well equipped for diving mishaps, including cuts, bites and stings. It also has a **decompression chamber** (☏03-2014117), where the staff are trained to deal with diving accidents. The reputable dive centres are equipped with emergency oxygen tanks, a first-aid kit and a mobile phone.

DIVE SAFE CHECKLIST

Before You Go

Are you insured? If things go wrong underwater, treatment in the decompression chamber can cost thousands. If you hadn't planned to dive before arriving in Jordan, many of the better dive centres can provide insurance.

Have you informed your doctor? Diving can affect your metabolism and, if you're on medication, your dosage of prescription drugs might need to be changed.

Have you been drinking? Alcohol dehydrates, especially in Jordan's dry climate, and increases susceptibility to decompression sickness.

During the Dive

Do you know your diving depth limit? The Red Sea's clear waters and high visibility often lure divers into going too deep. The depth limit for casual divers is 30m – stick to it.

Will you remember what your boat looked like? Some dive sites get crowded and boats can look similar from underneath. It's not unknown for divers to be left behind because they didn't realise that their boat was leaving.

After Care

Have you allowed 24 hours before flying? Divers are in serious danger of decompression sickness if they attempt to fly too soon.

Have you allowed 12 hours before leaving Aqaba? As most routes out of town involve an uphill drive, the change in altitude may trigger decompression sickness. If you're heading for Petra or Wadi Rum, leave your journey until tomorrow.

Jordan's Best Dives

The Power Station

Location: Around 500m south of Aqaba

Rating: Intermediate

Access: Shore or boat

From a shallow fringing reef of fire coral, a sloping plateau of coral and sand patches leads to a 200m sheer wall, dropping from 12m to a narrow shelf at 40m.

First Bay

Location: Next to the Marine Science Station

Rating: Novice

Access: Shore or boat

First Bay is a shallow reef plateau with lagoons and sandy channels leading to a fringing reef of fire coral. Just south is Cazar Reef, noted for black coral trees.

Cedar Pride

Location: 5km north of the Royal Diving Club

Rating: Intermediate

Access: Shore or boat

Intact and festooned with soft corals, the wreck of the *Cedar Pride* is a true highlight with magnificent sea fans, basket stars and rainbows of fish caught in the sunlight.

Japanese Garden

Location: 4km north of the Royal Diving Club

Rating: Novice

Access: Shore or boat

Just south of the *Cedar Pride,* this reef sports large coral heads, including black coral. Lionfish, angelfish and schools of snapper and butterfly fish inhabit the magnificent colourful reef.

Gorgonian I and II

Location: 3km north of the Royal Diving Club

Rating: Novice

Access: Shore or boat

PLAN YOUR TRIP RED SEA DIVING & SNORKELLING

RED SEA ROYALS

Sultan Ibrahim, king fish and king soldier bream are not the only royals in the water. Diving in Jordan enjoys support from the very top, with King Abdullah II reported to be an avid diver. In fact his patronage was instrumental in the establishment of Jordan's premier artificial reef, the wreck of the *Cedar Pride.* Running aground after a fire in the engine room, this Spanish-built cargo ship was towed back out to sea in 1986 by the World Wildlife Fund (WWF) and sunk as an artificial reef. Today, the freighter lies on her port side at a depth of 25m, within easy reach of the shore, and is now one of the premier dive sites in the Red Sea.

Gorgonian I and II take their names from large, solitary fan corals. Nearby wonders include giant cabbage corals and green turtles that feed on the sea grass.

Big Bay

Location: 2km north of the Royal Diving Club

Rating: Intermediate

Access: Shore or boat

There are four sites in Big Bay – Blue Coral, Kalli's Place, Moon Valley and Paradise – which feature lacy blue and black coral. The 'long swim' (1km) to the Royal Diving Club is popular.

The Aquarium & Coral Gardens

Location: Offshore from the Royal Diving Club

Rating: Intermediate

Access: Shore or boat

The Aquarium is home to a spectacular fringing reef with a giant wall of fire corals. Immediately south lies Coral Gardens, home to lots of reef fish, seahorses and moray eels.

Plan Your Trip

Travel with Children

Children are universally adored in Jordan so you'll find that taking the kids adds a welcome dimension to your trip. Children are instant ice-breakers and will guarantee contact with local people, especially as foreign families are still something of a novelty.

Best Regions for Kids

Jerash, Irbid & the Jordan Valley
Kids studying the Romans will love Jerash, where centurions bring history alive and there are chariot races.

Dead Sea
The kids will love swimming with extra buoyancy in the very salty water.

Madaba & the King's Highway
With tunnels and passageways, there's heaps to explore at Karak while the Islamic Museum (p144) makes sense of Crusader history.

Petra
The horse rides are fun but a pre-trip viewing of *Indiana Jones & the Last Crusade* should nail it.

Aqaba
Teenagers can learn to dive while younger kids paddle in the temperate sea.

Wadi Rum
Camel rides, 4WD adventures and sandboarding make Wadi Rum a hit. Get the guide to spin the kids a Bedouin yarn.

Azraq & the Eastern Desert Highway
Search for oryx and ostriches on the Shaumari Wildlife Reserve (p236) night safari.

Jordan for Kids

Expect a Warm Welcome

While few concessions are made for youngsters, except the occasional high chair in a restaurant and baby-changing facilities in modern city malls, you'll find people go out of their way to make your family feel welcome, especially on buses and in shops, hotels and restaurants.

The Jordanian Family Way

Child-oriented activities are still a novel concept in Jordan, as normally kids are included in adult outings and entertainments. Jordanians enjoy socialising in groups so there's usually an extra pair of hands to mind the kids. As a result of this child-inclusive approach, most adult highlights are treated as children's highlights too.

Cultural Highlights a Hit

Feedback from parents on Lonely Planet's Thorntree forum is very positive about the experience of taking children to Petra, Jerash, Karak and Wadi Rum, although it pays to get the family curious about the destination in advance. Jordan is a gold mine for school projects on the Romans, for example.

Children's Highlights

Dining Experiences

Jordanian sweet shops A treat for all the family with honey-drenched pastries and giant, colourful platters of *kunafa* – shredded dough with cream cheese.

Fruit juice stalls A healthy way to beat the heat – watermelon and pomegranate juices are favourites.

Wild Jordan Café Brunch at this cafe in Amman (p61) offers opportunities for eco-education.

Rainy-Day Activities

Haya Cultural Centre (p56) Includes an interactive eco-museum.

Amusement Parks

Amman Waves (p56) A Western-style water-park between the airport and Amman is a hit with all ages.

Luna Park Rides (p56) Offers rides and amusements for kids.

Planning

When to Go

Spring is the best time for a family visit. The weather is great, attractions are open and evening amusements are on offer.

The heat of summer (mid-May to mid-September) is difficult for children to tolerate, restricting your activities to early morning and late afternoon. Winter months (mid-November to mid-February) can be freezing and many activities are restricted or too cold to be enjoyable. The risk of flash floods in wadis is an added anxiety.

Coping with High Temperatures

At any time of year, temperatures are comparatively high, particularly around noon. Trips to Petra and Wadi Rum involve long periods of sun exposure and it's not always easy to find shade: plan visits around early mornings and late afternoons. Follow local custom and take a family nap after lunch: this has the advantage of keeping the kids out of the worst of the sun and ensuring they're fresh for an evening out.

Avoiding Sickness

To prevent stomach complaints, children should stick to bottled mineral water, which is readily available, and avoid peeled fresh fruit and washed salads.

Fresh and powdered milk is available but it's worth checking that fresh dairy products (such as milk, cream, yoghurt and cream cheese) are made with pasteurised milk. Ice cream is usually best avoided in rural areas where the electricity supply is often unreliable, leading to frozen goods defrosting and refreezing.

General hygiene may not be the priority it is in many Western countries; carrying a hand sanitiser is a good idea in case the local water supply is suspect.

Nursing Infants

Breast-feeding in public is culturally acceptable providing you are reasonably discreet. Carrying an extra garment, like a shawl or a cardigan, to tuck around you and the babe may help keep male curiosity at bay.

What to Pack

Disposable nappies (diapers) are not readily available outside Amman and Aqaba. Come prepared with plastic bags to avoid contributing to Jordan's ubiquitous litter problem.

Mosquito nets and repellent are handy in the warmer months; malaria is not an issue in Jordan but itchy bites can easily become infected in the heat.

Car seats are not a big thing in Jordan so bring one with you. Pavements, or lack of, will be challenging for most prams but the locals seem to cope with them!

Jordanians are tolerant of Western norms but you will earn local respect if the kids dress appropriately. This is particularly the case with teenage girls: skimpy clothing, however fashionable elsewhere, will bring unwanted attention and stares.

Safety Check

Travelling in Jordan is generally safe for the family, with low incidences of crime.

Further Reading

Comprehensive advice about travelling with children can be found in Lonely Planet's *Travel with Children*.

PLAN YOUR TRIP TRAVEL WITH CHILDREN

Regions at a Glance

Petra is the natural focus of a visit to Jordan and for good reason. The ancient city of the Nabataeans, set in spectacular scenery, is one of the world's wonders. With beautiful Wadi Rum nearby, Red Sea diving and the holiday vibe of Aqaba, southern Jordan is a destination in its own right.

For adventure-seekers, hiking is recommended in the nature reserves along the Dead Sea and along the legendary King's Highway. Striking east, the desert castles – a motley assortment of old buildings from the region's glory days – make a good off-the-beaten-track excursion.

A circuit around the semi-arid highlands of the north is especially lovely in spring when wildflowers bloom at Jerash, Jordan's Roman gem, and at the biblical sites around Madaba.

Let's not forget the capital, Amman! With Roman ruins downtown and a youthful cafe culture pulsing in hilltop neighbourhoods, the city showcases modern Jordan.

Amman

Roman Ruins
Modern Middle East
Shopping

Ancient Downtown
The Roman antiquities of the Citadel and Roman Theatre define the heart of the city and are well worth exploring. Amman's museums give context to the experience of Jordan's major historical attractions.

Capital Cafe Culture
Sophisticated malls, buzzing coffee shops and happening nightlife challenge the regional perception of Jordan as a sleepy backwater. Values are conservative and there is plenty of evidence of the traditional Middle East, but for feeling the pulse of the country's youthful, well-educated and techno-savvy population the capital is the place to be.

Souvenir Hunting
From gold bangles to Iraqi currency bearing Saddam Hussein's image, Amman's souqs and streets are full of intriguing souvenirs. To make your spending mean more, root out the neighbourhood cooperatives.

p42

Jerash, Irbid & the Jordan Valley

Roman Ruins
Hiking
Scenic Views

Outposts of Empire

Don't think twice about visiting Jerash: this remarkably well-preserved outpost of the Roman empire has been wowing visitors for centuries and is one of the top three highlights of Jordan. Spare time for the lesser antiquities at atmospheric Umm Qais. Archaeology buffs will love Pella.

Sustainable Tourism

The socially and environmentally aware nature reserve at Ajloun is a byword for sustainable tourism. Hikes from here take you through the heartland of rural Jordan, passing traditional communities and providing an opportunity to see rare strawberry tree woodlands.

Rural Rides

Take any route from the juniper uplands of Jerash, Salt or Umm Qais to the fertile and subtropical Jordan Valley and a natural-history lesson awaits.

p75

Dead Sea Highway

Spas & Springs
Hiking
Dramatic Drives

Dead Sea Float

No one should come to Jordan and miss out on the extraordinary experience of a Dead Sea float. With luxury spas along the sea's eastern shore, this is the place to schedule some serious R&R. Nearby hot springs complete the opportunity for healthy treatments.

Wild Water

With unexpected waterfalls, oases and glimpses of wildlife, Mujib Biosphere Reserve is a great place for outdoor adventures. Expect to get wet in year-round pools. Further along Wadi Araba, Dana Biosphere Reserve has good sea-level trails and vegetarian feasting at Feynan Ecolodge.

Switchback Drives

Snaking from the vineyards of the King's Highway to the tomato fields and potash plants of the Dead Sea Highway, this region is peppered with exciting drives.

p106

Madaba & the King's Highway

Religious Relics
Handicrafts
Hiking

Soul Searching

Moses, Elijah, Jesus Christ and John the Baptist are some of many biblical figures that blessed Jordan's soil, and Mt Nebo remains a place of pilgrimage today. Crusader castles at Karak and Shobak and the Christian town of Madaba show how this inheritance has been embraced over centuries.

Made in Jordan

Some of the best handicrafts in Jordan are made in cottage industries in and around Madaba. Traditional weaving near Mukawir and mosaic-making along the King's Highway are two of many crafts helping sustain rural communities.

Winter Wonders

The best and arguably the most beautiful hikes in Jordan are to be had in the upper wadis of Wadi Mujib and Dana Biosphere Reserve, despite winter snows.

p121

Petra

Ancient Ruins
Hiking
Stunning Scenery

Ancient Architecture

The ancient city of Petra is a world wonder. Allow enough time to reach the Treasury in early morning, picnic at a High Place by noon, watch the sunset at the Monastery and walk the Siq by candlelight at night – at least two days, in other words.

Hikes to High Places

Petra has some of the best and most accessible hikes in Jordan. Engaging a local Bedouin guide will help bring the recent history of Petra to life. Avoid the oven-baking summer months when the heat is overbearing. Some hikes are restricted after winter rains.

Natural Decor

Outrageously colourful sandstone, wind-eroded escarpments and oleander-trimmed wadis make the landscape of Petra a worthy consort of the ancient architecture. Don't forget your camera!

p155

Aqaba, Wadi Rum & the Desert Highway

Red Sea Diving
Desert Camping
Stunning Scenery

Red Sea Spectacle

Whether you dive, snorkel or simply swim, Jordan's Gulf of Aqaba gives easy access to the delights of the Red Sea. Early spring and late autumn offer the most comfortable temperatures.

Bedouin Encounter

You don't have to be a *Lawrence of Arabia* fan to enjoy hanging up your boots with the Bedouin after a day's camel trek. Desert camps are comfortable but can be freezing in midwinter and stifling in midsummer.

Desert Landscape

Even if you don't stay overnight, it's worth driving as far as the Wadi Rum visitor centre. From here you can see the Seven Pillars of Wisdom and it'll be instantly clear why the desert is a highlight of Jordan.

p193

Azraq & the Eastern Desert Highway

Architecture
Wildlife
Remote Travel

Pleasures Domes

The Umayyad bathhouses, hunting lodges and caravan staging posts of the Eastern Desert are collectively known as the 'desert castles'. It's not so much the buildings as the arid desert context that make visiting these outposts of civilisation worth the effort.

Jordan's Wildlife

The oasis at Azraq, while only a shadow of its former glory, is still a top spot for birdwatching. Visits to the reserve help to ensure that the remaining wetlands, together with the reversal of water drainage for urban use, are maintained.

Extreme Desert

Few make it to the black wastelands of the Badia, but if you're happy to spend some days tackling the extreme desert then head for Burqu Reserve, which redefines the term 'remote'.

p227

On the Road

Amman عمان

🔖 06 / POP 2.8 MILLION / ELEV 850M

Best Places to Eat

➡ Hashem Restaurant (p60)

➡ Afrah Restaurant & Coffeeshop (p60)

➡ Sufra (p61)

➡ Fakhr El-Din Restaurant (p62)

➡ Romero Restaurant (p62)

Best Places to Stay

➡ Jordan InterContinental Hotel (p58)

➡ Hisham Hotel (p57)

➡ Jordan Tower Hotel (p56)

➡ Caravan Hotel (p57)

➡ Palace Hotel (p57)

Why Go?

As Middle Eastern cities go, Amman is a relative youth, and though it lacks the storied history and thrilling architectural tapestry of other regional capitals, there's plenty here to encourage you to linger awhile before making for Petra, the Dead Sea or Wadi Rum. In fact, Amman is one of the easiest cities in which to enjoy the Middle East experience.

The city has two distinct parts: urbane Western Amman, with leafy residential districts, cafes, bars, modern malls and art galleries; and earthy Eastern Amman, where it's easier to sense the more traditional and conservative pulse of the capital.

At the heart of the city is the chaotic, labyrinthine 'downtown', an Amman must-see. At the bottom of the city's many hills, and overlooked by the magisterial Citadel, it features spectacular Roman ruins, an international-standard museum and the hubbub of mosques, souqs and coffeehouses that are central to Jordanian life.

When to Go

➡ The capital's hilly location brings sharp winds (and even the occasional day of snow) during cold winters, making March to May and October to November the best time for a visit.

➡ If you can bear the claustrophobic heat of mid-summer, which radiates off densely packed buildings and lurks in breezeless alleyways, then July and August are recommended for the annual Jerash Festival. At this time the Roman Theatre comes alive and the capital's penchant for an evening promenade comes into its own.

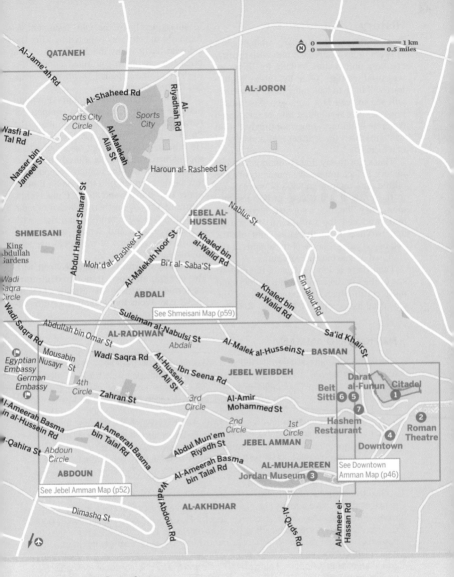

Amman Highlights

1 Visit the ruins (and museum) of the ancient **Citadel** (p45).

2 Admire the engineering precision of the **Roman Theatre** (p48).

3 Explore the breadth of Jordanian history at the superb **Jordan Museum** (p45).

4 Stroll **downtown** and rub shoulders with Amman's immigrant population.

5 See an exhibition at **Darat al-Funun** (p50), and sip tea amid the Byzantine ruins.

6 Learn to cook like a local with a class at **Beit Sitti** (p54).

7 Queue at **Hashem Restaurant** (p60), a legendary felafel eatery.

8 Cycle in countryside around Amman on a **Bike Rush** (p55) day trip.

9 Lunch in **Fuheis** at the excellent Zuwwadeh Restaurant and amble through **Wadi as-Seer**.

History

Despite its ancient lineage, Amman as it appears today is largely a mid-20th-century creation, and visitors looking for the quintessential vestiges of a Byzantine Middle East will have to look quite hard. What they will see instead is a homogeneous, mostly low-rise, cream-coloured city of weathered concrete buildings, some sparklingly clad in white marble, others rather grey and in need of a facelift.

That's not to say that Amman is without history. In fact, impressive remnants of a Neolithic settlement from 8500 BC were found in the 1970s at Ain Ghazal in Eastern Amman. They illustrate a sophisticated culture that produced the world's earliest statues and carvings from limestone and plaster. Today you can see some of these finds at the National Archaeological Museum.

Then there is Jebel al-Qala'a, the present site of the Citadel, and one of the oldest and most continuously inhabited parts of the city, established around 1800 BC. Referred to subsequently in the Old Testament as Rabbath, the city was besieged by King David who burnt many inhabitants alive in a brick kiln. Rabbath continued nonetheless to flourish and supplied David with weapons for his ongoing wars.

Visitors bump into Amman's Egyptian heritage each time they see a company or restaurant called Philadelphia, after the Ptolemy ruler Philadelphus (283–246 BC). He rebuilt the city during his reign and it was named Philadelphia after him. It was one of the cities of the Roman Decapolis before being assumed into the Roman Empire under Herod in around 30 BC. Philadelphia, meaning 'City of Brotherly Love', was redesigned in typically grand Roman style, with a theatre, forum and Temple to Hercules, the striking remains of which can be seen to this day.

The city's fortunes largely declined with the empire, although it regained some of its former glory after the Muslim invasion in AD 636. From about the 10th century lit-

---

NAVIGATING AMMAN

Like Rome, Amman was originally founded on seven major hills, but today it spreads across more than 20. It's not really a city to explore on foot, apart from the downtown area – known by locals as *il-balad*. A straight, flat road is almost unheard of, so the only way to make any sense of Amman in a short time is to pick out the major landmarks on the hills (jebels).

The main hill is Jebel Amman, home to several embassies, a few hotels and trendy restaurants. The traffic roundabouts in this central area (some now replaced with tunnels and major intersections) are numbered west of downtown from 1st Circle to 8th Circle. Rainbow St leads east off 1st Circle. If you're travelling in a taxi, street names will mean little, so ask for the nearest 'circle' and walk from there, or give the driver a nearby landmark (like an embassy or hotel).

Slightly northwest of downtown is the up-and-coming area of Weibdeh, with plenty of places to eat, have a coffee in funky surroundings and enjoy the area's slightly arty vibe. Further out in the same direction is Jebel al-Hussein, notable for the Housing Bank Centre; its mossy, terraced facade sticks out a mile. This also marks the start of the upmarket Shmeisani area, which stretches out to the north as far as the leafy Sports City. It has plenty of restaurants, shops, top-end hotels and a few nightclubs. Another trendy and affluent area is Abdoun, south of 4th Circle and the location of supercool cafes and several embassies.

Closer to downtown is the grittier Abdali area, with its large bus terminus. A few budget hotels are in the area. It can be readily identified by the distinctive blue dome of the King Abdullah Mosque.

In the far west is swanky Sweifieh, a booming shopping area. Further out, the city's outlying towns, suburbs and refugee camps have now pretty much merged into one sprawling urban area.

If you plan to stay for some time, or intend to visit places out of the centre, the free *Amman & Jordan* map is available at many hotels and car-hire offices, and will suit most people. The more comprehensive *Maps of Jordan, Amman and Aqaba* published by Luma Khalaf is also worth picking up, and is available from most bookshops.

tle more is heard of Amman until the 19th century when a colony of Circassians settled there in 1878.

You might not think it if you visit the sleepy tracks of Amman train station today, but the Hejaz Railway led to an early-20th-century boom in the city's fortunes when it became a stopover on the new 'pilgrimage route' between Damascus and Medina (Saudi Arabia). King Abdullah chose Amman as the headquarters of the new state of Trans-Jordan in 1921; it was officially declared the capital of the Hashemite kingdom two years later.

Over the intervening years, the city has weathered successive waves of immigration (from Palestine and in the last decade from Iraq and now Syria), sprawling well beyond its original seven hills. As a result Amman has had to contend with severe water shortages, compounded by the lack of urban planning.

Despite the challenges, the citizens of Amman are ever-optimistic, many grateful for the opportunity of rebuilding their lives in a generous and stable environment. This is best evidenced by the almost continual expansion, embellishment and development projects that besiege the city, most of which take longer to complete than anticipated. No one complains, however, as the capital plays an ever-increasing role on the regional stage. Only minimally troubled by the Arab Spring of 2011, it remains a vibrant, open-minded city, famed in the region for its educational institutions and confident about the future.

Dangers & Annoyances

Amman is a safe city for visitors. Although there are security guards and metal detectors in and around tourist sites and top-end hotels, most people see this as a positive response on behalf of the government to protect foreigners in the capital.

In fact, crime of any sort in Amman is extremely rare, and Jordanians take pride in reminding foreigners that their country remains an oasis of peace in a notoriously belligerent region.

Sights

A largely modern construction, Amman is home to few vistas that evoke images of grand empires. That said, scattered amid the concrete streetscapes are several spectacular remnants of Philadelphia, particularly the ruins on top of Jebel al-Qala'a, and the

Roman Theatre downtown. The most interesting part of this open-hearted city, however, is the chance that it affords to meet its cosmopolitan inhabitants – in the souqs of downtown, for example, or in the coffeehouses and modern malls of its fashionable hilltop neighbourhoods in Jebel Amman and beyond.

Downtown

★ Jordan Museum MUSEUM
(Map p52; www.jordanmuseum.jo/en; btwn Omar Matar & Ali Bin Abi Taleb Sts ; admission JD5; ⊙10am-2pm Sat-Mon, Wed & Thu) The Jordan Museum, located next to the City Hall, is a museum of international standard. Housed in a beautiful modern building, a series of beautifully presented and informative displays tell Jordan's historical epic from the first people through the Nabataean civilisation to the cusp of the modern era. Highlights include the oldest-known human statues (the spookily modern 8000-year-old mannequins of Ain Ghazal), Jordan's share of the Dead Sea scrolls, and a host of remains from Petra and surrounds.

The upstairs galleries, featuring Islamic Jordan to the Arab Revolt, were still to open when we visited, but either way, this museum is a must.

★ Citadel RUIN
(Map p46; ☑4638795; Jebel al-Qala'a; admission JD2; ⊙8am-4pm Sat-Thu Oct-Mar, to 7pm Sat-Thu Apr-Sep, 10am-4pm Fri year-round) The area known as the Citadel sits on the highest hill in Amman, Jebel al-Qala'a (about 850m above sea level), and is the site of ancient Rabbath-Ammon. Occupied since the Bronze Age, it's surrounded by a 1700m-long wall, which was rebuilt many times during the Bronze and Iron Ages, as well as the Roman, Byzantine and Umayyad periods. There's plenty to see, but the Citadel's most striking sights are the Temple of Hercules and the Ummayad Palace.

Artefacts dating from the Bronze Age show that the hill was a fortress and/or agora (open space for commerce and politics) for thousands of years.

The two giant standing pillars are the remains of the Roman Temple of Hercules. Once connected to the Forum (downtown), the temple was built during the reign of Roman emperor Marcus Aurelius (AD 161–80). The only obvious remains are parts of the podium and the columns, which are visible

Downtown Amman

AMMAN

JEBEL WEIBDEH

52

59 Al-Malek al-Hussein St

JEBEL AL-QALA'A

13

Al-Malek Ali bin al-Hussein St

JEBEL AL-QALA'A

4

49

15

Nimer bin Adwan St

5

1 *Citadel*

Omar al-Khayyam St

51

50 53

48 56

23

18

Cinema al-Hussein St

Yaqout al-Hamawi St

Sa'id Khair St

Shabsough St

Service Taxi 4 26

22

16

28 17

Al-Amir Mohammed St

Service Taxi 2

6 54

Al-Malek Faisal St

31

47

Service Taxi 7

58

27

Service Taxi 6

Hashemi St

Mu'ath bin Jabal St

57

Othman bin Affan St

Moh'd al-Shabeebi St

Fawzi al-Malouf St

Rainbow St (Abu Bakr as-Siddiq St)

Basman St

21

Al-Qabartay St

Service Taxi 3

Service Taxi 38

Service Taxi 1

36

34

Ibn al-Atheer St

3

Fruit & Vegetable Souq

10

Italian St

24

Hardware Souq

Petra St

43 29

12

38

41

46 25

19

37

45

Al-Mahmoud Taha St

14

33

40

35

44

42

39

Khirfan St (Al-Malek Faysal al-Awal St)

Omar bin al-Khattab St (Mango St)

See Jebel Amman Map (p52)

60

Quraysh St

Service Taxi 35

Fruit & Vegetable Market

Service Taxi 27

Al-Malek Talal St

Quraysh St

Italian St

Service Taxi 25 & 26

Italian Hospital

Hashemi St

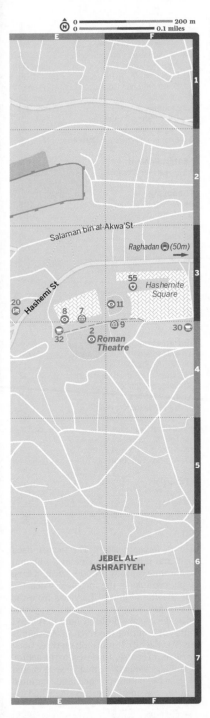

from around town. There's also a rather touching remnant of a stone-carved hand, which shows the level of detail that would have adorned the temple in its glory days. Nearby is a lookout with sweeping views of the downtown area.

The Citadel's most impressive series of historic buildings is focused around the **Umayyad Palace**, behind the National Archaeological Museum. Believed to be the work of Umayyad Arabs and dating from about AD 720, the palace was an extensive complex of royal and residential buildings and was once home to the governor of Amman. Its lifespan was short – it was destroyed by an earthquake in AD 749 and was never fully rebuilt.

Coming from the south, the first major building belonging to the palace complex is the domed audience hall, designed to impress visitors to the royal court. The most intact of the buildings on the site, the hall is shaped like a cross, mirroring the Byzantine church over which it was built. After much debate as to whether the central space had originally been covered or left open to the elements, consensus came down on the side of the ceiling dome, which was reconstructed by Spanish archaeologists.

A courtyard immediately north of the hall leads to a 10m-wide colonnaded street, lined with numerous arches and columns, and flanked by residential and administrative buildings. Further to the north is the former governor's residence, which includes the throne room.

East of the audience hall is the **Umayyad Cistern**, an enormous circular hole with steps leading down to the bottom, which once supplied water to the palace and surrounding areas. The small disc on the floor in the centre once supported a pillar that was used for measuring water levels.

Near the museum to the south is the small **Byzantine Basilica**, most of which has been destroyed by earthquakes. It dates from the 6th or 7th century AD, and contains a few dusty mosaics.

The **Citadel ticket office** is located on the road leading up to the Citadel's entrance. Fully licensed multilingual guides (up to JD15 per hour) usually congregate near the ticket office and can really enhance your visit.

The only access roads to the Citadel are from Al-Malek Ali bin al-Hussein St. It's better to hire a taxi for the trip up (around

Downtown Amman

JD1 from downtown), and save some energy for the recommended walk down. Steps lead from east of the Citadel complex, past a viewing platform to Hashemi St, opposite the Roman Theatre. This makes a fine start to a walking tour of downtown (see p50).

★ **Roman Theatre**   THEATRE
(Map p46; admission incl Folklore Museum & Museum of Popular Traditions JD1; ◷ 8am-4pm Sat-Thu & 9am-4pm Fri Oct-Mar, 8am-7pm Apr-Sep) This magnificently restored theatre is the most obvious and impressive remnant of Roman Philadelphia, and is the highlight of Amman

for most foreign visitors. The theatre itself is cut into the northern side of a hill, and has a seating capacity of 6000. The best time for photographs is the morning, when the light is soft – although the views from the top tiers just before sunset are also superb.

The theatre was probably built in the 2nd century AD during the reign of Antoninus Pius (AD 138–61). It was built on three tiers: the rulers, of course, sat closest to the action, the military secured the middle section, and the general public perched and squinted from the top rows. Theatres often had religious significance, and the small shrine above the top row of seats once housed a statue of the goddess Athena (now in the National Archaeological Museum), who was prominent in the religious life of the city.

Full restoration of the theatre began in 1957. Unfortunately, non-original materials were used, which means that the present reconstruction is partly inaccurate. However, the final product is certainly impressive, especially considering that the theatre has again become a place of entertainment in recent years. Productions are sometimes put on here in July and August – check with the tourist office or ask at your hotel.

Folklore Museum MUSEUM
(Map p46; ☑4651742; Roman Theatre complex; admission incl in Roman Theatre ticket; ⊗8am-7pm Sat-Thu & 10am-4pm Fri May-Sep, 8am-5pm Sat-Thu & 10am-4pm Fri Oct-Apr) Immediately to the right as you enter the Roman Theatre, this small museum houses a modest collection of items illustrating traditional Jordanian life. It includes a Bedouin goat-hair tent complete with tools; musical instruments such as the *rababa* (a one-stringed Bedouin instrument); looms; *mihbash* (coffee grinders); some weapons; and various costumes, including traditional Circassian dress. Don't miss the black-and-white photos of old Amman by the entrance.

Museum of Popular Traditions MUSEUM
(Map p46; ☑4651670; Roman Theatre complex; admission incl in Roman Theatre ticket; ⊗8am-7pm Sat-Thu & 10am-4pm Fri May-Sep, 8am-5pm Sat-Thu & 9am-4pm Fri Oct-Apr) This small museum, immediately to the left as you enter the Roman Theatre, has well-presented displays of traditional costumes, jewellery and face masks. A separate gallery displays mosaics from Jerash – your best chance to get up close, as little remains on site.

Forum ROMAN PLAZA
(Map p46) The row of columns immediately in front (north) of the Roman Theatre is all that's left of the forum, once one of the largest public squares (about 100m by 50m) in Imperial Rome. Built in AD 190, the square was flanked on three sides by columns, and on the fourth side by the Seil Amman stream, though almost everything lies underneath the modern streets. The current plaza project, which is nearly complete, will help bring back something of the sense of grand public space, albeit with a modern aesthetic.

Odeon THEATRE
(Map p46; ⊗daylight) FREE On the eastern side of the forum stands the 500-seat Odeon. Built in the 2nd century AD, it served mainly as a venue for musical performances. It was probably enclosed with a wooden roof or temporary tent roof to shield the performers and audience from the elements. Like its bigger sibling, the nearby Roman Forum, it is seasonally used for performances.

Nymphaeum FOUNTAIN
(Map p46; Quraysh St; ⊗daylight Sat-Thu) FREE Built in AD 191, this elaborate public fountain was once a large, two-storey complex with water features, mosaics, stone carvings and possibly a 600-sq-metre swimming pool – all dedicated to the nymphs. Excavations started in earnest in 1993, and restoration will continue for many years. Except for a few columns, an elegant archway and a few alcoves, there is little to see, though the workers toiling away may yet reveal hidden treasures in the years to come.

Al-Husseiny Mosque MOSQUE
(Map p46; Hashemi St) FREE Built by King Abdullah I in 1924, and restored in 1987, this compact mosque is in the heart of downtown on the site of an earlier mosque built in AD 640. The mosque is more interesting as a hive of activity than for any architectural splendour – the precinct is a popular local meeting place. Non-Muslims are not normally admitted.

Duke's Diwan MUSEUM
(Map p46; Al-Malek Faisal St; ⊗dawn-dusk) FREE This historic townhouse, built in 1924, has served as a post office (Amman's first), the Ministry of Finance and a hotel. Today, it has been restored with period furnishings by a

---

TUNNEL UNDER AMMAN

In ancient Roman Philadelphia, royalty considered it beneath them to mingle with the general public unless they had to. To ease their path between the major sites, an underground tunnel was built to connect the Citadel high on the hill with the Nymphaeum and the Theatre. While modern visitors to Amman might welcome having such access without having to negotiate the streets of downtown, the tunnel's precise location and state of repair is a closely guarded secret.

prominent Jordanian businessman, who is also the duke of the village of Mukhaybeh. There's not much to see, and the staircase has seen better days, but it gives an interesting glimpse of a bygone age.

Darat al-Funun   GALLERY
(House of Arts; Map p46; ☑ 4643251; www.daratal-funun.org; 13 Nadim al Mallah St, Weibdeh; ☺ 10am-7pm Sat-Thu) **FREE** On the hillside to the north of the downtown area, this cultural haven is dedicated to contemporary art. The main building features a small art gallery with works by Jordanian and other Arab artists, an art library, and workshops for Jordanian and visiting sculptors and painters. A schedule of upcoming exhibitions, lectures, films and public discussion forums is available on the website and in the *Jordan Times* newspaper.

Almost as significant as the centre's artistic endeavours are the architectural features of the site. At the base of the complex, near the entrance, are the excavated ruins of a 6th-century Byzantine church. Buildings further up the hill are mostly restored residences from the 1920s – it was in one of these that TE Lawrence wrote part of *Seven Pillars of Wisdom*. There is also a peaceful cafe and gardens with views over Amman.

Access is easiest on foot. From near the southern end of King Hussein St, head up the stairs under the 'Riviera Hotel' sign. At the top of the stairs, turn immediately right onto Nimer bin Adwan St and walk uphill for 50m where you need to take the left fork. The entrance gate (no English sign) is on the right after a few metres.

◉ Jebel Amman & Around

Rainbow Street   STREET
(Abu Bakr as-Siddiq St; Map p46) This street in Jebel Amman is a destination in itself. Ammanis come here every evening to promenade, and visit the many great cafes and restaurants – to see and be seen. There are plenty of shops if you come in the daytime (the area is good for souvenirs), but either way it's best explored by foot, as the narrow one-way street easily clogs with traffic any time of day or night.

King Abdullah Mosque   MOSQUE
(Map p52; ☑ 5672155, ext 219; Suleiman al-Nabulsi St, Jebel Weibdeh; admission incl museum JD2; ☺ 8-11am & 12.30-2pm Sat-Thu) Completed in 1989 as a memorial by the late King Hussein

🚶 City Walk
Highlights of Amman

START CITADEL
END HASHEM RESTAURANT
LENGTH 3KM; TWO HOURS

The best way to experience the key sights of Amman, which are largely clustered in downtown, is on foot. Go in the morning, when the light is best for photos, or early evening when the souqs are at their liveliest.

Begin at the hilltop ❶ **Citadel** (p45). The pillars of the Temple of Hercules are the best place to gain a sense of Amman's ancient Philadelphian roots and to survey how the city has spread beyond the original seven hills.

Follow Al-Qalat St round the edge of the Citadel walls. Steps (by a school with a flag) lead down to Salah bin Al-Akwa St; this is the shortcut locals take to reach downtown. A ❷ **viewpoint** to the right offers great views of the Roman Theatre. A further flight of stairs leads steeply downtown, past the Amman Panorama Art Gallery.

Head gingerly across the busy main road at the bottom (Hashemi St), cross Hashemite Sq, and climb the hill to the left of the theatre. Take in the view of the Citadel and the hotchpotch of facades that line the main road, most of which date from the mid-19th to the mid-20th centuries. Follow the stairs in front of the coffeehouse and pass by the souvenir shops en route to the theatre complex.

The small building on your right is the Roman ❸ **Odeon** (p49), but it's somewhat overshadowed by the neighbouring ❹ **Roman Theatre** (p48), which seems to extend indefinitely up the hillside. Walk between the Theatre and the Roman columns, all that remains of the ❺ **forum** (p49); the newly rebuilt plaza here provides space for the traditional Ammani evening stroll. From here you're ready to plunge into the heart of downtown.

Cross the road onto Hashemi St, passing nut shops, perfumeries and a store selling mosque accessories such as brass crescents for minaret tops. Turn left at the traffic lights to come to the ❻ **Nymphaeum** (p49). It takes imagination to resurrect this Roman fountain complex from the remain-

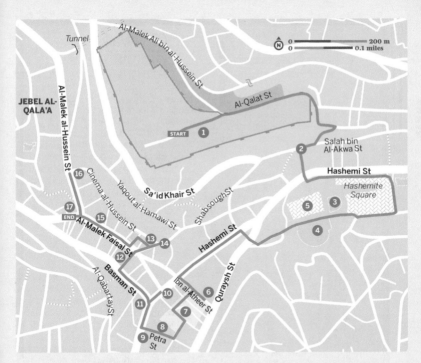

ing ruins and even more imagination to picture the stream that ran nearby until recently and which now flows under the road.

Pluck up courage and dive into the 7 **fruit and vegetable souq** opposite. It's possible to travel the Middle East in this part of the souq as you pass sticky mounds of Saudi dates, Iranian pistachios and Syrian olives.

Turn left at the yellow shop, passing flat-bread bakeries, and then right, through the 8 **hardware souq** of aluminium kettles and giant ladles. Turn right into Petra St (spelt 'Be-tra') and take in the gorgeous aroma of spices and coffee. On either side of the road are tradi-tional 9 **Arabic medicine stalls**, recognisable by the dangling dried alligators, trays of star-fish and drawers of herbs and henna.

A right turn onto Hashemi St takes you to 10 **Al-Husseiny Mosque** (p49). At Friday lunchtime hundreds of men stream out of the mosque after the weekly sermon. In the precinct in front of the mosque craftsmen sit behind their tools waiting for their next job.

Cross the street and enter the tiny 11 **Al-Afghani souvenir store**. Every con-ceivable space is occupied by chess sets, old postage stamps, plastic mosque clock-radios and odd ephemera.

Turn left into Basman St, passing Palestini-an embroidered dresses, and turn right down a flight of stairs just before House 22. The 12 **women's souq** here challenges any pre-conceptions about prudish Arab women: the alleyways flutter with risqué lingerie. It may be no accident that the 13 **gold souq**, where Arab men are expected to spend a portion of their salary, sits opposite, on the other side of Al-Malek Faisal St (King Faisal St). If you divert up Shabsough St, you can find the tiny 14 **Souq Al-Sri Lankiyitat**, a cluster of shops serving Amman's South Asian immigrant community (and a good place for a curry).

Continue along Al-Malek Faisal St and you'll come to the 15 **Duke's Diwan** (p49). The city is enjoying a renaissance at present and old establishments like this are being highlighted with signs in English along the length of Al-Malek Faisal St. Just past the or-nate Arab Bank, for example, a sign indicates a short diversion to 16 **Habibah** (p60), the perennially popular sweetmeat store with its brass platters of *kunafa* (shredded wheat and syrup dessert). After stocking up on desserts, return to Al-Malek Faisal St and the legendary 17 **Hashem Restaurant** (p60) for Amman's best hummus and felafel platters.

AMMAN

Jebel Amman

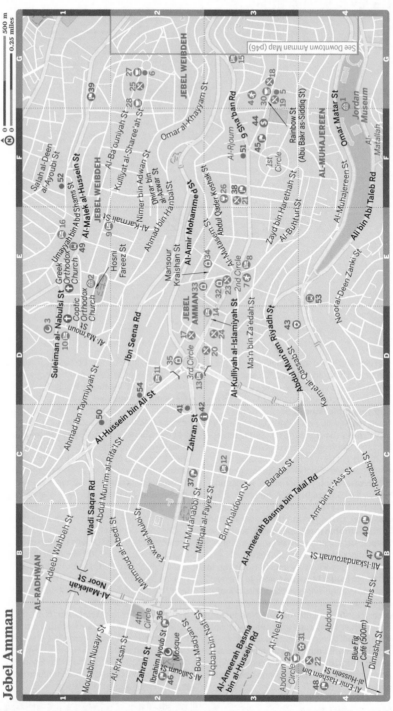

0 500 m
0 0.25 miles

See Downtown Amman Map (p46)

AL-RADHWAN

JEBEL WEIBDEH

JEBEL WEIBDEH

JEBEL AMMAN

AL-MUHAJEREEN

Jordan Museum

Al-Matallah

Mousabin Nusayr St
Adeeb Wahbeh St
Al-Ri'Asah St
Al-Malekah Noor St
Zahran St
Ibrahim Ayoub St
Al-Mumtaz St
Abu Madyan St
Al-Salloum St
Mosque
4th Circle

Ahmad Ibn Taymiyyah St
Abdul Mun'im al-Rifa'i St
Wadi Saqra Rd
Al-Hussein bin Ali St
Al-Rifa'i St

Suleiman al- Nabulsi St
Al-Ma'moun St
Coptic Orthodox Church
Greek Umayyah St
Orthodox Church

Salah al-Deen al-Ayoubi St
Al-Malek al-Hussein St
Al-Karmali St
Abd Shams St

Hosni Fareez St

Ibn Seena Rd

Zahran St
Al-Mutanabbi St
Mithqal al-Fayez St
Bin Khaldoun St
Fawzi al-Maloof St

Al-Amir Mohammed St
Mansour Kraishan St
Ahmad bin Hanbal St
Dhfar bin al-Anwar
Nimer bin Adwan St
Kulliyat al-Sharee'ah St
Al-Ba'ouniyah St
Omar al-Khayyam St

3rd Circle
Al-Kulliyyah al-Islamiyah St
Jebel Amman
2nd Circle
Abdul Qader Koshak St
Al-Mutasem St
Al-Rioum
1st Circle
9 Sha'ban Rd
Rainbow St (Abu Bakr as-Siddiq St)
Zayd bin Harethah St
Al-Buhturi St

Ma'n bin Za'edah St
Abdul Mun'em Riyadh St
Kamtelar- Qassab St

Al-Ameerah Basma bin al-Hussein Rd
Al-Ameerah Basma bin Talal Rd
Barada St
Amr bin al-'Ass St
Al-Rawabi St

Noof al-Deen Zanki St
Al-Muhajereen St
Omar Matar St
Ali bin Abi Taleb Rd

Abdoun Circle
Al-Neel St
Al-Emir Hashim bin al-Hussein St
Dimashq St
Hims St
Ali-Iskandarounah St

Blue Fig Café (500m)

Jebel Amman

to his grandfather, this blue-domed landmark can house up to 7000 worshippers, with a further 3000 in the courtyard. There is also a small women's section for 500 worshippers, and a much smaller royal enclosure. The cavernous, octagonal prayer hall is capped by a magnificent blue dome 35m in diameter, decorated with Quranic inscriptions. This is the only mosque in Amman that openly welcomes non-Muslim visitors.

The Islamic Museum inside the mosque houses a small collection of photographs and personal effects of King Abdullah I. Shards of ancient pottery are also on display together with coins and stone engravings.

A Friday visit may be possible if you avoid prayer time, but call ahead to be sure. Women are required to cover their hair – headscarves are available at the entrance to the mosque together with *abeyyas* (black, full-length outer clothing) to cover bare arms, legs or jeans. Shoes must be removed before entering the prayer hall.

Jordan National Gallery of Fine Arts   GALLERY
(Map p52; ☑ 4630128; www.nationalgallery.org; Hosni Fareez St, Jebel Weibdeh; admission JD5; ☉ 9am-5pm Wed-Mon) This small but impressive gallery is a wonderful place to gain an appreciation of contemporary Jordanian painting, sculpture and pottery. Renovated in 2005, the attractive space highlights contemporary art from around the Middle East and the greater Muslim world. Temporary exhibitions here are of high quality, and serve as a valuable introduction (or refresher) to the world of Islamic art.

The gallery is signposted from Suleiman al-Nabulsi St, opposite the King Abdullah

Mosque. It is housed in two buildings, separated by a small park – Building 1, on the north side of the park, is the smaller but holds an excellent gift shop; Building 2 opposite contains the bulk of the collection and a cafe.

☉ Other Suburbs

Military Museum   MUSEUM
(Map p59; ☎ 5664240; ⊙ 9am-4pm Sat-Thu) **FREE** The simple and solemn Martyr's Memorial houses a small but interesting collection of documents, chronicling Jordan's recent military history, from the Arab Revolt in 1916 (in which 10,000 Arab fighters were killed) through to the Arab-Israeli Wars. The intention, however, is a focus on remembrance rather than historical verisimilitude.

The memorial is on the road to Zarqa, 1km east of the Sports City junction, in the grounds of the Sports City. A private taxi from downtown costs around JD6.

Hejaz Railway   TRAIN STATION
(☎ 06-4895412; King Abdullah I St; admission JD2; ⊙ dawn-dusk) Except for the occasional cargo train, only the breeze rolls through this historic old station at present. For years speculation has been that a functioning passenger service to Aqaba would return to the tracks of the Hejaz Railway, made famous in the West by the pursuits of TE Lawrence. There's a small on-site museum and you can sit in the elaborately decked Royal Carriage. The station is 2.5km east of the Roman Theatre, on the edge of the downtown area.

Abu Darwish Mosque   MOSQUE
On top of Jebel al-Ashrafiyeh, this attractive mosque was built in 1961 with alternating layers of black and white stone. Non-Muslims are generally not permitted inside. Take service taxi 25 or 26 from Italian St in downtown to the mosque, or charter a taxi. It's a very long and steep climb southeast of downtown if you decide to walk.

Royal Automobile Museum   MUSEUM
(☎ 5411392; www.royalautomuseum.jo; King Hussein Park; admission JD3; ⊙ 10am-7pm Wed-Mon, 11am-7pm Fri) Car enthusiasts will like this display of over 70 classic cars and motorbikes from the personal collection of King Hussein. It's in the northwestern suburbs, north of 8th Circle. The best way to reach the museum from downtown is to take a taxi.

🏃 Activities

The top-end hotels offer a day rate to nonguests for use of their **swimming pools** and other facilities (from around JD25).

Sports City   SWIMMING
(Map p59; ☎ 5667181; incl locker JD15) This complex in northern Amman has an Olympic-sized pool. Admission prices for non-members decrease as the day goes on. Note that women may feel uncomfortable swimming here. The Sports City complex also has tennis courts, which you can rent for JD4 per hour.

Royal Racing Club   CAMEL RACES
(☎ 5850630) Horse and camel races take place in spring and summer and horse-riding lessons are available. The club is located off the Desert Hwy on the way to Queen Alia airport.

🗫 Courses

Amman has become an increasingly popular place to take an Arabic course, attracting students who might have opted for Cairo or Damascus in quieter times.

★ Beit Sitti   COOKING COURSE
(Map p46; ☎ 077-7557744; www.beitsittijo.com; from JD30) If you want to learn the secrets of Jordanian cooking, head for 'Grandmother's House' (Beit Sitti's literal meaning), a villa on the edge of Weibdeh, where ebullient chef-sisters Maria, Dina and Tania Haddad have opened the kitchen of their old family home to eager students. You'll tackle a handful of classic and lesser-known recipes, then sit down to a mouth-watering feast at the end of it, prepared by your own hands. Prices vary according to the size of the group; advise ahead of time if you're vegetarian.

Shababeek   LANGUAGE COURSE
(☎ 5822158; www.shababeekcenter.com; 23 Baris St, Sweifieh) Prices vary according to numbers of students and hours per week: 10 hours (per hour JD5.500 to JD9), 20 hours (per hour JD4.500 to JD7).

Ahlan World   LANGUAGE COURSE
(Map p46; ☎ 4612371; www.ahlan-world.org; 8 Fou'ad Slim St, Weibdeh; 2-week course from JD140) Residential options are also available.

Institut Français   LANGUAGE COURSE
(Map p52; ☎ 4612658; www.ifjordan.com/; Kulliyat al-Sharee'ah St, Weibdeh; 45hr course JD170; ⊙ 9am-6.30pm Sat-Wed, 9am-3pm Thu) Offers Arabic classes.

BATHING WITH BRUISERS IN AMMAN'S HAMMANS

If you thought you felt sore after walking up and down Amman's multiple hills, then just wait until you see what they do with you at the local hammam (Turkish bath). The large, muscular attendants (male or female, depending on your sex) could easily retrain as Sumo wrestlers and you can rely on them to find parts of the body you didn't know you had. In fact, they'll remove parts of the body you didn't know you had, as the art of extreme exfoliation counts as one of their many talents.

A largely Ottoman creation, based no doubt on a Roman obsession with communal bathing, Turkish baths have existed as places of social gathering and ritual cleansing across the Middle East for centuries. Amman's bathhouses, despite being largely modern affairs, belong to this decidedly masochistic tradition. Think we're exaggerating? Then pay a visit to the **Al-Pasha Turkish Bath** (Map p46; ☏ 4633002; www.pashaturkishbath.com; Al-Mahmoud Taha St; JD25; ⊘ 9am-2am, last booking midnight) or **Marrakech Hammam** (Map p52; ☏ 4615551; Bldg 45, 2nd Circle; JD30; ⊘ women 9am-4pm, men 5pm-1am) and you can make up your own mind about this quintessential Middle Eastern experience.

The torture begins with a brief spell in the steam room: while you meekly sip ice-cold *karkade* (sweetened hibiscus tea), you'll be scalded with missile precision by occasional boiling-hot drops of condensed water from the ceiling. The next ordeal is a dip in the Jacuzzi, softening you up with dislocating jets of water for the scrubbing to come. Don't even think about backing out now as the bathhouse attendant will have spotted you, waiting to beckon you to an alcove in the wall.

Using what can only be described as a glorified Brillo pad, the attendant will quite literally scour the visible surface area of your body. For a few extra dinars, he or she will even set to work on your callused feet with a precision file! Don't expect phrases like 'no' and 'please don't' – uttered in either Arabic or English – to help you. More often they invite an almost sadistic acceleration of pummelling, pounding and slapping, accompanied by snorts of laughter. In fact, a sense of humour seems to be a prerequisite on both sides of the fluffy white towels handed out so thoughtfully in the antechamber of the baths: in emergencies (as when a nose hair is plucked without warning or two ears are lifted independently of the scalp) these towels can be used as a flag of surrender by battered bathers to signal that enough is enough.

After five to 10 minutes (which will feel like a lifetime), you'll be led to marble slabs for an olive-oil massage. If you opt for an additional full-body mud pack, then prepare to be pinched as the masseur checks you're still breathing under the caking armour. This is not the moment to try to strut off with attitude, nor to look back in anger, as there is enough olive-oil soap on the marble tiles to make sure you aren't the one having the last laugh.

If, by now, the prospect of being bullied in the bath is putting you off the idea altogether, don't let it. The bizarre part about the experience is that the moment you step out of the steaming pools of indistinct water and are laid to rest on the marble platform, or the moment you expose your newly scraped and kneaded flesh to the outside air, you'll feel so rejuvenated that you'll be booking your next appointment before you leave.

Generally speaking, women are welcome during the day, while evenings are men only. Book ahead as, believe it or not, this is a very popular pastime. Also, be sure to bring a modest swimming or underwear – women may go topless, but it's not the done thing to strip off to absolutely nothing.

☞ Tours

The main backpacker hotels all offer a variety of day trips from Amman.

Bike Rush   CYCLING
(Map p52; ☏ 079-9454586; www.facebook.com/bikerush; ⊘ Sat-Thu 12pm-9pm) Day trips cost around JD18, including transport out to the area you'll explore. Most destinations are a short drive from Amman: the Dead Sea, Madaba and Mt Nebo are commonly offered destinations, but they vary according to the time of year – heading north to the green hills is a popular option in spring.

Custom trips are also offered, as well as straight bike hire (you'll even be delivered to where you're staying). The shop is a minute's walk downhill from Rainbow St.

Tropical Desert ADVENTURE TOUR
(☎079-5431616; www.tdtrips.com) If you have a taste for adrenalin, this respected Amman tour company has scheduled trips every weekend, including rock-climbing, canyoning and hiking. Adventure specialists with well-trained guides.

Wild Jordan ECOTOUR
(Map p46; ☎4616523; www.rscn.org.jo; Othman Bin Affan St, downtown) There are no nature reserves within the capital area, but Amman is the best place to organise trips to any of Jordan's Royal Society for the Conservation of Nature (RSCN) reserves. Accommodation in most reserves has to be booked in advance. Tour destinations include Mujib Biosphere Reserve, Dana Biosphere Reserve, Ajloun Forest Reserve and Azraq Wetland Reserve.

Festivals & Events

Concerts, plays and performances are occasionally held at the Odeon and the Roman Theatre in July and August. The Ministry of Tourism office (p68), near 3rd Circle, is the best source of information, but also check out the English-language newspapers and posters in the cafes along Rainbow St.

The Jerash Festival (p85) is Jordan's best-known cultural event (generally visited as a day trip from Amman).

Regional and international musicians take part in the **Amman Jazz Festival** (www.ammanjazzfestival.com; ⏲Apr), with concerts held in Amman and occasionally at some of the Dead Sea resorts.

The **Hakaya cultural project** (☎5687557; www.hakaya.org/en; ⏲Sep) connects organisations and individuals from around the Mediterranean who believe in the power of story-telling to effect positive cultural change. Its annual festival is held in Amman every September.

Sleeping

There are two main areas for hotels: Jebel Amman, where there's a range of top-end and midrange accommodation close to downtown; or in downtown itself, where most of the budget options are located. The five-star hotels compete favourably with others in the region and represent reasonable value for money. The midrange options include wi-fi, air-conditioning and satellite TV and are usually tucked into quieter suburbs away from the noisy main streets. The budget hotels downtown vary considerably in cleanliness and facilities, but all those recommended here sport clean linen, at least a fan, and friendly, experienced management. In addition, most can arrange onward connections. Most hotels include breakfast in their room rates.

Downtown

★ **Jordan Tower Hotel** HOTEL $
(Map p46; ☎4614161; www.jordantoweramman.com; 50 Hashemi St; male & female dm JD13, s/d/tr JD28/39/46; ❄@📶) This warm and friendly hotel has a winning location: you couldn't be closer to the key sights without offering beds in the Forum. Rooms are bright and snug with flat-screen TVs, though the bathrooms are small; there's also a big, bright

AMMAN FOR CHILDREN

While Amman is not exactly the most exciting city for kids, they will feel welcome, even in a restaurant late at night.

Amman Waves (☎4121704; www.ammanwaves.com; Airport Rd, Amman; adult/child JD14/8; ⏲10am-7pm) This Western-style water park is about 15km south of town on the highway to the airport. Note that adults should respect local sensibilities and wear appropriate swimwear (no Speedos or bikinis).

Haya Cultural Centre (Map p59; ☎5665195; Ilya Abu Madhi St, Amman; ⏲9am-6pm Sat-Thu) Designed especially for children, this centre has a library, playground, an interactive eco-museum and an inflatable castle. It also organises regular activities and performances for kids.

Luna Park (Map p59; ☎5698925; Khaled bin al-Walid Rd, Amman; admission JD3; ⏲10am-10pm) Has rides and amusements for the kids. Another branch is located at King Abdullah Gardens.

Jordan Bowling Centre (☎5512987; Makkah al-Mukarramah Rd; game JD3) For tenpin bowling come to the Mecca Mall in the northwestern suburbs.

and homely reception-cum-lounge area and rooftop restaurant. Offers day trips to the Dead Sea, Petra and other sites.

Farah Hotel
HOTEL $

(Map p46; ☎4651443; www.farahhotel.com.jo; Cinema al-Hussein St; 4- to 6-bed dm JD6, s/d/tr JD22/30/39, without bathroom JD14/20/27; @🗟) A firm favourite with travellers, this this well-managed establishment downtown has a shady garden and a homely, tranquil atmosphere, unlike its neighbours off the high street. A roof terrace offers great views of downtown, and the hotel owners have many years of experience in onward transport and tours to the major tourist sites.

Palace Hotel
HOTEL $

(Map p46; ☎4624326; www.palacehotel.com.jo; Al-Malek Faisal St; s/d/tr JD20/26/40, without bathroom JD18/28/30; ✳@🗟) The Palace offers good-value budget accommodation and its location in the heart of King Faisal St can't be bettered (look for the entrance on the pedestrianised sidestreet). Some of the basic, airy rooms have tiny balconies from which to enjoy the bustle of the street below. Guests can add their name to the lists for onward transport options and tours to top sites outside Amman

Cliff Hotel
HOTEL $

(Map p46; ☎4624273; Al-Malek Faisal St; s/d/tr/q without bathroom JD8/10/12/15, breakfast JD1.500; 🗟) This long-standing shoestring favourite has basic and quite dark rooms, but there's a big bright lounge area that acts as a sociable meeting place (don't be put off by the grungy hotel entrance). The shared bathrooms have hot water. A popular choice among younger travellers, the Cliff also offers a mattress on the roof in summer. Has day trips to the Dead Sea, Petra and other sites.

Sydney Hostel
HOTEL $

(Map p52; ☎4641122; sydney_hostel@yahoo.com; 9 Sha'ban St; dm JD7, s/d JD27/35; ✳🗟) Set aside a little from the other downtown options, this hotel nonetheless boasts big rooms, which are something of a pleasant novelty. There's a huge communal area surrounding reception. Better than expected for the price. Breakfast isn't included for the dorm rate.

★ Art Hotel
HOTEL $$

(Map p46; ☎4638900; www.facebook.com/ArtHotelDowntown; 30 Al-Malek Faisal St; d around JD70; ⊖✳🗟) On the cusp of opening during research, this stylish new hotel looks to be a great addition to the downtown scene. Rooms are well-finished in crisp white with good fittings. It has a deli-counter in the lobby and a restaurant in the works. An informal atmosphere is encouraged, but it's the breezy roof terrace overlooking downtown that really seals the deal.

🛏 Jebel Amman & Around

Caravan Hotel
HOTEL $

(Map p52; ☎5661195; caravan@go.com.jo; Al-Ma'moun St; s/d/tr/q JD22/28/33/38; @) On a quiet side street location near the King Abdullah Mosque, this place is an excellent choice. The big clean rooms have a bright aspect and en-suite toilets and showers. With 45 years' experience helping travellers, the Caravan also offers a comprehensive transport service with English-speaking drivers. It costs JD3 for a taxi to the north bus station.

Canary Hotel
HOTEL $

(Map p52; ☎4638353; canary_h@hotmail.com; 17 Al-Karmali St; s/d JD24/32; @) In the leafy Jebel Weibdeh area, the cosy B&B-style Canary feels a million miles from the chaos of downtown. The rooms are more comfortable than luxurious, although everything is kept spick and span, including the bathrooms. There's a pleasant garden area in front of the hotel.

Heritage House
HOTEL $$

(Map p46; ☎4643111; www.heritageamman.com; Rainbow St; r JD90; 🗟) It's taken a while for the hotel scene to catch up with what's happening around Rainbow St, but Heritage House has managed to take advantage of its location. Compact, subtle and modern, it's a useful getaway from city life, with a series of small rooms and studios.

Toledo Hotel
HOTEL $$

(Map p52; ☎4657777; www.toledohotel.jo; Umayyah bin Abd Shams St; s/d/tr from JD70/80/90; ✳@🗟⊠) The Moorish-style Toledo offers a quality experience on the cusp of the top-end sector. Modern rooms with soft and subdued lighting boast business-friendly amenities, and the bathrooms are pleasingly spacious. The big draw of the hotel, however, is the ornate foyer with its Moroccan-style tiles and keyhole arches, and free wi-fi access.

Hisham Hotel
HOTEL $$$

(Map p52; ☎4644028; www.hishamhotel.com.jo; Mithqal al-Fayez St; s/d from JD80/102; ✳@🗟)

This delightful hotel in a leafy embassy district of Jebel Amman is an excellent choice if you're looking for a hotel removed from the hustle and bustle of the city while still within easy reach of downtown. The rooms are comfortable with flat-screen TVs and minibars, and are brought to life with small, personal touches.

The family atmosphere, attractive decor and convivial Seven Barrels bar next door make this a frequent haunt of discerning travellers.

Hotel Le Royal
HOTEL $$$

(Map p52; ☑ 4603000; www.leroyalamman.com; Zahran St, 3rd Circle; r from JD180; ✳@🛜✹) Amman doesn't get more ostentatious than this huge drum of a hotel on top of Jebel Amman, currently the tallest building in the capital. A favourite of visiting sheikhs and dignitaries (the Pope stayed on his recent Jordan tour), this is not the place for intimacy, but it is an address that will impress. Opulent rooms incorporate traditional Middle Eastern design elements, though the highlight of the property is its award-winning health-and-beauty spa, which is the biggest in Amman.

Jordan InterContinental Hotel
HOTEL $$$

(Map p52; ☑ 4641361; www.intercontinental. com; Al-Kulliyah al-Islamiyah St; r from JD190; ✳@🛜✹) The grandaddy of luxury hotels in Amman, the much-loved InterCon has been hosting foreign dignitaries since the early days of Jordan's founding. A great favourite for local weddings, complete with traditional drumming, and with excellent Jordanian and Lebanese restaurants, and quality craft and antique shops, this is as good a place as any for an introduction to local city culture.

While it's certainly not the newest hotel, nor the most expensive on the block, there is an aged grace here not found at other top-end properties.

Grand Hyatt Amman
HOTEL $$$

(Map p52; ☑ 4651234; www.hyatt.com; Al-Hussein bin Ali St, 3rd Circle; r from JD180; ✳@🛜✹) An enormous complex with hundreds of rooms, suites and apartments as well as restaurants, bars, clubs, swimming pools and even a shopping mall, the Grand Hyatt is truly a class act. The majority of the hotel is constructed from polished Jerusalem sandstone, an elegant touch that tones down the sheer extravagance of it all.

Belle Vue Hotel
HOTEL $$$

(Map p52; ☑ 4616144; www.bellevue.com.jo; 2nd Circle, Jebel Amman; s/d JD85/95; ✳🛜) Towering over 2nd Circle, the Belle Vue is both a handy landmark to navigate by and a comfortable place to rest your head. It punches above its weight in terms of value for money and has many rooms with good views over Amman.

🛏 Shmeisani

AlQasr Metropole Hotel
HOTEL $$$

(Map p59; ☑ 5689671; www.alqasrmetropole.com; 3 Arroub St, Shmeisani; s/d JD100/110; ✳@🛜) Straddling the boundary between midrange and top-end in terms of facilities if not price, this hotel is the closest thing to a boutique establishment in Amman, with large contemporary paintings making a splash in the foyer. Located in fashionable Shmeisani, AlQasr has only 66 rooms, each artistically designed with wood floors, crown moulding and soft lighting. The hotel has an excellent range of restaurants and bars, including Vinaigrette (p62).

Kempinski Amman
HOTEL $$$

(Map p59; ☑ 5200200; www.kempinski.com; Abdul Hamid Shouman St, Shmeisani; r from JD210; ✳🛜✹) Amman's most chic and sophisticated accommodation option, this European-styled hotel is right at home in Shmeisani with immaculate rooms, designer furnishings and positively regal bathrooms. Offering a wide range of upmarket bars and restaurants, there's also an impressive list of entertainment, including a bowling alley, a cinema, and a games centre for the kids.

Le Meridien
HOTEL $$$

(Map p59; ☑ 5696511; www.lemeridien.com; Al-Malekah Noor St, Shmeisani; r from JD120; ✳@✹) For those vital first impressions, Le Meridien is grand and stylish. While it primarily targets business travellers, the hotel is considerably more affordable than the competition, yet still manages to win guests over with its flawless rooms and world-class service. Like other hotels in this upmarket category, the Meridien has a private gym, swimming pools and a health spa.

🍴 Eating

Amman has a wide range of eating options, with budget places concentrated in downtown, while the more upmarket restaurants serving Arab and international cuisine are

Shmeisani

Shmeisani

concentrated in Jebel Amman, Weibdeh and Shmeisani. If you fancy taking the local approach to choosing a dinner venue, then promenade Rainbow St in Jebel Amman, Culture St in Shmeisani or Waqalat St around the 7th Circle in Sweifieh, and just pop into whichever of the many restaurants appeals the most.

Many of the pubs and bars in Amman also serve food. Although there are small grocery stores throughout the capital, you can find larger supermarkets located in the more affluent districts like Sweifieh and Abdoun.

Downtown

★ Hashem Restaurant   FELAFEL $

(Map p46; Al-Malek Faisal St; the works JD3; ☺24hr) You haven't tried felafel until you've eaten here. This legendary eatery, run for half a century by a Turkish family, is so popular with locals and visitors alike that there's stiff competition for tables, many of which overflow into the alleyway. Aim for an early lunch or supper if you want to avoid the queues, although it has to be said that Hashem does a fantastic job of feeding the multitude in record time. Mid-afternoon, it makes a great place to sup a mint tea and watch downtown slide towards siesta.

Restaurant Mohammed Malik   INDIAN $

(Map p46; ☑079-5440715; 56 Shabsough St; curries JD3) Tucked away in tiny Souq Al-Sri Lankiyat, this Pakistani-run cafeteria serves up generous plates of excellent curries, biryanis, dal, samosas and the like to Amman's South Asian community. It's a little down-at-heel, but like the masala movies trilling on the TV in the corner, the food can't help but raise your spirits.

Cairo Restaurant   MIDDLE EASTERN $

(Map p46; ☑4624527; Petra St; meals JD2-5; ☺6am-10pm) Recommended by travellers, this simple restaurant serves good local food at budget prices. Most locals opt for the mutton stew and boiled goat's head, but you may prefer the *shish tawooq* with portions of grilled chicken large enough for two.

Habibah   DESSERTS $

(Map p46; Al-Malek al-Hussein St; pastries from 500 fils) This legendary shop is a good bet for Middle Eastern sweets and pastries. Sweet tooths of all ages line up for honey-infused, pistachio-topped and filo-crusted variations on the region's most famous desserts. There is another branch on Al-Malek Faisal St.

Afrah Restaurant & Coffeeshop   MIDDLE EASTERN $$

(Map p46; ☑4610046; Al-Malek Faisal St; mains from JD5; ☺9am-1am) This popular restaurant in the heart of downtown is more about the ambience than the food. Squeezed into every nook and cranny of the renovated upper storeys of this typical townhouse, the tables fill up quickly in the evening, particularly those with a balcony view of Al-Malek Faisal St below. Live Arab pop entertainment is offered nightly from around 9pm. Old coffee pots, brass trays and other Eastern bric-a-brac are strewn in various alcoves, suspended from pillars and strung from the ceiling, recalling days of yore. Access is via a steep staircase up an alleyway, next to the Farah Hotel.

Al-Quds Restaurant   JORDANIAN $$

(Jerusalem Restaurant; Map p46; ☑4630168; Al-Malek al-Hussein St; pastries from 800 fils, mains from JD6; ☺7am-10pm) The Jerusalem Restaurant specialises in sweets and pastries, but it has a large, good-value restaurant at the back that provides a great opportunity to try typical Jordanian dishes. The house speciality is *mensaf*, a Bedouin dish of lamb on a bed of rice, and *maqlubbeh* (upside-down rice) is frequently on the menu.

Sara Seafood Restaurant   SEAFOOD $$

(Map p46; ☑4561115; Al-Malek Faisal St; fish dishes from JD5; ☺10am-1am) This restaurant doesn't look much from the outside and looks positively uninviting from the street entrance (next to Cliff Hotel), but it turns out some of the best seafood in the neighbourhood. There's a tiny balcony overlooking busy Al-Malek al-Hussein St or quieter tables inside. The restaurant offers n decent choice of salads, whipped up at the micro-shop opposite the entrance downstairs.

Jebel Amman, Jebel Weibdeh & Abdoun

Al Quds   FELAFEL $

(Map p52; Rainbow St; felafel 500 fils) It's the kind of question that could lead to arguments – where is the best felafel in Amman? – but we're happy to nail our colours to the mast and vote for this tiny, spotlessly clean place on Rainbow St, which has been serving them up for over 50 years. Tasty sandwiches (with tomato and pickles) are served up as fast as you like, but watch out for lunchtime queues when the officeworkers descend. Trust us, you'll go back for more.

Volk's Burger
BURGERS $

(Map p52; ☑4622020; www.facebook.com/VolksBurger.Jo; Paris Circle, Weibdeh; burgers from JD3.750; ⊙ noon-1am Sat-Thu, 6pm-1am Fri) Our favourite place in Amman to get a burger – fat juicy patties and good bread with a side of peppery fries. The fillings are excellent, including the Wonderland (mushrooms, emmental, beef bacon and salad) and the Blue Cheese (blue cheese with sautéed onions and honey mustard).

Reem Cafeteria
MIDDLE EASTERN $

(Map p52; ☑4645725; 2nd Circle; shwarma from 850 fils) There are hundreds of shoebox-sized shwarma kiosks in Amman but few that have the customers queuing down the street at 3am. Having had one of Reem's delicious shwarmas (and a second and third), we know exactly why. Look for the red-and-white awning (with milling crowds) on 2nd Circle.

Blue Fig Café
FUSION $$

(☑5928800; Al-Emir Hashem bin al-Hussein St; mains JD4-8; ⊙8.30am-1am) If you're wondering where Amman's fashionable set go to escape their own cuisine, look no further than this supercool, glass-and-steel restaurant near Abdoun Circle. Offering an extensive and imaginative mix of world fusion dishes (try a crème brulée flavoured with Kyoto green tea and mint), the Blue Fig creates its ambience with seductive world music and the occasional Arabic poetry reading.

Abu Ahmad Orient Restaurant
MIDDLE EASTERN $$

(Map p52; ☑3522520; 3rd Circle; mains JD5-11; ⊙noon-midnight) This excellent midrange Lebanese place has a leafy outdoor terrace that bustles with life during the summer months. The standard fare comprises grilled meats, but the real highlights are the hot and cold mezze – try a *buraik* (meat or cheese pie) or the *yalenjeh* (stuffed vine leaves).

Ararat
ARMENIAN $$

(Map p52; ☑4601097; Rainbow St; mains JD6-12; ⊙11am-11.45pm) Wondering what Armenian cuisine is like? Head to Ararat and leave with a belly full of great food. Try *sini kufta* (lamb and wheat casserole) and a variety of tasty cooked salads, or go for a selection of smaller starters (JD2.250 to JD4.500) – we were particularly taken with the *lemajoun* (Armenian 'pizza'), *mante* (baked dumplings), *buererg* (cheese pastries) and *makanek* (spiced sausages). The menu leans heavily towards the carnivorous.

Wild Jordan Café
CAFE $$

(Map p46; ☑4633542; Othman Bin Affan St; mains JD7-12; ⊙11am-midnight; ☎☑) At wonderful, ecofriendly Wild Jordan Café, the emphasis is on locally sourced produce, healthy wraps, organic salads and locally plucked herbs. Smoothies are a welcome change from the ubiquitous coffee of cafes elsewhere. The glass walls and open-air terrace offer vistas of the Citadel and the downtown area – a great way to gain a perspective of Amman's main sights. The weekend brunch is always popular.

Noodasia
ASIAN $$

(Map p52; ☑5936999; Abdoun Circle; mains JD5-10) The shiny chrome and dark woods of this stylish pan-Asian diner feel like they have been lifted straight from the cooler quarters of Shanghai. However, the menu stretches across the Asian continent, and includes Chinese, Thai and Japanese snacks and main dishes such as green curries, sushi combos and the obligatory Chinese noodle dish.

★Sufra
JORDANIAN $$$

(Map p46; ☑4611468; www.facebook.com/Sufra-Restaurant; 28 Rainbow St; starters from JD3.350, mains from JD10; ⊙1-11.30pm Sun-Thu, 9.30am-11.30pm Fri & Sat) How good is Sufra when it comes to traditional Jordanian cuisine?

AMMAN'S STREET FOOD

Amman's street food has two jewels in the crown: its felafel and its shwarma. But where do you find the best? Everyone has their own answer of course, but after exhaustive research, we think we've got it covered.

For our favourite felafel, take yourself to the tiny Al Quds (p60), for the freshest and tastiest sandwiches. If it's meat you're hankering for, Reem Cafeteria is frequently acknowledged as having the most delicious shwarma in the city. Like Al Quds, it's a blink-and-miss-it sort of place, but if you're trying to find both, you can generally pick them out by the hungry queues they attract.

Like our recommendations, or think you found better? Get in touch and let us know!

Well, if the royal family are fans, we're hardly ones to argue. Housed in a lovely old villa with a terrace garden, this really is the place to eat well. The signature *mansaf* (lamb with rice and nuts, with a yoghurt sauce) is a delight.

Romero Restaurant
ITALIAN $$$

(Map p52; ☑4644227; www.romero-jordan.com; Mohammed Hussein Haikal St; mains JD10-18) Established half a century ago in an elegant traditional townhouse, Romero comes complete with period furniture, Venetian chandeliers and a roaring fire in winter. With intimate tables tucked in unexpected corners, a fine wine list to savour and succulent homemade pasta, this venue is just the place to come for a celebration. Book in advance.

Cantaloupe
INTERNATIONAL $$$

(Map p46; www.cantaloupe.jo; 10 Rainbow St; mains JD10-16; ☺1pm-1am) A self-styled gastropub, this restaurant-lounge is a lovely place for a splurge. While you can eat inside, the treat here is the rooftop terrace, with quite breathtaking views over downtown Amman. The menu is largely international (the steaks are good), the wine list broad, and the music softly jazzy.

Bonita Inn
SPANISH $$$

(Map p52; ☑4615060; mains JD12-25; ☺noon-midnight) If you're looking for a change from Middle Eastern fare but still want to mix with a Jordanian clientele, this primarily Spanish restaurant, off Al-Kulliyah al-Islamiyah St, is a great favourite with locals. The authentic paella Valenciana and gazpacho soup are recommended. The restaurant is located in a typical Jebel Amman townhouse (opposite the InterCon), lending a cosy charm to the venue. Don't eat too many tapas if you want to do justice to the paella!

Fakhr El-Din Restaurant
MIDDLE EASTERN $$$

(Map p52; ☑4652399; 2nd Circle; mains JD8-15) Tastefully decorated and with crisp, white linen tablecloths, this fine-dining restaurant is located in a 1950s house with a beautiful little garden. Over 10 years, countless guests have visited this establishment in search of what the proprietor terms 'genuine Arabic cuisine and hospitality'. A range of raw meat dishes, including lamb fillet, make an interesting addition to all the familiar Middle Eastern favourites.

Shmeisani & Other Suburbs

Vinaigrette
FUSION $$$

(Map p59; ☑5695481; AlQasr Metropole Hotel, 3 Arroub St, Shmeisani; mains JD8-15) Located on the top floor of the AlQasr, and in keeping with the hotel's boutique theme, this restaurant offers trend-setting Middle Eastern fusion food and gourmet sushi and salads – build your own salad and sushi combo, or let the house choose for you. Mellow jazz complements the superb views over the city.

La Terrasse
JORDANIAN $$$

(Map p59; ☑5601675; 11 Aug St, Shmeisani; mains JD10-25; ☺1pm-1am) This Shmeisani favourite offers some delicious local dishes and soups in a cosy, relaxed upper-storey dining area. The wine list is extensive, with labels representing Jordan and Tunisia (JD30 to JD40 a bottle). Most nights, after 10.30pm, the tiny stage is given over to live Arab singers and musicians, making it a popular venue for locals.

Diwan al-Sultan Ibrahim Restaurant
MIDDLE EASTERN $$$

(☑5517383; Ocean Hotel, Shatt al-Arab St, Umm Utheina; mains JD10-15; ☺noon-midnight) The Diwan comes highly recommended by locals and expats for its high-quality Lebanese food. The fresh fish is the speciality with options arrayed on ice. A whole Ibrahim fish (JD30) is fun for a party. The ambience in the cavernous dining area is good if there's a crowd but a bit impersonal if you arrive early.

Kan Zeman
JORDANIAN BUFFET $$$

(☑4128391; dinner buffet JD23; ☺7.30pm-midnight) Located in a historic inn with a vaulted ceiling, this restaurant is brought to life each night when traditional live music fills the ancient halls. On-site workshops housed in old stable blocks sell glass, rugs and jewellery among other souvenirs. It's aimed primarily at tour groups, and at around 15km south of 8th Circle in the village of Al-Yadoudeh – 3km east of the Desert Hwy – it's only worth the effort if you happen to be in the area. A taxi fare from downtown costs around JD15 each way.

Drinking & Nightlife

There is plenty of nightlife in Amman. The areas to head for are Jebel Amman, Shmeisani and the western suburbs, where numerous fashionable cafes and bars abound, as well as a few nightclubs and live houses that stay open until the early hours. For an authentic local experience, several grubby bars in downtown, patronised almost exclusively by men, are tucked away in the alleys near Al-Husseiny Mosque. Almost all bars serve food of some description.

Downtown, around Hashemite Sq and along Hashemi St, the dozen or more cafes attract locals and tourists alike, especially in summer. The place to be seen at night is anywhere around Abdoun Circle, where there are plenty of cool cafes. Take local advice – fashions change frequently in this part of Amman.

Orient Bar & Restaurant BAR
(Map p46; ☑ 4636069; beer from JD3; ☺ 11am-late) Also known as Al-Sharq, this spit-and-sawdust (and testosterone) bar in downtown, off Al-Amir Mohammed St, serves a range of beers, spirits and the local arak (if you dare). If you've had a bit to drink, mind your head on the stairs on the way down.

Al-Rashid Court Café CAFE
(Map p46; ☑ 4652994; Al-Malek Faisal St, downtown; tea or coffee from JD3; ☺ 10am-midnight Sat-Thu, 1-11pm Fri) The 1st-floor balcony here is *the* place to pass an afternoon and survey the chaos of the downtown area below, though competition for seats is fierce. Also known as the Eco-Tourism Café, this is one of the best places for the uninitiated to try a nargileh (JD2). Although you won't see any local women here, it's well accustomed to foreign tourists. To find it, look for the flags of the world on the main facade; the entrance is down the side alley.

Auberge Café COFFEEHOUSE
(Map p46; Al-Amir Mohammed St, downtown; ☺ 10am-midnight) One floor below the Cliff Hotel, this gritty Jordanian spot is popular with local men. Make your way through the tobacco haze to reach the balcony, which overlooks the main street. You'll have to fight with the regulars to sit there, mind.

Living Room COCKTAIL BAR
(Map p52; ☑ 4655988; Mohammed Hussein Haikal St, Jebel Amman; drinks JD4-8, mains JD8-20; ☺ 1pm-1am) Part lounge, part sushi bar and part study (think high-backed chairs, a fireplace and the daily newspaper), the Living Room is so understated that it's easily missed. It offers quality bar meals, fine music and delicious iced tea with lemon grass and mint. Non-teetotallers can enjoy the full

complement of expertly crafted cocktails on offer, which are served up deliciously strong. Book tables in advance at the weekend.

La Calle BAR
(Map p46; ☑ 077-7266928; Rainbow St; ☺ noon-1am) One of the few proper drinking holes on Rainbow St, La Calle has a couple of decent-sized bar areas, and a small but breezy terrace on the 3rd floor that's great for cooling off with a glass of wine or a chilled bottle of local Carakale ale. Food (burgers, pizzas, salads and the like) is available, while if you want to drink early, the daily happy hour (6pm to 8pm) takes the sting out of Jordan's generally high alcohol prices.

Darat al-Funun Café CAFE
(Map p46; Nimer bin Adwan St, downtown; snacks from JD1; ☺ 10am-7pm Sat-Thu; ☎) In the heart of a cultural centre, this is a peaceful place to escape from downtown, especially as it's surrounded by a garden and the ruins of a Byzantine church. Lawrence wrote part of *Seven Pillars of Wisdom* in the neighbouring house, so who knows what creative spirits linger here. Closed during Ramadan.

Peace Café COFFEEHOUSE
(Map p46; ☑ 079-5297912; Al-Amir Mohammed St, downtown; ☺ 9am-midnight) Try to ignore the filthy staircase on your way up to this utterly basic smoking den. If you can land one of the two balcony tables overlooking the street, you'll have one of the prime vantage points in downtown. As with the Auberge Café, do it like the locals – puff at a nargileh (JD2.500) and just watch the world go by.

Kepi CAFE
(Map p52; ☑ 077-5456850; www.facebook.com/CafeKepi; Paris Circle, Weibdeh; ☺ 7.30am-1am Sun-Thu, 8.30am-1am Fri; ☎) This corner cafe is a refreshing mix of traditional and modern: the old wood and high ceilings give it the air of a place where old Ammani men congregate to play dominoes, but you're just as likely to see trendy young urbanites with laptops. Large windows keep things breezy and fresh, and there's a good menu if you fancy lunch (there's even a passable stab at Tex-Mex food).

Rumi CAFE
(Map p52; www.facebook.com/rumicafejo; 14 Kulliyat al-Sharee'ah St, Weibdeh; ☺ 7am-midnight Sun-Thu, 9am-midnight Fri & Sat; ☎) This small café, named for the poet and liberally decorated

with his writings, is a charming new addition to the Weibdeh scene. There's plenty of coffee on offer, but the tea is the thing here: choose from a menu that includes blends from Bahrain (flavoured with rosewater), Iraq (cardamom), Morocco (mint), and more besides. There's a simple breakfast menu, plus cakes and sandwiches on offer throughout the day.

Turtle Green
CAFE

(Map p52; 46 Rainbow St; ⊘ 8am-midnight Sat-Thu, 10am-midnight Fri; 🔊) Named for the two terrapins in a terrarium in the shop window, this tea shop is a good place to refuel halfway down Rainbow St. As well as hot drinks and juices, the pitchers of iced tea (in eight varieties) are very refreshing, and Turtle Green does a good line in *manaeesh* (flatbread topped with thyme, cheese and more), salads and sandwiches. At busy times, the upstairs area can be rather smoky.

Grappa
BAR

(Map p52; 🖉 4651458; Abdul Qader Koshak St, Jebel Amman; beer JD4-5; ⊘ 6pm-1.30am) Stylish wooden benches and black-and-white photos on the wall give this rustic bar a hip feel, but it's the huge windows with views and the summer terrace seating that really draw the crowds.

Books@café
CAFE

(Map p46; 🖉 4650457; Omar bin al-Khattab; mains JD5-12; ⊘ 10am-midnight; 🔊) You may need to keep your sunglasses on when you enter this establishment – the retro floral walls and beaded curtains in psychedelic colours are a fun if dazzling throwback to the '70s. This is typical modern Jordanian coffeehouse chic, and the tasty global food is far less interesting than the hip young Jordanians lounging on sofas in corners or typing furiously on their laptops. Alcohol is served, but only with a food order.

Shaher's Penthouse Cafeteria
CAFE

(Map p46; Sahat al-Malek Faysal al-Awal St, downtown; coffee JD3; ⊘ 9.30am-11pm) This cosy cafe has a traditionally decorated indoor dining area as well as an outdoor terrace overlooking the street far below. Hussein, the resident musician, will happily play the oud (lute) or violin to provide a cultured counterpoint to the street noise below.

Rovers Return
PUB

(🖉 5814844; Ali Nasouh al-Taher St, Sweifieh; drinks JD3-5, meals JD5-8; ⊘ 1pm-late) A godsend for homesick *Coronation St* fans, this popular, cosy English pub in Sweifieh near the 7th Circle has wood panelling and a lively atmosphere. The comfort food includes authentic fish and chips, and roast beef with gravy. The entrance is round the back of the building and can be hard to find – look for the red 'Comfort Suites' sign.

Blue Fig Café
BAR

(🖉 5928800; Al-Emir Hashem bin al-Hussein St; mains JD5-11; ⊘ 8.30am-1am; 🔊) A convivial place to spend an evening, with a chic crowd, pleasant atmosphere (the terrace is lovely in summer evenings) and occasional live music.

Al Hail Restaurant & Café
CAFE

(Map p46; Hashemite Sq, downtown; ⊘ 9am-midnight) A glass of mint tea (JD3) here comes with perhaps the best view of the Citadel on offer downtown. It's an unpretentious place, despite the decorative well in the front garden, and it's popular with locals in the evening when the neighbouring theatre is illuminated.

Al-Sendabad Coffee Shop
CAFE

(Map p46; 🖉 4632035; Hashemite Sq, downtown; ⊘ 10am-midnight) About 150m west of the Roman Theatre, this place has good views over the city (though not of the theatre itself). You can sit on the roof in summer.

Tche Tche Café
CAFE

(Map p52; 🖉 5932020; Abdoun Circle, Jebel Amman; snacks JD1-3; ⊘ 10am-11pm) You'll have to arrive early to get a seat in this bright and buzzing cafe, one of a chain that stretches across the Middle East. Far from a traditional coffeehouse, it's a hit with Jordanian women who come to smoke nargileh and enjoy the Arabic pop.

☆ Entertainment

Cinemas

There are several modern cinema complexes that offer recent releases. Ticket prices vary. Programs for cinemas are advertised in the English-language newspapers. Note that the less-than-salubrious cinemas downtown usually feature Arabic, Indian and Thai films subtitled in Arabic and may not be of much interest to Western visitors.

Royal Film Commission
CINEMA

(Map p46; 🖉 4642266; www.film.jo; 5 Omar bin al-Khattab Street) The home of the Jordanian film industry, the commission holds regular screenings and festivals featuring the best of local and international cinema. The outdoor amphitheatre looking over downtown is a great place to see a film, while the stylish on-site **Montage** (Map p46; 5 Omar bin al-Khattab Street; ⊙9am-11pm; 🕿) cafe is worth a visit at any time of day.

Cinema City CINEMA
(☑5527948; Mecca Mall) Popular multiplex cinema, showing new Hollywood and Bollywood movies.

Galleria CINEMA
(Map p52; ☑5934793; Abdoun Circle, Jebel Amman) Western and Bollywood new releases.

Exhibitions & Music
Various foreign cultural centres organise lectures, exhibitions and musical recitals. Darat al-Funun (p50) often features recitals of classical and traditional music. The Jordan National Gallery of Fine Arts (p53) sometimes has visiting exhibitions of contemporary art.

For the exquisite Arabic art of calligraphy, you can watch a master at work in **Hassan Ali Hassan Kanaan's workshop and gallery** (☑077 7888007) downtown. Call ahead for an appointment to view.

Events are advertised in the local English-language newspapers, and on flyers posted along Rainbow St.

Sport
Football (soccer) is followed religiously by most locals. The capital's two main teams, playing in Jordan's Premier League, are Wahadat (generally supported by Palestinians, as it was originally formed in refugee camps), who play at the **Amman International Stadium** (Map p59; Sports City, Shmeisani; ticket JD3), and arch-rivals Faisaly (Jordan's most successful club), who play at **King Abdullah Stadium** (Qwesmeh; ticket JD3). The games are mostly played on Friday.

 Shopping
Jordan has a rich craft tradition and there are several quality craft centres where you can buy handmade items and antiques on Rainbow St and near the InterContinental Hotel. Many of these outlets are run by women's cooperatives to benefit threatened communities and help preserve the environment. Lots of souvenir shops selling sand bottles, headdresses, miniature brass coffee pots and Bedouin jewellery are dotted around the tourist sights of downtown.

AMMAN SHOPPING

ARTISTIC AMMAN

In more ways than one, Amman is a young city. Not only does the capital mostly date from the middle of the 20th century, but around half of its population is aged under 30. A highly educated population, combined with high youth unemployment and Jordan's status as a safe haven in a tough regional neighbourhood, have all helped give birth to a lively arts scene with a young, cool vibe.

The regeneration of Rainbow St was a key moment in providing a hub for artistic endeavours in the capital, and there are plenty of cafes where you can spot trendy youth tapping away at laptops while smoking on a nargileh, or you can find them at the hipster fashion outlet Mlabbas (p66). There's also the cool movie crowd at the Royal Film Commission (p64). Flyers along Rainbow St will alert you to concerts and art gatherings, as well as events you might not immediately associate with the region, such as video-game and digital-animation events.

Amman's artistic quarter has since migrated over the hill to the upcoming district of Weibdeh, leaving a great trail of street art behind it (before you leave Rainbow St, check out Amman's Wall of Fame, aka the British Council parking lot, which has become the hub for Jordan's graffiti scene). Outfits like Photograffiti have given Amman a flourishing street art scene, which has matured to include **An Urban Reflection** (www.facebook.com/anurbanreflection), a non-profit arts residency program that invites artists to work with local communities in the city to produce site-specific art and wall paintings.

If you're spending an extended period in Amman, check out art space the **Studio** (☑4646367; www.facebook.com/thestudiojo; Prince Mohammed St), where you can take printing classes, meet and collaborate with young artists and connect to the local scene. For those who prefer pens to paint, **Project Pen** (http://projectpen.me) is another great way to connect with local creatives.

Mall mania has swept through Amman in recent years. Popular malls include **City Mall** (☎5868500), **Mecca Mall** (☎5527948; Makkah al-Mukarramah Rd) and **Abdoun Mall** (☎5920246; Al Umawiyeen St, Zahran), but there are many others. Expect cinemas, local and international chain stores, restaurants and coffee shops. They're incredibly popular among the city's middle classes, and are an oddly fascinating reflection of modern Jordanian culture

There are several bookshops selling English-language publications and there's at least a kiosk for maps, guidebooks and newspapers in each top-end hotel. Books@ café (p64) has a reasonable stock, although you're better off heading to a mall for a wider selection.

Jordan River Foundation   HANDICRAFTS
(Map p46; ☎5933211; www.jordanriver.jo; Bani Hamida House, Fawzi al-Malouf St, Jebel Amman; ⊙8.30am-7pm Sat-Thu, 10am-5pm Fri) Supporting top-notch worthy causes by selling equally top-notch crafted items, this shop has become an institution in Amman. The showroom supports handloomed rugs from Bani Hamida and exquisite Palestinian-style embroidery. Cushions, camel bags, embroidery, baskets and Dead Sea products make it an excellent place to buy items of stylish decor. Only the highest-quality pieces make it into the showroom (reflected in the prices).

Wild Jordan Centre   HANDICRAFTS
(Map p46; ☎4633718; Othman bin Affan St, downtown; ⊙10am-10pm) The nature store at the Wild Jordan Centre sells products made in Jordan's nature reserves, including silver jewellery, organic herbs and jams from Dana, and candles made by Bedouin women as part of an income-generating project in Feynan. Decorated ostrich eggs are another speciality. All profits are returned to the craftspeople and to nature-reserve projects.

Mlabbas   CLOTHING
(Map p46; www.mlabbas.com; 28 Rainbow St) Want to look like a hip urban Jordanian? Head to this cool-as-you-like T-shirt shop on Rainbow St for an amazing array of screen-printed tees by local artists. Styles range from big-brand pastiches through to graffiti art, manga and cartoons, as well as a witty line in Arabic puns (ask the staff for translations). Prints, postcards and stickers are also available.

Balian   CERAMICS
(Map p46; 8 Rainbow St) The Balian family came to Amman from Jerusalem in the early 1920s, and have been selling their traditional hand-painted tiles ever since. The decor is popular with wealthy Ammanis eager to show off their good taste, and while you might be able to trick out an entire room, their individual decorative tiles make lovely souvenirs.

Soap House Trinitae   BEAUTY
(Map p46; 4633953; 8 Rainbow St) There's more to pampering yourself in Jordan than just Dead Sea mud. Up an alley at the bottom of Rainbow St, you'll find this lovely old villa and garden offering the best in organic luxury, with a gorgeous range of soaps and skincare products.

Souk Jara   MARKET
(Map p46; www.facebook.com/soukjara; Rainbow St; ⊙10am-10pm Fri) A weekly open-air flea market run by the Jebal Amman Residents' Association (JARA), selling a variety of handicrafts. It's good fun to browse, and there are some great food and drink stalls and occasional live music to add to the atmosphere.

Ola's Garden   HANDICRAFTS
(Map p46; ☎079 5390136; www.facebook.com/ola.garden; Khirfan St; ⊙11am-5.30pm) The home of beautiful handcrafted fashion, from clothes to jewellery. Owner-designer Ola Mubaslat showcases her creations in the most welcoming way (we particularly love the scarves and necklaces), and even offers classes in embroidery and jewellery design.

Love on a Bike   ART
(Map p46; ☎079 6433311; www.facebook.com/loveonabike; Khirfan St) Young artist Rima Malallah has her own unique take on what it means to be a modern Ammani, with her brightly decorated shop full of quirky cartoony prints, and hand-painted ceramics and wooden boxes.

Beit Shocair   HANDICRAFTS
(Map p46; 38 Khirfan St) A large villa on one of Amman's oldest streets, Beit Shocair offers space to artists and artisans to sell their wares. Traditional Jordan handicrafts dominate, but there's usually enough variety to find something that catches the eye. The building is worth a visit in itself, and there's a rooftop restaurant as well, with great views to downtown.

Jacaranda
ART GALLERY

(Map p46; ☑ 4644050; www.facebook.com/Jacarandalmages; 18 Omar bin al-Khattab St) One of Amman's leading contemporary-art galleries, Jacaranda holds regular exhibitions of excellent regional artists, and is particularly strong in its print and photographic offerings.

Bawabet al-Sharq
HANDICRAFTS

(Map p46; ☑ 4637424; Rainbow St, downtown; ⊗ 9am-7pm) The 'Gate of the Orient' has locally made (some on site) home decor items tending towards the kitsch. Sales benefit several Jordanian women's groups.

Al-Alaydi Jordan Craft Centre
HANDICRAFTS

(Map p52; ☑ tel/fax 4644555; Jebel Amman; ⊗ 9am-6pm Sat-Thu) Spread over several floors, just off Al-Kulliyah al-Islamiyah St, this vast showroom includes jewellery, Hebron glassware, Palestinian embroidery, kilims, wood carvings, old kitchen implements and Bedouin tent accessories.

Al-Burgan
HANDICRAFTS

(Map p52; ☑ 4652585; www.alburgan.com; 12 Tala't Harb St, Jebel Amman; ⊗ 9.30am-6.30pm Sat-Thu) Al-Burgan has a small but good selection of handicraft, but the staff is knowledgeable and prices are reasonable. It's behind Jordan InterContinental Hotel.

Oriental Souvenirs Store
SOUVENIRS

(Map p52; ☑ 4642820; 3rd Circle, Jebel Amman; ⊗ 8am-7pm Sat-Thu) This friendly, family-run store is more rustic than many others, but it's something of an Aladdin's Cave.

Artisana
SOUVENIRS

(Map p52; ☑ tel/fax 4647858; Mansour Kraishan St, Jebel Amman; ⊗ 9.30am-6pm Sat-Thu) This excellent small showroom has a wide range that includes scarves, bottles of holy water from the Jordan River and spooky reproductions of the famous 6000-year-old statues from Ain Ghazal.

Beit al-Bawadi
CERAMICS

(☑ 5930070; www.beitalbawadi.com; Fawzi al-Qawuqji St, Jebel Amman; ⊗ 9am-6pm Sat-Thu) Quality ceramics bought here support local artisans, whom you can see working in the basement. Designs are both traditional and modern, some decorated with Arabic calligraphy, and pieces cost around JD50 to JD80.

Silsal Ceramics
CERAMICS

(☑ 5931128; Innabeh St, North Abdoun; ⊗ 9am-6pm Sat-Thu) Has a small showroom of superb modern pottery. If you're coming along Zahran St from 5th Circle, it's the third small street on the right.

ℹ Information

EMERGENCY

Tourist Police (Map p52; ☑ 4603360, ext 254; Ministry of Tourism & Antiquities, ground fl, Al-Mutanabbi St, Jebel Amman; ⊗ 8am-9pm) As well as this office, there is a small tourist-police booth (Map p46; Hashemi St) near the Roman Theatre.

INTERNET ACCESS

Amman has plenty of internet cafes, particularly in downtown, and wi-fi is increasingly widespread in cafes and coffeeshops.

AMMAN INFORMATION

ℹ CROSSING THE STREET IN AMMAN

When you first arrive in Amman, one of your greatest challenges is likely to be making it safely to the other side of the street. This is especially true of the downtown area, although the faster-moving thoroughfares elsewhere also pose a serious hazard to your health. Contrary to what you may think, Amman's drivers have no desire to run you over; they just want to get to their destination as quickly as possible.

The installation of more traffic lights has made the situation a little easier, but you'll still have a better chance of survival if you follow a few simple 'rules'. In slow-moving traffic, the name of the game is brinkmanship – whoever yields last will win. A car missing you by inches may scare the hell out of you but is actually a normal and precisely calculated course of events.

Cross wide roads a lane at a time – if you wait for a big gap you'll be there all day. Some unscrupulous travellers have even been known to hail a taxi so that it will block traffic and give them a lane's head start. Make your decision and then don't hesitate – Amman's drivers will make their decisions based on a reasonable assumption of what you'll do next.

Above all, have patience; an extra minute's wait is infinitely preferable to a nasty accident. And if all else fails, put your pride behind you and ask some old lady to lead you by the hand – or at least follow in her slipstream.

Internet Yard (Map p46; ☑ 5509569; dweib@
joinnet.com.jo; Al-Amir Mohammed St, downtown; per hr JD1; ☺ 9.30am-midnight)

Meeranet (Map p59; ☑ 5695956; Ilya Abu
Madhi St, Shmeisani; per hr JD2; ☺ 24hr)

Welcome Internet (Map p46; ☑ 4620206;
Al-Amir Mohammed St, downtown; per hr JD1;
☺ 10.30am-1am)

MEDIA

The **BeAmman** (www.beamman.com) listings
website is a great guide for all that's fresh and
happening in Amman.

Jordan Today is a free monthly booklet that
includes a Yellow Pages listing of embassies, airlines, travel agencies and car-rental companies
in both Amman and Aqaba, as well as restaurant
listings and news of upcoming events.

The monthly *Where to Go* includes a useful
collection of Amman restaurant menus. To track
down a copy of either, ask at one of the tourist
offices or at top-end hotels and restaurants.

The English-language *Jordan Times* and *Star*
newspapers both print entertainment listings
and useful phone numbers.

MEDICAL SERVICES

Amman has more than 20 hospitals and some
of the best medical facilities available in the
Middle East. The English-language *Jordan Times*
and *Star* list hospitals and doctors on night duty
throughout the capital. They also publish a list of
pharmacies open after-hours.

Italian Hospital (Map p46; ☑ 4777101; Italian
St, downtown)

Palestine Hospital (Map p59; ☑ 5607071;
Al-Malekah Alia St, Shmeisani)

MONEY

Changing money in Amman is quick and easy,
especially since there are dozens of banks downtown and in Jebel Amman, the two areas in which
most visitors are likely to find themselves. The
Arab Bank, Jordan Gulf Bank and the Housing
Bank for Trade & Finance are among those with
widespread ATMs for Visa and MasterCard, while
Jordan National Bank and HSBC ATMs allow you
to extract dinars from your MasterCard and are
Cirrus-compatible. The Housing Bank has an
ATM in the arrivals hall at Queen Alia International Airport after passing through customs.
Although there's a bank before immigration, it
is not always open, so make sure you have some
local currency to buy your Jordanian visa.

Many moneychangers are located along
Al-Malek Faisal St in downtown. For changing
travellers cheques, try **Sahloul Exchange Co**
(Map p46; ground fl, Aicco Bldg, Al-Malek
Faisal St, downtown; ☺ 9am-7pm Sat-Thu).
There is also **Musharbash Exchange** (Map
p52; Rainbow St),

POST

There are lots of small post offices around town
(ask your hotel for the nearest), including at the
Jordan InterContinental Hotel between 2nd and
3rd Circles in Jebel Amman, and in the Housing
Bank Centre in Shmeisani.

If you wish to send a large parcel home by post,
you must first weigh the item at the Parcel Post
Office, in an alleyway behind the central post
office in downtown (it looks more like a shop,
so look out for the weighing machine on the
counter). Then take it unwrapped to the nearby
Customs Office, diagonally opposite (look for
the sign with the word 'Customs' in English on
the crest), where a customs declaration must
be completed. Then take the parcel back to the
Parcel Post Office for packing and paying.

Central Post Office (Map p46; Al-Amir
Mohammed St, downtown; ☺ 7.30am-5pm Sat-
Thu, 8am-1.30pm Fri)

Customs Office (Map p46; Omar al-Khayyam
St, downtown; ☺ 8am-2pm Thu-Sat)

Parcel Post Office (Map p46; Omar al-
Khayyam St, downtown; ☺ 8am-3pm Mon-Thu
& Sun, to 2pm Sat)

TELEPHONE

The private telephone agencies around downtown Amman are the cheapest places for international and domestic calls.

TOURIST INFORMATION

Ministry of Tourism & Antiquities (Map p52;
☑ 4603360, ext 254; fax 4646264; ground fl,
Al-Mutanabbi St, Jebel Amman; ☺ 8am-9pm)
The most useful place for information is this
office, southwest of the 3rd Circle, which is also
the centre for the tourist police. The staff is
friendly, and speaks good English.

Wild Jordan Centre (Map p46; ☑ 4616523;
www.rscn.org.jo; Othman Bin Affan St, downtown) Provides information and bookings for
activities and accommodation in any of Jordan's nature reserves, including Dana and Wadi
Mujib. The centre is run by the Royal Society for
the Conservation of Nature (RSCN). There are
also a small crafts shop and organic cafe here.

⊕ Getting There & Away

AIR

Amman is the main arrival and departure point
for international flights, although some touch
down in Aqaba as well.

Royal Jordanian Airlines (Map p59;
☑ 5100000; www.rj.com; Al-Malekah Noor St,
Shmeisani)

BUS, MINIBUS & SERVICE TAXIS

There are two main bus and minibus stations in
Amman: the North Bus Station (serving northern destinations and sometimes referred to as

Tabarbour) and the South Bus Station (serving southern destinations and sometimes referred to as Wahadat).

In addition, there are smaller bus stations serving specific destinations such as the Dead Sea, as well as private coaches from the JETT and Trust offices.

Service taxis are generally faster, but they don't always follow fixed schedules. They depart from the same stations as the minibuses.

All departures are more frequent in the morning, and most dry up completely after sunset.

Main Public Bus Stations

Located in the northern suburbs, the **North Bus Station** (Tabarbour) offers services to the north. A taxi to this station from downtown costs from JD3. Fairly regular minibuses and service taxis leave between 7am and 6.30pm for the following destinations: Ajloun (JD1, every 30 minutes, two hours), Jerash (900 fils, hourly, 1¼ hours) and Madaba (800 fils, every 10 minutes from 6am to 8pm, 45 minutes). Services are also available

to Deir Alla (for Pella, one hour), Fuheis (45 minutes), Irbid (two hours), Ramtha (two hours), Salt (45 minutes) and Zarqa (for Azraq, 30 minutes); all these services cost under JD1.

From the North Bus Station, **Hijazi Travel & Tours** (☏ 02-7240721) runs daily buses to Irbid (JD2, every 15 to 20 minutes from 6am to 7pm, 1½ hours).

There's also a daily airport bus (JD3, every 30 minutes from 6.15am to midnight, 45 minutes).

Almost all buses and service taxis heading south leave from **South Bus Station** (Wahadat) in the southern suburbs by Middle East Circle (Duwaar Sharq al-Awsat). A taxi to this station from downtown costs from JD2.500.

For Petra, minibuses and service taxis (JD5, four hours) depart for Wadi Musa when full from the far corner of the lot between about 7am and 4pm (but travel early in the day where possible). Buses to Aqaba (JD5.500, five hours) leave every two hours or so until 9pm. There are regular buses to Karak (JD1.650, two hours) until 5pm, Shobak (JD4, 2½ hours) and Ma'an

---

ⓘ WHEN CIRCLES ARE SQUARES

With its endless one-way streets, stairways, narrow lanes and jebels, Amman is confusing enough to get around anyway, but the ambiguous names for the streets and circles would challenge the navigational skills of even the most experienced explorer. We try to use the more common names on maps and in the text, but if street signs (handily written in English as well as Arabic), directions given by locals and queries from taxi drivers are still confusing, refer to the list below.

Don't forget that Al-Malek means King, so King Faisal St is sometimes labelled Al-Malek Faisal St. Similarly, Al-Malekah is Queen and Al-Emir (Al-Amir) is Prince. And don't be too surprised that some 'circles' *(duwaar)* are now called 'squares' *(maidan)*...

Circles

➡ 1st Circle – Maidan al-Malek Abdullah

➡ 2nd Circle – Maidan Wasfi al-Tal

➡ 3rd Circle – Maidan al-Malek Talal

➡ 4th Circle – Maidan al-Emir Gazi bin Mohammed

➡ 5th Circle – Maidan al-Emir Faisal bin Hussein

➡ 6th Circle – Maidan al-Emir Rashid bin al-Hassan

➡ 7th Circle – Maidan al-Emir Talal bin Mohammed

➡ Weibdeh Circle – Duwaar al-Baris (Paris Circle)

➡ Ministry of the Interior Circle – Maidan Jamal Abdul Nasser

➡ Sports City Circle – Maidan al-Medina al-Riyadiyah

Streets

➡ Rainbow St – Abu Bakr as-Siddiq St

➡ Zahran St – Al-Kulliyah al-Islamiyah St

➡ Mango St – Omar bin al-Khattab St

➡ Saqf Sayl St – Quraysh St

➡ Police St – Suleiman al-Nabulsi St

(JD2.750, three hours). Most services stop running around 4pm.

For Dana there are three buses a day from 11am for Qadsiyya (JD3, three hours); otherwise take a bus to Tafila (JD2.750, 2½ hours) and change.

There are semiregular service taxis to Karak (JD3, 2½ hours), Ma'an (JD6, three hours) and also infrequently to Aqaba (JD10, five hours).

Other Public Bus Stations

Abdali Bus Station (Map p52; Al-Malek al-Hussein St, Jebel Amman) This station is a 20-minute walk (2km uphill) from downtown; service taxi 6 or 7 from Cinema al-Hussein St goes right by. This is the station to use for air-conditioned buses and service taxis for international destinations. The bus station is transformed into a giant flea market on Fridays and there are plans to redevelop the entire site as part of an ambitious urban-regeneration project.

Muhajireen Bus Station (Map p52; Al-Ameerah Basma bin Talal St) This small station is opposite the Muhajireen police station. Minibuses to Wadi as-Seer leave frequently from here during daylight hours. There are also services to Madaba and Mt Nebo (500 fils, 45 minutes) between 6am and 5pm.

Minibuses for the Dead Sea leave from here. There are no direct services: the route involves a minibus to Shuneh al-Janubiyyeh (South Shuna, JD1, 45 minutes) and then a wait for another minibus to Suweimeh. At Suweimeh, you'll have to hire a taxi or hitch for the last stretch. It has to be said that few will want to attempt this route, which is unreliable and can leave you stranded in the Jordan Valley. It's better to take a taxi or a tour straight to the Dead Sea from one of the downtown hotels in Amman (or the Black Iris Hotel or Mariam Hotel in Madaba).

Raghadan Bus Station In downtown Amman a few minutes' walk east of the Roman Theatre, this station is mainly used for service taxis to surrounding suburbs, although there is talk of widening the network with minibuses to nearby towns.

Private Coach Stations

The domestic **JETT office** (Map p59; ☑5664146; www.jett.com.jo; Al-Malek al-Hussein St, Shmeisani) is about 500m northwest of the Abdali bus station. Passengers board the bus outside the office. There are six buses daily to Aqaba (JD7.500, five hours, 7am, 9am, 11am, 2pm, 4pm and 6pm), and one bus to King Hussein Bridge (JD7.250, one hour, 7am), for entry into Israel and the Palestinian Territories. There are daily services to Irbid (JD1.900, every 30 minutes from 6am to 7.30pm, two hours).

A daily JETT bus connects Amman with Petra, largely designed for those wanting to visit on a day trip. The service leaves at 6.30am (single/ return JD9.500/19, four hours) and drops passengers off at Petra Visitor Centre in Wadi Musa at 9.30am. The return bus leaves between 4pm and 5pm, so bear in mind this option leaves very little time for visiting the sites of Petra.

A weekly Jett bus departs for Amman Beach at the Dead Sea (single JD8) on Fridays at 8am and returns at 4pm. If there are insufficient passengers, however, the service is cancelled.

CAR

There are many car-rental agencies to choose from in King Abdullah Gardens, where there is a collection of around 50 car-rental companies.

ℹ TAKING A TAXI IN AMMAN

Only the brave or the foolhardy would sit behind the wheel in Amman, where driving is complicated by extremely complex roads twisting around the contours of the city's many hills, and is further made miserable by dense, unpredictable traffic. Buses are slow and unreliable and you need to be in the right place at the right time to rely on a service taxi. Without doubt, therefore, the best way of getting around is to do what the locals do and hop in a cab.

Most drivers of private taxis use the meter as a matter of course, but some may refuse to do so – or may simply refuse the ride. This is not necessarily indicative of an intention to overcharge: meter charges are set by the government and often don't reflect the realities of petrol price rises and the unprofitable business of waiting in long traffic queues, especially in congested downtown traffic.

If you're in town for a couple of days, it's well worth identifying a taxi driver who speaks English and who is used to working with tourists. These gear-stick warriors of the city have knowledge to rival a London cabby, knowing every shortcut and unusual attraction in town and ensuring you don't get stuck for hours in a queue. They'll drop you off and pick you up at the time of your choice and if they're on another fare when you call, they'll often send a reliable friend. Many of these drivers are willing and able to take visitors on longer trips around Amman, to Jerash, the Dead Sea or the desert castles. If you find a driver you like, grab his number, or ask at your hotel for a recommendation.

ℹ️ SERVICE TAXI ROUTES

Service taxi 1 From Basman St for 4th Circle.

Service taxi 2 From Basman St for 1st and 2nd Circles.

Service taxi 3 From Basman St for 3rd and 4th Circles.

Service taxi 4 From the side street near the central post office for Jebel Weibdeh.

Service taxi 6 From Cinema al-Hussein St for the Ministry of the Interior Circle, past Abdali station and JETT international and domestic offices.

Service taxi 7 From Cinema al-Hussein St, up Al-Malek al-Hussein St, past Abdali station and King Abdullah Mosque, and along Suleiman al-Nabulsi St for Shmeisani.

Service taxis 25 & 26 From Italian St, downtown, to the top of Jebel al-Ashrafiyeh and near Abu Darwish Mosque.

Service taxi 27 From Italian St to Middle East Circle for Wahadat station.

Service taxi 35 From opposite the Amman Palace Hotel, passing close to the Muhajireen Police Station.

Service taxi 38 From downtown to Makkah al-Mukarramah Rd.

Avis (Map p59; ☑ 06-5699420, 24hr 777 397405; www.avis.com.jo; King Abdullah Gardens, Amman) Offices at King Hussein Bridge and Aqaba; branches at the airport, Le Royal Hotel and Jordan InterContinental Hotel in Amman. The biggest car-hire company in Jordan.

Budget (Map p59; ☑ 06-5698131; www.budget. com; 125 Abdul Hameed Sharaf St, Amman)

Europcar (Map p59; ☑ 06-5655581; www. europcar.middleeast.com; Isam Al-Ajlouni St, Amman) Branches at Radisson SAS, King Abdullah Gardens and in Aqaba.

Firas Car Rental (Map p52; ☑ 4612927; 1st Circle, Jebel Amman) The agent for Alamo Car Rental.

Hertz (Map p59; ☑ 06-5920926; www.hertz. com; King Abdullah Gardens, Amman) Offices at the airport, Grand Hyatt Amman, Sheraton and in Aqaba.

National Car Rental (Map p59; ☑ 24hr 5591731; www.1stjordan.net/national; Le Meridien, Amman) Also has offices at Amman Marriott and Sheraton hotels.

Reliable Rent-a-Car (☑ 06-5929676; www. rentareliablecar.com; 19 Fawzi al-Qawuqji St, Amman)

ℹ️ Getting Around

TO/FROM THE AIRPORTS

Queen Alia International Airport (p319) is 35km south of the city. The **Airport Express Bus** (☑ 4451531, 0880 022006) runs between the airport and the North Bus Station (Tabarbour), passing through the 4th, 5th, 6th and 7th Circles en route. This service runs hourly between 7am and 11pm, and at 1am and 3am, from the airport daily. From Amman, it runs from 6am to 10pm hourly and at 2am and 4am.

Sariyah buses (JD3, 45 minutes) run every 30 minutes between 6.15am and midnight. From the airport, buses depart from outside the arrivals hall of Terminal 2. Buy your ticket from the booth at the door.

There are branches of Avis and Hertz and other car-rental companies. Those that don't have an office at the airport will meet you at the airport or otherwise will arrange for you to pick up a car from there.

The quickest and easiest way to reach the airport is by private taxi (JD20 to JD25 from downtown).

To get to Marka Airport, take a service taxi for 200 fils from Raghadan station.

TAXI
Private Taxi

Private taxis are painted yellow. They are abundant, can be flagged from the side of the road and have cheap fares. A taxi from downtown to Shmeisani, for example, costs JD2.500 and it's JD3 to Tabarbour. For longer journeys around town, you're best off agreeing a price per hour (JD10 was the current going rate at the time of writing).

Service Taxi

These white cabs are shared taxis that stick to specific routes and are not permitted to leave the city limits. Fares cost from 400 fils per seat, and you usually pay the full amount regardless of where you get off. After 8pm, the price for all service taxis goes up by 25%.

There can be long queues at rush hour (8am to 9am and 5pm to 6pm). The cars queue up and usually start at the bottom of a hill – you get into the last car and unusually the whole line rolls back a car space and so on.

AROUND AMMAN

With the exception of downtown, uncovering remnants of the ancients is no easy task in Amman as the capital is largely a 20th-century creation. However, you don't have to look far beyond the city limits for historical reminders of the country's illustrious past. Indeed, the outskirts of the capital are home to Roman ruins, biblical landmarks, Byzantine churches and Ottoman structures, all of which are set against beautiful landscapes that are a world apart from the streets of Amman. Most destinations can be reached on a half-day trip from Amman.

Wadi as-Seer & Iraq al-Amir

وادي السير & عراق الأمير

West of the capital lies the fertile Wadi as-Seer, standing in marked contrast to the treeless plateau surrounding Amman. The stream-fed valley is lined with cypress trees, and dotted with fragrant orchards and olive groves. In the springtime, particularly April and May, as-Seer plays host to spectacular wildflower blooms that include the Jordanian national flower, the black iris.

The village itself, which is largely Circassian in origin, is now virtually part of sprawling western Amman. However, there still remains a sense of distinct community, especially in the Ottoman stone buildings and mosque that lie at the centre of the village. The main attractions of the area, however, lie further down the wadi.

About 4km past Wadi as-Seer, on the road to the village of Iraq al-Amir, you can spot part of an ancient **Roman aqueduct**. Shortly past the aqueduct, look up to the hillside on the left to a facade cut into the rock. Known as **Ad-Deir**, it most likely served as an elaborate medieval dovecote.

If you continue for a further 6km, you'll come to the caves of **Iraq al-Amir** (Caves of the Prince). The caves are arranged in two tiers – the upper tier forms a long gallery (partially damaged during a mild earthquake in 1999) along the cliff face. The 11 caves were once used as cavalry stables, though locals have taken to using them to house their goats and store fodder. Steps lead up to the caves from the paved road – keep an eye out for the ancient Hebrew inscription near the entrance.

Opposite the caves is the village of Iraq al-Amir, home to the **Iraq al-Amir Handicraft Village** (⊙8am-4pm Sat-Thu), selling handmade pottery, fabrics, carpets and paper products. The project was founded by the Noor al-Hussein Foundation, and employs many women from the surrounding area. Profits are returned to the community.

About 700m further down the road, just visible from the caves, is the small but impressive **Qasr al-Abad** (Palace of the Slave; ⊙daylight) **FREE**. Despite appearances and indeed its name, it was most likely built as a fortified villa rather than a military fort. Its precise age isn't known, though it's thought that it was built by Hyrcanus of the powerful Jewish Tobiad family sometime between 187 and 175 BC. Although never completed, much of the palace has been reconstructed, and it remains an impressive site.

The palace was built from some of the biggest blocks of any ancient structure in the Middle East – the largest is 7m by 3m. The blocks were only 20cm or so thick, making the whole edifice quite flimsy, and susceptible to the earthquake that flattened it in AD 362. Today, the setting and the animal carvings on the exterior walls are the highlights. Look for the carved panther fountain on the ground floor, the eroded eagles on the corners and the lioness with cubs on the upper storey of the back side.

The gatekeeper will open the interior, as well as a small museum (which includes drawings of what the complex once looked like) for a tip of JD1. If he's not around, ask for the *miftah* (key) at the small shop near the gate.

ℹ Getting There & Away

Minibuses leave regularly from the Muhajireen bus station (p70) for Wadi as-Seer village (300 fils, 30 minutes) and less frequently from the Raghadan bus station (p70) in downtown. From Wadi as-Seer, take another minibus – or walk about 10km, mostly downhill – to the caves. Look for the signpost to the Iraq al-Amir Handicraft Village, which is virtually opposite the stairs to the caves. Alternatively take bus 26 from Shabsough St in downtown to its terminus and then change to a bus for Wadi as-Seer or take a taxi. From the caves, it's an easy stroll down to the *qasr* (but a little steep back up).

If you're driving, head west from 8th Circle and follow the main road, which twists through Wadi as-Seer village.

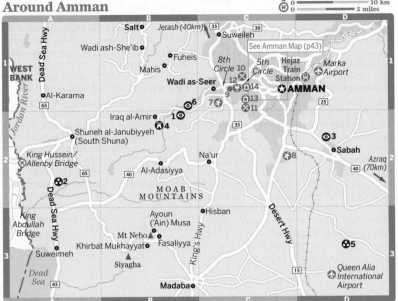

Cave of Seven Sleepers (Ahl al-Kahf) أهل الكهف

The legend of the 'seven sleepers' has several parallels throughout literature. It involves seven Christian boys who were persecuted by the Roman Emperor Trajan, then escaped to a cave and slept there for 309 years. This is one of several locations (the most famous being Ephesus in Turkey) that claim to be that cave. Inside the **main cave** (Ahl al-Kahf; ⊘8am-6pm) **FREE** – also known as Ahl al-Kahf (Cave of the People) – are eight smaller tombs that are sealed, though one has a hole in it, through which you can see a creepy collection of human bones. Above and below the cave are the remains of two mosques. About 500m west of the cave is a large **Byzantine cemetery**, the tombs of which are sadly full of rubbish.

The cave is to the right of a large new mosque complex in the village of Rajib, off the road from Amman to Sabah. Buses from Amman to Sabah pass 500m from the mosque; catch them at South bus station (p69); the journey costs less than 500 fils and takes 15 minutes. Alternatively, take a minibus from Quraysh St in downtown, ask for 'al-Kahf' and the driver will show you where to get off to change for a Sabah bus. The easiest way there is by chartered taxi (around JD8 each way).

Around Amman

Fuheis

فحيص

🎵 06 / POP <5000 / ELEV 1050M

Just 15km northwest of Amman, this pleasant village is famous for fruit growing and, somewhat incongruously, cement production. First built in about 2000 BC, Fuheis is now a largely Christian village, with several Orthodox and Catholic churches. The main reason for a visit, however, is to have lunch or dinner in the town's celebrated restaurant.

The Jordanian cuisine at the **Zuwwadeh Restaurant** (📞 4721528; mains JD6-14; ⏰ 10am-midnight) is delicious, especially the *fatteh* (fried bread with hummus, meat or chicken and pine nuts) – the 'wedding *fatteh*' is complemented by tomato and cardamom. You can choose between shady outdoor tables or an intimate indoor dining area, and most nights there are live oud performances upstairs (after 7pm). Highly popular with locals and discerning expats from Amman, the ambience is lively and warm, helped much by the jovial, attentive staff. Alcohol is served.

ℹ Getting There & Away

Fuheis is easy to reach by minibus from Abdali bus station (p70) in Amman (500 fils, 40 minutes). The town is also connected to Wadi as-Seer, making it possible to visit both destinations as a day trip from Amman. If you're dining at the restaurant, it's best to pre-arrange a chartered taxi back to Amman for around JD12.

The minibus stop in the older Al-Rawaq neighbourhood (also known as *il-balad*) is at a roundabout, close to the Zuwwadeh Restaurant and marked by a statue of St George (known locally as Giorgis) slaying a dragon.

Jerash, Irbid & the Jordan Valley
جرش & إربد & الشمال

Best Places to Stay

➡ Hadrian Gate Hotel (p84)

➡ Olive Branch Resort (p84)

➡ Biscuit House Bed & Breakfast (p90)

➡ Qalet al-Jabal Hotel (p88)

Best Places to Eat

➡ Lebanese House (p85)

➡ Umm Qais Resthouse (p98)

➡ Bethany Touristic Restaurant (p105)

Why Go?
The far north of Jordan is frequently eschewed by visitors, in favour of Petra's grandeur and the splashy attractions of the Dead and Red Seas. However, this is a region rich in ancient ruins and biblical associations, all set in rolling countryside that's ablaze with wildflowers in springtime.

The epic Roman city of Jerash is the north's big hitter, a world-class destination without the crowds. Its contemporary, Umm Qais, is smaller but offers views of three countries from its ruins. At Bethany, you can visit the spot on the River Jordan where Christ was said to have been baptised, while Jordan's Islamic history is well-represented by the castle of Qala'at ar-Rabad, perched atop an imposing hill, and the well-preserved Ottoman trading town of Salt. If all this history feels like too much, you can easily get away from it all on the hiking trails of the Ajloun and Dibeen forest reserves.

When to Go

➡ The natural time to visit the northern part of Jordan is in spring (March to mid-May) when the black iris, the country's national flower, puts in a shy appearance along roadsides and a profusion of knee-high wildflowers spill across the semi-arid hillsides.

➡ For culture vultures, the hot summer months of July and August bring music and poetry to the Roman ruins in the Jerash Festival of Culture & the Arts.

➡ From early November to January, sub-tropical fruits ripen in the Jordan Valley while the region's hill towns shiver through winter.

Jerash, Irbid & the Jordan Valley Highlights

❶ Wander the colonnaded streets of **Jerash** (p79), a spectacularly well-preserved Roman provincial city.

❷ Hike along the trails of **Ajloun Forest Reserve** (p88) in the shade of trees.

❸ Visit the fairy-tale castle of **Qala'at ar-Rabad** (p87), one of Jordan's most impressive Islamic structures.

❹ Survey views of three countries from the basalt ruins of **Umm Qais** (p96).

❺ Discover the richness of Jordan's flora at the **Royal Botanic Garden** (p86).

❻ Peruse the exhibits at the **Museum of Archaeology & Anthropology** (p91), within the vibrant campus of Yarmouk University in Irbid.

❼ Travel the subtropical **Jordan Valley** (p94), sampling seasonal fruits.

❽ Scoop water from the River Jordan at **Bethany** (p103), where Jesus was reputedly baptised.

❾ Amble by traditional houses in the souq town of **Salt** (p101) and discover how the town came by its name.

History

When travelling around the far north of Jordan, you may notice the name 'Gilead' crop up from time to time. This was the region's name in biblical times, defined by the sculpting waters of the Yarmouk River to the north and the once mighty River Jordan to the west. The hills of Gilead have been occupied since antiquity, and were home to the Roman Decapolis. Largely established during the Hellenistic period, these 10 city-states flourished along the boundaries of the Greek and Semitic lands. The Romans transformed these cities into powerful trading centres – the torchbearers of Roman culture at the furthest reaches of the empire.

If you're wondering where these cities are today, chances are you are walking on them! Northern Jordan is the most densely populated area in the country, and is home to the major urban centre of Irbid as well as dozens of small towns and villages which have largely engulfed many of the ancient sites. With a bit of amateur investigation it's easy to make out the ancient tells (mounds) and archaeological remains of the Decapolis, scattered among Gilead's rolling hills. If you haven't the time or inclination for such sleuthing, just head for Umm Qais (Gadara), Pella and most especially Jerash, where there are enough clues among the standing columns, amphitheatres and mosaic floors to conjure the full pomp and splendour of the Roman past.

Nature Reserves

There are two reserves in the north of Jordan, both encompassing rare woodland. Ajloun Forest Reserve (p88) is the more developed of the two, with excellent hiking trails and accommodation options. The Dibeen Forest Reserve (p86) is a popular spot for weekend picnics. Not strictly a nature reserve, but worth checking out, is the soon-to-be-opened Royal Botanic Garden (p86) at Rumman.

Dangers & Annoyances

This region is bordered by Israel and the Palestinian Territories to the west and by Syria to the north. Given the sensitivity of relations between these countries, a bit of discretion is advised when travelling near the Yarmouk or Jordan Valleys. There are many checkpoints, particularly around the convergence of those two valleys near Umm Qais, so it is imperative to carry your passport and, if driving, your licence and car-rental details. Don't hike too close to either border. Avoid taking photographs near the border area – this includes photographing the River Jordan near checkpoints.

ⓘ Getting There & Away

Amman is the gateway to the north so most public transport from other regions transits through the capital, though there are connections from Madaba and Aqaba directly to Irbid. There are four international borders in the north with public transport to Israel and the Palestinian Territories. It was once also possible to cross directly into Syria, but the conflict there has long closed this option. By car, you can enter the region either via Jerash from Amman or along the Jordan Valley from the Dead Sea.

ⓘ Getting Around

Compared with other parts of Jordan, the north is well-served by public transport. Minibuses link most towns and villages (and the main city of Irbid), and run at irregular intervals along the Jordan Valley. A bit of patience is required waiting for buses to fill up and forget trying to establish the 'correct fare'; that said, no journey in the north is likely to cost more than JD1. Driving in this region is very rewarding, but requires a few navigational skills as promising rural roads often lead to dead ends due to steep-sided wadis.

JERASH & AROUND

Often referred to as the 'Pompeii of Asia', the ruins at Jerash (known in Roman times as Gerasa) are one of Jordan's major attractions, and one of the Middle East's best examples of a Roman provincial city. Remarkably well preserved through the centuries by the dry desert air, Jerash comprises a collection of triumphal arches, two amphitheatres, a hippodrome where live chariot races are conducted each day, temples and a spectacular colonnaded forum. Whether you're an aspiring archaeologist, an admirer of the ancients or simply a visitor looking for a morning's diversion, the ruins at Jerash cannot fail to impress.

Although the ruins are the undoubted key attraction in the area, there is more to Jerash (which also comprises a thriving modern town) and the surrounding area than just the ruins. Nearby Ajloun, for instance, has a grand castle and offers hiking trails, picnic opportunities and lots of places to buy fresh fruit from the surrounding hillside

orchards. As such, although Jerash is usually visited as a day trip from Amman, there's more than enough of interest in the area to warrant at least one overnight stop.

Jerash   جرش

📍 02 / POP 123,190 / ELEV 618M

Arriving in the modern town of Jerash today, with its provincial streets and small market gardens, there's little to suggest its illustrious past. But the moment you cross from the new town into the ancient city boundaries, marked by the imposing Hadrian's Arch, it becomes immediately apparent that this was once no ordinary backwater but a city of great wealth and importance. And how did Jerash, which was never on a major trade route, come to be so important? The answer lies in the soil. Whatever route you take to reach the town, and at whatever time of year, you will pass the ubiquitous fruit stalls that characterise the area. Figs, apples, plums, berries, and most especially olives all grow prodigiously in the surrounding hillsides, and the surplus of crops helps the local farming communities to prosper just as in ancient times.

Jerash is cleaved in two by a deep and cultivated wadi. Today, as in the days of the Romans, the bulk of the town's inhabitants live on the eastern side of the wadi. The walled city on the west side of the wadi, graced with grand public monuments, baths and fountains, was reserved for administrative, commercial, civic and religious activities. The two were once linked by causeways and processional paths, and magnificent gates marked the entrance. Access to the remains of this walled city today is through the most southerly gate, known as Hadrian's Gate or the Arch of Triumph.

While there are certainly other surviving Roman cities that boast similar architectural treasures, the ancient ruins at Jerash are famous for their remarkable state of preservation. Enough structures remain intact for archaeologists and historians, and even the casual visitor, to piece together ancient life under the rule of an emperor.

History

Although inhabited from Neolithic times, and settled as a town during the reign of Alexander the Great (333 BC), Jerash was largely a Roman creation and well-preserved remains of all the classic

Jerash

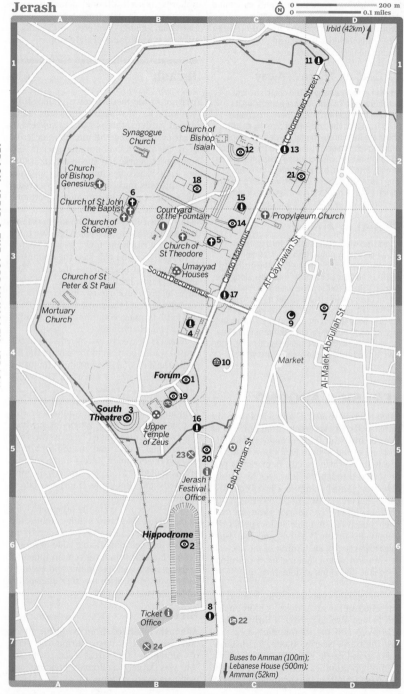

0   200 m
0   0.1 miles

Irbid (42km)

11

(Colonnaded Street)

Church of Bishop Isaiah

Synagogue Church

12

13

21

Church of Bishop Genesius

18

Church of St John the Baptist

6

15

Courtyard of the Fountain

Propylaeum Church

Church of St George

14

Church of St Theodore

5

Cardo Maximus

Church of St Peter & St Paul

Umayyad Houses

South Decumanus

Al-Qayrawan St

9

7

Mortuary Church

17

Al-Malek Abdullah St

4

10

Market

Forum

1

19

South Theatre

3

Upper Temple of Zeus

16

Bab Amman St

23

20

Jerash Festival Office

Hippodrome

2

Ticket Office

8

22

24

Buses to Amman (100m);
Lebanese House (500m);
Amman (52km)

Jerash

Roman structures – forum, cardo maximus, hippodrome, nymphaeum – are easily distinguishable among the ruins.

Following General Pompey's conquest of the region in 64 BC, Gerasa became part of the Roman province of Syria, and then a city of the Decapolis. Over the next two centuries, trade with the Nabataeans (of Petra fame) flourished, and the city grew extremely wealthy, thanks to local agriculture and iron-ore mining. In the 1st century AD the city was remodelled on the grid system with a colonnaded main north–south street (the cardo maximus – one of the great highlights of the site today) intersected by two side streets running east–west.

The city was further enhanced in AD 106, under Emperor Trajan, and the triumphal arch at the far southern end of the city (through which the site is accessed today) was constructed in AD 129 to mark the important occasion of Emperor Hadrian's visit. Jerash's fortunes peaked around the beginning of the 3rd century, when it was bestowed with the rank of Colony and boasted a population of 15,000 to 20,000 inhabitants.

The city declined with a devastating earthquake in 747 and its population shrank to about one-quarter of its former size. Thereafter, apart from a brief occupation by a Crusader garrison in the 12th century, the city was completely deserted until the arrival of the Circassians from Russia in 1878. The site's archaeological importance was quickly realised, heralding over a century of excavation and restoration and the revival of a new town on the eastern flank of the ruins.

⊙ Sights

The Jerash **ruins** (admission JD8; ⊙8am-4.30pm Oct-Apr, to 7pm May-Sep) cover a huge area and can seem daunting at first, especially as there is virtually no signage. To help the ruins come alive, engage one of the knowledgable guides (JD20) at the ticket checkpoint to help you navigate the main complex. The whole route, walking at a leisurely pace and allowing time for sitting on a fallen column and enjoying the spectacular views, takes a minimum of three to four hours; there are, however, a couple of opportunities to cut the visit short. The theatre is a 10-minute walk back to Hadrian's Arch, while the Temple of Artemis is a 20-minute walk back. In the hot months, start your visit as early as possible in the morning, as there's little shade at the site.

The entrance to the site is south of the ancient city, close to Hadrian's Arch. The **ticket office** (☏6351272) is in a modern souq with souvenir and antique shops, a post office and a semi-traditional coffeehouse. Keep your ticket as you will have to show it at the South Gate.

Hadrian's Arch   MONUMENT
There's no better way of gaining a sense of the pomp and splendour of Rome than walking through the triumphal, 13m-tall Hadrian's Arch at the entrance to Jerash, built to honour the visiting emperor. From here you can see a honey-coloured assortment of columns and walls, some delicately carved with acanthus leaves, some solid and practical, extending all the way to a pale view of hills in the distance – just as the Roman architects intended.

The gateway was originally twice this height and encompassed three enormous wooden doors.

★ Hippodrome
STADIUM

Built sometime between the 1st and 3rd centuries AD, this ancient sports field (244m by 50m) was once surrounded by seating for up to 15,000 spectators, 30 times the current seating capacity, and hosted mainly athletics competitions and chariot races at Jerash. Recent excavations have unearthed remains of stables and pottery workshops, plus indications that it was used for polo by invading Sassanians from Persia during the early 7th century. The stadium currently hosts twice-daily re-enactment shows (p81).

The show, a joint Swedish-Jordanian venture, has become one of the highlights of a modern visit to the ancient city and is simply too good to miss. It begins with the parading of 40 Roman legionnaires (Jordanian special forces) who complete a range of military drills, from the tortoise manoeuvre to the use of a catapult, and is followed by gladiators fighting it out with tridents, nets and *gladius* (swords) and four chariots racing seven laps around the hippodrome's central wooden *spina*.

South Gate
MONUMENT

Two hundred metres north of the Hippodrome in Jerash is the South Gate, which was most likely constructed in AD 130 and originally served as one of four entrances along the city walls. Along the way you can see how the Roman city, then as now, spilt over both sides of Wadi Jerash, with most of the residential area lying east of the wadi. The visitor's centre is on the right before the gate and is the place to hire a guide.

One square kilometre of the city is encased by the 3m-thick, 3.5km-long boundary walls. Don't forget to look up as you pass under the South Gate: like Hadrian's Arch, the columns bear elaborately carved acanthus-leaf decorations and would once have supported three wooden doors. Framed by the archway is the first hint of the splendours ahead – the columns of the forum start appearing in ever greater profusion as you walk towards them.

Vaulted Gallery
MUSEUM

The vaulted passageway, under the courtyard of the Temple of Zeus, is a good starting point in Jerash's ancient city. When your eyes become accustomed to the gloom, you'll see a superb display of columns, pediments and masonry carved with grapes, pomegranates and acanthus leaves. This is a good place to brush up on the three main column styles: Doric, Ionic and Corinthian.

It is the gallery here that's worth seeing: the legacy of Rome has endured because of the 'built to last' quality of each structure. Take a look at the model of the Temple of Zeus as it will help to recreate the ruins in your mind later.

★ Forum
ROMAN PLAZA

Whatever the light and whatever the weather, the forum, with its organ-pipe columns arranged around an unusual oval-shaped plaza, is always breathtaking and is one of Jerash's undisputed highlights. This immense space (90m long and 80m at its widest point) lies in the heart of the city, linking the main thoroughfare (the cardo maximus) with the Temple of Zeus. It served as a marketplace and the main locus of the city's social and political life.

Today it still draws the crowds, with Jordanian families picnicking and site guards napping among the columns. And what superb columns they are! Constructed in the middle of the 1st century AD, the forum is surrounded by 56 unfluted Ionic columns, each constructed from four solid cuts of stone that appear double in number because of their shadow. The plaza itself is just as spectacular, paved with extremely high-quality limestone slabs. The slabs, which increase in size as they radiate from the middle, create a sense of vortex that draws your eye to the centre point. To appreciate this effect fully you need an aerial view, which can be gained from climbing the steps to the Temple of Zeus.

Temple of Zeus
TEMPLE

Built in AD 162 over the remains of an earlier Roman temple, the Temple of Zeus in Jerash was once approached by a magnificent monumental stairway, leading from the temenos (sacred courtyard). Today, lizards sun themselves in the cracks of pavement, oblivious of the holy sacrifices that used to take place here. The temple, on the summit of the hill, towers above the city. Enough of this once beautiful building remains, despite erosion and earthquakes, to understand its former importance.

A path leads from the temenos to the temple, via a welcome stand of trees. You can pause here for a panorama of the forum

SALUTE THE TROOPS AT JERASH'S CHARIOT RACE

Have you ever considered how and why Rome managed to conquer the lands of the Middle East so easily? Pay a visit to the spectacular ruins at Jerash, and you may just find the answer.

The answer doesn't lie in the ruins of empire scattered around the site but in the novel re-enactment, held twice daily at the hippodrome. Bringing entertainment back to the playing field for the first time in 1500 years, the **Roman Army & Chariot Experience** (www.jerashchariots.com; admission JD12; ⊘ shows 11am & 2pm Sat-Wed, 11am Fri) is faithful to history, right down to the Latin commands.

Visitors will have a chuckle at the lively repartee of the master of ceremonies, one Adam Al-Samadi, otherwise known as Gaius Victor. Dressed as a Roman legionnaire with a feather pluming from his helmet, he stands erect like a true centurion. 'Salute the troops,' he demands in a cockney English accent as he hitches his tunic and raises a spear to the amassed veterans of the Jordan army – in their new uniform of the Sixth Roman Legion.

'These men,' Gaius says imperiously to the huddled audience on the bleachers, 'they didn't want to die in some godforsaken battlefield. They wanted to go home to their wives and mistresses in civilised Rome and draw their pensions.' That's why, he argues, the Roman soldiers were the best in the world: 'Get in, get out, stop messing about – eight minutes of fighting, then fresh men for the next eight minutes of fighting.'

A trundle of soldiers shuffles into formation and slams down gleaming shields; they advance across the arena like a gleaming, metal-plated, human tank, impervious to the lances of the leather-clad natives – if rather more vulnerable to the giggles from spectators. 'So Gaius Victor,' I ask after the show. 'What is it that makes such an erudite fellow like you do a job like this?' 'Call it bread and circuses,' he says. 'That's what kept people happy under the Romans and I guess that's what keeps us happy today.'

That sounds like a logical enough answer, but then his eyes mist over and he adds: 'You know, there's the moment in the performance when you say "Salute the troops" and watch them salute you back. To this day, it gives me a thrill that I can't explain.' Forget the disciplined armies; forget the orderly organisation of labour and provisions – local people fell under the magic of Rome. As a spare soldier blasts the horn from atop Jerash's triumphal arch, his scarlet cloak furling behind him and the flag of Jordan blowing in the wind, it's easy to see how.

Jenny Walker

and a small hill of pines, home to the site museum (p84). As you walk from the trees to the temple, notice the intricate friezes of floral and figurative motifs unearthed by French excavations. The delicacy of the design contrasts strikingly with the massive size of the building blocks that comprise the inner sanctum of the temple.

★ South Theatre   ROMAN AMPHITHEATRE
Entering the South Theatre at Jerash through a wooden door between the arches, there's little to suggest the treasure encased by the plain exterior. But then suddenly you emerge in the upper seating and you can't help but be impressed. Built between AD 81 and 96 and once housing 5000 spectators amid two storeys of seating (only one tier of which remains), the theatre is almost perfect.

Sit in Row 30 of the 32 rows of seats (if you can read the Greek numbers) and you'll see how the elaborately decorated stage is just a foreground for the backdrop of ancient and modern Jerash. At sunset, the lighting melts the stage surface. Cue music? That's provided by the visitors who whisper experimental choruses and the members of the Jordanian Scottish bagpipe band who, with less subtlety, blast sporadic tunes to the four winds to illustrate the excellent acoustics.

The theatre comes into its own during the Jerash Festival of Culture & Arts (p85) when it proves as worthy a venue today as it was to the ancients 2000 years ago.

South Decumanus   STREET
The south decumanus at Jerash once served as the Roman town's main east–west axis. At the eastern end is a modern **mosque**,

a fitting reminder of how Jordan has embraced many different religions over the years and continues to tolerate different forms of worship to this day.

But tolerance hasn't always been a given, as you'll see if you take the left fork from the street's western end up to what might be termed 'Church Hill', where a number of ancient churches lie in ruins. A path that runs between the theatre and the Temple of Artemis offers a good vantage point of the south decumanus' double colonnade stretching to the south.

Church of St Cosmos & St Damianus
CHRISTIAN

When Christianity became the official state religion under Emperor Constantine in AD 324, all Roman monuments that were tainted by so-called pagan practices were abandoned. These structures were subsequently pilfered for building materials as Roman cities competed with one another to build glorious churches and cathedrals. A total of 15 churches lie among Jerash's ruins, with the Church of St Cosmos & St Damianus (look for a complex with four bulbous columns and a thick outer wall) one of the best-preserved.

Consecrated in 533 in memory of twin brothers – both doctors, who devoted themselves to the care of the poor and the needy, and who were martyred during the reign of Diocletian – the church boasts the best-preserved mosaics at Jerash. Stand above the retaining wall and you can clearly make out zoomorphic figures, geometric designs and medical symbols. Some of the mosaics from this church are now housed in the Museum of Popular Traditions (p49) in Amman.

Continue up the hill and just before you reach the great temple in front of you, sit on the stone sarcophagus nearby and survey the view: this is one of the best vantage points in Jerash, showing the extent of the ruins from North Gate to Hadrian's Arch.

THE DECAPOLIS

The Roman commercial cities within modern Jordan, Syria and Israel and the Palestinian Territories became known collectively as the Decapolis in the 1st century AD. Despite the etymology of the word, it seems that the Decapolis consisted of more than 10 cities, and possibly as many as 18. The league of cities served to unite Roman possessions and to enhance commerce in the region. In Jordan the main Decapolis cities were Philadelphia (Amman), Gadara (Umm Qais), Gerasa (Jerash), Pella (Taqabat Fil), and possibly Abila (Qweilbeh) and Capitolias (Beit Ras, near Irbid).

Rome helped facilitate the growth of the Decapolis by granting the cities a measure of political autonomy, within the protective sphere of Rome. Each city operated more like a city-state, maintaining jurisdiction over the surrounding countryside and even minting its own coins. Indeed, coins from Decapolis cities often used words such as 'autonomous', 'free' and 'sovereign' to emphasise their self-governing status.

The cities may have enjoyed semi-autonomy but they were still recognisably Roman, rebuilt with gridded streets and well-funded public monuments. A network of Roman roads facilitated the transport of goods from one city to the next, and the wheel ruts of carriages and chariots can still be seen in the paving stones at Umm Qais and Jerash. The so-called imperial cult, which revolved around mandatory worship of the Roman emperor, helped unify the cities in the Decapolis while simultaneously ensuring that its residents didn't forget the generosity of their Roman benefactors.

Wandering the streets of the ruined cities today, it's easy to imagine life 2000 years ago: the centre bustling with shops and merchants, and lined with cooling water fountains and dramatic painted facades. The empty niches would have been filled with painted statues; buildings clad in marble and decorated with carved peacocks and shell motifs; and churches topped with Tuscan-style terracotta-tiled roofs.

The term Decapolis fell out of use when Emperor Trajan annexed Arabia in the 2nd century AD, although the sister cities continued to maintain connections with one another for another 400 years. Their eventual demise was heralded by the conquest of the Levant in 641 by the Umayyads. Political, religious and commercial interests shifted to Damascus, marginalising the cities of the Decapolis to such an extent that they never recovered.

Temple of Artemis TEMPLE

Dedicated to Artemis, the goddess of hunting and fertility and the daughter of Zeus and Leto, this temple was built between AD 150 and 170, and flanked by 12 elaborately carved Corinthian columns (11 still stand). The construction is particularly impressive given that large vaults, housing temple treasure, had to be built to the north and south to make the courtyard level. The whole of the building was once clad in marble and prized statues of Artemis would have adorned the niches.

If you're lucky enough to visit on a partially cloudy day, you're in for a treat as the sandstone pillars of the temple light up like bars of liquid gold each time the sun comes out of the clouds. It's a magical sight, and magic, or a sense of the world beyond, was exactly what the architects of this gem of a building would have been trying to capture in the temple design.

Alas, the edict of Theodorius in AD 386, permitting the dismantling of pagan temples, led to the demise of this once-grand edifice as the temple was picked apart for materials to construct new churches. The Byzantines further disgraced the site by converting it to a mere artisan workshop for kitchenware and crockery. In the 12th century the structure was temporarily brought back to life as an Arab fortification, only to be destroyed by the invading Crusaders.

If your energy is starting to flag, this is a good place to turn back. You can descend through the **propylaeum**, built in AD 150 as the monumental gateway to the Temple of Artemis, and originally flanked by shops. If you want to get a sense of the complete extent of Jerash, head towards the North Gate and be rewarded by one or two extra surprises.

North Theatre ROMAN AMPHITHEATRE

Just downhill from the Temple of Artemis is the beautiful little North Theatre. Built in about AD 165 and enlarged in 235, it was most likely used for government meetings rather than artistic performances. Originally it had 14 rows of seats with two vaulted passageways leading to the front of theatre, as well as five internal arched corridors leading to the upper rows. Many of the seats are inscribed with the names of delegates who voted in the city council.

Like many of the grand monuments at Jerash, the North Theatre was destroyed by earthquakes and then partially dismantled for later Byzantine and Umayyad building projects. However, in recent years it has been magnificently restored and still maintains a capacity of about 2000 people. The theatre may not have been used for performances but there's still plenty of rhythm in the design details, with round niches and inverted scallop shells, and exuberant carvings of musicians and dancers at the base of the stairs.

North Gate MONUMENT

Built in about AD 115, the North Gate forms an impressive full stop at the northern limit of the Jerash ruins. Commissioned by Claudius Severus, who built the road to Pella, it still makes a fine, if somewhat neglected, frame for the cardo maximus which stretches in all its glory along the entire length of the ancient walled city. If you've reached the North Gate, you deserve a pat on the back because very few visitors bother to walk this far.

The good news is it's all downhill from here on the 35-minute nonstop walk back to Hadrian's Gate; if you want to savour the many monuments on the way, however, it will take at least an hour.

Cardo Maximus STREET

Jerash's superb colonnaded cardo maximus is straight in the way that only a Roman road can be. This is one of Jerash's great highlights and the opportunity to walk along its entire 800m length from North Gate to forum well rewards the effort.

Built in the 1st century AD and complete with manholes to underground drainage, the street still bears the hallmarks of the city's principal thoroughfare, with the ruts worn by thousands of chariots scored into the original flagstones.

The 500 columns that once lined the street were deliberately built at an uneven height to complement the facades of the buildings that once stood behind them. Although most of the columns you see today were reassembled in the 1960s, they give an excellent impression of this spectacular thoroughfare.

There are many buildings of interest on either side of the cardo maximus, in various states of restoration and ruin. From north to south, the highlights include the **northern tetrapylon** (archway with four entrances), built over the intersection with the north decumanus (one of two main streets running east to west). Rebuilt in 2000, the latter was probably designed as a gateway to the North Theatre.

Western Baths
BATHHOUSE

On the eastern side of the cardo maximus at Jerash lie the earthquake-stricken remains of the Western Baths – once an impressive complex of hot- *(calidarium)*, warm- *(tepidarium)* and cold-water *(frigidarium)* baths. In Roman times, public bathing fulfilled the role of a social club and attracted a wide variety of people who gathered to exchange news and gossip as well as to enjoy music, lectures and performances.

Dating from the 2nd century AD, the Western Baths represent one of the earliest examples of a dome atop a square room. The **Eastern Baths** lie outside the gated city on the other side of the wadi in the modern town of Jerash. They are lit up at night and are interestingly juxtaposed with a modern mosque.

Nymphaeum
FOUNTAIN

On the western side of the cardo maximus is the elegant nymphaeum, the main ornamental fountain of Jerash, dedicated to the water nymphs. Built in about AD 191, the two-storey construction was elaborately decorated, faced with marble slabs on the lower level, plastered above and topped with a half dome. Water cascaded into a large pool at the front, with the overflow pouring out through seven carved lions' heads.

Although it's been quite some time since water poured forth, the well-preserved structure remains one of the highlights of Jerash. Several finely sculpted Corinthian columns still frame the fountain, and there is a lovely pink-granite basin at its base, which was probably added by the Byzantines. At one point the entire structure was capped by a semi-dome in the shape of a shell, and you can still make out the elaborate capitals lining the base of the ceiling.

Cathedral
CHURCH

South of the nymphaeum, an elaborate staircase rises from the cardo maximus to Jerash's only cathedral. Little more than a modest Byzantine church, it was constructed in the second half of the 4th century on the site of earlier temples. At the height of its glory, the cathedral consisted of a soaring basilica supported by three naves, and boasted a magnificent portal that was finely decorated with elaborate marble carvings.

Southern Tetrapylon
MONUMENT

Marking the intersection of the cardo maximus with the south decumanus (p81), this four-pillared structure is in good repair.

Nearby on the western side of the cardo maximus is the **agora** or macellum, where people gathered for public meetings around the central fountain.

Museum
MUSEUM

(☑ 6312267; ⊘ 8.30am-6pm Oct-Apr, to 5pm May-Sep) **FREE** Before you finish exploring the ancient city of Jerash, visit the small museum just above the forum. It houses a small but worthwhile selection of artefacts from the site, such as mosaics, glass, gold jewellery and coins found in a tomb near Hadrian's Arch. Almost as good as the exhibits is the view the hill affords of Jerash, ancient and modern, spread across either side of the town's defining wadi.

🛏 Sleeping

Many people visit Jerash as a day trip from Amman, which is possible on a tour but quite difficult using public transport unless you make a very early start. An overnight stop is more rewarding: the modern town of Jerash, which encompasses the ruins of the Eastern Baths, comes to life after sunset and is a pleasant place to explore in the early evening. With only one hotel in the middle of the town, and only one other place to stay nearby, it is important to book ahead. If you have a car, Ajloun has more accommodation and is only about a 20-minute drive away.

Olive Branch Resort
HOTEL **$$**

(☑ 6340555; www.olivebranch.com.jo; s/d/tr incl breakfast from JD35/50/60, camping own tent/hired tent JD12/14; ☒) Around 7km from Jerash on the road to Ajloun, this hilltop countryside hotel is situated amid olive groves and pine trees. The spacious rooms have some oddities, such as a bathtub in the bedroom, but the balconies with rural views compensate. Country fare, including kebab suppers and *labneh* (yogurt) breakfasts, are served in the poolside garden or in the modest restaurant.

Unstructured camping is possible in the grounds. A taxi from Jerash costs JD3. By car, drive from Jerash towards Ajloun for 5km; turn right and continue steeply uphill for 1km. Turn right again at the bend in the road – it is signposted but it's hard to read the signs at night.

Hadrian Gate Hotel
HOTEL **$$**

(☑ 077 7793907; s/d/tr/penthouse from JD25/40/50/70; ☒) Run by the always friendly and accommodating Ismail Khasim and

JERASH FESTIVAL OF CULTURE & ARTS

If you happen to be in Jordan in the middle of summer, it's worth catching a show in one of the Roman amphitheatres. Since 1981 the ancient city of Jerash has hosted the annual **Jerash Festival of Culture & Arts** (www.jerashfestival.jo; ☉ Jul), under the sponsorship of Queen Noor. Events are held in the South Theatre, North Theatre and Oval Plaza in Jerash, as well as the Royal Cultural Centre in Amman, and other places like Umm Qais and Mt Nebo. Special programs for children are also held at the Haya Cultural Centre in Amman.

The festival is held over 17 days from mid-July to mid-August, and features an eclectic array of performances including plays, poetry readings, opera and musical concerts from around the world. Events are listed in English in the official souvenir news sheet, the *Jerash Daily*, printed every day of the festival, and the English-language newspapers published in Amman.

Tickets cost around JD10 for events in Jerash, and around JD30 for more formal events in Amman and elsewhere. Since the events change from year to year, it is best to check online regarding the locations of ticketing venues. There is also a festival office next to the visitor centre near the South Gate, though it's only open during the festival. Several bus companies, including JETT, offer special transport to Jerash, which is useful considering public transport usually finishes early in the evening.

his son Walid, Jerash's only hotel boasts a spectacular location overlooking Hadrian's Gate. Breakfast is served on the rooftop terraces with a panoramic view of the Temple of Artemis to the west and Jerash's market gardens to the east.

A range of private rooms with shared bathrooms are humble but spotless; more commodious is the en-suite penthouse with air-con. The host's hospitality makes up for the simple amenities.

✖ Eating

Modern Jerash is a bustling town with several outdoor markets, as well as the obligatory smattering of kebab and felafel shops. It is also home to one of Jordan's best-loved restaurants, the Lebanese House. There's a string of no-fuss restaurants on the main street opposite the visitor's centre. Around the entrance to the ruins there are some eating options, but there is only one place to buy refreshments inside the ruins proper.

Jerash Rest House   BUFFET **$**
(☎ 077 217584; buffet JD5; ☉noon-8pm) The only restaurant inside the ruins, this is a welcome stop for weary visitors. Located near the South Gate it attracts large volumes of tourists, but service is quick and efficient and it serves alcohol. The lunch buffet and barbeque is more conducive to an afternoon nap than a jaunt round the ruins, but it's tasty nonetheless.

★ **Lebanese House**   LEBANESE **$$**
(☎ 6351301; mains JD4-9; ☉noon-11pm; ✦) Nicknamed 'Umm Khalil', this rambling restaurant, which has served more than five million customers since 1977, is a national treasure. Try the fresh almonds while you wait for sizzling mezze and fresh-baked bread. If you can't decide what to sample, try the regular meal (JD15) or the house special (JD22) for a selection of the best dishes.

The indoor and outdoor seating gets busy with local families after 9pm. It's a five- to 10-minute walk from Jerash's centre.

Jordan House Restaurant   BUFFET **$$**
(☎ 077 217584; buffet JD6; ☉8am-9pm; ✦) Serving a comprehensive buffet between 11am and 5pm, this friendly establishment at the entrance to the ruins is a good place for a Turkish coffee before starting out, and a fresh lemon and mint drink over lunch on your return.

ℹ Information

BOOKS & MAPS

Published by the Jordan Tourism Board, the free *Jerash* brochure includes a map, some photos and a recommended walking route. It can be found at the visitor centre in Jerash or the Jordan Ministry of Tourism & Antiquities (p316).

Anyone with a particular interest in the history of Jerash should pick up one of the three decent pocket-sized guides: *Jerash: The Roman City; Jerash: A Unique Example of a Roman City;* or the most comprehensive and readable *Jerash*.

JORDAN'S ROYAL BOTANIC GARDEN

Several years in the making, with an anticipated soft opening in 2015, the new **Royal Botanic Garden** (RBG; www.royalbotanicgarden.org; Rumman) aims to showcase Jordan's surprisingly varied flora and highlight best practices in habitat conservation. The site, which overlooks the King Talal Dam, spreads over 180 hectares, with a variation of 300m of elevation, allowing it to reproduce Jordan's main habitat zones – pine forest, oak forest, juniper forest, the Jordan Valley and freshwater wadi. A large display botanic garden is also planned.

The RBG aims to become a key scientific research foundation, with a seed bank and herbarium (set up with the help of Kew Gardens; its virtual version can be browsed online), as well as teaching organic farming and permaculture techniques. The RBG also has a large community outreach to local farming communities. Volunteers who wish to work at the garden are welcomed. Check the website for details and more on the exact opening date.

All three are available at bookshops in Amman. *Jerash* by Iain Browning gives a more detailed historical account.

TOURIST INFORMATION
Next to the South Gate, the visitor centre has informative descriptions and reconstructions of many buildings in Jerash, as well as a good relief map of the ancient city. Toilets are available at the entrance (in the middle of the souvenir souq), at Jerash Rest House and at the visitor centre.

Allow at least three hours to see everything in Jerash, and make sure you take plenty of water, especially in summer. It's best to avoid walking around the site in the middle of the day between April and September, as there is little shade from the sun. It's possible to leave limited luggage at the Jerash Rest House, for no charge, while you visit the site.

❶ Getting There & Away
Jerash is located approximately 50km north of Amman, and the roads are well signed from the capital, especially from 8th Circle. If you're driving, be advised that this route can get extremely congested during the morning and afternoon rush hours.

From the North Bus Station (Tabarbour) in Amman, public buses and minibuses (800 fils, 1¼ hours) leave regularly for Jerash, though they can take up to an hour to fill up. Leave early for a quick getaway, especially if you are planning a day trip.

Jerash's bus and service-taxi station is a 15-minute walk southwest of the ruins, at the second set of traffic lights, behind the big white building. You can pick up a minibus to the station from outside the visitor centre for a few fils. From here, there are also plenty of minibuses travelling regularly to Irbid (JD1, 45 minutes) and Ajloun (600 fils, 30 minutes) until around 4pm. You can normally flag down the bus to Amman

from the main junction in front of the site to save the trek to the bus station.

Transport drops off significantly after 5pm. Service taxis sometimes leave up to around 8pm (later during Jerash Festival) from the bus station, but it's not guaranteed.

A private taxi between Amman and Jerash should cost around JD18 to JD25 each way, with a bit of determined bargaining. From Jerash, a taxi to Irbid costs around JD14 to JD20.

Dibeen Forest Reserve
متنزة دبين الوطني

Established in 2004, this small **nature reserve** (☎ 02-6370017; ⊙ year-round) **FREE** consists of around 8 sq km of Aleppo pine and oak forest. Managed by the Royal Society for the Conservation of Nature (RSCN), Dibeen is representative of the wild forests that once covered much of the country's northern frontiers but which now account for only 1% of Jordan's land area. Despite its small size, Dibeen is recognised as a national biodiversity hotspot and protects 17 endangered animals (including the Persian squirrel) and several rare orchids.

As Dibeen is still very much a work in progress, facilities are currently limited compared with other RSCN reserves. There are some short marked (but unmapped) **hiking trails** through the park. In March and April carpets of red crown anemones fill the meadows beneath the pine-forested and sometimes snow capped hills. Most trails are either small vehicle tracks or stony paths, some of which continue beyond the park's boundaries. The area is very popular with local picnickers on Fridays, and litter is a problem.

Impinging on the park is a seven-star hotel financed by an Emirati national, which is expected to be completed by 2015. There is currently no other place to stay.

The park is only usefully accessed by car. Follow the signs from Jerash and expect to get lost! Keep heading for the obvious hillside woodland as you pass through nearby hamlets and you will eventually stumble on the entrance.

Ajloun عجلون

☑ 02 / POP 94,458 / ELEV 744M

It may look a bit rough around the edges, but Ajloun (or Ajlun) is founded on an ancient market town and boasts a 600-year-old mosque with a fine stone-dressed minaret. Most visitors, however, don't come to experience this chaotic little hub and its limited attractions. They come for the impressive castle that perches on top of a nearby hill, where it has commanded the high ground for nearly 1000 years.

With the biblical site of Mar Elias and one of Jordan's best nature reserves in the vicinity, Ajloun makes a good base for a couple of days of exploration. It is also reasonably close to Jerash (30 minutes by minibus, 20 minutes by car), offering alternative accommodation and making a rewarding weekend circuit from Amman.

◉ Sights

Qala'at Ar-Rabad (Ajloun Castle)　CASTLE

This historic castle was built atop Mt 'Auf (1250m) between 1184 and 1188 by one of Saladin's generals (and nephew), 'Izz ad-Din Usama bin Munqidh. The castle commands views of the Jordan Valley and three wadis leading into it – making it an important strategic link in the defensive chain against the Crusaders, and a counterpoint to the Crusader Belvoir Fort on the Sea of Galilee (Lake Tiberias) in present-day Israel and the Palestinian Territories.

It was enlarged in 1214 with the addition of a new gate in the southeastern corner, and once boasted seven towers as well as a surrounding 15m-deep dry moat. With its hilltop position, Qala'at ar-Rabad was one in a chain of beacons and pigeon posts that enabled messages to be transmitted from Damascus to Cairo in a single day. The rearing of pigeons in the area is still a popular pastime.

After the Crusader threat subsided, the castle was largely destroyed by Mongol invaders in 1260, only to be almost immediately rebuilt by the Mamluks. In the 17th century an Ottoman garrison was stationed here, after which it was used by local villagers. The castle was 'rediscovered' by the well-travelled JL Burckhardt, who also just happened to stumble across Petra. Earthquakes in 1837 and 1927 badly damaged the castle, though slow and steady restoration is continuing.

Note that there is a useful explanation in English just inside the main gate, and a small museum containing pots, snatches of mosaic and some intriguing medieval hand grenades. Apart from this, nothing else in the castle is signposted, although not much explanation is needed to bring the place to life, especially given that the views from these lofty heights are nothing short of spectacular.

The castle is a tough (3km) uphill walk from the town centre, but minibuses very occasionally go to the top (about 100 fils). Alternatively, take a taxi from Ajloun (JD1 to JD2 each way). A return trip by taxi from Ajloun (JD7 to JD10), with about 30 minutes to look around, is money well spent. The visitors centre and ticket office is about 500m downhill from the castle entrance; there is a small scale model of the castle on display here and, perhaps more usefully, clean toilets.

Mar Elias　ARCHAEOLOGICAL SITE

(☉8am-7pm Apr-Oct, to 4pm Nov-Mar) FREE

This little-visited **archaeological site**, believed to be the birthplace of the prophet Elijah, gives you just the excuse you need to explore the countryside around Ajloun. To be honest, it's not a spectacular site by any stretch of the imagination, though it's worth checking out for its religious and historical significance.

Elijah (also known as Elias) is mentioned in both the Quran and the Old Testament, and is thought to have been born around 910 BC in the village of Lesteb, next to Mar Elias. The prophet died not far away in Wadi al-Kharrar, before supposedly ascending to heaven on a flaming chariot. During Byzantine times, a pilgrimage site grew up around Mar Elias under the guidance of the nearby Bishopric of Pella. In 1999 excavations unearthed a church complex dating back to the early 7th century.

From the car park, stairs lead up above the ruins of the earliest church, the apse of which has a tree growing directly above it. The foundations of the main cross-shaped church are easy to make out and are decorated with wonderfully fresh floor mosaics. Look for the tomb chambers to the back right of the church, and an earlier chapel with plain white tiles to the south. Water cisterns and bits of masonry dot the rest of the site.

There's no public transport to the site. From Ajloun take a right by the Qalet al-Jabal Hotel, climb the hill for 1km and take a left at the junction, heading downhill after this for 2.7km. At the junction/army post take a right for another 1.8km until you see a signpost pointing left (the right branch leads to Ishfateena and the Ajloun Forest Reserve). After 1km take the paved track on the left for 400m up to the site (a total of 8.3km from Ajloun).

If you're heading on to Ajloun Forest Reserve, take a left when you get back to the junction, 1.4km from the site, and head towards Ishfateena. After 1.6km you'll reach the main road; take a right here and after 5km the reserve is signposted to the left, 300m above the main Irbid–Ajloun highway.

Mar Elias can also be reached by foot along the spectacular Prophet's Trail, which connects the site to the Ajloun Forest Reserve.

🛏 Sleeping & Eating

There are two hotels on the road up to the castle, either of which are a good option if you want to enjoy the sunset from the castle ramparts.

There are a few places for a snack and a drink inside Ajloun Castle. For something more substantial, both **Abu-Alezz Restaurant** (meals JD2-3) and **Al-Raseed** (meals JD2-3) near the main roundabout in Ajloun offer standard Jordanian fare, including chicken, hummus and shwarma. Alternatively, pick up some supplies in the many Ajloun grocery stores, supplement your rations with freshly picked fruit from the many roadside fruit stands, and head into the surrounding hills for a picnic.

Qalet al-Jabal Hotel   HOTEL $
(☑6420202; www.jabal-hotel.com; s/d/tr from JD28/38/48) About 2km downhill from Ajloun Castle, this busy little hotel boasts a gorgeous garden of flowering jasmine, grapevines and roses. The decor is a tad tired

and the furnishings on the minimal side but there are expansive views from many of the rooms. The highlight of the hotel is the outdoor terrace where meals are served.

Ajloun Hotel   HOTEL $
(☑6420524; r incl breakfast from JD25) Located just 1km down the road from the castle, this is a handy option for an early morning visit to the castle. There's a comfortable lounge area in the foyer, and the rooms were being re-done and improved when we visited. Choose a top-floor room for grand views of the countryside.

ℹ Information

Just south of the main roundabout in Ajloun, the Housing Bank changes money and has an ATM.

ℹ Getting There & Away

Ajloun is approximately 75km northwest of Amman and 30km northwest of Jerash. The castle can be clearly seen from most places in the area. If you're driving or walking, take the signposted road (Al-Qala'a St) heading west at the main roundabout in the centre of Ajloun. The narrow streets of the town centre can be horribly congested at times.

From the centre of town, minibuses travel regularly to Jerash (600 fils, 30 minutes along a scenic road) and Irbid (JD1, 45 minutes). From Amman (900 fils, two hours), minibuses leave half-hourly from the North Bus Station.

Ajloun Forest Reserve
محمية عجلون الطبيعية

Located in the Ajloun Highlands, this small (just 13 sq km) but vitally important **nature reserve** (☑02-6475673; ⊙year-round) **FREE** was established by the RSCN in 1988 to protect oak, carob, pistachio and strawberry tree forests. The reserve also acts as a wildlife sanctuary for the endangered roe deer (which is being brought back from the brink of extinction through captive breeding programs) as well as wild boar, stone martens, polecats, jackals and even hyena and grey wolves.

The RSCN has worked hard to develop tourist infrastructure within the reserve and woodland cabins are perfect for a romantic retreat. Of course, the real appeal of the reserve is its good network of **hiking trails**, with a variety of paths suited to hikers of all fitness levels. The landscape of rolling hills and mixed forest is lovely, especially if you've been spending a few too many hours in Jordan's barren deserts or congested capital. Even if you don't complete any of the hiking trails, it's worth entering the woodland at the start of the Roe Deer Trail just to enjoy the strawberry trees, so named because of their vivid, strawberry-red peeling bark.

⊙ Sights

The RSCN supports a number of local community projects in and near the reserve to help develop new sources of income for the local population. These small-scale, high-value projects include three workshops that produce olive-oil soap, screen-printed items and traditional Jordanian cuisine, all of which can be purchased on site or in the reserve's Nature Shop. The three houses are free to visit and are within a 10-minute drive of the reserve (follow the signposts from the main road near the reserve) or, more rewardingly, can be reached via a hiking trail. Pick up a map from the visitors centre before you set out.

The Soap House   WORKSHOP
(Orjan Village; ⊙9am-4pm) 🏃 Ever wondered what pomegranate soap smells like? Local women demonstrate the art of making all kinds of health-promoting soaps using natural local ingredients and comprising 90% pure olive oil. Pomegranate is one of a dozen exotic fragrances.

House of Calligraphy   WORKSHOP
(⊙9am-4pm) 🏃 You don't have to be a linguistic scholar to enjoy and appreciate the dynamic rhythms of Arabic script. Reinforcing their Islamic heritage, the women operating in this workshop aim to educate visitors about Arab culture and there is even an opportunity to try your hand at calligraphy using a reed to write your name in Arabic.

The Biscuit House   WORKSHOP
(Orjan Village; ⊙9am-4pm) 🏃 Delicious Jordanian delicacies are prepared for sale in RSCN Nature Shops here in this cottage-industry kitchen. With an on-site cafe selling locally produced herbal teas, olive-oil crisps and molasses and tahini sandwich cookies, it's tempting to stay until morning – quite possible at the Biscuit House Bed & Breakfast.

JERASH, IRBID & THE JORDAN VALLEY AJLOUN FOREST RESERVE

LOVING THE LAND

It's easy to spot a guide at one of the six flagship nature reserves run by the Royal Society for the Conservation of Nature (RSCN) – they exude such a passion for their place of work. This is hardly surprising when you consider that, as part of the RSCN's far-sighted policy to involve local people, the rangers are almost all born and raised nearby.

Take Majid, a ranger at Ajloun. He loves the evergreen oak forests because he played in them when he was young; he remembers village grandfathers harvesting the strong strawberry-tree timber to build houses and local grandmothers using the fruit to settle stomach ailments. There were also hunts for roe deer and wild boar – the same species Majid is now helping to reintroduce and protect today.

Hunting may be banned within the parks, but local communities are still given a vested interest in the land they call their own. At Ajloun, six of the surrounding villages are involved in the maintenance of the reserve: 'Our families want to protect their sons' employment,' says Majid, 'so they are keen to support the reserve and make it work for the benefit of the whole community.'

Naturally, not everyone is equally committed and the reserve faces problems such as illegal cutting of wood for valuable oils and the odd attempt at poaching. The clever part of the RSCN philosophy, however, is that villagers are not banned from exploiting their birthright resources without being offered an alternative income. At Ajloun, for example, a guided trail offers visitors a chance to meet with the area's soap makers: these enterprising women make their ecofriendly products from natural resources in low-impact cottage industries and sell them at fair prices in the Ajloun Reserve shop.

At each of the reserves, the challenges may be slightly different (extraction of water in Mujib and Azraq, overgrazing in Dana), but the story of culturally sensitive and sustainable development is the same. To quote Chris Johnson, director of Wild Jordan (the marketing arm of the RSCN), it is this 'amazing relationship between landscape and people' that is securing Jordan's ancient wild lands for future generations – indeed, saving them for the sons of Majid.

🏃 Activities

It's important to arrange return transport at the reserve visitor centre before you leave on any hike except the Roe Deer and the Rockrose trails. Trails are maintained by the RSCN, and each has a specific fee to hike. The majority require you take a guide (included in the fee).

Roe Deer Trail HIKING
(JD9; ⊘ year-round) If you're just stopping by for the day, the 2km Roe Deer Trail takes about an hour and can be self-guided. It starts from the accommodation area, looping over a nearby hill – past a 1600-year-old stone wine press and lots of spring wildflowers (April) – and returning via a roe deer enclosure.

Soap House Trail HIKING
(JD14; ⊘ year-round) This guided 7km trail (three hours) combines a visit to the reserve's oldest strawberry tree with a panoramic vista at Eagle's Viewpoint. Descending from the 1100m lookout, the trail leads through evergreen woodland to the soap house where enterprising women make natural olive-oil soap.

Houses Trail HIKING
(JD23; ⊘ year-round) This guided 7km trail (three hours) links the three RSCN handicraft workshops – the Soap House, the House of Calligraphy and the Biscuit House. Pause at the Biscuit House for coffee and home-baked delights. Allow extra time for visiting each workshop.

Orjan Village Trail HIKING
(JD22; ⊘ Apr-Oct) A guide is needed for this rural 12km trail (six hours) that weaves alongside a brook, following poplar trees and fruit orchards. The olive trees at the end of the hike date back to Roman times.

Rockrose Trail HIKING
(JD14; ⊘ Apr-Oct) This scenic 8km trail (four hours) involves some steep scrambling and requires a guide. The route passes through heavily wooded valleys, rocky ridges and olive groves and offers sweeping views of the Palestinian West Bank.

Prophet's Trail HIKING
(JD19; ⊘ year-round) Terminating at the archaeological site of Mar Elias, where the prophet Elijah was reportedly born, this 8.5km guided route (five hours) winds through fig and pear orchards. At Wadi Shi-teau the trail plunges into a dense forest of oak and strawberry trees.

Ajloun Castle Trail HIKING
(JD27; ⊘ year-round) With prior arrangement it's possible to continue hiking from Mar Elias for another 9.5km through Wadi Al-Jubb to Ajloun Castle – a tough extra four hours over rough and steep terrain. The trail is 'donkey-assisted', which helps considerably on the difficult final ascent towards the castle.

🛏 Sleeping & Eating

★ Biscuit House Bed & Breakfast B&B $$
(📞 6475673; s/d incl breakfast JD49/70) ◢ This wonderful B&B is situated in a lush wadi with its own orchards. All the furniture is made from recycled wood. The highlight, however, is breakfast, rustled up by the ladies of the cooperative who run a commercial kitchen here producing goods for the RSCN's Wild Jordan Nature Shops. The thyme, olives, cheese and jam are all locally sourced.

It's an experience just getting to this rural homestead in the village of Orjan, where a stream, olive groves and ancient poplars make a welcome contrast to the dry and dusty hills of Ajloun. Just about negotiable by car along a very steep but graded road.

Ajloun Reserve Tented Bungalow BUNGALOW $$
(📞 6475673; s/d/tr/q incl breakfast JD52/63/75/87) ◢ The reserve encompasses luxury tents perched on a treehouse-style wooden platform and light and breezy canvas bungalows (open April through October). Both are a short walk from an ablution block containing environmentally sound composting toilets and solar-heated showers. Bring plenty of mosquito repellent during the summer months.

Ajloun Reserve Cabin CABIN $$$
(📞 6475673; s/d/tr/q incl breakfast from JD81/92/104/116, luxe s/d/tr/q JD90/116/127/139) ◢ These rustic cabins equipped with terraces overlooking a patch of forest make for a delightful retreat. Regular cabins share a toilet and shower block; the newer luxe cabins are ensuite.

Meals (lunch and dinner) are available by reservation in the tented **rooftop restaurant** (buffet JD14) by the visitors centre, though you can always cook for yourself on the public barbecue grills.

From the rooftop, there are wonderful views of snowcapped Jebel ash-Sheikh (Mt Hermon; 2814m) on the Syria–Lebanon border; snow is common in the reserve between December and February.

ℹ Information

At the entrance to the reserve is a modest **visitor centre** (⊙ dawn-dusk) with a helpful reception where you'll find information and maps on the reserve and its flora and fauna. There is also a Nature Shop selling locally produced handicrafts.

You should book accommodation and meals in advance through the RSCN via its Wild Jordan Centre in Amman. If you're planning to take a guided hike, you must book 48 hours ahead. Guided hikes require a minimum of four people and start from JD9 per person, depending on the choice of trail.

ℹ Getting There & Away

You can reach the reserve by hiring a taxi from Ajloun (9km) for around JD5 to JD7; ask the visitor centre to book one for your departure. If you're driving, take the road from Ajloun towards Irbid and take a left turn by a petrol station 4.8km from Ajloun towards the village of Ishfateena. About 300m from the junction take a right and follow the signs 3.8km to the reserve, which is next to the village of Umm al-Yanabi.

IRBID & AROUND

Jordan's far-flung northern hills were once popular with those heading overland to Syria, but these days see relatively few travellers. This is a shame as the region's rolling hills and verdant valleys are home to characterful rural villages, country lanes overrun by goats, and ubiquitous olive groves among whose ancient trunks lie the scattered remains of forgotten eras.

And then, of course, there is Irbid. This thriving university town is generally overlooked by visitors, despite some national treasures; in this densely populated part of the country, Irbid is a key place in which to feel the pulse of modern Jordan.

All minibuses, in whatever village you find them, appear to make a beeline for Irbid, from where connections can be made to almost anywhere in the country. With a car, it's possible to visit the remote battleground of Yarmouk or the ruins of the Decapolis city of Umm Qais as a day trip from Irbid.

Irbid إربد

📄 02 / POP 751,634 / ELEV 582M

Jordan's second-largest city is something of a glorified university town. Home to Yarmouk University, which is regarded as one of the most elite centres of learning in the Middle East, Irbid is in many ways more lively and progressive than staid Amman. The campus, which is located just south of the city centre, is home to shady pedestrian streets lined with outdoor restaurants and cafes. Since the start of the Syria crisis, Irbid has taken in large numbers of refugees, both living in the city itself or the large camp on the outskirts.

Historians and archaeologists have identified Irbid as the Decapolis city of Arbela. The area, in all likelihood, predates the Romans with significant grave sites suggesting settlement since the Bronze Age. Aside from the tell lying at the centre of town, however, there is little evidence today of such antiquity.

◉ Sights

Museum of Archaeology & Anthropology   MUSEUM

(📄 7211111; ⊙ 10am-1.45pm & 3-4.30pm Sun-Thu) FREE This recommended museum features exhibits from all eras of Jordanian history. The collection opens with 9000-year-old Neolithic statuettes found near present-day Amman, covers the Bronze and Iron Ages, continues through the Mamluk and Ottoman occupations, and closes with modern displays on rural Bedouin life. One of the highlights is a reconstruction of a traditional Arab pharmacy and smithy. The Numismatic Hall has some fascinating displays on the history of money over 2600 years. All displays are labelled in English.

Jordan Natural History Museum   MUSEUM

(📄 7211111; ⊙ 8am-5pm Sun-Thu) FREE Encompassing a range of stuffed animals, birds and insects, as well as rocks from the region, this may not be to everybody's taste but it is at least a good place to identify some of Jordan's most elusive species. The museum is in the huge green hangar No 23.

Dar As Saraya Museum   MUSEUM

(📄 7245613; Al Baladia St; ⊙ 8am-6pm) FREE Located in a stunning old villa of basaltic rock, just behind the town hall, this museum is a real gem. Built in 1886 by the Ottomans, the building is typical of the caravanserai established along the Syrian pilgrimage

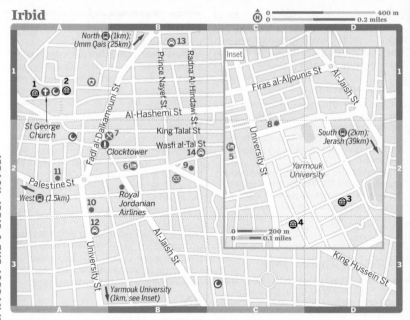

Irbid

⊚ Sights
1 Beit Arar A1
2 Dar As Saraya Museum A1
3 Jordan Natural History Museum D2
4 Museum of Archaeology &
Anthropology C3

🛏 Sleeping
5 Al-Joude Hotel C2
6 Omayah Hotel B2

⊗ Eating
Alia Supermarket .... (see 6)
Al-Joude Garden Restaurant ...... (see 5)
7 Clock Tower Restaurant B2
News Café .... (see 5)

ⓘ Transport
8 Minibus & Service Taxis to
Downtown C2
9 Minibus to South Bus Station B2
10 Minibus to University A2
11 Minibus to West Bus Station A2
12 Service Taxi to University A3
13 Service Taxis to North Bus
Station B1
14 Service Taxis to South Bus
Station B2

route with rooms arranged around a paved internal courtyard. It was used as a prison until 1994 and now houses a delightful col-lection of local artefacts illustrating Irbid's long history.

Don't miss the olive press in the court-yard, or the impressive basalt doors with 'iron' bolts carved in stone.

Beit Arar MUSEUM
(off Al-Hashemi St; ☺9am-5pm Sun-Thu) **FREE**
Set up to host cultural events, Beit Arar is located in a superb old Damascene-style house. The rooms are set around a courtyard paved with volcanic black stones, and there are manuscripts and photo displays of Arar, one of Jordan's finest poets.

🛌 Sleeping

It has to be said that the standard of hotels in Irbid is not great. The redeeming feature, especially among the budget options, is the great friendliness of the welcome.

Al-Joude Hotel HOTEL $
(☎7275515; off University St; s/d/tr incl buffet breakfast from JD30/35/60; 🕸@🕸) Located near Yarmouk University, Irbid's only mid-range hotel has seen better days. Rooms are clean and spacious but sparse, noisy and tired. The good part is that you don't have to go looking for nightlife – in an evening, half of Irbid pours into the hotel's popular News Cafe or the Al-Joude Garden Restaurant.

Omayah Hotel HOTEL **$**

(☎ 7245955; omayahhotel@yahoo.com; King Hussein St; s/d JD20/30; ❄) Fair value for money, this recently renovated budget hotel boasts satellite TV, as well as large picture windows overlooking the heart of the city. The friendly proprietor is kind and helpful and solo women will feel comfortable here.

Rooms towards the back of the property are a bit quieter – a good choice for light sleepers who don't want to be woken by the sounds of honking car horns.

✕ Eating

It's hard to imagine how the restaurants along the length of University St all make a living. Every other establishment along the 'Champs Elysées of Irbid' (so-called by one hotel proprietor) is dedicated to some kind of eatery or other. And then you remember that there are 22,000 hungry students living just over the road. The fare is pretty standard but the attraction is not the food but the evening vibe: after 9pm the streets swell with gregarious crowds looking for a good night out and seeming to find it on the promenade between roundabouts.

Self-caterers and would-be picnickers should head to the **Alia Supermarket** (King Hussein St) near the Omayed Hotel, which has a good selection of local produce, including the region's justifiably famous olives. The nearby street market sells all manner of fresh fruits from northern orchards.

Clock Tower Restaurant JORDANIAN **$**

(Al Jaish St; meals JD3-5; ☺8.30am-9.30pm) The name of this popular local is written in Arabic but as it's right next to the clock tower and has a huge spit of shwarma roasting in the window, it's hard to miss. There's a family seating area upstairs for a bit of peace and quiet, and the Jordanian staple dishes are cheap, cheerful and delicious.

This is one budget restaurant where you won't have to worry about a stomachache in the heart of downtown.

News Café CAFE **$**

(off University St; pizza JD2.500) Downstairs from the Al-Joude Hotel, this is one of the most popular gathering places for Irbid's cool set. Styled along the lines of a Western-style coffee shop, the News Café is warm and inviting, offering coffee, milkshakes, pizza and other snacks.

True to its Middle Eastern roots, however, you can also indulge in the obligatory nargileh (water pipe), which is a great way to lose an afternoon or evening to smoke-induced bliss.

Al-Joude Garden Restaurant JORDANIAN **$$**

(off University St; mixed grill meals JD6-10) Students, visiting parents and local families crowd into the courtyard outside Al-Joude Hotel to sip fresh fruit juices and smoke a strawberry nargileh. The waiters are kept in a constant state of rush in this teeming venue as they are summoned for hot embers and top-ups of Turkish coffee – expect long waits for food orders.

Chilly even in the summer once the moon comes up, the management thoughtfully provides Arab overcoats – strictly, mind, for the ladies as the lads are expected to tough it out. Dessert is best had in one of the many juice and cake shops in the neighbouring streets.

ⓘ Information

Irbid has plenty of banks for changing money and most have ATMs. The police station is above the market area and offers great views of the city. There are literally dozens of internet cafes along the southern end of University St (Shafeeq Rshaidat St) near Yarmouk University; most are open year-round.

Post Office (King Hussein St; ☺7.30am-5pm Sat-Thu, to 1.30pm Fri)

Royal Jordanian Airlines (☎ 7243202; cnr King Hussein & Al-Jaish Sts)

ⓘ Getting There & Away

Approximately 85km north of Amman, Irbid is home to three main minibus/taxi stations.

From the **North Bus Station** (Tabarbour), there are minibuses to Umm Qais (45 minutes), Mukheiba (for Al-Himma; one hour) and Quwayliba (for the ruins of Abila; 25 minutes) for between 400 fils and JD1.

From the large **South Bus Station** (new Amman bus station; Wahadat), air-conditioned Hijazi buses (JD2, 90 minutes) leave every 15 to 20 minutes between 6am and 7pm for Amman's north bus station. There are also less comfortable buses and minibuses from Amman's north bus station (less than JD1, about two hours) and plenty of service taxis (JD1). Minibuses also leave the South Bus Station for Ajloun (45 minutes), Jerash (45 minutes) and the Syrian border for around 800 fils.

From the **West Bus Station** (Mujamma al-Gharb al-Jadid), about 1.5km west of the centre, minibuses go to Al-Mashari'a (45 minutes) for the ruins at Pella, Sheikh Hussein Bridge (for Israel and the Palestinian Territories; 45 minutes) and Shuneh ash-Shamaliyyeh (North Shuna; one hour) for between 800 fils and JD1.200.

❶ Getting Around

Getting between Irbid's various bus stations is easy, with service taxis (200 fils) and minibuses (100 fils) shuttling between them and the centre. Service taxis and minibuses to the South Bus Station can be picked up on Radna al-Hindawi St; for service taxis to the north bus station head to Prince Nayef St. For the west bus station take a bus from Palestine St, just west of the roundabout.

The standard taxi fare from the centre (al-Bilad) to the university (al-Jammiya) is 500 fils; few taxis use meters in Irbid. A minibus from University St to the university gate costs 200 fils. Otherwise it's a 25-minute walk.

Irbid's traffic is notoriously bad. If you have a car, be aware that the congestion, one-way roads and lack of parking can make driving a stressful experience.

Abila (Quwayliba) (قويلبا) أبيلا

Lying just 10km north of Irbid, between the twin hills of Tell Abila and Tell Umm-al-Amad, are the ancient remains of the Decapolis city of Abila. At first glance you'd be forgiven for thinking that this site could only be enjoyed by the committed ruin hunter or the aspiring archaeologist. Indeed, little remains of this once-great city, especially since the earthquake of AD 747 did a pretty thorough job of turning Abila into a rock-strewn field.

To date, much of Abila remains largely unexcavated and the site certainly isn't set up for visitors. Of course, you don't need a guide to find the Roman-Byzantine **theatre** or the scattered remains of **columns** from the markets, temples and baths lying around the site.

However, if you're looking for a real Indiana Jones experience and have a torch, explore the eerie **tomb caves** that are carved into the hillsides surrounding the site. At one point the caves were full of corpses, but tomb raiders stripped them clean over the millennia. However, the spectacular **frescoes** adorning the walls and ceilings are marvellously intact, and made all the more dramatic by their remoteness.

The Abila site is close to the village of Quwayliba, located about 10km north of Irbid. Buses leave from the North Bus Station in Irbid (less than JD1, 25 minutes) for Quwayliba; ask the driver to drop you off at the ruins.

Yarmouk Battleground

If you have a car and are intrigued to know why all roads out of Irbid seem to lead to **Yarmouk Battleground**, then follow the signs northeast towards the village of Saham Al Kfarat. The site is of great significance to Muslim Arabs as this was where, on the 12th of August in AD 636, an army of 40,000 Arabs confronted 125,000 Byzantine fighters and emerged victorious. A lot of blood was spilled that day with 4000 Muslims and 80,000 of their adversaries killed, and the battleground remains something of a pilgrimage site to this day.

The signposted road from Irbid leads not to the battleground itself but to a spectacular viewpoint, high above the Yarmouk River which marks the border with Syria. The battle took place in the valley below but from this vantage point it's easy to see how the disciplined, motivated, mobile and homogenous Arabs, united by faith and good leadership, were able to overcome the mercenary Byzantine groups. The latter, who had no belief in the fight, lacked strategy and were ill-disciplined, were particularly disadvantaged by their heavy armour – as can easily be imagined on a hot August day overlooking the steep, sun-parched hillsides opposite the viewpoint.

The viewpoint, which has an interpretive plaque and a monument but no facilities, is not accessible by public transport. By car, it is a 30-minute drive from Irbid; don't give up on the signs – they're just widely spaced. A shortcut to Umm Qais is signposted halfway between the viewpoint and Irbid.

THE JORDAN VALLEY

When Moses reputedly surveyed the Promised Land from Mt Nebo, surely it wasn't the semi-arid hills surrounding the Dead Sea that gave hope for the future, but the great green ribbon of fertility extending from the sea's northern shore towards the distant mountains. The River Jordan has supported human settlement since antiquity, sustained by the rich soil that to this day makes farming an obvious pursuit.

Visitors will be struck by the contrast between the olive-growing hillsides and the subtropical Jordan Valley; they will also probably be struck by the heavily policed border with Israel and the Palestinian Territories which runs along the length of the River Jordan. The valley has been the site of fight and flight for centuries and is still a sensitive area as disputes about territory give way to concerns over water.

Despite the frisson of political friction, there is absolutely no danger in visiting the area and indeed there are many worthwhile sights, from the Roman ruins of Umm Qais in the north to the assumed baptism site of Jesus at Bethany-Beyond-the-Jordan. The valley itself, with commercial farms of bananas, papayas, potatoes, tomatoes and aubergines rubbing alongside market gardens of locally sold produce, is worth a trip in its own right, especially when the valley's many flame trees are in full, glorious flower. At sunset, the encasing hills turn an extraor-dinary colour of pink and egrets flap across the reed beds, oblivious of the border. Incidentally, the only place where you can actually see the River Jordan is at Bethany, as the demands of irrigation have reduced this once mighty river to a mere brook, hidden between the fields.

There is plenty of public transport plying the valley from village to village. With a car, however, it is considerably easier to make the side trips from the valley floor (which is at an altitude well below sea level) to places of interest above sea level, such as the ruins at Pella or the bustling town of Salt. It takes about an hour and a half to drive the full length of the valley, with accommodation possible in Umm Qais at the northern end, Pella in the middle and the Dead Sea in the south. A sample of the valley can also be included in a roundtrip from Amman and Jerash. Don't forget your passport to show in the numerous police checkpoints.

THE JORDAN VALLEY

Forming a part of the Great Rift in Africa, the fertile valley of the Jordan River was of considerable significance in biblical times, and is now regarded as the food bowl of Jordan.

The hot dry summers and short mild winters make for ideal growing conditions, and (subject to water restrictions) two or three crops are grown every year. The main crops are tomatoes, cucumbers, melons and citrus fruits, many of which are cultivated under plastic.

The Jordan River rises from several sources, mainly the Anti-Lebanon Range in Syria, and flows south into the Sea of Galilee (Lake Tiberias), 212m below sea level, before draining into the Dead Sea. The actual length of the river is 360km, but as the crow flies the distance between its source and the Dead Sea is only 200km.

It was in the Jordan Valley, some 10,000 years ago, that people first started to plant crops and abandon their nomadic lifestyle for permanent settlements. Villages were built and primitive irrigation schemes were undertaken; by 3000 BC produce from the valley was being exported to neighbouring regions, much as it is today.

The Jordan River is highly revered by Christians, mainly because Jesus was said to have been baptised in its waters by John the Baptist at the site of Bethany-Beyond-the-Jordan. Centuries earlier, Joshua also supposedly led the Israelite armies across the Jordan near Tell Nimrin (Beth Nimrah in the Bible) after the death of Moses, marking the symbolic transition from the wilderness to the land of milk and honey:

> And while all Israel were passing over on dry ground, the priests who bore the ark of the covenant of the Lord stood on dry ground in the midst of the Jordan, until all the nation finished passing over the Jordan.

Joshua 3:17

Since 1948 the Jordan River has marked the boundary between Jordan and Israel and the Palestinian Territories, from the Sea of Galilee to the Yarbis River. From there to the Dead Sea marked the 1967 ceasefire line between the two countries – it now marks the continuation of the official frontier with the Palestinian Territories.

During the 1967 war with Israel, Jordan lost the West Bank, and the population on the Jordanian east bank of the valley dwindled from 60,000 before the war to 5000 by 1971. During the 1970s, new roads and fully serviced villages were built and the population has now soared to over 100,000.

Al-Himma (Mukheiba)

الحمى (مخيبا)

☑ 02 / POP <5000 / ELEV -130M

If you have just paid a visit to the Yarmouk Battleground viewpoint you may be interested to descend to the hot springs of Al-Himma in the village of Mukheiba. At the confluence of the Yarmouk and the Jordan Rivers, you can gain a good idea of the battle site from the ground, although access to the site proper is currently restricted. The hills (almost an escarpment) up which the conflicting armies had to run look considerably steeper from here and make the Muslim victory all the more impressive.

In Roman and Byzantine times, al-Himma was the site of Gadara's bath complex, famous throughout the empire for its lavish design and architecture. Most of the ruins today lie across the border in the Israeli-occupied Golan Heights and the modern incarnation of the baths has not endured the downturn in tourism of the past decade.

Mukheiba marks the northernmost reach of Jordan's portion of the Jordan Valley, 10km north of Umm Qais. This edgy border town can be reached via a scenic road (with checkpoints) giving views of the Golan Heights in Syria and the Sea of Galilee (Lake Tiberias) in Israel and the Palestinian Territories. Public transport is not reliable here and the village is not a good place to be marooned.

Umm Qais (Gadara)   أم قيس

☑ 02 / POP <5000 / ELEV 310M

And when he came to the other side, to the country of the Gadarenes, two demon-possessed men met him, coming out of the tombs, so fierce that no one could pass that way. And behold, they cried out, 'What have you to do with us, O Son of God? Have you come here to torment us before the time?' Now a herd of many swine was feeding at some distance from them. And the demons begged him, 'If you cast us out, send us away into the herd of swine'. And he said to them, 'Go.' So they came out and went into the swine; and behold, the whole herd rushed down the steep bank into the sea, and perished in the waters.

Matthew 8:28-32

In the northwest corner of Jordan, in the hills above the Jordan Valley, are the **ruins** (admission JD3; ⊘ 24hr) of the Decapolis city of Gadara (now called Umm Qais). Although the site is far less complete than Jerash, it is nonetheless striking due to the juxtaposition of Roman ruins with an abandoned Ottoman-era village. Umm Qais is especially attractive in spring when an explosion of wildflowers adorns the fallen masonry.

Umm Qais has another claim to fame as the site where, according to the Bible, Jesus performed one of his greatest miracles: casting demons from two men into a herd of pigs. Since the first millennium, Gadara has resultantly been a Christian place of pilgrimage, though an alternative Israeli site on the eastern shore of the Sea of Galilee also claims to mark the spot.

The site boasts spectacular views of three countries (Jordan, Syria, and Israel and the Palestinian Territories), encompassing the Golan Heights, Mt Hermon and the Sea of Galilee (Lake Tiberias). Over the past decade or more, Umm Qais has become a rallying point for homesick Palestinians (many of whom are now Jordanian nationals), yearning for a glimpse of their former homeland. The Resthouse (p98), a popular restaurant located amid the ruins, is a particular favourite with families congregating to swap stories of the Holy Land.

History

The ancient town of Gadara was ruled by a series of powerful nations, including the Ptolemies, the Seleucids, the Jews and, from 63 BC, the Romans who transformed the town into one of the great cities of the Decapolis.

Herod the Great was given Gadara following a naval victory and he ruled over it until his death in 4 BC – much to the disgruntlement of locals who tried everything to put him out of favour with Rome. On his death the city reverted to semi-autonomy as part of the Roman province of Syria and it flourished under various guises until the 7th century when, in common with other cities of the Decapolis, it lost its trading connections and became little more than a backwater.

The town was partially rebuilt during the Ottoman Empire and many structures from this period, built in the typical black basaltic rock of the region, remain well preserved alongside the earlier Roman ruins.

In 1806 Gadara was 'discovered' by Western explorers but excavation did not

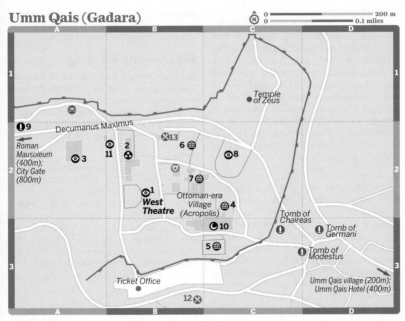

Umm Qais (Gadara)

commence in earnest until the early 1980s. Thanks to German funding, considerable restoration of the Roman ruins has taken place, but much remains still to be excavated.

◉ Sights

★ West Theatre
AMPHITHEATRE

Entering Umm Qais from the south, the first structure of interest is the well-restored and brooding West Theatre. Constructed from black basalt, it once seated about 3000 people. This is one of two such theatres – the **North Theatre** is overgrown and missing the original black basalt rocks which were recycled by villagers in other constructions.

Basilica Terrace
RUIN

The remains of this 6th-century **church**, with an unusual octagonal interior sanctum, are marked today by the remaining basalt columns. The church was destroyed by earthquakes in the 8th century. A bit of imagination is needed to reconstruct the colonnaded courtyard opposite, the western section of which housed a row of **shops** (the shells of which remain).

Decumanus Maximus
STREET

The main road passing through the site, and still paved to this day, once linked Gadara

with other nearby ancient cities such as Abila and Pella. In its heyday, the road extended as far as the Mediterranean coast.

Baths
BATHHOUSE

West along the decumanus maximus are the overgrown public baths. Built in the 4th century, this would once have been an impressive complex of fountains (like the nearby **nymphaeum**), statues and baths, though little remains today after various earthquakes.

Roman Mausoleum   TOMB

The decumanus maximus continues west of the main site for 1km or so, leading to some ruins of limited interest, including **baths**, **mausoleums** and **gates**. Japanese and Iraqi archaeologists are currently excavating here. Most interesting is the basilica built above one of the Roman mausoleums. You can peer down into the subterranean tomb through a hole in the basilica floor. The sarcophagus of Helladis that once lay here can be seen in the Museum of Anthropology and Archaeology (p91) in Irbid.

Museum   MUSEUM

(☑7500072; ☉8am-6pm Sat-Thu, to 4pm Fri) **FREE** Housed in Beit Russan, a former residence of an Ottoman governor, this modest museum is set around an elegant and tranquil courtyard of fig trees. The main mosaic on display (dating from the 4th century and found in one of the tombs) illustrates the names of early Christian notables. Another highlight is the headless white marble statue of the Hellenic goddess Tyche, which was found sitting in the front row of the West Theatre.

Ottoman Village   RUIN

Surrounding the museum are the comprehensive ruins of an Ottoman village dating from the 18th and 19th centuries. Two houses, **Beit Malkawi** (now used as an office for archaeological groups) and the nearby **Beit Heshboni**, are still intact. An **Ottoman** **mosque** and the remains of a **girls' school** are also worth a cursory visit if you choose to amble around the derelict lanes.

🛏 Sleeping & Eating

Not many people spend the night in Umm Qais, especially since the ruins can easily be accessed on a day trip from Jerash or Irbid. Staying here does give the option, though, of making a full day's excursion along the Jordan Valley the following day.

Umm Qais Hotel   HOTEL $

(☑7500080; www.umqaishotel.com; s/d incl breakfast from JD15/20) With extremely modest rooms above a bakery (guess where bread for breakfast comes from) and a stone's throw from the ruins, this family-run hotel makes up for the lack of attractions with hearty hospitality. Home-cooked Jordanian food is available on request from the landlady. Half-day trips into the local countryside can be organised from here.

Shine Cottage Grilling   CAFE $

(meals JD2-4; ☉9am-9pm) A small open-air cafe that has great views from the terrace and is one of only two places for casual refreshments near the ruins. It is opposite the parking lot.

★ Umm Qais Resthouse   JORDANIAN $$

(☑7500555; meals JD3-8; ☉10am-7pm, to 10pm Jun-Sep; ☑) Without doubt, one of the best parts of the Umm Qais site is pausing to take

---

FORBIDDEN FRUIT IN THE JORDAN VALLEY

This is border country, historically disputed land, where the names alone (Golan Heights, West Bank) cast a long shadow over the fields of onions and tomatoes. Mr Abu Eiad, in this year of drought, casts an eye up to the cloudless sky and pronounces with profound stoicism, 'It's God's will'. He is happy, he says. With two wives, four sons and two daughters, why shouldn't he be? It also transpires that he has something else to smile about. Hidden between the limes and lemons of his family plot, water gushes into a beautiful vale of emerald green. It's a far cry from the plastic-sheeted fields of corporate neighbours, some dry-baked like old leather, others artificially green under their polythene coating.

The spring is diverted by stones into the orchard one day and the potato fields the next, the excess siphoned off to help neighbours. Abu Eiad's wife wants help for new technologies to develop their enterprise. Casting a look at the Garden of Eden in front of us, with its plump, organic fruit and glossy aubergines, it's hard to imagine that anything could improve on their winning formula.

'Take a picture!' Abu Eiad insists, as he stands in waving distance of the Jordan River – and the armed border guard who thankfully is looking the other way. But it isn't the border that's the focus of the shot: the focus is on two farmers, either side of the thin ribbon of reeds, plucking weeds from their onion beds, just as other *fellaheen* (subsistence farmers) have been doing in the Jordan Valley for centuries.

refreshment at the Umm Qais Resthouse, perched atop a small hill in the heart of the ruins. With stunning views over Galilee, the Golan and the peaks of Lebanon, it's the perfect venue for lunch or an early dinner.

Located inside a converted Ottoman house, the restaurant is part of a famed consortium of top-notch restaurants in Jordan and offers an impressive seasonal menu highlighting fresh produce, local wines and locally raised meats. The open-air terrace is surrounded by flowers in spring that look good enough to sprinkle on the salad.

ℹ Information

The easiest way to enter ancient Gadara is from the western end of the car park. There are minimal signs in the site so it's worth collecting the brochure about Umm Qais from the ticket office. *Umm Qais: Gadara of the Decapolis* (JD3), published by Al-Kutba, is ideal for anyone who wants further information. Guides (JD10) are available from the ticket office.

There are toilets at the Umm Qais Resthouse. The tourist police are along the lane between the museum and the Resthouse.

ℹ Getting There & Away

Umm Qais village, and the ruins 200m to the west, are about 25km northwest of Irbid and about 110km north of Amman. Minibuses leave Irbid's North Bus Station (800 fils, 45 minutes) on a regular basis. There's no direct transport from Amman.

With a car you can descend to the Jordan Valley road via the village of Adasiyyeh. The occasional minibus runs down this road to Shuneh ash-Shamaliyyeh, but if you are relying on public transport to get to Pella from here it's easier to backtrack via Irbid.

Pella (Taqabat Fahl)   بيلا

In the midst of the Jordan Valley are the ruins of the ancient city of **Pella** (Taqabat Fahl; ☉8am-6pm) FREE, one of the 10 cities of the fabled Roman Decapolis. Although not as spectacular as Jerash, Pella is far more important to archaeologists as it reveals evidence of 6000 years of continuous settlement. In fact, it's regarded as the most historically significant site in all Jordan. Centred on a large tell and surrounded by fertile valleys that together comprise a rich watershed, Pella has fostered human civilisation from the Stone Age to medieval Islamic times.

Pella (Taqabat Fahl)

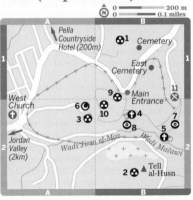

Pella (Taqabat Fahl)

◎ Sights
1	Abbasid Settlement B1
2	Byzantine Fort B2
3	Canaanite Temple A2
4	Civic Complex Church (Middle Church) B2
5	East Church B2
6	Mamluk Mosque A2
7	Nymphaeum (Baths) B2
8	Odeon (Theatre) B2
9	Roman Gate B1
	Roman Temple .... (see 2)
10	Umayyad Settlement B2

✕ Eating
11	Pella Rest House B1

Many of the ruins are spread out and in need of excavation, so some walking and a bit of imagination are required to get the most from the site. Unlike Jerash, which overwhelms visitors with its monumental grandeur, Pella is harder to visualise, but the superb setting just above the Jordan Valley can be reward enough, particularly when the land blooms in spring.

History

Pella was inhabited a million years ago by hunters and gathers who followed herds of game animals through the Stone Age forests and savannahs. By 5000 BC permanent Neolithic farming villages had sprung up around the tell and attracted the attention of the Egyptians, who referred to the site in written texts in the 2nd millennium BC.

Pella thrived due to its strategic position on the trade routes running between Arabia, Syria, Egypt and the Mediterranean. Luxury items, including ivory sculpture and gold jewellery, have been excavated from the site, suggesting that Pella was a prosperous settlement throughout the Bronze and Iron Ages.

Under the Greeks, the settlement earned the name 'Pella' after the birthplace of Alexander the Great. The Jews largely destroyed Pella in 83 BC as the inhabitants were not inclined to adopt Jewish customs. Twenty years later, the legions of Roman emperor Pompey swept into the Levant and rebuilt it, along with neighbouring cities in the Decapolis. Life under the Romans was embraced in Pella and the city enjoyed an era of political autonomy and economic stability; it even had the power to mint its own coins.

It was to Pella that Christians fled persecution from the Roman army in Jerusalem in AD 66. Although they later returned to Jerusalem, they left a strong mark on Pella, helping to ease the city's adoption of Christianity a few centuries later.

Pella reached its peak during the Byzantine era, and by the year 451 the city was influential enough to warrant its own bishop. The population at this time may have been as high as 25,000, and there is evidence that Pella was part of an expansive trade route that encompassed most of Asia Minor as well as North Africa.

The city was virtually destroyed by the earthquake that shook the whole region in 747. The last occupiers of Pella were the Mamluks of the 13th and 14th centuries. While Pella enjoyed a brief renaissance, the defeat of the Mamluks by the Ottomans caused the residents of Pella to flee, ending more than 6000 years of continuous settlement. Today the ruins of Pella lie a few kilometres away from the modern Arab village of Taqabat Fahl.

◉ Sights

At the base of the main mound (on your right as you pass through the main entrance) are the limited remains of a **Roman gate** to the city. Atop the hill are the ruins of an **Umayyad settlement**, which consisted of shops, residences and storehouses. The small, square **Mamluk mosque** to the west dates from the 14th century. Carved into the southern side of the hill is the recently excavated **Canaanite temple**, which was con-

structed in around 1270 BC, and dedicated to the Canaanite god Baal.

The main structure, and indeed one of the better preserved of the ruins at Pella, is the Byzantine **civic complex church** (or middle church), which was built atop an earlier Roman civic complex in the 5th century AD, and modified several times in the subsequent two centuries. Adjacent is the **odeon** (a small theatre used for musical performances). It once held 400 spectators, but you will need considerable imagination to picture this now. East of the civic complex church are the low-lying remains of a Roman **nymphaeum** (public fountain).

Up the hill to the southeast is the 5th-century **east church**, which has a lovely setting perched high above the lower city. From there a trail leads down into Wadi Malawi and then climbs **Tell al-Husn** (note the remains of tombs cut into the hillside), atop which are the stones of a **Byzantine fort** and **Roman temple**. There are good views of the Jordan Valley from here.

Outside the main site, there are the ruins of a small **Abbasid settlement** about 200m north of the main entrance. There are also a few limited **Palaeolithic ruins** (4km), **Roman baths** and a **rock bridge** (3km) reached via the road past the turn-off to the Pella Rest House.

Enquire at the rest house about how to get to the rubble of a **Hellenistic temple** high on Jebel Sartaba to the southeast. From there, Jerusalem is visible on a clear day. The return hike takes a good couple of hours.

🛏 Sleeping & Eating

Pella Countryside Hotel　　　　B&B $
(☑ 079 5574145, 077 6184337; dheebjawahreh575@ hotmail.com; s/d incl breakfast from JD30/40) This B&B has lovely rural views from a shared guest lounge. The seven comfortable rooms, with private bathrooms, have plenty of country-style flourishes. It's a good place to relax for a couple of nights and the owners can arrange picnics in the surrounding hills. From February to May, black irises, the national flower of Jordan, bloom in the garden.

The hotel is signposted off the road to the ruins.

Pella Rest House　　　　JORDANIAN $$
(☑ 079 5574145) Closed when we visited, this famous restaurant is renowned for its exceptional views over Pella and the Jordan Valley: Israel and the Palestinian Territories is

visible to the right of the communications towers, the West Bank is to the left, and the Jenin Heights and Nablus are in the middle. Hopefully it is due to reopen before too long.

ℹ Information

The site can be entered for free at several points, including next to the (closed) Pella Rest House on the hill.

Anyone with a specific interest should buy *Pella* (JD3), published by Al-Kutba and available in major bookshops around Jordan.

ℹ Getting There & Away

From Irbid's West Bus Station, minibuses go to Al-Mashari'a (800 fils, 45 minutes), though be sure to get off before Al-Mashari'a at the junction. Pella is a steep 2km walk uphill from the signposted turn-off, but occasional minibuses ascend to the rest house if they see visitors heading for the ruins. Minibuses and service taxis travel regularly from Amman's north bus station to Deir Alla (800 fils, one hour) close to the Pella junction.

With your own car, the ruins are an easy day trip from Irbid, Jerash or Amman. Exploring the scenic back roads to Ajloun (25km) takes a bit of a nose for navigation but is worthwhile for the insights into rural life among the olive groves that it affords.

Salt السلط

🗹 05 / POP 70,000 / ELEV 814M

Progressing along the Jordan Valley in either direction, it is worth taking a 30-minute detour into the hills to visit the characterful old town of Salt. Part of the fun of the visit is climbing to a viewpoint and marker, 10 minutes from the valley floor, which indicates sea level. If you were just about anywhere else on the planet, you'd be surfacing for air at this point.

The town itself is set in a steep-sided, narrow valley. During Ottoman rule, Salt was the region's administrative centre, but was passed over as the new capital of Trans-Jordan in favour of Amman. Consequently, Salt never experienced the intense wave of modernisation that swept across the capital, and as a result has retained much of its historic charm. Today, much of Salt's downtown is a living museum of Ottoman-period architecture.

Salt is visited by few foreign tourists and remains one of the undiscovered highlights of the Jordan Valley area. A multimillion-dollar aid package awarded to

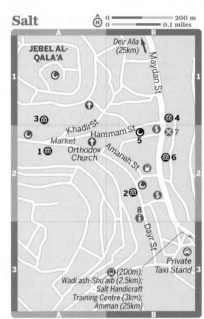

Salt

◉ Sights
1 Beit Abu Jaber	A2
Beit Mismar	(see 8)
2 Beit Muasher	B2
3 English Hospital	A1
4 Muhammed al-Bashir's House	B1
5 Ottoman Mosque	B2
6 Salt Archaeological Museum	B2

🍴 Eating
7 Al-Salam Restaurant	B2

ℹ Information
8 Tourist Office	B2

the city in 2004 by Japan has been used to preserve many of the city's old buildings and to create facilities for tourists. While infrastructure is still largely lacking, it's heartening to see that the residents of Salt have embraced their city's architectural heritage in a country where concrete urbanisation is the norm.

History

While you'd be forgiven for thinking that the town was named after the table condiment, Salt was either named after the Greek word *saltus* meaning 'forests' (although these are long gone) or from *sultana* for the grapes that were once abundant in the region.

Construction began on Salt's characteristic limestone buildings in the late 19th century thanks to the arrival of merchants from Nablus. Over several decades, Salt began to thrive as trade networks sprang up between the city and neighbouring Palestine.

Following the establishment of Trans-Jordan, the new emir chose Amman as his capital due to its proximity to the railway. Almost overnight, Salt went into decline. War with Israel separated Salt from the port of Haifa in 1948, and later from its trading partner of Nablus in 1967, ending Salt's significance as anything more than a rural town above the Jordan Valley.

◎ Sights & Activities

There are some fine examples of **Ottoman architecture** in town dating from the late 19th and early 20th century. Few of these gracious limestone buildings are open to the public, but some of the elegant facades are worth viewing. Stairways lead up to fine views from atop Jebel al-Qala'a.

Salt Archaeological Museum   MUSEUM
(⏏ 3555651; admission JD1; ◎ 8am-6pm May-Oct, to 4pm Nov-Apr) This delightful little museum is located in a well-restored Ottoman-era building and covers the local history of the Jordan Valley area with excellent information boards in English. The downstairs rooms focus on glass and pottery (some dating back 5000 years), spanning the Roman, Byzantine and Islamic eras, mostly from around Salt but also from Deir Alla and Tell Nimrin (from where Joshua is thought to have led the Israelites across the River Jordan into the Promised Land).

Upstairs are some examples of local traditional dress, displays on traditional farming activities and mosaic fragments from churches around Salt.

**Salt Handicraft
Training Centre**   WORKSHOP
(⏏ 3550279; Nageb al-Daboor district; ◎ 8am-3pm Sun-Thu) Visitors can watch weaving, pottery, mosaics and other handicrafts being made at this women's cooperative, 3km out of town. The centre specialises in both training and production and has a showroom for displaying the finished products. A taxi here costs JD1 to JD2 from the centre; ask for the Balkhar Islamic School (Bejanib Maddaris al-Balkhar al-Islamiy). The turn-off is at a set of traffic lights by a bridge, 2km from Salt along the road to Amman.

Wadi ash-Shu'aib   HIKING
If you have a car it's worth exploring Wadi ash-Shu'aib, a refreshing valley named after the prophet Jethro ('Shu'aib' in Arabic).

DISCOVERING SALT ON FOOT

Salt is one town that really rewards a bit of on-foot exploration, as much of the old quarter can only be accessed by stairways and the best of the souq area is clustered into pedestrian-only alleyways. The following 3km route, which takes about 90 minutes to complete, leads you on a circular tour of Salt's backstreets, taking in its bazaars and old Ottoman architecture.

From Salt bus station walk up Dayr St, past the impressive doorway of **Beit Mismar** and the lovely balcony columns of **Beit Muasher**, both grand old Ottoman residences. Continue along Dayr St as it passes the curved walls of Salt's Orthodox church to the recently restored **Beit Abu Jaber**, which houses a small local-history museum. Head across the plaza and take the stairs up to the right of the mosque, curving round to the entry of the former **English Hospital** (look for the letters 'EH' on the green gate). From here you can wind your way uphill for fine views over the town and descend along a neighbouring staircase.

Alternatively, return to the plaza and head down **Hammam St**, Salt's most atmospheric backstreet, past the ornate **Ottoman mosque** to the junction with Maydan St. Across the street is the colonnaded entry of **Muhammed al-Bashir's House** (built between 1890 and 1910), now a traditional coffeehouse (with a tree in front). Next door is Beit al-Sulibi (built between 1920 and 1930).

Break for lunch at the **Al-Salam Restaurant** and end your tour at the **archaeological museum**.

There are some hiking opportunities here and interesting caves. It's 2.5km southeast of Salt.

🛌 Sleeping & Eating

The northern end of Maydan St is lined with traditional cafes, full of men drinking tea and smoking nargileh. Basic restaurants along the same street and by the bus station have kebabs, though the best place in town for Arabic food is the **Al-Salam Restaurant** (🕿 3552115; Maydan St; meals JD3-5; ⊙ 7am-10.30pm Sat-Thu), which serves up rotisserie chicken and good shish kebab meals.

Saltus Hotel   HOTEL **$$**
(🕿 079 5421790; www.facebook.com/Saltus Hotel; r JD40-70) Currently Salt's only hotel, the Saltus sits on the outskirts of town and operates in part as a vocational school for the hospitality industry – staff are eager to please. The hotel itself is a relatively modest affair, with simple contemporary rooms, restaurant and views across the hills.

ℹ Information

The friendly **tourist office** (🕿 3555652; Dayr St; ⊙ 8am-3pm Sun-Thu) is upstairs in the impressive old residence of Beit Mismar, but catching it open as per the advertised hours is something of an art. Try to pick up a copy of the excellent *Salt Heritage Trail* pamphlet, which has a useful map and guide to the town's history and architecture.

ℹ Getting There & Away

The bus station is on the main road south of the town centre. There are minibuses to Salt (JD1, 45 minutes) from Amman's North Bus Station, via the University of Jordan, and occasional service taxis from Raghadan. From Salt, minibuses head fairly regularly down to the Jordan Valley to Shuneh al-Janubiyyeh (South Shuna; 800 fils, 45 minutes). Minibuses also go to Wadi as-Seer (600 fils, 30 minutes) and Fuheis (600 fils, 30 minutes), with which Salt can be combined as a day trip from Amman. Taxis can be chartered to Amman for around JD10 to JD15.

The drive to Salt from the Jordan Valley, along either the road south of Deir Alla or from South Shuna, is spectacular. The 30-minute route winds through Bedouin encampments to the coniferous and windswept hillsides of the Zay National Park (little more than a municipal picnic spot) and affords many panoramic views of the Jordan Valley.

Shuneh al-Janubiyyeh (South Shuna) الشونة الجنوبية

🕿 05 / POP 6000 / ELEV -240M

Serving as a junction for public transport along the Jordan Valley and King Hussein Bridge, as well as for the Dead Sea, this town is well connected by minibus with Amman's Muhajireen bus station (800 fils, 45 minutes), as well as Madaba (600 fils, 45 minutes) and Salt (500 fils, 45 minutes). There are also frequent minibuses to Suweimeh, 3km from the Dead Sea resorts.

A few simple restaurants and grocery stores are scattered around town. Consider chartering a taxi (if you can find one) for a few hours from Shuneh al-Janubiyyeh to places like Bethany-Beyond-the-Jordan (JD15) and Amman Beach (JD15).

Bethany-Beyond-the-Jordan (Al-Maghtas) المغطس

> Then Jesus came from the Galilee to the Jordan to be baptised by John.
>
> *Matthew 3:13*

> This took place in Bethany beyond the Jordan, where John was baptising.
>
> *John 1:28*

Whatever one's religious persuasions, it's hard not to be moved by this minimal pile of ruins with its preposterously long name, lying at the end of the Jordan Valley near the Dead Sea. This is the site, archaeologists assure us, where John the Baptist preached, where Jesus was baptised, where the first five apostles met and where, thereby, the foundations of the early Christian faith were laid. They chose an auspicious spot, as many also believe that this was the place from where prophet Elijah (who was born in Mar Elias in north Jordan) ascended to heaven in a whirlwind:

> And as they still went on and talked, behold, a chariot of fire and horses of fire separated the two of them. And Eli'jah went up by a whirlwind into heaven.
>
> *2 Kings 2:11*

Although John was later beheaded by Herod at Machaerus and Jesus was crucified in Jerusalem, the meeting between the two men at this spot in the fertile Jordan Valley was one of hope and new beginnings. It is little surprise, then, that it became a focus for early pilgrimage, and remains so to this day.

History

The name Bethany comes from the Aramaic Beit Anniya (House of the Crossing). As you stand by the near-stagnant river, Israel and the Palestinian Territories is almost within arms' reach. Pilgrim churches, guesthouses and a 6th-century pilgrim road developed around the crossing as pilgrims broke their journey between Jerusalem and Mt Nebo. Today, there's little visible evidence of the early passage of pilgrims but the sense of crossing is still disturbingly apparent.

The sense of fight and flight at this point is captured in the famous mosaic map of Madaba where a gazelle turns towards a lion (identifiable only by its tail) in hot pursuit. They're running through the Jordan Valley towards the Dead Sea, just above the place where John baptised Jesus, and are symbolic, perhaps, of the human flight that has marked this poignant patch of land for centuries.

The site has only relatively recently been identified. Some ancient ruins were discovered in 1899 but it wasn't until the clearing of landmines (following the 1994 peace treaty with Israel and the Palestinian Territories) that the remains of churches, caves, extensive wells and several baptism pools were unearthed. After much debate, scholars identified the site of John the Baptist's mission and Jesus' baptism from descriptions in the Bible and from 3rd- to 10th-century pilgrim accounts. Pope John Paul II sanctified the claim with an open-air mass at the site in the spring of 2000.

◎ Sights

Entry to the **baptism site** (www.baptismsite.com; JD12; ⊙ 8am-6pm Apr-Oct, to 4pm Nov-Mar) includes a one-hour guided tour (in seven languages) and shuttle-bus service which departs every 30 minutes to the main complex, close to the sensitive border with Israel and the Palestinian Territories. The following sites are all part of the tour.

Tell Elias   RUIN
Tell Elias is where Elijah is said to have ascended to heaven, although there is little to see here. The rebuilt arch marks the 5th- to 6th-century pilgrim chapel, where Pope John Paul II authenticated the site in March 2000. The nearby 3rd-century rectangular prayer hall is one of the earliest Christian places of worship ever discovered, dating from a period when Christianity was still illegal.

The bus continues to a modern baptism pool with filtered water from the Jordan River (the river is badly polluted).

Spring of John The Baptist   SPRING
Accessible on foot (hot in summer so take a hat and water), this is one of several places where John is believed to have carried out baptisms. Most baptisms were conducted in the spring-fed waters of Wadi al-Kharrar rather than in the Jordan River. The path leads through thickets of tamarisk and *argul* (wild cherry) and the yellow rose of Jericho in spring.

Site of Jesus' Baptism   RUIN
The main archaeological site comprises the remains of three churches, one on top of the other. Steps lead down to the original water level and a building nearby marks the likely **site of Jesus' baptism**. Byzantine churches were built to mark the site during the 5th and 6th centuries, and rebuilt on the same site after they were destroyed by flooding. All that remains today are traces of original mosaic.

Jordan River   RIVER
The walking trail passes a golden-roofed Greek Orthodox church and leads, under the watchful eye of border guards, to the river – little more than a stagnant ditch. It's not very inviting but you can be baptised in the Jordan if accompanied by a priest. Across the river (and the border) is a rival Israeli baptism complex. This is the only place where civilians can currently touch the Jordan River as the remainder runs through a military no-man's-land.

House of Mary the Egyptian   RUIN
Mary the Egyptian was a 'reformed sinner' who lived and died in a two-room house, now a ruin, in the 4th century. The trail continues left, up some wooden stairs to a two-room **hermit cave** burrowed into the soft rock.

Rhotorios Monastery   HISTORICAL BUILDING
The hill behind the House of Mary the Egyptian holds the presumed cave of John the Baptist, a 5th-century monastery (built around the site) and the ruined Rhotorios Monastery, which has a mosaic floor with Greek inscriptions. In the 3rd to 4th century, the plaster-lined pools were used by pilgrims for bathing. In the early years of Christianity, John was a more celebrated figure than Jesus and this was the more important of the two pilgrimage sites.

Eating

Bethany Touristic Restaurant   FISH **$$$**
(☑ 079 6076060; fish JD12; ☺ 10am-midnight)
Attached to a thriving fish farm, this res-
taurant specialises in excellent tilapia (*tal-
loubi* in Arabic), locally known as baptism
fish. The fish is fried, or baked with sweet
peppers and fresh coriander. It's a popular
spot at weekends, particularly at dusk when
the sun sets over distant Jerusalem. Look for
signs along the road halfway between the
baptism site and the main Amman–Dead
Sea road. This was the only place to eat near
Bethany at the time of writing.

ℹ Information

Collect a brochure and map at the main gate,
where there are toilets and a few desultory
souvenir shops. The flies here can be of plague
proportions in spring so bringing repellent is a
good idea, along with a hat since the site is very
exposed to the sun.

ℹ Getting There & Away

The site is located near South Shuna, which
is at the southern end of the Jordan Valley. If
you're coming from Amman, follow signs to the
Baptism Site along the main road to the Dead
Sea. Tours from the budget hotels in Amman and
Madaba often include this site in a Dead Sea day
trip from around JD50 for a maximum of four
people. Getting to Bethany-Beyond-the-Jordan
by public transport is more difficult. Take any
minibus to Suweimah and ask to be dropped at
the Al-Maghtas junction. The Dead Sea is to the
left of the junction, the baptism site to the right.
There's no public transport for the 5km trip to
the visitor centre. Take plenty of water if you
intend to walk or hitch.

Dead Sea Highway
الطريق البحر الميت

Best Places to Stay & Eat

➡ Mövenpick Resort & Spa (p112)

➡ Dead Sea Marriott (p113)

➡ Mujib Biosphere Reserve (p117)

➡ Panorama Restaurant (p116)

➡ Feynan Ecolodge (p116)

Best Spas

➡ Zara Spa (p111)

➡ Anantara Spa (p111)

➡ Dead Sea Marriott Spa (p112)

➡ Evason Ma'In Hot Springs Six Senses Spa (p117)

Why Go?

Sometimes you've got to get down low to find the real highlights. The Dead Sea is the example par excellence – to be found quite literally at the lowest point on earth. Taking a dip takes on a new meaning here, as the intensely salty water keeps you so buoyant you'll be bobbing about like a cork rather than gracefully swimming a few strokes. Dead Sea mud famously doubles as a skincare product, but you can take things to a more luxurious level at one of the many high-end spas that line the coast here.

The region is more than just brine and therapeutic massages, however. Stretch your legs by hiking in the beautiful nature reserve of Wadi Mujib, and sleep in a candlelit eco-resort, or get to know the local Bedouins by joining a pioneering community-tourism project.

When to Go

➡ Blisteringly hot and humid from May to October, and chilly from December to January, the best time to enjoy the Dead Sea pleasure domes is around February and November – perfect for sunny swims and balmy dining al fresco. Catering to the peak tourist season at this time, resorts offer live entertainment.

➡ Those looking for adventure should aim for spring: the Dead Sea Ultra Marathon brings physical activity to a seashore more famous for sunning than running, and hikes along water-bound Wadi Mujib are free from the danger of flash flooding.

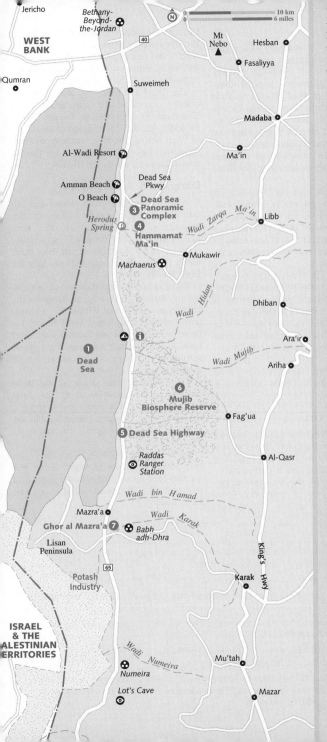

Dead Sea Highway Highlights

❶ Descend to the depths for a bob in the **Dead Sea** (p109), the lowest land elevation on earth, before scaling the heights with a cocktail at a lavish spa resort.

❷ Relax mind and body at a famous **Dead Sea spa** (p116), applying mud used for cosmetic purposes since the time of Herod.

❸ Place the Dead Sea in historical and geographical context at the informative **Dead Sea Panoramic Complex** (p115).

❹ Wallow in hot springs at **Hammamat Ma'in** (p116), one of the region's thermal oases.

❺ Drive from high ground to low ground towards the **Dead Sea Highway** (p114) for the best views in Jordan.

❻ Splash through the canyon pools of **Mujib Biosphere Reserve** (p117), keeping an eye open for ibex.

❼ Get a taste of traditional village life at the **Zikra Initiative** (p109) community-tourism project.

History

It's easy to sense the antiquity of a region that has supported human endeavour for thousands of years. All along the highway, freshwater springs bring a hopeful abundance of life (as at Wadi Mujib) in vivid contrast to the surrounding barren escarpment. In season, the parched soil is threaded with crates of blood red tomatoes and glossy-coated eggplants (aubergines), proving the unexpected fecundity of a region that looks to all intents and purposes like a desert.

Belying its name, even the Dead Sea has contributed to the pattern of human civilisation. Known to the ancients as the Sea of Asphalt, it produced bitumen, creating a nascent oil industry, as it was harvested by the Nabataeans and sold to neighbours for embalming processes.

Travel along the Dead Sea Highway today, with its proximity to the Israel and Palestinian Territories, and you'll quickly feel how division defines the territory to this day. Police checks, border posts, cautious eyes across the Rift Valley – this is disputed soil, a land cleaved in two, geologically, historically and politically. You may try to float in peace in a Dead Sea spa, but you can't help but be aware that the calm has been bought at a high price.

Nature Reserves

One of the most delightful wilderness areas in Jordan, Mujib Biosphere Reserve lies just around the corner from the Dead Sea resorts. Unfortunately this is partially why there are concerns for the long-term viability of the reserve, as the water that flows through the wadi is siphoned off to supply the demands of tourism. Whatever the future of the reserve, for now the area offers waterfalls, canyon adventures and a chance to catch sight of the elusive ibex.

The Dead Sea Highway also gives secondary access to the spectacular Dana Biosphere Reserve and to Dana's Feynan Ecolodge (p116) – the only accommodation in Wadi Araba. The main entrance to Dana Biosphere Reserve, however, is via the village of Dana off the King's Highway.

Dangers & Annoyances

Due to the proximity of the Israel and Palestinian Territories border, there are numerous police checkpoints in the area. Keep your passport, driver's licence, rental contract and *ruksa* (car registration card) handy on any of the roads near or along the Dead Sea Highway.

There are few petrol stations in the vicinity, and little accommodation (except at the Dead Sea resorts and within the national parks of Wadi Mujib and Wadi Dana). It's therefore important you honour the desert code and fill up each time you see a petrol station or you stand a very real chance of getting stranded.

There is very little shade at the Dead Sea or indeed anywhere along the Dead Sea Highway, so it is important to bring a hat and plenty of water, particularly in the summer when temperatures can soar to an intolerable 50°C.

On Friday and public holidays the hotels and public areas are crowded. Some will see this as a good thing; others might find the typically Jordanian noise levels an annoyance!

FAST FACTS

➡ The Dead Sea is part of the Great Rift Valley; it is the lowest land elevation on earth at 408m below sea level and more than 390m deep.

➡ It is not actually a sea but a lake filled with incoming water with no outlet.

➡ It is the second-saltiest body of water on earth (after Lake Aral in Djibouti), with a salt content of 31%.

➡ Egyptians used Dead Sea mud (bitumen) in their mummification process; the last lump of floating bitumen surfaced in 1936.

➡ The majority of Dead Sea minerals (including calcium and magnesium) occur naturally in our bodies and have health-giving properties.

➡ The Dead Sea is 3 million years old but has shrunk by 30% in recent years (half a metre per year) due to evaporation and the demands of the potash industry, one of Jordan's most valuable commodities.

COMMUNITY TOURISM ON THE DEAD SEA

While luxury spas are the face of Dead Sea tourism, the Zikra Initiative (www.zikraini-tiative.org) has been pioneering an alternative approach: community-exchange tourism. Visitors can arrange to spend the day in the farming community of Ghor al Mazra'a at the southern tip of the Dead Sea, learning how to tend gardens, make handicrafts and bake bread, or how to cook the delicious local dish *galayat bandora* (tomato in a pan). Locals can also take you on hikes in the surrounding hills.

It's a relaxed and low-key approach to tourism, allowing you to make a direct person-al connection to rural Jordanians and learn about their lives. The visitor fees (usually around JD35) are ploughed directly back into the community in the form of microloans for local families, and social development projects. Visits must be arranged in advance.

❶ Getting There & Away

The Dead Sea Highway is most easily reached by road from Amman but other access points include Madaba, Karak and Wadi Mousa, all of which make suitable bases for exploring the region. Although the Dead Sea Highway (Hwy 65) ends in Aqaba, there's not much to see or explore along the southern reaches of the highway, and there's no public transport. It's just about possible to get to the Dead Sea resorts with a frustrating and unreliable combination of minibuses and taxis, but tours offer the most realistic way of reaching the area.

❶ Getting Around

Pretty much the only way to explore the Dead Sea Highway (Hwy 65) is with a car; there are effectively no public-transport options. The Dead Sea Highway runs along the edge of the Dead Sea, between the honey-coloured Moab Moun-tains and the distant cliffs of Judaea on the West Bank, and offers an interesting alternative to the Desert Highway between Amman and Aqaba.

If you're not in a hurry, there are some spec-tacular roads that link the Dead Sea Highway with the King's Highway. With the intimate insight these roads afford into Bedouin commu-nities and striking desert landscape, they are almost destinations in their own right.

Dead Sea   البحر الميت

⏹ 05 / POP >5000 / ELEV -400M

It would be a travesty to come to Jordan and miss the Dead Sea. At 400m below sea lev-el, this extraordinary body of intense blue water, polished smooth like oiled skin on a windless day in winter or ruffled into salty whitecaps during the summer winds, lies at the lowest point on earth. The extreme sa-linity of the water has nothing to do with the Dead Sea being below sea level; rather it comes about because of the high evapora-tion rate. This salinity makes for an almost intolerable environment for all but the most microscopic of life forms. Indeed, the only things you're likely to see in the Dead Sea are a few buoyant tourists.

Dead Sea salts and minerals have long been exploited for their skin-friendly prop-erties – although they don't always feel that friendly. While swimming in the sea, you'll discover cuts you never knew you had (don't shave before visiting), and if any water gets in your eyes, be prepared for a few minutes of agony. In fact, 'swimming' is probably a misnomer – bobbing is nearer the mark as the buoyancy experienced in the Dead Sea makes it difficult to move through the water.

The best way to visit the Dead Sea is to stay at one of the luxury resorts at the north-eastern end of the sea. Here you can enjoy a spa treatment, watch the sunset across the water and toast the rising night lights of Jerusalem, perched 1200m above the West Bank.

Alternatively, the Dead Sea can be reached as a day trip from Amman or Madaba.

History

The Dead Sea has been called many names in its time, including the logical 'Salt Sea' and the less flattering 'Stinking Sea' (slap a little Dead Sea mud on your face and you'll soon see why). A Greek traveller, Pausanias, first gave it the current name, noticing that the extreme brackishness of the water made it unsupportive of life. The high salinity is due to the fact that the sea has no outlet and the high summer temperatures evaporate the fresh water more quickly than it is re-plenished. Each year, due to intensive irri-gation in the Jordan Valley, the sea shrinks. This, together with the potash industry on the southern shore, has caused many en-vironmentalists to lament the imminent death of this extraordinary stretch of water.

DEAD SEA HIGHWAY DEAD SEA

🏃 Activities

People come to the Dead Sea to engage with the sea and its mineral properties, either by taking a dip or by wallowing in a spa. About the only other activity on offer is a chance to ride on a camel or a horse. The Bedouin bring their magnificently liveried animals to the corniche between the resorts and pace them up and down the pavement between ad hoc tea stalls. A five-minute ride or photo opportunity costs around JD2.

A huge new development currently under construction is Porto Dead Sea, an Egyptian-led project carrying a JD800-million-price tag, which will include another five-star hotel, shopping mall, entertainment and sport facilities. Porto Dead Sea is just south of the current resort area. Expect the first stages to be opening by 2016.

Swimming

Although technically you can take a dip anywhere along the Dead Sea coast, unless you are staying at one of the resorts it can be surprisingly difficult to reach the sea. This is especially the case as each year the sea retreats further from the shore, making it less and less accessible from the cliffs. Also, after a dip in the Dead Sea you'll find yourself coated in uncomfortable encrustations of salt that are best washed off as soon as possible. And then, there's the utter lack of privacy to consider: the road follows

THE DEAD SEA IS DYING

The Dead Sea is the lowest place on earth, and probably one of the hottest. The resulting evaporation produces an astonishing salinity of 31%, about nine times higher than the oceans, making a dip in the Dead Sea a very salty experience. The high mineral concentrations mean incredible buoyancy and great photo opportunities – get a snapshot of your travel companions happily sitting upright on the water reading newspapers. The water's oily minerals also contain salubrious properties. German health insurance covers periodic visits to the Dead Sea for psoriasis patients to visit and luxuriate in the healing waters.

Sadly, no natural resource in the Middle East shows more signs of relentless population growth and economic development than the Dead Sea. Technically, the sea is a 'terminal lake' into which the Jordan River, along with other more arid watersheds, deposit their flow. Despite the folk song's characterisation of the River Jordan as 'deep and wide', in fact it has never been much of a gusher. When Israeli and Jordanian farmers began to divert its water to produce a new agricultural economy in the 1950s, the flow was reduced to a putrid trickle and the Dead Sea began to dry up.

In 1900, the river discharged 1.2 trillion litres a year into the Dead Sea, but water levels in the river today are hardly 10% of the natural flow. The Jordanian and Israeli potash industries in the southern, largely industrial Dead Sea region exacerbate the water loss by accelerating evaporation in their production processes. The impact is manifested in sink holes, created when underground salt gets washed away by the infiltrating subsurface freshwater flow. Particularly ubiquitous on the western (Israeli side) of the sea, the ground literally opens up – with people, farming equipment and even trucks falling in. Perhaps the most acute environmental consequence though is the 27m drop in the sea's water level, and the long and discouraging walks now required to reach the edge of the retreating beach.

Several solutions have been considered to bring back water to the Dead Sea. A 'Med-Dead' canal utilising the height drop from the Mediterranean Sea was discarded because of the prohibitively expensive price tag. But a similar pipeline from the Red Sea is seriously being considered. Dubbed the 'Peace Conduit', the project would pipe water from the Gulf of Aqaba to the Dead Sea's southern shore, producing hydroelectricity as well as a desalination plant that would provide water to Amman. Environmentalists question the anticipated unnatural water chemistry reaction and the seismic instability of the area. The World Bank, however, recently decided that the US$5 billion project was sufficiently serious to justify a $15 million feasibility study.

Dr Alon Tal is a professor in the Desert Ecology Department at Israel's Ben-Gurion University.

the shoreline closely, and so do the border police! For these three reasons, it's better to reserve your swim for the comfort of the Dead Sea resorts or day beaches, where freshwater showers are available and where access to the sea is generally cleared of sharp and lethally slippery rocks.

In addition to the day beaches below, the resorts offer day rates outside holiday periods.

Al-Wadi Resort
SWIMMING

(adult/child JD25/18; ⊙9am-6pm Sat-Thu, to 7pm Fri) This privately run resort has a variety of water games, including a wave machine and slides, in pleasantly landscaped surroundings. There are two restaurants (open 10am to 5pm), one selling snacks and the other offering an Arabic menu. Children are measured on entry: those under 95cm are admitted free! The resort is about 500m north of the Convention Centre at the head of the resort strip.

Amman Beach
SWIMMING

(☑3560800; adult/child JD20/10, restaurant buffet JD14; ⊙9am-8pm, restaurant 11am-5pm) This public facility goes under the full title of Amman Beach Tourism Resort, Restaurant & Pools. The beach, 2km south of the main resort strip, gives affordable access to the Dead Sea. The grounds are attractively landscaped and the beach is clean, with sun umbrellas, freshwater showers and a vibrant local flavour.

Locals generally swim fully clothed, though foreigners shouldn't feel uncomfortable in a modest swimming costume. Women alone may attract less unwanted attention by wearing shorts and a T-shirt.

There are also a number of swimming pools, a restaurant, some drinks stalls, basketball courts and an amusement park next door. It gets very busy at weekends (especially Friday afternoon and Saturday morning).

Amman Beach is the finishing line for the annual **Dead Sea Ultra Marathon** (http:// deadsea.runjordan.com) in April.

O Beach
SWIMMING

(☑3492000; www.obeach.net; adult/child with lunch JD25/20; admission only JD15/10; ⊙9am-6pm) This private beach, stepped down the hillside in a series of landscaped terraces and infinity pools, is a great way to enjoy the Dead Sea in comfort without paying for a night in the neighbouring hotels. If you're looking for an extra-restful experience, VIP areas are provided for an extra JD30 (couples only) with king-sized beds. A range of spa treatments and massages is also available. There are several restaurants and bars and a weekend buffet.

Mud Bathing

Most beaches have mud pots by the sea's edge where you can self-administer a full-body mud-pack. Leave it in place to bake under the sun for five to 10 minutes and then wash it off in the sea. It tightens the skin and leaves it feeling smooth, tingly and refreshed.

Spa Treatments

Many people go to the Dead Sea area for the therapeutic treatments on offer in the Dead Sea spas. The low levels of UV rays and high oxygen levels are good for the health, and the Dead Sea mud contains high concentrations of minerals. These include calcium and magnesium, helpful remedies against allergies and bronchial infections; pungent bromine, which promotes relaxation; iodine, which alleviates certain glandular ailments; and bitumen, which has skin-rejuvenating properties. Many of these Dead Sea properties are made into easy-to-use preparations such as soaps, shampoos and lotions, and are sold at the Dead Sea spas and in tourist shops throughout Jordan.

Of course, you don't need to be under-the-weather to enjoy the benefits of a spa treatment. If you feel like a scrub or a massage, or just a bit of pampering, it's easy to book in for an hour or two.

Anantara Spa
SPA

(☑3568888; www.spa.anantara.com/deadsea; Kempinski Ishtar Hotel; ⊙10am-10pm) The highlight of this highly luxurious and architecturally striking spa is the Royal Hammam Ritual (JD130, 90 minutes), touted as 'pure bliss for mind and body'. It includes massage, body scrub and body wrap applied with traditional Jordanian-style vigour.

Zara Spa
SPA

(☑3491310; www.zaraspa.com; Mövenpick Resort & Spa; guests/nonguests JD20/50; ⊙8.30am-8.30pm) One of the largest spas in the Middle East, Zara Spa offers a range of facilities and treatments in a beautiful environment. Rates include access to a gym, private beach, pool, sauna, steam room and foot-massage pool, and an infinity pool and aqua-pressure

BRAVING LUXURY IN A DEAD SEA SPA

You can't come to the Dead Sea and not try a spa. Even if you're a die-hard, old-school traveller who feels that sleeping on a bed with a soft mattress is a sign of weakness, there's a certain gratification to succumbing to the spa experience. You'll be in good company: Herod the Great and Cleopatra, neither noted as wimpish types, both dipped a toe in spa waters. So ditch the hiking boots for a day, step into a fluffy bathrobe and brave the clinically white, marble entrance hall of a Dead Sea pleasure dome.

The spa experience (from around JD30) usually begins with a mint tea and a spa bag to stow your worldly goods – this isn't going to be a chlorinated swim in the municipal pool back home. You'll then be shown to the mirrored changing rooms, with Dead Sea soaps and shampoos and more towels than you'll have body to towel down. This marks the point of no return: the silent-padding assistants waft you from here along marble corridors to the opulent bathhouses.

All the spas offer a range of cradling Dead Sea waters with different levels of salinity. There's usually a foot spa and a float in a Damascene-tiled Jacuzzi. Outside pools assault visitors with a variety of bullying jet sprays. Best of all are the little pots that bubble when you sit in them and ought to be X-rated.

Luxury of this kind is an extreme sport and by the time you reach the spa's private infinity pool, you'll be so seduced by the ambience you won't have the energy to try the saunas, steam rooms or tropical sprays, let alone the gym. Lie instead under an oleander by the pool, sip a chilled carrot juice and wonder why you resisted the spa experience for so long.

pool too. Extra services include a mud wrap (JD60, one hour), dry flotation, hot-stone therapy, shiatsu and other massages (from JD60 for 50 minutes). A day package costs JD190 for 3½ hours of treatments; a three-day package is JD365.

Dead Sea Marriott Spa SPA
(☑ 3560400; Dead Sea Marriott; basic entry guests/nonguests JD20/30; ☺ 8.30am-8.30pm) The spa here includes a heated pool, Dead Sea saltwater pool, Jacuzzi, steam room and sauna. Treatments include massage (JD75, 55 minutes), body wraps, salt scrubs, phytomer facials, mud facials, dry flotation and hydro baths. An Arabic loofah experience (JD95, 75 minutes) has to be tried to be believed!

Dead Sea Spa SPA
(☑ 3561000; www.deadseaspahotel.com; Dead Sea Spa Hotel; ☺ 8am-6pm) This spa focuses primarily on medical rather than recreational treatments, with an in-house dermatologist and physiotherapist. Entry to the beach, pools and spa costs JD30 at weekends (JD25 on weekdays) and includes a fitness room, solarium and Dead Sea saltwater pool. A full-body Swedish massage (JD25) and mud application (JD30) are also available.

🛏 Sleeping & Eating

Along the Dead Sea Highway, about 5km south of Suweimeh, there are a number of first-class resorts. They don't look much from the highway, but once you're inside you'll see that they tumble into landscaped gardens, terraced sun spots, cascading pools and pristine Dead Sea beaches. They all have excellent restaurants and offer vantage points for watching the sun set over the hills of Judaea. Reservations are necessary at weekends (Friday and Saturday). At other times, discounts are often offered for walk-in customers. Unfortunately, there are no budget or midrange hotels in the vicinity. Madaba is the nearest town for cheaper accommodation, but public transport to or from Madaba is impractical, so you'll spend more time on the road than you will in the sea – unless you take a tour.

A new Hilton is due to open in 2015.

★ **Mövenpick Resort & Spa** RESORT $$$
(☑ 3561111; www.moevenpick-hotels.com; r from JD215; ❉ @) This wonderfully planted haven boasts a river that ambles through the village-style complex of rustic two-storey apartments. Wooden screens and balconies allow guests to enjoy sea or garden views in private, while secluded seating areas around

a superb infinity pool add to the ambience. The Zara Spa is renowned as one of the best in the Middle East.

Culinary high points include Al-Saraya buffet, a Thursday night barbecue and a prodigious Friday brunch. The Mövenpick charges JD50 for access to the pools, beach and buffet (couples and families only) and an extra JD50 for access to the spa.

Kempinski Hotel Ishtar   RESORT $$$

(☑3568888; www.kempinski.com; s/d from JD200/220; ✸@✉) This grand resort isn't shy in its bid to be the best. Floor-to-ceiling windows stretch the length of the Dead Sea vista, a Sumerian-style lobby overlooks a spectacular, circular infinity pool, and a series of water features tumbles down to the Dead Sea. Each of the modern rooms has a semi-shaded balcony and semi-sunken bath. A palace among hotels.

Champagne is served with breakfast and the restaurant cuisine, including Thai and Mediterranean, is excellent.

Dead Sea Marriott   RESORT $$$

(☑3560400; www.marriott.com; s/d from JD175/190; ✸@✿✉) Polished marble floors, brass fixtures and fittings, and spacious rooms contribute to the general opulence of this much-loved resort. Eating spots include sea-view cafes and a brasserie-style French restaurant. Two cinemas, high-speed internet access, a jungle playground, mini-waterfall and family pool ensure the kids are kept happy while parents luxuriate in the spa.

The Marriott charges JD60 for use of its pools and access to the beach, with JD25 of that redeemable against food and drink in its restaurant.

Crowne Plaza   RESORT $$$

(☑3494000; www.crowneplaza.com/deadsea-jordan) The newest international brand to stake its towel on the shores of the Dead Sea, the Crowne Plaza feels like a small town, with several blocks of rooms circled around the immense central pool area. Rooms are large and comfortable, if you can drag yourself away for long from the spa and several restaurants.

Holiday Inn Resort Dead Sea   RESORT $$$

(☑3495555; www.ichotelsgroup.com; s/d from JD100/120; ✸@✉) This excellent resort with plenty of pools will appeal to families,

with its easier access to the Dead Sea. It is located at the far northern end of the hotel strip, well away from the current construction boom.

The Holiday Inn charges JD25 on weekdays and JD45 at weekends and holidays for access to its beach and pools.

Dead Sea Spa Hotel   RESORT $$$

(☑3561000; www.deadseaspahotel.com; r from JD120; ✸✉) Not as refined as its neighbours, this hotel is pleasant nonetheless. It has a medical/dermatological spa, private beach access, a big pool and a separate kids' pool with slides. Choose from rooms in the main block or bungalows. There's a restaurant complex at the northern end of the hotel with some chain outlets and a sea view

The Dead Sea Spa Hotel charges JD25 for day entrance to its resort and beach facilities, with a snack and a drink thrown in.

❶ Getting There & Away

BUS & MINIBUS

JETT buses offer a Friday-only service to the resort strip south of Suweimeh from Amman (JD8 return) at 8am, returning at 4pm if there are sufficient passengers. The bus leaves from the JETT office near Abdali bus station. Check with the JETT office (p70) in Amman for the latest timetable.

Minibuses from Muhajireen bus station only run as far as Suweimeh.

CAR

From Amman, it takes about an hour to reach the Dead Sea resorts, along Hwy 40 and Hwy 65. Alternatively, you can drive from Madaba via Mt Nebo. If you choose this route, your first view of the Dead Sea will be a spectacular blue lozenge beyond the iron-coloured hills.

TAXI

A return taxi from Amman to the resort strip costs about JD50 including three hours' waiting time (minimum required to make the trip worthwhile) or JD15 for a one-way journey. From Shuneh al-Janubiyyeh, taxis cost from JD30, including side trips to Bethany-Beyond-the-Jordan and the Dead Sea Panoramic Complex. If you take a taxi from Shuneh to the Dead Sea in only one direction (JD10 depending on your negotiation skills), bear in mind that it's very hard to find an onward taxi from the beach area.

Some budget hotels in Amman and Madaba organise day trips via Mt Nebo, the Dead Sea Panoramic Complex and Hammamat Ma'in.

Herodus (Zara) Spring

نبع هيرودس

These hot springs, around 5km south of Amman Beach, have been famous for centuries, and are even marked on the Madaba mosaic map. Indeed, nearby is the site of ancient Callirhöe, a favourite spa of the ancients. Herod came here in 4 BC to find treatment for, according to Josephus, 'an unbearable itching all over his body' – quite possibly psoriasis. Little remains to be seen at the archaeological site (discovered in 1807) other than remnants of Roman bathhouses and the ancient harbour from which Herod's boats sailed. But with a bit of imagination, it's easy enough to conjure poor Herod's itching form being led to the therapeutic hillside.

Despite the popularity of the spot with locals, especially on Friday, it's hard to recommend swimming here either in the hot-spring pools (which are unclean), or at the beach, which affords no privacy from the road.

The site is adjacent to the police station. Follow the sign for Mukawir and Dhiban uphill for 300m and the Callirhöe ruins are on the left. There is no public transport.

DRIVING BELOW ZERO

The switchback roads that link the high ground with the low ground (often below sea level) are a highlight of Jordan, especially if you are driving and can stop to admire the panoramic views. The roads twist through terraced fields of onions, hug contours of sheep-cropped hills, and edge past nomadic communities of Bedouin with their black tents and attendant goats, before spiralling into a painted desert, vermilion with iron ore, olive green with copper oxides and laced with hanging gardens. Here is a summary of the best of these drives. You won't find the roads indicated on all maps, but they are all well paved, suitable for a 2WD car (beware sharp bends) and usually marked 'Dead Sea' or 'Wadi Araba' on signs. Remember to carry your passport with you as there are numerous checkpoints along the roads to the Jordan Valley and Dead Sea Highway.

Salt to Dead Sea

1½ hours, 23km descent and 60km along the Jordan Valley

A varied drive along a busy road of Aleppo pines, red-barked strawberry trees and gardens of early-summer hollyhocks, giving way to tamarisks and acacias. Let your brakes cool at the sea-level marker and enjoy the view of the fertile Jordan Valley, lit up with flowering flame trees in May.

Follow signs for Zay National Park and Deir Alla on Hwy 30 from Salt. Watch out for truck drivers on their mobile phones on the hairpin bends! Add a 14km detour (well signposted) to Mountain Breeze Country Club for a tea break. Notice the humidity and heat as you approach the Dead Sea.

Mt Nebo to Dead Sea Resorts

30 minutes, 21km

An easy drive, passing wildflowers and clumps of prickly pear, and driving through Bedouin grazing grounds before descending to a colourful, semi-arid desert with spectacular Dead Sea views.

The start of the descent is to the left of the Mt Nebo entrance gate. After 14.5km, turn left for the Dead Sea resorts or right for Bethany-Beyond-the-Jordan.

Madaba to Dead Sea Panoramic Complex

50 minutes (half-day with stops), 30km plus 5km return trip to Hammamat Ma'in

The best of the Dead Sea drives, through avenues of windswept junipers and firs, vines and olive groves, and alongside a wadi decorated with flowering oleander. Don't miss the steep descent of the sulphurous hillside to Hammamat Ma'in. Recover at the aptly named Panorama Restaurant. Follow signs for Hammamat Ma'in from King's Highway, 1km south of

Dead Sea Panoramic Complex البحر الميت بانوراما

Walk among the cacti to this **lookout** (admission per person JD2; ⊘8am-10pm), high above the Dead Sea, watch the raptors wheel in the wadis below and you will have to pinch yourself to think that you are standing at sea level. This wonderful museum and restaurant complex offers some breathtaking views, especially on a crisp day in winter when the Judaea Mountains across the water seem as if they are an arm's stretch away.

For an excellent introduction to the geology, history and environment of the Dead Sea, spare an hour for the **Dead Sea Museum** (⊘9am-4pm) FREE. Drive the roads in the area and you'll notice the rich pattern, texture and hue of the exposed rocks alongside the road. This is particularly the case on the Dead Sea Parkway, which extends above the Dead Sea Panoramic Complex to Hammamat Ma'in and Madaba, or below to the Dead Sea Highway. Along the cut of the steepest section of road, rich layers of sedimentary rock create natural murals that add to the beauty of the journey. In the museum, you can identify and touch specimens of this geological treasure.

A short hiking trail called the **Zara Cliff Walk** (1.4km; easy) follows the edge of the

Madaba. The road, sometimes referred to as the 'Dead Sea Parkway', is incorrectly shown on most maps. Use low gear if you're making a detour to Hammamat Ma'in. Continue to the Dead Sea resorts (7km), Bethany-Beyond-the-Jordan (25km) or Amman (60km).

Karak to Safi

30 minutes, 40km

This is an easy drive along steep-sided wadi, with expansive views of potash production. Take a side trip to Lot's Cave.

Time this drive for midafternoon, when the sunset turns the sandstone to molten gold. Follow signs from the King's Highway in Karak to Mazra'a or 'Dead Sea' along Hwy 50. Turn left at the Dead Sea Highway for Safi.

Tafila to Fife

40 minutes, 26km

Descend from cypress woodland, through weather-beaten rock formations and palm oases to tomato fields at Fifa.

Give extra time to this trip – it's a veritable geography lesson in habitats at different altitudes. Take Hwy 60 from the centre of Tafila, following signs for Wadi Araba; take care on the sharp bends.

Little Petra to Wadi Araba

One hour 15 minutes (half-day with stops), 45km plus 2km return to Little Petra and 20km return to Feynan Ecolodge

This fantastic drive begins with Nabataean sites such as the Elephant Rock and a side trip to the Siq at Little Petra. Look out for rock-cut wine presses and dams through Siq Umm Al-Alda, decorated with ancient carob trees. Pass through the psychedelically green landscape surrounding a reclaimed-water project and visit a pre-pottery Neolithic tell (ancient mound) – look for a wire fence on the left of the road – at Shkarat Msaiad. The mountain road thereafter twists through magnificent rainbow rocks before gliding into Wadi Araba, dotted with Bedouin camps, acacia trees and sand dunes.

Head through Umm Sayhoun to Little Petra. Turn right to Hesha and Bayder and immediately left, following signs to Wadi Araba. The road, which doesn't appear on most maps and isn't numbered, is damaged but not impassable at the bottom. At the junction in Wadi Araba, turn right to Qurayqira to stay at Feynan Ecolodge or left to reach the Dead Sea Highway. From the highway junction, it is 130km to Aqaba.

> **DON'T MISS**

FEYNAN ECOLODGE

There are virtually no eating or sleeping stops along the southern part of the Dead Sea Highway. However, the exception – the Feynan Ecolodge – truly is exceptional, and is a destination in and of itself.

Owned by Dana Biosphere Reserve and privately managed, Feynan Ecolodge is the only sleeping option south of Wadi Mujib. More usually found at the end of a long, hard day's hike through the Dana Biosphere Reserve, this lodge is more grail than guesthouse. Set in magnificent multihued desert, the lodge lies 22km off the Dead Sea Highway, via the Bedouin village of Greigra. Park at the office on the edge of the reserve and you'll be transported the rest of the distance by 4WD. For more information on staying at the lodge, see p152.

For a pit stop an hour's drive north of Aqaba, **Beir Mathkour** has a restaurant, craft shop and petrol station within a garden of palms.

wadi and highlights local flora and fauna. You will hear the Tristram's grackles before you see these birds as they screech across the wadi. Hyrax can also be spotted here.

To recharge, try at least one mezze in the **Panorama Restaurant** (☑3245500; mains JD10-18; ⊙noon-10pm; 🍴), which more than lives up to its name. The excellent cuisine makes it a popular venue for weekend lunch and dinner. Try the ground-walnut (JD3) or *shanklish* (local cheese, rolled in thyme and mixed with tomatoes, onion and parsley; JD2), and follow it up with marinated, locally reared lamb chops (JD12) or *sawda dajaj* (chicken livers with grenadine syrup and lemon), which are a meal in themselves (JD4).

The complex is clearly signposted off the Dead Sea Highway, about 10km south of the Dead Sea resorts. The Dead Sea Panoramic Complex makes a worthwhile stop on a day circuit from Madaba, Mt Nebo, Bethany-Beyond-the-Jordan, the Dead Sea and Hammamat Ma'in, either by hired car or taxi (JD50 through Charl at the Mariam Hotel in Madaba). There is no public transport.

Hammamat Ma'in

حمامات ماعين (زرقاء ماعين)

☑ 05 / ELEV -90M

Drive anywhere in the hills above the Dead Sea and you'll notice occasional livid-green belts of vegetation, a trickle of water as it catches the sunlight, or a curtain of ferns across a disintegrating landscape of sulphurous rock. On closer inspection, you may catch a puff of steam and the hiss of underground water. These hills are alive with the sound of thermal springs – about 60 of

them suppurate below the surface, breaking ground with various degrees of violence.

The most famous spring is **Hammamat Ma'in** (admission per person JD15; ⊙9am-9pm), a spectacular resort in Wadi Zarqa Ma'in. The water, ranging from 45°C to a blistering 60°C, tumbles off the hillside in a series of waterfalls and less assuming trickles, and is collected in a variety of pools for public bathing. It contains potassium, magnesium and calcium.

The entrance fee permits use of the Roman baths at the base of the waterfall closest to the entrance and a swimming pool. Visitors are requested not to bring their own picnic, but this is rarely enforced. The valley is hugely popular on Friday during spring and autumn.

🏃 Activities

Thermal Bathing

Two main baths are open to the public. The **Roman baths** have clean, indoor hot baths (separate for men and women). There is also a small **family pool** beside a waterfall (turn left after the entrance), restricted to women, families and couples.

The large, clean, cold-water **swimming pool** closes around 4pm. A steaming waterfall downstream makes a striking backdrop for tea on the terrace of the hotel.

Spa Treatments

The exquisite little **Six Senses Spa** (☑3245500; www.sixsenses.com; ⊙9am-8pm) offers a range of different treatments and experiences. There are two thermal pools naturally hovering at 42°C and a natural sauna cave (65°C to 70°C) buried discreetly in the heart of the wadi. It's a beautiful place to relax with grouse scuttling over the rocks and eagles wheeling above. In addition, there is a dry sauna and treatment rooms, each with a private garden. Use of the facilities costs JD40 including towels and green tea. A range of treatments include a one-hour Dead Sea body wrap (JD70) and the signature 90-minute holistic massage (JD95). If you book in at the spa, the JD15 admission fee to Hammamat Ma'in is waived.

Hiking

It's possible to hike the 8km from the springs through Wadi Zarqa Ma'in to Herodus Spring on the Dead Sea Highway. The moderate to hard trail involves negotiating deep pools, reed beds and slippery surfaces and is closed after rains. The hike requires a guide (JD120 for a minimum of two people), which can be organised through the resort reception if you book one day ahead. The fee includes the price of transport to collect you from the end of the trail.

Another small trail leads from the security guard hut, above the main waterfall. It is an easy hike. There is no need for a guide, but you are requested to let the resort reception know that you are attempting it. If you prefer a guide to manage the small steep section, it costs JD35 per person for a minimum of two people. For JD65 the price includes breakfast, which is winched across the wadi in a basket to a shaded picnic spot in full view of the main waterfall.

🛏 Sleeping & Eating

Evason Ma'In Hot Springs
Six Senses Spa   RESORT **$$$**
(☑ 3245500; www.sixsenses.com/evason-ma-in; s/d JD270/350; ❄@☎) This luxurious resort is shaded with mature trees and made characterful with extravagant Arabesque features. Many of the rooms – with sumptuous bathrooms – share a view of the piping, sulphurous hillsides. Windows onto the waterfalls from the restaurant bring the hot springs to your table. Fine dining includes home-grown herbs and vegetables from the hotel's organic garden.

The hotel organises daily excursions to the Dead Sea, but chances are you'll find it hard to leave the sanctuary of the resort's own intimate spa.

ⓘ Getting There & Away

The resort is 18.5km from the Dead Sea resorts and 27km from Madaba, and well signposted in either direction. If you're driving, the 2.5km descent into Hammamat Ma'in is scenic (with bands of green, yellow and red streaking the hillside) but very steep, so use low gear.

From Madaba a taxi costs around JD15 one way, or JD25 for a return journey including around an hour's wait. Alternatively, take a tour from the Black Iris Hotel in Madaba for JD28 with a three-hour waiting time. There is no public transport.

Mujib Biosphere Reserve

محمية الموجب

Straddling the Dead Sea Highway, this wonderful reserve, which ranges from 900m above sea level to 400m below, was originally established by the Royal Society for the Conservation of Nature (RSCN) for the captive breeding of the Nubian ibex. It now supports a surprising variety of over 400 species of plants (including rare orchids), 186 species of birds and 250 animal species, including Syrian wolves, striped hyenas, caracals and Blandford's fox. It's also an important staging post for migratory birds travelling between Africa and Europe.

The reserve faces several challenges. Water in the permanently flowing wadis of the reserve has significantly reduced as water is siphoned off for use in Amman and the Dead Sea resorts. With illegal hunting, overgrazing of livestock and the demands of mining companies for licences to start mineral extraction, the future of the park is looking precarious. Against all the odds, the RSCN is doing a first-class job in managing the 215 sq km reserve and it can only be hoped that increased tourism to the reserve – with its crystal-clear pools of water, hanging gardens and desert escarpments – will increase the pressure on the government to guarantee its long-term protection.

🏃 Activites

Siq Trail   HIKING
(per person JD13) The easiest hike on offer, this exciting self-guided 2km wade and scramble into the gorge ends at a dramatic waterfall.

Malaqi Trail   HIKING
(per person JD47) This wet trail is the reserve's most popular hike. It's a half-day trip involv-

A WALK ON THE WET SIDE

If you're in the vicinity of the Mujib Biosphere Reserve and fancy a walk on the wild side, then try the 2km Siq Trail (p117), the shortest hike in the reserve. Late spring and summer are the perfect times for hiking, at least for the reserve's so-called 'wet trails'. And by wet, they really mean wet, as you have to wade through the wadi's permanent standing pools of water. After rains, water height can reach well over 1m and may make the wadi inaccessible.

Leave your valuables behind (you can leave a locked backpack at reception), wrap your camera in a watertight bag, wear hiking sandals rather than leather hiking boots and brave the surprisingly noisy rush of water.

The Good Bits

➡ 'Petra with water' is how the reserve ranger described the Siq Trail, and the comparison is a fair one.

➡ Beautiful pockets of lime-green reeds harbour toads and the occasional snake.

➡ The wadi is decorated with outrageously banded rock, scooped out and smoothed by the water.

➡ Being pushed by the water from one rock pool to the next has its moments.

➡ The adrenalin rush as the water thunders past a precarious foothold is exhilarating.

➡ Relief on surfacing easily from the bubbling cauldrons of water is almost worth the fear of leaping in.

➡ You'll be happy the pictures came out even though the camera didn't make it.

The Bad Bits

➡ Even on a summer morning it gets surprisingly cold wading between the canyon walls.

➡ Ignore the macho types telling you it's just a 'gentle splash': depending on water levels, it's more like an assault course.

➡ There are three or four points where you need a steadying hand to help cross fast-moving water (ask for a guide if you're on your own).

➡ Several giant, slippery boulders or obstructions at best require inelegant scrambling, shunting and stretching, and at worst invite a dislocated hip or shoulder.

➡ On the descent, the leap of faith into a deep pool of water takes quite a bit of courage.

So is it worthwhile? Without doubt! If you're fit but not a great water-goer, you'll be surprised by how benignly exciting it is to be alone in a raging torrent, bounced down small waterfalls and flipped into gorgeous pools of sunlight in what must be one of the region's most accessible little adventures.

---

ing a hot and unremitting climb into the wadi, a visit to the natural swimming pools of Wadi Hidan and a descent (often swimming) through the siq (gorge). The finale involves rappelling down the 18m waterfall (not suitable for non-swimmers or vertigo sufferers).

If you have limited time, tackle the wet Canyon Trail instead. The trails start 3km south of the visitor centre.

Ibex Trail　　　　　　　　　　　HIKING
(per person JD25) This dry winter trail is a half-day guided hike that leads up to a Nubian ibex enclosure at the Raddas ranger station, along a ridge with views of the Dead Sea, and an optional excursion to ruined Qasr Riyash.

🛏 Sleeping & Eating

Mujib Chalets　　　　　　　　　　CHALET
(☑079 7203888; www.rscn.jo; s/d/tr JD55/65/75) The Mujib Biosphere Reserve operates 15 chalets on the shores of the Dead Sea. Book in advance, either by calling the manager directly, or when booking your hike with the RSCN. The chalets have twin beds, a fridge and a shaded patio overlooking the Dead Sea in a plot that is still being developed. The communal shower block has hot and cold water, and there are freshwater showers by the beach. The small restaurant serves early breakfast (7am to 8.30am) for hikers. Guests can also order a simple lunch or dinner (JD11).

ℹ️ Information

The **visitor centre** (📞 079 7203888) is along the Dead Sea Highway, about 20km south of the Dead Sea resorts, beside a suspension bridge across Wadi Mujib. Guides are compulsory for all but the Siq Trail and should be booked in advance through the RSCN's Wild Jordan Centre (p306). Only 25 people per day are allowed on each trail and there's a minimum group size of five on the guided trails. Apart from the Ibex Trail, children under 18 years are not allowed. Life jackets are provided.

There are three wet trails (open between 1 April and 31 October) and two dry (1 November to 31 March). The best time to visit is April and May, although February and March, and October and November, are the high seasons. The region is extremely hot and dry for most of the year, so guided treks usually begin early in the morning. For the wet trails, you may be wading up to your chest in water (or swimming), so bring a swimming costume, towel, walking shoes that can get wet, and a waterproof bag for your valuables and camera. A spare set of clothes is also recommended.

ℹ️ Getting There & Away

There's no public transport to the reserve: hire a car or take a taxi from Amman (125km), the Dead Sea resorts, Madaba or Karak.

Lisan Peninsula

ليسان شبه جزيرة

From Wadi Mujib, the Dead Sea Highway continues along the remaining length of the sea until it veers inland at the Lisan Peninsula. This area, together with the shallow waters of the Southern Ghor (Depression), is now dominated by the potash plant. Huge quantities of potassium chloride (Jordan's most valuable commodity), calcium and bromine are reclaimed from the Dead Sea through solar evaporation, leaving piles of discarded rock salt along the shoreline. The area was once settled during the early-Byzantine period and a number of minor ruins are scattered across the landscape.

The fields to the south of the Lisan Peninsula are highly fertile and produce tomatoes in biblical quantities, as well as eggplants (aubergines), cucumbers and potatoes, groves of bananas and date palms. It's a colourful region to visit during the winter harvest (January) when trucks, laden with produce, lumber up the mountain roads, leaving a trail of off-loaded vegetables strewn behind them.

Lot's Cave

كهف لوط

> Now Lot went up out of Zo'ar, and dwelt in the hills with his two daughters, for he was afraid to dwell in Zo'ar; so he dwelt in a cave with his two daughters.
>
> *Genesis 19:30*

Lot, the nephew of Abraham, features repeatedly in the colourful annals of the Dead Sea's southern shores. Lot's Cave (☼ daylight) **FREE**, just past the Lisan Peninsula, is where he and his daughters apparently lived after fleeing the destruction of Sodom and Gomorrah. Lot's wife famously turned into a pillar of salt after looking back at the smouldering city.

In an eyebrow-raising incident that's remarkable even for the Bible, Lot's two daughters spiked their father's drink, had sex with him and then nine months later gave birth to his grandsons/sons Moab and Ben-Ammi, the forefathers of the Moabite and Ammonite peoples.

The cave, a stiff 10-minute climb up a steep flight of steps, is surrounded by the ruins of a small Byzantine church (5th to 8th centuries), a reservoir and some mosaics, which were excavated by the British Museum. Remains from the cave date to the early Bronze Age (3300–2000 BC) and an inscription in the cave mentions Lot by name.

Near the start of the climb up to the cave is the literally titled **Lowest Point on Earth Museum** (📞 03-2302845; Safi) **FREE**. Shaped like a giant stone comma, it contains beautifully displayed remains excavated from the site, including mosaics, 4500-year-old pottery, and ancient textiles. Other displays explain the area's importance for sugar production during the Mameluke period, and artefacts that illustrate the region's story up to the Bedouin tribes of today. A café and crafts shop run by **Safi Crafts** (www.saficrafts.blogspot.com/), a local women's cooperative, rounds out the experience.

The cave is 2km northeast of Safi and well signposted from the Dead Sea Highway. Look for the circular museum building on the hillside. Regular minibuses run between Karak and Safi (800 fils, one hour). If you're relying on public transport, be prepared for a 2km walk from the highway.

IN SEARCH OF SODOM

Say the words 'Sodom and Gomorrah' and dens of iniquity spring to mind. The Book of Genesis (Gen 19:24–25), responsible for the wicked reputation of these two terrible towns, describes the last straw – namely, when local Sodomites demanded to have sex with the angels sent by God to visit Lot. In response 'the Lord rained upon Sodom and upon Gomorrah brimstone and fire...and he overthrew those cities, and all the plain, and all the inhabitants of the cities, and that which grew upon the ground...'

Fanciful legends of a fevered biblical imagination? Not necessarily. The edge of Wadi Araba is located on a major fault line, and it's possible that the towns were swallowed up by collapsing soil. Another possibility is that an earthquake released large amounts of underground flammable gas and bitumen (the infamous 'slime pits' referred to in the Old Testament), which were ignited by fire or a lightning strike.

Whatever the cause of their demise, archaeologists have long speculated about the location of the world's most sinful cities. Many archaeologists favour the southern shore of the Dead Sea. But there's also the Bronze Age site of Babh adh-Dhra, on the edge of Wadi Karak. This town (population roughly 1000) was destroyed in 2300 BC, but intriguingly it holds the remains of 20,000 tombs, containing an estimated half a million bodies – as such it's odds-on favourite for Sodom. Both Babh adh-Dhra and the nearby site of Numeira, believed to be Gomorrah, are covered in a 30cm-deep layer of ash, suggesting the cities ended in a great blaze.

Natural disaster or the wrath of God? Some believe it amounts to the same thing.

Wadi Araba   وادى عربة

Beyond the town of Safi, the Dead Sea Highway enters the arid landscape of Wadi Araba, and the desert quickly reasserts its dominance. The odd sand dune encroaches upon the road, the escarpment recedes to the distance and the sky assumes the epic quality of uninterrupted space. As such, there is not much to see along the final run into Aqaba – although the sensation of driving uphill to the Red Sea is an odd one. You can make the journey more interesting by diverting to the King's Highway, along the remarkable roads to Karak, Tafila or Little Petra.

Madaba &
the King's Highway
مأدبا & الطريق الملوكي

Best Places to Stay

➡ Black Iris Hotel (p128)

➡ Mariam Hotel (p130)

➡ Al-Nawatef Camp (p150)

➡ Dana Guest House (p151)

➡ Feynan Ecolodge (p152)

Best Places to Eat

➡ Haret Jdoudna Complex & Cafe (p131)

➡ Adonis Restaurant (p131)

➡ Nebo Restaurant & Terrace (p135)

➡ Feynan Ecolodge (p152)

Why Go?

Occupying the central highlands and interrupted by the mighty Wadi Mujib, Madaba and the points of interest that punctuate the King's Highway lie at the heart of ancient Jordan. With prehistoric dolmens in rolling pastureland, panoramic sites of biblical importance, exquisite Roman mosaics and well-preserved Crusader castles, there is something fascinating to see along the entire length of this central region.

That doesn't mean to say that the region is only of interest to history buffs or religious pilgrims. As home to diverse communities, including Jordan's Christian minority, and encompassing dramatic and highly varied landscapes, this is quintessential Jordan. With good accommodation, traditional Jordanian dining and opportunities for hiking and canyoning, it's easy to engage with both town and country in a region that is still surprisingly off the beaten track for most visitors.

When to Go

➡ Enjoyable year-round, the higher altitude towns along the King's Highway often experience snow in winter providing a spectacular backdrop to Crusader castles. The cold air brings cut-glass clarity to the region's sweeping panoramas by day, and chilly nights inspire huddles around wood fires in true Arab tradition.

➡ For hiking, the season extends from March (when trail-side flowers are at their best) until 30th October. While Jordan's lowlands shrivel in the heat, this region's uplands offer relative cool, grapes and figs in abundance, raptor migration and grand sunsets.

Madaba & the King's Highway Highlights

1 Piece together early Christian history in the mosaics of **Madaba** (p123).

2 Take shade under an ancient stone dolmen in **Wadi Jadid** (p137).

3 Survey the Promised Land from Moses' memorial at **Mt Nebo** (p134).

4 Splash through permanent pools of water in one of the regions many **canyons** (p130).

5 Dance in Salome's footsteps at **Mukawir**, where Herod allegedly beheaded John the Baptist (p137).

6 Watch the ladies at **Bani Hamida** (p138) weave their past into a prosperous future.

7 Enjoy the eagle-eye vista of **Wadi Mujib** (p140) from the viewpoint.

8 Listen to the thunder of ghostly hooves at **Karak Castle** (p143). and **Shobak Castle** (p153), Jordan's most impressive Crusader remains.

9 Hike from the temperate uplands to the scorching desert floor of Wadi Araba in **Dana Biosphere Reserve** (p147).

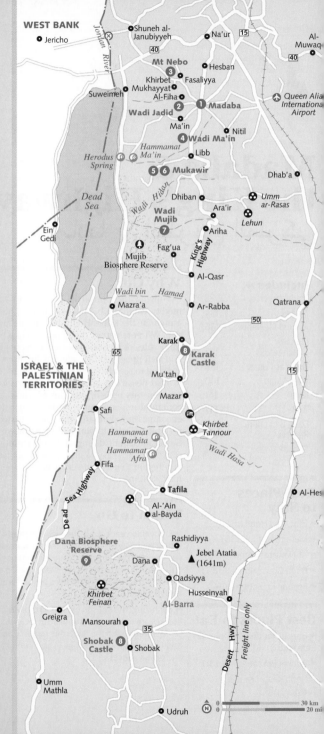

History

The landscape either side of the great yawning gap of Wadi Mujib is identical. There are neat olive groves, avenues of poplars, prickly pear fences, gently undulating hills, sheep driven along a network of paths, villages of flat-roofed houses – and occasional piles of fallen masonry from antiquity. North and south of the divide, the rural communities seem to form part of a seamless continuum along the surface of the upper plateau and, unless you have driven along the King's Highway, you might never guess at the great hiatus that divides the region in two.

There is surely no better metaphor for the continuity of human life along this ancient trade route. For the past 3000 years, the King's Highway has been traversed by the Israelites en route to the Promised Land; by Nabataeans to and from their sacred city at Petra; by Christian faithful on pilgrimages to Moses' memorial at Mt Nebo; by Crusaders to their castle fortifications; and by Muslim pilgrims heading to and from Mecca. Travel the road today, with all its difficulties, and you follow in the path of history.

Nature Reserves

The Royal Society for the Conservation of Nature (RSCN) runs two nature reserves straddling the central plateau, wedged between the King's Highway and the Dead Sea Highway. **Mujib Biosphere Reserve** is more usually accessed from the Dead Sea and is covered in that chapter. **Dana Biosphere Reserve** is accessed via the small upland village of Dana, just off the King's Highway. Protecting a rich diversity of flora and fauna, Dana Biosphere Reserve offers the visitor a chance to camp and hike in the reserve's striking landscape.

Dangers & Annoyances

Hiking and canyoning in any of the wadis that criss-cross the region from November to February should be approached with caution, if not avoided, because of the danger of flash floods. After rains, walls of water roll out of the canyons without warning, even on a cloudless day, uprooting trees and strewing boulders in their wake. Take advice before setting out and inform the hotel where you are heading.

It can get seriously cold here in winter with snow and hailstones. Many visitors get caught without adequate clothing as the daytime temperatures may still be beguilingly warm.

There is no public transport that crosses Wadi Mujib on the King's Highway, making it easy to get stranded – especially dangerous in high summer temperatures.

🛈 Getting There & Away

Of Jordan's three highways running north to south, the King's Highway is by far the most interesting, with a host of historical attractions lying on the road or nearby. The highway, which is little more than a rural road for most of its length, connects Madaba to Petra via Crusader castles, Roman forts, biblical sites, a windswept Nabataean temple and some epic landscapes – including the majestic Wadi Mujib.

The King's Highway is connected with the Dead Sea Highway via spectacular hairpin roads that are a highlight in their own right. Most public transport, however, connects with the King's Highway via the Desert Highway. Madaba is directly accessible from the main international airport (without the need to enter Amman).

🛈 Getting Around

It's not possible to travel the length of the King's Highway by public transport. This is because Wadi Mujib gets in the way. Minibuses serve the communities on either side of the wadi, but through traffic uses the Desert Hwy. Chartering a taxi for the day, however, is feasible.

The most convenient way to explore the King's Highway is to hire a car. You can drive the whole route from Madaba to Petra in a day. Allowing time to stop at all the places of interest and with a return along the Dead Sea Highway takes four to five days.

Hotels in Madaba and downtown Amman run minibus tours that stop in Wadi Mujib and Karak (and sometimes Dana and Shobak) en route to Petra.

At the time of writing, the conflict in neighbouring countries and the attendant refugee crisis made hitchhiking unsafe.

Madaba

مأدبا

🖉 05 / POP 156,300 / ELEV 800M

The amiable market town of Madaba is best known for a collection of Byzantine-era mosaics. The most famous of these is the mosaic map on the floor of St George's Church, but there are many others carpeting different parts of the town, many of which are even more complete and vibrant in colour.

Wonderful though they are, the mosaics are not the only reason to pay Madaba a visit. A traveller in the early 20th century

MADABA & THE KING'S HIGHWAY MADABA

Madaba

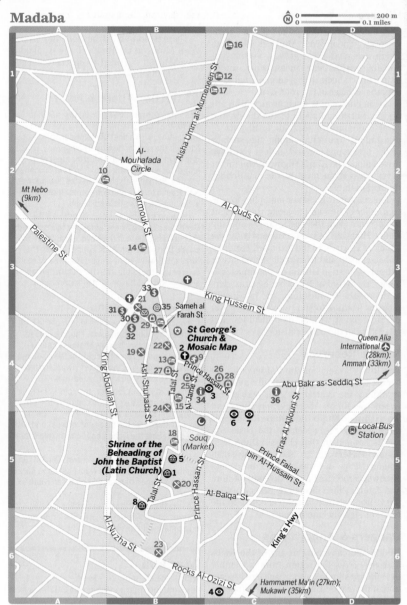

described being shot at by the people of Madaba just so they could bring him back to town as 'their guest and to eat their food'. No one is likely to shoot at you today, but the town remains one of the most traveller-friendly in Jordan.

Madaba has an interesting cultural mix. One-third of the population is Christian (the other two-thirds are Muslim), making it one of the largest Christian communities in Jordan. The town's long tradition of religious tolerance is joyfully – and loudly –

Madaba

expressed on Friday. This is one day when you shouldn't expect a lie-in. The imam summons the faithful to pray before dawn, the carillon bells bid the Orthodox Christians to rise at first light, and finally Mammon gets a look in with the honks and groans of traffic. The rest of the day is punctuated with yelps to buy apricots, bleats from passing herds of sheep, and friendly greetings from children.

Madaba is easily and best explored on foot. With its lively shops dangling with strings of shoes, skinned goats tended by men in white Wellington boots, sewing machines rattling off repairs by the roadside, piles of fat cabbages, and giant aluminium pots and pans, Madaba is a typical King's Highway town. Unlike most other towns along the highway, however, it has a good choice of hotels and restaurants.

Less than an hour by public transport from Amman, Madaba makes an alternative base for exploring King's Highway and Dead Sea highlights. By taxi, you can even travel directly from Queen Alia International Airport in around 20 minutes, bypassing Amman altogether.

History

The region around Madaba has been inhabited for around 4500 years and was one of the towns divided among the 12 tribes of Israel at the time of the Exodus. The region passed from Ammonites to Israelites, Nabataeans and eventually, by AD 106, to Romans, under whom Madaba became a prosperous provincial town with colonnaded streets and impressive public buildings. The prosperity continued during the Christian Byzantine period, with the construction of churches and the lavish mosaics that decorated them.

The town was abandoned for about 1100 years after a devastating earthquake in AD 747. In the late 19th century, 2000 Christians from Karak migrated to Madaba after a bloody dispute with Karak's Muslims. The new arrivals found the town's signature mosaics when they started digging foundations for houses. News that a mosaic map of the Holy Land had been found in St George's Church in Madaba reached Europe in 1897, leading to a flurry of excavation that continues to this day. Various NGOs have assisted

MADABA & THE KING'S HIGHWAY MADABA

in restoration and rejuvenation projects in Madaba; at the time of writing, US Aid was taking an active initiative in this field. To find out more, see www.usaid.gov/jordan.

◉ Sights

Madaba is sprinkled over the top of a tell. The most interesting part of town is the old quarter on top of the hill, rather than the new developments along the King's Highway. Follow signs for the 'Visitors Centre', or any of the hotels, to reach the centre of town.

Most tourists file dutifully in and out of St George's Church and pay scant attention to the rest of Madaba. This is good news for the discerning visitor who can pore over the town's other stunning mosaics, untroubled by the crowds. The Archaeological Park, Madaba Museum and Church of the Apostles are all covered by the same combined ticket.

★ **St George's**
Church & Mosaic Map   CHURCH
(Talal St; adult/child under 12yr JD1/free; ⊙ 8am-5pm Sat-Thu Nov-Mar, 8am-6pm Sat-Thu Apr-Oct, 9.30am-5pm Fri year-round) This rather modest 19th-century **Greek Orthodox church** houses a treasure of early Christianity. Imagine the excitement in 1884 when Christian builders came across the remnants of an old Byzantine church on their construction site. Among the rubble, having survived wilful destruction, fire and neglect, the flooring they discovered wasn't just another mosaic, it was one with extraordinary significance: to this day, it represents the oldest map of Palestine in existence and provides many historical insights into the region.

Crafted in AD 560, the map has 157 captions (in Greek) depicting all the major biblical sites of the Middle East from Egypt to Palestine. It was originally around 15m to 25m long and 6m wide, and once contained more than two million pieces. Although much of the mosaic has been lost, enough remains to sense the complexity of the whole.

On Friday and Sunday morning the church opens at 7am for Mass (visitors welcome); viewing the map at these times is not

---

NAVIGATING THE MADABA MAP

It takes some orientation to be able to 'read' the Mabada Map spread across the floor of St George's Church. Chances are you will intuitively look at the mosaic expecting north to be in front of you, towards the altar. In fact, the map, and indeed the church itself, is oriented towards the east. Imagine, therefore, as you approach the map, that you are in the hills west of Jerusalem, looking over the crenulated tops of the great city residences towards the Dead Sea and follow the guide below for the highlights.

North (top left)

In the most touching part of the mosaic, fish in the Jordan River scamper back upstream from the lethal waters of the Dead Sea, swimming under the cable-drawn ferries of the river crossing (marked today by King Hussein Bridge). A bodiless lion pursues a gazelle just above Bethany, the supposed site of Jesus' baptism (marked as 'Sapsafas' on the map).

East (straight ahead)

The most exquisitely detailed part of the map depicts Jerusalem, complete with city walls, gates and the central road (cardo). Becalmed on the waters of the Dead Sea, their oars at the ready, lie two boats going nowhere. Perhaps they were trying to ferry Herod to the spa at Callirhöe (Zara), marked by three springs and two palm trees. Lot's Cave, where the old man was seduced by his two daughters, lies just above the oasis of Safi (Balak or Zoara). The walled town of Karak appears in the uppermost portion of the map, at the end of vertical Wadi Al-Hasa.

South (far right)

Mt Sinai is recognisable by the multicoloured mountains from which Moses descended with the Ten Commandments. Look for fish in the mosaic fingers of the Nile Delta; they swim towards the Mediterranean, only a snippet of which remains. Almost fragmented from the rest of the Holy Land by damage, but resolutely connected to Egypt and the Mediterranean Sea, is Gaza. This accident of history gives the map a kind of presentiment that matches its historical vision.

permitted. A small shop by the exit sells copies of the map and reproduction Orthodox icons.

Before viewing the map, take a look at the full-size replica in the ticket office, making it easier to spot the details that you want to focus on in the church. The ticket office doubles as a small interpretative centre. The centre offers visitors the chance to watch a free seven-minute video explaining the mosaic map in several languages.

Visitors Centre   HISTORIC BUILDING

(☑3253563; Abu Bakr as-Seddiq St; ⊗8am-6pm Oct-Apr, to 7pm May-Sep) This helpful interpretative centre makes a good starting point for visiting the highlights of Madaba. It is worth a visit in its own right as it is housed in a beautifully restored traditional house from the late 19th century, belonging to the al-Batjali family. Two of the rooms contain interesting information panels in English on the history of Madaba, and there's a 10-minute film that sets the town in its historical context.

Note the open central courtyard – unusual in Jordan where the predominantly Muslim culture normally dictates a closed, interior space to protect family privacy. The shady courtyard of plumbago and geraniums offers a respite from a hot day's sightseeing; there are clean toilets next to the centre's car park.

Madaba Institute for Mosaic Art & Restoration (MIMAR)   MOSAIC WORKSHOP

(☑3240723; Abu Bakr as-Seddiq St; ⊗8am-3pm Sun-Thu) FREE Originally set up as a school in 1992 by the Jordanian Government, this institute trains Jordanian artists in the production and restoration of mosaics, spreads awareness of mosaics in Jordan and actively preserves mosaics throughout the country. The restoration work of the school's artisans is evident in the Archaeological Park, the Church of the Apostles and at Khirbet Mukhayyat. Visit the administration office to arrange a workshop visit and an appreciation of the painstaking nature of mosaic making.

Madaba Archaeological Park I & Virgin Mary Church   ARCHAEOLOGICAL SITE

(☑3246681; Abu Bakr as-Seddiq St; combined ticket/child under 12yr JD2/free; ⊗8am-4pm Oct-Apr, to 5pm May-Sep) Some careful restoration and excavation in the early 1990s led to the creation of this open-air museum which

houses a collection of ruins and fine mosaics from the Madaba area. The Church of the Virgin Mary is also included in the site; built in the 6th century and unearthed beneath the floor of someone's house in 1887, the church boasts a central mosaic, thought to date from AD 767, that is a masterpiece of geometric design.

As you enter the complex, you'll see a 1st-century BC mosaic from Machaerus, which is said to be the oldest mosaic found in Jordan. Follow the walkway to the right, above the Roman street. This street once ran east to west between the Roman city gates and was lined with columns. Continue past the faded but elegant mosaics of the Church of the Prophet Elias (built AD 607), pausing to enjoy the details (such as the fine green bird), and then descend to the crypt (AD 595).

The large roofed structure in front of you contains some of the most impressive mosaics on the site, including those of Hippolytus Hall, an early-6th-century Byzantine villa. Spot the four seasons in each corner and notice the beautiful depictions of flowers and birds. The middle section shows characters from the classic Greek Oedipal tragedy of Phaedra and Hippolytus. The upper image shows Adonis and a topless Aphrodite spanking naughty, winged Eros, while the Three Graces (daughters of Zeus, representing joy, charm and beauty) float nearby.

Archaeological Park II (Burnt Palace)   ARCHAEOLOGICAL SITE

(Prince Hassan St; ⊗8am-3pm Sun-Thu Oct-Apr, to 5.30pm Sun-Thu May-Sep) FREE Walkways lead around the ruins of this late-6th-century luxury private mansion, destroyed by fire and earthquake around AD 749. From this vantage point, there's a good view of assorted mosaics, the best of which are the hunting sequences in the east wing, and the lion attacking a bull in the west wing. It's probably fair to say that the site takes more imagination than most.

Look out for the continuation of the ancient Roman road that runs through what is now the Archaeological Park, as well as the 6th-century Martyrs Church, which was destroyed in the 8th century. If the on-site guard is willing, ask to see the buried mosaics of the church: protected from the light by sand until restoration takes place, the few tesserae (squares) of buried mosaic that he'll expose for you are astonishing in the vibrancy of their colour.

Dar Al-Saraya   HISTORIC BUILDING
(Talal St) Built in the late 19th century as the administrative centre of the Ottomans, this grand old building was subsequently used as the headquarters of the British administration in 1922. It was recently renovated and is tipped to open soon as a restaurant. In the meantime, the adjacent hillside plaza makes a good place to catch the breeze.

★ **Shrine of the Beheading of
John the Baptist (Latin Church)**   MUSEUM
(☑ 3244065; Talal St; adult/child under 12yr JD1/free; ⊙ 9am-5pm Oct-Apr, to 7pm May-Sep) This operational early-20th-century Roman Catholic Church has been transformed into an intriguing destination for visitors and pilgrims by the restoration of the ancient sites upon which the church sits. The gem of the complex is the **Acropolis Museum**, housed in the ancient, vaulted underbelly of the church. Here, an ancient well dating to the Moabite era, 3000 years ago, is still operational.

The church facade was built with ancient stones, and Roman columns with Corinthian capitals dot the courtyard. In the 19th-century chapel, which now acts as a visitors centre and gift shop, there is a fascinating exhibition of photographs dating from 1902 to 1911. Spare some time and energy to scale the belfry. The last section involves steep metal ladders with handrails and a bit of dexterity manoeuvring around the bells and bell ropes, but it's worth the effort for the best panorama in Madaba.

The church is closed to visitors during Mass and for occasional events on Sundays. Handcrafted roseries from the Holy Land are on sale and there are spotlessly clean toilets in the visitors centre.

Madaba Museum   MUSEUM
(☑ 3244189; Haya Bint Al-Hussin St; combined ticket/child under 12yr JD2/free; ⊙ 8am-5pm, to 7pm May-Sep) Housed in several old Madaba residences, highlights of this museum include a 6th-century mosaic depicting a naked satyr, a saucy (and partially damaged) mosaic of Ariadne dancing with cymbals on her hands and feet, and a mosaic in the courtyard depicting two rams tied to a tree – a popular image recalling Abraham's sacrifice. A small, dusty Folklore Museum is included in the admission price, featuring jewellery, traditional costumes and a copy of the Mesha Stele.

There have long been plans to move the museum to Dar Al-Saraya, but nothing has come of this yet. It may explain, however, why the museum is rather under par. The open courtyard with grape vines, palms and a view makes a pleasant place to sit.

Church of the Apostles   CHURCH
(King's Highway; combined ticket/child under 12yr JD2/free; ⊙ 9am-4pm Oct-Apr, 8am-5pm May-Sep) This insignificant-looking church contains a remarkable mosaic dedicated to the Twelve Apostles. The embroidery-like mosaic was created in AD 568 and is one of the few instances where the name of the craftsman (Salomios) is included. The central portion shows Thalassa, a female personification of the sea, surrounded by fish and slippery marine creatures. Native animals, birds, flowers, fruits and cherubic faces decorate the corners.

🛏 **Sleeping**

Madaba has a good range of hotels, mostly run by Christian families and all within easy walking distance of the town's main sights. Prices include breakfast and private bathroom unless otherwise noted. A Best Western is the only chain hotel in town.

★ **Black Iris Hotel**   GUESTHOUSE $
(☑ 3241959; www.blackirishotel.com; near Al-Mouhafada Circle; s/d/tr JD25/30/40; 🖥) For a 'home away from home' feeling, it's hard to beat this family-run hotel. The rooms are cosy and there's a spacious communal sitting area. The 'very special breakfast' includes date cake and homemade fig jam, and the owner (trained hotelier and former chef in Switzerland) makes home-cooked Jordanian suppers on request, garnished with home-grown herbs from his garden.

The kindly and knowledgeable assistance in organising onward travel (as shown in the hotel website) makes the Black Iris ever popular with readers; women travelling alone will feel comfortable here. The hotel is easy to spot from Al-Mouhafada Circle.

Queen Ayola Hotel   HOTEL $
(☑ 3244087; www.queenayolahotel.com; Talal St; s/d JD25/30, s/d with shared bathroom JD10/18; 🖥) With happy hour from 6pm to 10pm and good food, this is a popular travellers haunt. The rooms are simple but clean and two have balconies onto the street – fun for people-watching in the heart of town. The

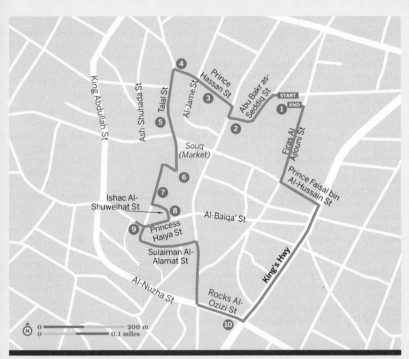

Town Walk
Mosaics & Museums in Madaba

START VISITORS CENTRE
END VISITORS CENTRE
LENGTH 3KM; THREE HOURS

From the ❶ **visitors centre** (p127) leave via Abu Bakr as-Seddiq St, pausing at the bend to admire the town view. Call in ❷ **Archaeological Park I** (p127), catching topless Aphrodite spanking Eros. Turn right and immediately left along colourful, pedestrianised 'Artisan St' (Prince Hassan St), with its flapping kilims. Duck into ❸ **Archaeological Park II** (p127) for a preview of yet-to-be-restored mosaics. The antique shop opposite is an Aladdin's cave of copper coffee pots.

At the T-junction with Talal St, turn right for ❹ **St George's Church** (p126), famed for its mosaic map, and visit cosy Ayola Coffeeshop opposite. Backtrack along Talal St. The renowned restaurant ❺ **Haret Jdoudna** (p131) is tucked into a traditional Madaba residence on the right; the craft shop here supports good causes. Continue uphill along Talal St towards ❻ **Dar Al-Saraya** (p128), rumoured to become Madaba's main museum. The road curves uphill to the ❼ **Shrine of the Beheading of John the Baptist** (p128), a Catholic church constructed with Roman fragments. Compare the modern town vista from the belfry with the photographs in the gallery.

From the church, turn left along Ishac Al-Shuweihat St, passing ❽ **Adonis Restaurant** (p131). Turn right on Princess Haiya St to ❾ **Madaba Museum** (p128) – a shady spot to absorb Madaba's layered history.

Backtrack to Sulaiman Al-Alamat St and pass an unexcavated cathedral and fine houses. Turn right at the T-junction and head downhill, turning left onto Rocks Al-Ozizi St. Call into the tiny ❿ **Church of the Apostles** (p128) to see imagined marine creatures in mosaic.

Walk north along the King's Highway past hardware stores abuzz with Bedouin shoppers in traditional headdresses. Turn uphill along Prince Faisal bin Al-Hussain St, noting the mosque's minaret rising majestically above Madaba's skyline. At the crossroads, adorned with gold shops, tailors and haberdashers, turn right onto Firas Al Ajlouni St and make your way back to the visitors centre.

hotel facilitates local trips, such as half- and full-day hiking and canyoning.

Salome Hotel
HOTEL $

(☎ 3248606; www.salomehotel.com; Aisha Umm al-Mumeneen St; s/d/tr JD25/30/36; ❄ @ 🛜) With the family-run appeal of a small residential hotel, the Salome is a good choice for a quiet stay. It has a welcoming reception-cum-lounge, a licensed restaurant and an ever-charming owner. It's located next to the Mariam Hotel, an easy five-minute walk from the town centre.

Rumman Hotel
HOTEL $

(☎ 3252555; www.rummanhotel.com; Aisha Umm al-Mumeneen St; s/d/tr JD24/30/38; ❄ @ 🛜) A friendly owner, spacious rooms and the only bathtubs in town, Rumman lives up to the Twal family reputation for hospitality and visitor assistance.

St George's Church Pilgrim House
GUESTHOUSE $

(☎ /fax 077 5364218; pilgrimshousemadaba@gmail.com; Talal St, entry via Prince Hassan St; s/d/tr JD25/35/45; 🛜) Although it receives mainly Christian pilgrims, travellers can expect a warm welcome at this guesthouse. Rooms are ascetically simple. If you encounter the patron, the urbane and charming Father Innocent, then your stay will be extra blessed! Profits from the guesthouse are invested in the neighbouring church school.

Moab Land Hotel
GUESTHOUSE $

(☎ /fax 3251318; moabland_hotel@orange.jo; Talal St; s/d/tr JD30/35/40) With grand views of St George's Church and beyond, this family-run hotel couldn't be more central. The prize draw, apart from the welcome, is the glorious rooftop terrace where breakfast is served in summer. The reception is on the upper floor.

★ Mariam Hotel
HOTEL $$

(☎ 3251529; www.mariamhotel.com; Aisha Umm al-Mumeneen St; s/d/tr/q JD30/40/50/60; ❄ @ 🛜 ☒) The Mariam has built a prodigious reputation over the years, offering good facilities including a bar, pool-side restaurant and a cheerful communal area. A restaurant and bar on the 5th floor offers

OFF THE BEATEN TRACK

CANYONING

The central part of Jordan is riven with wadis and canyons, some of which only come alive during a flash flood and others which are home to permanent watercourses that push their way through the rocky landscape to the Dead Sea. Along the way the presence of water creates beautiful semitropical oases of palms, oleandar and ferns. Often hidden from the road, these secret gardens are one of the treasures of Jordan.

While thankfully the most spectacular canyons (such as those of the lower Wadi Mujib) are protected and made safely accessible by the Royal Society for the Conservation of Nature (RSCN), there is nothing to stop a visitor exploring other canyons off the beaten track. The Upper Hidan Gorge and the Canyon of Zarqa Ma'in near Madaba, together with Wadi ibn Hammad and Wadi Labun near Karak, offer a range of outdoor adventures from casual splashing through shallow pools to technical routes involving abseiling and swimming across deep pools with points of no return.

It's worth bearing in mind with any veering off the beaten track in Jordan that canyoning is not yet an established sport here and you're more likely to bump into shepherds than fellow adventurers. You must be self-sufficient and aware of the potential dangers involved.

To go it alone, the essential companion for canyoning is the widely available hikers' bible, *Jordan: Walks, Treks, Caves, Climbs & Canyons,* by Di Taylor and Tony Howard (4th edition 2007). For escorted trips (recommended given the unpredictability of flash flooding), contact the RSCN (p318) at Wadi Mujib or Dana, the **Feynan Ecolodge** (☎ 079 9599507; rkhawaldeh@rscn.org.jo), or the Black Iris Hotel (p128) in Madaba.

The Queen Ayola Hotel (p128) in Madaba offers trips to the Canyon of Zarqa Ma'in through the characterful, bilingual, local taxi driver-guide Mr Odtllah. The four-hour trip (only possible if there is no rain) is manageable without any special levels of fitness or experience and includes luxuriating in the warm-water pools emanating from the famed hot springs. A helpful traveller's video in the hotel sets the scene: the application of mud, pool-side, by the guide might just be the clincher!

views across town. Reservations are recommended. The hotel arranges transport to/from the airport (around JD14) and to Petra (among other destinations) for hotel guests.

Ask Charl Twal, the friendly owner who is a keen advocate of responsible tourism involving interaction with locals, about a trip to see the local dolmens – a subject he is knowledgeable and passionate about.

Mosaic City Hotel HOTEL $$
(☎ 3251313; www.mosaiccityhotel.com; Yarmouk St; s/d JD44/53, extra bed JD15; ❄ ☎) This attractive family-run hotel has bright, spacious rooms. Some have balconies overlooking lively Yarmouk St but windows are double-glazed, keeping street noise to a minimum. The reception at this central hotel is ever amiable and facilities include a cool new bar, pool table and hand-crafted soap shop. A family room sleeps four, with a double-size bathroom (JD87).

St John Hotel HOTEL $$
(☎ 3246040; www.saintjohnmadaba.com; Talal St; s/d/tr JD45/55/65; ❄ ☎) ✎ This central and attractive new hotel has cosy, modern rooms, many with balconies. The hotel has been designed with ecofriendly features such as solar panels and energy-efficient bathrooms. In addition, the already popular Rabwat Madaba Skybar and Restaurant offers wonderful views and a convivial atmosphere. A gym and free bicycle use help work off a night on the roof.

Madaba Inn Hotel HOTEL $$
(☎ 3259003; www.madaba-inn.com; Talal St; s/d/tr JD45/70/80; ❄ ☎) Though needing refurbishment, this 33-room hotel is in a good central position and has car parking. Wi-fi is restricted to the lobby.

🍴 Eating & Drinking

Madaba is a good place to sample traditional Jordanian food. Most of Madaba's restaurants serve beer, some interesting local wines and the local firewater, arak.

There are a number of snack shops along Yarmouk St and the King's Highway, selling felafel, shwarma and roasted chicken. For freshly baked Arabic bread, head for the ovens opposite the Church of the Apostles. There are several grocery stores in the centre of town. Fresh fruit and veg for a picnic can be bought along King Abdullah St.

There's little going on in Madaba after dark except drinking and eating: for the liveliest bars, head for the Queen Ayola, Ayola Coffeeshop, Mosaic City Hotel, the Skybar at St John's Hotel or poolside at the Mariam Hotel.

Abu Yousef JORDANIAN $
(Ash Shuhada St; JD 2; ◷ 8am-1pm; ✎) Little more than a hole in the wall, Abu Yousef's establishment is part of the fabric of the town, serving fresh hummus and felafel daily to those in the know. Found opposite the parking lot of Haret Jdouna, this modest restaurant has supported the owner Abu Yousef (now in his dotage) and his family for over 30 years.

Ayola Coffeeshop & Bar CAFE $
(☎ 3251843; Talal St; snacks around JD2.500; ◷ 8am-11pm; ☎ ✎) If you want a toasted sandwich, Turkish coffee, glass of arak with the locals, or simply a comfortable perch on which to while away some time with fellow travellers, then this is the place to come. There's free internet access if you have a laptop.

Al-Baraka Sweets BAKERY $
(cnr Sameh al-Farah & King Abdullah Sts; ◷ 10am-10pm) Don't miss out on Arabic bakeries, like Al-Baraka Sweets, where you'll find round trays of honey-drizzled pastries, some filled with local cheese, other with nuts and sugar.

★ Haret Jdoudna Complex JORDANIAN $$
(☎ 3248650; Talal St; mains JD8-15; ◷ noon-midnight; ✎) Popular with locals and discerning diners from Amman, and set in one of Madaba's restored old houses, this restaurant is a Madaba favourite. Sit indoors by a roaring fire in winter or in the shaded courtyard in summer and sample the traditional Jordanian dishes such as *mutaffi bethanjan* (fried eggplant with sesame).

Other popular dishes include *fatteh* (fried bread with garlic-laced yoghurt and hummus, sometimes with chicken) and *sawani* (meat or vegetables cooked on trays in a wood-burning oven). Buy a souvenir of a good night out from the handicraft shop within the complex and you'll have the added satisfaction of contributing to a good cause.

★ Adonis Restaurant & Cafe JORDANIAN $$
(☎ 3251771; Ishac al-Shuweihat St; mixed grill JD7; ◷ 11am-2am) Housed in a beautifully restored typical Madaba residence and run by one of

MADABA & THE KING'S HIGHWAY MADABA

the town's returning sons, this excellent restaurant has quickly become the place to be at weekends. Serving typical Jordanian fare in a space that expands almost magically into unseen corners, Adonis has the added charm of live music on Thursday and Friday nights.

Bowabit Restaurant   CAFE $$

(✆ 3240335; Talal St; mains JD7.500; ⏱ 10am-midnight) With two tables overhanging the road opposite St George's Church, photographs of old Madaba on the wall and excellent Italian-style coffee, this is a number-one place to relax after strolling round town. Alternatively, make a night of it over a dish of Madaba chicken and a beer (JD4).

Dana Restaurant   BUFFET $$

(✆ 3245749 3245452; bassamtwal@hotmail.com; Rocks Al-Ozizi St; lunch buffet JD10; ⏱ noon-3pm) Popular with tour groups, this restaurant serves a good-quality buffet in a pleasant dining hall. It makes a useful stop if you've worked up an appetite on the walking tour.

🛍 Shopping

You can visit private mosaic workshops (with no obligation to buy) around town and purchase your own copy of the Madaba map or a more modest Tree of Life (from JD15, depending on the size).

Madaba is also famous for its colourful hand-loomed kilims (rugs), which flap and dance outside shops throughout town (especially between the Burnt Palace and St George's Church on pedestrianised 'Artisan St'). Buying one of these rugs is more than just a purchase, it's a great way to get under the skin of the town: chats and tea with the rug-sellers are de rigueur.

Spare some time to amble along Yarmouk St: here you will find water pipes, women's headscarves and shops selling Jordanian sweets. The street comes alive at night and it's a good place to mingle with local shoppers to get a flavour of the town.

There are several warehouse-like emporia selling handicrafts but they are mainly intended for tour groups and lack the personal touch of shops in town. If you are into one-stop shopping, however, you can find these outlets along the road to Mt Nebo.

Haret Jdoudna Complex   HANDICRAFTS

(✆ 3248650; Talal St; ⏱ 10.30am-11pm) Selling an extensive range of crafts, including mosaics, ceramics, textiles and clothing, this shop, attached to the restaurant of the same name,

stocks particularly exquisite embroidery. Many of the items for sale are sponsored by the Arab Cultural Society, which supports Jordanian war widows. Indeed, most items come from local nonprofit organisations, including the Jordan River Foundation which supports marginalised communities.

Hanania Silver Shop & Rafidi for Silver   JEWELLERY

(Prince Hassan St; ⏱ 10am-1pm & 4pm-7pm) There are a number of quality jewellery shops in town including these locally renowned master silversmiths along Prince Hassan St. There is little on display in the windows but every piece is handcrafted to the highest standards.

Holy Treasures Centre   SOUVENIRS

(✆ 3248481; Talal St; ⏱ 10am-1pm & 4pm-7pm) Opposite St George's Church, this shop has an extensive range of Dead Sea products. It also sells consecrated holy water from the Jordan River.

Spice   FOOD

(Sameh al-Farah St; ⏱ 8am-8.30pm) For an unusual present, take back a selection of spices or freshly ground coffee beans from this aromatic grocers.

Madaba Studio & Lab   ELECTRONICS

(✆ 3245932; Talal St; ⏱ 8am-8.30pm) Has memory cards and batteries.

Rosa Silver   HANDICRAFTS

(Prince Hassan St; ⏱ 10am-1pm & 4pm-7pm) There are a number of quality shops in town where locally renowned master silversmiths make chains, pendants and rings.

Carpet City   HANDICRAFTS

(✆ 3244397; Al-Jame St; ⏱ 10am-1pm & 4pm-7pm) Be warned! It's notoriously difficult to leave a carpet shop in Jordan empty-handed. This is partly due to the skill of the salesmen and partly because the rugs are so desirable. This family-run enterprise made the camel bags that feature in the film *Lawrence of Arabia*: if their rugs don't win favour, the stories they weave surely will.

Jordan Jewel   HANDICRAFTS

(✆ 3241364; Mt Nebo Road; 10am-1pm & 4pm-7pm) A large handicraft centre specialising in mosaics, located 1km before Mt Nebo on the road from Madaba. The owner of this large emporium employs a large number of physically challenged locals to help offer marginalised people a way back into society.

ℹ Information

Collect a brochure called *Madaba and Mount Nebo*, summarising Madaba's attractions, from the visitors centre. Other good Jordan Tourist Board brochures include *Madaba Mosaic Map* and *Mount Nebo*.

The American Center of Oriental Research publishes the definitive *Madaba: Cultural Heritage* (around JD20). More portable is the *Mosaic Map of Madaba* by Herbert Donner (JD10), with a fold-out reproduction of the map and detailed text. Also recommended is the pocket-sized *Madaba, Mt Nebo* published by Al-Kutba (JD3). All of these are also available at the visitors centre.

The bookshop opposite the Burnt Palace sells a range of international newspapers.

Arab Bank (Sameh al-Farah St; ☺ 8.30am-3pm Sun-Thu) Accepts Visa and MasterCard, and has an ATM.

Bank of Jordan (cnr Palestine & King Abdullah Sts; ☺ 8.30am-3pm Sun-Thu) Changes cash and travellers cheques.

Housing Bank (Sameh al-Farah St; ☺ 8.30am-3pm Sun-Thu) Accepts Visa; has an ATM.

Jordan National Bank (cnr King Abdullah & Talal Sts; ☺ 8.30am-3pm Sun-Thu) Changes cash and travellers cheques.

Ministry of Tourism & Antiquities (☑ 3252687; www.tourism.jo; ☺ 8am-3pm Sun-Thu) Has an office above the Burnt Palace for specialised information about Madaba's preservation efforts.

Post Office (Sameh al-Farah St; ☺ 8am-5pm) Long-distance telephone calls can be made here.

Tour.Net Internet (Talal St; per hr 500 fils; ☺ 9am-2am)

Tourist Police Office (☑ 191; Talal St; ☺ 24hr) Just north of St George's Church and in the visitors centre.

Visitors Centre (☑ 3253563; Abu Bakr as-Seddiq St; ☺ 8am-6pm Oct-Apr, to 7pm May-Sep) This helpful information office has a range of brochures and some informative displays. Ask to see the 10-minute film that sets Madaba in the context of the surrounding highlights. There are toilets and a handy car park.

ℹ Getting There & Away

The bus station is about 15 minutes' walk east of the town centre on the King's Highway. Most attractions around Madaba (with the exception of Mt Nebo and Mukawir) are time-consuming if not impossible to reach by public transport. It's easy, however, to charter a taxi in Madaba or take one of the well-thought-out tours or transport options from the Black Iris Hotel (available to all) or the Mariam Hotel (available to residents of the hotel only); both these hotels have a wealth of experience in organising trips for independent travellers.

ℹ MA'AN NOT AMMAN!

If you're brave enough to try travelling by public transport in the region, be careful how you pronounce the transport hub of Ma'an. If you don't get your gutturals worked out, you may just find yourself heading back to the capital – no laughing matter if you've just spent a day of your trip trying to edge along the King's Highway.

TO/FROM THE AIRPORT

If you want to bypass the bustle of Amman, it's possible to reach Madaba from Queen Alia International Airport by private taxi (daytime JD22-25) in under half an hour. Most hotels in Madaba can arrange a taxi from the airport if you contact them in advance (JD14 to JD20). Taxis from Madaba to the airport cost a couple of dinars less.

TO/FROM AMMAN

From the Muhajireen, South (Wahadat) and North (Tababoor) bus stations in Amman, there are regular buses and minibuses (JD1, one hour) throughout the day for Madaba. Minibuses return to Amman until around 8pm (earlier on Friday). Taxis cost a minimum of JD15 during the day, JD20 at night.

TO/FROM THE DEAD SEA

It's really not feasible to rely on public transport to reach the Dead Sea as the route involves two minibus rides, which are unreliable at best, and a taxi ride from Suweimah that can cost almost as much as a taxi from Madaba. If you're determined, check with your hotel for the latest information on these ad hoc services. To visit the Dead Sea by taxi with enough time for a swim, you need to factor in three hours' waiting time. The Black Iris offers this trip for JD28.

One popular trip from Madaba to the Dead Sea is via Mt Nebo and Bethany, returning via the Dead Sea Panoramic Complex and Hammamat Ma'in (around JD50).

With your own transport, you can drive to the Dead Sea via Mt Nebo and return along the Dead Sea Panoramic Complex road. Branch off to Hammamat Ma'in and the new Mukawir road for a spectacular detour. Alternatively, you can make a longer but equally stunning drive via Karak.

SOUTH ALONG THE KING'S HIGHWAY

There is no public transport linking Madaba with Karak along the King's Highway as scaling the banks of Wadi Mujib on a regular basis costs more in vehicle maintenance than it earns in fares. Trying to get there on a sequence of local minibuses and taxi hire is made problematic by the lack of taxis to charter across Wadi Mujib from Dhiban to Ariha. Even if you find a taxi, they are likely to charge you as much as the taxi fare from Madaba to Karak so you gain little by the enterprise. From Karak minibuses run to Tafila, where you can find transport for Qadsiyya (access to Dana). Public transport south of Qadsiyya is infrequent, so you may need to take a minibus to Ma'an and then another to Wadi Musa (Petra).

A much easier option is to take the daily service organised for residents by the Mariam Hotel (p130). Leaving at 10am, it goes to Petra (arriving around 6pm), with a stop at Wadi Mujib for photos, and an hour in Karak. You can get off at Dana, but you may have to pay the full fare. The service requires a minimum of three people (the hotel will link you with other passengers staying at the hotel) and a maximum of four, and costs JD20 per taxi. The Black Iris Hotel offers a similar service for the same price for nonresidents. Other hotels offer similar deals though with less frequency. A normal taxi fare for this service is between JD90 to JD120 per car.

TO/FROM MUKAWIR

From the local bus station in Madaba, minibuses go to Mukawir (for Machaerus castle; JD1, one hour) several times a day (not Fridays). The last minibus leaves at around 5pm. The service isn't wholly reliable – it will only run if there are enough passengers. A taxi costs JD20 with one hour of waiting time.

❶ Getting Around

The walk from the bus station to the centre of town is quite a hike with bags, but taxis (costing around JD1) are plentiful. If you are driving, note that it is not possible to park outside some of the cheaper hotels as they are on busy, narrow streets.

Mt Nebo   جبل نيبو

Go up unto...Mount Nebo in Moab, across from Jericho, and view Canaan, the land I am giving the Israelites as their own possession. There on the mountain that you have climbed you will die.

Deuteronomy 32:49-50

Mt Nebo is where Moses is said to have seen the Promised Land, a land he was himself forbidden to enter. He died (allegedly aged 120) and was later buried in the area, although the exact location of the burial site is the subject of conjecture. The site flickered briefly into the international spotlight with the visit of Pope John Paul II in 2000.

The Mt Nebo region features several rocky outcrops, including Siyagha (the local name of the site, meaning 'monastery'). The Moses Memorial Church is perched on the summit, commanding sweeping views of the Dead Sea, and Israel and the Palestinian Territories beyond.

A pleasant side trip from Madaba, just 9km away, the church with its magnificent mosaics is the centrepiece of a small hilltop complex, signposted from the Madaba–Dead Sea road.

History

A Roman nun, Etheria, stumbled across the original three-apsed church on this site during a pilgrimage in AD 393. A nave was added in the 5th century, the first baptistery chapel (with the mosaic) in 530, and the main basilica in 597, together with a large monastery.

By this time Nebo had grown into an important pilgrimage site, even earning a signpost off the main Roman road through the region (a Roman mile marker lies in the museum). Pilgrims would travel to Jerusalem, Jericho, Bethany, Ayoun Musa and Mt Nebo, before descending to Hammamat Ma'in for post-pilgrimage bathing.

◉ Sights

Moses Memorial Church   CHURCH
(Mt Nebo; admission JD1; ⊘8am-4pm Oct-Apr, to 6pm May-Sep) On top of Mt Nebo, this modest church, or more accurately basilica, was built around 4th-century foundations in AD 597 and has just undergone a major reconstruction project. It houses important mosaics (from around AD 530), which rank as some of the best in Jordan. The masterpiece is a hunting and herding scene interspersed with an assortment of African fauna, including a zebu (humped ox), lions, tigers, bears, boars, zebras, an ostrich on a leash and a camel-shaped giraffe.

The church was abandoned by the 16th century and only relocated in the 20th century, using 4th- and 5th-century pilgrim travelogues. The Franciscans bought the site in 1932 and were responsible for excavating most of the ruins of the church and the monastery, as well as reconstructing much of the basilica.

The church is part of a functioning monastery, off limits to visitors. Smoking and mobile phones are not allowed in the vicinity of the church. Toilets can be found next to the on-site museum. Expect a rise in admission charge (which covers both the church and the neighbouring Memorial Viewpoint) when the work is complete.

★ **Memorial Viewpoint** VIEWPOINT
(admission JD 1, included in Moses Memorial Church admission; ⊙ 8am-4pm Oct-Apr, to 6pm May-Sep) Moses' view of the Promised Land towards ancient Gilead, Judah, Jericho and the Negev is marked by an Italian-designed bronze memorial, next to the Moses Memorial Church. The ironwork, symbolising the suffering and death of Jesus on the cross and the serpent that 'Moses lifted up' in the desert, stands in the middle of an invariably windy viewing platform. Markers indicate notable points in the often-hazy distance, including the Golan Heights, Jerusalem (just 46km away) and the Dead Sea.

A small museum near the viewpoint has some interesting milestones and a 3D map of the area.

To enjoy similar views away from the crowds, pack a picnic and hike along the road downhill from Mt Nebo (towards the Dead Sea) for 100m and take the track to the left to the nearby hilltop.

La Storia Tourism Complex MUSEUM
(Ethnographic Diorama; ☑ 3241119; www.lastoria-nebo.com; admission JD2; ⊙ 9am-5pm) This new ethnographic diorama, 2km before Mt Nebo on the Nebo–Madaba road, features an exhibition of tableaux billed as depictions of the major religious, historical and cultural highlights in the heritage of Jordan. Noah's Ark, complete with stuffed badger and ducks, marks the entrance of this fun, eccentric exhibit that is already proving a big attraction with nationals. The evocation of Bedouin and village life in the ethnographic scenes provide an interesting commentary on fast-disappearing Jordanian traditions.

An on-site handicraft shop sells some quality items, such as mosaics and olive wood carvings, some of which are produced by artisans attached to the complex.

✗ Eating

★ **Nebo Restaurant & Terrace** BUFFET $$
(☑ 3242442; buffet JD10; ⊙ 11.30am-6pm Sat-Thu, until late Fri) The spectacular view and warm welcome from the patrons makes this restaurant worth a trip to Mt Nebo in its own right. Panoramic windows and a roof terrace make the very best of the vista and the restaurant has its own ovens for fresh Arabic bread.

Asa Moses Restaurant BUFFET $$
(Siyagha Restaurant; ☑ 3250226; Opp Ayoun Mousa junction; buffet JD10; ⊙ noon-4.30pm; ☑) If you visit Mt Nebo at lunchtime, call into this recommended trestle-tabled restaurant. It produces a daily buffet of traditional Jordanian dishes (including *maqlubbeh*, if ordered an hour in advance). The stone pillars and reed ceiling add to the 'been here forever' ambience. Try a local 'Mt Nebo' wine and sink into the *majlis* cushions for a nap.

MADABA & THE KING'S HIGHWAY MT NEBO

DON'T MISS

MAKING MOSAIC HISTORY

In a bid to be registered in the Guinness World Records, the Madaba Tourism Development & Heritage Preservation Association has enlisted visitors to the region to participate in the creation of the **King's Highway Portrait** (La Storia Tourism Complex, Mt Nebo; ⊙ 9am-5pm), the largest mosaic in the world – appropriate for a region famed for its mosaic-making heritage. Included in the admission price to the neighbouring La Storia Tourism Complex on the road towards Mt Nebo, the activity involves placing one tile into a mosaic depiction of the King's Highway.

The finished 'portrait' will measure 6m by 30m long, with a total area of 180 sq meters. Around four million marble, granite and limestone tesserae, or tiles, each just 2cm in size, will be required to finish the project. Already, thanks to the help of Jordanian royalty, ambassadors, celebrities and 58,000 visitors, the mosaic is one-third complete. Charl Twal, one of the founders of this elaborate and engaging project, encourages all visitors to Madaba and Mt Nebo to participate: 'By placing a tile in the King's Highway,' he claims, 'you are not just visiting Madaba but becoming part of its future.'

ℹ️ Information

The authoritative *Town of Nebo* by Fr Sylvestre J Salter and Fr Bellarmiro Bagatti details Mt Nebo and other Christian sites in Jordan. More portable is *Mount Nebo* by Michelle Piccirillo. Both are usually available for sale inside the church. The Jordan Tourism Board publishes an excellent pamphlet entitled *Mount Nebo*, which summarises the site's significance. The encyclopaedic *Mosaics of Madaba* is on display inside the church.

ℹ️ Getting There & Away

From Madaba, shared taxis to Mt Nebo cost around JD1; a private taxi from Madaba costs JD5 (or JD8 return, with one hour waiting time).

From Mt Nebo the road continues for 17km into the Jordan Valley to meet the main Amman–Dead Sea Highway, offering grand views of the Dead Sea. The drive takes you from the tree line of olives and root vegetables, past a rocky landscape of prickly pears, to the ochre-coloured hills of the Dead Sea depression. The yellow turns to red as the road twists past iron-rich escarpments and finally descends to the extreme green of the Jordan Valley, dotted with greenhouse plastic. There is no reliable public transport along this route.

Around Mt Nebo

The hills and wadis (dry valleys) around Mt Nebo are peppered with ancient sites that are seldom visited except by archaeologists, sheep, goats and the occasional lost rambler. Though needing a bit of perseverance to find, and imagination to make the ruins and their historical context come alive, these sites are intimations of the complexity of this region's multi-layered past. They also show the rural beauty of today's Jordan that lies just off the beaten track.

👁 Sights

Church of SS Lot & Procopius   MOSAIC
(Khirbet Mukhayyat; ☉ daylight hours) FREE
Originally built in AD 557, this church houses a remarkable mosaic with scenes of daily life such as agriculture, fishing and wine making (in particular the cutting and carrying of grapes). The mosaics have recently been painstakingly restored after damage by rainwater. Look for the on-site caretaker to unlock the door for you; a tip of JD1 is appropriate in return.

The church is near the village of Khirbet Mukhayyat, the original site of ancient Nebo village as mentioned on the 9th-century BC Mesha Stele and in the Bible. The turn-off to

Khirbet Mukhayyat is signposted 'Al-Makhyt', about 6km from Madaba and 3km before reaching the church complex at Mt Nebo. A sealed road leads 2.5km along the edge of the village to a rugged car park surrounded by juniper trees. There is no public transport.

Moses' Spring   RUIN
(Ayoun Musa; ☉ 24hr) This spring is one of two places where the prophet is believed to have obtained water by striking a rock. Six giant eucalyptus trees mark the spot and there's an occasional waterfall over the lip of the rocks if it's been raining, but there's little to see except the low-lying ruins of a couple of churches nearby. There is no public transport to the site. Walking down from the main road is easy; coming back up is the killer.

To reach the site, turn right at the sign about 1km before the church at Mt Nebo. A 2.4km switchback road to the spring is steep (but sealed) and offers a close-up view of Bedouin encampments, hunkered down against the elements. Arums grow in abundance among the rocky patches of tilled ground, and small, fertile wadis bristle with citrus and olive trees. Sadly, the littered site is disfigured by discarded concrete buildings and is badly in need of a clean up.

Tell Hesban   RUIN
(Hesban; ☉ daylight hours) FREE Amateur archaeologists will like Tell Hesban, 9km north of Madaba. Over the centuries this strategic hill has been a Bronze Age settlement, an Amorite capital (900–500 BC), a Hellenistic fortress (198–63 BC), a Roman settlement called Esbus (63 BC–AD 350), a Byzantine ecclesiastical centre (AD 350–650), an Umayyad market town (650–750), a regional capital of the Abbasids (750–1260) and Mamluks (1260–1500) and, finally, an Ottoman village. All these layers of history are on view, albeit faintly.

The site is well signed, indicating the remains of a Byzantine church (the mosaics are displayed in Madaba), a Roman temple and a Hellenistic fort. There are lots of caves and cisterns both here and in neighbouring Wadi Majar. The largest Bronze Age cave can be explored with a torch (flashlight). Minibuses run frequently from Madaba (300 fils, 20 minutes) to Hesban or otherwise take a taxi for JD6. Coming from Madaba, the tell is on the left side of the road; if you are driving, turn left at the first set of traffic lights after the pedestrian bridge in the modern town of Hesban and follow your nose up the hill.

Wadi Jadid   وادي جديد

More terraced fields than wadi, Wadi Jadid is locally renowned for its remarkable collection of early Bronze Age burial chambers and stone memorials. Known as **dolmens**, these stone structures date back to around 5000 to 3000 BC and consist of two upright stones capped by a bridging stone. The term 'dolmen' means stone table and it remains a mystery as to how the huge bridging stones were winched into position: little wonder that social anthropologists regard them as proof of early social cohesion.

◉ Sights

★ **Dolmen Field**   ARCHAEOLOGICAL SITE
(⊘24hr) There are about 40 dolmens scattered across this unmarked site, with at least 12 in good condition. There are thousands more scattered across Jordan, especially around ar-Rawdah.

From the road, it takes about 30 minutes to walk to the nearest dolmen, and an hour to reach more distant groups. The site is near the village of Al-Fiha, 10km southwest

of Madaba, but you need to be 'in the know' to find it. The best way to visit is by checking on directions with the Mariam Hotel (p130) in Madaba, downloading a map from its website or joining a tour (JD12 plus JD3 for each hour spent at the site).

With your own vehicle, you can continue downhill to the Dead Sea (30 minutes) after Wadi Jadid. The road is narrow and potholed towards the end but it threads through beautiful and varied terrain, with Bedouin camps, green valleys of grapevines, olive groves and citrus orchards. As it descends to the desert floor, the road passes a spring with a small waterfall – almost miraculous in the arid landscape.

Mukawir (Machaerus)
مكاور (مكاريوس)

☑ 05 / POP <5000 / ELEV 700M
Just beyond the village of Mukawir (pronounced 'mu-*kar*-wir') is the spectacular 700m-high hilltop perch of Machaerus: the castle of Herod the Great and the place where Salome is said to have danced for the head of John the Baptist.

MADABA & THE KING'S HIGHWAY WADI JADID

LOCAL KNOWLEDGE

DOLMENS IN DANGER

There are not many people who are moved to tears by the fate of a pile of old rocks, but Charl Twal of the Mariam Hotel and the Madaba Tourism Development & Heritage Preservation Association is not like many people. Not content to manage one of the most successful tourist enterprises in Madaba, he also finds time to take an active interest in the geological and historical heritage of the local landscape. He was the first to highlight the remarkable dolmens of Wadi Jadid for tourists, and he has been trying to raise awareness of their existence in a bid to ensure their preservation.

The strategy was working well, with a steadily increasing number of appreciative tourists visiting the site and calls for some kind of official recognition of the dolmens' value... until the summer of 2014. Alarmed by the increased visibility of the ancient heritage on their plot of land, some locals have come to the conclusion that the dolmens may represent more trouble than they are worth. Afraid of losing their land to tourism, acts of vandalism have been reported increasingly on the site culminating in the complete destruction of one of the biggest monoliths. Clearly distressed by this turn of events, Charl described being summoned to Wadi Jadid by a well-wisher to witness the final blows of the jackhammer.

An advocate of responsible tourism, Charl is now seeking the support of visitors to help win government protection for the embattled dolmens. He encourages tourists to contribute to his 'Save the Dolmen Campaign' by sharing a picture of Wadi Jadid on social media, registering concern on Lonely Planet's Thorntree forum or blogging on review sites. By demonstrating the dolmens are of global interest, Charl hopes he can obtain government protection for these ancient monuments.

Concerns about the dolmens, or indeed any positive or negative feedback regarding sights and facilities in Jordan, can be registered with the **Ministry of Tourism** (info@mota.gov.jo) and the **Jordan Tourism Board** (info@visitjordan.com).

The pudding basin of a hill was first fortified in about 100 BC, and expanded by Herod the Great in 30 BC. The ruins themselves are of minor interest, but the setting, with the wind blowing through the columns like one of Salome's seven veils, is both haunting and beautiful. Most days you'll be alone with the ghosts.

There was nowhere to stay in Mukawir at the time of writing, but a hotel is rumoured to open near to the ruins – check for an update at the visitors centre in Madaba. In the meantime, water, tea and coffee (and tickets to the castle) are sold from a Bedouin tent at the entrance to the castle.

◉ Sights & Activities

★ **Castle of Herod the Great**   CASTLE

(admission JD1.500; ☺ 8am-6pm) Machaerus is known locally as Qala'at al-Meshneq (Castle of the Gallows), a fitting name given that it is renowned as the place where John the Baptist was beheaded by Herod Antipas, the successor of Herod the Great. The castle is about 2km past Mukawir village and easy to spot. If you don't feel in the mood for a climb, it's worth coming this way just to see the hilltop fortress framed by sea and sky beyond.

From the car park, a stone staircase leads down to the main path, which climbs the hill in a clockwise direction. Near the base of the climb, a small track leads around the main hill to the right, past a number of caves. Legend has it that it was in one of these that the gruesome execution took place. Flocks of choughs wheel through the air in suitably ominous fashion.

The main path climbs eventually to the castle. At the top, the modest ruins are unlabelled, but you can just about make out the low-lying remains of the eastern baths and defensive walls.

The reconstructed columns southwest of the deep cistern mark the site of Herod Antipas' palace triclinium; this is the site where Salome reputedly danced. According to the Bible, John the Baptist had denounced Herod Antipas' marriage to his brother's wife, Herodias, as Jewish law forbade a man marrying his brother's wife while he lived. Bewitched by his stepdaughter Salome's skill as a dancer, the king promised to grant her anything she wished. To take revenge on the Baptist, Herodias told her daughter to ask for his head on a platter:

And she went out, and said to her mother, 'What shall I ask?' And she said, 'The head of John the Baptiser.'

Mark 6:24

So, at the request of Salome, John was killed at Herod's castle, Machaerus. Provocative Salome has inspired painters and writers ever since.

The Romans built a siege ramp on the western side of the hill when taking the fort from Jewish rebels in AD 72; the remains are still visible.

Dead Sea and Hammamat Ma'in Trails   HIKING

(with guide from JD50) Mukawir is a great hiking area, with plenty of shepherds' trails snaking around hilly contours. One particularly worthwhile track leads steeply down the west side of the castle hill from the top and along a ridge towards the Dead Sea. It's also possible to follow shepherds' trails (or the 4WD road) to the hot springs at Hammamat Ma'in.

You must exercise extreme caution if taking any of these trails as the terrain falls steeply away and many paths are only for the sure-footed. Women are advised not to hike alone. You can arrange with a private tour operator to hike from Mukawir to Zara/Herodus Hot Springs, a strenuous three- to four-hour trek. On any of these trails the views are magnificent, particularly at sunset.

🛍 Shopping

★ **Bani Hamida Weaving Centre & Gallery**   HANDICRAFTS

(☎ 3210155; www.jordanriver.jo; ☺ 8am-3pm Sun-Thu, 10am-6pm Fri, to 4pm winter) This women's cooperative in Mukawir village (by the side of the road leading to the castle) is run by the Bani Hamida Centre and is a good place to buy gorgeous, colourful kilims and cushions. The colour-ways are constantly updated to reflect contemporary tastes while traditional Bedouin patterns continue to inspire the weavers.

An elaborate 100cm by 50cm kilim costs around JD75; prices are fixed. The women who run the centre speak little English, but welcome you to the workshop. For an excellent anthropological perspective on the Bani Hamida story, it's worth picking up a copy of *A Bedouin Perspective* (JD5) by Sue Jones, who worked with the Jebel Bani Hamida women in the early 1990s. This booklet is on sale in the showroom.

WEAVING A FUTURE: THE WOMEN OF BANI HAMIDA

The Bani Hamida rug-making initiative was established in 1985, with help from Save the Children, to bring paid work to the newly settled Bedouin women of Mukawir district. The project began with only 12 women, all experienced hand-loom weavers. Ten years later, the cooperative involved 1500 women from the surrounding hillsides washing, carding, spinning and dyeing sheep's wool, and weaving the rugs. All these activities took place around the usual business of looking after husband, family and home. Now supported by the Jordan River Valley Foundation, the project employs 24 full-time staff who are responsible for the coordination of the project, carrying out international marketing and promoting the vision of the enterprise.

There have been challenges (such as competition, cheap imports and failing tourism) but the project continues to be a success, empowering women in proportion to their involvement. Earning even a little extra money has brought independence and social manoeuvrability, allowing women to change their lives and, most significantly, those of their children. When asked what the project meant for her family, one weaver at the showroom in Mukawir explained that she could afford to buy new pans from Madaba; another had funded a university education for her son.

These changes have been achieved by harnessing, rather than rejecting, the traditional skills that have been handed from mother to daughter since the days of Abraham, and which have helped define the Bedouin identity. As such, buying a Bani Hamida rug is more than just making a purchase; it is affirming an ancient but evolving way of life.

❶ Getting There & Away

Frequent minibuses (650 fils, one hour) leave from outside the local bus station in Madaba for the village of Mukawir, via Libb (the last is around 5pm). From there, it's a pleasant downhill stroll to the foot of the castle, or ask the minibus driver to take you the extra distance for a few fils more. There is no return traffic between the castle car park and the village, although one delighted traveller reported that the bus driver kindly waited for her while she spent 30 minutes looking round the ruins.

By car, the road from the King's Highway snakes along a ridge with spectacular views. An impressive sealed road links the site with Hammamat Ma'in and the Dead Sea.

Umm ar-Rasas   أم الرصاص

Despite looking rather unpromising from the outside, Umm ar-Rasas is one of those delightful surprises that crops up along the King's Highway. Designated a Unesco World Heritage site in 2004, it acquired a visitor centre in 2008, though it provides little context. Visitors are accompanied to the ruins by tourist police; although kind and friendly, they are not able to give much in the way of interpretation.

About 1.5km north of the ruins is an enigmatic 15m-tall **stone tower**, the purpose of which baffles archaeologists as there are no stairs inside but several windows at the top.

It was most likely a retreat for stylites, early Christian hermits who lived in seclusion on the top of pillars. Crosses decorate the side of the tower and several ruined monastery buildings lie nearby.

As part of the development of facilities at Umm ar-Rasas, a new museum is planned for the archaeological site of **Lehun**. Lehun was a garrison town built in AD 300 to house the 4th Roman Legion, forming part of a line of Roman forts called the Limes Arabicus, which defended the most remote borders of Rome. The site is 7km east of Dhiban and is worth a visit not so much for the random excavations as for the panoramic view across Wadi Mujib.

Church of St Stephen   MOSAIC

(⊙8am-4pm) **FREE** The ruined Church of St Stephen, protected by an ugly hangar, is one of four churches in the original village of Umm ar-Rasas. Inside, the magnificent **mosaics** date back to about AD 785. If you have mosaic fatigue after Madaba and Mt Nebo, try to muster up one last flurry of enthusiasm for this well-preserved masterpiece.

There are depictions of hunting, fishing and agriculture; scenes of daily life (such as boys enjoying a boat ride, a man astride an ostrich); and the names of those who helped pay for the mosaic. A panel consisting of 10 cities in the region includes Umm ar-Rasas, Philadelphia (Amman), Madaba, Esbounta

THE MESHA STELE

If you're travelling along the King's Highway, you'll keep coming across references to the Mesha Stele, but chances are you'll find little opportunity to discover what it is. Here's a quick ready reference to this significant artefact.

What is a stele? It's an ancient upright stone, usually decorated in some way.

And the Mesha Stele? It was a chest-high, black basalt tablet of stone carved with inscriptions.

Who discovered it? It was found by a missionary at Dhiban in 1868.

Why was it so famous? It provided historical detail of the battles between the Moabites and the kings of Israel and was also the earliest example of Hebrew script to be unearthed at that time.

Why was it made? It was commissioned by King Mesha of Moab to advertise his successes against Israel.

What happened to it? After surviving intact from about 850 BC to AD 1868, it quickly came to a rather unfortunate end. After finding the stele, the missionary reported it to Charles Clermont-Ganneau at the French consulate in Jerusalem, who made a mould of the tablet and returned to Jerusalem to raise the money to buy it. While he was away, local families, arguing over who was to benefit from the sale, lit a fire under the stone and poured water over it, causing it to shatter. Although most pieces were recovered, inevitably some were lost.

Where is it now? The remnants were collected and shipped off to France, and the reconstructed stone is now on display in the Louvre in Paris. Copies can be seen in the museums at Amman, Madaba and Karak.

(Hesban), Belemounta (Ma'in), Areopolis (Ar-Rabba) and Charac Moaba (Karak). A northern panel depicts Jerusalem, Nablus, Casearea, Gaza and others.

Kastron Mefaa   RUIN
(⊙8am-4pm) FREE The Umm ar-Rasas site spans the expansive ruins of Kastron Mefaa (mentioned in the Bible as the Roman military outpost of Mephaath). The ruins encompass four churches (including the Church of Lions with impressive namesake mosaics) and city walls. Arches rise up randomly from the rubble like sea monsters and you can spot cisterns and door lintels everywhere, although a lack of signposts makes it hard to grasp the structure of the ancient town.

ℹ Getting There & Away

As with all points along the King's Highway, the easiest way to get to either Umm ar-Rasas or Lehun is to drive or charter a private taxi from Madaba, 32km to the north. The turning is clearly signposted off either the King's Highway or the Desert Highway (Umm ar-Rasas lies halfway between the two).

A few minibuses go directly to Umm ar-Rasas via Nitil from the local bus station in Madaba.

Alternatively, catch anything going to Dhiban, and try arranging a taxi (if you can find one) from there. It costs around JD12/20 one way/return, including waiting time.

Wadi Mujib   وادي الموجيب

Stretching across Jordan from the Desert Highway to the Dead Sea (covering a distance of over 70km) is the vast Wadi Mujib, proudly known as the 'Grand Canyon of Jordan'. Aside from being spectacular, it is also significant as the historic boundary between the ancient Amorites (to the north) and the Moabites (to the south). Moses is believed to have walked through Wadi Mujib, when it was known as the Arnon Valley. The King's Highway crosses the upper reaches of the wadi while the lower reaches fall within the Mujib Biosphere Reserve – normally accessed from the Dead Sea Highway.

The canyon measures 1km deep and 4km wide, but it takes the King's Highway 18km of road to switchback down one wall of the wadi, across the dam at the bottom and up the other side. From the picturesque olive groves of the upper plateau, on either side of the wadi, there is no hint of the upheaval that renders the land in two.

Travelling south, **Dhiban** is the last town you'll pass through before the descent into Wadi Mujib. Once the powerful capital of an empire carved out by King Mesha in the 9th century BC, Dhiban is where the Mesha Stele was discovered. There is nothing left of the ancient city and it's hard to imagine this unexceptional little town had such an illustrious past.

Even if you are not intending to make the crossing, it's worth travelling to the canyon rim. Past Dhiban, the road descends after 3km to a **lookout** over Wadi Mujib. Some enterprising traders have set up a tea stall here and an assortment of fossils and minerals from the canyon walls are for sale. This is the easiest point on the road to stop and absorb the view, take a photograph and turn around if you're heading back to Madaba (there are no turning points after that until you reach the dam at the bottom).

Ariha is the nearest village to the canyon rim on the southern side of Wadi Mujib, although the village is about 2.5km off the main King's Highway.

Eating

There's nowhere between Madaba and Karak to stay and few places to find refreshment, except one or two ad hoc outposts on the southern walls of Wadi Mujib which sell tea and make the most of the views.

Trajan Rest House & Restaurant   BUFFET $$
(☎079 5903302; trajan_resthouse@yahoo.com; JD10; ☺noon-3pm) Climbing out of Wadi Mujib gorge on the southern side, you come to this strategically placed restaurant, perched like an eyrie on the canyon rim. Every day Mr Awad and his family prepare open buffets (mostly intended for tour groups) of spicy meatballs and herb chicken in a cavernous grotto of Bedouin artefacts, rugs and long trestle tables.

Getting There & Away

Dhiban is where almost all transport south of Madaba stops. The only way to cross the mighty Wadi Mujib from Dhiban to Ariha is to charter a taxi (if you can find one) for JD15 each way but be warned, finding an onward taxi in Ariha is even harder. At the time of writing, hitching was not recommended; if you don't have a hire car, the best option is to take a taxi from Madaba or Karak.

Ar-Rabba عرابه

The holy and historic city of Ar-Rabba came under the rule of King Mesha (9th century BC), then Alexander the Great (mid-4th century BC) and later the Nabataeans (from the 2nd century BC to the 2nd century AD). The Greeks named it Areopolis after Ares, the god of war, and the Romans based their Arab governorate here.

◉ Sights

Ar-Rabba Ruins   RUINS
(☺daylight hours) FREE At the northern end of town are the minimal ruins of a Roman temple from the end of the 3rd century AD (two niches contained statues of the Roman emperors Diocletian and Maximilian), and other Roman and Byzantine buildings. None of the ruins are signposted. The site is accessible by minibus from Karak, 16km to the south, but is best visited on a 15-minute stop en route between Madaba and Karak.

Karak الكرك
☑03 / POP 77,400 / ELEV 1000M

The ancient Crusader stronghold of Karak (or Kerak) lies within the walls of the old city and is one of the highlights of Jordan. The fortified castle that dominates the town was a place of legend in the battles between the Crusaders (Franks) and the Islamic armies of Saladin (Salah ad-Din). Now one of the most famous Crusader castles, in its day Karak was just one in a long line of Frank defences, stretching from Aqaba in the south to Turkey in the north.

Often ignored by travellers speeding south towards Petra, Karak deserves a detour.

History

Karak lies on the ancient caravan routes between Egypt and Syria, and was used by the Greeks and Romans. The city is mentioned several times in the Bible as Kir, Kir Moab and Kir Heres, capital of the Moabites, and later emerges as a Roman provincial town, Charac Moaba. The city also features in the famous mosaic map in St George's Church in Madaba.

The arrival of the Crusaders gave the city renewed prominence, especially after King Baldwin I of Jerusalem built the castle in AD 1142. Standing midway between Shobak and Jerusalem, Karak's commanding

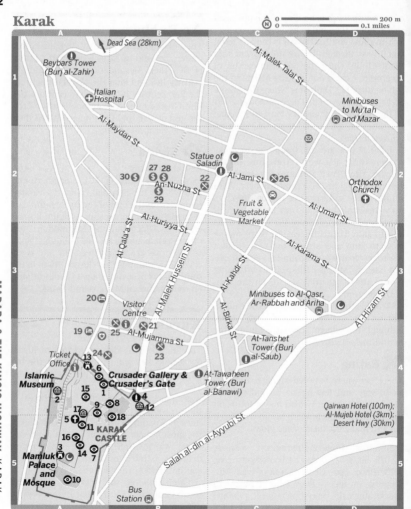

position and strategic value are obvious even today: unsurprisingly it soon became the capital of the Crusader district of Oultrejourdain and, with the taxes levied on passing caravans and food grown in the district, helped Jerusalem to prosper.

Saladin's Muslim armies took the castle in 1183 after an epic siege. The Mamluk sultan, Beybars, took the fort in 1263 and strengthened the fortress, deepening the moat and adding the lower courtyard, but three towers collapsed in an earthquake in AD 1293.

Little more is known of the castle until Jean Louis Burckhardt (the Swiss explorer who rediscovered Petra) passed through Karak in 1812, describing the castle as 'shattered but imposing'.

In the 1880s, religious fighting compelled the Christians of Karak to flee north to resettle in Madaba and Ma'in; peace was only restored after thousands of Turkish troops were stationed in Karak.

◉ Sights

Karak's friendly, busy and chaotic town centre radiates around the statue of Saladin. The plaza near the entrance to the castle has been redeveloped, and it is in the surround-

Karak

⊙ Top Sights
1 Crusader Gallery & Crusader's
   Gate A4
2 Islamic Museum.. A4
3 Mamluk Palace and Mosque A5

⊙ Sights
4 Carved Figure B4
5 Crusader Church A5
6 Dry Moat A4
7 Glacis A5
8 Greek Inscriptions B4
9 Kitchen A4
10 Mamluk Keep.. A5
11 Marketplace A5
12 Northeast Tower....................................... B4
13 Ottoman's Gate... A4
14 Prison Cells... A5
15 Residences A4
16 Rosette Gallery... A5
17 Sacristy A4

18 Soldiers' Barracks & Kitchen................ B5

⊙ Sleeping
19 Karak Rest House...................................... A4
20 Towers Castle Hotel................................. A3

⊗ Eating
21 Al-Fid'a Restaurant B4
22 Al-Motaz Sweets B2
23 Al-Shubba.. B4
24 King's Castle Restaurant........................ A4
25 King's Restaurant.................................... B4
   Kir Heres Restaurant .... (see 20)
   Shehab Restaurant .... (see 20)
26 Shwarma Stands...................................... C2

ⓘ Information
27 Arab Bank.. B2
28 Housing Bank.. B2
29 Jordan Islamic Bank............................... B2
30 Jordan National Bank B2

ing streets that you'll find most of the tourist hotels and restaurants. Qala'a St is also known by the English name, Castle St.

Look for signs in the suburbs for a panorama viewpoint just outside town; apart from providing grand views of the castle, it is the location of the town's only new hotel in a decade (not yet open). Ignore the signs for the 'sound and light show' which was not functioning at the time of writing.

⊙ Karak Castle

Karak Castle   CASTLE
(☏ 2351216; admission JD1; ☺ 8am-4pm Oct-Mar, to 7pm Apr-Sep) The entrance is at the southern end of Al Qala'a St. Throughout the castle, informative display boards give detailed descriptions of the history and function of each structure. Bring a torch (flashlight) to explore the darker regions, and watch your head on low doorways. Reconstruction and excavation work within the castle is ongoing. Beware touts at the entrance offering to guide you – they will expect a tip (JD5 to JD10) whatever they may say in advance!

➡ **Ottoman's Gate**
The main entrance to Karak Castle is Ottoman's Gate which is reached via a bridge. The Crusader's Gate would once have been the main thoroughfare but is currently awaiting restoration and remains closed to the public. Take time to pause on the bridge before Ottoman's Gate: on a windy day, high

above the **dry moat**, it is a struggle and a relief to reach the gate's shelter.

➡ ★**Crusader Gallery & Crusader's Gate**
The Crusader Gallery functioned as the stables of Karak Castle. Near the far end of the gallery, steps lead down to the Crusader's Gate. Those entering the castle did so via a narrow winding passage, separated from the Crusader Gallery by a wall. This restrictive access is typical of Crusader castles, ensuring the entrance could be easily defended.

On the north wall of the gallery is a (now headless) **carved figure** that local legend claims to be Saladin, but which actually dates from the 2nd century AD and is believed by scholars to be a Nabataean funerary carving. A small staircase leads up to the site of the ruined **northeast tower** while a long passageway leads southwest to the soldiers barracks.

➡ **Soldiers' Barracks & Kitchen**
The Karak Castle barracks are notable for the small holes used for light, the walls of limestone and straw, and a few Byzantine rock inscriptions on the walls. Across the corridor is the kitchen, which contains large, round stones used for grinding olives, and huge storage areas for oil and wheat. In a dark tunnel (only visible with a torch) are some **Greek inscriptions** of unknown meaning. A door from the **kitchen** leads to a giant oven.

⇒ ★ Glacis & Upper Court

Beyond the parapet at Karak Castle is the glacis, the dizzyingly steep rocky slope that prevented invaders from climbing up to the castle and prisoners from climbing down. This is where Renauld de Châtillon delighted in expelling his enemies.

The overgrown upper court has a large cistern and the largely unexcavated domestic **residences** of the castle. At the northern end of the castle is the terrace, directly above the Crusader Gallery, with fine views. Above the far (southern) end of the castle rises Umm al-Thallaja (Mother of Snows), the hill which posed the greatest threat to the castle's defences during times of siege. To the west is the village of Al-Shabiya, which was once called Al-Ifranj because many Crusaders (Franks) settled here after the fall of the castle.

⇒ Crusader Church

Karak Castle's main Crusader church was built with a **sacristy** down the stairs to the right (north). Note how in this lowered room there are arrow slits in the walls, suggesting that this originally formed part of the castle's outer wall. The neighbouring tower is believed to have been a Mamluk mosque.

⇒ Mamluk Keep

A keep is a refuge of last resort and it was here that the defences of Karak Castle were strongest, with 6.5m-thick walls, arrow slits on all four levels and a crenellated section at the top. The keep was built from 1260 by the Maluk sultan Beybars.

From the keep, stairs lead down to the Mamluk Palace.

⇒ ★ Mamluk Palace and Mosque

Built for Sultan al-Nasir Muhammad in 1311, the open-air reception hall of this palace is a variation of the classic Islamic design of four *iwans* (chambers) off the main hall; there are barrel-vaulted rooms on two sides. The mosque here, with a clearly visible mihrab (niche) facing Mecca, was probably reserved for palace notables.

Pause near the top of the stairs for good views of Wadi Karak and the alleged site of the condemned cities of Sodom and Gomorrah. Return to the main Crusader church.

⇒ Prison and Rosette Gallery

At the main Crusader church in Karak Castle you will find two corridors. The left (east) corridor leads past seven prison cells and the prison administration office. The right (west) corridor leads from the foot of the stairs through the Rosette Gallery, named after the carved rosette at the bottom of the staircase.

⇒ Marketplace

From the main Crusader church you can take a passage to the left of the steps, which leads northwest through the bowels of Karak Castle, roughly underneath the church. The corridor turns right (north) and emerges into the better-lit areas of a delightful underground marketplace with various shops and cellars.

At the northern end of the market, a path leads back to the entrance (also the exit).

⇒ ★ Islamic Museum

(⊙ 8am-3pm Oct-Mar, to 6pm Apr-Sep) `FREE`
Down the hill by the Mamluk ruins is the excellent Islamic Museum. In a semisubterranean part of Karak Castle, with a vaulted ceiling, this evocatively lit collection houses some of the finds from the castle and excavations in the surrounding area.

🛏 Sleeping

Qairwan Hotel
BOUTIQUE HOTEL $

(Cairwan Hotel; ☑/fax 2396022; King's Highway; s JD27, without bathroom JD10, d/tr JD30/40, 5-bed jacuzzi suite with kitchen JD44; ❋🐕) This homely family-run establishment is Karak's answer to a boutique hotel. Each of the nine rooms is unique, with quirky decoration. Unexpectedly, stairs lead to a cavernous disco. The hotel is 500m from the bus station, just outside Karak town. Breakfast costs JD4, dinner JD7, wi-fi JD3 and hotwater is available from 6am to 10am and 6pm to 8pm.

Towers Castle Hotel
HOTEL $

(☑/fax 2354293; Al-Qala'a St; s/d/tr JD20/30/35) Near the castle, this friendly budget hotel is a good meeting place for younger travellers. Don't be put off by the dingy reception area: the rooms, with floral motifs, are clean and many open onto balconies with views across Wadi Karak. You can find help with onward travel from here.

Karak Rest House
HOTEL $$

(☑2351148; moaweyaf@gmail.com; Al-Qala'a St; s/d incl breakfast JD28/47) Next door to the castle, with sweeping views of Wadi Karak from many of the rooms, this tired hotel with its faded lobby is at least conveniently located. The owners are responsible for building the new Falcon Hotel with a swimming pool and panoramic view of the castle (not yet open).

Al-Mujeb Hotel
HOTEL **$$**

(2386090; almujeb_hotel@yahoo.com; King's Highway; s/d/tr incl breakfast JD30/45/60; ❄) This sprawling, three-storey hotel attracts an assortment of interesting guests who huddle round the gas heater in the foyer on a cold winter's evening. The hotel is around 5km from Karak, by the junction on the road to Ar-Rabba. If you are driving, consider parking here and taking a taxi (JD5 to JD6 one way) into town.

✗ Eating

Most restaurants are near the castle on Al-Mujamma St or near the statue of Saladin. Shwarma stands are clustered around Al-Jami St.

King's Restaurant
JORDANIAN **$**

(2354293; Al-Mujamma St; mezze 500 fils, mains from JD4; ⊘8am-10pm) Opposite an open area called Castle Plaza, this restaurant with tables on the pavement attracts travellers at all times of the day and night. It offers grills, pizzas and sandwiches, and local, home-cooked Jordanian dishes such as *maqlubbeh* (steamed rice with meat, grilled tomato and pine nuts). The freshly squeezed orange juice is welcome after hot climbs up and down Al-Qala'a St. It's open for breakfast in Ramadan.

Al-Fid'a Restaurant
JORDANIAN **$**

(079 5037622; Al-Mujamma St; mains JD5; ⊘8am-10pm) This popular, unsophisticated eatery sells standard local fare of chicken, hummus and salad.

Al-Motaz Sweets
SWEETS **$**

(2353388; An-Nuzha St; ⊘8am-10pm) This Arabic pastry shop is a must for those with a sweet tooth.

Shwarma Stands
SHWARMA **$**

(JD1; ⊘4pm-10pm) These popular shwarma stands are in a busy part of town, making it easy to strike up conversation with hungry shoppers in the queue.

Kir Heres Restaurant
JORDANIAN **$$**

(2355595; Al-Qala'a St; mains JD5-7; ⊘Noon-10pm; 🍴) A popular meeting point for travellers, this restaurant serves ostrich steaks, chicken with local herbs, fried *haloumi* (salty cheese) and mushrooms with garlic and thyme – a welcome change from the usual grilled goat. Try the locally produced sweet white wine (not available in Ramadan) in the upper gallery at lunchtime and you can forget about visiting the castle afterwards!

King's Castle Restaurant
BUFFET **$$**

(2396070; buffet JD10; ⊘noon-4pm) The daily lunch buffet here is popular with tour groups. With pleasant outdoor seating, castle views and over 20 salads to choose from, it's easy to understand why. The eastern building is worth a visit for its impressive relief display of the castle.

Shehab Restaurant
CAFE **$$**

(9513803; Al-Qala'a St; mains JD6; ⊘noon-8pm) If you're tired from a long walk up Castle Hill, this is a good place to pause before your reach the castle entrance.

Al-Shubba
SUPERMARKET

(Al-Mujamma St; ⊘10am-10pm) Try Al-Shubba if you need to stock up on supplies for the next leg of the King's Highway.

🛍 Shopping

While there is a small selection of souvenirs around the castle area, for an idea of how the people of Karak like to spend their money, take a walk down Al-Malek Hussein St – the road that leads from Castle Plaza to the Saladin statue. Here you will find tailors stitching fake fur to collars; leather jackets and red woollen sweaters dangling in the wind; vendors with rakishly tied headscarves and broken-backed shoes (the local answer to slip-ons); bushy green bundles of coriander hanging from butchers' shops; fennel, turnips and shaggy-mopped carrots begging to be bought for a picnic; and locally gathered herbs in textile bags flagging the outside of spice and coffee bean shops. There is even a small gold souq – selling mostly silver.

ℹ Information

There are at least four banks that change money on An-Nuzha St, one block south of the Saladin roundabout, and most have an ATM for Visa and MasterCard.

Italian Hospital (Al-Maydan St; ⊘24hr)

Post Office (Al-Khadr St; ⊘7am-6pm Sat-Thu) In the lower (northern) part of town.

Tourist Police (191; Al-Qala'a St; ⊘24hr)

Visitor Centre (2354263; Al-Qala'a St; ⊘8am-4pm Sat-Thu) Active in high season only.

ℹ Getting There & Away

Karak is difficult but not impossible to reach by public transport, accessed from the Desert Highway. The main bus station is outside the town, at the bottom of the hill by the junction of the King's Highway. If you are driving, there is a highly scenic road (Rte 50) that leads from Karak down to the Dead Sea.

BUS & MINIBUS

From the main bus station, several daily buses go direct to Amman's south bus station (JD2, around two hours) via the Desert Highway. Minibuses also run about every hour along the King's Highway from Karak to Tafila (JD1.500, one hour), the best place for connections to Qadsiyya (for Dana Biosphere Reserve) and Shobak. To Wadi Musa (for Petra), take a minibus to Ma'an (JD2.500, two hours) which leaves around 1pm daily, and change there. Alternatively, leapfrog on minibuses to Tafila, Shobak and Wadi Musa.

Buses to Aqaba (JD5, three hours) travel in the mornings via the Dead Sea Highway about four times a day. In the afternoon it's better to take the Amman bus to Qatrana on the Desert Highway and change to a southbound bus to Aqaba.

There are smaller minibus stands around town for services to Safi (JD1) and Mazra'a (600 fils) on the Dead Sea Highway, south along the King's Highway to Mu'tah (500 fils) and Mazar (400 fils), and north to Al-Qasr, Ar-Rabba and Ariha.

TAXI

From Amman it's possible to charter a taxi to Karak via the Desert Highway for about JD50 one way. From Amman via the King's Highway, with a stop at Madaba and Wadi Mujib, it costs at least JD80.

From Karak, taxi fares cost around JD50 to Amman or Madaba, JD45 to Dana and JD65 to Petra.

❶ Getting Around

The old city of Karak is easy to get around on foot but has a maddening system of narrow one-way streets. If you're driving, consider parking outside town and taking a taxi.

Wadi Hasa & Khirbet Tannour خربة التنور

Travelling south from Karak, the King's Highway gradually descends from a brooding piece of black volcanic hillside into the impressive but arid Wadi Hasa (the biblical Zered Valley). Attempts at tomato growing are in evidence but it's hard to encourage the rocky topsoil into production in an otherwise wild and thermally active landscape.

The highway skirts a reservoir, above which looms a small, conical hill. A track leads off to the right of the highway from where a steep 15-minute hike heads to the top of the hill for panoramic views and the ruined temple of Khirbet Tannour.

Nearby, lying along a potholed, winding road off the main highway, are two popular picnic spots, the hot springs of Hammamat Burbita and Hammamat Afra.

Access to the whole area is only feasible with private transport.

◉ Sights & Activities

Khirbet Tannour Temple   RUIN
(☉ daylight hours) FREE The neglected ruins of the 2000-year-old Nabataean temple of Khirbet Tannour are worth the hike up the hill for the view, if nothing else. A famous statue of Nike was found here, a copy of which is housed in Amman's National Archaeological Museum; the original is in Cincinnati. A statue of the goddess Atargatis (currently in Amman's National Archaeological Museum) was also unearthed from this auspicious little hilltop.

In truth there's not much to see here except for column bases and the outlines of a temple courtyard with adjoining rooms. Despite this, most people will relish the windswept site and epic location. In fact the term 'most people' is misleading: there is the strong suggestion among the scampering lizards and the desert larks that no one ever comes up here – except a conscientious travel writer or two. Even the dogs herding sheep along the fertile wadi to the south keep their distance, running in contours around the lower hills.

The turn-off to the ruins is 36km south of Karak town, at the crest of the hill – a dam is clearly visible at the bottom. It is marked as 'AT TA NO I QUI ES SI', which isn't a Latin inscription but a weather-beaten version of 'At-Tannour Antiquities Site'. The 1.5km access road is potholed, but you can park off the track quite easily. Walk up to the communication tower and the path up the hill becomes obvious.

Hammamat Burbita   BATHHOUSE
(Hammamat Burbayta; JD5; ☉ 8am-8pm) Recently renovated, this modest pool complex (closed during Ramadan) is fed from natural hot springs at the bottom of a reed-filled wadi. Popular with locals, especially at weekends, the oasis is a welcome sight amid the arid landscape. There are changing facilities and a separate pool for women. The spring is 13km off the King's Highway; the turning is signposted about 23km north of Tafila.

There is no public transport but it is adequately signposted if you are driving. A chartered taxi from Tafila to Burbita or neighbouring Afra costs around JD30 return, including waiting time.

Hammamat Afra   BATHHOUSE
(JD7; ⊘8am-10pm) Facilities at this large thermal spring (open daily, including Ramadan) include private pools for men and women, changing rooms and picnic areas. Admission is paid at the entry gate to the spring, 5km from neighbouring Hammamat Burbita. You must show your passport before continuing the extra 1km to the rock pools, built against the canyon walls. You can't see the springs from the road. Women on their own are likely to feel conspicuous.

There is quite a rowdy atmosphere at weekends and there's little chance of escaping the party as wardens prohibit you exploring the wadi upstream.

Tafila   الطفيله

📞03 / POP 87,500 / ELEV 1050M

Wrapped around a steep-sided wadi, Tafila (also spelled Tafileh) is a busy market centre and transport junction. There is nothing to see, except the decrepit exterior of a ruined Crusader castle (closed to visitors). It was in Tafila that one of the Prophet Mohammed's emissaries was beheaded, leading to the military conquest by the Islamic armies from AD 632.

The only reason to come here is to change minibuses. They leave almost hourly from Karak (JD1, one hour), crossing the inspiring desert scenery of Wadi Hasa. There are also direct minibuses to/from Wahadat station in Amman (JD2.800, 2½ hours) via the Desert Highway; Aqaba (JD2.500, 2½ hours) via the Dead Sea Highway; Ma'an (JD1.500, one hour) via the Desert Highway; and Shobak (JD1.500, one hour) and Qadsiyya (for Dana Biosphere Reserve; JD1.300, 30 minutes) along the King's Highway.

Dana Biosphere Reserve
محمية دانا الطبيعية

📞03 / ELEV 1250M

Dana Biosphere Reserve (adult/student per day JD8.200/JD4.100, with RSCN lodging free) is one of Jordan's hidden gems. The focal point is the charming 15th-century stone village of Dana, which dangles beneath the King's Highway on a precipice, commanding exceptional views of the valley below. The reserve extends to the valley floor, the centre point of which is the reserve's famed Feynan Ecolodge. For wildlife enthusiasts it's a must, but it is also a wonderful place to spend a few days hiking or simply relaxing en route along the King's Highway.

The reserve is the largest in Jordan and includes a variety of terrain, from sandstone cliffs over 1700m high near Dana to a low point of 50m below sea level in Wadi Araba. Sheltered within the red-rock escarpments are protected valleys that are home to surprisingly diverse ecosystems. About 600 species of plants (ranging from citrus trees and juniper to desert acacias and date palms) thrive in the reserve, together with 180 species of birds. Over 45 species of mammals (25 of which are endangered) also inhabit the reserve, including caracal, increasing herds of ibex, mountain gazelles, sand cats, red foxes and wolves. The installation of night traps has given reserve wardens a better understanding of the movement of these rarely spotted animals.

The best time to visit Dana is in the spring, when the hillsides bloom with flowers, or during the autumn, when the auburn foliage thins out, making it easier to spot wildlife. That said, while the winter can be bitterly cold in the upper part of the reserve (some of the trails will close), this is a good time to explore the Feynan area in the lower part of the reserve. Similarly, when it is sweltering in summer in the lower reaches of the wadi, there's seldom need of air-con in Dana.

The visitor centre (p152) at Dana is the first port of call for a visit to the reserve, unless you are staying at the Rummana Campground. The ticket office closes at 3pm, so if you are planning a sunset hike make sure you arrive before then.

History

Dana village dates from the Ottoman period, but was abandoned less than a generation ago as locals moved to nearby Qadsiyya in search of jobs. Farmed by only a handful of remaining residents, the neighbouring terraces, which once grew pistachio, almond, walnut, pomegranate, lemon and apple crops, are slowly slipping back to nature. Ongoing attempts by various parties to entice the villagers back into the reserve are hampered by the fact that housing with utilities, schooling and basic infrastructure is to be had in nearby towns that are far more accessible. That said, there are signs of green shoots in the village, thanks to the persistent efforts of the Royal Society for the Conservation of Nature (RSCN) and the tourism it promotes. Several old houses are being renovated and shopkeepers, barbers and bakers are being invited to return.

About 50 Bedouin families drift in and beyond the lower reaches of the reserve. They are only permitted to herd their livestock in the Dana Valley at certain times of the year to allow the vegetation to recover.

The RSCN assumed control of the reserve in 1993 in an attempt to promote ecotourism, protect wildlife and improve the lives of local villagers in an integrated project. The reserve directly or indirectly employs locals from nearby villages, and income from tourism is helping to sustain a number of families beyond the reserve and provide environmental education in local schools.

Dana is unique because it has four ecosystems ranging from altitudes of 1700m to minus 50m, all of which occur within a very compact distance. For this reason Dana has now achieved official 'biodiversity reserve' status.

◉ Sights

Dana Museum
MUSEUM

(www.rscn.org.jo; ⊙8am-3pm) FREE Spare 20 minutes for the RSCN's wonderful little museum, next to the Dana Guest House. It illustrates the various wildlife at 1500m on the King's Highway, at 1100m at Dana Village and 50m below sea level in Wadi Araba. It also explains the peculiar challenges to the ecosystem in a reserve that experiences 350mm of rain per year in winter on the mountaintops, and soaring desert temperatures and 10mm of rain per year at sea level.

It makes a good place to begin an exploration of the area, helping to give context to the various treasures of the reserve to look out for during a hike.

✦ Activities

Dana Biosphere Reserve begs to be explored on foot. It's only by getting out in the thick of it that you feel the special beauty of the terrain and invite the chance encounter with Dana's diverse wildlife.

The RSCN organises a series of established hikes ranging from a couple of hours of easy ambling to strenuous overnight trips. In addition, there are hikes taking in the wadis adjacent to the reserve including a two-day hike to Feynan Ecolodge, via Wadi Ghuweir, overnighting at the lodge and returning via Wadi Dana. The visitor centre (p152) can give information on the full range of hikes. The trails from Al-Barra require a short drive to get to the trailhead (RSCN charges JD11.600 for a shuttle).

RSCN guides are available (and compulsory on most hiking trails) to give visitors a deeper understanding of the reserve. They cost (for a minimum of four people) JD10 per person for up to two hours, JD13 for three to four hours and JD17 for five to six hours. It costs JD17 per person for a guide for a full day. Discounts are available for groups of five or more (maximum 20 people).

Hotels in Dana can help organise longer treks to Shobak (two days) via Wadi Feynan, Wadi Ghuweir and the village of Mansourah, and even on to Petra (four days).

Al-Nawatef Camp organises several excellent guided hikes in Wadi Ghuweir and Wadi Hamra. Ask about Ali's Walk, a three-day hike to Petra (JD180 to JD200 per person for a minimum of two people), including guide, camping facilities, all meals and transportation of luggage.

Easy Hiking Trails

Rummana Campground Trail
HIKING

(1-2hr, self-guided; ⊙15 Mar-31 Oct) This spectacular walk traces the fluted edge of Wadi Dana's canyons, circling through the trees and rock formations around the campground, and giving plenty of opportunities for a quiet sit among untroubled wildlife.

Look out for griffon vultures wheeling above the stone turrets of Wadi Dana, brilliant turquoise agamas (a type of lizard) basking on rocks, jewel beetles and, if you get really lucky, an early-morning ibex in the creases and folds of neighbouring canyons.

★ Wadi Dana Trail
HIKING

(16km, 6hr, self-guided; ⊙year-round) Although this is the most popular trail, you are still likely to have this long hike through majestic Wadi Dana to yourself. The trail is easy to follow, partially along a disused road and partially via Bedouin grazing paths. Although no scrambling is involved, be aware that the trail involves a relentless one-hour descent at the beginning of the hike that gives toes, calves and knees a good bruising.

It's not feasible to complete the walk in both directions in a day unless you are super fit or plainly masochistic. Either stay the night at Feynan Ecolodge at the bottom of the walk, or arrange with the RSCN office for a car (JD52.200) to bring you back to Dana either via Tafila (2½ hours) or Shobak (2¾ hours).

Moderate Hiking Trails

Rummana Mountain Trail HIKING
(2.5km, 1-2hr, self-guided; ⊘ 15 Mar-31 Oct) From Rummana Campground to the nearby Rummana (Pomegranate) Peak, this trail gives great views over Wadi Araba. One Rummana receptionist, Mahmoun, described the trail as a good metaphor for life: lots of ups and downs, but greatly rewarding when you reach your goal.

Nawatef Trail HIKING
(2.5km, 2½hr, guide required; ⊘ year-round) This great short walk, from Al-Barra to the luscious springs and Nabataean ruins of Nawatef, involves a steep uphill walk back to Dana.

White Dome Trail Hiking HIKING
(8km, 3hr, guide required; ⊘ 15 Mar- 31 Oct) Taking you past dramatic wadi escarpments surrounding Rummana Campground and past the beautiful terraced gardens of Dana village, this trail leads through waist-high vegetation to Dana Guest House.

THE WADI DANA TRAIL: A WALK IN THE PARK

One of the most popular trails at Dana is the 'easy hike': the 16km Wadi Dana Trail, from Dana to Feynan Ecolodge (p152). As it's downhill all the way, it ought to be a mere walk in the park, but don't be deceived – it's not as easy as it sounds! Start the walk after lunch: that way you'll reach the hotter part of the walk in the cooler part of the day. Take more water than you think you'll need and wear a hat. Don't forget in your planning that it takes three hours, partly by 4WD, to return to Dana by road.

The Bad Bits

➡ Interminable initial descent on a potholed vehicle track, wishing you'd worn thicker socks

➡ Blazing heat with little shade (there's only one tree in the first hour)

➡ Not having time to stop to chat with the Bedouin (some JD1 notes for tea would've been handy)

➡ The end of the wadi is nowhere near where you think it is

➡ Being overtaken by an encouraging old couple on a donkey saying '*Funduq* (hotel) – only five minutes', when you're still an hour's walk from Feynan

➡ The prospect of no beer and no meat at the inn – the Feynan Ecolodge is dry and vegetarian-only

The Good Bits

➡ A lizard sunning itself in the ash of an old fireplace

➡ A crest of goats marshalled into camera by an entrepreneurial herdsman

➡ Carnival-pink oleander flowers, waving like bunting along the entire lower wadi

➡ Secret gardens of reeds and oleander and huge, spreading trees

➡ A barefoot race by local lads conducted for the sheer fun of running

➡ A Sinai agama (lizard), whose brilliant turquoise livery demanded a second look

➡ The same encouraging couple returning on the donkey saying '*Funduq* – only five minutes'

➡ The sampling of delicious cool water and superb vegetarian food at Feynan Ecolodge

So is it worthwhile? Without doubt! Chances are that even in peak season you'll have the reserve to yourself. Anyone who has hiked main trails in other popularly visited destinations will know what a treat that is.

WORTH A TRIP

ANCIENT DANA

There's something rather magical about coming across a pile of smelted fragments and realising that this is evidence of industry, not from any industrial revolution, but from the activities of communities 6000 years ago.

There are almost 100 archaeological sites in the Dana Reserve, most still being excavated by British teams. The ruins of **Khirbet Feynan**, at the mouth of Wadi Feynan and Wadi Ghuweir, are particularly interesting: the 6000-year-old copper mines here were once the largest metal-smelting operations in the Near East and are mentioned in the Bible. The Romans later worked the mines using Christian slaves.

The hills of Dana still contain copper, but despite lobbying from mining companies, the Jordanian government has agreed not to allow mining in the reserve. A growing cement factory which quarries along the rim of the reserve is the nearest incursion permitted in this wildlife haven.

Copper Mines Trail (☑ 64645580; www.ecohotels.me/Feynan; JD13, minimum 2 adults; ☉ Sep-Jun) You can explore the slag heaps of the main mines of Umm al-Amad, together with the ruins of three churches, Iron Age sites and a Roman tower, on a fascinating hike in the hills offered most days from Feynan Ecolodge (three to four hours). The tour is very hot for much of the year so carrying water and wearing a hat is essential.

Strenuous Hiking Trails

Fida Canyon Trail   HIKING
(2.5km, 2hr, guide required; ☉ year-round) This short but strenuous hike leads from Al-Barra to Shaq al-Reesh and is not for the faint-hearted.

Hammam Al-Dathnah Trail   HIKING
(17km, 9hr, guide required; ☉ year-round) A spectacular but highly taxing trail, it leads from Al-Nawatef, crossing Hamra Valley and Palm Tree Valley to Feynan Ecolodge.

Al-Ghuweir Trail   HIKING
(16km, 6-7hr, guide required; ☉ year-round) This demanding hike leads along river beds and through a siq (canyon) and a valley of palm trees to arrive at Feynan Ecolodge. It is to be avoided if rain is expected or has recently fallen because of flash floods. Transport to the start of this trail, near Shobak, costs JD25.

Cycling

Mountain Bike Trail   CYCLING
(☑ 079 9599507; www.ecohotels.me/Feynan; ☉ Sep-Jun) A mountain-bike trail offers cyclists opportunities to explore the lower Dana area on saddleback: a four-hour ride costs JD18 (JD29 with a guide); a full day's ride costs JD29 (JD47 with a guide). The trail starts at Feynan Ecolodge and uses gravel tracks past the archaeological site of Khirbet Feynan, ending at the villages of Rashaydeh and Greigra. There are opportunities to stop en route to hike or have tea with the Bedouin. The lodge has 10 bikes available.

🛏 Sleeping & Eating

The RSCN operates two excellent places to stay, Dana Guest House and Rummana Campground, both of which should be booked in advance through the Wild Jordan Centre (p306) in Amman. In addition, the RSCN owns the award-winning Feynan Ecolodge at the bottom of the valley, a two- to three-hour drive or day's hike from Dana. In Dana village, there are three privately run budget hotels and there's a private camp just outside the reserve. Each arranges transfers and hiking but make sure you pay your reserve fees as it is illegal to walk in the reserve without a ticket, and besides money from tourism is the main hope for the long-term survival of this reserve. Camping in the reserve, except at the Rummana Campground, is not permitted.

★ **Al-Nawatef Camp**   CAMP $
(☑ 079 6392079, 2270413; www.alnawatefcamp. com; half board in tented chalets with shared shower block JD15) Perched on the edge of an escarpment and surrounded by black iris, this wonderful camp is run by a hospitable local who knows the area. The goat-hair chalets with beds, linen and blankets boast balconies with exceptional views. The camp is signposted 2km off the King's Highway, 5km south of the Dana turning in Qadsiyya.

Tea and coffee is available all day, delicious dinners are rustled up from the ground oven and a free transport service is offered to Dana village. You can set your own tent up in the grounds for JD5 and order dinner (JD5) or breakfast (JD2) to suit. The owner can collect you from the main road. He also organises onward travel via local buses and will drop you at the relevant junction. The camp organises some excellent hiking opportunities.

Dana Tower Hotel GUESTHOUSE $

(077 7514804, 079 5688853; www.dana-tower-hotel.com; half board per person JD15; with shared bathroom JD11; summer rooftop camping JD3) Free transfer to/from the main road, a quirky assembly of small, unheated rooms called 'Flying Carpet' and 'Crazy Camel', leafy courtyards, a *majlis* (Arab-style sitting area) draped in memorabilia and rooftop seating make this a winner with younger backpackers. Added perks: a dinner of 22 dishes, free tea, a washing machine and hot showers.

Onward transport (JD17 to Petra, JD45 to Feynan by 4WD) is available.

Dana Moon Hotel GUESTHOUSE $

(079 7533581; dana.moonhotel@hotmail.com; half board per person JD15) Simple rooms with shared bathrooms characterise this guesthouse and the *majlis* under the pine trees is an attractive feature. The hotel runs the neighbouring Feynan Way Restaurant.

★**Dana Guest House** ECOLODGE $$

(2270497; www.rscn.org.jo; s/d/tr/q with shared bathroom incl breakfast & park entry fee JD68/85/102/120, d with private bathroom JD96) With panoramic views across the reserve, a roaring fire in winter and enthusiastic park rangers, this ecolodge is run by the RSCN. The lodge has minimalist, stone-walled rooms, all but two of which have a balcony with exceptional views from which to shiver in the dawn. Heating and hot water are provided by solar panels.

Breakfast and delicious local suppers (JD14) are shared around trestle tables.

Dana Hotel BOUTIQUE HOTEL $$

(079 5597307, 2270537; www.suleimanjarad.webs.com; half board per person in villas JD25, s/d JD12/20; dinner JD5) A warm welcome is assured from the patrons of this hotel, run by the Sons of Dana, a cooperative that claims to provide social programmes to around 150 local residents. It's the oldest established hotel in Dana and, thanks to the assistance of USAid, it has recently expanded into a number of attractively renovated old houses in the village.

Rummana Campground CAMP $$

(s/d/tr/q tent incl breakfast & park entry fee JD52/64/75/87; 20% student discount; 15 Mar-31 Oct) Prices at this camp may seem steep given the minimal facilities, but waking up to the sound of Dana's wildlife, it's easy to see why reservations are necessary. With great hiking trails just beyond the tent pegs, you can step into the cloudscape as the mist rises from the valley floor. Tents come with mattresses and bedding.

You can drive here in 30 minutes or hike in three hours from Dana village. Barbecue grills are available if you bring your own food and fuel. Dinner (JD15) and breakfast (included in the camp fee) are whisked up by a jolly cook intent on beefing you up for another day's exertions.

Feynan Way Restaurant JORDANIAN $

(dinner JD3-10; 7am-midnight) Occupying a tree-shaded terrace, this simple restaurant provides an opportunity for breakfast or lunch after the long hike from the campground, or a welcome chance to 'go out' from your hotel in the evening.

🛍 Shopping

RSCN Craft Shop HANDICRAFTS

(Dana Guest House; 9am-5.30pm) With a wide range of quality crafts inspired by nature, workshops (closed by 3.30pm) and a food-drying centre for making organic food, the craft shop is well worth a visit. Villagers are given the opportunity to make quality local crafts (organic herbs, fruit rolls, jams, olive-oil soaps, candles and silver jewellery) that are sold by the RSCN throughout Jordan.

The leather goods and candles produced by local Bedouin women at Feynan Ecolodge, in particular, give local women a degree of economic independence and an incentive to move away from goat rearing, which is detrimental to the fragile environment.

Village Shop FOOD & DRINK

(Feynan Ecolodge; 9am-noon) Apart from stocking up on water and juice for hikes here, you can also get lunch boxes (JD4) of bread, egg and fruit that will be welcome in the wilds. The shop stocks locally produced honey and jam as well. Opening hours are erratic!

GREEN LODGING

The one-of-a-kind **Feynan Ecolodge** (☎ +962 6 464 5580; www.ecohotels.me/feynan; Wadi Feynan; half board incl park entry fee from s/d/tr JD101/127/170; ☺ Sep-Jun), owned by the RSCN, is accessible on foot from Dana (a day's hike) or by 4WD from the Dead Sea Highway (see p116). Powered entirely by solar energy, Feynan features mud-rendered architecture and the candle-lit nights at the lodge, with its caravanserai ambience, vegetarian suppers and guided star-gazing, are a real highlight.

The lodge lives up to its mantra of 'helping nature, helping people' through its commitment to the environment and community-based projects. Local people are directly involved (as drivers, guides, bakers and candlemakers), directly benefiting 80 local families; around half of all revenue from tourism is returned to the community. Waste is recyled and the use of traditional water filtration saves the equivalent of 10,000 plastic bottles a year.

It gets very hot here in summer (air-conditioning is available in extreme temperatures only) and you should bring a torch and mosquito repellent. The hot water (available between 11am and 7pm) is solar-heated. Dinner comprises a delicious vegetarian feast of potato, rice, eggplant (aubergine), tomato and bean dishes, garnished with local herbs and served with wafer-thin Arabic bread. Staff are recruited from local Bedouin tribes, food and supplies are purchased locally and a share of profits from tourism is invested in the care of Dana Biosphere Reserve.

Feynan Ecolodge runs a number of scheduled hiking, canyoning and special-interest tours that allow guests to experience the best of the lower reaches of the reserve, as well as providing unique opportunities to engage with the seminomadic Bedouin people. There can't be too many hotels where you can learn breadmaking, coffee-pounding and kohl-crushing. Better yet, pack a knapsack of supplies and some cool water and spend the day with a shepherd.

❶ Information

Visitor Centre (☎ 2270497; www.rscn.org.jo; ☺ 8am-3pm) The visitor centre in the Dana Guest House complex (p151) is the place to obtain further information about the reserve and its hiking trails and to arrange a guide. Reservations for guides are advisable in spring and autumn as there is a daily maximum number of people permitted on certain trails. Admission fees are included in the price of RSCN accommodation.

❶ Getting There & Away

The easiest way to get to Dana by public transport is from Tafila. Minibuses run every hour or so between Tafila and Qadsiyya (JD1, 30 minutes). The turn-off to Dana village is 1km north of Qadsiyya; from here it's a steep 2.8km downhill walk to Dana village (there's no bus). Alternatively, you can take a private car with one of the locals in Qadsiyya for JD4. There are three early morning buses to Amman (JD3, three hours); the first bus leaves Qadsiyya at 4.30am, the next at 5am and the third at around 6am.

A taxi to Dana from Karak costs around JD40 one way. A taxi to Petra costs JD36 or JD12 in a shared taxi from the hotel. The Dana Tower Hotel organises a bus from Amman's south bus station for JD5 if you book with the hotel in advance.

If you're driving from Tafila or Karak, the first signpost you'll see off to the right goes to the Rummana Campground. The turn-off to the Dana Biosphere Reserve is signposted just before the village of Qadsiyya. Beware, it is a steep descent: use low gear instead of relying on your brakes.

To get to Rummana Campground from Dana village, head 4.5km north of Qadsiyya along the King's Highway and turn left at the signpost. The campground is 6km along a road partially shared by cement-factory traffic. The RSCN can arrange transport from Dana village for JD10.500 (for one to four people).

Shobak شوبك

☑ 03

Semi-arid for most of the year, the striking white-stone hills and wadis of Shobak make for a dramatic landscape, particularly on a crisp winter's day when the sky is cobalt blue. Most people visit Shobak not so much for the sleepy town but rather its eponymous castle. It is also the start or end point of some spectacular hikes towards Dana in the north and Petra in the south.

⊙ Sights & Activities

★ **Shobak Castle** CASTLE
(Mont Real or Montreal; ⊙ daylight hours) FREE
Perched in a wild, remote landscape, Shobak Castle wins over even the most castle-weary, despite being less complete than its sister fortification at Karak. Formerly called Mons Realis (the Royal Mountain), it was built by the Crusader king Baldwin I in AD 1115. Restoration work is ongoing and hopefully this will include some explanatory signs. In the meantime, the caretaker shows visitors around for about JD10. Bring a torch for exploring the castle's many dark corners.

Built on a small knoll at the edge of a plateau, Shobak Castle is especially imposing when seen from a distance. It withstood numerous attacks from the armies of Saladin before succumbing in 1189 (a year after Karak), after an 18-month siege. It was later occupied in the 14th century by the Mamluks, who built over many of the Crusader buildings. As you climb up from the entrance, there are some **wells** on the left. Soon after passing these, you'll see the reconstructed **church**, one of two in the castle, down to the left. It has an elegant apse supported by two smaller alcoves. The room leading off to the west was the **baptistery**; on the north wall there are traces of water channels leading from above.

Returning to the main path, turn left. After passing under the arches, a door leads into the extensive **market**. Turn left and descend 375 steps into an amazing secret passageway that leads to a subterranean spring, finally surfacing via a ladder outside the castle, beside the road to Shobak town. Tread carefully, use a torch and don't even think about coming down here if you're claustrophobic. Alternatively, continue past the tunnel for 50m and you'll pass a large two-storey building with archways, built by the Crusaders but adapted by the Mamluks as a school. At the northern end of the castle is the semicircular **keep** with four arrow slits. Outside, dark steps lead down to the **prison**. Head to the northeast corner of the castle to see Quranic inscriptions, possibly dating from the time of Saladin, carved in Kufic script around the outside of the keep.

Following south along the eastern perimeter, you'll pass the **entrance to the court** of Baldwin I, which has been partly reconstructed. The court was later used as a Mamluk school. Continuing south, you'll pass some baths on the right. Off to the left

is a reconstructed **Mamluk watchtower**. Just past the tower is the second church. In a room to the left as you enter, you can see above a door in the east wall a weathered carving of a Crusader cross. In the **church** proper, the arches have been reconstructed. Beneath the church are **catacombs**, which contain Islamic tablets, Christian carvings, large spherical rocks used in catapults and what is said to be Saladin's very simple throne. From the catacombs, the path leads back to the gate.

Jaya Camp Hiking HIKING
(☑ 079 5958958; www.jayatouristcamp.yolasite.com; per person from JD35) Jaya camp offers day trips and overnight camping trips from Shobak to Feynan Ecolodge or to Little Petra with longer trips possible. Guided trips cost JD70 per day and the camps can arrange the transportation of luggage (JD70 per day). Visits to a local Bedouin family (JD5; JD30 to stay overnight) are popular.

For interesting cultural insights, the owner also runs a two-day 'Food & Training' experience on site, introducing guests to coffee-grinding, handlooming, pottery and the preparation of a traditional Bedouin meat and rice dish, *mansaf* (JD50 per person, including one night's camping).

Historical Re-enactment CULTURAL
(Jordan Heritage Revival Company; ☑ 077 7606052, 079 6606052; www.jhrc.jo) Not yet running on a routine basis, this show has plans to bring the history of Shobak Castle to life. Check the website for updates or ask the guide at the castle entrance to see if the promised daily shows have become a reality.

🍴 Sleeping & Eating

There is limited accommodation in Shobak village (properly known as Musallath); all options have fine views of the castle.

There are a few grocery stores and cheap restaurants in the village.

Jaya Tourist Camp CAMP $
(☑ 079 5958958; www.jayatouristcamp.yolasite.com; half board per person JD20) 🅿 With 15 tents in a tranquil spot on high ground opposite Shobak Castle, this friendly campsite set in a garden of hollyhocks has a clean shower block and Bedouin goat-hair tents for relaxing. To reach the camp, follow the signs from the King's Highway. The road passes Montréal Hotel and ends after 1km at the camp, which also offers hiking.

Showbak Camp & Caves Zaman Motel
GUESTHOUSE $

(☑077 7996834; showbakcavehotel@yahoo.com; half board per person with shared bathroom JD35) These refurbished caves at the foot of the castle have been in the owner's family for generations; he can remember his grandparents living here. Warm in winter and cool in summer, the caves give visitors a feel for an ancient way of life. They are located at the bottom of the castle hill, marked by trestle tables displaying local fossils.

Montréal Hotel
HOTEL $$

(☑077 6951714; www.jhrc.jo; r JD50, ste JD90; ☎) This hotel, which has a spectacular view of the castle, offers guests some lovely features, including a stylish lounge around a central gas fire. The rooms are simple but comfortable. The hotel takes a sustainable approach and has solar panels for hot-water heating and electricity. Dinner is available (JD9).

ⓘ Information

Shobak Castle Visitor Centre (☉9am-5pm Nov-Mar, to 7pm Apr-Oct) Situated at the bottom of the castle hill, the visitor centre has limited facilities (and no telephone), but there are at least great views of the castle. The caretaker can rustle up a Turkish coffee in the attractive courtyard and there are functioning toilets.

It's worth a stop for a perusal in the little Bedouin shop that displays an assortment of rocks, fossils and 'buried treasure', much of which should probably have stayed that way!

ⓘ Getting There & Away

Occasional buses link Shobak village with Amman's south bus station (JD5, 2½ hours, 5.30am daily), Aqaba and Karak. Some minibuses travelling between Wadi Musa and Ma'an also pass through Shobak. For the 3km from Shobak village to the castle, you can charter a taxi (around JD6 return including waiting time) or walk.

If driving, there are two well-signposted roads from the King's Highway to the castle and there are signs from Shobak village.

Petra

بترا

Best Places to Eat & Drink

➡ Cave Bar (p187)

➡ Sahtain (p187)

➡ Petra Kitchen (p179)

➡ Red Cave Restaurant (p186)

➡ Basin Restaurant (p176)

Best Places to Stay

➡ Mövenpick Hotel (p183)

➡ Amra Palace Hotel (p184)

➡ Taybet Zaman Hotel & Resort (p186)

➡ Petra Palace Hotel (p183)

➡ Petra Guest House Hotel (p183)

Why Go?

The ancient Nabataean city of Petra, with its elaborate architecture chiselled out of the pink-hued cliffs, is not just the leading highlight of a country blessed with more than its fair share of top sites: it's a wonder of the world. It lay forgotten for centuries, known only to the Bedouin who made it their home, until the great Swiss explorer, Jean Louis Burckhardt, happened upon it in 1812.

Built partly in honour of the dead, the Petra necropolis retains much of its sense of hidden mystery thanks to its inaccessible location in the heart of a windblown landscape. Reached via the Siq, a narrow rift in the land whose cliffs cast long shadows across the once-sacred way, the path suddenly slithers into sunlight in front of the Treasury – a spectacle that cannot fail to impress. Add to this the cheerfulness of the Bedouin, and it's easy to see what makes Petra a must.

When to Go

➡ March to May is peak tourist season in Petra and for good reason. Hiking is at its safest, the wadis are seamed with prolific pink-flowering oleander, and climbs to the High Places are accompanied by spears of flowering aloe.

➡ Mid-October to the end of November, Petra's second high season, offers a last chance to visit in good weather before rains put some routes off-limits. Bitterly cold by night with bright blue skies by day, Petra is almost empty in winter, allowing for a more intimate engagement with the 'Pink City'.

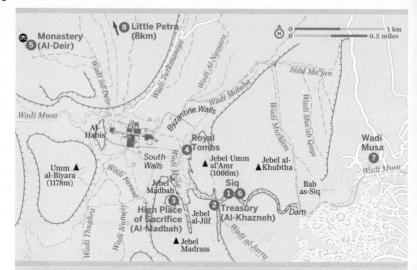

Petra Highlights

❶ Tread the path of history by winding through the **Siq** (p159), the sheer-sided chasm leading to an ancient world.

❷ Catch the early-morning sun slanting off the pillars of the **Treasury** (p160), the sublime spectacle at the end of the Siq.

❸ Climb the processional way to the **High Place of Sacrifice** (p161), pause for tea with the Bedouin and return to the valley floor through a garden of wildflowers.

❹ Search the **Royal Tombs** (p164) for spirits, lurking in the rainbow-coloured hollows.

❺ Make the pilgrimage to the **Monastery** (p169) and watch the weather-burnished stones catch alight at sunset.

❻ Let your soul glide through the Siq's shadows, guided by music and candlelight on tour with **Petra by Night** (p181).

❼ Prepare your own traditional Jordanian supper at **Petra Kitchen** (p179).

❽ Visit **Little Petra** (p190) and enjoy Nabataean tombs and temples in a miniature siq without the company of tour groups.

History

Think of Petra and you will inevitably think of the Nabataeans, the nomadic tribe from western Arabia who built most of the monuments in the ancient city that are visible today. They were not the first inhabitants of the region, however. In fact, neolithic villages dating from around 7000 BC are in evidence in the surrounding wadis and hillsides of Petra. Remains of the most famous of these, excavated in the 1950s, can be seen at Al-Beidha, just north of Petra. Built at the same time as Jericho on the West Bank, Al-Beidha is one of the earliest known farming communities in the Middle East.

The Nabataeans arrived in a region around the 6th century BC. They were organised traders and over the next 500 years

they used their wealth to build the city of Petra. In its heyday, under King Aretas IV (8 BC–AD 40), the city was home to around 30,000 people, including scribes (the Nabataeans created their own cursive script, the forerunner of Arabic) and expert hydraulic engineers who built dams, cisterns and water channels to protect the site and its magnificent buildings.

By AD 106, as trade routes shifted from Petra to Palmyra and new sea trade routes via the Red Sea to Rome bypassed Petra altogether, the Romans had assumed control of the weakened Nabataean empire. Far from abandoning the city of Petra, however, the invaders recast the ancient city with familiar Roman features, including a colonnaded street and baths. The city was honoured by a visit from Emperor Hadrian in AD 131, and in the 3rd century Petra once again became a capital city – this time of the newly created province of Palaestrina Tertia.

Earthquakes in 363 and 551 ruined much of the city and Petra became a forgotten outpost, a 'lost city' known only to local Bedouin who preferred to keep its whereabouts secret. In 1812, however, a young Swiss explorer, Jean Louis Burckhardt, ended Petra's splendid isolation, riding into the abandoned ancient city disguised as a Muslim holy man.

Throughout the 19th century, Petra became the focus of the Western European obsession with the Arabic Orient and the site was pored over by numerous archaeologists, travellers, poets and artists (including the famed British painter David Roberts in 1839). The first English archaeological team arrived in 1929 and excavations have continued unabated to the present day. In 1992 the mosaics of the Petra Church were unveiled and in 2003 a tomb complex was found underneath the Treasury. Part of the continuing allure of the 'rose red city' is that despite years of scrutiny, Petra still has many secrets yet to be discovered.

Nature Reserves

Petra is a protected area, although it is administered differently than Jordan's other nature reserves. Given the number of visitors it hosts each year, the area has its own challenges, particularly erosion and damage to antiquities. For this reason, it's important to pay it the same respect you would any other reserve and avoid littering, wandering off paths, picking flowers, marking the monuments or disappearing behind a rock instead of using the toilet facilities.

Dangers & Annoyances

Some travellers have complained of over-charging and hard-sell techniques (not to mention persistent local children!). This is rarely aggressive, and waxes and wanes with the fortunes of local traders. If you visit in winter, people are too busy keeping warm to worry about sales. In the competitive high season, however, traders and animal handlers make up for lost time. Invariably, after establishing contact with a smile, greeting or snippet of conversation, you'll find almost all will reciprocate in kind.

When hiking from September to March, pay careful attention to the weather as the wadis are susceptible to flash flooding. This is where great walls of water pulse along the narrow defiles, sweeping aside everything in their path.

Many visitors are distressed by the perceived harsh treatment of some of the animals used for transportation, particularly by the younger boys. The use of camels, donkeys and mules is an important part of the community livelihood and most owners take their responsibilities seriously. If you do witness cruelty, however, report the incident to the tourist police or contact the Brooke Hospital for Animals, near the visitor centre.

ℹ Getting There & Away

Petra is a three-hour drive from Amman, two hours from Aqaba and 1½ hours from Wadi Rum. If driving to or from the Dead Sea, consider travelling along the spectacular and seldom-used road that links Little Petra with Wadi Araba.

PETRA

ℹ NAVIGATING PETRA

The town of Wadi Musa is the transport and accommodation hub for Petra, as well as for other attractions in the vicinity, such as Little Petra. The town is split roughly into three parts. The upper part comprises a few top-end hotels lining the main road, each of which has spectacular views of the weathered sandstone landscape (although not of Petra itself). The town centre is where most of the cheaper hotels, the bus station and shops are located. The lower part of town, a 10-minute walk from the town centre, is where you'll find most of the top-end and midrange hotels, together with souvenir shops, tourist restaurants and the famed Cave Bar.

Beyond this is the Petra Visitor Centre (p177) and entrance to Petra. The ancient city is reached on foot via the Siq, or gorge, which begins after a 15-minute walk (or horse ride) from the entrance and takes a further 20 minutes on foot. There is another seldom-used entrance near the village of Umm Sayhoun, but tickets (p176) can only be bought from the main visitor centre.

ℹ FINDING YOUR OWN PACE IN PETRA

Instead of trying to tick off all the top spots (the quickest way to 'monument fatigue'), make Petra your own by sparing time to amble among unnamed tombs, have a picnic in the shade of a flowering oleander or sip tea at a stall on the valley floor and watch everyone else toiling to 'see it all'.

The following suggestions combine some of the obvious highlights with off-the-beaten-track exploration.

Half Day (five hours) Amble through the Siq, absorbing its special atmosphere and savouring the moment of revelation at the Treasury. Resist the temptation to head for the Theatre; instead, climb the steps to the High Place of Sacrifice. Pause for tea by the Obelisk and take the path into Wadi Farasa, enjoying wildflowers and the Garden Tomb en route. The path reaches the Colonnaded Street via a paintbox of rock formations. If there's time, visit the Royal Tombs then return to the valley floor for a chat with Bedouin stallholders and a hunt for the perfect sand bottle.

One Day (eight hours) Spend the morning completing the half-day itinerary, but pack a picnic. After visiting the Royal Tombs, walk along to Qasr al-Bint and hike along the broad wadi that leads to Jebel Haroun as far as Snake Monument – an ideal perch for a snack and a snooze. Return to Qasr al-Bint and slip into the nearby Nabataean Museum to find out more about the snake you shared lunch with. Save some energy for the climb to the Monastery, a fitting finale for any visit to Petra.

Two Days Spend the second day scrambling through exciting Wadi Muthlim and restore your energy over a barbecue in the Basin Restaurant. Walk off lunch exploring the hidden beauty of Wadi Siyagh with its pools of water before strolling back along the Street of Facades. Sit near the Theatre to watch the sun go down on the Royal Tombs opposite – the best spectacle in Petra.

ℹ Getting Around

There are usually plenty of private (yellow) un-metered taxis travelling up and down the main road of Wadi Musa towards the entrance for Petra, especially in the early morning and late afternoon. The taxi fare around central Wadi Musa is JD2 to JD3; it costs a little more if you go as far as 'Ain Musa.

Within Petra, the only way to reach most sites is by walking (strong, comfortable shoes are essential!) or by taking a camel, donkey or mule to more distant and uphill sites.

The Ancient City

The ancient city of Petra is strewn over a vast area of mountains and wadis, but there's only one main access point. Be careful not to underestimate the amount of time it takes to walk between sights, nor the uphill return journey when you're tired.

Petra is open every day unless it rains heavily – rare but disappointing occasions if you only allow one day for your visit in winter. Sturdy footwear, a hat, sunscreen and water are essential at any time of year and a warm coat is needed in winter. Take spare batteries and memory cards with you as supplies are limited beyond the Siq.

Start your visit to Petra at the visitor centre plaza in Wadi Musa, across from the Mövenpick Hotel. This is where you can buy tickets, get leaflets and a map, and use the toilets (although there are several inside the ancient city).

◉ Sights

There are over 800 registered sites in Petra, including some 500 tombs, but the best things to see are easy to find and easy to reach. From the gate, a path winds 800m downhill through an area called **Bab as-Siq** (Gateway to the Siq), punctuated with the first signs of the old city.

There are signs in English throughout Petra, helping to identify the main monuments.

A word of caution: the ancient city is strewn with High Places, once used for sacrifice or other ritual. These locations, all of which afford magnificent views and are a highlight of a visit, usually involve a steep hike up steps to a hilltop where there is no railing or other safety features. Some readers have expressed dismay at this.

Djinn Blocks   MONUMENT

(Map p164) Just past the entrance, look out for three enormous, squat monuments, known as Djinn Blocks or God Blocks. Standing guard beside the path, they take their name from the Arabic word for spirit, the source of the English word *genie*. Other than the fact they were built by Nabataeans in the 1st century AD, little is known about their why or wherefore – they could have been tombs, funerary dedications, or related to the worship of water and fertility.

Whatever their intended function, they are the lodestar for the modern visitor – a tantalising taste of the monuments to come, or announcing journey's end on your weary return.

Obelisk Tomb &
Bab as-Siq Triclinium   TOMB

(Map p164) Near the entrance, along the path to the left, is a tomb with four pyramidal obelisks, built as funerary symbols by the Nabataeans in the 1st century BC. The four obelisks, together with the eroded human figure in the centre, probably represent the five people buried in the tomb. The monument comes into its own at sunset when the obelisks are thrown into relief.

The obelisk tomb at first appears to be multistorey. In fact it was built on top of a much earlier structure, with a Doric columned facade. This building is known as a triclinium, or dining room, and is one of several in Petra. This is where annual feasts were held to commemorate the dead, although it's hard to imagine the conviviality of a banquet in the silent hollow that remains.

Near the Obelisk Tomb, further down the track towards the Siq, a signposted detour to the right leads to several stepped tombs carved into the tops of domed hills. It's a secret little place, missed by almost everyone in their rush to get to the Siq.

★ Siq   CANYON

(Map p164) The 1.2km Siq, or canyon, with its narrow, vertical walls, is undeniably one of the highlights of Petra. The walk through this magical corridor, as it snakes its way towards the hidden city, is one full of anticipation for the wonders ahead – a point not wasted on the Nabataeans who made the passage into a sacred way, punctuated with sites of spiritual significance.

The Siq starts at an obvious bridge, beside a modern dam. The dam was built in 1963, on top of a Nabataean dam dated AD 50, to stop floodwater from Wadi Musa flowing through the Siq. To the right, Wadi Muthlim heads through a Nabataean tunnel – the start (or finish) of an exciting hike (p170). The entrance to the Siq was once marked by a Nabataean monumental arch. It survived until the end of the 19th century, and some remains can be seen at twin niches on either side of the entrance. Many people charge through the Siq impatient to get to Petra. That's a pity because the corridor of stone is worth enjoying for its own sake and the longer you take to travel through it, the more you can savour the final moment of arrival.

Technically, the Siq, with its 200m-high walls, is not a canyon (a gorge carved out by water), but a single block that has been rent apart by tectonic forces. At various points you can see where the grain of the rock on one side matches the other – it's easiest to spot when the Siq narrows to 2m wide. The original channels cut into the walls to bring water into Petra are visible, and in some places the 2000-year-old terracotta pipes are still in place. A section of Roman paving was revealed after excavations in 1997 removed 2m of soil accumulation.

Some historians speculate that the primary function of the Siq was akin to the ancient Graeco-Roman Sacred Way. Some of the most important rituals of Petra's spiritual life began as a procession through the narrow canyon, and it also represented the end point for Nabataean pilgrims. Many of the wall niches that are still visible today along the Siq's walls were designed to hold figures

---

DON'T MISS

LIVING HISTORY

Included in the price of the entry ticket to Petra is a chance to see the Jordan Heritage Revival Company in action with **History of Petra** (Jordan Heritage Revival Company ; ☑ 077 7606052, 079 6606052; www.jhrc.jo; ☺ Sat-Thu). Dressed as Roman centurions, some in full armour on horseback, their steel helmets glinting in the sun, the actors in this dramatic re-enactment cut quite a dash against the normally imperturbable ancient city monuments. Ask at the visitors centre about the current schedule. There are no shows on Friday or during Ramadan.

or representations (called *baetyls*) of the main Nabataean god, Dushara. These small sacred sites served as touchstones of the sacred for pilgrims and priests, offering them a link to the more ornate temples, tombs and sanctuaries in the city's heart, reminding them that they were leaving the outside world, and on the threshold of what was for many a holy city.

At one point the Siq opens out to reveal a square tomb next to a lone fig tree. A little further on, look for a weathered carving of a camel and caravan man on the left wall. The water channel passes behind the carving. Hereafter, the walls almost appear to meet overhead, shutting out the sound and light and helping to build the anticipation of a first glimpse of the Treasury. It's a sublime introduction to the ancient city.

★ **Treasury (Al-Khazneh)** TOMB
(Map p164) Known locally as the Treasury, this tomb is where most visitors fall in love with Petra. The Hellenistic facade is an astonishing piece of craftsmanship. Although carved out of iron-laden sandstone to serve as a tomb for the Nabataean King Aretas III (c 100 BC–AD 200), the Treasury derives its name from the story that an Egyptian pharaoh hid his treasure here (in the facade urn) while pursuing the Israelites.

Some locals clearly believed the tale because the 3.5m-high urn is pockmarked by rifle shots. As with all rock-hewn monuments in Petra, the interior is unadorned. The Treasury is at its most photogenic in full sunlight between about 9am and 11am.

Diagonally opposite the Treasury is a **Sacred Hall** (Map p164), which may have had ritual connections with the Treasury.

Street of Facades TOMBS
(Map p164) From the Treasury, the passage broadens into what is commonly referred to as the Outer Siq. Riddling the walls of the Outer Siq are over 40 tombs and houses built by the Nabataeans in a 'crow step' style reminiscent of Assyrian architecture. Colloquially known as the Street of Facades, they are easily accessible, unlike many tombs in Petra.

A couple of tombs are worth exploring here. The first tomb (number 67) is unusual

---

THE TOMBS OF PETRA

There are more tombs dotted around Petra than any other type of structure; for years visitors assumed that the city was a vast necropolis. One plausible reason why so few dwellings have been discovered is that many of the Nabataeans lived in tents, much like some Bedouin do today.

Petra's earliest rock tombs date from the 3rd century BC. The size and design of the tombs depended on the social status and financial resources of the deceased, ranging from simple cave-like tombs to the ornate facades of the Royal Tombs, the high point of Nabataean funerary architecture.

More sculptors than architects, the Nabataeans quickly realised that it was easier to carve tombs out of the soft sandstone rock than to build free-standing structures that were vulnerable to earthquakes. The larger tombs were carved out of the rock from the top down, using scaffolding support, and the facades were then plastered and painted (almost none of this decoration remains).

The dead were buried in *loculi* (small, separate cavities) carved from the plain walls inside the tomb, while the exterior decoration was made to represent the soul (and sometimes likeness) of the deceased. All but the most simple tombs contained banqueting halls where funerals and annual commemorative feasts were held. Some rooms were frescoed and you can still see traces of coloured decoration in Wadi Siyagh's Painted House and in Siq al-Barid (Little Petra).

The Nabataeans were a nomadic desert people without an architectural heritage of their own, but as traders they were cosmopolitan enough to borrow elements of art and architecture from neighbours. Thus you'll see Egyptian, Assyrian, Mesopotamian, Hellenistic and Roman styles throughout Petra, as well as unique local architectural inventions such as the Nabataean horned column. If you combine this eclecticism with the organic nature of Petra's cave-like tombs, the stunning natural colour of the rock and natural grandeur of the landscape, it's easy to see how Petra has captured the imagination of generations of travellers.

in that it has a funeral chamber in the upper storey. The low entryway highlights how the valley floor has risen over the centuries thanks to the debris washed down during flash floods. Nearby, tomb 70 is unusual in that it is freestanding, with a ziggurat-style top that makes it look like a miniature fort.

★**High Place of Sacrifice**   VIEWPOINT
(Map p164) The most accessible of Petra's High Places, this well-preserved site was built atop Jebel Madbah with drains to channel the blood of sacrificial animals. A flight of steps signposted just before the Theatre leads to the site: turn right at the obelisks (Map p164) to reach the sacrificial platform. You can ascend by donkey (about JD10 one way), but you'll sacrifice both the sense of achievement on reaching the summit and the good humour of your poor old transport.

The obelisks are over 6m high; they are remarkable structures because they are carved out of the rock face, not built upon it: looking at the negative space surrounding them, you can understand the truly epic scale of excavation involved. Dedicated to the Nabataean gods Dushara and Al-'Uzza, their iron-rich stone glows in the sun and they act like totems of this once-hallowed ground.

The altar area includes a large rectangular triclinium, where celebrants at the sacrifice shared a communal supper. In the middle of the High Place, there's a large stone block preceded by three steps. This is a *motab* (repository), where the god statues involved in the procession would have been kept. Next to it is the circular altar, reached by another three steps; stone water-basins nearby were used for cleansing and purifying.

The faint bleat of sheep or the clunk of a goat bell evokes the ancient scene – except that no ordinary person would have been permitted to enter this holy of holies at that time. Cast an eye across the superb panorama in front of you – far above the mortal goings-on of both ancient and modern city – and it's easy to see how this site must have seemed closer to the sky than the earth.

The steps to the High Place of Sacrifice are well maintained, if unremitting, and it takes about 45 minutes up through the crevices and folds of the mountain to reach the obelisks from the Theatre. From here you fork right to reach the altar area. The route is steep but not unduly exposed, so is manageable (unless you suffer from severe ver-

ⓘ BACK DOOR TO PETRA

In the 1980s many of the Bdoul Bedouin, who had lived in Petra for generations, were resettled in villages such as neighbouring Umm Sayhoun. At the end of this village is an access road into the old city of Petra. It would be a pity to enter Petra this way on your first day, as the Siq is Petra's most spectacular highlight. But if you want a shortcut to the Monastery thereafter, take a taxi to the gate at the top of this road and walk down to the museum (20 minutes). From there it's a 40-minute walk to the Monastery. This is 45 minutes shorter than the alternative walk via the Siq. Note that you can't buy tickets here and you can't enter without one so don't forget to bring your ticket with you.

tigo) even without a head for heights. From the altar area, descend the shelves of rock to a broad rim: about 50m down are regal views of the Royal Tombs.

It's worth sitting here for a while. From this lofty vantage point you can watch the everyday dramas of camel handlers arguing with their mounts, young children moving goats from one patch of sparse vegetation to the next and Bedouin stallholders regaling the unsuspecting traveller. They each move beyond the languishing tombs of ordinary folk, far too mindful of the needs of the living to worry much about the forgotten hopes of the ancient dead.

From the obelisks it's possible to continue to the city centre via a group of interesting tombs in beautiful Wadi Farasa (p171).

Theatre   THEATRE
(Map p164) Originally built by the Nabataeans (not the Romans) over 2000 years ago, the Theatre was chiselled out of rock, slicing through many caves and tombs in the process. It was enlarged by the Romans to hold about 8500 (around 30% of the population of Petra) soon after they arrived in AD 106. Badly damaged by an earthquake in AD 363, the Theatre was partially dismantled to build other structures but it remains a Petra highlight.

The seating area had an original capacity of about 3000 in 45 rows of seats, with three horizontal sections separated by two corridors. The orchestra section was carved from the rock, but the backdrop to the *frons*

PETRA THE ANCIENT CITY

Petra

WALKING TOUR

Splendid though it is, the Treasury is not the full stop of a visit to Petra that many people may imagine. In some ways, it's just the semicolon – a place to pause after the exertions of the Siq, before exploring the other remarkable sights and wonders just around the corner.

Even if you're on a tight schedule or worried the bus won't wait, try to find another two hours in your itinerary to complete this walking tour. Our illustration shows the key highlights of the route, as you wind through Wadi Musa from the **Siq** ❶, pause at the **Treasury** ❷ and pass the tombs of the broader **Outer Siq** ❸. With energy and a stout pair of shoes, climb to the **High Place of Sacrifice** ❹ for a magnificent eagle's-eye view of Petra. Return to the **Street of Facades** ❺ and the **Theatre** ❻. Climb the steps opposite to the **Urn Tomb** ❼ and neighbouring **Silk Tomb** ❽: these Royal Tombs are particularly magnificent in the golden light of sunset.

Is the thought of all that walking putting you off? Don't let it! There are donkeys to help you with the steep ascents and Bedouin stalls for a reviving herb tea. If you run out of steam, camels are on standby for a ride back to the Treasury.

TOP TIPS

» **Morning Glory** From around 7am in summer and 8am in winter, watch the early morning sun slide down the Treasury facade.

» **Pink City** Stand opposite the Royal Tombs at sunset (around 4pm in winter and 5pm in summer) to learn how Petra earned its nickname.

» **Floral Tribute** Petra's oleanders flower in May.

Treasury
As you watch the sun cut across the facade, notice how it light up the ladders on either side of Petra's most iconic building. These stone indents were most probably used for scaffolding.

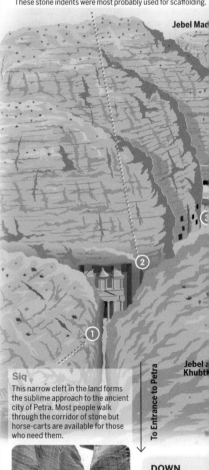

Jebel Mad

Jebel a Khubth

To Entrance to Petra

Siq
This narrow cleft in the land forms the sublime approach to the ancient city of Petra. Most people walk through the corridor of stone but horse-carts are available for those who need them.

DOWN DIFFERENTLY

A superb walk leads from the High Place of Sacrifice, past the Garden Tomb to Petra City Centre.

igh Place of acrifice

aagine the ancients eading the stone eps and it'll take ur mind off the steep scent. The hilltop atform was used for cense-burning and ation-pouring in nonour of forgotten ods.

Outer Siq

Take time to inspect the tombs just past the Treasury. Some appear to have a basement but, in fact, they show how the floor of the wadi has risen over the centuries.

Street of Facades

Cast an eye at the upper storeys of some of these tombs and you'll see a small aperture. Burying the dead in attics was meant to deter robbers – the plan didn't work.

s to High Place

⑤

⑥

Souvenir shops, teashops & toilets

Wadi Musa

Wadi Musa

To Petra City Centre →

⑦

⑧

Jebel Umm al'Amr (1066m)

Royal Tombs

Royal Tombs

HEAD FOR HEIGHTS

For a regal view of Petra, head for the heights above the Royal Tombs, via the staircase.

rn Tomb

arning its name om the urn-shaped nial crowning the ediment, this grand difice with supporting rched vaults was erhaps built for the aan represented by ne toga-wearing bust a the central aperture.

Silk Tomb

Perhaps Nabataean builders were attracted to Wadi Musa because of the colourful beauty of the raw materials. Nowhere is this more apparent than in the weather-eroded, striated sandstone of the Silk Tomb.

Theatre

Most stone amphitheatres are freestanding, but this one is carved almost entirely from the solid rock. Above the back row are the remains of earlier tombs, their facades sacrificed in the name of entertainment.

Petra

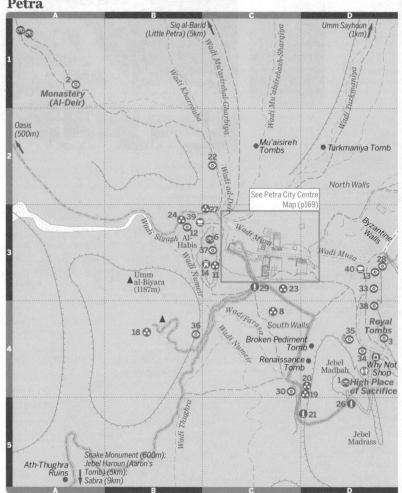

scaenae (stage, which is no longer intact) was constructed, as opposed to carved, in three storeys with frescoed niches and columns overlaid by marble. The performers entered through one of three entrances, the outlines of which are still partially visible.

To make room for the upper seating tiers, the Romans sliced through more tombs. Under the stage floor were storerooms and a slot through which a curtain could be lowered at the start of a performance. From near the slot, an almost-complete statue of Hercules was recovered.

With a backdrop worthy of a David Roberts canvas, the Theatre now offers a vantage point from which to watch a modern tragicomedy of the ill-costumed, cursing their high-heeled footwear; the ill-cast, yawning at tedious tour guides; and the ill-tempered – mainly in the form of irritable camels and their peevish owners.

★ **Royal Tombs**   TOMB
(Map p164) Downhill from the Theatre, the wadi widens to create a larger thoroughfare. To the right, the great massif of Jebel al-Khubtha looms over the valley. Within

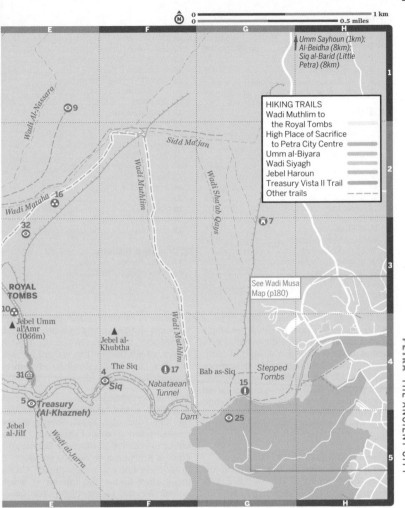

its west-facing cliffs are burrowed some of the most impressive burial places in Petra, known collectively as the 'Royal Tombs'. They look particularly stunning bathed in the golden light of sunset.

The Royal Tombs are reached via a set of steps that ascends from the valley floor, near the Theatre. A fantastic hike from the Royal Tombs leads up to the numerous places of worship on the flattened High Place of Jebel Khubtha, together with a spectacular view of the Treasury. The steps are easily visible between the Palace and Sextius Florentinus tombs. The Royal Tombs also can be reached via the adventurous hike through Wadi Muthlim.

➡ Urn Tomb

(Map p164) The most distinctive of the Royal Tombs is the Urn Tomb, recognisable by the enormous urn on top of the pediment. It was built in about AD 70 for King Malichos II (AD 40–70) or Aretas IV (8 BC–AD 40). The naturally patterned interior of the Urn Tomb measures a vast 18m by 20m.

Part of what makes the Urn Tomb such a grand structure is the flanking Doric portico cut into the rock face on the left of the tomb,

Petra

and the huge open terrace in front of it – a feature that encouraged its use, according to a Greek inscription inside the tomb, as a cathedral in AD 447. The double layer of vaults was added at a later date by the Byzantines. Look towards the top of the building and you'll see three inaccessible openings carved between the pillars. These are also tombs, the central one of which still has the closing stone intact, depicting the king dressed in a toga.

➜ Silk Tomb & Corinthian Tomb

Next to the distinctive Urn Tomb in the Royal Tomb group is the so-called **Silk Tomb** (Map p164), noteworthy for the stunning swirls of pink-, white- and yellow-veined rock in its facade. The badly damaged **Corinthian Tomb** (Map p164), immediately adjacent, is something of a hybrid, with Hellenistic decorative features on the upper level and a Nabataean portico on the lower level. The tomb gets its name from the Corinthian capitals adorned with floral motifs.

➜ Palace Tomb

(Map p164) The delightful three-storey imitation of a Roman or Hellenistic palace, known as the Palace Tomb, is distinctive among the Royal Tombs for its rock-hewn façade, the largest in Petra. The doors lead into typically simple funerary chambers

while the 18 columns on the upper level are the most distinctive and visually arresting elements of the tomb. Notice the top-left corner is built (rather than carved) because the rock face didn't extend far enough to complete the facade.

Sextius Florentinus Tomb　　　TOMB
(Map p164) A few hundred metres around the hill from the Royal Tombs is the seldom-visited Sextius Florentinus Tomb, built from AD 126 to 130 for a Roman governor of Arabia, whose exploits are glorified in an inscription above the entrance. Unlike many other tombs, the interior is worth a look for the clearly discernible *loculi* (graves); there are five carved into the back wall and three on the right as you enter.

Have a cup of tea with the Bedouin grandmother who has set up shop here and you can admire the dazzling veining of the tomb in peace. The gorgon's head in the centre of the facade above the columns is eroded, but it's still possible to distinguish the vine tendrils emanating from the head. The horned capitals are a uniquely Nabataean creation.

Colonnaded Street　　ANCIENT THOROUGHFARE
(Map p169) Downhill from the Theatre, the Colonnaded Street marks Petra's city centre. The street was built around AD 106 and follows the standard Roman pattern of an

east–west *decumanus,* but without the normal *cardo maximus* (north–south axis). Columns of marble-clad sandstone originally lined the 6m-wide carriageway, and covered porticoes gave access to shops.

At the start of the Colonnaded Street is the **Nymphaeum** (Map p169), a public fountain built in the 2nd century AD and fed by water channelled from the Siq. Little can be seen today, although it's recognisable by the huge 450-year-old pistachio tree, giving welcome shade in summer.

Also along the Colonnaded Street are the limited remains of the market area and the unrecognisable ruins of the **Royal Palace** (Map p169).

The street ends at the **Temenos Gateway** (Map p169). Built in the 2nd century AD, the gateway originally had huge wooden doors and side towers. It marked the entrance to the **temenos** (sacred courtyard; Map p169) of the Qasr al-Bint, separating the commercial area of the city from the sacred area of the temple. Look closely for the few remaining floral friezes and a figure with an arrow, which suggest that this was once a very grand structure. Opposite are the minimal ruins of the **Nabataean baths** (Map p169).

Great Temple
TEMPLE

(Map p169) A major Nabataean temple of the 1st century BC, this structure was badly damaged by an earthquake not long after it was built, but it remained in use (albeit in different forms) until the late Byzantine period. A *theatron* (miniature theatre) stands in the centre. The temple was once 18m high, and the enclosure was 40m by 28m. The interior was originally covered with striking red-and-white stucco.

The first set of stairs was fronted by a **monumental propylaeum** (gateway) while the courtyard at the top of the first stairs marked the **lower temenos**, flanked by a triple colonnade. The upper level housed the temple's sacred enclosure, with four huge columns (made from stone discs and clad in marble) at the entrance.

Qasr al-Bint
TEMPLE

(Map p169) One of the few free-standing structures in Petra, Qasr al-Bint was built in around 30 BC by the Nabataeans. It was later adapted to the cult of Roman emperors and destroyed around the 3rd century AD. Despite the name given to it by the local Bedouin – Castle of the Pharaoh's Daughter – the temple was originally built as a

PETRA THE ANCIENT CITY

ⓘ TOP TIPS FOR MAKING THE MOST OF PETRA

Petra at Dawn The Treasury is sunlit in the morning; you may have seen photos but the real thing is indescribably magical.
Tip: Go before the 8am tours arrive.

Photogenic Petra By midafternoon most of Petra's weary guests have returned to base. Those who linger catch the Royal Tombs turn pink at sunset.
Tip: The sun sets around 6pm in summer and 5pm in winter.

Petra on High The Siq, Street of Facades and museum all lie brooding in the wadi bottom. Climb a few steps, hike to a High Place, sit on a camel and you'll find a whole new dimension to Petra.
Tip: The Theatre seats give grandstand views.

Hidden Petra Petra doesn't give up its secrets easily and most visitors leave without discovering the exquisite Monastery, at the top of 800 hand-hewn steps.
Tip: Best seen in the full sun of afternoon, beautiful views of Wadi Araba are just a 15-minute stroll from the Monastery to the lookouts. Use the 'back door' from Umm Sayhoun to save time.

Green Petra Explore a parallel world along the hidden wadis of Petra; lizards, snakes and scorpions are common but shy residents beside the rocky pools.
Tip: Magnificent pink oleander blossoms stripe the wadis in profusion in May.

Living Petra Petra may be a pile of ruins to some, but for others it's home; take Raami's Tours to see how the Bdoul Bedouin interact with their famous monuments.
Tip: Say yes to tea with the Bedouin and participate in Petra's age-old ritual.

Petra by Night (p181) Catch the spirit of Petra by candlelight.
Tip: Warm coat needed in winter.

dedication to Nabataean gods and was one of the most important temples in Petra.

The temple once stood 23m high and its features included marble staircases, imposing columns, a raised platform for worship, and ornate plaster and stone reliefs – examples of which are housed in the modest Nabataean Museum nearby. The central 'holy of holies', known as an *adyton,* would have housed an image of the deities. The sacrificial altar (Map p169) in front, once overlaid with marble, indicates that it was probably the main place of worship in the Nabataean city and its location at street level suggests that the whole precinct (and not just the temple interior) was considered sacred.

Temple of Winged Lions   TEMPLE

(Map p169) The recently excavated Temple of the Winged Lions, built around AD 27, is named after the carved lions that once topped the capitals of each of the columns. The temple was probably dedicated to the fertility goddess, Atargatis, the partner of the male god Dushara. Fragments of decorative stone and painted plaster found on the site of this once important temple are now on display in the Nabataean Museum.

The fragments suggest that both the temple and entry were handsomely decorated with a colonnaded entry of arches and porticoes that extended across the wadi.

Petra Church   CHURCH

(Map p169) An awning covers the remains of Petra Church (also known as the Byzantine Church). Inside the church are some exquisite Byzantine floor mosaics, some of the best in the region. The mosaics originally continued up the walls. A helpful map and explanations in English are also located inside the church.

The structure was originally built by the Nabataeans, and then redesigned and expanded by the Byzantines around AD 530. It eventually burned down, and was then destroyed by repeated earthquakes. It was recently restored by the American Center of Oriental Research in Amman.

Al-Habis   VIEWPOINT

(Map p164) Beyond Qasr al-Bint is the small hill of Al-Habis (the Prison). From the Nabataean Tent Restaurant, steps lead up the hill to the small Al-Habis Museum (Map p169; ☺8am-4pm) FREE, the smaller of Petra's two museums. The classical statues, tiny figurines

and painted stuccowork on display lend a human dimension to the huge scale of the site.

If you continue up the steps, beyond the museum, a little-used path leads around the back of Al-Habis, with striking views of fertile Wadi Siyagh and the junction with Wadi Numeir. The path soon skirts the teahouse and comfortable cave home of Bdoul Mofleh, one of the last residents of Petra. Asked why he didn't leave when the rest of his family were relocated to Umm Sayhoun, he replied, 'Why would I? This is my home; I've always lived here.' With a view to die for and a garden of flowering jasmine, it's easy to see why this hardy resident chose to stay. Notice the red-capped aloe, standing to attention in early summer, billeted across the cliffs opposite.

The path continues around the hill, past the Convent Group (Map p164) of tombs to a flight of steps. These lead in turn (via a wooden plank bridge) to the top of Al-Habis, another of Petra's many High Places. At the summit (allow 10 to 15 minutes to reach the top) are the limited ruins of a small Crusader fort (Map p164), built in AD 1116 by Baldwin I. The ruins are not impressive, but the views across the city certainly are.

From here you can either hike via the Pharaun Column (Map p164) – a good landmark – to Snake Monument in Wadi Thughra, or along Wadi Farasa to the High Place of Sacrifice.

Alternatively, complete the circuit of Al-Habis by descending the hill behind Qasr al-Bint. On your way down, look out for the Unfinished Tomb (Map p164). It offers a rare glimpse of the way the Nabataeans constructed their rock tombs, starting at the top on a platform of scaffolding and working their way down. Nearby is the enigmatic Columbarium (Map p164), whose multiple niches remain a mystery; some suppose they housed votive images or urns, others say this was a dovecote for pigeons.

Nabataean Museum   MUSEUM

(Petra Archaeological Museum; Map p169; ☺9am-5pm Apr-Sep, to 4pm Oct-Mar) FREE The small Petra Archaeological Museum, usually referred to as the Nabataean Musuem, has an interesting display of artefacts from the region, including mosaics. Explanations are in English. The museum, together with a shop selling detailed maps and fixed-price, handmade jewellery sponsored by the Queen Noor Foundation, shares the same building as the Basin Restaurant (p176).

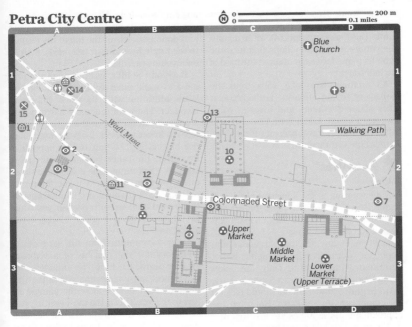

Petra City Centre

⚐ 0 ⎯⎯⎯⎯⎯⎯⎯ 200 m
Ⓝ 0 ⎯⎯⎯⎯⎯⎯⎯ 0.1 miles

Walking Path

⭐ Monastery (Al-Deir)   TOMB

(Map p164) Hidden high in the hills, the Monastery is one of the legendary monuments of Petra. Similar in design to the Treasury but far bigger (50m wide and 45m high), it was built in the 3rd century BC as a Nabataean tomb. It derives its name from the crosses carved on the inside walls, suggestive of its use as a church in Byzantine times.

The cave teahouse opposite is a good vantage point for admiring the Monastery's Hellenistic facade – particularly spectacular bathed in midafternoon sunlight. The courtyard in front of the Monastery was once surrounded by columns and was used for sacred ceremonies.

Behind the teahouse, tomb 468 is worth exploring for another fine facade, some defaced carvings and excellent views. A trail leads up to stunning **viewpoints** over Wadi Araba, Israel and the Palestinian Territories and south to the peak of Jebel Haroun, topped by a small white shrine.

The easy-to-follow trail to the Monastery starts from the Nabataean Museum and takes about 40 minutes (if in doubt, look for weary hikers coming down). Alternatively, donkeys (with a guide) can be hired for about JD30 return depending on your negotiation skills; you're better off walking

coming down as the donkeys travel fast and the way is steep and slippery, making for an uncomfortable and at times dangerous journey for both you and your mount. The trip is best started in midafternoon when there is welcome shade and the Monastery is at its most photogenic. The remarkable ancient rock-cut path of more than 800 steps follows the old processional route and is a spectacle of weird and wonderfully tortured stone. There are several side paths to explore, including a detour to the **Lion Tomb** (Lion Triclinium; Map p164), set in a gully. The two weather-beaten lions that lend the tomb its name face each other at the base of the monument.

An exciting 6km hike leads from the Monastery to Siq al-Barid (Little Petra; it takes about 2½ hours and involves some easy scrambling). Ask at Petra Visitor Centre (p177) or at local travel agencies for a guide as the route is difficult to find.

🏃 Activities

Hiking

Anyone wanting to see some stunning landscapes, explore unexcavated tombs and meet the Bedouin should pack an extra bottle of water and go hiking.

Most hikes are not that strenuous and none are overnight trips (camping is not permitted within Petra). Only the hikes along Wadi Muthlim and to Sabra or Little Petra require a guide. Hikers should pick up the contoured *Map of Petra*. Note that the approximate hiking times are just that and do not include time for pottering.

Experienced multilingual guides can be hired from the Petra Visitor Centre from JD50 (for one to nine people) for a simple route to the Museum, or from local travel agencies. It costs an extra JD20 for a guide to either the High Place of Sacrifice or to the Monastery. Unofficial Bedouin 'guides' may charge considerably less than the official rates: occasionally they are very good but there's no guarantee. Women on their own should be cautious of hiking with unregistered guides, particularly as most of the hikes involve spending time in isolated parts of Petra.

Please stick to trails, use only the toilets provided and remove your litter to avoid degradation of the area.

Short Hikes

Wadi Muthlim to Royal Tombs   HIKING
(moderate; guide mandatory, JD50; ⊙1½hr one-way) This adventurous 1½-hour canyon hike is an exciting alternative route into Petra if you've already taken the main Siq path. Flash floods are a serious issue in the area and a guide is mandatory. The hike is not difficult or too strenuous, but there are several boulder blockages and in winter you may need to wade through pools of water.

The trail starts from the dam, just before the entrance to the Siq. Before entering the

ancient, 88m-long Nabataean tunnel, it's possible to make a short detour (veer right and double-back over the top of the tunnel) to the **Eagle Monument** (Map p164), with its eponymous carvings.

Back on the hike, walk through the tunnel and you'll emerge into the sunlight of Wadi Muthlim with its thick ribbon of oleander. The wadi gradually narrows into a metre-wide siq and in three places you'll have to lower yourself down 2m-high boulder blockages. The first is easy enough to negotiate; the other two take a bit more strategy – not impossible if you have someone to lean on, but tricky if you attempt it on your own. If you're not comfortable on the second boulder, turn back or you could get stuck between boulder blockage two and three!

After 25 minutes from the start of the hike, look for the remains of a Nabataean dam above the trail. Five minutes later, you'll meet a T-intersection where the trail joins Wadi Mataha. Follow the painted arrow to the left. This is the most exciting part of the hike as the canyon narrows to little more than a crack in the rock. You can see here how treacherous this hike would be in a flash flood as there is little space between you and the parallel walls. At certain times of the year you may have to splash through residual pools of water here until at length you pass into the perfect picnic point. Surrounded by Nabataean niches, and shaded on two sides almost all day, this little square of ancient Petra has a presence far bigger than its dimensions.

From here, follow the cliff face to the left, past a series of little-visited tombs, including **Dorotheos' House** (Map p164) and the Sextius Florentinus Tomb (p166), until you reach the Royal Tombs. Alternatively, you can turn northeast on a small track that begins from the wadi almost opposite the Tomb of Sextius Florentinus, and explore the interesting so-called **Christian Tombs of Moghar al-Nassara** (Map p164) where excavations are ongoing.

Some parts of the canyon may be impassable if it's been raining. Flash floods occur along Wadi Muthlim because the dam at the start of Petra's main Siq deliberately diverts water along this wadi. As such, it's imperative that you don't start this trek if it's been raining, is raining or is likely to rain soon. Your guide should have the latest information on the condition of the route.

'IBRAHIM' BURCKHARDT: EXPLORER EXTRAORDINAIRE

There can't be many explorers in history who can match the remarkable exploits of Jean Louis Burckhardt. Born in 1784 in Lausanne, Switzerland, he studied Arabic and attended lectures on science and medicine at Cambridge University in the UK before moving to Aleppo in 1809. Here he converted to Islam and took the name Sheikh Ibrahim bin Abdullah. Over the next two years he became a master of disguise, adopting local customs and putting his alias to the test among local Bedouin.

In 1812, travelling between Damascus and Cairo, he heard locals tell of fantastic ruins hidden in the mountains of Wadi Musa. Determined to see for himself, he had to think of a ploy to allay the suspicions of his guide and porters:

I, therefore, pretended to have made a vow to have slaughtered a goat in honour of Haroun (Aaron), whose tomb I knew was situated at the extremity of the valley, and by this stratagem I thought that I should have the means of seeing the valley on the way to the tomb.

Jean Louis Burckhardt, Travels in Syria and the Holy Land

The plan worked and soon he was riding down the Siq, trying hard to hide his astonishment. His guide wasn't fooled for long, and imagined that the pale Syrian had come hunting for treasure, declaring: 'I see now clearly that you are an infidel, who have [sic] some particular business amongst the ruins.' To avoid occasioning more suspicion, Burckhardt had to confine his curiosity to the briefest examination of the ancient monuments – enough, however, to conclude that this was Petra, a place which he understood 'no European traveller has ever visited'. Despite being a man not given to literary flourishes, his journals reveal something of the excitement of his discovery:

The situation and beauty of [the Treasury] are calculated to make an extraordinary impression upon the traveller, after having traversed...such a gloomy and almost subterranean passage [the Siq]...it is one of the most elegant remains of antiquity existing.

For many an explorer, this expedition would have been a lifetime's achievement – but not for Burckhardt. He went on to find the source of the Niger, stumbled on the magnificent Ramses II temple at Abu Simbel in Egypt, and still under disguise explored Mecca and Medina. In 1815 he contracted dysentery in Cairo which returned with fatal consequences in 1817. He was buried as a Muslim in the Islamic Cemetery in Cairo. He was only 33 years old.

High Place of Sacrifice to Petra City Centre HIKING

(moderate; self-guided; ⏱1hr one way) This one-hour hike starts from the High Place of Sacrifice (p161) and passes through a less visited but beautiful part of Petra. It's also possible to do this hike in reverse, making for a grand afternoon exit from the site.

From the top of the High Place path, near the obelisks, a trail with steps heads down towards Wadi Farasa. The start of the trail is not obvious, so look for the helpful piles of stones indicating the trail, or ask for directions at the drinks stand. The hike is immediately rewarding with magnificent veined rock formations and wild gardens of flowers. After about 10 minutes of descent, you'll come to the 5m-long **Lion Monument** (Map p164), where water was channelled to pour out of the lion's mouth from the rock face

above – an example of Nabataean engineering at its most sophisticated. A stone altar diagonally opposite suggests the fountain had some religious function. The steps wind further down the side of the cliff to the **Garden Tomb** (Map p164) – more likely to have been a temple – and the remains of a giant water cistern.

A little further down, on the left, is the elegant **Roman Soldier's Tomb** (Map p164), named after the statue over the door. Almost opposite is the **Garden Triclinium** (Map p164), a hall used for annual feasts to honour the dead placed in the Soldier's Tomb. The hall is unique in Petra because it has carved decoration on the interior walls. The tomb and triclinium were once linked by a colonnaded courtyard.

Hereafter, the trail branches to the right, above the dry wadi floor. A teahouse here

KATSIUBA VOLHA/SHUTTERSTOCK ©

1. Petra (p155)
Chiselled into out-of-the-way cliffs, the buildings of Petra lay forgotten for centuries.

2. Camels
Riding a camel is a good way to reach Petra's more remote and uphill sites.

3. Treasury (Al-Khazneh; p160)
The tomb of Nabataean King Aretas III is lit up with candles on an atmospheric night tour of Petra.

4. Rock tombs (p160)
Petra's oldest rock tombs were carved into the sandstone in the 3rd century BC.

JPRICHARD/SHUTTERSTOCK ©

sells handmade strings of cloves, a good sniff of which is surprisingly reviving. The path forks at the ridge ahead. The right fork leads past some outrageously colourful but dilapidated tombs and descends eventually to the Colonnaded Street (p166). The left fork passes **Az-Zantur** (Map p164), a 1st-century AD palace that's still under excavation. Nearby is a collection of ruined **Nabataean and Roman houses** (Map p164), one of the few traces of habitations so far discovered in Petra. The trail continues west along the ridge to the **Pharaun Column**, the lone surviving column of another Nabataean temple. From here you can turn left to Snake Monument for a longer hike or go straight on for Qasr al-Bint and Al-Habis. If you're disoriented, look for Petra Church, north of the Colonnaded Street: its pale green awning makes a good landmark.

Wadi Siyagh   HIKING
(easy; self-guided; ☻1hr return) For a leg-stretcher that doesn't require a vertical take-off, try the trail that follows the dry riverbed of Wadi Siyagh beneath Al-Habis hill. Once a residential suburb of Petra, the wadi and the nearby slopes have unexcavated tombs and residences to explore and offer some peaceful picnic spots once you pass the noisy restaurant generator.

Enter Wadi Siyagh opposite the Basin Restaurant. You'll soon see steps on the right leading to the **Painted House** (Map p164), one of the very few tombs in Petra that still has traces of Nabataean frescoes. Further down, at a bend in the valley, is a **Nabataean quarry** (Map p164).

The main attraction further along the valley is the dense oasis of green bushes, water pools and even waterfalls (in winter). In spring, the flowers are beautiful and in May and June it's worth making the hike just to enjoy the oleander and seams of aloe.

The trail along Wadi Siyagh is easy to follow, but becomes a bit rough in parts as it ascends the wadi walls. Don't attempt the hike if rain is imminent because flash floods are possible.

Treasury Vista I   HIKING
(strenuous; guide mandatory, JD80; ☻1hr return) Leading steeply up from the trailhead opposite the Treasury, this trail is generally closed to casual visitors as the handkerchief-sized lookout above the vertical cliff is extremely dangerous. Check with the visitor centre to see if the trail is currently open.

Treasury Vista II   HIKING
(moderate; self-guided; ☻1½hr return) Offering a dramatic and unusual view of the Treas-

---

LOVING PETRA TO DEATH

It seems ironic that after 1000 years of obscurity, if not neglect, Petra owes its current fragility to a renaissance of interest. In a 'good' year half a million people visit, putting a huge strain on the management of one of the world's best-loved antiquities. The combination of thousands of footprints a day, increased humidity levels from the breath of tourists in tombs, and erosion caused by adventurous travellers clambering over monuments and steep hillsides combine to threaten Petra's longevity.

Acutely aware of the problems, a number of local, national and international bodies have been cooperating for more than a decade to protect and enhance the 853 sq km site. For the most part Petra is now spotlessly clean, thanks to constant maintenance, improved toilet facilities and a shift in attitude from visitors, who largely carry their rubbish back out with them.

Other improvements include the use of an invisible mortar to conserve fragile masonry and replace unsightly cement used in previous restoration attempts; major shoring up of the Siq; and ongoing conservation of tomb facades. Rampant development in Wadi Musa has also been checked, an infrastructure of drainage and sewerage systems installed and a moratorium enforced on the building of unsightly hotels that impinge on the sense of seclusion in Petra. Better signage and trail markers are yet to appear.

These conservation measures, however, will only save Petra for future generations with the cooperation of visitors. Each visitor can play a part by sticking to trails, not clambering over the monuments, resisting the temptation to touch crumbling masonry, removing litter and using designated toilet facilities. These things sound obvious, but judging by a piece of graffiti that reads 'David 2014' on top of one of the High Places, responsible tourism may still be a long time coming.

ury, this hike ascends processional steps about 150m northeast of the Palace Tomb. The stiff climb leads to a hilltop Nabataean cistern and a dramatic lookout about 200m above the entrance to the Siq. Start this hike in the early morning to catch the Treasury in sunlight.

A recently renovated set of processional steps leads steeply uphill from about 150m northeast of the Palace Tomb (they are signposted). The stiff climb takes about 20 minutes and flattens out at a hilltop Nabataean cistern (Map p164). Along the way there are wonderful views of the Theatre.

Continue south from the cistern (currently occupied by a helpful Bedouin teahouse owner) along a less obvious dirt path. Descend through the dry wadi for about 15 minutes and then pass into a small ravine; suddenly you will reach a dramatic lookout about 200m above the Treasury, with fantastic views of the mighty edifice. Watch your step and look out for landmarks on the way down as it is hard to find the path back to the top of the steps.

Back at the cistern, a tiny cleft in the rock reveals worn steps leading down a gully and along the rock face to a point next to the Urn Tomb. The trail isn't all that clear (and is rather dirty at the outset), but it is navigable with a bit of common sense. The author, lacking in this quality, ended up on a Nabataean drain dangling over a vertical drop. Of course, you can always return the way you came.

Long Hikes

Umm al-Biyara HIKING

(strenuous; self-guided; ⊘3hr one-way) The strenuous hike from Qasr al-Bint to Umm al-Biyara (1178m) offers stunning mountaintop views. Legend has it that the flat-topped mountain was once the Edomite capital of Sela, from where the Judaean king Amaziah (r 796–781 BC) threw 10,000 prisoners to their deaths over the precipice.

> He the Judaean king, Amaziah was the one who defeated ten thousand Edomites in the Valley of the Salt and captured Sela in battle...
>
> *2 Kings 14:7*

There are ruins of a 7th-century BC Edomite village (Map p164) at the top as well as several cisterns. There are also many unexcavated tombs (Map p164) along the base of the eastern cliffs.

The return trip from Qasr al-Bint to Umm al-Biyara (the Mother of Cisterns) takes about three hours and offers stunning mountaintop views over Petra (you can even spot the Monastery). It's a fairly strenuous hike up hundreds of steps, but the trail is easy to follow. Start the hike in the midafternoon when most of the path is in shade but don't leave it too late as you don't want to be coming down in poor light.

From behind Qasr al-Bint, head to the Pharaun Column and descend to the road that leads along Wadi Thughra towards Snake Monument. The path up the rock face starts from the left of the largest of the rock-cut tombs on the southeast face of the mountain.

Jebel Haroun HIKING

(strenuous; self-guided or JD150 with guide; ⊘6hr return) This hike via Snake Monument starts from Qasr al-Bint. Jebel Haroun (1350m) is thought to be the biblical Mt Hor – the burial site of Moses' brother Aaron; a white shrine built in the 14th century marks the site.

> Aaron will be gathered to his people: he will die there. Moses did as the Lord commanded: they went up to Mount Hor in the sight of the whole community.
>
> *Numbers 20:26-27*

Some people (Muslims as well as Christians) consider the shrine as a place of pilgrimage. For many, however, the big drawcard of Jebel Haroun is the superb panoramic view from the top.

It's possible to hire a guide with a donkey or even a camel for the trip, but if you're reasonably fit and not fazed by working out your own route from the network of goat tracks that head in the general direction, then this really isn't necessary.

The trail to Jebel Haroun starts at Pharaun Column, and follows the dirt road past Bedouin settlements to Snake Monument, a curled stone that resembles a snake on a rock pedestal. Continue to the southwest towards the obvious white shrine (which looks deceptively close); the trail is not as steep as it looks. At the bottom of the mountain, find the caretaker if you want to enter the shrine.

Sabra HIKING

(strenuous; guide advisable, JD150; ⊘5hr return) The trip from Qasr al-Bint to the remote Nabataean suburbs of Sabra follows the path of ancient trade caravans that once unloaded their precious cargoes at the fringes of the main city.

The remains at Sabra include some ruined walls, temples, bridges and a small Roman theatre. A guide is needed even to find the trail from Snake Monument. A return trip on donkey costs from around JD80, depending on your powers of negotiation.

An exciting option offered by some travel agencies is the adventurous two-day hike from Tayyibeh, through the Siq-like Wadi Tibn to Sabra, camping overnight and continuing on to Petra the next day.

Horse Riding

For those who know how to ride, it costs from around JD40 for a two- to three-hour horse ride around the surrounding hills. A particularly exciting ride leads across a plateau at the top of the Treasury – definitely not one for the faint-hearted as the horses pull up from a gallop to a stop at the vertiginous cliff edge. Book a ride through one of the tourist agencies in town or, for more of an adventure, ask the animal handlers near the entrance to Petra to take you to their favourite haunt.

✕ Eating and Drinking

There are lots of ways to enjoy alfresco dining in Petra, from a simple take-your-own picnic to fine dining (well nearly) at a buffet restaurant.

For breakfast, spread your cloth in the little opening at the end of Wadi Muthlim; it's overlooked by god niches and as this is, after all, a necropolis, you may host unexpected guests of the ethereal kind. Entertain the wind for lunch on top of Umm al-Biyara and have high tea (or at least tea-on-high) with the Bedouin stallholder above the Royal Tombs. For dinner with a difference, choose a Nabataean dining room (the Garden Triclinium is a good bet) or share a candlelight supper. For the latter, join the Petra by Night Tour and spread your tablecloth in the middle of the Siq while the crowds race to the Treasury.

If a picnic takes too much forethought, snacks (including sandwiches, biscuits, fruit, ice cream) are sold at kiosks with outside tables and chairs throughout the site.

In the neighbouring village of Umm Sayhoun, north of the city centre, you can try the original flavours of Petra in a Bedouin family home, prepared by the mother of the house. Not content just to watch? Then cook the food yourself at Petra Kitchen in Wadi Musa.

Throughout Petra, including at the High Place of Sacrifice and the Monastery, stalls sell bottled water, soft drinks and snacks. Best of all they sell sweet black tea laced with herbs; sharing a quiet conversation with the aged or infant vendor is a guaranteed highlight of the ancient city.

Nabataean Tent Restaurant   BUFFET $$
(Map p169; lunch buffet JD10, drinks JD2; ⏱11am-3pm) With simple Jordanian dishes and one or two international favourites, this casual restaurant occupies a lovely spot under blue-flowering jacaranda trees (they flower in May). The proprietors rustle up a generous pack lunch with a sandwich, boiled egg, yoghurt and cake for a bargain JD6; you can eat it on the spot with a Turkish coffee if you wish.

★ Basin Restaurant   BUFFET $$
(Map p169; lunch buffet JD17, fresh orange juice JD4; ⏱noon-4pm; ✐) The Basin serves a wide spread of international dishes, including a healthy selection of salads, fresh felafel and barbecued spicy sausage. Lots of desserts are also on offer, including fruit and *umm ali* (a bread-pudding-like dessert). There's a fully air-conditioned interior seating area or groups sit by the ravine under canvas while independent travellers are given tables under the trees.

Bdoul Mofleh Tea Shop   TEAHOUSE
(Map p164; ☎077 6094797; lunchbox JD4, tea by donation; ⏱10am-4pm) This long-term Petra resident, Bdoul Mofleh, rustles up ad hoc tea for those passing his 'unofficial' cave house on Al-Habis.

Have a Break Tea & Coffee   CAFE
(Map p164; water JD2, coffee JD3; ⏱9am-6pm) With a view of the Royal Tombs, this Bedouin-run establishment can muster sandwiches, snacks and milkshakes. With a permanent awning and nascent garden, this is in just the right spot to enjoy sunset.

❶ Information

Ticket Office (☎/fax 2156044; 1-/2-/3-day pass JD50/55/60; admission free for children under 15 years; ⏱6am-4pm, to 6pm in summer) The ticket office is in the visitor centre (p177) at the entrance to Petra. Although tickets are not sold after 4pm, you can remain in Petra until sunset (5pm in winter). Entry fees

A DOZEN UNUSUAL WAYS TO ENJOY PETRA

→ Enter Petra via the narrow Wadi Muthlim (p170) instead of the Siq (best kept for the second day of a visit).

→ Gain an eagle's-eye view of the Treasury from a path above the Royal Tombs (p174).

→ Gallop across a plateau on horseback, high above the Treasury.

→ Descend from the High Place of Sacrifice (p171) via the garden valley of Wadi Farasa.

→ Take tea with one of the few remaining residents of Petra behind Al-Habis (p168).

→ Unfurl a portable feast in a triclinium, a banqueting hall for honouring the dead.

→ Hike with a guide to Little Petra (p191) from the Monastery.

→ Find your own secret garden beyond the Siq at Little Petra (p190).

→ Saddle up a donkey for the two-day hike to Sabra (p175) via Wadi Tibn.

→ Leave Petra with the Bdoul Bedouin via the road to Umm Sayhoun.

→ Walk between Umm Sayhoun and Wadi Musa for a sublime view of Petra at sunset.

→ Stop at the viewpoint on the scenic road to Tayyibeh for the ultimate Petra panorama.

are payable only in Jordanian currency and multiday tickets are nontransferable. If visiting Petra as a day trip from Israel and the Palestinian Territories the entry fee is JD90.

If you're contemplating trying to enter Petra without paying, please don't. The preservation of Petra depends on the income from tourists and this is where responsible tourism begins.

You can hire an **official guide** (JD50 for one to nine people) from the visitor centre to explain the sights between the entrance and the museum; these guides have a lot of knowledge and experience and can bring a different dimension to your visit. Guided tours, which last three hours, are available in English, Spanish, French, German, Russian, Arabic and Hebrew. It costs an additional JD20 to take a guide to any of the High Places and a further JD30 to engage the guide for the descent through Wadi Farasa. Sufian Amarat of Jordan Beauty Tours at the Petra Visitor Centre is a helpful source of information about guides.

TOILETS

There are reasonable toilets at the visitor centre, before the Theatre and near the Basin Restaurant. Teahouses provide clean portable toilets throughout the site – most people give a tip of JD1 to the caretakers who maintain them. Please keep to these facilities to avoid spoiling the site for others.

TOURIST INFORMATION

Petra Visitor Centre (☑ 2156020; www. visitpetra.jo; ⊙ 6am-6pm May-Sep, to 4pm Oct-Apr) Information is available at the Petra Visitor Centre, just before the entrance. It houses the

ticket office (p176) and a helpful information counter and is surrounded by souvenir shops.

WEBSITES

American Museum of Natural History (www. amnh.org/exhibitions/petra) See an online Petra exhibition.
Brown University (www.brown.edu/Departments/Joukowsky_Institute/Petra) Take an online tour of the excavations of the Great Temple.
Complete Petra (www.isidore-of-seville.com/petra) A great collection of current and archived links on Petra.
Go 2 Petra (www.go2petra.com) For background and general travel info on Petra.
Nabataea Net (http://nabataea.net) Everything you could want to know about the Nabataean empire.

ⓘ Getting Around

If you buy your ticket at the Petra Visitor Centre, a return horse ride for the 800m stretch between the main entrance and the start of the Siq is included in your ticket (arrange a return time with the handler). A tip of JD3 or JD4 is appreciated. If you walk down you can usually find a ride back to the entrance for around JD8. Horses and carriages with drivers travel between the main entrance and the Treasury (2km) for JD20, and to the museum for JD40 per carriage (which seats two people), plus JD5 per person in tips.

Unofficial donkey and mule rides (with handlers) are available all around Petra for negotiable prices. Donkeys can reach the High Place of Sacrifice (from JD10 one way) and the top of the Monastery (JD30 return). Mules can also be rented for longer trips to the Snake Monument (from JD25), Jebel Haroun (JD50) and Sabra (JD80). Leading donkeys, mules and camels is a genuine occupation for local Bedouin, who prize their animals as an important part of their livelihood; that said, some of the younger animal handlers can be seen using a stick or whip with unnecessary aggression – perhaps in a misguided bid to look manly. If you have hired animal transport, don't feel shy to intervene if you feel the treatment is inappropriate. There is an animal clinic near Petra Visitor Centre called the Brooke Hospital for Animals and you can report mistreatment of animals to www.pdtra. gov.jo.

Magnificently bedecked camels are available for rides between Qasr al-Bint and the Treasury (one way/return about JD15/25) and they will pause for a photograph near the Theatre. You may be able to hitch a ride on something four-legged back along the Siq for a few dinars at the end of the day.

WALKING TIMES TO KEY SIGHTS IN PETRA

To make the most of Petra you need to walk. The good news is that you don't have to be a serious hiker with a week to spare to have a 'Burckhardt moment' in the ancient city – you just need to know where to go and when. Times in the following table indicate one-way walks (unless stated otherwise) at a leisurely pace. At a faster pace without stopping, you can hike from the Petra Visitor Centre to the Treasury in 20 minutes and the museum in 40 minutes along the main thoroughfare. Don't forget to double the time for the uphill return journey, particularly if you're tired after a day's sightseeing. A variety of animal transport is usually on hand to get you back to base if you're seriously flagging: for example, you can take a donkey from the Monastery to the Museum, a camel to the Treasury, a horse carriage to the Siq entrance and a horse to the visitor centre.

DIRECT ROUTE	TIME	DIFFICULTY	ALTERNATIVES & INTERESTING DETOURS
Visitor Centre to Siq Entrance	15 minutes	Easy	**Horse ride** Ponies are for hire to help you reach the dam near the Siq entrance – useful on the uphill return journey.
Siq Entrance to Treasury	20 minutes	Easy	**Hike** Clamber above the Royal Tombs to a Treasury viewpoint and look down on everyone else looking up (one hour; strenuous).
Treasury to Royal Tombs	20 minutes	Easy	**Hike** Climb the steps between the Royal Tombs and Sextius Florentinus tomb for a regal-eyed view of Petra. Continue to the cistern and descend to the Urn Tomb (one to 1½ hours; strenuous). **Hike** As an alternative to the Siq, squeeze through sinuous Wadi Muthlim to reach the Royal Tombs (1½ hours; moderate, guide required).
Treasury to Obelisk at High Place of Sacrifice	45 minutes	Moderate	**Walk** Go beyond the High Place altar onto the solitary edge of the escarpment for a wide-angle view of Petra (15 minutes from Obelisk; easy).
Obelisk to Museum (via main thoroughfare)	45 minutes	Easy	**Hike** Instead of returning down the steps you ascended, hike via enchanting Wadi Farasa, passing rainbow-coloured rocks, Lion Monument and Garden Tomb (one hour from Obelisk; moderate).
Treasury to Museum	30 minutes	Easy	**Walk** Trace the path around the base of the Royal Tombs to Dorotheos' House, explore the rarely visited Christian Tombs and follow Wadi Mataha to the Museum (one hour; easy)
Museum to Monastery	40 minutes	Moderate	**Walk** Get a head-start to the Monastery via Umm Sayhoun access road (one hour; moderate), pausing at Turkmaniya Tomb, famous for its long Nabataean inscription (20 minutes from Umm Sayhoun to museum; easy). **Hike** For a rare glimpse of how tombs such as the Monastery were cut, walk around Al-Habis to see the Unfinished Tomb (40 minutes return to museum; moderate).

Wadi Musa   وادي موسى

🔲 03 / POP 30,050 / ELEV 1150M

The village that has sprung up around Petra is called Wadi Musa (Valley of Moses). It's an easy-going assemblage of hotels, restaurants and shops stretching about 5km from 'Ain Musa (Moses' Spring) to the main entrance of Petra at the bottom of the wadi.

Wadi Musa's fortunes depend almost entirely on tourism. Dozens of new hotels were hastily erected in the late 1990s (after the peace treaty with Israel), often with no aesthetic or social sensitivity. Many locals bought into the new opportunities that mass tourism offered only to be stung in the tourism slumps that have followed hostilities among Jordan's neighbours. A moratorium on hotel building remains in place in an effort to curb rampant expansion and to shift the focus to improving services rather than simply 'packing them in'.

Prices in Wadi Musa are inevitably higher than in other tourist destinations in Jordan, reflecting its status as guardian to one of the 'New Seven Wonders of the World', identified by an international public poll in 2008.

🏃 Activities

Hammams

Those in the know head for a Turkish bath: the perfect way to ease aching muscles after a long day's walk in Petra. This time-honoured bathing experience is enjoying a current resurgence of popularity and many new baths have appeared in Wadi Musa, most attached to hotels, including the Amra Palace Hotel (p184) and the Petra Palace Hotel (p183). The service on offer at a hammam typically includes steam bath, massage, hot stones, scrubbing and 'body conditioning'. The baths are popular with tourists and locals alike so it's best to book ahead, especially if requesting a female attendant (women only). Prices typically range from JD15 to JD30, depending on the combination of services on offer. Check with your hotel for local discounts.

Petra Turkish Bath   BATHHOUSE
(🔲 2157085; ⊙ 3-10pm) In the passage under the Silk Road Hotel, near the entrance of Petra, this hammam has a completely separate bath area for women, with female attendants.

🛈 NAVIGATING WADI MUSA

The commercial centre of Wadi Musa is Shaheed roundabout, around 3km uphill from the entrance to Petra. There is a second collection of midrange and top-end hotels, restaurants and souvenir shops 2km downhill, closer to the Petra entrance. There are also a number of four- and five-star hotels on the 'rim' of Wadi Musa, on the road towards Wadi Rum, all of which have wonderful views – not of Petra but of the unique surrounding landscape.

Salome Turkish Bath   BATHHOUSE
(🔲 2157342; ⊙ 4-10pm) Entered via a grotto displaying old farming implements, this bathhouse has an atmospheric sitting area for relaxing with herbal tea after bathing. It's located near Al-Anbat II Hotel.

Sella Turkish Bath   BATHHOUSE
(🔲 2157170; www.sellahotel.com; ⊙ 5.30-10pm) The Sella bathhouse has a comprehensive list of services including sauna and separate baths for men and women. Dead Sea products are on sale here.

🎓 Courses

⭐ **Petra Kitchen**   COOKING COURSE
(🔲 2155700; www.petrakitchen.com; cookery course per person JD35; ⊙ 6.30-9.30pm) If you've always wanted to know how to whip up wonderful hummus or bake the perfect baklava, Petra Kitchen is for you. Located 100m up the main road from the Mövenpick Hotel, Petra Kitchen offers nightly cookery courses for those wanting to learn from locals how to cook Jordanian mezze, soup and main courses in a relaxed family-style atmosphere.

A local Jordanian chef is on hand to make sure you don't make a goat's ear of the authentic Jordanian dishes. The menu (including delicious vegetarian fare) changes daily. The experience starts at 6.30pm (7.15pm in summer) and the price includes the printed recipes, food and soft drinks. Better still, buy a bottle of St George wine to share with your fellow apprentice chefs. Reservations are recommended.

🧭 Tours

A couple of the budget (and a few midrange and top-end) hotels can arrange simple day trips around Petra and further afield.

Wadi Musa

PETRA WADI MUSA

N
0 400 m
0 0.2 miles

Al-Anbat Hotel (1km); 'Ain Musa (2km); Post Office (2km)

Upper Wadi Musa and luxury hotels (2km); Tayyibeh (10km)

Police Roundabout

Main Police Station

Shaheed Roundabout

Tourist Rd (Wadi Musa Main St)

Hertz Rent-a-Car

Al-Wu'ira (1.5km); Sayhoun (3km); Al-Beidha (8km)

Jett Bus Stop

Tourist Police Station

Visitor Centre
Post Office

Entrance To Petra

Brooke Hospital for Animals

Petra (2.5km)

Bus Station

Wadi Musa

There are many excellent **local guides** working independently in the Petra area. These include **Mahmoud Twaissi** (077 254658; mat65petra@yahoo.com), who has a well-earned reputation not just as a guide but also as a fixer for large-scale projects throughout the country. Equally well regarded is **Mohammed Al-Hasanat** (2156567; explorerone69@yahoo.com), who has been a licensed national guide since 1979. He has a passion for hiking and has had plenty of practice: 'I took my first steps [hiking] aged six,' he says, 'and I've been walking ever since.' Both these guides are reliable, knowledgeable both of the historical and cultural contexts of the areas they cover, and experienced in catering to the needs of individual or groups with special interests. They can organise camping tours over several days including camel and horse safaris. Similarly recommended is **Ogla Nawafleh** (o_nawafleh@yahoo.com).

★**Petra by Night**   TOUR
(adult/child under 10yr JD12/free; 8.30-10.30pm Mon, Wed & Thu) If you have been wondering what Petra would be like under the stars, then you're not alone. The extremely popular Petra by Night Tour was introduced in response to numerous requests from visitors wanting to see the the Siq and Treasury by moonlight. The 'tour' starts from Petra Visitor Centre (cancelled if raining) and lasts two hours.

Readers express a mixed response to the experience, which allows you to walk along the Siq (lined with 1500 candles) as far as the Treasury in as much silence as is possible given the crowds. Here, traditional Bedouin music is played and mint tea served. Clearly, given the popularity of the tour, this isn't going to be the moment to commune with history in awed solitude, but night certainly brings a different perspective to the Siq that many feel is

PETRA WADI MUSA

PETRA UNDER THE STARS

Like a grumbling camel caravan of snorting, coughing, laughing and farting miscreants, 200 people and one jubilantly crying baby make their way down the Siq 'in silence'. Asked to walk in single file behind the leader, breakaway contingents surge ahead to make sure they enjoy the experience on their own. And eventually, sitting outside the Treasury, the collected company shows its appreciation of Arabic classical music by lighting cigarettes from the paper bag lanterns, chatting energetically, flashing their cameras and audibly farting some more.

Welcome to public entertainment in the Middle East! If you really want the Siq to yourself, come in the winter, go at 2pm or take a virtual tour on the internet.

Despite the promotional literature to the contrary, silence and solitude is not what the Petra by Night tour (p181) is all about. What this exceptional and highly memorable tour does give you is the fantastic opportunity to experience one of the most sublime spectacles on earth in the fever of other people's excitement. Huddles of whispering devotees stare up at the candlelit god blocks, elderly participants are helped over polished lozenges of paving stones, the sound of a flute wafts along the neck-hairs of fellow celebrants – this is surely much nearer to the original experience of the ancient city of Petra than walking reverentially through the icy stone corridor alone.

worthwhile. The performance of Bedouin storytelling at the Treasury depends on the mood of the raconteur. Tickets are available from travel agencies in town, or from the Petra Visitor Centre before 6pm. See boxed text, p182.

Petra Moon Tourism Services TOUR
(☑ 07-96170666; www.petramoon.com) Petra Moon is the most professional agency in Wadi Musa for arranging trips inside Petra and around Jordan (including Wadi Rum and Aqaba). The office is on the main road to Petra. It can arrange horses to Jebel Haroun, fully supported treks to Dana (four to five days), hikes from Tayyibeh to Petra and camel treks to Wadi Rum.

This agency runs a popular 14-day tour around Jordan for 10 to 18 people.

Raami Tours TOUR
(☑ 2154551, 2154010; www.raamitours.com) This tour company, based on the main road in the Bedouin village of Umm Sayhoun, organises traditional meals for visitors who want to try genuine homecooking. They also design tailor-made tours to fit all schedules, special interests and budgets (email at least three days ahead of arrival).

The owner is the son of Marguerite van Geldermalsen, author of *Married to a Bedouin* – an expatriate who married into the Bdoul and who brought young Raami up in a Petra cave for the first few years of his life. Guided tours into Petra, therefore, don't come any more authentic than this!

Jordan Travel & Tourism TOUR
(www.jordantours-travel.com) In addition to local tours, Jordan Travel organises daily trips to Jerusalem. Near the Sella Hotel.

Jordan Experience TOUR
(☑ 2155005; www.jordan-experience.com) On the main road to Petra.

La Beduina CULTURAL TOUR
(☑ 06-5541631; www.labeduinatours.com) Specialist tours including hiking, cooking, horse- and camel-riding, and yoga tours.

Petra Night Tours TOUR
(☑ 2154010; www.pntours.com) Not to be confused with the Petra by Night tour, this well-established, family-run agency organises a variety of tours in Petra and beyond. It also sells tickets for the candle-lit tour of the Siq!

Zaman Tours & Travel ADVENTURE TOUR
(☑ 2157723; www.zamantours.com; Wadi Musa) Adventure tours, camping, camel treks and hiking.

🛏 Sleeping

The 1908 Macmillan's guide *Palestine and Syria* had the following advice:

At Petra, there is no sleeping accommodation to be found, and travellers therefore have to bring with them camp equipment, unless they prefer to put up with the inconvenience of sleeping in the Bedwin huts at Elji, half an hour distant from Petra, or spend the night in some of the numerous temples. Such a course cannot be recommended to European travellers, especially if ladies are in the party.

Even as recently as 1991, there were only four official places to sleep in Wadi Musa. Visitors now have a choice of over 70 hotels (none of which are inside the ancient city itself) and camping is no longer permitted.

The high season is generally from April to mid-May and October to November (check the heating works!). Outside these times, prices can drop quickly from the official rates, especially if you're staying more than a couple of nights. Most hotels have a variety of rooms in a variety of sizes; some have a balcony, while others have no natural light, so ask to see some options. Most accommodation prices include a private bathroom and come with breakfast – the norm in Wadi Musa, unlike in the rest of Jordan. Note that the views advertised by some hotels are of Wadi Musa valley, not of Petra itself.

Women travelling alone need to be more on their guard in budget hotels in Wadi Musa than in other towns (make sure doors lock properly and there are no peep holes).

If you get off the minibus at the Shaheed roundabout in Wadi Musa with a backpack, then you will be besieged by persuasive touts. Decide on your choice of hotel in advance if you want to be left alone.

🛏 Lower Wadi Musa

Most hotels are located at the bottom end of town, within walking distance to the entrance to Petra.

★ Petra Palace Hotel   HOTEL $$
(🖉 2156723;   www.petrapalace.com.jo;   s/d/tr JD49/70/95; ❄@🏠🏊) Located on the main street, 500m from the entrance to Petra, this attractive and well-established hotel – with its palm-tree entrance, big bright foyer and helpful management – is an excellent choice. A whole suite of rooms open onto the outdoor swimming pool. The lively bar and restaurant are also drawcards.

The hotel is home to one of the better Turkish baths (JD20 per person), open from 3pm to 9pm. This establishment also runs the Rock Camp (p191) near Little Petra.

Silk Road Hotel   HOTEL $$
(🖉 2157222; www.petrasilkroad.com; s/d/tr JD40/65/85; P❄) Hand-painted panels of Bedouin camps stretch across the foyer and restaurant walls of this old favourite, 300m from the en-

trance to Petra. The lavender hued common areas may not be to everyone's taste but the rooms all have decent furniture and big bathtubs. Some rooms are very dark, so ask for one with a view. The buffet in the outside restaurant (JD10) is popular with tour groups.

La Maison   HOTEL $$
(🖉 2156401;   www.lamaisonhotel.com.jo;   s/d/tr JD70/80/90; ❄) The brass jardinières decorating the foyer set the tone for this good-value hotel, just uphill from the entrance to Petra. With quality furniture, generous fluffy duvets and a stylish makeover in black and white, La Maison is a comfortable option, tucked up a quiet road behind the main street. Ask about the brighter end rooms, which offer 120-degree views. The roof terrace is a great place to catch the sunset in summer.

★ Petra Guest House Hotel   HOTEL $$$
(🖉 2156266;   www.guesthouse-petra.com;   s/d/tr JD90/105/125;   P❄🏠) You can't get closer to the entrance to Petra without sleeping in a cave – and indeed the hotel's bar (the famous Cave Bar, p187) is located in one. Choose from spacious, motel-like chalets or sunny (if cramped) rooms in the main building. The staff are unfailingly delightful and the breakfast buffet is superior to most. Offers excellent value for money.

★ Mövenpick Hotel   LUXURY HOTEL $$$
(🖉 2157111; www.moevenpick-hotels.com; r from JD185; ❄@🏠🏊) This beautifully crafted Arabian-style hotel, 100m from the entrance to Petra, is worth a visit simply to admire the inlaid furniture, marble fountains, wooden screens and brass salvers. As the hotel is in the bottom of the valley there are no views, but the large and super-luxurious rooms all have huge windows regardless. The buffet breakfast and dinner are exceptional.

Petals are floated daily in the jardinière, a roaring fire welcomes winter residents to the Burckhardt Library (a lounge on the upper floor) and there's a pleasant ambience on the roof garden in summer.

Petra Moon Hotel   HOTEL $$$
(🖉 2156220;   www.petramoonhotel.com;   s/d/tr JD108/120/150; ❄@🏠🏊) On the hill, this establishment is run by two brothers who have transformed this once modest plot into a luxurious complex of modern rooms, sumptuous bathrooms and a rooftop swimming pool and terrace. The terrace is the place for splendid sunset views and a popular nightly barbecue (7pm to 11pm).

PETRA WADI MUSA

📖 Wadi Musa Town Centre

The hotels in the town centre are most convenient for the bus station and shops. It's just about possible to walk downhill to Petra from here, but if you want to save your energy for the ancient city itself enquire about free transport to and from the gate (usually offered by hotels once a day in each direction).

★ Cleopetra Hotel   HOTEL $

(📞 2157090; www.cleopetrahotel.com; s/d/tr JD20/30/40; @ 🛜) This continues to be the friendliest and most efficiently run budget hotel in town. The hotel has bright, fresh rooms with private bathrooms and hot water. There's a communal sitting area in the lobby which is ideal for meeting fellow travellers and rooftop developments are planned. Wi-fi is available for JD2.

The hotel can organise overnight 4WD trips to Wadi Rum (JD40 per person for a minimum of three) that travellers repeatedly recommend. Talk with the ever-helpful Mosleh about other possibilities for transportation. The hotel offers a competitive laundry service.

Al-Rashid Hotel   HOTEL $

(📞 2156800; www.alrashidhotel.com; s/d/tr from JD28/38/50; ❄🛜) This well-run, friendly hotel has an attractive, marble-floored lobby and elegant furniture. The newly painted rooms all offer satellite TV.

★ Amra Palace Hotel   HOTEL $$

(📞 2157070; www.amrapalace.com; s/d/tr JD44/64/84; ❄@🛜❄) This lovely hotel with its pretty garden of roses and jasmine, marble-pillared lobby, giant brass coffeepots and homely furniture offers a more Jordanian sense of hospitality than many of the rather bland hotels in town. The brothers who have run this establishment for many years take a personal interest in the details and it shows.

Each room has spotless linen that's changed every day (there's a laundry on site), wooden headboards, upholstered furniture and satellite TV. Most rooms have views across the valley. Services include a pool heated to 28°C, jacuzzi, summer terrace and Turkish bath (JD15 per person). There's also a cafe on the ground floor with unlimited internet access and free wi-fi. With a strong sense of family prevailing, this is undoubtedly one of the best hotels

in Wadi Musa. Ask about packages from the hotel to its camp in Wadi Rum.

Seven Wonders Hotel   HOTEL $$

(📞 2155156; www.sevenwondershotel.com; s/d JD58/77; @🛜❄) A relative newcomer to the hotel scene in Wadi Musa, the rooms at this hotel are decked with unsullied thick carpets and some have balconies with good views over the town and surrounding landscape. There's a terrace with a 'dry' bar (no alcohol served).

Book two hours ahead for the hotel's Afra Turkish bath (JD35 per person). Open from 5pm to 10pm, the baths are good with sauna, jacuzzi, steam room and massage.

Al-Anbat Hotel II   HOTEL $$

(📞 2157200; www.alanbat.com; s/d/tr JD25/40/50; 🛜) The cavernous, dark lobby of this hotel is less than welcoming but the rooms on offer are large and comfortable. There are good views across Wadi Musa and the surrounding hills from many of the rooms and the roof terrace. There's an excellent Turkish bath opposite.

📖 Upper Wadi Musa

The luxury hotels in Upper Wadi Musa are located at the top end of town, on the scenic road between the town centre and Tayyibeh, a 10- to 15-minute drive from the Petra Visitor Centre. Perched at around 1400m above sea level, they offer fine views over the Rift Valley and most have beautiful terraces for a sunset drink. Unfortunately, the hotels have somewhat blighted the once-secluded view from inside Petra. Some good budget and midrange options are available on the road from 'Ain Musa into town.

Rocky Mountain Hotel   HOTEL $

(📞 2155100; rockymountainhotel@yahoo.com; s/d/tr/q JD26/39/50/60, buffet dinner JD8; ❄@🛜) This backpacker-friendly hotel near the junction with the main road into town has caught just the right vibe to make it a successful travellers' lodge. The hotel focuses on cleanliness and has a cosy communal area with free tea and coffee. The *majlis*-style roof terrace makes the most of the impressive sweeping views.

The Anglo-Jordanian couple who run the hotel take their responsibility towards guests seriously and can advise on onward travel. A free shuttle service to the Petra entrance runs at 7.30am and 8.30am, returning at 5pm and 6pm.

Al-Anbat Hotel I   HOTEL **$**
(☑ 2156265; www.alanbat.com; s/d/tr JD20/35/45, buffet lunch or dinner JD10; ✿@🛜🛏) Located some way out of town on the road between 'Ain Musa and Wadi Musa, this three-storey resort offers midrange quality for budget prices and features a beautiful, brand-new lobby with sofas spanning the magnificent view. The large rooms (many with gorgeous sunset views) have satellite TV and come with a balcony. The rooms in the extension are particularly attractive.

Other facilities include a Turkish bath (JD15 for guests) and small pool, but the best feature of the hotel is the restaurant, perched like a nest on top of the new block and with extensive views of the Petra landscape from all windows. Free transport to/from Petra is available. Campers (JD7 per person) can use a designated area with showers and a kitchen, and you can park a campervan. A laundry service is available.

Sella Hotel   HOTEL **$$**
(☑ 2157170; www.sellahotel.com; s/d/tr JD40/66/85; ✿@🛜) About to reopen at the time of writing, this newly renovated hotel has luxurious rooms, decked in stylish stone tiles with split ceilings and marble sinks in the bathrooms – almost boutique for Wadi Musa. There are good views and the hotel runs the spotless Turkish baths (p179) opposite. The rates may change to reflect the added features.

★**Taybet Zaman Hotel & Resort**   HOTEL **$$$**
(☑ 2150111; www.jordantourismresorts.com; r from JD125; ✿@🛏) 🖊 With the rose-tinted sandstone typical of Petra's famous landscape spread beneath the lintels of this unusual hotel, you won't mind being a half-hour drive from the entrance to the site. Indeed, the sequestered nature of the accommodation, in renovated local village houses, is part of its unique appeal. The hotel is perched above expansive views of the Rift Valley in Tayyibeh village.

With luxurious rooms, handicraft shops, a swimming pool and Turkish bath set in tranquil gardens of fig trees and flowering plumbago, the hotel offers something of a rural idyll, a place to retreat to, perhaps, after the rigours and crowds of Petra. The hotel houses the highly recommended terrace restaurant Sahtain (p187). If you want to be closer to Petra, ask about its sister hotel in Wadi Musa, Beit Zaman. A taxi from Petra (10km) costs about JD15

one way. Ask to pause at the spectacular viewpoint, just below the junction for the hospital.

Petra Panorama Hotel   HOTEL **$$$**
(☑ 2157393; www.petrapanorama.com; s/d JD75/85; ✿🛜🛏) Popular with European tour groups, this hotel was designed for package tourists with its cavernous corridors, unsubtle touches and a *Mary Celeste* atmosphere during the day. That said, the rooms, which cascade in tiers down the mountain, are bright and spacious; all come with uninterrupted views.

Most rooms open on to terraces where you can enjoy your own private sunset and, for this, the hotel is a recommended choice.

Nabataean Castle Hotel   HOTEL **$$$**
(☑ 2157201; www.movenpick-hotels.com; r incl half board from JD164; ✿🛜🛏) Mövenpick runs this often fully booked hotel. It is an opulent choice, although it plays second fiddle to its sister hotel (p183) near the entrance to Petra. Most rooms have views over the valley, but the windows are surprisingly small. There's a free daily shuttle bus to and from Petra.

Petra Marriott   HOTEL **$$$**
(☑ 2156407; www.marriott.com; r from JD145; ✿@🛜🛏) One of the most elegant hotels in the area, though remote in every sense from the experience of Petra. Services include a pool, several restaurants, a Turkish bath and even a cinema for free use by guests.

> **MOSES' SPRING**
>
> Then Moses raised his arm and struck the rock twice with his staff. Water gushed out, and the community and their livestock drank.
>
> *Numbers 20:11*
>
> 'Ain Musa (Moses' Spring) is one of two possible locations in Jordan for the site where Moses supposedly struck the rock with his staff and water gushed forth to the thirsty Israelites (the other possible site is near Mt Nebo). The simple site is marked by a modern three-domed building occasionally visited by local pilgrims. The site is located near the King's Way Hotel, alongside the King's Highway at the main junction into Wadi Musa from the north.

PETRA WADI MUSA

✗ Eating

The main road through Wadi Musa is dotted with grocery stores where you can buy picnic necessities; there's also a supermarket next to Al-Anbat Hotel I, slightly out of town on the road to 'Ain Musa. Some hotels can arrange snack boxes with a boiled egg, bread and tomato. A felafel sandwich travels well and makes a filling lunch. Buy your dessert course at **Sanabel Bakery** (⊙ 5am-midnight), which sells a delicious range of Arab sweets on Shaheed roundabout.

After a hot day's hiking in Petra, it's hard to resist a Swiss ice cream (JD2.800) from the foyer cafe of the Mövenpick Hotel.

If you're climbing the hill between the Petra Visitor Centre and Shaheed roundabout, you might like to stop for a simple Jordanian buffet at the **Sand Hills Restaurant** (mains from JD4; ⊙ 8am-midnight), a halfway house with a small craft shop, cafe with seating on the pavement, and four clean loos!

The cheapest places to eat are around Shaheed roundabout and Sanabel Bakery. Most are similar in menu and price. More midrange options with a wider selection of dishes are near the entrance to Petra. Fine dining is confined to the five-star hotels.

Al-Wadi Restaurant   JORDANIAN $
(☑ 2157151; salads JD1, mains JD4-5; ⊙ 7am-late) Right on Shaheed roundabout, this lively spot offers pasta and a range of vegetarian dishes and local Bedouin specialities such as *gallaya* (meat, rice and onions in a spicy tomato sauce) and *mensaf* (lamb on a bed of rice topped with a lamb's head), most of which come with salad and rice.

Al-Arabi Restaurant   MIDDLE EASTERN $
(☑ 2157661; mains from JD4; ⊙ 6am-midnight) Located off the Shaheed roundabout, this spot offers hummus, felafel and shwarma.

Cleopatra Restaurant &
Coffee Shop   BUFFET $
(☑ 079 5318775; mains JD3, buffet JD6; ⊙ 6am-11pm) This canteen musters a reasonable open buffet, with a range of Bedouin specialities.

Bukhara Restaurant   KEBAB $
(mains JD4; ⊙ 11am to midnight) Selling rotisserie-style barbecued chicken and kebabs, this popular restaurant on Shaheed Roundabout (opposite Petra Butchery BBQ) is just the place to satisfy an appetite after the long slog up from Petra.

★ Red Cave Restaurant   JORDANIAN $$
(☑ 2157799; starters JD1, mains from JD5; ⊙ 9am-10pm) Cavernous and friendly, this restaurant serves local Bedouin specialities including *mensaf* and *maqlubbeh* (steamed rice with meat, grilled tomato and pine nuts). It's a popular travellers' meeting point and a cosy

---

DAVID ROBERTS: PAINTING PETRA

Stand in certain parts of Petra and Little Petra and it's almost impossible not to imagine striped-robed Arabs from the 19th century lounging languidly in the foreground. Sit in the cafes and hotel lobbies of Wadi Musa and you'll see the same characters and landscapes writ large across otherwise vacant walls. And who do we have to thank for this 'picturesque' peopling of ancient Petra? The culprit is one David Roberts: artist, Scot and much-beloved topographer of the late Romantic era.

Given the continuing popularity of his images with tourists, it's safe to say that Roberts (1796–1864) had the common touch. This may have had something to do with his seven-year apprenticeship as a housepainter, or perhaps his stint as a scenery painter at the Theatre Royal in Edinburgh. Whatever the reason, his compositions are full of human interest – an unloaded caravan, friends waving across a wadi, a quarrel between traders cast against a backdrop of exaggerated landscape.

Roberts visited the region in 1839 dressed as an Arab, in the tradition of Burckhardt just two decades earlier, and travelled with a caravan of 20 camels and local bodyguards. Petra was the high point of his journey, despite having to cut short his visit due to trouble with local tribes. On his return to Britain, his watercolours, magnificently interpreted in lithograph by the Belgian engraver Louis Haghe, were exhibited in 1840 and won instant critical acclaim.

Roberts' images have now passed into the visual vocabulary of one of the world's most treasured sites. For a shoemaker's son with no formal art training who began life painting houses, that's a formidable legacy.

place to come on a chilly evening or to catch the breeze on a hot summer's day.

Oriental Restaurant JORDANIAN $$
(☑2157087; mains JD6; ⊙11am-9.30pm) Together with the neighbouring **Sandstone Restaurant** (☑079 5542277; mains JD8), this main-street favourite offers simple fare of tasty mixed grills, salad and mezze with pleasant outdoor seating. Both are good places for a beer and a good-natured chuckle at the menu.

★Sahtain JORDANIAN, INTERNATIONAL $$$
(☑2150111; buffet JD20; 🖫☑) This delightful restaurant at the Taybet Zaman (p186) is as much an experience as a seriously tasty supper. With a cavernous, vaulted interior and a flower-bedecked terrace, the restaurant specialises in traditional Arabic and international home-cooked specialities. The dinner buffet allows the chance to try a variety of local favourites, including more than 20 different salads.

Simpler fare for lunch includes a tasty chef's salad and sandwiches that are more like main meals between slices of bread.

Al-Saraya Restaurant INTERNATIONAL $$$
(☑2157111; lunch/dinner JD20/JD25; 🖫☑) Serving a top-notch international buffet in an elegant banquet hall, this fine-dining restaurant offers a quality of dishes that matches the general opulence of the Mövenpick Hotel in which it is located. Leave time for a nightcap in the grand, wood-panelled bar afterwards which sports a roaring fire in the hearth in winter.

🍸 Drinking

★Cave Bar BAR
(☑2156266; ⊙4-11pm) You can't come to Petra and miss the oldest bar in the world. Occupying a 2000-year-old Nabataean rock tomb, this blue-lit Petra hotspot has been known to stay open until 4am on busy summer nights. Sit among the spirits, alcoholic or otherwise, and you'll soon get a flavour of Petra you hadn't bargained on (not least the 26% tax and service charge!).

The menu includes delicious comfort food such as potato wedges and fish and chips that you may feel you've earned after a day's exercise in Petra. Don't be put off by the loud music at the entrance: the noise stops there. The restaurant and bar is next to the entrance to Petra Guest House Hotel, behind the Petra Visitor Centre.

Al-Maqa'ad Bar BAR
(☑2157111; ⊙4-11pm) The Mövenpick Hotel bar has a superb Moroccan-style interior with carved wooden grills and a chandelier. It's worth having a cocktail or an ice-cream special just to enjoy the ambience. A 26% tax and service charge is applied.

Wranglers Pub BAR
(☑2156723; ⊙2pm-midnight) The Petra Palace Hotel runs this sociable bar, decorated with assorted local memorabilia.

☆ Entertainment

There's not a lot to do in the evening other than take a bath in the hammam and plan your next day in Petra. Some hotels organise DVDs or other entertainment, but only when there are enough takers.

🛍 Shopping

There are many souvenir shops near the entrance to Petra and ad hoc stalls run by local Bedouin inside Petra. Throughout Wadi Musa you'll see craftsmen patiently pouring coloured sand into glass bottles; they will write your name if you give them time. Top-end hotels sell good-quality handicrafts, though few pieces in their collections are local to Petra and prices tend to be inflated (as expected in the country's top tourist destination). Ask for Umm Raami's concession inside Petra where you can buy contemporary silver jewellery inspired by ancient Nabataean designs and crafted by local women originally trained through a Noor al-Hussein Foundation project.

The **Wadi Musa Ladies Society** (⊙6am-9pm) and the **Society for the Development and Rehabilitation of Rural Women** (⊙6am-9pm) both have shops at the visitor centre selling a range of souvenirs, books and crafts.

Books on Petra can be found in the shops at the visitor centre and along the main road through Wadi Musa.

Made in Jordan HANDICRAFTS
(☑2155700) This Wadi Musa shop sells quality crafts from local enterprises. Products include olive oil, soap, paper, ceramics, table runners, nature products from Wild Jordan in Amman, jewellery from Wadi Musa, embroidery from Safi, camel hair shawls, and bags from Aqaba as well as Jordan River Foundation goods. The fixed prices reflect the quality and uniqueness of each piece; credit cards are accepted.

PETRA WADI MUSA

BOOKS & MAPS

A Good Read

There is some interesting literature about Petra, together with beautiful souvenir books, available at shops and stalls around Wadi Musa and Petra.

One of the best guidebooks, *Petra: A Traveller's Guide* by Rosalyn Maqsood, covers the history and culture of the site and describes several hikes. The pocket-sized *Petra: The Rose-Red City,* by Christian Auge and Jean-Marie Dentzer, provides excellent historical context. Jane Taylor's *Petra* is another good paperback introduction to the site. Taylor also wrote the authoritative *Petra & the Lost Kingdoms of the Nabataeans*. There's a chapter on hiking in Petra in Tony Howard and Di Taylor's *Jordan – Walks, Treks, Climbs & Canyons*.

For an engaging account of the Bdoul Bedouin who once lived in the caves surrounding the Petra valley and who now live on the rim of the ancient city, *Married to a Bedouin* is a recommended read. The author, Marguerite van Geldermalsen, raised three children among the Bdoul and ran the local health clinic. Since the book's publication in 2006, Marguerite has become a local celebrity in Jordan, has received the Queen of the United Kingdom and Queen Noor in her cave, and her son now runs tours for those wanting to gain an understanding of Bedouin life in the area. She continues to live in the Bdoul community at Umm Sayhoun.

Finding Your Way

Very little in Petra is signposted or captioned, so a map and guidebook are essential.

If you plan to hike long distances in Petra without a guide, the best map is the Royal Jordanian Geographic Centre's contoured 1:5000 *Map of Petra* (2005; JD5). It's usually available at bookshops in Wadi Musa and at the stand outside the Nabataean Museum.

The *Petra* brochure, published by the Ministry of Tourism & Antiquities, has an easy-to-read map with useful photos that help identify certain monuments. Pick one up before coming to Petra as the visitor centre often runs out.

City of Wonders Bazaar   SOUVENIRS
(☺8am-10pm) Has a good selection of hand-blown glass bottles displayed in the window. Prices range from JD8 to JD35.

Indiana Jones Gifts Shop   GIFTS
(☎2155069; ☺8am-10pm) Good place to buy a video of the main sites in Petra.

Rum Studio & Labs   PHOTOGRAPHY
(☎2157467; ☺8.30am-10pm) A range of digital accessories is available here; the shop is located in front of the Silk Road Hotel on the main road.

ⓘ Information

EMERGENCY

Main Police Station (☎2156551, emergency 191) In Wadi Musa, adjacent to the police roundabout.

Tourist Police Station (☎2156441, emergency 196; ☺8am-midnight) Near Petra Visitor Centre. A few tourist police can be found lounging around in the shade inside Petra.

INTERNET ACCESS

There are lots of internet cafes around the town centre, including **Rum Internet** (per hour JD1; ☺10am-midnight), located downhill from Shaheed roundabout. **Seven Wonders Restaurant** (per hour JD3.500; ☺9am-11pm), near the entrance to Petra, also serves a luxury hot chocolate (JD2.500).

LAUNDRY

Most hotels will do laundry for around JD2 per piece, through the drycleaners at Amra Palace Hotel.

MEDICAL SERVICES

The **Queen Rania Hospital** (☎2150628) offers high-standard health care and is open for emergencies without referral. It's located 5km from the police roundabout on the road to Tayyibeh.

The **Wadi Musa Pharmacy**, located near the Shaheed roundabout, has a wide range of medications and toiletries.

MONEY

Many hotels will change money, albeit at a poor rate. The Housing Bank and Jordan Islamic Bank up from the Shaheed roundabout are good for money exchange; both have ATMs. The Arab Bank is downhill from the roundabout. Closer to the Petra entrance, the Cairo-Amman Bank in the Mövenpick Hotel and the Arab Jordan Investment Bank both change cash. The banks are open from about 8am to 2pm Sunday to Thursday and (sometimes) 9am to 11am on Friday. A couple of moneychangers near the Silk Road Hotel keep longer hours.

POST

Visitor Centre Post Office (⊘7.30am-5pm) The attraction of using the small post office by the Petra Visitor Centre is that mail is postmarked 'Petra Touristic Post Office', rather than Wadi Musa.

TELEPHONE

International telephone calls can be made from private agencies along the main streets of Wadi Musa. The cheapest and easiest way to make a call is to buy a prepaid phonecard.

TOURIST INFORMATION

Information and tickets are available at the visitor centre (p177), just before the main entrance to Petra.
Jordan Jubilee (www.jordanjubilee.com) The author of this celebrated website, Ruth, is a long-term resident of Wadi Musa and local guru.

❶ Getting There & Away

Public transport to and from Wadi Musa is less frequent than you'd expect, given that it's the top tourist attraction in Jordan. The best place to find information about minibuses and other transport is to ask at your hotel or one of the restaurants around the Shaheed roundabout.

BUS & MINIBUS

A daily JETT bus connects Amman with Petra, largely designed for those wanting to visit on a day trip. The service leaves at 6.30am from the JETT office, near Abdali Bus Station (single/return JD9.500/19, four hours) and drops off passengers at Petra Visitor Centre in Wadi Musa. The return bus leaves at 5pm.

Minibuses leave from the bus station in central Wadi Musa. Most minibuses won't leave unless they're at least half full, so be prepared for a wait. If there are insufficient passengers, they may not leave at all, or you may be approached to pay for the empty seats. This is not a scam: it's just an attempt by the driver to cover the cost of the journey. You should establish the fare you are being charged before departing. There are far fewer services on Fridays.

Regular minibuses travel every day between Amman's South Bus Station (Wahadat) and Wadi Musa (JD7, four hours) via the Desert Highway. These buses leave Amman and Wadi Musa when full every hour or so between around 6am and noon. From Amman there are services up until around 4pm; from Wadi Musa there may be an additional journey or two depending on demand. Schedules change frequently so ask at your hotel for the latest information.

Minibuses leave Wadi Musa for Ma'an (JD1.500, 45 minutes) fairly frequently throughout the day (more often in the morning), stopping briefly at the university, about 10km from Ma'an. From Ma'an there are connections to Amman, Aqaba and (indirectly) Wadi Rum. Minibuses also leave Wadi Musa for Aqaba (JD7, 2½ hours) at about 6am, 8.30am and 3pm – ask around the day before to confirm or check through your hotel.

For Wadi Rum (JD7, two hours) there is a daily minibus around 6am. It's a good idea to reserve a seat the day before – your hotel should be able to ring the driver. If you miss this bus or the service isn't operating, take the minibus to Aqaba, get off at the Ar-Rashidiyyah junction and catch another minibus (hitching is not recommended though possible) the remainder of the journey to Rum. You may well be charged extra for luggage

PETRA WADI MUSA

PETRA: PUBLIC TRANSPORT AT A GLANCE

TO/FROM	DURATION	FREQUENCY	NOTES
Amman (210km) via Desert Highway	4 hours	1 bus daily/11 minibuses daily	**JETT Bus** Leaves 6.30am from Amman's JETT bus office near Abdali Bus Station. Returns 4pm (summer 5pm) from Petra Visitor Centre. **Minibus** Leaves (only when full) between 6am and noon to/from the south bus station (Wahadat) in Amman and Wadi Musa bus station.
Wadi Rum (90km)	2 hours	1 daily	**Minibus** Leaves 6am from Wadi Musa bus station. Leaves 8.30am from Petra Visitor Centre. May only leave if full: ask hotel/camp owner to contact bus driver in advance.
To/from Aqaba (120km)	2½ hours	4 daily	**Minibus** Leaves between 6.30am and 8.30am, with one midafternoon to/from Wadi Musa bus station and Aqaba minibus station. Leaves only when full.

(around JD3), especially if it takes up a seat that could be used for a paying customer. Buy water for your journey in advance and make provisions for a Wadi Rum tour either from your hotel, a travel agent or on arrival in Rum to avoid falling victim to opportunistic touts at the station. Cleopatra Hotel, among other hotels, organises competent overnight tours to Wadi Rum.

To Karak, a minibus sometimes leaves at around 7am and sometimes at noon (JD7), but demand is low so it doesn't leave every day and there is no service on Fridays. Alternatively, travel via Ma'an.

CAR

Hertz Rent-a-Car (☑2156981; ⊘8am-6pm) rents out cars from JD45 per day. A 4WD costs around JD160 per day.

Petra and Wadi Musa are well signposted along the main highways. The road from Petra to Little Petra extends to the Wadi Musa–Shobak road offering a scenic alternative route out of town. A spectacular road winds into Wadi Araba for direct access to the Dead Sea Highway (damaged by flooding but passable with extreme care and a good head for heights at the time of writing). The road to Tayyibeh is also particularly scenic.

TAXI

Private (yellow) taxis are easy to find in Wadi Musa. A few 4WD taxis are available for much the same cost, but they are not of much benefit as you will still have to join a 4WD tour from the Wadi Rum Visitor Centre if you want to explore the protected area. One-way taxi fares cost JD40 to Wadi Rum (one hour) or Aqaba (1½ hours); JD10 to Shobak (JD15 return including a one-hour wait); and JD50 to Karak (1½ hours). If you want to travel to Madaba or Amman via the King's Highway, with stops at Shobak, Dana and Karak, the fare is around JD90.

Siq al-Barid (Little Petra)
سيق البيضاء (البتراء الصغيرة)

Siq al-Barid (Cold Canyon) is colloquially known as **Little Petra** and is well worth a visit. It was thought to have served as an agricultural centre, trading suburb and re-supply post for camel caravans visiting Petra. The surrounding area is picturesque and fun to explore, especially as it is home to some of the oldest settlements in the world, including Al-Beidha.

◉ Sights

★Little Petra Siq   RUIN
(⊘daylight hours) **FREE** From the car park, an obvious path leads to the 400m-long siq,

which opens out into larger areas. The first open area has a **temple**, which archaeologists know little about. Four **triclinia** – one on the left and three on the right – are in the second open area, and were probably used as dining rooms to feed hungry merchants and travellers. About 50m further along the siq is the **Painted House**, another small dining room, which is reached by some exterior steps.

The Painted House is worth a closer look as faded but still vivid frescoes of vines, flowers and birds on the underside of the interior arch are a rare example of Nabataean painting, though the walls have been blackened by Bedouin campfires. Cut into the rock opposite the room is a large cistern; there are also worn water channels at various points along the siq.

At the end of Siq al-Barid are some steps. You can climb to the top for great views and plenty of picnicking opportunities. With extra time and interest you can explore the Nabataean quarries and cisterns of Umm Qusa, located just before the entrance to Siq al-Barid.

Al-Beidha   RUIN
(⊘daylight hours) **FREE** The Neolithic ruins of **Al-Beidha** date back 9000 years and, along with Jericho, constitute one of the oldest archaeological sites in the Middle East. The remains of around 65 round (and later rectangular) structures are especially significant because they pinpoint the physical transition from hunter-gatherer to settled herder-agriculturalist communities. The settlement was abandoned around 6000 BC, keeping the site intact.

A 15-minute walking trail, starting to the left of the entrance to Little Petra, leads to the site.

It's important to keep to the marked trails at Al-Beidha as the site is fragile. It's fair to say that for the casual visitor, the ruins require imagination.

Al-Wu'ira   CASTLE
(Map p164; ⊘daylight hours) **FREE** Built by the Crusaders in AD 1116, **Al-Wu'ira** was overrun by Muslim forces 73 years after construction. An impressive old bridge (previously a drawbridge) leads over the gorge to a gatehouse and the limited ruins.

Look for the unsigned turn-off, about 1.5km north of the Mövenpick Hotel. The castle is on the left side of the road leading to Siq al-Barid (Little Petra).

🏃 Activities

Little Petra to the Monastery
HIKING
(moderate; guided; from JD45; ⏱4hr) If you come prepared, it's possible to hike from Siq al-Barid to Petra's Monastery (Al-Deir), or to Petra centre via Wadi Mu'aisireh al-Gharbi-ya. You'll need a guide for the four-hour trek (from JD45 – ask at the car park by the entry to Siq al-Barid or at one of the camps below) as route-finding is tricky. You must also have a valid ticket to Petra (not available from Siq al-Barid).

🛏 Sleeping & Eating

There are several camps in the area which make a rural retreat from the slightly claustrophobic atmosphere of Wadi Musa. If travelling with family, ask about discounts for children – some camps offer half price for kids under 12 years of age.

Seven Wonders Bedouin Camp
CAMP $
(📱079 7958641; rockymountainhotel@yahoo.com; half board per person in tent JD30, B&B JD20) Signposted along a track off the road to Little Petra and tucked discreetly into a hillside, this relaxed and good-value camp looks particularly magical at night when the open fires are burning and the rocks behind the camp are illuminated. Accommodation is in simple but cosy cabins with electric light, carpets and mosquito nets. Hot water and towels are available.

Tasty traditional fare is served from a *zerb* oven and *mehndi* (barbecue) pits while wholesome vegetarian soups are made on the premises by an experienced chef. The camp offers both the usual guided hike to Petra (JD45 for up to four people) and an interesting two-hour 4WD and hiking excursion (JD60) to a local wadi with impressive rock formations. The camp is run by the same management as the popular Rocky Mountain Hotel (p184) in Wadi Musa.

The Rock
CAMP $$
(📱079 777589; www.therockpetra.com; half board in Bedouin/army tent JD33/JD40 per person) This relaxed camp in Ba'ja has a gorgeous location on a small plateau with typical wind-blown rocks as a backdrop and an unusually green vista (thanks to the neighbouring farming project) stretched across the plain below. There is a choice between white army-style tents or more traditional hand-woven goat-hair tents and a variety of cosy perches for traditional suppers.

> ## BEDOUIN HUMOUR
>
> While you're in Petra, look out for the funny side of your visit. Locals are famous for their mischievous sense of humour, offering camels as 'air-conditioned taxis' and donkeys as 'Mercedes Benz'. Handicrafts are often prefaced with the words 'buy one for the wife and one for the girlfriend'. However, you may not see the funny side of 'happy hour prices' charged for souvenirs in the evening which may well mean they cost double!

If you sup a glass of wine from the outdoor bar (JD5) you'll be partaking in an ancient tradition as you'll see from the Nabataean wine press within the camp grounds. Remains of a dam and water channels are also visible. A two-hour walk and scramble in the adjacent Siq Ba'ja brings you to the ruins of a well-preserved 9000-year-old neolithic village.

To reach the camp, follow the Rock Camp signs from Little Petra towards Wadi Araba. The last 200m is just about accessible in a 2WD vehicle if you drive slowly over the rutted track.

Ammarin Bedouin Camp
CAMP $$
(📱079 5667771; www.bedouincamp.net; half board per person in tent JD52) A 10-minute walk from Little Petra and signposted off the approach road, this camp is in Siq al-Amti, hidden in a spectacular amphitheatre of sand and hills, and run by the local Ammarin tribe. Accommodation comprises mattress and blankets in a sectioned Bedouin tent with concrete floors, with a clean shower and toilet block. Reservations are essential.

You can pitch your own tent and use the camp's facilities (JD20 per person) and there's space to park a campervan (JD32 per night per vehicle, with power). *Zerb* dinners (meat cooked in a pit in the ground) can be prepared on request (JD30 extra). The camp offers guided hikes and camel trips in the surrounding hills. A Bedouin guide is JD100 per day or JD50 for the hike to Petra.

Spare time for a wonderful little ethnographic museum on site, spotlighting the local Ammarin tribe. In particular, it is interesting to read the story of Torfa Bint Saleh

PETRA SIQ AL-BARID (LITTLE PETRA)

Al-Ammarin for an idea of the everyday hardships of a life on the fringe.

The camp offers transfers from Petra (JD10 one way).

Little Petra Bedouin Camp CAMP **$$**
(☑077 6331431, 079 5300135; per person JD25, half board per person JD40, minimum 2 people) Signposted just off the main road to Little Petra, this secluded complex in a basin surrounded by mountains brings a touch of class to the rural retreat. It offers camping with army tents that sport proper beds with linen and mattresses, and full-length wood-rimmed mirrors. Dinner is prepared in a cave and served among the rocks or in romantic caverns.

ℹ Getting There & Away

Some hotels in Wadi Musa organise tours to Little Petra. Private taxis cost about JD22 one way or JD32 return, including an hour's wait. An accompanying guide costs JD50 from the visitor centre.

If you're driving, take the road north of the Mövenpick Hotel and follow the signs to 'Beda' or 'Al-Beidha'. Turn left at the junction from where it's just under 1km to the car park.

Alternatively, it's a pleasant 8km walk following the road. The route passes the village of Umm Sayhoun, the 'Elephant Rock' formation and then 'Ain Dibdibah, which once supplied Petra with much of its water. You can shortcut across fields to the left about 1km before the junction to Al-Beidha.

Aqaba, Wadi Rum & the Desert Highway
العقبة وادي رم & الطريق الصحراء

Best Places to Stay

➡ InterContinental Hotel (p202)

➡ International Arab Divers Village (p208)

➡ Bait Ali Lodge (p221)

➡ Rum Stars Camp (p220)

Best for History

➡ Aqaba Fort (p198)

➡ Ruins of Ayla (p197)

➡ Lawrence's House (p215)

➡ Humaiyma Ruins (p225)

Why Go?

Southern Jordan is the home of the Bedouin, whose legendary courage and bravado were made famous by TE Lawrence in *Seven Pillars of Wisdom*. They inhabit the unforgiving Southern Desert, a quintessential landscape of sand dunes, oases and weathered escarpments, beautiful at sunset and awe-inspiringly extreme in midsummer. A trip to Wadi Rum makes all but the most unromantic at heart long to leave the modern world behind and attempt the life of a nomad. And that's possible – at least for a day or two amid the camps of Rum and Diseh, on camel back, by 4WD or floating above in a hot-air balloon.

Nearby Aqaba and the neighbouring diving centres give access to another of Jordan's natural splendours: the coral gardens of the Red Sea. Even if wet suits aren't your thing, Aqaba is a relaxed and pleasant destination in which to wash off the desert dust and plan your onward journey.

When to Go

➡ Aqaba enjoys year-round warmth, even in winter, and a crystal clear sea. This brings holidaymakers from the chilly uplands to the shore in large numbers – especially during national holidays and religious festivals.

➡ The desert springs to life after rain, making February to May and October to November the perfect time for desert adventure in Wadi Rum. With temperate days and balmy nights, camping is blissful.

➡ Despite high temperatures, the all-night music festival Distant Heat attracts party-goers to Wadi Rum in mid-summer.

➡ Beware! Mid-winter brings bitter evening temperatures to the desert.

History & Culture

There is a magnificent road (A35) that leads from Wadi Musa, with westerly glimpses across expansive Wadi Araba, to the escarpment of Jebel Batra. Here the road joins the Desert Highway and hand in hand they sweep onto the majestic floor of what is commonly called the Southern Desert. For centuries this has been the home of the Bedouin, whose tribes rallied together in the most convincing expression of the pan-Arab ideal during the 20th-century Arabic Revolt. The cry of 'to Aqaba' still rings between the towering walls of Wadi Rum, carried in the whistle of the freight train as it winds along the now-placid tracks of the Hejaz Railway.

As romantic as the nomadic life may seem, in the past two or three decades many of the Bedouin tribes have turned to a settled life. The desert, much of which is characterised not by the picturesque features of Wadi Rum but by inhospitable plains, doesn't take prisoners. Life to this day is hard here, even for the Bedouin and, in the words of Lawrence, 'a death in life' for strangers. Take the journey along the Desert Highway, along the edge of the mighty Badia, and you'll quickly learn a new respect for this extreme environment – and for the people and wildlife who have adapted to its privations.

Nature Reserves

There are two reserves in the south of Jordan. On land, the **Wadi Rum Protected Area**, run by the Aqaba authorities, offers desert adventure such as camping, camel treks, hiking, ballooning and off-road driving, amid beautiful sand dunes and sandstone landscapes.

Offshore, the **Red Sea Aqaba Marine Park** (part of the bigger, cross-border Red Sea Marine Peace Park) was established in 1997 to protect the complex marine environment of the Red Sea south of Aqaba. It is best accessed through one of the diving clubs in the area. The park stretches from the Marine Science Station to the Royal Diving Club, and extends about 350m off the coast. Enforced by rangers, there's a ban on fishing and boating is limited within the park. Jetties enable divers and snorkellers to jump into the water rather than wade out over coral from the beach.

Dangers & Annoyances

The Red Sea is home to a number of hazards that with common sense can be avoided. For divers, it's important to remember that most

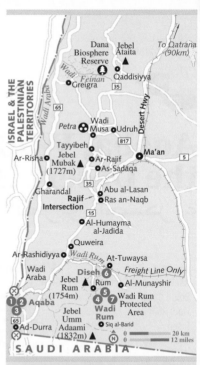

Aqaba, Wadi Rum & the Desert Highway Highlights

1 Don mask and flippers and hover with the pipe fish over spectacular coral gardens in the **Red Sea** (p29).

2 Taste fresh tuna steaks in one of the fish restaurants of **Aqaba** (p195), and ruin your love for the tinned version.

3 Relax at one of Jordan's southerly **coastal resorts** (p208) and enjoy the three 'S's (sun, sea and sand).

4 Live a 'Lawrence moment' by riding through Wadi Rum on a **camel** (p217), visiting the places made famous in *Seven Pillars of Wisdom*.

5 Enjoy the banter between Bedouin drivers on a **4WD excursion** (p216) through Wadi Rum.

6 Book a private tent and personally delivered dinner on your own sand dune in **Diseh** (p224) for the ultimate candlelit supper.

7 Camp with the Bedouin in a goat-hair tent in **Wadi Rum** (p220) and experience the night sky in all its glory.

roads out of Aqaba lead uphill. This means that 'the bends' are a serious concern if you fail to acclimatise in Aqaba before heading on to Wadi Rum or Petra.

ℹ️ Getting There & Away

Aqaba is well served by public transport from Amman and even has an international airport. The city is a gateway to Egypt, usually by boat to Taba, Nuweiba and Sharm El Sheikh. At the time of writing, there were security issues in many parts of the Sinai and it remains important to check the latest travel advisories issued by your consulate before deciding on travel to this region. Aqaba is also a gateway to Israel and the Palestinian Territories through the blissfully straightforward Wadi Araba border crossing. This crossing presented no security threat at the time of writing, but with the general tension in Israel at present, you should be aware that there are only limited transport options from Eilat, many of which involve transiting through Jerusalem.

Wadi Rum is not as easy to get to without your own transport or without taking a tour from Aqaba or Petra. With a car it's possible to link this region with the Eastern Desert via Hwy 5.

ℹ️ Getting Around

It's possible to make a roundtrip of this most southerly part of Jordan by public transport from Aqaba in three to four days. Hiring a car from Aqaba makes accessing the South Coast and Wadi Rum much easier. You don't need a 4WD for Wadi Rum as you can drive to the Visitors Centre on tarmac. From there, unless you are an expert sand driver, it's advisable to take an excursion with a Bedouin driver.

AQABA & AROUND

Perched on the edge of the Gulf of Aqaba, ringed by high desert mountains and enjoying a pleasant climate for most of the year, Aqaba has what it takes to make a major resort – a fact not lost on developers: the glamorous US$2.5 billion Saraya Project, which includes lagoons, a marina, a golf course and a British university, is well on the way to completion.

The Tala Bay development has already given Aqaba and its surrounding coastline a facelift, but it's also fair to say that there's still a long way to go before Aqaba rivals Egypt's Sharm el Sheikh or Israel's Eilat. Hit hard by conflict in neighbouring countries, Jordan's tourism projects are often on hold. Not everyone will feel sad at

this: many like the sleepy atmosphere and the fact that Aqaba has remained a seaside destination largely catering to Jordanian holidaymakers.

Aqaba العقبة

☑ 03 / POP 136,200 / ELEV 50M

Aqaba, with its infectious 'on holiday' atmosphere, retains the relaxed small-town atmosphere of a popular local getaway, despite the growing developments and the unsightly port nearby. For the visitor, although there's not much to 'do' as such, the town offers a sociable stopover en route to the diving and snorkelling clubs to the south and the big destinations of Wadi Rum and Petra. It's also an obvious place to break a journey to/from Israel and the Palestinian Territories or Egypt, security situation permitting.

The winter temperature in Aqaba rarely goes below 20°C and is often quite a few degrees warmer. In summer the weather is hot, with daytime temperatures over 35°C, but the sea breezes make it bearable. It also helps to follow the traditional siesta: everything shuts down around 2pm and re-opens after the afternoon nap, around 6pm.

History

> And king Solomon made a navy of ships in Ezion-Geber, which is beside Eloth (Eilat), on the shore of the Red Sea, in the land of Edom.
>
> *1 Kings 9:26*

In the 10th century, a Muslim traveller described Aqaba as 'a great city' and a meeting place of pilgrims en route to and from Mecca. Indeed, from as early as the 10th to 5th centuries BC, it was at the heart of ancient trade routes transporting copper ore, smelted from mines in Wadi Araba, and transported by King Solomon's fleets to far-flung destinations. Ceramics from China and coins from Ethiopia highlight the cosmopolitan nature of the port throughout its early history. Thereafter the Egyptians, Nabataeans and Romans all found their uses for 'Ayla', as it came to be known, and the discovery of a late-3rd-century purpose-built church – one of the oldest in the world – is suggestive of a prosperous community, embracing of change.

In AD 1068 the town's fortunes changed when a huge earthquake split the old city of Ayla in two. The shifting of trade routes to Baghdad in the middle of the 16th century

Aqaba

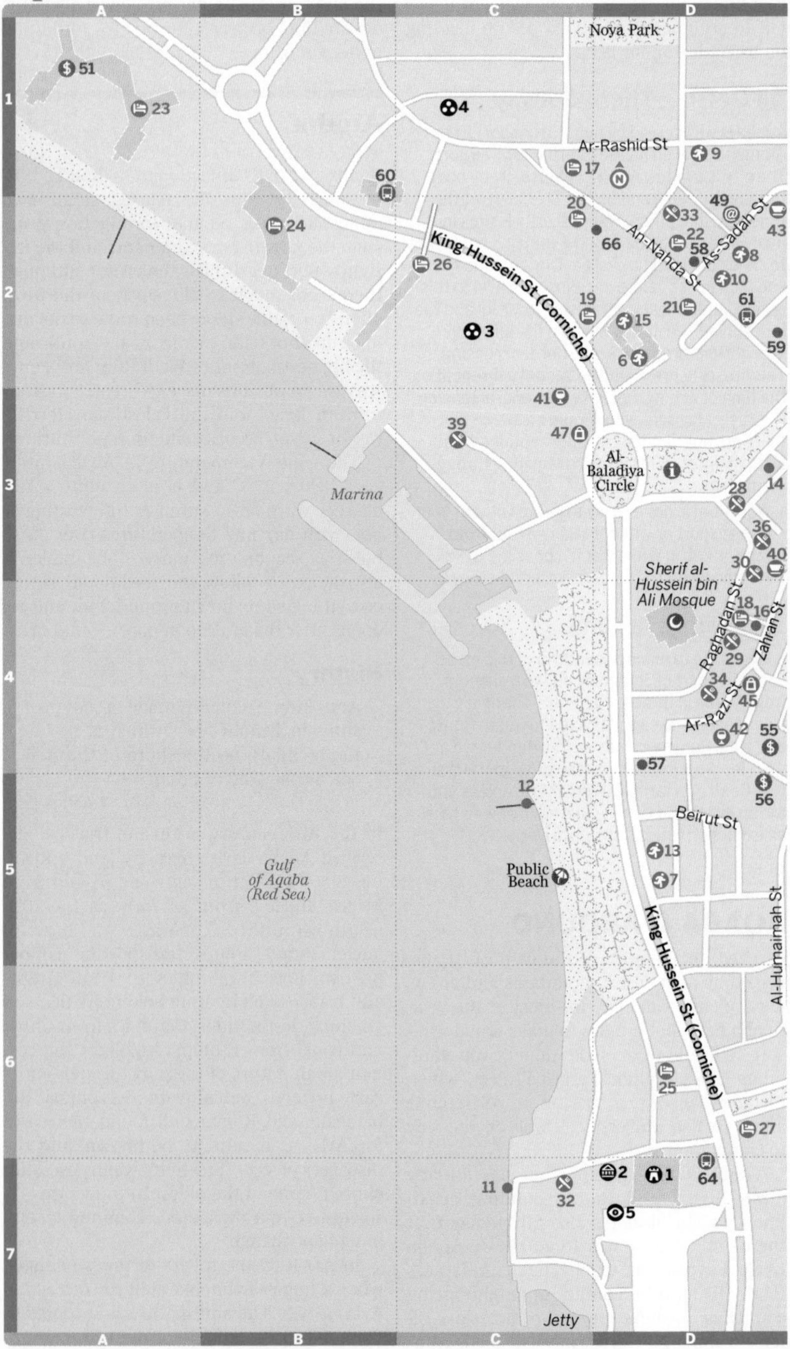

Noya Park

51

23

4

Ar-Rashid St

60

17

9

24

20

33

49

43

@

26

66

An-Nahda St

58

8

King Hussein St (Corniche)

22

10

19

61

3

15

21

59

6

41

47

Al-Baladiya Circle

28

14

39

36

Marina

30

40

Sherif al-Hussein bin Ali Mosque

18

16

Raghadan St

Zahran St

29

34

45

Ar-Razi St

42

55

57

56

Gulf of Aqaba (Red Sea)

12

Beirut St

13

Public Beach

7

King Hussein St (Corniche)

Al-Humaimah St

25

27

11

32

2

1

64

5

Jetty

led to the final eclipse of the port, which dwindled to an insignificant fishing village for the next 500 years.

Aqaba returned to the spotlight during the Arab Revolt in the early 20th century when Ottoman forces were ousted after a raid by the Arabs (and TE Lawrence) in 1917. Thereafter the British used the town as a supply centre from Egypt to support the assault on Damascus.

After WWI, the border between Trans-Jordan and Saudi Arabia had not been defined, so Britain arbitrarily drew a line a few kilometres south of Aqaba. The Saudis disputed the claim but took no action. As the port of Aqaba grew, the limited coastline proved insufficient, so in 1965 King Hussein traded 6000 sq km of Jordanian desert for another 12km of coastline with Saudi Arabia. Today, with the value of tourism to the gross national product, that has proven to be a very farsighted deal.

⊙ Sights

To be fair, there isn't too much to see and most people come to Aqaba to relax by the beach or go snorkelling or diving. The one or two sights here are best enjoyed as part of a stroll around town (p200). Alternatively, take a **horse and cart** (JD15 for 30 minutes) from outside Aqaba Gulf Hotel.

King Hussein St (written in full as King Al-Hussein bin Talal St, or referred to simply as the Corniche) is the main axis of Aqaba. It follows the languid gulf from the border with Israel and the Palestinian Territories to the border with Saudi Arabia. In the centre of town a walking path parallels King Hussein St along the beach, ending at a huge flag – the location of Aqaba Fort and the tourist office. The disappointingly obtrusive port is a few kilometres south of the centre of Aqaba.

Ayla   RUIN
(Corniche; ⊙24hr) **FREE** Located along the Corniche and incongruously squeezed between the marina and the Mövenpick Resort, Ayla is the site of the ancient port of Aqaba. The ruins are limited, but fading noticeboards in English pinpoint items of interest. At the back of the parking space behind the JETT bus office is another small section of the old city, including the city wall and the ruins of an **ancient church** (⊙daylight hr) **FREE**.

Aqaba

◎ Sights

◉ Activities, Courses & Tours

▣ Sleeping

✹ Eating

◯ Drinking & Nightlife

⬡ Shopping

❶ Information

❶ Transport

Aqaba Fort   FORT

(off King Hussein St; admission incl Aqaba Museum JD1; ⊗ 8am-4pm Sat-Thu, 10am-4pm Fri) The fort was built between 1510 and 1517, as attested by the Arabic inscriptions inside the monumental gateway, and was used as a khan (travellers' inn) for pilgrims on their way to Mecca. The Ottomans occupied the castle until WWI when, in 1917, the fortress was substantially destroyed by shelling from the British Royal Navy. The Hashemite coat of arms above the main entrance commemorates the Arab Revolt that swept through Aqaba, ousting the Turks.

This squat fortification, at the other end of the Corniche near the **giant flag**, measures around 50m by 50m, and is unusual in having sides of slightly uneven length.

Aqaba Museum MUSEUM

(Museum of Aqaba Antiquities; West of King Hussein St; admission JD1; ⊙8am-4pm Sat-Thu, 10am-4pm Fri) The museum, part of the Aqaba Fort complex, was previously the home of the great-great-grandfather of the present king, Abdullah II. The collection of artefacts includes coins, ceramics and 8th-century Islamic stone tablets. Anyone who has travelled the King's Highway may be interested to see an inscribed milestone from the Trajan Rd (the Roman incarnation of this famous thoroughfare). There's a small tourist information centre housed at the museum.

🏃 Activities

Beaches

The main free **public beach** is the stretch of sand lined with cafes between the marina and Aqaba Fort. Women may feel more comfortable swimming at a hotel beach or at Berenice Beach Club (p207) on the South Coast.

Mövenpick Resort Hotel SWIMMING

(☑/fax 2034020; www.moevenpick-hotels.com; King Hussein St; day use JD40; ⊙8am-sunset) Day use of a clean beach, three pools, health club, sauna and jacuzzi; includes a JD5 drink voucher.

InterContinental Hotel SWIMMING

(☑2092222; www.intercontinental.com; King Hussein St; day use JD25; ⊙8am-sunset) Day use of beautiful gardens, pools and beach.

Water Sports

The top-end hotels are well equipped for various water sports (prices start from around JD15 per hour). Waterskiing, jet-skiing, windsurfing and kayaking are some of the water sports on offer between March and October. All hotels can organise snorkelling and diving, although these activities are best carried out from the diving clubs south of town (see p29).

Cruises

Each of the big hotels has a cruise boat for swimming and lunch by day, or sundowners and belly dancing by night. In addition, several boats moor by the harbour office in the marina waiting for sufficient customers to leave.

Sindbad CRUISE

(☑2050077; www.berenice.com.jo; Marina) Operates a number of popular cruises around the Gulf of Aqaba either from the marina or from Berenice Beach Club. Prices range from around JD20 to JD40 depending on choice of cruise. Most cruises operate daily and can be booked through any hotel.

Sample trips include a four-hour snorkelling cruise (child under 12yr/adult JD12/20); sunset cruise from 6pm to 9.30pm including a BBQ dinner on the beach (child/adult JD12/29); day-trip from 10am to 4pm to Pharaoh's Island in Egypt with a BBQ lunch (child/adult JD15/37).

Glass-Bottom Boats

If you don't have time to go diving or snorkelling, the next best thing is a glass-bottom

---

WORTH A TRIP

SUN & SAND COMBO TOURS FROM AQABA

Many come to Aqaba with limited time and try in vain to juggle a snorkle in the Red Sea with a trip to Wadi Rum. Given the lack of public transport, one way to do both in 36 hours is by using a single tour company.

With four or five boats operational in Aqaba, **Aquamarina Transportation Company** (☑2058557; www.aquamarina-aqaba.com; As-Sadah St; 1hr sunset cruise per person JD10) is leading the way in boat rides. It offers trips to Pharaoh Island (child under 12yr/adult JD12/35), three-hour glass-bottom boat rides between 3pm and 6pm (child/adult JD12/22) and popular one-hour sunset trips at 6pm (child/adult JD6/10). The price includes soft drinks.

The company also runs recommended overnight tours to its well-run Rahayeb Desert Camp (p224) in Diseh, near Wadi Rum. The tour leaves at 2pm and returns the next morning at 10am. The price (from JD60 per person, for one or more) includes a three-hour 4WD drive in the desert, dinner in a *zerb* oven, accommodation in a tented cabin with en-suite toilet, and a camel ride. This is perhaps the easiest and cheapest way to visit Rum from Aqaba in a short time period without your own transport.

Town Walk
Discovering Aqaba on Foot

START MÖVENPICK RESORT HOTEL
END MÖVENPICK RESORT HOTEL
LENGTH 3KM; TWO HOURS

Gain a sense of Aqaba's antiquity in the ❶ **ruins of Ayla** (p197): there has been a port at the mouth of the gulf for many centuries. From the Corniche, enter the ❷ **marina** to understand the town's strategic location, with Israel and Egypt just across the water and Saudi Arabia 14km to the south.

Returning to the Corniche, walk to the majestic ❸ **Al-Sharif Al-Hussein bin Ali Mosque**, recently renovated by the current king, and take the path opposite through the carefully tended allotments of spinach and radish to the ❹ **beach**. During holidays, the beach comes alive with picnicking locals; off season, you'll have the sand to yourself. Continue south to the large plaza at the base of the giant flag and cut inland to the ❺ **Aqaba Fort** (p198). Catch the cry of 'To Aqaba' as you pass through the giant wooden gates: this is where the Arab Revolt memorably ousted the Turks, with TE Lawrence in tow. Stand in the big man's shoes (or at least in his celebrity sandals) under the courtyard tree and watch the mountains turn ruby red at sunset.

Turn left onto the busiest section of the Corniche, dodging the invitations to snack at the town's popular shwarma vendors. Turn right up Ar-Razi St and first left, doglegging through the ❻ **fruit & vegetable souq** selling monumental mounds of eggplants. Turn left on Zahran St – or be led by your nose to the spice shops. ❼ **Trinket shops** punctuate the parade. Duck left through one of the alleyways and turn right onto Raghadan St for desserts from the famous pastry shops at the bend in the road or mezze at ❽ **Ali Baba Restaurant** (p203).

Cross the busy Amman Hwy to An-Nahda St, the teeming centre of modern Aqaba. Choose a fish restaurant for the catch of the day or share ❾ **coffee** and sheesha with locals along As-Sa'dah St. Turn left onto Ar-Rashid St by the ruins of an ❿ **ancient church**; a few paces will bring you to the Mövenpick Resort Hotel – a grand place for an end-of-tour ice cream.

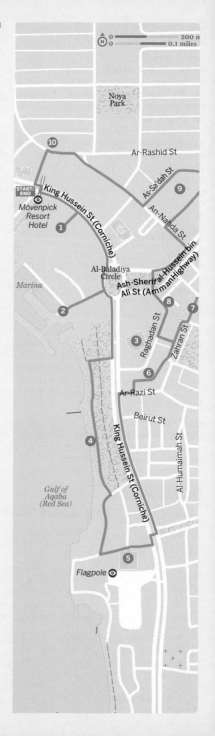

boat. The ride is fun, but the amount of fish and coral on view is usually disappointing unless you get away from central Aqaba. This entails hiring a boat for at least two to three hours.

Glass-Bottom Boat Dock BOAT TOUR
(from ½hr/1hr JD25/45; ☺6am-sunset) Boats congregate along the jetty in front of Aqaba Fort. The rate charged is per boat which holds about 10 people. Prices reflect demand so be prepared to bargain when it's busy. During any of the trips, you can swim, snorkel or fish (bring your own equipment).

Boats also leave from the **central public beach** and from Berenice Beach.

Neptune Submarine Vision BOAT TOUR
(☑9430969; www.aqababoat.com) A glass-bottom boat with a difference, the Neptune has a glass hull that is fully submersed allowing for a 360° view in what the company describes as a dry-dive experience. The self-styled 'underwater observatory' leaves daily from the Tala Bay marina, on the south coast.

Discounts are available from the Tala Bay Beach Club.

Hammams

Bab Al-Hara BATHHOUSE
(☑079 9663800; Ar-Rashid St; JD25; ☺9am-10pm) This spotlessly clean, friendly establishment offers steam bath, jacuzzi, foot and body massage and sauna, and there's a separate pool for women and families. The masseur and owner, Mr Raid, has years of experience and trained in Dubai and China. He describes his establishment as 'very safe for ladies' and women tourists have recommended him.

A one-hour oil massage costs an additional JD25.

Aqaba Turkish Baths BATHHOUSE
(☑2031605; King Hussein St; JD15; ☺10am-10pm) Offers the full works – massage, steam bath and scrubbing. The bath caters mainly for men although special arrangements can be made if women call in advance.

👉 Tours

There are a number of reliable travel agents in town offering diving and snorkelling trips and tours in Jordan. Some agencies organise day trips to Wadi Rum and Petra (from JD145 per person for a minimum of two; JD200 for one including entry tickets). The amount of time at either site is disappoint-

ingly brief but more rewarding than spending half the day waiting for public transport. Some of the more experienced agencies include the following.

International Traders TOUR
(☑2013757; www.traders.com.jo; Al-Hammamat al-Tunisieh St; ☺8.30am-11pm) Reliable and quality service.

Nyazi Tours TOUR
(☑2022801; www.nyazitours.com; King Hussein St; ☺8.30am-11pm) Recommended adventure tour company run by Nyazi Shaba'an, former director of Antiquities & Tourism in Petra. Camping, hiking, jeep tours and camel trips along Wadi Umran.

Wadi Rum Desert Services TOUR
(☑2063882; http://wadirumdesertservice.tripod.com; ☺8.30am-11pm) Located next to Al-Shami Restaurant, off Zahran St.

🛏 Sleeping

Aqaba is a popular place for Jordanian and Saudi tourists in winter (October to March), with the season and hotel rates peaking in April, May, October and November. Holidaymakers also flock to Aqaba from northern Jordan during long weekends and public holidays, especially around Eid al-Adha (immediately after the hajj). At these times, prices may increase by as much as 30% and you must book in advance.

Campers, overlanders and dive enthusiasts should consider staying at one of the camps along the beach south of Aqaba. The long-established camps have the budget sector well weighed off here.

Most hotels include satellite TV, air-conditioning and private bathroom with hot water. Most cheaper hotels don't include breakfast but can usually rustle up something uninspiring for around JD2 to JD5; better still, go for beans and *labneh* in the nearest cafe. On the whole, midrange accommodation in Aqaba offers better value for money. As for top-end accommodation, don't dismiss the big hotels as characterless chains: in Aqaba, as at the Dead Sea, each of these luxury complexes involves stunning design and pleasant landscaping.

Most hotels are on the free shuttle bus route to the Berenice Beach Club (p207).

Moon Beach Hotel HOTEL $
(☑2013316; ashrafsaad77@yahoo.com; King Hussein St; s/d/tr with sea view JD18/30/35; ❄) Near the fort, this is undoubtedly the best budget

option. The foyer is a welcoming mixture of heavy wooden furniture and photographs of old Aqaba. Most rooms have sea views, though the faded furnishings won't be to everyone's liking. The delightful family-run management easily makes up for the dodgy decor. Ask about the two-bedroom family suites for longer stays.

Al-Shula Hotel
HOTEL $

(📞 2015153; alshulahotel@yahoo.com; Raghadan St; s/d/tr JD25/30/35; ❄) With its black-and-white marble reception desk and painted mirrors, the Al-Shula makes quite a statement. Most rooms have views to the sea across the mosque complex – good for a 4.30am wake-up call! The hotel is in the heart of one of Aqaba's busiest restaurant streets.

Aqaba Gulf Hotel
HOTEL $$

(📞 2016636; www.aqabagulf.com; King Hussein St; r JD84; ❄@🛜☗) This tired old favourite (the only hotel in Aqaba with a tennis court) is just across the road from the Aqaba Gateway complex. The first hotel to be built in Aqaba, it has quite an honour roll of guests. The stained-wood, split-level dining room looks thoroughly dated, like the rest of the common-use areas, but this is not a criticism.

Captain's Hotel
BOUTIQUE HOTEL $$

(📞 2060710; www.captains.jo; An-Nahda St; s/d JD75/85; ❄@🛜☗) Aqaba's version of a boutique hotel, the Captain's began life as a fish restaurant (p204) – still flourishing on the ground floor – and evolved, one storey at a time, into this stylish accommodation. With copper-tiled flooring and compact rooms with Arabian-style furniture, this is an upmarket choice for a midrange price. Other facilities include sauna and jacuzzi.

Yafko Hotel
HOTEL $$

(📞 2042222; www.yafko.com; cnr Corniche & Prince Mohammed St; s/d JD25/45) Although not directly on the coast, you can sit in bed at this newly opened hotel and enjoy the sea views. Some rooms are an odd shape but the furnishings and stone trim make this an attractive choice. It is conveniently located near the fort, transport hubs and the road leading to the southern beaches.

Golden Tulip
HOTEL $$

(📞 2051234; www.goldentulipaqaba.com; As-Sadah St; s/d JD65/80, low-season weekdays JD35/50; ❄) This thoroughly recommended hotel in the centre of town is comfortable and modern. The foyer comes complete with a vocal African Grey parrot and karaoke bar. The rooms are cosy and bright but beware knees and elbows in the surprisingly small bathrooms. The reception desk is manned by a uniformly charming staff.

Al-Cazar Hotel
HOTEL $$

(📞 2014131; alcazarhotel.co; An-Nahda St; s/d/tr from JD35/40/50; ❄☗) If you're looking to stay somewhere with character, then book into this faded old grand dame of Aqaba, with its two dozen overgrown Washington palms in the front garden, an enormous empty lobby and a bar with outrageous filigree plaster. The spacious rooms have bathrooms with multiple mirrors and marble surfaces that must have looked grand in their day.

Aquavista Hotel
HOTEL $$

(📞 2051620; humanehabco@gmail.com; An-Nahda St; s/d incl breakfast JD45/55; ❄) The rooms in this functional, nondescript hotel are clean and comfortable – if you can look beyond the lime green walls and yellow ceilings. The staff are helpful, though, and the hotel is well-located for Aqaba's restaurants and nightlife.

★ InterContinental Hotel
RESORT $$$

(📞 2092222; www.intercontinental.com; King Hussein St; r from JD119; ❄@☗) An imposing full stop at the end of the bay, the InterCon boasts less of an infinity pool than an infinity sea: on a calm day, the Gulf of Aqaba stretches in one seamless ripple all the way to Egypt. With exceptional landscape gardening, pools and a lazy river, the InterCon has stolen the top spot in Aqaba's luxury accommodation.

Providing the kind of practical service that has made this chain a favourite throughout the Middle East, and with six restaurants and a shopping arcade among its many amenities, you won't want to move on in a hurry.

Mövenpick Resort Hotel
RESORT $$$

(📞 2034020; www.moevenpick-hotels.com; King Hussein St; r from JD196; ❄@☗) Spreadeagled across the main road, this stylish hotel has a palatial interior decorated with mosaics and Moroccan lamps. The huge pool and beach complex has three pools, a gym (open 6am to 10pm), lovely gardens and the Red Sea Grill. Other dining options include the Palm

Court, and Italian and Lebanese restaurants, both with outdoor terraces.

Kempinski Hotel
RESORT $$$

(☑ 2090888; www.kempinski.com; King Hussein St; r from JD245; ✳ @ ☒) Lavish, multilayered swimming pools, six restaurants and bars (including the renowned Fish Inn and Black Pearl) and a spa make this super-luxury hotel worth top dollar. Despite being more angular and austere than its neighbours, the service is flawless. A comprehensive tour service covers camping and balloon trips at Wadi Rum and overnight trips to Petra.

✗ Eating

Aqaba has a large range of places to eat to suit all budgets. The seafood is particularly delicious: try Aqaba's signature dish of *sayadieh* (fish layered onto rice with a tomato, onion and pepper sauce). For shwarma (meat sliced off a spit and stuffed in a pocket of pita-type bread with chopped tomatoes and garnish), grills and snacks, the dusty array of stalls and restaurants along King Hussein St spill onto the pavement and are popular with locals. For a wider choice of budget meals, have a prowl along Raghadan St – the eateries range from little more than a collection of open-air tables serving tea, hummus, fuul (fava-bean paste) and felafel, to larger restaurants.

There are plenty of modern and sophisticated restaurants in the newer part of town, especially along either side of As-Sadah St. Note that many restaurants do not have a license to sell alcohol.

On a hot day, stop by **Hani Ali** (Raghadan St) for traditional sweets and delicious ice cream, or **Gelato Uno** (off An-Nahda St) behind the Hertz car-rental office. For something similarly tasty, check out the **ice-cream parlour** and **cake shop** at the Mövenpick Resort Hotel and order a 'special' (from JD2.700 – you don't have to enter the hotel – there's access from King Hussein St).

Syrian Palace Restaurant
SYRIAN $

(☑ 2014788; Raghadan St; mains JD3-10; ⊘ 10am-midnight) As the name implies, this is a good option for Syrian and Jordanian cuisine, including fish. It's next to the Al-Amer Hotel.

Al-Tarboosh Restaurant
PASTRY $

(☑ 2018518; Raghadan St; pastries around 200 fils; ⊘ 7.30am-midnight) With the Arabic Moon, this is one of two neighbouring pastry shops

that offer a great range of meat, cheese and vegetable sambusas. Order a bag for takeaway or sit and eat them straight from the oven at the tables outside.

Cafes
CAFES $

(sandwiches JD2; ⊘ 10am-10pm (seasonal)) There are popular beachfront cafes between Aqaba Fort and the marina. The front-row seats are so close to the water that you can wet your toes while you whet your appetite. No alcohol is served at these public places. Some close in the low season.

★ Ali Baba Restaurant
JORDANIAN $$

(☑ 2013901; Raghadan St; mains JD9; ⊘ 8am-midnight; ✳ ☑) With its wooden awning, leafy cannas and potted palm trees, this favourite still draws the crowds. The outdoor seating area wrapped around the corner facade is a good vantage point for people-watching. In the evening the Ali Baba is more than just a restaurant – it's the amiable heart of old town Aqaba with alcohol served upstairs (available even in Ramadan).

Formosa Restaurant
CHINESE $$

(☑ 2060098; Aqaba Gateway complex; mains JD6-10; ⊘ noon-11pm; ✳ ☑) For an excellent Chinese perspective on Aqaba's seafood (and with plenty of meat and vegetable options on the menu too), you can't top this cosy, intimate restaurant. 'Our guests are part of the Formosa family', claim the Jordanian owner and his Taiwanese wife – a point proved by the many regulars who enjoy the atmosphere as much as the cuisine.

Rakwet Kanaan Restaurant & Cafe
JORDANIAN $$

(As-Sadah St; mains JD7.500; ⊘ 10am-1am) Selling a delicious range of Oriental pastries, cooked over firewood and liberally sprinkled with thyme, rosemary and sage, this restaurant is wrapped around the bend in the road where its pavement divans catch the breeze. The savoury dough platters are very filling so it's worth casting an eye at the size of the neighbour's portion before ordering your own!

Al-Mabrouk Beach Touristic Restaurant
SEAFOOD $$

(☑ 2063304; Raghadan St; mains JD10; ⊘ 9am-11.30pm; ✳) This attractive restaurant is a friendly and popular place for a large fish supper, with glass-top tables decorated with shells outside, or air-conditioned dining indoors. A local favourite is a pot of Al-Mabrouk fish, mussels, calamari and tomatoes (JD13).

Floka Restaurant SEAFOOD $$$
(☑ 2030860; An-Nahda St; mains JD8-15; ⊙ 12.30-11.30pm; ❋) Choose from the catch of the day (which normally includes sea bream, silver snapper, grouper and goatfish) and select how you would like it cooked. Service can be a little slow but it's a friendly, unpretentious establishment. There's indoor and outdoor seating.

★ **Royal Yacht Club Restaurant** ITALIAN $$$
(☑ 2022404; www.romero-jordan.com; Royal Yacht Club; mains JD10-18; ⊙ noon-11pm; ❋ ☑) With views of the marina, this elegant, wood-panelled restaurant is the place to savour a romantic sunset and mingle with Aqaba's nouveau riche. The mostly Italian menu includes Mediterranean favourites like crab, avocado, shrimp and artichoke salad, mussels Provençale and homemade vegetarian pasta. Making a reservations is recommended. Tax of 17% is added to the bill.

★ **Captain's Restaurant** SEAFOOD $$$
(☑ 2016905; An-Nahda St; mains JD8-15; ⊙ 8am-midnight; ❋) Serving consistently good quality seafood, including *sayad-ieh* (fish served with rice in an onion and tomato sauce) and seafood salad, this is a perennially popular choice for locals with something to celebrate. The stylish and amiable restaurant was so successful the owners built an entire hotel (p202) on the same site for those too full to make it home!

Self-Catering

Bakery BAKERY
(Al-Hammamat al-Tunisieh St; ⊙ 9am-9pm) One among many bakeries in town producing Arabic flat bread, biscuits and sometimes pastries and samosas.

Fruit and Vegetable Souq FRUIT MARKET
(Raghadan St; ⊙ 10am-7pm) The fruit and vegetable souq, hidden at the southern end of Raghadan St, is the best place to buy healthy, locally grown items for a picnic.

Humam Supermarket SUPERMARKET
(☑ 2015721; Al-Petra St; ⊙ 8.30am-2.30pm & 4-11pm) The best supermarket in town.

Safeway SUPERMARKET
(⊙ 8am-midnight) Quite a hike from downtown, located 750m north of Princess Haya Hospital.

♟ Drinking & Nightlife

Many of the midrange and all the top-end hotels have bars, and most offer some kind of happy hour from 6pm to 7.30pm. Around the As-Sadah St loop are a number of open-air coffeehouses with armchairs on the pavement, selling nargileh, coffee and soft drinks.

Juice Stands JUICE
(Ar-Razi St; ⊙ 10am-11pm) The juice stands on Ar-Razi St are popular meeting places for travellers.

Al-Fardos Coffee Shop COFFEEHOUSE
(⊙ 10am-midnight) Just off Zahran St, this is a traditional coffeehouse where local men sip *qahwa,* play backgammon and stare open-mouthed at Arabic music videos. It has a pleasant outdoor setting, and foreign women are welcome.

Rovers Return PUB
(☑ 2032030; Aqaba Gateway; ⊙ 12.30pm-12.30am) An aerial version of the Amman expat favourite (it's located in a mock lighthouse), this pub attracts a young crowd. If you're British and feeling homesick, stay for fish and chips or roast beef (JD9.500) and watch three-screen football. The only downside is that the compact space can get oppressively smoky.

Royal Yacht Club Bar BAR
(☑ 2022404; ⊙ 5-11pm) Above the Romero Restaurant in the marina, this is an elegant rendezvous with a harbourside view of the sunset.

Wisalak Cafe CAFE
(☑ 2022600; ⊙ 3pm-midnight) If you want to get off the road for a bit of peace and quiet, try this cosy cafe, which has an upstairs seating area.

Aqaba Gateway MALL
(☑ 2012200; Al-Baladiah Circle; ⊙ 10am-midnight) There's not too much in the way of entertainment in Aqaba but this mall at least offers a popular meeting point in the evening with a bar, a collection of restaurants, fast-food outlets and shops.

WORTH A TRIP

ON A WINTER'S DAY SOUTH OF AQABA YOU CAN...

➜ Snorkel or dive in safe hands at the Royal Diving Club (p31). The club offers a day rate of JD15 (child JD7) to use the beach, pool and other facilities – free if you're coming to dive.

➜ Learn about what's under the sea without getting your feet wet at the **Aquarium** (☑ 20 15145; admission JD3; ⊘ 8am-5pm). Part of the Marine Science Station complex (7.5km south of Aqaba), the aging and dated tanks nonetheless provide a colourful glimpse of coral, moray eels, turtles and stonefish.

➜ Laze under a sunshade on the free public beach at the **Marine Park Visitors Centre** (☑ 2035801). As the headquarters of the Aqaba Marine Park (12km south of Aqaba), it has a jetty, museum, cafe, gift shop and park office. It gets busy on Friday and overrun on public holidays.

➜ Mull over fishermen's tales and a mint-and-lime juice at Berenice Beach Club (p207). This diving centre (13.5km south of Aqaba) offers a good beach, swimming pools, showers, bar and restaurant.

➜ Explore a Crusader castle on **Pharaoh's Island** (safe to visit at the time of writing but check with the tour operator for the latest advice). Hotels can book day trips to the island (off Egypt's coast) for around JD40 per person, which includes the entrance fee to the island, Egyptian visa, lunch and transport.

🛍 Shopping

Aqaba is a fun place to shop, especially at night when Jordanian holidaymakers treat the shops as an excuse to cruise around in large groups, enjoying the company of strangers. Head for the souq in the older part of town, where shops are bulging at the seams with loofahs, colourful Arab headscarves, Dead Sea products and nuts and spices.

Aqaba is also a good place to buy jewellery, with a few gold and silver shops in the souq and several shops between King Hussein St and An-Nahda St selling beads of turqoise, amber and lapis lazuli. Red and pink beads of coral are also common components of local jewellery: these are usually sourced, as they have been for centuries, from the northern Mediterranean or from the Far East. If they are perfect, they are most likely synthetic. Check the provenance of the beads with the vendor to ensure they have not been sourced locally from rare stone corals, protected in the marine reserves.

South Kingdom Bazaar   SOUVENIRS
(Aqaba Gateway; ⊘ 9am-midnight) Selling all the old local favourites, from ostrich eggs and camel bone boxes to Dead Sea products.

Eibal Coffee   FOOD
(☑ 2035555; As-Sadah St; 1kg nuts from JD8.500; ⊘ 10am-midnight) For upmarket nuts scooped from wooden drawers, this is the place to come. Try the smoked nuts: the mixed pistachio, cashew and almonds are irresistibly moreish. Ask for a kilo of nuts to be bagged in 250g bags so that they don't go soft in the humidity.

Photo Hagop   PHOTOGRAPHY
(☑ 2012025; opposite Orange Telecom/Downtown; ⊘ 8.30am-11pm) Branches around town offer digital accessories.

Redwan Bookshop   BOOKS
(☑ 2013704; redwanbook@hotmail.com; Zahran St; ⊘ 7.30am-12.30pm & 4-9pm) One of the best bookshops in Jordan with an extensive selection of newspapers, hard-to-find Jordanian titles, Lonely Planet guidebooks, and English, German and French novels.

Yamani Library   BOOKS
(☑ /fax 2012221; Zahran St; ⊘ 9am-2.30pm & 6-10pm) Has a range of English novels.

ℹ Information

DANGERS & ANNOYANCES

Women travellers have reported varying degrees of harassment from local lads on the public beaches. Foreign women may feel less conspicuous wearing loose shirts and baggy shorts over a swimsuit, or, better still, using the facilities of one of the beach-side hotels in town or Berenice Beach along the southern coast. Bikinis are acceptable in either of the latter locations.

EMERGENCY

Police Station (☑191, 2012411; Ar-Reem St) Opposite the bus station.

Princess Haya Hospital (☑03-2014111; Ash-Shrif al-Hussein bin Ali St) Well-equipped and modern. It's just north of Princess Haya Square roundabout.

INTERNET ACCESS

Aqaba has a good sprinkling of internet cafes, particularly along As-Sadah St, most of which charge around JD1 to JD2 per hour.

10zll Internet Cafe (☑2022009; As-Sadah St; per hr JD2; ☺24hr) Next to Days Inn, this large establishment offers a reliable, fast and continually updated service. In fact this is not your average net cafe: with fish, budgies and potted cacti, it lives up to the owner's vision of a 'beautiful net experience'.

MONEY

There are dozens of banks and ATMs around the city. Many are located along the southern side of Al-Hammamat al-Tunisieh St.

Numerous moneychangers are congregated around the corner of Zahran and Ar-Razi Sts. They keep longer hours than the banks.

POST

DHL (☑2011385, 2012039; Al-Petra St)

General Post Office (☺7.30am-7pm Sat-Thu, to 1.30pm Fri) Opposite Zahran St in the centre of town.

TELEPHONE

There are a number of telephone booths outside the general post office, and several stalls nearby sell telephone cards. Other private telephone agencies are located on the main streets, and some moneychangers also offer telephone services. Note that international calls from Aqaba are up to five times cheaper than in Wadi Rum.

TOURIST INFORMATION

Tourist Office (☑/fax 2013363; Baladiya Circle; ☺8am-2.30pm Sun-Thu) Located in a kiosk in the middle of a new park between carriageways, the tourist office just east of the roundabout has lots of leaflets and precious little else despite friendly staff. There's another branch inside Aqaba Museum.

VISA EXTENSIONS

Aqaba Special Economic Zone Authority (ASEZA; ☑2091000; www.aqabazone.com; Ash-Sherif al-Hussein bin Ali St-Amman Hwy) Opposite Safeway. You need to register here if you were given a free visa on arrival in Aqaba and plan to stay in Jordan for more than 14 days. The website has some useful information about Aqaba. You can also extend visas at the police station (p206).

❶ Getting There & Away

AIR

King Hussein International Airport

(☑2034010; www.aac2.info) Aqaba has Jordan's only commercial airport outside Amman, although it only awakes from slumber when a flight is about to leave or arrive. It's located 10km north of town. There's no bus to the airport, so take service taxi 8 (15 minutes, around JD2) from the main bus/minibus station, or take a taxi for around JD8 to JD10.

There are daily flights to Amman and intermittent charter flights.

Royal Jordanian (☑2018633; www.rj.com; Ash-Sherif al-Hussein bin Ali St; ☺9am-5pm Sun-Thu) Operates daily flights to Amman's Queen Alia International Airport. Its office at the airport is the place to buy, confirm or change Royal Jordanian or Royal Wings air tickets. Tickets to Amman cost from JD64 one way, JD139 return.

Royal Wings (www.royalwings.com.jo) A subsidiary of Royal Jordanian, offering expensive charter flights.

BOAT

At the time of writing, it was safe to travel to Sharm El Sheikh. Travel to Nuweiba and Taba, however, was considered inadvisable due to the heightened security threat in the upper part of Sinai. The situation changes rapidly, so check the latest advisories issued by your consulate before travelling.

Buy your ticket at the ferry terminal when departing, except during hajj when you may need to book in advance. See Getting There & Away in the Transport section for further information.

Sindbad Marine Transportation (☑079 6608084; www.sindbadjo.com) This private company offers a 30-minute shuttle service by high-speed catamaran to Taba (not running at the time of writing due to political instability in the area and flood damage) and to Sharm el Sheikh. Bookings are best made through a local travel agent in Aqaba.

BUS

JETT Bus Office (☑2015222; King Hussein St) Next to the Mövenpick Resort Hotel, buses run five times daily to Amman's North Station (JD9, five hours), between 7am and 5pm. The office is a 10-minute walk from the centre. Book tickets for these at least a day in advance. Buses leave from outside the office.

JETT Bus Office (☑2032200; just off An-Nahda St) More of an office than a bus station, it operates one of two JETT bus services in Aqaba. There are five daily buses to Amman's south station (JD7, four hours) between 8am and 9pm. Book a day in advance.

CAR

Aqaba has branches of all the major car-hire agencies. Most charge a 'drop fee' (JD35) if you wish to leave the car in Amman or at Queen Alia International Airport. Hiring in Aqaba makes some sense as public transport in the south of the country is less frequent and requires more connections than in the north. Aqaba is also far easier to drive around than Amman. The cost of car hire is between JD35 to JD45 for a small- or medium-sized car per day, plus a collision damage waiver (average JD10-12 per day). Enquire about seasonal discounts. Reservations are necessary.

Al-Cazar Car Rental (☑ 2014131; An-Nahda St)

Avis (☑ 2022883; www.avis.com.jo; King Hussein St) Located inside the Housing Bank Centre.

Europcar (☑ 2019988; www.europcar.com.jo; An-Nahda St)

Hertz (☑ 2016206; www.hertz.com.jo; An-Nahda St)

Thrifty (☑ 2030313; An-Nahda St) Opposite the Al-Cazar Hotel.

MINIBUS

To Wadi Musa (for Petra) two minibuses (JD5, 2½ hours) leave when full, departing between 6am and 7am and between 11am and noon; the exact departure times depend on the number of passengers and you may have a long wait as very few locals use this service. Drivers often offer passengers the option, however, to leave with a minimum of four to five people providing each passenger pays extra.

Two minibuses go to Wadi Rum (JD3, one hour) at around 6.30am and, more reliably, 11am.

Minibuses to Amman's south station (JD6, five hours) leave when full – approximately every three hours throughout the day.

All of the above minibuses leave from the **main Aqaba bus/minibus station** (Ar-Reem St). Minibuses to Karak and Tafila (JD3.500, three hours), via Safi and the Dead Sea Highway, are the exception, leaving from the small station next to the mosque on Al-Humaimah St.

TAXI & SERVICE TAXI

From the main bus/minibus station, service taxis head to Amman (JD11, five hours), but far less regularly than buses and minibuses. To Karak (JD6, three hours) they leave from the small station on Al-Humaimah St. Service taxis start lining up at either station at 6am and many have left by 8am, so get there early. Chartering a taxi costs around JD60 one way to Petra (JD80 return) and JD40 to Wadi Rum (JD50 with two hours of waiting time).

Chartering a taxi to the south coast beaches costs JD12, and between Aqaba and the Israel and the Palestinian Territories border it costs around JD10.

ⓘ Getting Around

TO/FROM THE AIRPORT

Aqaba's King Hussein Airport (p206) is located 10km north of town, close to the border with Israel and the Palestinian Territories. There's no bus to the airport, so take service taxi 8 (around JD2, 15 minutes) from the main bus/minibus station, or take a taxi for around JD8 to JD10.

TO/FROM THE FERRY TERMINAL & SOUTHERN COAST

Minibuses (JD1) leave from near the entrance to Aqaba Fort on King Hussein St for the Saudi border via the southern beaches, camps, dive sites and Royal Diving Centre, passing the ferry terminal for boats to Egypt. Minibuses returning to Aqaba can be full of construction workers heading off shift from 2pm to 3pm. A taxi from central Aqaba to the ferry terminal costs around JD8 (JD12 to the southern beaches).

TAXI

Hundreds of private (blue-green) taxis cruise the streets beeping at any tourist (Jordanian or foreign) silly enough to walk around in the heat rather than take an air-conditioned taxi. Taxis are unmetered so prices are entirely negotiable, and the drivers in Aqaba enjoy the sport. Most rides cost from JD3 to JD5. A horse-drawn 'taxi' costs around JD25 for a 30-minute ride.

South Coast

There is only 27km of Jordanian coastline between Israel and the Palestinian Territories and Saudi Arabia. Much of the northern section of shoreline is paved over by the town and container ports of Aqaba. The shore south of the port is protected within the **Red Sea Marine Peace Park**, and is run in cooperation with Israel and the Palestinian Territories; it is managed locally by the Aqaba Marine Park. Resorts and dive centres are scattered along this precious seaside and the reefs here are in good condition. The Red Sea in this northern end of the Gulf of Aqaba is highly saline; this, together with winds from the north and minimal tides, means the water stays crystal clear, while the average water temperature is 22.5°C in winter and 26°C in summer.

🏃 Activities

★**Berenice Beach Club**   WATER SPORTS
(www.berenice.com.jo; JD15; ⊙ 9am-sunset) The only dedicated, private beach club on the south coast, Berenice has pools, a jetty giving

access to a coral reef, a dive centre, watersports, restaurants and spotless changing rooms. It attracts record crowds on Fridays. It offers a 50% discount for guests of many Aqaba hotels and operates a regular free shuttle bus service (check the website for current schedule).

As part of the Sindbad group, it also organises a variety of boat trips, including to Pharaoh Island. The club is not open to single men.

Tala Bay Beach Club WATER SPORTS
(☑ 9430949; www.aqababoat.com; JD10) With three pools, a pool bar, restaurants, waterskiing, jet-skiing, parasailing, windsurfing, kite boarding, kayaking, sailing, diving and snorkelling, this beach club, within the Tala Bay complex, caters to all levels of energy. Day entry to the beach includes transport on the shuttle bus from Aqaba.

🛏 Sleeping & Eating

There are three main types of accommodation along the South Coast: the hotel attached to the Royal Diving Club at the far southern end of the beach, the budget and traveller-friendly camps clustered around the Bedouin Garden Village, and the luxury hotels of the Tala Bay complex. All include breakfast and have on-site bars and restaurants. They usually provide a free daily shuttle service into Aqaba for their guests. Snorkelling gear can be hired from each hotel for around JD5 for all-day use, and hotels can arrange water-bound activities with the neighbouring dive centres.

Bedouin Garden Village HOTEL $
(☑ 079 5602521; camping per person JD15, s/d/tr/q JD26/40/50/60, meals JD5-9; 🕸 🎧 🕸) Only a 50m walk from a dive site, this funky little spot offers a clutch of cosy rooms and camping pitches. The highlight is swapping stories with fellow travellers beneath the Bedouin tent. This is one of the few places where caravans are catered for: a surcharge of JD10 per night covers parking fees and use of the hotel's wash room and other facilities.

Coral Bay Resort RESORT $$
(☑ 2015555; s/d on weekdays JD70/75, weekends JD75/85; 🕸 @ 🎧 🕸) ✈ Part of the Royal Diving Club, this is a popular, eco-friendly dive centre with a good reputation. If you're planning on taking a dive course or arranging a lengthy dive package, this makes a good base. Accommodation is in simple rooms with bright motifs and there's a sociable bar.

★**International Arab Divers Village** GUESTHOUSE $$
(☑ 2031808; www.aqabadive.com; dm/s/d/tr/family JD15/35/45/60/80, meals JD12-15; 🕸 🎧 🕸) Up hill from the hurly-burly of the coast and with great views across the Gulf of Aqaba from the rooftop terrace, this competent, homely place attracts those with a serious interest in exploring the Red Sea and returning to relax over a beer in the garden. The attached dive centre has a very good reputation.

Marina Plaza Hotel BOUTIQUE HOTEL $$$
(☑ 2092900; www.marinaplazahotel.com; r from JD85; 🕸 @ 🎧 🕸) ✈ This luxury hotel is located within the Tala Bay complex, which comprises five-star hotels, residences, a

---

STONE CORALS – UNIQUE TO AQABA

A quick peak at the Aquarium (p205) along the South Coast quickly establishes the pedigree of underwater wildlife along this part of the Red Sea. It won't come as any surprise that this part of the coast attracts international underwater photographers, drawn to the clarity of a sea with almost no current, and the relative ease of filming colourful sea slugs, frog fish and seahorses while standing in the shallows.

What is less anticipated is that this part of the coast attracts those in the know for another reason: it is home to a great diversity of stone corals. According to local experts, there are over 100 different varieties of these marine creatures visible in local dive sites.

Corals, which are generally classified into two main categories, hard and soft, are living marine invertebrates whose exoskeletons fuse together to form coral reefs. Stone corals have been used in the crafting and carving of jewellery for thousands of years and it remains a respected occupation of local master jewellers. The trade in this natural gem, however, is on the decline as attention turns towards preservation and protection of corals in their natural habitat. Growing in dark shady places on the ocean floor, these remarkable corals take some skill in identification – ask at International Arab Divers (p208) for a guide to their location.

marina, a golf course and a water-sports club. The developers have worked hard to minimise their impact on the environment, as demanded by the Red Sea Aqaba Marine Park, and the complex is well landscaped.

As is often the case with these complexes, however, it is detached from any sense of being in Jordan, except on public holidays when Jordanians flood in!

❶ Getting There & Around

If you're staying in Aqaba and planning on going diving, most operators will arrange transport to the dive sites and there are free shuttle buses to Berenice Beach from many hotels.

Minibuses (JD2) leave from near the entrance to Aqaba Fort on King Hussein St for the Saudi border via the southern beaches, camps, dive sites and Royal Diving Club, passing the ferry terminal for boats to Egypt. A taxi from central Aqaba to the ferry terminal costs JD8.

WADI RUM & AROUND

Western visitors have been fascinated by the magnificent landscape of Wadi Rum ever since TE Lawrence wrote so evocatively about its sculpted rocks, dunes and Bedouin encampments in *Seven Pillars of Wisdom* in the early 20th century:

> The crags were capped in nests of domes, less hotly red than the body of the hill; rather grey and shallow. They gave the finishing semblance of Byzantine architecture to this irresistible place: this processional way greater than imagination... Our little caravan grew self-conscious, and fell dead quiet, afraid and ashamed to flaunt its smallness in the presence of the stupendous hills.

The name Wadi Rum lends itself not just to the broad valley of Lawrence's description, but to a whole series of hills and dunes stretching north to south for over 100km. The central valley, 900m above sea level, fans into an arena dominated by Jebel Rum (1754m), once considered the highest peak in Jordan – an accolade that actually belongs to Jebel Umm Adaami (1832m) on the Saudi border.

The area has been protected since 1988 and is controlled by the Aqaba Special Economic Zone Authority (ASEZA), which has a mandate to promote tourism for the benefit of local communities while protecting the fragile desert environment. With over 100,000 visitors per year using 600 4WDs, this is no mean feat.

Of course, the stewardship of the desert is shared with the local Bedouin who have been roaming the area for centuries. Many of the 5000 Bedouin remaining in the area have now opted for a settled life in the villages of Rum, Diseh and Shakriyyeh but, certainly as far as they are concerned, that does not make them any less Bedouin.

Although not part of the Wadi Rum protected area, the desert spills in equal magnificence into neighbouring areas including Diseh. The sandstone monuments and intervening sand dunes are a feature of Jordan's Southern Desert that stretches right to the Saudi border to the south while running out into the plains of the Badia in the northeast.

The most comfortable months for a visit are early spring (March and April) and late autumn (October and November). Winter (December to February) is bitterly cold and summer (May to September) miserably hot: with temperatures of 40°C, this is when you really come to know the meaning of desert! Nighttime temperatures can fall to 0°C throughout the year, so come prepared if you're camping or watching the sunset.

Wadi Rum   وادي رم

🗓 03 / ELEV 950M

Wadi Rum is everything you'd expect of a quintessential desert: it is extreme in summer heat and winter cold; it is violent and moody as the sun slices through chiselled siqs (canyons) at dawn or melts the division between rock and sand at dusk; it is exacting on the Bedouin who live in it and vengeful on those who ignore its dangers. For most visitors, on half- or full-day trips from Aqaba or Petra, Wadi Rum offers one of the easiest and safest glimpses of the desert afforded in the region. For the lucky few who can afford a day or two in their itinerary to sleep over at one of the desert camps, it can be an unforgettable way of stripping the soul back to basics.

History

With its many wells and springs, Wadi Rum has been inhabited since prehistoric times. Petroglyphs and burial mounds appear throughout the area, indicating its importance as a hunting and meeting point in ancient times. It was referred to by the Greeks and Romans, who noted its vineyards (now gone), and olive and pine trees (some of

LAWRENCE OF ARABIA

You can't visit Wadi Rum and fail to bump into Lawrence. The legacy of the esoteric Englishman is everywhere – there's even a mountain named *Seven Pillars of Wisdom*, after his famous account of the Arab Revolt. Lawrence's ubiquitous local evocation is something of a cynical one, mind, designed to cash in on the chiefly foreign fascination with this legendary figure.

Lawrence the Legend

It was largely thanks to the promotion of *Seven Pillars of Wisdom* by an American journalist in 1926 that the Lawrence legend was born. In this adventurous account of derring-do, much of which takes place in the desert in and around Wadi Rum, Lawrence casts himself in the role of trusted adviser, brave soldier and ultimately a messiah figure of the Arab cause. However, that was not necessarily how he was regarded from an Arab perspective. Indeed for some he was 'Lawrence Who?' – one among 100,000 Arabs, 10% of whom died in their epic struggle to build a nation.

The Man Behind the Myth

So what are the facts? Born in 1888 into a wealthy English family, Thomas Edward Lawrence ('TE' to his friends) nurtured an early passion for the Middle East. He studied archaeology at Oxford and became bewitched by the region in 1909 while researching his thesis on Crusader castles. With the outbreak of WWI, Lawrence became a natural choice for the intelligence service in Cairo, where he became attached to the Hejaz Expeditionary Force. Lawrence felt a natural sympathy towards the fomenting Arab Revolt, the objective of which was to oust the Turks and create an Arab state. Learning to ride camels with the best of them, and wearing Arab clothing like so many other English adventurers before him, Lawrence accompanied the armies of the great Arab warrior (and later statesman) Emir Faisal in 1917 and learned a respect for his comrades that lasted a lifetime. Lawrence died in a motorcycle accident in 1935 – a lone and isolated figure, by all accounts, who never fully found in peacetime the sense of purpose and passion he experienced with his Arab comrades in the desert.

Lawrence's Legacy

Some say that Lawrence was embarrassed by the hero status conferred upon him by an adoring English public (in 1927 he changed his name to Shaw and chose to enrol as a private in the RAF); others say he did nothing to put his contribution into a more historically accurate perspective. But Lawrence's legacy is best judged not so much in terms of his disputed military accomplishments, eccentric and brave though they may be, but in the way he immortalised (at least for Western readers) some of the great characters of modern Arab history. It is not just the hallowed names of Auda and Faisal that ring out of the desert at Wadi Rum; to his credit, Lawrence also describes with great tenderness the ordinary foot soldiers of the Arab cause who gave their lives for a brave new world. In the process, Lawrence immortalised forever the magnificence of the Bedouin landscape from which these soldiers hailed, inspiring generations of visitors to see for themselves the wonder of Rum.

which remain on the mountaintops). Some Islamic scholars claim that this is the location of an ancient Arab tribe, the Ad, described in the Quran.

About 30,000 inscriptions decorate Wadi Rum's sandstone cliffs. They were made first by tribes from Southern Arabia and later by the Nabataeans who settled in Wadi Rum around the 4th century BC. The two tribes lived peacefully side by side, honouring the same deities of Lat and Dushara.

The region owes its fame, however, to the indefatigable TE Lawrence, who stayed here in 1917 during the Arab Revolt – a campaign led by King Hussein bin Ali against the Ottoman Turks in a bid to establish an independent Arab nation. The king's camel- and horse-mounted troops passed through Wadi Rum on their way to conquer Aqaba and some units (including that of Lawrence) returned to use the area as a temporary base before moving north towards Damascus.

The discovery of a Nabataean temple (behind the Rest House) in 1933 briefly returned the spotlight to the desert. A French team of archaeologists completed the excavations in 1997.

Flora & Fauna

Despite its barren appearance, Wadi Rum is home to a complex ecosystem. Small medicinal plants dot the desert and are used to this day by the Bedouin, and during the infrequent rains parts of the desert bloom with over 200 species of flowers and wild grasses. Around the perennial springs, hanging gardens of fig, fern, mint and wild watermelon topple over the rocks, creating shaded lairs for small mammals, birds and reptiles.

For most of the year, the extreme heat and lack of ground water mean that animals only venture out at night. If you sit tight, you may well see a hedgehog, hare or hyrax (a small furry animal implausibly related to the elephant). If you're extremely lucky, you could catch a glimpse of a jackal, wolf, caracal or giant-horned ibex. Sadly, you are not likely to see the highly endangered Arabian oryx, a small group of which were released into Wadi Rum in 2002 but which didn't like the new accommodation and set out for the rocky plains of neighbouring Saudi Arabia. A new program of reintroduction in a less sandy neighbourhood of Rum, supported by the United Arab Emirates, is so far meeting with more success.

This is big-bird country and there is usually a raptor or two (including sooty falcons, kestrels and eagle owls) circling on the thermals above the desert floor, on the lookout for the desert's plentiful geckos, agamas and lizards. If you see a scorpion, snake or camel spider, count yourself lucky, as they are all shy residents of Rum.

⊙ Sights

Visitor Centre Museum   MUSEUM
(⊙8am-6pm) **FREE** While you are buying your ticket to enter Wadi Rum, spare half an hour to visit the informative museum (next to the restaurant) which helps to give a human context to the desert. The displays also explain environmental issues through information panels in English and natural-history exhibits. Ask to see the 10-minute film on some of the highlights of Wadi Rum, shown in the purpose-built cinema.

Seven Pillars of Wisdom   ROCK FORMATION
Named in honour of Lawrence's book, this large rock formation, with seven fluted turrets, is easy to see from the road. If you fancy a closer look, a rewarding hike circumnavigates the mountain via **Makharas Canyon**.

WADI RUM ITINERARY BUILDER

Even with only have a few hours to spend, you can enjoy some of what Wadi Rum has to offer. Below is a suggestion of what you can do in a given time under your own steam. Obviously, the longer you stay, the more your eyes (and heart) open to the desert. For more on hitching, see p222.

WITH THIS TIME...	YOU CAN GO THIS FAR...	AND DO THIS MUCH
En route to elsewhere	Visitor Centre	Have a panoramic view of Wadi Rum (lit up magnificently at sunset).
One hour	Visitor Centre	Enjoy a leisurely lunch overlooking Wadi Rum, then visit the museum.
Two hours	Rum Village	Walk through Wadi Rum on the tarmac road (7km) as far as Rum Village, snack at the Rest House and hitch a lift back.
Three hours	Lawrence's Spring	Hitch a ride to Rum Village and hike through the sand to Nabataean Temple & Lawrence's Spring.
Half day	Al-Hasany Dunes	Time your hike from Rum Village to the sands to coincide with sunset.
Overnight	Desert Camp	Book your accommodation at a Wadi Rum camp through the visitor centre (4WD transport included) or pay extra to ride there by camel.
Two days	Wadi Rum & Diseh Area	Choose a Wadi Rum camp near Barrah Canyon, then hike through the canyon (5km) to a Diseh camp for the following night.

Wadi Rum

	0	5 km
	0	2.5 miles

Desert Hwy (5km)

15

16

17 Shakariya Village

Abu Hawl (7km)

Jebel Amud

Jebel Umm Salab

Wadi Rum Protected Area

Freight line only

Diseh

Permanent Campsite
Temporary Campsite

25
12 Tell Hassan

Wadi Leyyah

Makharas Canyon

24

21
13
18 Umm Nfoos
5

Thamudic & Kufic Rock Art

(1753m)

Jebel Umm al-Ishrin

Wadi Umm al-Ishrin

Jebel Rum (1754m)

22

Rakhabat Canyon

Kharazeh Canyon

Jebel Barrah

Jebel Abu Judayda

11

9 Rum Village

Jebel Umm Ejil

Jebel Faishiyya

7

Al-Hasany Dunes
6

Al-Hasany Dunes
1

Wadi al-Kheweimilat

4

Jebel Umm Ulaydiyya

8

Wadi al-Bgaina

Barrah Canyon

Jebel Mahraq

Khazali Siq 3

10

23

Jebel Qattar

19 Jebel Khazali

20

Umm Sabatah

Jebel Qaber Amra

Jebel Burdah

Wadi Rum Protected Area

14

2 Burdah Rock Bridge

Jebel Umm Fruth

Jebel Umm Adaami

Wadi Rum

Jebel Umm al-Ishrin　　　　　　MOUNTAIN

The deeply crevassed 'Mother of Twenty', a 20-domed mountain forming the east flank of Wadi Rum, is connected to the Seven Pillars of Wisdom formation. The mountain acquired its name, according to local legend, after a woman killed 19 suitors; she was outwitted by the 20th, so she married him. The whole range turns a magnificent white-capped auburn during sunset.

Jebel Rum　　　　　　MOUNTAIN

The western flank of Wadi Rum is formed by Jebel Rum (1754m) which towers over Wadi Rum village. It is a popular destination for scramblers and climbers who tackle parts of the ancient Thamudic Way to the summit (guide required – ask at the visitor centre; see p219 for more info). Similar pathways, once used for hunting ibex and collecting medicinal plants, link one massif to another throughout the area giving limitless scope for hiking, scrambling and climbing.

Rum Village & Village Plaza　　　VILLAGE

Rum village, in the middle of Wadi Rum, houses a small community of Bedouin who have chosen to settle rather than continue a more traditional nomadic life. The village has a rest house, restaurants and a couple of grocery shops. It also has the last piece of tarmac before the desert proper. The small, squat Rum Fort is currently closed to the public.

Nabataean Temple　　　　　　RUIN

On a small hill in Rum village, about 400m behind the Rest House (follow the telephone poles), are the limited ruins of a 2000-year-old temple, dedicated to the deity Lat. Inside the Rest House an information board describes the temple and its excavation. The ruins are important because they are evidence of a permanent Nabataean settlement, built on the earlier foundations of a temple built by the Arab tribe of Ad.

The baths in a villa behind the temple are the earliest so far discovered in Jordan. Near the temple are some inscriptions by hunters and nomads dating back to the 2nd century BC.

**Lawrence's Spring
(Ain Ash-Shallalah)**　　　　　SPRING

This spring, on the edge of the open sands, is a regular stop on the 4WD circuit. Alternatively, it can be reached on a soft sand hike from the Rest House; the walk takes about 1½ hours return. Look for a white water tank at the opening of Wadi Shallalah. After the tank, a path climbs the hill to the spring.

The spring was named in honour of Lawrence's evocative description in the *Seven Pillars of Wisdom*:

> In front of us a path, pale with use, zigzagged up the cliff-plinth... From between [the] trees, in hidden crannies

NAVIGATING WADI RUM

Highway to Visitor Centre

Wadi Rum is accessed from a tarmac road off the main Desert Highway, an hour's drive from Aqaba. The road is flanked at first by fields of watermelons, but shortly after crossing the Hejaz railway line the splendid scenery begins, becoming increasingly spectacular as you reach the mouth of Wadi Rum. The road passes a police post and the junction for the small village of Diseh and continues towards the visitor centre (p222). This is where all visitors to Wadi Rum must report before venturing further into the valley.

Even if you don't have time to spend a whole day at Wadi Rum, it is worth coming as far as the visitor centre. From this attractive complex you can see Lawrence's **Seven Pillars of Wisdom** (a striking rock formation at the head of the valley), visit the museum, watch a short film about the desert, have lunch and get an idea of what Rum is all about. This is also where you pay the admission fee if you want to proceed further into the valley.

Visitor Centre to Rum Village

Beyond the visitor centre, the road is initially lined by a battered set of 4WDs, accompanied by their Bedouin drivers awaiting the next fare in rotation. The tarmac road continues for 7km to the village of Rum. The village, wedged between the towering dome-capped pillars of Wadi Rum, has a few concrete houses, a school, some shops and the Beau Geste–style fort, headquarters of the much-photographed Desert Patrol.

Again, if you don't have much time or can't afford one of the 4WD tours, consider at least reaching the village (you can drive in your own car, hitch or walk after paying the entrance fee). In the village, there's a pleasant rest house with an outside terrace and basic camping facilities.

Rum Village to Desert Interior

To penetrate the desert beyond the village of Rum, you must either have organised a 4WD trip from the visitor centre, booked a camel or be prepared for an exhausting hike through soft sand. With your own 4WD you can make your own way in, provided you know how to drive and navigate off-road in sand.

Beyond the village of Rum, the tarmac runs out and numerous tracks take over, slithering through the soft sand of Wadi Rum to an open area of converging valleys. From here, tracks lead to various points of interest such as rock bridges, desert mushrooms and yardangs. Most 4WD and camel tours make a circular route through the intersecting wadis of the area before returning to the visitor centre.

Outside this heavily visited area is a portion of desert known as the **Wilderness Area**. It is forbidden to take a 4WD into this protected zone but you can hike there with a guide.

For overnight stays, there are several Bedouin campsites with rudimentary facilities within Wadi Rum and the neighbouring Diseh area, on the rim of the reserve.

Books & Maps

If you are planning any hikes and scrambles, bring a detailed guidebook and map; if you plan to do some serious hiking and rock climbing, it's vital to organise a guide in advance.

British climber Tony Howard has spent a lot of time exploring Wadi Rum, and has co-written with Di Taylor the excellent and detailed *Treks & Climbs in Wadi Rum, Jordan* and a pocket-sized version called *Walks & Scrambles in Wadi Rum*. Treks and climbs around Wadi Rum are also mentioned in Howard and Taylor's *Walking in Jordan*. Buy these books before arriving in Wadi Rum.

The free Wadi Rum brochure has a map showing the major sites and is available from the visitor centre. The 1997 *Map of Rum* is contoured and detailed for a small section of northern Wadi Rum (ie around Rum village). The most detailed and informative map is *Wadi Rum Tourist Plan*, published by International Traditional Services Corp, but it's not widely available.

of the rock, issued strange cries; the echoes, turned into music, of the voices of the Arabs watering camels at the springs which there flowed out three hundred feet above ground.

Together with other springs in the area, this natural water spout that tumbles into a leafy 'paradise just five feet square' allowed Rum to become an important waterhole for caravans travelling between Syria and Arabia. Look out for a small shrine dedicated to Lat, an aqueduct used to channel the water from the spring and inscriptions on the rock face. Notice too the aroma of mint in the air: it grows wild among the ferns and trees of this shady place.

Ain Abu Aineh   SPRING
Often mistaken for Lawrence's Spring, the 'Father of Aineh Spring' is piped down the mountain into a large tank for Bedouin sheep, goats and camels. Look out for a large boulder near the tank: it is covered with Thamudic inscriptions, proving the spring has been used for a similar purpose for millennia. To reach Ain Abu Aineh, head south from the Rest House and follow the eastern side of Jebel Rum for 3km (a 1½-hour walk in soft sand).

The site in itself is not particularly special but the views across to Jebel Khazali are wonderful, especially at sunset when the whole amphitheatre of stone and sand turns orange.

Lawrence's House (Al-Qsair)   RUIN
There is little left of this building, erected on the Nabataean ruins of a water cistern. Nonetheless, legend has it that Lawrence stayed here during the Arab Revolt and that makes it a must on the regular 4WD circuits of the area. Near the building is a Nabataean inscription that mentions the area's ancient name of Iram. The remote location and uninterrupted view of the **red sand dunes** are the main attraction.

★Al-Hasany Dunes   SAND DUNES
While there are dunes in several places around Wadi Rum, the most striking are the red sands that bank up against Jebel Umm Ulaydiyya. If you are on a 4WD tour, drivers will stop near a pristine slope for you to plod your way to the crest of the dune. To reach the dunes on foot from the visitor centre takes three hours, partly through soft sand. They're particularly lovely at sunset.

Alameleh Inscriptions   PETROGLYPHS
Thamudic and Nabataean inscriptions, depicting camel caravans, hunting warriors and various animals, are common throughout the Wadi Rum area. The Alameleh inscriptions, near the Seven Pillars of Wisdom and on the edge of the Diseh district, are some of the most comprehensive and best preserved.

Anfaishiyya Inscriptions   PETROGLYPHS
The Anfaishiyya inscriptions are scratched into the smooth surface of a huge, vertical rock face.

Rock Bridges
There are many chiselled rock formations in the area, where the wind has whittled away the softer parts of the sandstone, leaving the tortured forms of harder rock behind. The most striking of these formations are the natural bridges that arch from one rock mass to another. You can see several of these bridges around the area, but there are three famous ones known as Burdah, Umm Fruth and Little Rock Bridge.

★Burdah Rock Bridge   ROCK FORMATION
The largest of Rum's three arches is the Burdah Rock Bridge, precariously perched about 80m above surrounding rock. There's a precipitous hike to the summit.

Umm Fruth Rock Bridge   ROCK FORMATION
Best seen in the late afternoon light, Umm Fruth Rock Bridge is tucked away in a remote corner of the desert and can be easily climbed without gear or a guide.

Little Rock Bridge   ROCK FORMATION
(Rakhabat al-Wadak) Easy to climb, this bridge offers great views across a broad expanse of desert.

Siqs & Canyons
★Khazali Siq   CANYON
An easy siq to explore is the narrow fissure that cuts into Jebel Khazali. You can explore on foot for about 150m, far enough to appreciate the cool shade and to see inscriptions made by the ancients who used the siq for the same purpose. Look out for drawings of ostriches, pairs of feet and a woman giving birth. You need ropes and a guide to penetrate further and 4WD transport to reach the siq.

Siq Umm Tawaqi   CANYON
A popular destination by 4WD is Siq Umm Tawaqi, a beautiful area with mature trees

sprouting apparently from the rock face. Locals have carved the humorous likeness of TE Lawrence (complete with Arab headdress) and two other prominent figures of the Arab Revolt into a stone plinth in the middle of the siq.

Barrah Canyon CANYON
One of the most visited of numerous canyons that riddle Wadi Rum, this 5km-long corridor of rock through the mountains offers opportunities for hiking, camel trekking, climbing or simply napping in the shade and absorbing the special atmosphere of Wadi Rum's hidden heartland.

🏃 Activities

Although you could have a pleasant day out in the Wadi Rum area by calling in at the visitor centre and ambling along to the village of Rum, you will have a more interesting experience if you penetrate deeper into the desert. This requires leaving the tarmac behind and going off-road. You can do this most effectively by hiring a 4WD vehicle with driver; by hiring a camel or a horse with a mounted escort; or by hiking, scrambling or climbing with or without a guide.

If you are an experienced sand-driver, you can hire a self-drive 4WD from the visitor centre for JD35 or take your own vehicle into the reserve for JD20.

4WD Excursions

The easiest way to see the largest number of sights in the least amount of time is to arrange a 4WD trip. This is easily done through the excursion office at the visitor centre on arrival.

Rates for 4WD excursions are fixed and listed on a board outside the excursion office at the visitor centre. The prices are per vehicle, not per person, so it can help with costs if you put together a group in Wadi

4WD EXCURSIONS AROUND WADI RUM

When booking a 4WD excursion at the Wadi Rum visitor centre you can either hire a driver for a whole day (make sure you agree on the destinations before leaving), or you can select a destination from two prescribed routes. 'Operator 1' routes cover the central areas of Wadi Rum; 'Operator 2' routes cover outlying (and equally beautiful) areas. Distances are measured from the visitor centre. Maximum times are given below: you could rush round the main sights of Wadi Rum in a few hours, but the trip will be much more rewarding if you get out of the vehicle and explore each of the sights on foot, or simply sit on a dune or rocky outcrop and enjoy the peace and quiet. Drivers are assigned in strict rotation so you may get a driver who speaks English and is knowledgeable about the desert or you may not. If you want a guide to accompany you, ask at the visitor centre or book one in advance.

SITE	DISTANCE	TIME	PRICE PER VEHICLE
Operator 1 Routes			
Lawrence's Spring	14km	1 hour	JD25
Khazali Canyon	30km	2 hours	JD35
Sunset sites of Rum	35km	2½ hours	JD44
Little Rock Bridge	35km	3 hours	JD44
Red Dunes	40km	3½ hours	JD51
Lawrence's House	45km	3½ hours	JD59
Umm Fruth Rock Bridge	50km	4 hours	JD67
Burdah Rock Bridge	60km	5 hours	JD75
Burdah Canyon	65km	8 hours	JD80
Operator 2 Routes			
Alameleh Inscriptions	15km	1 hour	JD25
Siq Umm Tawaqi	18km	2 hours	JD35
Sunset sites of Diseh	20km	2½ hours	JD44
Barrah Canyon	49km	3 hours	JD51
Burdah Rock Bridge	50km	4 hours	JD67
Full-day tour	60km	8 hours	JD80

Musa or Aqaba (not easy to do on arrival at Wadi Rum). Most 4WDs seat six people; some have bench seats in the back offering better views than the closed-in cabs but they are fearfully cold or boiling hot in extreme seasons.

If you take the vehicle for a day, don't forget to pack food and water for you and your driver. You can buy the basics of a rudimentary picnic in Rum village on your way into the desert.

It's unlikely that anything will go wrong with your trip as the drivers are highly experienced in the desert terrain. Some of the vehicles, however, have seen better days so if you are involved in a breakdown try to avoid heated confrontation: the Bedouin take their responsibility towards the visitor very seriously and they will quickly arrange for a replacement – if everyone remains amicable!

You may be approached by the odd freelance guide in Rum village. Prices may be cheaper but there are no guarantees regarding the safety or quality of the trip and, more importantly, it cheats the lads waiting patiently in line for a fare. In addition, 60% of the profit from excursions goes back to the cooperative: someone who jumps the queue robs the community of that revenue. Rangers tour the Wadi Rum area, checking that people have tickets. Entering without one is not only unethical, it is also illegal.

You can easily add on an overnight stay at a Bedouin camp (ask at the visitor centre when booking your vehicle). Your driver will simply drop you off in the afternoon and pick you up the next morning.

Camel Trekking

Travelling around Wadi Rum by camel is highly recommended. Apart from being ecologically sound, it enables you to experience Wadi Rum as the Bedouin have for centuries, and to appreciate the silent gravitas of the desert. That said, a ride of more than about four hours will leave you sore in places you never knew existed.

Rates for camel-trekking excursions are fixed and listed on a board outside the excursion office in the visitor centre. The prices are per person. You'll enjoy your ride much more if you ride yourself rather than being led. This will cost a bit more as you need to pay for your guide's camel, but it's well worth the extra cost.

You can easily add on an overnight stay at a Bedouin camp (ask at the visitor centre when booking your camel). If you want to return by 4WD then you have to pay the price of returning the camel to where you collected it from. If you have a lot of gear,

AQABA, WADI RUM & THE DESERT HIGHWAY WADI RUM

CAMEL TREKS AROUND WADI RUM

Camel routes are sorted into two circuits for operational purposes. Camel excursions normally begin from Rum village and distances are measured from the Rest House. Prices rise with the price of fodder and the routes on offer change from time to time.

SITE	DISTANCE	TIME	PRICE (MAX)
From Rum Village			
Nabataean Temple	1km	30 minutes	JD4
Lawrence's Spring	6km	2 hours	JD10
Khazali Canyon	14km	4 hours	JD20
Sunset sites	22km	4 hours	JD25
Red Dunes	25km	5 hours	JD20
Burdah Rock Bridge	40km	overnight	JD60
Full-day tour	unlimited	8 hours	JD30
Luggage camel	-	8 hours	JD30
From Alameleh			
Short Trip	2km	1 hour	JD10
Sunset sites	8km	2 hours	JD15
Siq Lawrence	9km	3 hours	JD20
Full-day tour	unlimited	overnight	JD60
Luggage camel	-	8 hours	JD30

ⓘ DESERT DANGERS

Before striking out alone, it's worth taking precautions against the following:

➡ Temperatures (cold as well as hot) can be extreme in midsummer (May to September) and midwinter (January).

➡ It's easy to get disoriented amid the craggy peaks and maps are often inaccurate.

➡ Passing traffic is rare.

➡ Natural water supplies are not common and sometimes undrinkable.

➡ Walking in sand is particularly exhausting.

it's better to hire an additional camel (at the same rate) to bear the load. It is also possible to arrange longer camel excursions from Wadi Rum to Aqaba (three to six nights depending on the route); or towards Wadi Musa (for Petra; about five nights).

The camel is no longer a common form of transport for Bedouin; most now prefer the ubiquitous pick-up truck – in fact, it's not unusual to see a Bedouin transporting a prized camel in the back of a Toyota. These grumpy but loyal animals, however, are still very much part of the Bedouin culture and camel races are held weekly in winter, generally on a Friday, at the camel track near Diseh. Ask at the visitor centre for details.

Horse Trekking

An alternative and memorable mode of four-legged transport through Wadi Rum and surrounding areas is by horse. Sample trips include a two-hour hack (around JD30), day-trips (from JD90) and overnight camping trips (from JD120 for a minimum of two people). These trips are for people who have riding experience – novices should not underestimate the challenge of riding high-spirited Arab horses in open country.

Rum Horses   HORSE RIDING
(☑ 079 5802108, 2033508; www.wadirumhorses.com) The highly recommended and long-established Rum Horses is the most professional camel- and horse-trekking agency. The stables are located on the approach road to the Wadi Rum visitor centre, about 10km from the Desert Highway. Look for a signboard beside the road.

The owner, Atallah Swillheen, trained and qualified in horse management and en-

durance racing in Europe. One of his horses, Sasha, is a five-time winner of the FEI endurance race in Jordan.

Hiking

For those who prefer 'Shanks' pony' to the real thing, there are many wonderful places to explore on foot and you can walk unguided to several of the main sights.

Makharas Canyon Hike   HIKING
(moderate; unguided; ⊘ 2½ hours return) This worthwhile canyon hike includes open vistas, canyon hiking and grand dune views. It begins at the visitor centre.

Hike southeast across the plain towards the Seven Pillars of Wisdom and then head up Makharas Canyon (take the left-hand wadi at the branch). The wadi narrows after about an hour from the visitor centre and then emerges onto a patch of gorgeous red sand with grand views of Jebel Barrah and Umm Nfoos to the east. From here, cut north over the sand dunes and plod around the northern tip of Jebel Umm Ishrin to return to the Seven Pillars of Wisdom.

Jebel Rum Round Trip   HIKING
(strenuous; unguided; ⊘ eight hours) This route offers stunning 'big country' scenery and begins at Rum village. Pass Lawrence's Spring and Ain Abu Aineh and circumambulate the southern half of Jebel Rum.

Jebel Umm Adaami Ascent   HIKING
(moderate; unguided; ⊘ two hours return) This route scales Jebel Umm Adaami (1832m), Jordan's highest peak on the rarely visited southern border with Saudi Arabia. It starts at Wadi Saabet, a 45-minute 4WD trip from the visitor centre.

The hour-long uphill hike is marked by cairns and offers sweeping views of Wadi Rum to the north and Saudi Arabia to the south and it can be unnerving in parts if you don't have a head for heights. On the way back, stop off at the rock carvings of nearby Siq al-Barid, a lovely spot for a picnic.

Scrambling

Scrambling lies somewhere between hiking and climbing. No technical skills are required, but you may have to pull yourself up short rock faces.

Burdah Rock Bridge Ascent   SCRAMBLING
(strenuous; guided; ⊘ one hour one-way) This popular scramble leads to the top of the bridge and fine views. There's nothing technical involved but you'll need a guide to

find the route and a head for heights on one spot just before the bridge. To continue beyond the bridge you'll need ropes and some climbing skills (one climber fell to his death here in 1999).

Rakhabat Canyon   SCRAMBLING
(moderate; guided; ⊙half-day) With a local guide or a copy of Tony Howard's *Walking in Jordan* you can navigate the labyrinthine siqs of Rakhabat Canyon for an exciting half-day trip through the heart of Jebel Umm al-Ishrin. The route starts at the western mouth of the canyon, just by Rum village.

At the far (eastern) end of the canyon you can hike across the valley to the Anfaishi-yya Inscriptions, and then return to Rum village via the southern point of Jebel Umm al-Ishrin, with a possible detour to Ain Abu Aineh en route. Alternatively, if you have abseiling (rappelling) experience, you can head west through the mountain ridge along the Kharazeh Canyon for a great loop route.

Rock Climbing
Wadi Rum offers some challenging rock climbing (up to Grade 8). Although the Bedouin have been climbing in the area for centuries, climbing as a modern sport is still relatively undeveloped. That said, there are now several accredited climbing guides, most of whom have been trained in the UK. To arrange a climbing trip, contact the visitor centre a few days in advance; they will put you in touch with a guide with whom you can negotiate the price and organise camping gear, equipment and transport. Costs start at around JD200 for one to two days' climbing.

Guides often suggest Jebel Rum for less experienced climbers: minimal gear is needed and it's close to the Rest House. Another popular climbing location is Jebel Barrah. For information on routes see Tony Howard and Di Taylor's books and check out www. wadirum.net.

Other Activities
For a magnificent eagle's-eye view of Wadi Rum, take to the air by balloon (JD130 per person for a minimum of two people). Trips take a minimum of two hours and are dependent on the weather. **Bait Ali Lodge** (☑079 5548133; www.baitali.com) acts as the local facilitator for the **Royal Aero Sports Club of Jordan** (☑2058052; www.rascj.com), providing the easiest way of making a booking for these sports. Bait Ali also rents out quad bikes (ATVs), along with maps of possible routes in the dry mud flats north of the camp.

The annual **Jebel Ishrin Marathon** takes place each September and the **Wadi Rum Endurance Race** (www.fei.org), a 120km-in-a-day FEI (Fédération Equestre Internationale) event, may interest horse enthusiasts.

Tours

If you have limited time, you may find it easier to arrange a tour to Wadi Rum from Aqaba. Prices start from around JD60 per

---

AGENCIES & GUIDES

Jeep drivers and camel escorts do a good job of looking after visitors, but if you want more detailed or specialised information about Wadi Rum, or help in organising a particular activity, you'll need to hire a guide. Staff at the visitor centre can help you locate a guide. Make contact around 48 hours to a week in advance and carry a copy of your email correspondence in case the staff at the visitor centre asks for it. For longer excursions, some planning is required on the part of the guide (eg buying provisions, arranging camels). April, September and October are the busiest seasons.

Prices per person per day for one to three people start from JD60 for a simple hike or scramble, and a discount is usually offered for groups of a minimum of four people (from JD50 per person).

Attayak Ali (☑079 5899723; www.bedouinroads.com) Well-respected climbing and adventure guide with many years of experience.

Attayak Aouda (☑079 5834736; www.rumguides.com) Experienced climbing guide.

Bedouin Adventures (☑Ahmed 079 5127025; www.bedouinadventures.com) Hiking, scrambling, camel trekking and three- to seven-night camping trips.

Eid Mohamed Al-Sowelleh (☑079 5624671) General guide.

Sabagh Eid (☑7891243, fax 2016238) General guide.

person per day (including transport, food and entrance fee) and can include an overnight stay in the desert (JD15 for facilities and breakfast). **Wadi Rum Safari** (☑ 20 63882) provides links to several Bedouin enterprises with good reputations.

Some tours overnight at Diseh and do not even enter the main protected area of Wadi Rum. Diseh has some good camps in beautiful scenery, but it is not part of the reserve area so you should be clear about what the tour entails to avoid disappointment.

🛏 Sleeping

There is no hotel in Wadi Rum, nor in the neighbouring village of Diseh, so if you want to spend time in the area, be prepared to camp. Camping can range from a goat-hair blanket under the stars at an isolated Bedouin camp or a mattress under partitioned canvas in a 'party tent' at Diseh to a comfortable cabin at Bait Ali, just outside Wadi Rum. You can even pitch your own tent in designated areas (enquire about locations at the visitor centre). Mattress, blankets and food are always provided, but not all camps provide linen or towels. Despite the online marketing literature, the camps all offer a very similar experience with a similar level of comfort and activities.

🛏 Rum Village

Rest House CAMPGROUND $
(☑ 2018867; mattress & blankets in 2-person tent per person JD5) The frayed tents at the back of the Rest House offer the most accessible accommodation, but they're only recommended if you arrive in Wadi Rum too late to head into the desert. You can pitch your own tent for JD3, which includes use of toilets and shower block.

🛏 In the Desert

The sky's the limit for those who stay in one of the Bedouin camps in Wadi Rum and this is definitely the best way to experience the desert. Unfurl your mat under the stars and let singing youths, together with the snorts of grumbling camels and the whistle of mint tea over the fire, lull you to sleep.

The Bedouin camps all conform to certain standards and are checked regularly. There are two types of camps – permanent (which usually have toilet-shower blocks and operate year-round) and temporary (used only occasionally by Bedouin groups or tourists). The

camps are only permitted in certain areas and these fall either within Wadi Rum or within neighbouring Diseh. The Wadi Rum camps are best booked through the visitor centre, either in advance (especially if you want to stay at a particular camp) or on arrival.

Accommodation in temporary camps is generally a mattress under the stars or a small two-person tent with a sewn-in ground sheet. Accommodation in permanent camps is in Rum tourist tents. These are tall enough to walk into and are made of goat-hair or other local fabric. The tents, like a small cabin, usually come with a camp bed, mattress and linen.

One or two camps offer en-suite loos attached to a larger version of the typical Rum tourist tent. These are probably the best bet if travelling with small children.

The price of accommodation in the standard permanent camp, including food, tents and bedding, is generally around JD30 per person per night and often includes transport by 4WD to the camp if you don't visit anywhere en route.

Camps advertising half board generally provide a simple barbecue supper with salads and Arabic bread, coffee or tea and a piece of fruit, and a breakfast of jam, cheese, bread and coffee. For groups staying in a temporary camp, there is an additional charge for the transportation of camping items to the campsite each day. If you have your own sleeping bag, tent and food, all you should have to pay is the cost of your four-wheeled or four-legged transport.

As there are many camps, all offering similar services in similarly beautiful parts of the desert, it is hard to recommend one over another.

Tour operators run their own camps scattered around the desert.

★ Rum Stars Camp CAMP $
(☑ 079 5127025; www.rumstars.com; half board in tent per person JD25) One of the camps situated deepest in the desert, it takes about 20 minutes by 4WD to reach. In a cosy location, tucked into the side of a mountain and overlooking quintessential Wadi Rum landscape, the camp is simple but well-run by Bedouin brothers. The owner, Ahmed Ogla Al Zalabeyh, speaks excellent English and is passionate about his Bedouin heritage.

The camp can arrange a number of activities including camel rides, 4WD trips, hiking and scrambling. Accommodation is in the typical Rum tourist tent with a shared toilet and shower block. A traditional Bedouin tent with cushions and carpets forms the social hub of the camp.

Bedouin Lifestyle Camp CAMP $

(☑ 077 9131803; www.bedouinlifestyle.com; half board in tent per person JD25) In operation since 2011, Atalla Ablawi operates this popular and well-run camp. Born in the desert, he moved to the village at age 10 and studied English and French at university. 'I'm like the fish,' he says, 'if you take me out of the desert, it's like being taken out of the water'.

Accommodation is in a typical Rum tourist tent but there is a range of other cabin tents, some with en suite loos, here and at the nearby sister camp, Shooting Stars, which has a fine sunset location.

Mohammed Mutlak Camp CAMP $

(☑ 077 7424837; www.wadirum.org; half board in tent per person JD30) In a beautiful spot overlooking Jebel Qattar, this camp is well established. Dinner may, if you're lucky, include delicious lamb cooked in a *zerb* (Bedouin oven buried in the sand). You can reach the camp by camel (from JD25, 2¼ hours). Hiking opportunities include a 45-minute hike to see the merging of red and white sand dunes.

Accommodation is in a sturdy and large version of the typical Rum tourist tent, raised off the ground. There's a large communal seating area. The camp offers daily onward transport to Petra, Aqaba and Amman.

Barrh Camp CAMP

(☑ 077 2220291; hzawaydeh@yahoo.com; half board per person JD25) Tucked discreetly at the end of Siq Umm Tawaqi, beside a giant vertical slice of rock in the heart of Wadi Rum, this camp is within walking distance of some fine rock inscriptions. The camp is run by Hilal Zawaedh, the president of the Diseh Village Touristic Cooperative, a group that ensures profits are returned to the local community.

Accommodation is in a compartmentalised Bedouin tent.

Around Wadi Rum

★ Bait Ali Lodge CAMP $$

(☑ 079 5548133, 079 9257222; www.baitali.com; half board in tent per person from JD35, in small/medium/large cabin JD 45/52/58, in deluxe chalet JD68; ☎⊠) ✐ If you want to stay in the desert but are not wild about roughing it, then Bait Ali offers a highly recommended compromise. Tucked behind a hill, with a fine view of the wilderness, this eco-friendly camp is clearly signposted just off the road, 15km from the Desert Highway and 9km from the Wadi Rum visitor centre.

Accommodation is in comfortable air-conditioned chalets, twin-bed cabins or in army tents with a shared shower block. Facilities include swimming pool, restaurant with nightly barbecue produced from an open *zerb*, a circular meeting hall with a central fire, a bar and a comfortable, cushion-filled Bedouin tent that adds an Arabian Nights atmosphere to the camp. The chef prepares delicious local, unleavened bread over a hot stone.

You can pitch your own tent (JD10) or park a camper van (JD10) and use the shower block. Advice is available on quad-bike rides (JD45 per person per hour), hikes, ballooning, skydiving (February and March) and other activities in the local area. The hike around Lion Mountain (12km, three hours) is particularly recommended.

GREENING THE DESERT

Arriving at Bait Ali, on the edge of Wadi Rum, you can't help but notice it's like an oasis in the middle of the desert. Commended as a Green Key Camp, the owners have always taken their responsiblity towards the environment seriously. Their latest venture in this regard was the creation of an organic farm on the camp premises. The cucumbers, tomatoes and aubergines that arrive on the table at night are grown in the camp's farm, established on sustainable, aquaponic principles and designed to work within the dry desert environment.

If you fancy getting more involved with this agro-venture then enquire after Bait Ali's Permaculture Courses. Four to six places on each course are offered at the camp each spring and autumn. The courses are run in conjunction with Alice Grey, a guru of dry climate agriculture and a director of **Byspokes** (www.byspokes.org), an innovative educational organisation dedicated to food and water security and sustainable community development.

✗ Eating

Apart from the good Rum Gate Restaurant at the visitor centre, there are limited eating options in Wadi Rum. The small grocery stores along the main road through Rum village have basic supplies and mineral water. The area around Diseh has some of the cleanest aquifer water in Jordan. While out in the desert you may be lucky enough to try a *zerb* – a Bedouin barbecue, cooked in an oven buried in the sand.

Rest House BUFFET **$$**
(☑/fax 2018867; breakfast JD5, lunch JD12, dinner buffet JD12; ⊙7am-8.30pm) Dining here is open-air and buffet-style. Sipping a large Amstel beer (JD5) while watching the sun's rays light up Jebel Umm al-Ishrin is the perfect way to finish the day.

Ali's Place CAFE **$**
(snacks JD4; ⊙6am-1am) Along the main road in Rum village, next to Alfi's climbing shop (a grocery store), this local place serves tea and snacks, and is where the younger Bedouin guides go to unwind.

Rum Gate Restaurant BUFFET **$$**
(☑2015995; Wadi Rum visitor centre; snacks JD5, buffet lunch JD12; ⊙8am-5pm; ✳☑) With 15 mixed salads and five hot dishes offered from noon to 3pm, the buffet at this restaurant is understandably popular. Outside lunchtime, the restaurant is a buzzing meeting place for guides, weary hikers and independent travellers who congregate over a non-alcoholic beer (JD2) and a chicken sandwich (JD5).

🛍 Shopping

Visitor Centre HANDICRAFTS
(☑2032918; Wadi Rum visitor centre; ⊙8am-5pm) This is a good place to look for local souvenirs. Most items are made by local women to whom most of the profits are returned. It's possible to visit the workshop in Rum village (closed Friday and Saturday) – ask for directions at the Rest House. There are also ceramics, textiles and Bedouin goat-hair rugs on sale.

ℹ Information

Admission to **Wadi Rum Protected Area** (per person JD5, children under 12 free) is controlled and all vehicles, camels and guides must be arranged either through or with the approval of the visitor centre. Essential items to bring include a hat, preferably with a brim to keep the sun off your neck and face, sunscreen, sturdy footwear and water. Warm clothing, including gloves, is essential in winter.

If you are camping (including at the Rest House), bring along a torch (flashlight), a book to read and a padlock (many tents are lockable).

The Bedouin are a conservative people, so dress appropriately. Long shorts and sleeveless T-shirts for men and women are just about acceptable around the Rest House, but baggy trousers/skirts and modest shirts/blouses will save you sunburn and earn you respect from the Bedouin, especially out in the desert.

The **Visitor Centre** (☑2090600; www.wadi-rum.jo; ⊙7am-7pm) is situated at the entry to the protected area, about 30km east of the Desert Highway and 7km north of Rum village. This is where you buy your entry ticket, book a 4WD or camel excursion, organise accommodation at a camp and book a guide. There are no ATMs or credit card payment facilities in Wadi Rum.

There is a restaurant, craft shops, an excellent museum, clean toilets and parking area. You can also ask to see a 10-minute film on some of the highlights of Wadi Rum, shown in the purpose-built cinema.

Police Station (☑2017050) Located in the old police fort 400m south of the Rest House. They will not receive complaints (go to the tourist police), but they will come looking for you if you get lost.

Tourist Police (☑2018215) At the visitor centre.

ℹ Getting There & Away

CAR
The most convenient way to get to Wadi Rum as an independent traveller is by car. You can hire a car in Aqaba and, if you intend to continue to Petra, you are well advised to keep it for the round-trip. This will save considerable time and frustration trying to fathom the limited public transport.

If you are accustomed to desert navigation and off-road driving in sandy conditions, you could hire a 4WD in Aqaba and drive into the desert yourself, providing you state your intention at the visitor centre at Wadi Rum and pay the JD5 (per person) entrance fee. Do not attempt this if you have no prior knowledge of desert driving.

Note that unless you book a 4WD excursion to Wadi Rum through the visitor centre, you can't guarantee that the vehicle (with or without a driver) is insured.

HITCHING
Because of the limited public transport to and from Rum village (which has only a small population), some travellers follow local custom

LOCAL KNOWLEDGE

AHMED OGLA AL ZALABEYH: STEWARD OF THE DESERT

Until he was seven years old, Ahmed lived the life of the nomad in Jordan's southern desert. His parents were keen for him to be integrated into the modern world so Ahmed and his siblings donned shoes for the first time and went to school. Over a decade later, after attaining a degree in English literature in Amman, Ahmed is back in Wadi Rum. Describing his four years in the big city as the worst of his life, he is relieved to come home to the desert and this is where he intends to stay. Married and now an established part of the tourist industry, Ahmed is both passionate and articulate about his Bedouin roots and he looks forward to bringing up his own family with a firm idea of what it means to be Bedouin.

What are the best places to visit in Jordan to have a Bedouin experience? There are many who claim to be Bedouin but who use the label for commercial ends. If you want to meet the real Bedouin, you must come to the desert – like here in Rum, or in Wadi Araba or in small pockets of the Eastern Desert. In these places you will encounter families who know what it means to live in the traditional nomadic way, moving with the seasons.

Where do the Bedouin go to escape the tourists? Ah, that's easier than you may think! We throw everything into the back of our pick-up truck and follow the camels into the desert, beyond the camps and the car tracks. That's our spiritual home and we return to it often.

How do the Bedouin find sustenance in the desert? Livestock are the key to survival. The Bedouin trade among themselves, exchanging camels and sheep for products such as goat-hair tents, rugs, milk and cheese or items of hardware from the market.

What does it mean to be Bedouin in the modern world? Life in the desert is about the basic origins of humanity. For us this includes the concept of hospitality which runs very deep in our culture. Increasingly, though, thanks to the need for education and access to better transport, it also means settlement – usually near to the desert's edge.

How will you ensure your children love the desert the way you do? I will take them, like my father took me, to all the places where our story can be told. Knowing that our grandfathers sat by this rock or under that tree helps us connect to the land and ensures our history is passed along.

What advice have you for the tourist wanting to meet the Bedouin? Don't be suspicious of our motives – just come and talk, or share tea with us. Yes we want to make a living but we want our culture to be understood more.

and hitch from the main road to the visitor centre. All transport heading along the Desert Highway will stop at Ar-Rashidiyya, 5km south of Quweira – with the exception of JETT buses. It is customary to pay the driver around JD3 for this ride. You can normally hitch a lift in a pick-up between the visitor centre and Rum village for around JD5. Travellers who choose to hitch should understand that they are taking a small but potentially serious risk; for more, see p326.

MINIBUS
At the time of research, there was at least one minibus a day to Aqaba (JD3, one hour) at around 7am. A second one may run at 8.30am, but check with your camp operator first. To Wadi Musa (JD7, 1½ hours) there is a fairly reliable daily minibus at 8.30am. Check current departure times at the visitor centre, Rest House or camp operator when you arrive in Wadi Rum.

For Ma'an, Karak or Amman, the minibuses to either Aqaba or Wadi Musa can drop you off at the Ar-Rashidiyya crossroads with the Desert Highway (JD2, 20 minutes), where it is easy to hail onward transport.

TAXI
Occasionally taxis hang around the visitor centre (and very occasionally the Rest House) waiting for a fare back to wherever they came from – normally Aqaba, Wadi Musa or Ma'an. It costs between JD30 to JD35 to Aqaba, and JD50 to JD55 to Wadi Musa (Petra). A taxi jeep from Rum village to the Ar-Rashidiyya crossroads with the Desert Highway costs around JD10. Some camps organise onward transport at competitive rates for their guests.

Diseh الديسي

Diseh is northwest of Rum village, about 12km as the vulture flies but 22km by road. The scenery is almost as spectacular as at Wadi Rum, and there are plenty of places to hike adjacent to the official Wadi Rum protected area. There are several camps in the desert near Diseh offering basic facilities. If you stay at one of these, you can organise transport to Wadi Rum visitor centre and book your desert excursion from there.

◉ Sights & Activities

The paved road to Diseh from the turn-off to Rum offers some interesting places to explore. For a negotiable price, locals will drive you out into the desert area north of the railway line, which is dotted with Nabataean and Roman dams, artificial rock bridges, rock carvings and inscriptions. The landscape around Jebel Amud is the most interesting. A longer trip could take in the 2m-high rock carvings at Abu Hawl (Father of Terror), 7km north of the Bait Ali camp, and on to a rock bridge at Jebel Kharazeh. A three-hour 4WD trip costs around JD55.

🛏 Sleeping

A number of camps near Diseh are popular, especially with sociable urbanites from Aqaba and Amman. The camps are roughly wrapped around a large hill with the first few camps adjacent to each other and accessible by 2WD (unless there's been heavy rain). They all offer traditional sitting areas with cushions and beds either in cramped individual tents or larger partitioned Bedouin tents. If you are looking for a quieter, more tranquil experience, the camps located in more isolated parts of the desert and requiring 4WD for access are a better bet – make sure you check on the location before you book to avoid disappointment.

Zawaideh Desert Camp CAMP $
(☎ 079 5840664; zawaideh_camp@yahoo.com; half board per person JD20) Close to the road and accessible by car, this simple but atmospheric camp is in the undercliff of the escarpment, on the edge of a wide plain. It has a reputation for providing a sociable experience around the lively campfire and is popular with Jordanians from the city looking to reconnect with the desert.

Rahayeb Camp CAMP $$
(☎ 079 6909030; www.rahayebcamp.com; half/full board per person JD32/38) Wedged into a secluded bend of the rocks, well away from the other Diseh camps, this is a well-run establishment. Two professional chefs rustle up traditional fare in the *zerb* oven while guests lounge under the stars around a central fireplace. Many tents (from JD45) are upmarket versions of the typical Rum tourist tent, with

---

WORTH A TRIP

BEDOUIN HISTORY & CULTURE

If you're keen to learn more about local Bedouin history and culture then two novel opportunities may be of interest.

Al-Hijaz Train Ride in Wadi Rum (Jordan Heritage Revival Company (JHRC); ☎ 077 7606052, 079 6606052; www.jhrc.jo; ⊙ 4.30pm Thu-Sat, Oct & Nov) Cast yourself as an extra in the Arab Revolt of 1917 on board an original Hijaz train. The action happens in the surrounding desert as members of the JHRC re-enact Bedouin skirmishes. The train (now diesel, not steam-driven) can be boarded at the station on the approach road to Wadi Rum. The train trip was temporarily suspended at the time of writing and ticket prices unavailable.

It was thanks in part to local Bedouin tribes, who joined Faisal's forces to defeat the Turks in a bid for Arab independence, that the leaders of the campaign were able to make a successful assault on Aqaba.

Rahayeb Desert Camp Activities (☎ 079 6909030; www.rahayebcamp.com; from JD50 per person) Brush up on your desert skills by being a 'Bedouin for a Day'. This camp arranges a day with a local family, sampling bread and coffee and learning how to milk sheep, goats and camels. It's harder than it looks and, unless you're a dairy farmer, is likely to elicit guffaws of laughter from your expert hosts.

Animal-print tracking, star gazing and Bedouin cooking lessons are also on offer.

their own toilets and showers, making this a convenient camp for families.

There are also super-secluded camping pitches near a miniature siq above the camp with nothing to disturb the peace but your own heartbeat.

A wellness programme with Dead Sea scrubs, massages, henna tattoos, hair braiding and yoga can give your stay at the camp an unusual (given the desert context) extra dimension. The camp is run in conjunction with Aquamarine Transportation Company in Aqaba and gives good advice for onward adventures.

Captain's Camp   CAMP $$
(☑ 079 5510432, 2016905; captains@jo.com.jo; half board per person JD35) A well-run midrange camp with hot showers, lots of snug seating areas and good buffets, this camp is popular with tour groups, especially as it's easily accessible from the road. The camp also offers a romantic tent for two (JD90 per person) in the middle of the desert, with a candlelit supper delivered to the tent flaps.

❶ Getting There & Away

You're unlikely to find a minibus or service taxi headed all the way to Diseh, so follow the instructions for getting to Wadi Rum as far as the turn-off to Diseh (the police checkpoint 16km after leaving the Desert Highway). From there you can ring ahead to one of the camps where someone is usually happy to come and collect you. If you get stuck, you can hitch the final 8km but be prepared for a wait. It's customary to give a few fils to the driver — JD1 should do it.

Minibuses often run from Diseh to the Desert Highway (JD2). A single bus runs to Aqaba daily at around 7am. Check at your camp for the latest information.

THE DESERT HIGHWAY

The Desert Highway, which follows the legendary tracks of the Hejaz Railway and a water pipeline, connects Aqaba in the south of Jordan with Damascus in Syria. The section between Amman and Aqaba is a road of very limited interest, poorly maintained and usually bearing heavy traffic. As such, it hardly ranks as one of Jordan's highlights. It is, however, the shortest route between Amman and southern Jordan and it's likely that you'll end up using the highway in one direction or another. This is the only road in Jordan that actually looks like a highway,

with dual carriageway for most of its length and lighting at main intersections.

There are very few places to sleep or eat along the Desert Highway and if you make it to Ma'an, you may as well continue on to Wadi Musa, Wadi Rum or Aqaba.

Humaiyma

Pressed up against the cliffs on the opposite side of the highway to Wadi Rum is the seldom-visited Bedouin district of Humaiyma. Curious visitors who notice the brown sign off the main Aqaba Hwy and struggle along the badly potholed access road are rewarded with a surprisingly large archaeological site.

The largely Nabataean site includes 27km of covered aqueducts, some of which are visible today; they are evidence of the Nabataean attitude towards water that it could be 'brought or caught' in channels from the mountains or in reservoirs on the plains. King Aretas III built Humaiyma around 80 BC as a trading post designed, according to archaeologists, to help settle nomadic tribes. His efforts, judging by the nomads camping nearby some 2000 years later, were not wholly successful. Trajan's army built a fort here in AD 106 and settlement continued into the Byzantine and early Islamic periods. In AD 750 the site was eventually abandoned.

There is a small visitors centre, but it was unmanned at the time of writing and there was no legible information at the site. A little more illuminating is the official website of the Canadian excavation team (http://web.uvic.ca/~jpoleson/Humayma/).

Ma'an   معان
☑ 03 / POP 118,800 / ELEV 1100M

With little of specific interest to visitors, Ma'an is one of the larger towns and administrative centres in southern Jordan and a useful transport junction. It has fulfilled this function for centuries as it lies on the main pilgrimage route from Jordan and Syria to Mecca in Saudi Arabia. The main north–south thoroughfare is King Hussein St, centred somewhere around the mosque and the communication tower. Here you'll find restaurants and several banks with ATMs. To get here from the bus station head two blocks west then one block north (a five-minute walk) to the southern end of King Hussein St, where it meets Palestine St.

❶ Getting There & Away

If you can't get a direct bus to where you want to go in Jordan, there's a good chance that you can find a connection in Ma'an.

The station for buses, minibuses and service taxis is a five-minute walk southeast of the centre. Departures from Ma'an start to peter out around 2pm and stop completely around 5pm.

There are regular minibuses (JD3, three hours) and less frequent service taxis (JD8, three hours) to/from Amman's South Bus Station (Wahadat). To Aqaba, minibuses (JD3, 80 minutes) and service taxis (JD3) are also frequent. For Wadi Rum, take an Aqaba-bound minibus to the junction at Ar-Rashidiyya (JD2) then take a minibus or hitch from here. For Petra, minibuses to Wadi Musa (JD1.500, 45 minutes) leave fairly frequently when full and stop briefly at the uni-versity en route. To Karak, there are occasional service taxis (JD 2.500, two hours) and three minibuses a day, via Tafila (JD2.500).

A chartered taxi to Petra/Wadi Musa costs around JD20, and JD35 to Karak or Aqaba.

Qatrana القطرانه

📞 03 / POP 8290 / ELEV 740M

One of the few towns along the Desert Highway is Qatrana, a couple of kilometres north of the turn-off to Karak, and a former stop on the pilgrim road between Damascus and Mecca. The only reason to stop here (if you have your own transport) is to have a quick look at **Qatrana Castle** FREE, built in 1531 by the Ottomans. It has been nicely restored, but there are no explanation boards.

Azraq & the Eastern Desert Highway
الأزرق & شرق الطريق الصحراء

Best Castles

→ Qasr al-Azraq (p234)

→ Qusayr Amra (p238)

→ Qasr Kharana (p239)

→ Umm al-Jimal (p244)

Best Views

→ Qasr Burqu (p245)

→ Qasr Aseikhin (p245)

→ Qasr 'Uweinid (p237)

→ Marsh Trail (p236)

Why Go?

Imagine a space so desolate that not even a boulder or a bush troubles the 360-degree horizon. Now add a carpet of ancient black volcanic rock, unnavigable even by camels. And finally, factor in a ravaging heat so overpowering in the summer that the ground pulses before your eyes and mirages appear in the distance. Welcome to the Eastern Desert!

So why, you might well ask, would anyone bother to come here? Although the Eastern Desert may look like uncharted territory, it has been inhabited by Bedouin, crossed by caravans and visited by migrating birds since recorded history. Today you can see evidence of this traffic in a string of intriguing ruined forts, hunting lodges and caravanserai, collectively known as the 'desert castles'. At the oases of Azraq and Burqu, birds still break their journey across the otherwise featureless desert.

When to Go

→ The best time to visit the remote plains of eastern Jordan is October to mid-April when temperate weather means getting stuck at a remote desert castle is merely inconvenient, not life-threatening.

→ With proper planning (including reliable transport, sufficient water supplies and a hat), May is another good time to visit. At this time, large numbers of raptors soar above the shimmering heat haze on their annual migration.

→ In winter, dust devils spiral on the plains as birds stop over in the Azraq wetlands en route between Europe and sub-Saharan Africa.

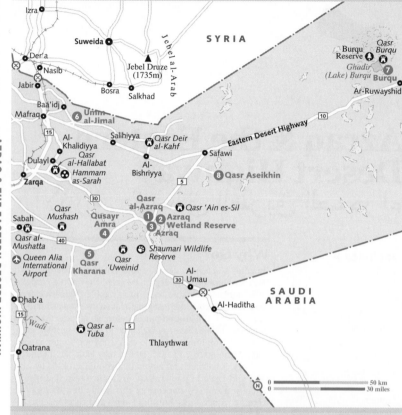

Azraq & the Eastern Desert Highway Highlights

1 Chase the ghost of Lawrence through **Qasr al-Azraq** (p234), the former headquarters of this enigmatic British officer.

2 Hunker down in the bird-hide at **Azraq Wetland Reserve** (p236) and watch the drama of a waterhole unfold.

3 Meet one of Jordan's ethnic minorities, the Chechens, at **Azraq Lodge** (p233) and enjoy a sumptuous dinner.

4 Admire the risqué frescoes in the bathhouse of **Qusayr Amra** (p238), a Unesco World Heritage site.

5 Wander the maze-like corridors of **Qasr Kharana** (p239), a mighty fortress in a lonesome desert.

6 Clamber through the basalt ruins of **Umm al-Jimal** (p244), an ancient town of shimmering black stone.

7 Use your off-road driving skills to reach **Burqu** (p245), an unlikely lake in the wilderness.

8 Understand why even camels find the black desert intimidating at **Qasr Aseikhin** (p245).

History

A string of ruined pavilions, caravanserai, hunting lodges and forts – known collectively (if erroneously) as the 'desert castles' – peppers the deserts of eastern Jordan, and is one of the country's most surreal attractions. Dating back to the Umayyads (AD 661–750) in the earliest years of Islam, the desert castles were once richly decorated with mosaics, frescoes, marble, plaster and painted stucco, providing oases of rest and refreshment in the harsh and inhospitable desert. Here, the elite could pursue their pastimes of hawking, hunting and horse racing during the day, while evenings were spent in wild festivities with wine, poetry and song.

The early Arab rulers were still Bedouin at heart, and their love of the desert may have led them to build these pleasure palaces, which once teemed with orchards and wild game. Or they may have come to avoid epidemics in the big cities, or to maintain links with, and power over, the Bedouin – the bedrock of their support in the conquered lands. The desert castles also served as staging posts for pilgrimages to Mecca, and along trade routes to Damascus and Baghdad: never underestimate the luxury of a hot bath in the desert!

Nature Reserves

Unlikely as it may seem on the road into the Eastern Desert from Amman, this region is home to three protected areas. The most developed is **Azraq Wetland Reserve**, which attracts many bird species around the gravely diminished oasis. **Shaumari Wildlife Reserve** protects endangered species such as the Arabian oryx but is currently closed to visitors (though you may be able to arrange a night safari through the RSCN), while **Burqu Reserve** is an undeveloped site in the middle of remote wilderness.

Dangers & Annoyances

The desert doesn't take prisoners. At any time of year, but particularly in the middle of summer, dehydration and the threat of heat exhaustion and heat stroke – a serious condition that requires immediate medical attention – are hazards of visiting remote desert locations. Minimise the risk by carrying and drinking plenty of water, wearing a hat, avoiding exertion in the middle of the day and planning an exit route if travelling by public transport. If driving off-road, be aware that you will have to be totally self-sufficient in the event of a puncture or mechanical failure.

During the spring, flies and mosquitoes are an annoyance. Bring repellent if visiting the oases.

ⓘ Getting There & Away

The easiest point of entry to the region is Amman and the towns of Zarqa and Mafraj. Desolate Hwy 5 from the south also leads into the area via Azraq. Trucks and some buses use the border crossing at Al-Umau with Saudi Arabia.

ⓘ Getting Around

Although minimal and intermittent minibuses ply the route to Azraq from Amman, some en route to the Iraqi border, it is very difficult to travel around this region by unreliable public transport. A better option is to take a tour from the capital, covering the main desert castles in a day trip. An even better bet is to hire a car for two days, which will allow for a stopover in Azraq. To make a comprehensive tour of the region, including Umm al-Jimal and Burqu along the remote Eastern Desert Highway, a 4WD with camping gear is recommended.

AZRAQ & AROUND

Azraq is the only town of any significance in the Eastern Desert and acts as a magnet for trans-continental traffic looking for refreshment and company after long desert drives. The name 'Azraq' is often loosely applied to all settlements directly east of Amman and the castles that are scattered across the desert plains here. Some of the best attractions of the region lie close to the town itself, including a fort and a wetland reserve. Beyond the fringes of the town, on the two main roads into Amman, there are several desert castles, including two of the most striking, Qasr Amra and Qasr Karana.

Azraq is the only place in the whole Eastern Desert where accommodation is available. To get a real sense of the desert, it is best to plan a trip around an overnight stop that allows at least for a picnic in the wilderness and a walk off-trail between castle-spotting.

A logical, clockwise sequence for sights can be followed by leaving Amman via Zarqa and taking Hwy 30 to Azraq. The return to Amman is via Hwy 40. This is the best route on which to visit the castles if you are travelling by public transport (which nonetheless involves some backtracking and taxi rides) and it is the usual route followed by tour companies on their day excursions. Don't use up all your energy on the outbound leg as two of the best castles, Qasr Amra and Qasr Kharana, lie along the inbound Hwy 40.

Zarqa الزرقاء

☑ 09 / POP 931,100 / ELEV 620M

The third-largest city in Jordan after Amman and Irbid, Zarqa is now virtually part of the continuous urban sprawl of northern Amman. There's not much to this gritty

ⓘ TOURING THE DESERT CASTLES

Jumping on an organised tour of the desert castles from Amman makes a lot of sense, especially if you're short of time or on a tight budget. Tours can be arranged at the Palace, Farah and Cliff hotels in Amman, which charge about JD15 to JD20 per person for a full-day trip with an hour at each site. You're unlikely to get a better deal by negotiating directly with the driver of a service taxi or private taxi in Amman, and regular taxi drivers are rarely keen on leaving the city. Tours by car (around JD45 for maximum of four people) can also be arranged from the Black Iris and Mariam hotels in Madaba.

working-class city that merits anything more than a passing glance, but you may have to change buses here if you're trying to visit the Eastern Desert on public transport.

In Zarqa, there are two terminals for buses, minibuses and service taxis. Transport to/from the north bus station (Tabarbour) in Amman (JD1, 30 minutes) uses the new (Amman) station. From the old station in Zarqa, there is public transport to smaller villages in the region, such as Hallabat (for Qasr al-Hallabat and Hammam as-Sarah) and Mafraq. Minibuses also leave intermittently for Azraq (JD1.500, 1½ hours). Minibuses shuttle between the two terminals in Zarqa every few minutes.

Hallabat   حلابات

The modest farming area of Hallabat is home to a fort of the same name and offers the first encounter with Umayyad architecture on the Desert Castle Loop.

◎ Sights

Qasr al-Hallabat Fort   CASTLE
(☉ daylight hours) FREE With a fair proportion of masonry still standing, some beautifully restored archways and a desolate perch on the edge of the Eastern Desert, this fort is a good introduction to the history of the region. Hallabat once boasted elaborate baths, intricate frescoes and mosaics, a mosque and several reservoirs, and served as a focus for a thriving farming community. Restoration of a substantial part of the site under

Spanish direction has restored an inkling of the castle's former stature.

As with all the castles in Jordan, it takes a bit of sleuthing to peel back the layers of history. In the case of Hallabat, you need only focus on three main eras – Roman, Byzantine and Umayyad.

Look first for a fine mosaic. This sits above a large central cistern and the ruins of the original fort. Built by the Romans during the reign of Emperor Caracalla (AD 198–217), the fort, like many in the region, was originally built as a defence against raiding desert tribes. As you survey the land from the castle hill, you can see why they picked this location, as it would have been easy to spot men on horseback darting across the rocky plain.

Now look for additions in basaltic rock, easily distinguished by its black colour. If you venture further into the Eastern Desert you'll find this volcanic rock scattered across vast plains providing a ready supply of building materials. In the 6th century the fort was converted by the Byzantines into a monastery for a short period, using the basalt blocks to expand the Roman structure.

Lastly, admire the decorated finesse of limestone walls (distinguished by their white colour), carved niches, reassembled arches and an elaborate porch with pillars. This is the work of the Umayyads (AD 661–750), who revisited the structure under the reign of the hedonistic caliph, Walid II and transformed the modest fort into an imposing three-storey complex with four large towers. Look for the remains of a large mosque with cusped arches, an agricultural enclosure fed by an elaborate irrigation system and the ruins of a village for palace servants that were included in the Umayyads' ambitious expansion project. Wondering where the baths are? You'll have to travel 3km east to see the remains of these, at Hammam as-Sarah.

Hammam as-Sarah   RUIN
(☉ daylight hours) FREE Part of the neighbouring fort complex in Hallabat, this hammam (bathhouse) has been extensively restored, revealing the underfloor piping system that was used to heat the hot and tepid bathing rooms. The hammam is located along the main road to Hallabat village, about 3km east of Qasr al-Hallabat and 5km from the main road. The minibus to Hallabat village drives past Hammam as-Sarah and can drop you off on request. The site is unlocked – just push open the gate.

There might have been considerably more to see at this hammam and hunting lodge complex, once linked to Qasr al-Hallabat, if locals hadn't taken a liking to the high-quality limestone blocks in the 1950s. It's hard to complain, though, as this kind of recycling has been traditional in the region since well before the Romans. Outside the main building is a well, nearly 20m deep, an elevated tank and the remains of a nearby mosque.

ℹ Information

Visitor Centre (⊘ daylight hours) This small visitor centre at the fort entrance houses a museum, guide post and toilets. While the inside portion of the musuem is yet to open to the public, the courtyard is adorned with reconstructed pillars and archways that give an idea of the decorative details bestowed on Qasr al-Hallabat by the Umayyads.

Arabic-speaking guides, most of whom were involved in the restoration work and knowl-edgeable about the castle, are available at the gate. Even without a common language, they can point you towards details otherwise missed and their enthusiasm for the project is infectious.

ℹ Getting There & Away

Close enough to Amman to be visited on a half-day excursion, Qasr al-Hallabat and Hammam as-Sarah are located near the village of Hallabat and are one of the few sites in the Eastern Desert that can be easily reached by public transport. From Amman's north bus station, take a minibus to the new (Amman) station in Zarqa, another minibus to the old station in Zarqa, and another to Hallabat village. To get from here to Azraq by public transport, your best bet is to return to Zarqa.

If you're driving, the castle takes a bit of liberal navigating off Hwy 30 (it is at least signposted) and makes a good first stop on the desert castle loop. It's a good hour's drive from here to Azraq, the main destination on the circuit.

WHICH CASTLES TO VISIT?

There are dozens of ruins belonging to the Umayyad dynasty scattered across the gravel plains of the Eastern Desert, so how do you choose which ones to visit?

Below is a list of the main castles and a guide to their accessibility. The castles fall into two convenient sets. The most famous ones lie on the so-called Desert Castle Loop. These are accessible on a day trip from Amman via Azraq, by tour or by car. Individual castles can be reached with more difficulty by a combination of minibus and taxi.

The other set lies on the so-called Eastern Desert Highway, or Hwy 10, which leads from the town of Mafraq to the Iraqi border. These are much more time-consuming to visit.

Each of the two sets takes a long, full day to cover. You can combine the two sets by staying the night in Azraq and using Hwy 5 to cut between the two.

Set 1: Desert Castle Loop

CASTLE NAME	PUBLIC TRANSPORT	4WD	BY TOUR	WORTHWHILE
Qasr al-Hallabat (p230)	Yes	No	Sometimes	✓✓
Qasr al-Azraq (p233)	Yes	No	Yes	✓✓✓
Qasr 'Uweinid (p237)	No	Yes	No	✓
Qusayr Amra (p238)	Taxi from Azraq	No	Yes	✓✓✓
Qasr Kharana (p239)	Taxi from Azraq	No	Yes	✓✓✓
Qasr Al-Mushatta (p240)	Taxi from Amman	No	No	✓✓

Set 2: Castles of the Eastern Desert Highway

CASTLE NAME	PUBLIC TRANSPORT	4WD	BY TOUR	WORTHWHILE
Umm al-Jimal (p242)	Yes	No	Sometimes	✓✓
Qasr Deir al-Kahf (p244)	No	No	No	✓
Qasr Aseikhin (p245)	No	No	No	✓
Qasr Burqu (p245)	No	Yes	No	✓✓

UMAYYADS? WHO WERE THEY?

If you had to guess the seventh-largest empire (and fifth-largest contiguous empire) the world has ever known, chances are you wouldn't think of the Umayyads. So why is it that this critically important dynasty, central to the modern shape of Islam and responsible for building some of the best loved expressions of Arab culture, is so unfamiliar to those outside the region? It could well be because the Umayyads belong to a Middle Eastern history, so often at odds with the crusading history of Western nations. It could be because the 8th century AD is generally associated, correctly or incorrectly, with the unenlightened Dark Ages, which tends to cast a long shadow over neighbouring cultures. Or it could be because the name Umayyad just doesn't roll off the tongue.

Whatever the reason, the Umayyads deserve the odds to be evened up a little. So, in the interests of fair play, here's a few fast facts to help understand who the Umayyads were and why they were important.

When were the Umayyads around? AD 661–750, in the early days of Islam.

This huge empire of theirs, where was it? From Portugal and Morocco in the west to Arabia and Persia in the east – about 9% of the world's land area.

So how big is that? 13 million sq km.

How many people were governed by this empire? At the time, around 30% of the world's population.

Where was the capital? Damascus.

What was their impact on Islam? Both positive and negative: they implemented a campaign of mass conversions to Islam but their dynasty was largely responsible for the damaging Sunni-Shiite split.

How were they regarded in their day? The minority Shiite resented the schism they caused by failing to uphold Prophet Mohammed's bloodline.

But the Sunnis supported them, presumably? Not exactly. Public Sunni opinion was that the Umayyad rulers were dim-witted sinners, preoccupied with earthly delights.

Is this what caused their demise? Partly. In 747 a rebellion of dissatisfied subjects on the fringe of the empire, combined with a huge earthquake in the region, led to a take-over of the empire by Shiite forces (known as the Abbasids) from Persia in 750.

Are the Umayyads remembered today? Yes! They established Arabic as the administrative language of the Middle East, their pan-Arab approach is used by nationalists to evoke an Arab Golden Age, and their association with the colour white is reflected in most modern flags of Arab countries.

Any other cultural legacies? They built the Dome of the Rock in Jerusalem and the Umayyad Mosque in Damascus, two of the great icons of Islamic art.

What was their significance in the area we now call Jordan? The string of hunting lodges, bathhouses and pleasure palaces known collectively as the 'desert castles' were built by the Umayyads – festive expressions of their creative and exuberant reign.

Azraq الأزرق

☑ 05 / POP 8000 / ELEV 510M

Meaning 'blue' in Arabic, Azraq once lived up to its name with a shimmering lake and extensive wetlands famed throughout the entire region. This magical oasis was both a refuge for wildlife in the middle of the arid Eastern Desert and a beacon for pilgrims and caravans plying the trade routes between Baghdad and Jerusalem. And then catastrophe struck: the wetlands were all but drained to supply the ever-increasing demands of the capital for water and the fortunes of the town and surrounding farming settlements withered.

That's not to say there is now no reason to visit. Azraq has reinvented itself as a pit stop for trucks pounding the Eastern Desert Highway between Amman and Baghdad, and for overland convoys from Saudi Arabia, and as such it has a frontier town atmosphere. The drivers who veer into this crossroads are all long-haul survivors who, in many cases, contend with the hazards not just of interminably tedious roads but also of ambush and the threat of violence. Have a cup of tea with any of these warriors of the long-distance road in the restaurants or mechanic workshops that line the roads of Azraq and suddenly your journey from Amman won't seem so far.

The modern reality of Azraq apart, the town neighbours one of the best of the desert castles, **Qasr al-Azraq**, and has the region's only accommodation. In the vicinity are the **Azraq Wetland Reserve** and the **Shaumari Wildlife Reserve**, making the most of what little remains of Azraq's once glorious natural inheritance.

History

As the region's most important permanent body of water and as a source for malachite, Azraq has been settled since neolithic times. The Romans, Mamluks and Ottomans each had turns controlling the area and in 1917–18 the town served as a staging post for the soldiers of Faisal's Arab Revolt. Lawrence of Arabia overwintered in the fort, using it as a temporary headquarter.

The town is home to two distinct communities. After WWI Druze refugees fleeing Syria settled in North Azraq, earning a living from salt production. South Azraq, meanwhile, was founded by Chechens fleeing Russian persecution, who eked out a living by farming and fishing on the shores of the oasis. Azraq Lodge is run by people from this community and the restaurant produces robust Chechen meals.

The recent settlement of Palestinian and Syrian immigrants has diluted ethnic distinctions and the virtual death of the oasis in the 1990s caused much of the local population to seek a living elsewhere. A brighter future appeared briefly on the horizon, with the increase in tourism to the Eastern Desert injecting extra life into the local economy, but now the region is more concerned with shoring up the new refugee camp. The prefabricated huts of Azraq Camp, which can be seen extending for miles across the desert midway between Amman and Azraq, was built by the United Nations in 2014 to house the burgeoning population of Syrian refugees escaping the conflict north of the border.

🛏 Sleeping & Eating

On a day trip it's difficult to cover anything more than the main desert castles that lie close to the highway. With an overnight stop in Azraq, you can also add a visit to Shaumari Wildlife Reserve, which is currently only possible on a pre-arranged night safari. Best of all, you can sample a Chechen dinner at Azraq Lodge.

★**Azraq Lodge** HOTEL **$$**
(📋3835017; s/d incl breakfast from JD70/82; ❄) This former British 1940s military hospital in South Azraq has been atmospherically renovated by the Royal Society for the Conservation of Nature (RSCN) as a base from which to explore the Eastern Desert. The RSCN has succeeded in preserving the historic building while incorporating modern facilities, so thankfully there's no need to rough it on bare stretchers.

There's an old field ambulance parked under a canvas porch and some period photographs (worth a visit in their own right) hung alongside paraffin lamps and gas masks to while away the hours before supper. While anyone raving about hospital food could normally expect to be admitted – or committed – at Azraq Lodge the traditional Chechen dishes served from the modernised hospital canteen are likely to be some of the best you sample in Jordan. Ring ahead to request lunch or dinner (around JD15) and come with a healthy appetite: the pomegranate salads and thyme-scented meat dishes arrive in generous portions on shared platters.

The lodge also houses a small handicraft workshop (9am to 4pm, Saturday to Thursday) where women from the local community make and sell silk screen prints, ostrich-egg paintings and recycled paper products.

Al-Azraq Resthouse HOTEL **$$**
(📋3895215; s/d/tr incl breakfast from JD45/55/65; ❄ 🅢 ⓢ) This poorly maintained hotel features unkempt rooms in need of maintenance, but with minimal local alternatives it's an option if Azraq Lodge is full. The pool is available for day use (JD10 for four hours) and there is a restaurant serving standard international fare. It's about 2km north of the Azraq T-junction and 1.5km along a local track.

Azraq Palace Restaurant JORDANIAN **$$**
(📋079 935070; buffet JD10; ⓣ11am-4pm & 6-11pm) Apart from Azraq Lodge, this is the best place to eat in town, which is why it

attracts tour groups on desert-castle excursions. The standard Jordanian fare of rice, grills, salads and dips is tasty and filling and the management helpful.

ℹ️ Getting There & Away

Minibuses run up and down the road along northern and southern Azraq in search of passengers before joining the highway to Zarqa (JD1.500, 1½ hours). If you are driving, you have the choice here of joining Hwy 5, which leads south after at least three or four hours of utter desolation to southern Jordan. The drive to Amman along either Hwy 30 or Hwy 40 takes around two hours. Make sure you obey the rules of desert driving and fill up with petrol when you see a station, as pumps are few and far between.

Qasr al-Azraq قصر الأزرق

It was to be Ali's first view of Azraq, and we hurried up the stony ridge in high excitement, talking of the wars and songs and passions of the early shepherd kings, with names like music, who had loved this place; and of the Roman legionaries who languished here as garrison in yet earlier times.

TE Lawrence, Seven Pillars of Wisdom

On the edge of dusty Azraq, this imposing fort is where TE Lawrence and Sharif Hussein bin Ali based themselves in the winter of 1917–18 during the Arab Revolt against the Turks.

Lawrence set up his quarters in the room above the southern entrance, while his loyal followers braved the elements in other areas of the fort. They were holed up here for several months in crowded conditions with little shelter from the intense cold – gaping holes in the roof were patched up with nothing but palm branches and clay.

Despite the hardships endured during his stay at Azraq, TE Lawrence writes fondly about the time spent with his men at arms. In the evenings everyone would assemble before a great fire in the open courtyard and break bread while swapping stories of war, peace and love. At the time, the castle also commanded sweeping views of the nearby palm-fringed oasis at Azraq.

History

Comparatively little is known about the history of Qasr al-Azraq, and there's been little excavation and renovation. Greek and Latin inscriptions date earlier constructions on the site to around AD 300, coinciding with Roman occupation.

The fort was renovated by the Umayyad caliph Walid II, who used it for hunting and as a military base. Its present form dates to 1237 when it was fortified by the Ayyubids as a defence against the Crusaders. The Turks subsequently stationed a garrison here in the 16th century. The tide turned in 1918, when it was from this building that the Arab Revolt launched an attack on Damascus that proved successful in ousting the Turks from the region.

◉ Sights

★ **Qasr al-Azraq** CASTLE
(admission JD1, ticket also valid for Qusayr Amra & Qasr Kharana; ⊙ daylight hours) Constructed out of black basalt stone, Qasr al-Azraq was originally three storeys high. Some paving stones in the main entrance have small indentations, carved by former gatekeepers who played a board game using pebbles to pass the time. By the courtyard entrance, look for the carvings of animals and various inscriptions.

Above the entrance is **Lawrence's Room**, strategically overlooking the entry and offset with arrow slits for defence. Opposite the entrance, and just to the left, are the remains of an **altar**, built in the 3rd century AD by the Romans. In the middle of the courtyard is a small **mosque**, angled as usual to face Mecca – it dates from the Ayyubid period (early 13th century), but was built on the ruins of a Byzantine church. In the northeast corner of the courtyard, a hole with stairs leads down to a **well**, full of water until about 20 years ago. In the northwest corner are the ruins of the **prison**.

The northern sections are residential areas with barely discernible ruins of a kitchen and dining room, and nearby storerooms and stables. The **tower** in the western wall is the most spectacular, and features a huge door made of a single massive slab of basalt. Lawrence describes in his book *Seven Pillars of Wisdom* how it 'went shut with a clang and crash that made tremble the west wall of the castle'.

ℹ️ Getting There & Away

The fort is situated on the edge of Azraq ash-Shomali (North Azraq), about 5km north of the Azraq T-junction. From the town centre, a taxi to the fort costs around JD2 (JD5 with a one-hour wait) – if you can persuade a taxi to bother with such a small commission.

Azraq Oasis محمية واحة الأزرق

For several millennia, the Qa'al Azraq (Azraq Basin) comprised a huge area of mudflats, pools and marshlands, which led to the establishment of Azraq as one of the most important oasis towns in the Levant. Although the basin was declared an 'internationally important wetland' by the Jordanian government in 1977, this largely token gesture failed to stop an environmental catastrophe. To provide fresh drinking water for the burgeoning cities of Amman and Irbid, the wetlands were all but drained by 1991.

◉ Sights & Activities

The Royal Society for the Conservation of Nature (RSCN) estimates that about 300 species of resident and migratory birds currently use the wetlands during their winter migration from Europe to Africa. They include raptors, larks, warblers, finches, harriers, eagles, plovers and ducks. A few buffaloes also wallow in the marshy environs, and jackals and gerbils are occasionally spotted in the late evening. The best time to see birdlife is in winter (December to February) and early spring (March and April). Large flocks of raptors steadily arrive in May. Ultimately, however, bird populations are dependent on the water levels in

DIARY OF AN ECOLOGICAL DISASTER

The **Azraq Oasis** and surrounding wetlands originally fanned out over 12,710 sq km, and was once regarded as the most important source of water in the region. Today it is considered one of the region's largest ecological disasters. The diary of this catastrophe makes for tragic reading.

200,000 BC Human settlement and herds of elephants, cheetahs, lions and hippos are evident around the Azraq Oasis.

8000 BC Age of the 'fossil water' collected in Azraq.

1950 Around 3000 cu metres of water fills the wetlands per year.

1960s Extraction of fossil water from the wetlands to the expanding cities of Amman and Irbid begins.

1967 On 2 February, 347,000 birds are recorded in the wetlands.

1975 Twice as much water is pumped from Azraq than the oasis can replenish in order to supply one-quarter of Amman's water demands.

1977 The Jordanian government signed an international wetlands-protection treaty that led to the establishment of the Azraq Wetland Reserve.

1980 Only 10 cu metres per year of water (compared with 3000 cu metres in 1950) fills the wetlands, exacerbated by the sinking of private, illegal wells for farming.

1991 The water table drops to over 10m below the ground, and the wetlands dry up completely.

1994 Funding and commitment from the UN Development Program (UNDP), Jordanian government and RSCN tries to halt the pumping of water from the wetlands to urban centres.

Mid-1990s Overpumping destroys the natural balance between the freshwater aquifer and the underground brine, resulting in brackish water unpalatable for wildlife, and hopeless for drinking and irrigation.

1998 Species of killifish (Aphanius sirhani), a small fish of only 4cm to 5cm in length and unique to Azraq, is brought to the edge of extinction.

2000 On 2 February, only 1200 birds are recorded in the wetlands.

2011 Around 1.5 million cu metres of fresh water is now being pumped back into the wetlands every year by the Jordanian Ministry of Water.

2015 Projected restoration of about 10% of the wetlands – providing the estimated 500 illegal deep wells operating in the area can be brought under control.

the reserve and as the water continues to be pumped out quicker than it is pumped in, the future of the oasis remains in jeopardy.

★ **Azraq Wetland Reserve**   NATURE RESERVE
(☑ 3835017; admission JD8.120; ⊙ 9am-6pm, to 4pm Sep-Feb) Administered by the RSCN, this small reserve is good for bird-watching. The Azraq Basin was originally 12,710 sq km (an area larger than Lebanon), but overpumping of ground water sucked the wetlands dry in the 1970s and '80s. In recent years, the RSCN has seized control of the wetlands and established a small nature reserve to help facilitate the recovery of the wetlands. Bird populations have returned but the wetlands remain a meagre reflection of their past glory.

An environmental recovery project of this magnitude is certainly worth support, and the on-site visitor centre has well-documented (if tragic and poorly maintained) exhibits detailing the history of the basin's demise.

Marsh Trail   HIKING
(easy; ⊙ 30min, unguided) The 1.5km pathway through the reserve gives an idea of the former beauty of the wetlands. Take a pair of binoculars and stop at the bird hide to spot ducks squabbling between the seasonal reed beds. A viewing platform overlooking the Shishan springs is worth noting: these springs once watered the entire wetlands.

Bring a bird book during migration as all sorts of unusual species turn up for a drink before heading across the surrounding desert plains. It takes a hard heart not to be moved by the scale of the ecological devastation visited on this former regional wonder.

❶ Getting There & Away

The Azraq Wetland Reserve is located 500m east of Azraq and is signposted off the main road.

Shaumari Wildlife Reserve

Established in 1975 by the RSCN, this 22 sq km reserve (Mahmiyyat ash-Shaumari; www. rscn.org.jo; ⊙ 8am-4pm) was created with the aim of reintroducing wildlife that has disappeared from the region, most notably the highly endangered Arabian oryx, Persian onagers (wild ass), goitered and Dorcas gazelles, and blue-necked ostriches.

At the time of research, the Shaumari Wildlife Reserve remained closed to visitors while it continues to undergo a radical overhaul. A night safari may be possible to arrange with advanced booking from the RSCN.

UNICORNS OF THE DESERT

The last time the Arabian oryx was seen in the wild in Jordan was in 1920 when hunting drove this magnificent, straight-horned antelope to local extinction. In 1972, the last wild Arabian oryx was killed by hunters in Oman, which led officials to declare the oryx extinct in the wild. However, in a remarkable conservation effort, the nine oryxes left in captivity (known now as the 'World Oryx Herd') were pooled together and taken to the Arizona Zoo for a captive breeding programme.

In 1978, four male and four female oryxes bred in Arizona were transported to Jordan in an effort to help re-establish the country's wild population. Under the auspices of the Royal Society for the Conservation of Nature (RSCN), the first calf, Dusha, was born at the Shaumari Wildlife Reserve the following year. Five years later, there were 31 oryxes at Shaumari. Since then, some have been released into the wild at Wadi Rum – a not altogether successful enterprise. The next step is to introduce oryx in other protected areas throughout the country. This has prompted the RSCN to overhaul their facilities at Shaumari significantly in the hopes of attracting greater interest and funding from tourists in their vital conservation project.

The return of the oryx to Jordan was the occasion of great national pride, which prompts the question: what is it about this antelope that provokes such emotion? Perhaps it's the uncanny resemblance of a mature bull, with rapier-like antlers, to the mythical unicorn. This is not as far-fetched as it seems. The ancient Egyptians used to bind the antlers of young oryx so they would fuse into one. Seeing a white, summer-coated herd-bull level up to a rival in profile, it's easy to confuse fact with fiction.

ⓘ Getting There & Away

The turning for Shaumari is well signposted, 7km from the Azraq T-junction, along the road to the Saudi border. A small potholed road leads a further 6km to the reserve. The last kilometre is gravel, but is easily manageable in a 2WD.

Qasr 'Uweinid   قصر عوينيد

If you can find this little scrap of history in the middle of the Eastern Desert, you deserve a medal! Once a robust and practical structure, built by the Romans in the 3rd century AD to protect the source of Wadi as-Sirhan (now in Saudi Arabia), this fort was abandoned less than 100 years later. All that remains now are the outline of the fort in broken walls and a couple of ruined wells and cisterns.

⊙ Sights

Qasr 'Uweinid   CASTLE
(⊘24hr) FREE You don't come to a fort like this to look at the pile of old stones, strewn across the wadi bottom – even though some of those stones have evocative inscriptions and even though you may well be one of only a handful of people to have stepped over the threshold in centuries. No, you come to a castle like this to enjoy the excuse it provides to encounter the desert.

A shallow wadi runs alongside the fort, home to stunted tamarisk trees and shrubs of stick-tight (a type of herb). From the top of the ruins, a vast sky opens up across the almost entirely flat horizon. The silence is almost audible as the nothingness pulses in your ears. This is why you attempt a visit to a castle like Qasr 'Uweinid, to experience the absence of all the usual clutter and noise. If you don't find it, it doesn't matter, but you will have gained a greater understanding of why for centuries visitors have been beguiled by the desert, sand or no sand!

ⓘ Getting There & Away

It's probably fair to say that you'll never find it without help (in researching Qasr 'Uweinid, a Bedouin sheikh and a police escort helped us locate the pile of greyish ruins on a small tell about 8km southwest of Shaumari). A 4WD isn't strictly necessary as the gravel plain is firm and when it stops being firm, you can get out and walk the last 500m.

Qusayr Amra   قصر عمرا

Today, Qusayr Amra appears randomly rooted on the parched desert plain, but in ancient times the site was carefully chosen for its proximity to a lush wadi famed for its wild pistachio trees. The bathhouse was supplied with underground water, tapped from the water table, which lay closer to the surface in former centuries. This potable water was accessed by deep masonry-clad wells – one of which can still be seen at the site a few metres north of the main building.

Adjacent to this 36m-deep well a restored *saqiyah* (a contraption activated by the circular pacing of a donkey), shows how the water would have been pumped to a cistern diverted either to the baths or to be siphoned off and traded to passing caravans.

The main three-vaulted structure is well-restored but what would otherwise be a fairly modest site is made remarkable by the high state of preservation of the floor-to-ceiling frescoes decorating the interior of Qusayr Amra. An impressive restoration effort has returned much of the vividness of colour to the Bacchanalian scenes of hunting, nude bathing and revelry.

History

The Umayyads built Qusayr Amra around AD 711 during the reign of Walid I (AD 705–15). Walid is most famous for launching a building campaign across the Umayyad empire that was crowned by the Umayyad Mosque in Damascus and the Dome of the Rock in Jerusalem.

In contrast to the religious solemnity of these grand projects, the bathhouse at Amra is devoted to more carnal subjects. Although Walid's disapproving successor ordered the destruction of all such imagery, fortunately for Amra, the far-reaching hand of Damascus spared this remote outpost of the Eastern Desert, allowing the modern visitor to appreciate a humour not normally associated with the early expressions of Islamic society.

Excavation at the site began in the mid-1970s under a team of Spanish archaeologists, and the frescoes were restored with funding from Austria, France and Spain. In 1985, the frescoes were formally recognised as important works, and Qusayr Amra became a World Heritage site.

⊙ Sights

★ Qusayr Amra   CASTLE
(admission JD1, ticket also valid for Qasr al-Azraq & Qasr Kharana; ⊗ 8am-6pm May-Sep, to 4pm Oct-Apr) One of the best-preserved desert buildings of the Umayyads, the Unesco World Heritage site of Qusayr Amra is the highlight of a trip into the Eastern Desert. Part of a much greater complex that served as a caravanserai, bathhouse and hunting lodge, the *qusayr* (little castle) is renowned for its rather risqué 8th-century frescoes of wine, women and wild times.

Walking downhill from the visitors centre towards the modest little structure, it's hard not to wonder what all the fuss is about. Even entering the main building into the **audience hall**, where meetings, parties, exhibitions and meals were once held, is decidedly underwhelming as the searing light of the surrounding desert all but obliterates the frescoes within.

But then your eyes grow accustomed to the light and you are greeted by two bare-breasted women painted on the arches, holding bowls of food (or money) against a blue background, draped in richly detailed cloth. Five centuries before the Early Renaissance in Europe, these frescoes depict a touchingly human quality – wrestlers warm up before the contest, a woman dressed in a mere strip of cloth bathes without coyness in a hinted patch of sunlight, the ear of a gazelle twitches as the herd surges ahead of the hunt, dogs pant as they race across the **west wall**, driving wild onagers into a trap of nets. Even the mundane construction of the baths is immortalised in the frescoes – in the compartmentalised images on the ceiling, depicting quarrying, moving the stones by camel, carpentry and plastering of the walls.

These are not the normal stylised images of the day, belonging to a religious canon of signs and symbols. Instead they appear to be a unique attempt to capture daily reality – quite unlike the geometric imagery that has come to be associated with early Islamic art.

That's not to say the frescoes fail to pay homage to more weighty subject matter. Look for the defaced image of the Umayyad caliph and you'll see he is surrounded by **six great rulers**, four of whom have been identified – a Byzantine emperor, Caesar; the Visigoth king, Roderick; the Persian emperor, Chosroes; and the Negus of Abyssinia. The fresco either implies that the Umayyad ruler was their equal or better, or it is simply a pictorial list of Islam's enemies.

And if the frescoes pay lip service to concerning matters of the day, they also encompass their own mostly forgotten symbolism too. A small doorway leads to the left through the three small rooms that made up the baths. The **apodyterium** (changing room) has three blackened faces on the ceiling, said to depict the three stages of man's life. Local Christians believe the central figure to be a depiction of Christ. The left wall has a hallucinogenic painting of an exuberant bear playing the banjo, egged on by an applauding monkey which no doubt would have suggested some political vanity of the day.

In the **tepidarium** (where warm water was offered and warm air circulated beneath the floor) naked women bathe a child while in the neighbouring hot-water **calidarium**, which is closest to the furnace outside, a whole Dome of Heaven spirals around the ceiling. This map of the northern hemisphere sky, accompanied by the signs of the zodiac, is among the earliest known attempts to represent the universe on anything other than a flat surface. Centaur-like Sagittarius, the Great Bear and several other zodiac signs (see the map in the visitor centre for details) would have been a fitting ultimate subject of contemplation for contemporary bathers.

ⓘ Information

Visitor Centre (⊗ 8am-6pm May-Sep, to 4pm Oct-Apr) Tickets and public toilets are available here. A relief map of the site, descriptions of the site's history and the plan of the frescoes help in identifying some of the key highlights that are hard to discern without an idea of what to expect. A Bedouin tent erected by enterprising locals sells mint tea, minimal refreshments and souvenirs.

Photography of the interior of Qusayr Amra is still unregulated, but bear in mind that flash photography, and indeed touching the walls, will harm the frescoes.

ⓘ Getting There & Away

Qusayr Amra is on the north side of Hwy 40, 26km from Azraq. It is only signposted coming from Amman, so keep an eye out if you are approaching in the other direction as the small, dune-coloured buildings are easy to miss. No minibuses travel this route and buses will not stop at Amra making it impossible to visit by public transport. Without a car, the only option is to hire a taxi from Azraq (from JD15 return if you can persuade one to take you!).

THE FRESCOES OF QUSAYR AMRA

The information boards in the visitor centre at Qusayr Amra assure the visitor that: 'None of the paintings of Qusayr Amra portray scenes of unbridled loose-living or carryings-on'. Given the context of early Islam's prohibition of any illustrations of living beings, it's difficult to agree.

Just how far these boundaries were pushed is evident on the western wall of the audience hall, where there is a depiction of a nude woman bathing. Some historians speculate that she may have been modelled on the favourite concubine of the ruler of Amra. The more your eyes roam the walls, past images of musicians, naked dancers, cherubs, baskets of fruit (and even a bear playing a banjo!) the more the heresy of the frescoes becomes apparent.

And the purpose of all these paintings? Some Islamic scholars blame the Ghassanids, a pagan Arab tribe that ruled the region at the time of Rome, others mumble about rogue rulers who were not true to Islam. But most admit privately that it seems as though the rulers were simply enjoying themselves on a boys' night out, away from the confines of the court.

Qasr Kharana قصر خرانه

Although it clearly isn't a castle, Kharana was a vital building for the Umayyads as evidenced by its dramatic size and shape. Despite the fact that it has the appearance of a khan (caravanserai), Kharana wasn't located on any major trade route, and there appears to be a total absence of structures for water storage. That just leaves the supposition that the building served as a meeting space for Damascus elite and local Bedouin.

Named after the *harra* (surrounding gravel plains), Kharana lords imposingly over a harsh and barren moonscape that appears inhospitable for human habitation. Inside, however, the internal courtyard provides a calm, protected space that even the wind fails to penetrate.

History

Very little is known about the origins of Qasr Kharana, although a painted inscription above one of the doors on the upper floor mentions the date AD 710, making it one of the earliest forts of the Islamic era. The presence of stones with Greek inscriptions in the main entrance also suggests it was built on the site of a Roman or Byzantine building, possibly as a private residence.

◉ Sights

★ **Qasr Kharana** CASTLE
(admission JD1, ticket also valid for Qusayr Amra & Qasr Al-Azraq; ⊘8am-6pm May-Sep, to 4pm Oct-Apr) Located in the middle of a vast, treeless plain, this imposing thick-walled structure

was the most likely inspiration for the 'desert castle' moniker and is arguably the most photogenic of all the desert castles. There is controversy about its function and purpose, but this important Umayyad structure remains an interesting sight for visitors, off the main Azraq–Amman road.

Despite its castle-like appearance, there is no evidence that the intimidating two-storey building, with what appear to be round, defensive towers and narrow arrow slits, was ever intended as a fort. In fact, the towers are completely solid, which means that they couldn't be manned by armed soldiers and it would be impossible to fire bows from the bizarrely shaped 'arrow slits', meaning that they most likely served as air and light ducts.

About 60 rooms surround the **courtyard** inside the castle, and most likely served as meeting spaces for visiting delegations. The long rooms either side of the arched entrance were used as **stables**, and in the centre of the courtyard was a basin for collecting rainwater. Remarkably, the interior is much smaller than you'd imagine as the walls are deceptively thick.

Climb the broad stairways and you'll find rooms on the upper storeys with vaulted ceilings. Some **carved plaster medallions**, set around the top of the walls, are said to indicate Mesopotamian influence.

Also in one of the rooms on the 2nd floor are a few lines of Arabic **graffiti**, which were crucial in helping to establish the age of the fortress. Above the door in simple black script is an inscription which translates to 'Abd al-Malik the son of Ubayd wrote it on

Monday three days from Muharram of the year 92'. Stairs in the southeast and southwest corners lead to the 2nd floor and the roof (closed to visitors).

ℹ️ Information

Visitor Centre (⊙ 8am-6pm May-Sep, to 4pm Oct-Apr) Entrance to the Kharana is through the visitor centre, which has some displays on local history. The hospitable owner of the adjacent Bedouin tent, which doubles as the site coffeehouse and souvenir stall, will brew you fresh mint tea and take time to discuss the issues of the day. Your patronage will be much appreciated if the current absence of tourism continues. Public toilets are available.

ℹ️ Getting There & Away

Kharana is 16km further west along Hwy 40 from Qusayr Amra. There's no viable public transport along the highway (although it could be included in a round trip by taxi from Azraq, from JD20) and the castle is only signposted coming from Amman. It's easier to spot than neighbouring Amra, especially as it's disappointingly close to a power station.

Qasr al-Mushatta قصر المشتى

The construction of Qasr al-Mushatta is believed to have started in about AD 743, under Caliph Walid II, who intended to establish a large city. Although the fort was planned as the biggest and most lavish of all the desert castles, it was never finished. In 744, Walid II was assassinated by angry labourers, many of whose colleagues had died during construction due to a lack of water in the area.

👁️ Sights

Qasr al-Mushatta   CASTLE
(⊙ daylight hr) **FREE** Of the five major desert castles, the 'winter palace' of Qasral-Mushatta is the most time-consuming to reach, and thus usually not part of most organised tours. But this is not to say that recently reconstructed Mushatta is located in the middle of nowhere – on the contrary, it's the closest of the desert castles to Amman. In fact, the ruins may be the last thing you see in the country as they're located right next to Queen Alia International Airport.

If you ignore the occasional sound of jumbo jets soaring overhead, the extensive ruins hint at the vast potential of the caliph's grand vision. Many pieces have disappeared over the years, ending up in museums around the world. The elaborate carving on the facade was shipped off to Berlin (it's now in the Pergamon Museum) after the palace was 'given' to Kaiser Wilhelm in 1903 by Sultan Abd al-Hamid of Turkey. Mushatta was also partially destroyed by earthquakes, and most of the columns and watchtowers have long since collapsed. However, the huge exterior wall and carved facades still hint at the original grandeur and beauty of the site.

Right of the entrance are the ruins of a mosque, with its obviously rebuilt mihrab (the niche in a mosque, indicating direction of Mecca). The northern sections have the remains of a vaulted audience hall and residences. Segmented pillars lie scattered around like broken vertebrae. One unusual feature of the site is that the vaults were made from burnt bricks (an uncommon material in buildings

---

ℹ️ VISITING THE DESERT CASTLES BY PUBLIC TRANSPORT

Although this is one region that really repays extra expenditure on a tour or on car hire, that doesn't mean the Eastern Desert is off limits to independent travellers on public transport. What it does mean is that you have to be selective about the castles you want to visit and be realistic about the time it takes to get there. There's no accommodation in the region except at Azraq, so early morning trips are best, giving you enough time to return to base. If you leave Amman (or Irbid) in the afternoon for the Eastern Desert, you run the risk of getting stranded.

You can visit the castles at **Umm Jimal**, **Hallabat** and **Azraq** by public transport, although it's almost impossible to travel between these sites without returning to Amman – or at least Zarqa. You shouldn't rely on hitching as there's little traffic and, at the time of writing, this was not recommended due to the number of refugees on the move.

Probably the most rewarding itinerary is to take the bus to Azraq (via Zarqa) and stay two nights. On the day of arrival you can walk from the town to **Qasr Azraq** and the following morning you can visit the **Azraq Wetland Reserve**. Take a taxi in the afternoon of the second day to **Qusayr Amra** and **Qasr Karana** and return to Azraq in the evening. On the third day, you can head back to Amman.

of this style) rather than black basalt. And of course, be sure not to miss the ancient toilets (complete with drains), which are located at the back of the hall.

ℹ️ Getting There & Away

Qasr al-Mushatta is impossible to reach by public transport. As the castle is located near sensitive areas – primarily the airport – make sure you have your passport ready to show the guards at the military checkpoints along the route.

If you're driving from Amman, head towards the Queen Alia International Airport, turn left off the Desert Highway to the airport, then turn right at the roundabout just past the Golden Tulip Airport Hotel. Leave your passport at the first security check and then follow the road for 12km around the perimeter of the airport, turning right by the second and third check posts.

An alternative is to charter a taxi from the airport (JD17) – an idea if you have a long wait for a flight – or combine a taxi to the airport with a visit to the ruins. A visit can be made from the airport in an hour.

EASTERN DESERT HIGHWAY

To the east of the town of Mafraq in northern Jordan, the scattered fields and settlements of Druze communities gradually peter out, replaced by a stony, black basalt desert that stretches intermittently to Syria in the north and Iraq in the east. The desolate region has long been criss-crossed by pilgrimage and trade routes to Mecca and Baghdad, and its position as a 'strategic corridor' continues today as the location of the Trans-Arabia Pipeline.

The region is best defined, however, by Hwy 10, otherwise known as the Eastern Desert Highway, which rolls in an interminable straight line all the way to the frontier with Iraq. Traversing the corridor between eccentric borders – known as 'Winston's Hiccup' – it thunders day and night with high-sided trucks, many of which travel in convoy for safety's sake. The highway is only occasionally punctuated by a town, developed to service the passing traffic. These sparse and gritty settlements are pretty much the only manmade features of a desert otherwise left to the Bedouin and their goats.

Jordan's harsh deserts make up 80% of the country's land, yet support only 5% of its population. The day trip along the formidable Eastern Desert Highway is almost worth the tedium of the journey to be reminded of that fact. Throw in a couple of atmospheric desert castles and the excursion to this little-visited corner of Jordan may well prove to be a highlight of your trip.

There is no accommodation along Hwy 10 and a 4WD is needed to reach Burqu, in the middle of the desert at the eastern reach of the highway. With your own vehicle, a two-day round trip from Amman or Irbid can be made via the town of Safawi at the junction with Hwy 5, with a night's stopover at Azraq. With public transport, you can just about reach Umm al-Jimal as a day trip from the nearest place to stay, but forget trying to get from here to anywhere else along the Hwy 10 corridor.

At the time of writing, the intensification of the civil war in Syria and the conflict in Iraq made straying too close to either border unwise. Take local advice (for example through your consulate or from your hotel in Amman or Madaba) before venturing into this area. It is inadvisable to hitch or pick up hitchhikers along this route at present.

Mafraq المفرق

📅 04 / POP 293,700 / ELEV 700M

There's nothing of obvious tourist interest in this dusty and congested frontier town. However, like Zarqa, you may have to change buses here if you're travelling on public transport.

Mafraq has two terminals for buses, minibuses and service taxis. The larger Bedouin station has minibuses and service taxis to the north bus station (Tabarbour) in Amman (JD1.300, one hour) as well as to Zarqa and Umm al-Jimal. Although occasional minibuses roam along the back roads to Deir al-Kahf (for Qasr Deir al-Kahf), bear in mind that as no accommodation is available in the area, you stand a high chance of being stranded. Equally, the minibus to Ar-Ruwayshid (nearest town to Qasr Burqu) won't help you as the castle site is utterly inaccessible without a 4WD from there.

From the Fellahin station, buses, minibuses and service taxis go to places in northern Jordan, such as Jerash and Irbid.

WINSTON'S HICCUP

When Winston Churchill was serving as British Colonial Secretary in the early 1920s, he once boasted that he had 'created Trans-Jordan with the stroke of a pen on a Sunday afternoon in Cairo'. As Churchill had something of a reputation for enjoying 'liquid lunches', a rumour started to fly that he had hiccuped while attempting to draw the border, and stubbornly refused to allow it to be redefined. The resulting zigzag in Jordan's eastern border subsequently became known as **Winston's Hiccup**.

Of course, Churchill was anything but drunk and foolish. The zigzag was precisely plotted to excise Wadi Sirhan, an age-old Incense Route and vital communication highway between French-controlled Syria and Arabia, from Jordan. The pen stroke also created a panhandle between Azraq and Iraq, which meant that the British now controlled an unbroken corridor between the Mediterranean Sea and the Gulf.

Today Jordan's erratic boundaries with Syria, Iraq and Saudi Arabia are of little political consequence, at least in comparison to the heightened emotions surrounding the border with Israel. However, Winston's Hiccup does stand as testament to a time when little to no lip service was given to the colonial division of occupied foreign lands.

Umm al-Jimal   أم الجمال

The famed American archaeologist HC Butler once wrote: 'Far out in the desert, in the midst of the rolling plain, there is a deserted city all of basalt, rising black and forbidding from the grey of the plain.' Indeed, Umm al-Jimal is one of the region's most captivating sites, and the opportunity to scramble across huge basalt blocks warmed by the heat of the desert sun is not to be missed.

It's best to visit early in the morning, or late in the afternoon, when the black basalt isn't too hot. Allow at least an hour or two to visit the site, although its enormous size (800m by 500m) invites lengthier exploration.

History

Supposedly founded in 1 BC by the Nabataeans, Umm al-Jimal (meaning 'Mother of Camels') is notable for the inverted V-shaped roofs, constructed from black basalt. The town was taken over by the Romans who used it as part of their defensive cordon against the desert tribes and it prospered as an important trading station for Bedouin and passing caravans. From Umm al-Jimal, roads led north to Bosra (in present-day Syria) and southwest to Philadelphia (modern Amman), which firmly established the town on most of the region's major trade routes.

The city grew during the Byzantine period when churches were constructed and Roman buildings demilitarised. At the peak of growth, this thriving agricultural city boasted some 3000 inhabitants. The key to Umm al-Jimal's prosperity lay in its sophisticated method of storing water, which was a necessity for surviving the long periods between rainfall and for irrigating staple crops. Even today, many of the ancient town's reservoirs are still virtually intact.

Umm al-Jimal declined in the early 7th century AD, coinciding with an outbreak of the bubonic plague and an earthquake in 747 which forced the remaining inhabitants to flee the city.

The ruins of Umm al-Jimal were briefly occupied by Druze refugees fleeing persecution in Syria in the early 20th century. Today, a small modern village has sprung up around the impressive ghost town which is now home to only a few stray dogs and children trotting through the ruins on a shortcut to school with their notebooks tucked under their arms.

⊙ Sights

★**Umm al-Jimal Ruins**   RUIN
(⊙daylight hours) `FREE` The unpretentious urban architecture of Umm al-Jimal, near the Jordanian–Syrian border, encompasses over 150 buildings standing one to three stories above ground, including 128 houses and 15 churches. Together, these buildings provide a fascinating insight into rural life during the Roman, Byzantine and early Islamic periods. Compared with other archaeological sites in the region, Umm al-Jimal was rarely looted or vandalised, which has left much of the original layout intact.

Comparatively little is known about the ruined city, referred to by archaeologists as the 'Black Gem of the Desert'. An extensive

Umm al-Jimal

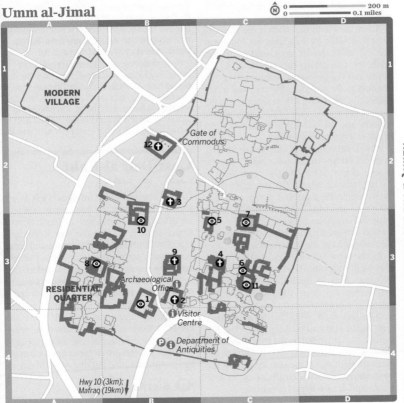

Umm al-Jimal

rural settlement in the lava lands east of Mafraq, the ruins are located on the edge of a series of volcanic basalt flows that slope down from Jebel Druze, providing high-quality building materials.

The large structure just past the southern entrance is the **barracks**, built by the Romans. The towers were added later and, like the castle at Azraq, it has a swinging basalt door that still functions. The **barracks chapel** was added to the east of the barracks during the Byzantine period (around the 5th century), and is inscribed with the names of the archangels Gabriel, Raphael, Michael and Uriel.

About 150m to the left (west) of the barracks is what some archaeologists believe is a **Nabataean temple** because of the altar in the middle. About 100m north of the barracks is the **Numerianos church**, one of several ruined Byzantine churches. Another 100m to the east is the **double church**, recognisable by its two semicircular naves, a wonderful structure that was renovated and extended several times over the centuries. About 80m to the right (east) is **house XVII**, whose double-door entrance, interior courtyard, fine corbelled ceilings, decorated doorways and carved pillars indicate that it was built by a wealthy family.

A few metres to the south is the **sheikh's house**, notable for its expansive courtyard, stables, black basalt door and stairways. Look for the gravity-defying stairs to the north and the precarious corner tower. You can just make out a double stairway to the east of the courtyard. After exiting the building you get a good view of the lovely arched window and vaulted semicircular basement in the exterior eastern wall.

About 150m north of the double church, steps lead down to the **main reservoir**, one of several around the city. Less than 100m to the left (west) is **house XIII**, originally a stable for domestic goats and sheep, and later renovated and used as a residence by Druze settlers. Here, take notice of the stone ventilation screen, which was used to separate the manger from the living space.

To the west (about 100m) is the **cathedral**, built in about AD 556, but now mostly in ruins – look for the lintel stone detailing the Roman emperors that ruled over the region. The **praetorium** (military headquarters) is less than 100m to the southwest. Built in the late 2nd century AD by the Romans, it was extended by the Byzantines and features a triple doorway. About 200m to the north through one of the old city gates is the **west church**, easily identifiable by its four arches and ornate Byzantine crosses.

❶ Information

Archaeological Office If someone hears your arrival, you'll be expected to sign the visitors' book. So few visitors come this way, however, you can excuse the warden for wandering off post now and again. While it is tempting to slip into the site incognito, it's probably worth letting someone in this office know that you have stepped into the site, just in case you break an ankle walking over the rubble. The site is so big and so deserted, you may not be discovered for days!

Visitor Centre (☉ daylight hours) More of a warden's post than a visitors centre, there are at least toilets at the entrance to Umm al-Jimal. For more details about the site, look for the hard-to-find booklet *Umm el-Jimal* (JD3), published by Al-Kutba and available sporadically at bookshops in Amman.

❶ Getting There & Away

Umm al-Jimal is about 20km east of Mafraq and only 10km from the Syrian border. With an early start, it is possible to do a day trip from Amman by public transport. From the Abdali or Raghadan bus stations in Amman, catch a bus or minibus to Bedouin station in Mafraq (possibly with a connection in Zarqa), and from Mafraq catch another minibus to Umm al-Jimal.

If you're driving, head 16km east of Mafraq along Hwy 10 towards Safawi, then take the signed turn-off north for 3km to Umm al-Jimal. If you have chartered a taxi from Amman for a day trip around the desert castles, it is possible to include Umm al-Jimal on the itinerary for a little extra (about JD10) – but start early to fit it all in.

Qasr Deir al-Kahf
قصر دير الكهف

One of the highlights of Qasr Deir is approaching it along the back roads that lead for 30km or so from Umm al-Jimal. Several Druze settlements dot the way with traditional basalt buildings still in use and small farms with active dovecotes staving off the northern reaches of the Eastern Desert.

The change in scenery is quite dramatic from here as the last of the irrigated farms are left behind on the rolling high ground, replaced by occasional Bedouin tents and herds of livestock. By the time you reach Hwy 10, the dust devils take over the plains and the land extends as far as the eye can see in an uninterrupted flat disc of nothingness.

◉ Sights

Qasr Deir al-Kahf CASTLE
FREE Built in the 4th century, the 'Monastery of Caves' is a purpose-built Roman fort that primarily served as a sentry post. Like its famous neighbour Umm al-Jimal, Deir al-Kahf is also constructed of black basalt, though the scattered ruins here are not nearly as extensive. There is an access road north of Hwy 10, or look for the signs along the back roads east of Umm al-Jimal.

❶ Getting There & Away

There's no reliable public transport to make a day trip from Amman or Irbid via Mafraq feasible. By car, the easiest way to be sure you are on the right road is to return to Hwy 10 and turn north at Salibayyah. After around 5km, veer right at the intersection with the road from Umm al-Jimal. There are intermittent signposts to Deir al-Kahf or follow your nose east for a further 25km, running parallel to the Syrian border. The fort is behind a police station. An access road leads for 10km south of the ruins to Al-Bishriyya on the Eastern Desert Highway.

FOR THE COMMITTED QASR-SPOTTER...

If the castles of the Zarqa-Azraq-Amman loop have whetted your appetite for Umayyad architecture, then you can earn your *qasr*-spotting badge by searching out one or two of the lesser *qasr* sites.

Qasr al-Tuba (⊙24hr) Easily the most impressive of the lesser-known castles, Tuba lies approximately 75km southeast of Amman and captures the sense of a staging post on long-forgotten incense routes. Tuba was erected by Caliph Walid II in about AD 743 and abandoned following his sudden assassination. Tuba is only accessible by 4WD along dirt tracks 50km south of Hwy 40, or 35km west of the Desert Highway.

The structure is unique for its sun-baked mud bricks and you can see an imposing doorway from the site at Amman's National Archaeological Museum. The sole nesting place in Jordan of the rare **Houbara bustard** is at nearby Thalathwat.

Qasr Mushash (⊙24hr) Once a grand Umayyad settlement, today Mushash lies in ruin. However, it's still possible to get a sense of the original layout, and there are a number of impressive buildings left standing including the remains of a palace, a large courtyard surrounded by a dozen rooms, baths, cisterns and walls built to protect against possible flooding. Only accessible by 4WD, Mushash can be reached via an access road along Hwy 40.

Safawi الطفاوي

📷 05 / POP 10,000 / ELEV 700M

A welcome sight along the Eastern Desert Highway is the small town of Safawi. In itself, the ramshackle collection of mechanic shops is unprepossessing to say the least but it does offer the chance to fill up with petrol, buy water and a snack and decide on whether you have enough energy to mount the assault on Qasr Burqu. Ar-Ruwayshid, the junction for Burqu, lies at least another hour and a half to the east (a round trip of four and a half hours from Safawi if you factor in the off-road visit to the lake).

Qasr Aseikhin قصر الشيخين

This small Roman **fort** (⊙24hr) FREE, built from basalt in the 3rd century over the ruins of a 1st-century Nabataean building, is an hour's detour from Safawi. The small structure is worth a visit for the commanding view of the plains, framed by a basaltic Roman arch. The surrounding vista gives you an idea of the struggle for survival endured by the Bedouin of the Badia – the local name for the Eastern Desert that stretches into Saudi Arabia; even camels are reluctant to pick their way across this rocky, basaltic plain.

The sealed access road to the ruins lies about 10km southwest of Safawi along Hwy 5. For some reason the access road stops about 1km short of the hilltop fort. The graded track thereafter is just about navigable in a 2WD vehicle but the walk is more rewarding if you want to get a sense of the utter remoteness of this former military outpost. From the junction with the main road, it is just 22km to Azraq.

Qasr Burqu قصر بورقو

You have to be a pretty dedicated castle spotter to visit this brooding black basalt fort, which stands guard over the silent shores of Ghadir (Lake) Burqu. Of course, the apparent incongruity of the lake in the harsh desert is what makes this place special. At the time of writing, it was only possible to organise trips to Qasr Burqu from the Royal Society for the Conservation of Nature (RSCN) base in Azraq by prior arrangement, though this may change in future.

⊙ Sights

Qasr Burqu CASTLE
(⊙24hr) FREE The Romans built the small fort at Burqu to protect a seasonal lake that provided precious water in a highly arid region. They helped conserve the water (run-off from the Haurun-Druze Plateau) by building a dam in the 3rd century, thereby securing water for caravans heading between Syria and Arabia. The fort became a monastery during the Byzantine period, and was later restored by the Umayyads in about AD 700.

Remarkably, an inscription on one of the walls of the fort suggests that it may have been occupied as late as 1409.

The lake, which often dries out in summer, is home to a number of bird species (including finches, storks, sandpipers, larks, cranes, buzzards, eagles and vultures) that come to roost because the water level rarely changes, even in summer. The harshness of the surrounding landscape, as well as the lack of properly graded roads, has acted as a strong deterrent against poaching, although the Bedouin occasionally fly their birds of prey in the area. Home to gazelles, desert hares, foxes, hyenas and even caracals this remarkable little oasis has all the makings of a national reserve.

Wild camping is possible out here (don't pitch too close to the lake for the sake of the wildlife – the winged, six-legged varieties bite viciously at dusk) but don't expect that your presence will go unnoticed. The local Bedouin are bound to find you and wonder what you are doing here, on the fringes of civilisation. They are also likely to insist you share tea with them.

With a tent, some basic survival gear and a reliable 4WD, you can enjoy a serious desert adventure out here which is precisely why the RSCN has been fighting to establish Burqu as a protected reserve, fitting nicely into its plans to develop tourism in the Eastern Desert. To see if it's possible to pre-arrange a guided tour to Qasr Burqu from Azraq, contact the RSCN at the Wild Jordan Centre in Amman.

ⓘ Getting There & Away

The good news for the flora and fauna – and the bad news for would-be visitors – is that Burqu is only accessible by 4WD. The lake and castle lie 22km northwest of Ar-Ruwayshid, a 45-minute drive across the desert on unmarked and unclear tracks from Hwy 10. The turn-off is about 3km west of Ar-Ruwayshid at a sign for Burqu spelt as 'Boarg'a'.

Although the driving is fairly straight forward, with a hard surface to within a few metres of the lake, you should not attempt to find the site without a guide unless you are confident of navigating off-road. If you have experience of desert driving, and provided you stick to the most obvious track, which is often routed between piles of white stone, the lake is fairly easy to find, although it takes quite a bit of nerve to stay your course across the barren land. More difficult is finding your way back to the highway from the lake – almost impossible if you haven't taken any reverse landmarks on the outbound journey (the pylons are helpful and so is the hint of a low, 1m-high embankment of a modern reservoir which you should keep on your left heading towards Burqu). The sense of satisfaction in finding this remarkable little oasis is worth all the anxiety and effort of getting there.

Understand Jordan

Jordan Today

For a country that only came into existence in its present form less than 100 years ago, Jordan has come far in terms of establishing an independent identity, distinct from neighbouring countries. Its citizens are proud of their nationality and the progress made, with relatively few resources, in developing modern infrastructure, health care and a regionally esteemed education system. It is this investment in human resources that has given Jordan the strength to thrive in a region of troublesome neighbours.

Best in Print

Married to a Bedouin (M van Geldermalsen; 2006) The author tells the story of her marriage to a local Bedouin man in Petra and how she brought her family up in a cave in the early years.

Into the Wadi (Michele Drouart; 2000) A readable account of an Australian woman's marriage to a Jordanian man.

Heroine of the Desert (Donya al-Nahi; 2006) The author of this true account describes her attempts to reunite children with their mothers after being abducted by their fathers in failed mixed-ethnicity marriages.

Nine Parts of Desire: The Hidden World of Islamic Women (Geraldine Brooks; 1995) One of the better books in a genre dominated by sensationalist writing.

Walking the Bible (Bruce Feiler; 2005) An enjoyable ramble through biblical locations in Jordan.

Best on Film

Lawrence of Arabia (1962) David Lean's classic.

A Dangerous Man: Lawrence after Arabia (1991) Starring a young Ralph Fiennes.

Indiana Jones and the Last Crusade (1989) Harrison Ford in Petra caper.

Jordan circa 2015

With so much history wrapped up in this tiny desert kingdom, it's easy to overlook the modern face of Jordan – something the government is trying to address by improving productivity, making Jordan a more attractive country for foreign investment, promoting Jordan as a high-tech service centre and by building ambitious tourist developments, including a 184-acre Star Wars theme park near Aqaba (announced formally in May 2013).

And 'ambitious' is an appropriate word. In a country of minimal resources – where water is in critically short supply, arable land accounts for just 2% of the landmass, and unemployment is hovering around 12% – the disproportionate investment in Jordan's coastal pleasure domes may appear somewhat reckless, especially given the precarious nature of tourism in the Middle East. Suffering under the burden of care towards incoming refugees and affected by the negative press regarding conflict in neighbouring countries, it's both surprising and refreshing that so many Jordanians remain optimistic about tourism in the current climate.

Home to a Seventh Wonder

When Petra was voted by popular ballot as one of the seven 'new' wonders of the world, it was a large accolade for a small country. But Jordan – straddling the ancient Holy Land of the world's three great monotheistic religions, and once an important trading centre of the Roman Empire – is no stranger to punching above its weight. Stand on Mt Nebo, consecrated by Pope John II, and survey the land promised to Moses; unfurl a veil at Mukawir, where Salome cast a spell over men in perpetuity; float in the Dead Sea beside a pillar of salt reputed to be Lot's disobedient wife – go just about anywhere in Jordan and you'll find every stone bares a tale.

The Arab Spring & Benign Dictatorship

For a brief moment in the spring of 2011, it looked as though Jordanians were set to join fellow protesters in Egypt, Tunisia, Libya and Syria in demonstrations popularly dubbed as the Arab Spring. Comprised largely of young students, and peaceful in their approach, Jordanian protesters argued on the streets of Amman for higher wages and a fuller embracing of democracy. The demonstrations soon petered out, however, leaving only weekly gatherings of die-hards after Friday prayers.

Democratic reforms have long been in place in Jordan. In November 1989 the first full parliamentary elections since 1967 were held, and women were allowed the vote. Four years later most political parties were legalised and able to participate in parliamentary and municipal elections.

Despite these concessions, democracy in Jordan is still something of an alien concept. Perceived as promoting the interests of the individual over those of the community, it runs against the grain of tribal traditions where respect for elders is paramount. In common with other parts of the Middle East, Jordan traditionally favours a strong, centralised government under an autocratic leader – what might be called benign dictatorship.

Of course, benign dictatorship is only as good as the leader. King Abdullah II is widely regarded both at home and abroad as both wise and diplomatic in his role – a modernising monarch in touch with the sensibilities of a globalised world, supportive of social and economic reform and committed to stamping out corruption.

Jordan's Troublesome Neighbours

Like his father, Abdullah II has proved adept at handling foreign affairs – imperative, considering the neighbourhood Jordan shares. Occupying the calm eye of the storm in the Middle East, the country has a long tradition of absorbing the displaced peoples of its troubled neighbours – so much so, in fact, that the demography of the country has changed forever with a majority population now comprising people of non-Jordanian origin.

While refugees of Palestinian origin belong to a prospering 'middle class', and wealthy refugees from the ongoing conflict in Iraq settle into permanent sanctuary in Jordan, the country is contending with a new and very different influx of refugees (the fourth influx in 50 years) from the civil war in Syria. These are not contributors to the political and economic fabric of Jordan but desperate, homeless people with little chance of repatriation in the foreseeable future. As of 2014 Jordan was host to the region's second-largest population of Syrian refugees and Za'atari camp, with its 120,000 residents, was equivalent in size to Jordan's largest cities.

POPULATION: **9.9 MILLION**

POPULATION GROWTH: **3.9%**

INFLATION: **3.2%**

GDP: **US$33.7 BILLION**

UNEMPLOYMENT: **12%**

AVERAGE ANNUAL INCOME:
LESS THAN US$5000

if Jordan were 100 people

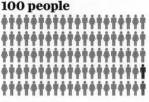

98 would be Arab
1 would be Circassian
1 would be Armenian

belief systems
(% of population)

| 92 | 6 | 2 |
| Sunni Muslim | Christian | Other |

population per sq km

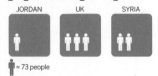

JORDAN   UK   SYRIA

≈ 73 people

Best Travellers' Tales

Travels in Syria and the Holy Land
(JL Burckhardt; 1822) Account of Petra's rediscovery.

The Desert and the Sown (Gertrude Bell; 1907) The 'brains behind Lawrence's brawn'.

Seven Pillars of Wisdom (TE Lawrence; 1926) The classic.

Extreme Rambling (Mark Thomas; 2011) Describes the author's attempt to walk the newly built wall surrounding Jerusalem.

Best Unesco Sites

Petra (1985) Needs no introduction!

Qusayr Amra (1985) Best of the Eastern castles.

Umm ar-Rasas (2004) Unique 1000-year-old mosaics.

Wadi Rum Protected Area (2011) Breathtaking desert.

Best to Avoid

Using the left hand when eating.
Pointing soles of the feet at someone.
Exposing shoulders or knees except at beach resorts.
Entering a mosque or someone's home wearing shoes.

Greeting People

Shake hands with women only if a hand is proffered.
Give things only with the right hand.
Baklava or dates make a good gift.

Speak Easy?

Jordan media Fairly free, tempered by local sensibilities.

Jordan Media City Transmits 247 channels.

Criticising the king Against the law.

With each new flood of asylum-seekers, Jordan's resources and the patience of its citizens are stretched to the breaking point with healthcare and education systems taking the brunt of the strain and housing prices driven up beyond the reach of many Jordanians. Added to this, a new wave of immigrants now looms over the country, following the threat from the self-styled Islamic State militants in Iraq; this time they bring with them a new spectre – the fear of alien and extremist ideologies.

Relationship with the West

During the most recent influx of refugees, provoked by the ongoing civil war in Syria, Jordan has repeatedly appealed for international aid to cope; this call to alms was taken up by Pope Francis during his visit in 2014, but as of yet has not been matched with a shared sense of responsibility from the international community. At the time of writing, there was a palpable sense of embittered resignation as Jordanians struggle to cope with high unemployment and the failing expectations of the tourism sector.

Despite the general sense of abandonment, Jordan remains a staunch ally of the West. It was one of the first nations to join a coalition of forces targeting Islamic State militants in air strikes, and signs are that Jordan will continue to walk the line between friendship with the West and a strong sense of kinship with moderate Arab states.

A Bright Future

Despite the mixed origins of its people, the current political and economic difficulties, and the insecurity of life in a volatile region, Jordanians are united in their pride for their country. And there's a lot to be proud of. The monarchy under King Abdullah II continues the acclaimed role of peacemaker between Arab and Western interests, Jordan is a regional leader in protecting the environment and promoting sustainable tourism, and its capital city is enjoying a modern renaissance.

In common with many Arab countries, Jordan is at a crossroads as it faces integration within the modern, democratic, global community. Unlike many of its neighbours, however, Jordan has recognised that the past is part of its future, and while the politicians plan a way to maximise on the country's unique legacy, the Bedouin still herd their sheep across an unchanged landscape in effortless continuity with the ancient past.

History

By default, a visit to Jordan involves engaging with history. But history in Jordan has a habit of coming alive and being instantly relevant to the present. Stub your toe on a ruin, find a Roman coin or hear the call to prayer, and you may just be glad to have a context in which to place that experience. Find out how the major events of the past have shaped Jordan's present.

Blending of Past & Present

Climbing off his donkey, a shepherd in a terraced field near Madaba tethers the animal to a giant thistle and seeks refuge from the noon heat under a dolmen. Stretched full length under the cold stone roof of this ancient burial chamber, he almost blends into the landscape – until his mobile phone erupts in a rendition of 'We wish you a merry Christmas'.

In Jordan, history is not something that happened 'before'. It's a living, breathing part of everyday life, witnessed not just in the pragmatic treatment of ancient artefacts but also in the way people live. Jordanians value their heritage and are in no hurry to eschew ways of life that have proved successful for centuries. The familiar linear approach to history, therefore, where one event succeeds another in an expectation of so-called progress, is almost irrelevant in a country where past and present merge together so seamlessly.

The very entity of Jordan is a case in point. The political state within its current borders is a modern creation, but it encompasses territory (east of the River Jordan) that has hosted the world's oldest civilisations. Egyptians, Assyrians, Babylonians, Greeks, Nabataeans, Romans, Crusaders and Turks all traded, built cities and fought wars here, leaving behind rich cultural influences – leaning posts upon which modern Jordanians have built a proud identity.

Main Periods of History

So are there any distinct historical periods? Not exactly. With some creativity, the abundant historical clues scattered across Jordan can be shuffled into several distinct blocks of time. Each period of history

Books on Jordan's History

....

The Middle East: A Brief History of the Last 2000 Years (Bernard Lewis; 1996)

....

History of the Arabs (Philip Hitti; 1937)

TIMELINE	c 250,000 BC	c 100,000 BC	c 20,000 BC
	With the aid of hand axes made of flint, early humans hunt elephants across the plains in the mild, wet climate of the Jordan Valley.	The Red Sea, lying in a branch of the Great Rift Valley, retreats from Wadi Araba, leaving the Dead Sea and the Sea of Galilee as two separate lakes.	Hunters and gatherers live in seasonal camps and rear their own livestock, with goats forming a substantial part of the diet in the early communities at Wadi Madamagh, near Petra.

features in the experiences of a visitor to the country, not only through a pile of fallen columns by the side of the road, but in the taking of tea with old custodians of the desert or the bargaining for a kilim with designs inherited from the Byzantine era.

In fact, just step foot in Jordan and you begin your encounter with history. Visit the dolmens near Madaba, for example, and you enter the cradle of civilisation; dating from 4000 BC, the dolmens embody the sophistication of the world's first villages. The era of trading in copper and bronze helped bring wealth to the region (1200 BC); you can find forgings from Jordan's ancient copper mines near Feynan Ecolodge in the Dana Biosphere Reserve. Travel the King's Highway and you'll not only be stepping in the path of royalty, but you'll see how this route helped unify city-states into a recognisable Jordan between 1200 BC and 333 BC.

The Greeks, Nabataeans and Romans dominated Jordan's most illustrious historical period (333 BC–AD 333), leaving the magnificent legacies of Petra and Jerash. The arrival of Islamic dynasties is evident from the 7th century onwards – in fact, the evidence is literally strewn over the deserts of Eastern Jordan in the intriguing Umayyad structures that dot the stark landscape. The conflict between Islam and Christianity, evident at Jordan's Crusader castles in Ajloun, Karak and Shobak, is a defining feature of the next thousand years.

British imperialism dominates Jordan's history prior to the Arab Revolt of 1914. Ride a camel through Wadi Rum and cries of 'To Aqaba' hang in the wind – and so does the name of Lawrence, the British officer whose desert adventures have captured the imagination of visitors to such an extent that whole mountains are named after him! Jordan's history is about independence, modernisation and cohabitation with difficult neighbours.

> From the earliest settlements, some people devoted themselves to animal husbandry, sustained by the meat, milk and wool of their livestock, while others planted olives, wheat and barley and farmed the land. This distinction between the 'desert and the sown' is apparent to this day.

Life in the Fertile Crescent (10,000–4000 BC)

Early Settlements

Stand on top of the knoll at Shkarat Msaiad, on the seldom-used road from Siq Al-Barid (Little Petra) to Wadi Araba, and survey the minimal mounds of stone and you could be forgiven for wondering what all the fuss is about. Despite the isolated beauty of the place, there isn't much to see but some stone walling. Yet this is the kind of place that archaeologists rave about because what you are looking at, they will solemnly tell you, is a 'PPN'.

A PPN, for the uninitiated, stands for Pre-Pottery Neolithic and is significant because such sites indicate a high degree of organisation among early communities. In fact, at this sheltered spot in the hills, you are look-

c 8000 BC	c 6000 BC	c 5000 BC	c 4000 BC
Some of the world's earliest settlements are established at Ain Ghazal and Al-Beidha and neighbouring Jericho. Inhabitants tame, breed and cook domestic animals.	The Ain Ghazal fertility sculptures (among the world's oldest sculptures) and wall paintings at Teleilat Ghassul in the Jordan Valley show that early inhabitants of the region value cultural activity.	Monumental stone dolmen near Ar-Rawdah indicate that burials are now linked to concepts of afterlife. The ingenious engineering is a wonder – and a mystery.	Permanent settlements are established in modern-day Amman and in the south, while copper is mined at Khirbet Feynan. Arts, such as pottery, illustrate the influence of powerful neighbours in Egypt.

ing at the very dawn of civilisation. If nothing else, the traces of shelter, water collection and farming demonstrate the basic immutability of life.

Jordan has a remarkable number of early settlements, largely thanks to its location within the fertile crescent – the rich arc of lands that included Mesopotamia, Syria and Palestine. The fecundity of the soil in this region allowed early humans to move from a hunter-gatherer existence to settlement in the world's earliest villages, dating between 10,000 and 8500 BC. One such village in Jordan is Al-Beidha, near Petra. It's tempting to think of our ancient forebears as simple people living simple lives, but the inhabitants of villages such as Al-Beidha built houses of stone and wood; they tamed, bred and cooked domestic animals; they planted wild seeds, grew crops, crushed grains and kept food in mud vessels hardened under the sun; and they began wearing and forming

THE RIFT VALLEY & THE BIOGRAPHY OF A SEA

You can't think about history in Jordan without factoring in its position on the edge of the ancient Rift Valley. Standing beside the apologetic trickle of water that runs through Bethany-Beyond-the-Jordan today, it's hard to imagine that some 100,000 years ago the entire Jordan Valley was under the fertile waters of the Red Sea. When the sea retreated it left two landlocked stretches of water – the Sea of Galilee (known in Jordan as Lake Tiberius) and the Dead Sea.

Despite its name – given by the Greek geographer and historian Pausanias, who noticed its life-defying salinity – the Dead Sea has long been associated with health-giving properties. Book into a Dead Sea spa and you will be part of a tradition begun in biblical times. Herod visited the spa at Callirhöe near Herodus Spring to treat itching skin, and Byzantine Christians followed suit along pilgrim roads to Bethany-Beyond-the-Jordan, Mt Nebo and Lot's Cave.

Useful in extending life, the Dead Sea has been useful in death, too. Study the haunting eyes of the Ain Ghazal statues in the National Archaeological Museum in Amman (dated from around 6000 BC, they're reputedly the oldest sculptures in the world) and you'll see that they are blackened with bitumen. The Greeks and Romans named the Dead Sea the 'Sea of Pitch' on account of the bitumen that used to float to the surface. This substance was harvested by the Nabataeans, who sold it to the Egyptians, who in turn used it for waterproofing funeral boats and for mummification. Ships laden with bitumen regularly crossed the sea in ancient times, as illustrated in the 6th-century Madaba mosaic map. The last piece of bitumen surfaced in 1936.

Today the area continues to contribute to health and wealth with important revenues from tourism and potash. Part of the western shore belonged to Jordan when the famous Dead Sea scrolls were discovered by a Bedouin shepherd at Qumran in 1947. Israel took control of the entire western shore in 1967 after the Six Day War, giving the term 'Rift Valley' a particularly modern resonance.

c 2900 BC	c 2300 BC	c 1500 BC	c 1200 BC
City-states emerge across the Middle East. Towns at Amman, Pella, Deir Alla and Tell Irbid are fortified and trade develops with neighbouring powers in Syria, Palestine and Egypt.	Sodom and Gomorrah, among the five so-called Cities of the Plain, are destroyed in a cataclysmic disaster on the southeast corner of the Dead Sea.	The Middle East enters a period of turmoil as Egypt's influence declines. The Philistines arrive west of the River Jordan, giving the land its current name of Palestine.	Ammon (Amman), Moab (Dhiban) and Edom (Buseira) emerge as the dominant kingdoms to the east of the Jordan River. Moses and the Israelites are refused entry to Edom.

decorative items – such as the astonishing fertility sculptures from Ain Ghazal dated around 6000 BC. These early settlers even left a record of their existence through wall paintings, such as those at Teleilat Ghassul in the Jordan Valley.

Complexity of Early Society in Jordan

If you have lingering doubts about the sophistication of the ancients, ponder the fields of dolmens (constructed between 5000 and 3000 BC) that are scattered throughout the country. Come across the local shepherds and they may well ask you: 'Why are you here? Is anything good here?' That would be a great question to pose to the ancients who carefully aligned their last resting places along the shoulders rather than the ridges of the semi-arid hills. As for us moderns, these highly charged sites force a reconsideration of these early people: how did they lever the monumental bridging stones into place and what power of belief prompted such laborious, collaborative effort? Many of Jordan's archaeological treasures provoke more questions than they answer in our human quest to understand more about our origins.

From Metals to Massacres (4000–1200 BC)

Invest enough importance in an object and someone else will inevitably want one as well. There's evidence that Jordan's first farmers swapped desirable items among themselves well before 4000 BC, perhaps triggering the rivalry to make and trade more accurate tools and more beautiful adornments. One commodity useful for both tools and adornments was copper – of which Jordan has plenty. Visit Khirbet Feynan in present-day Dana Nature Reserve and the vast areas of black copper slag illustrate the importance of copper mining for the ancient people of the region.

Within a thousand years, experimentation with metalwork led to the mixing of copper and tin to create bronze, a hardier material that allowed for the rapid development of tools and, of course, weapons.

During the Bronze Age (3200–1200 BC) the region's settlements showed greater signs of accumulated luxury items, growing rich on indigo, sulphur and sugar (which was introduced into Europe from the Dead Sea area). It is not by chance that the greater wealth coincided with a preoccupation with security, with defensive walls built around towns such as Pella. Early invaders included the Amorites, whose arrival in the area is often associated with the violent destruction of the five Cities of the Plain (near the southern end of the Dead Sea), including the settlements of Sodom and Gomorrah.

Invasion was not confined to the boundaries of modern-day Jordan. By the late Bronze Age (1500–1200 BC) the whole of the Middle East appeared to be at war. Wealthy city-states in Syria collapsed, Egyptians

According to a German survey, 15,000 to 20,000 tonnes of copper were produced from Feynan's copper-smelting sites – some of the oldest such sites in the region. This has left 150,000 to 200,000 tonnes of slag dotting the arid landscape.

850 BC	582 BC	c 500 BC	333 BC
The divided Israelite empire is defeated by Mesha, king of Moab, who recorded his victories in the famous Mesha Stele in the Moabite capital of Dhiban.	Ammon, Moab and Edom enjoy brief unity after near annihilation by the Israelites under King David and King Solomon. The union is short lived; they become Babylonian provinces under King Nebuchadnezzar II.	The innovation of the camel saddle transforms the lives of Arab nomads and eventually brings new caravans to Jordan's southern deserts en route to Damascus.	Alexander the Great wins the Battle of Issus, defeating Persian King Darius III. He moves on Syria and Palestine, which comes under the expansive empire of Greece.

THE CITY-STATE OF ISRAEL

The kingdoms of Edom, Moab and Ammon are mentioned in the Bible, especially in connection with the wandering Jews of the Exodus. According to the Old Testament, Moses and his brother, Aaron, led their people through Sinai in Egypt looking for a permanent territory to inhabit. They were forbidden entry to southern Jordan by the Edomites but managed to wind their way north, roughly along the route of the modern King's Highway, towards the Jordan River. Moses died on Mt Nebo, in sight of the Promised Land, and it was left to his successor Joshua to lead the Israelites across the river to the West Bank where they conquered the city of Canaan, which led to the establishment of the city-state of Israel in around 1436 BC.

retreated within their own borders from outposts in the Jordan Valley, and marauding foreigners ('Peoples of the Sea') reshaped the political landscape of the Eastern Mediterranean. The latter also brought the Philistines, who settled on the west bank of the Jordan and gave the land its current name of Palestine.

Unity in Adversity (1200–333 BC)

Emergence of a Recognisable 'Jordan'

It is difficult to talk about Jordan as a single entity for most of the country's history. That's because, at least until the latter part of the 20th century AD, its borders expanded and retreated and its peoples came and went, largely driven by the political ambitions and expediencies of more powerful regional neighbours.

Around 1200 BC, however, something akin to a recognisable 'Jordan' emerged from the regional mayhem in the form of three important kingdoms: Edom in the south, with its capital in Bozrah (modern Buseira, near Dana); Moab near Wadi Mujib; and Ammon on the edge of the Arabian Desert, with a capital at Rabbath Ammon (present-day Amman). It is unlikely that any of the three kingdoms had much to do with each other until the foundation of the new neighbouring city-state of Israel.

Succumbing to Powerful Neighbours

Israel quickly became a military power to be reckoned with, dominating the area of Syria and Palestine and coming into inevitable conflict with the neighbours. Under King David the Israelites wrought a terrible revenge on Edom, massacring almost the entire male population; Moab also succumbed to Israelite control and the people of Ammon were subject to forced labour under the new Jewish masters. However, Israelite

c 323 BC	c 100 BC	30 BC	9 BC–AD 40
Alexander dies in Babylon. The Greek inheritance gives access to the treasures of classical learning, and the cities of Philadelphia (Amman), Gadara, Pella and Jerash blossom under Hellenistic rule.	Greek generals squabble over who rules which parts of the Trans-Jordan while a tribe of nomadic Arabs quietly makes money from passing caravans. They establish their capital at Petra.	Herod the Great expands the castle at Mukawir, which will in a few years' time set the stage for Salome's dance and the beheading of John the Baptist.	Aretas IV, greatest of the Nabataean kings, presides over a city of wealth and beauty. The hidden cluster of tombs, temples and houses is adapted from Greek and Roman architecture.

might proved short-lived and, after King Solomon's brief but illustrious reign, the kingdom split into Israel and Judah.

By the middle of the first millennium BC – perhaps in response to Israelite aggression – Ammon, Moab and Edom became a unified entity, linked by a trade route known today as the King's Highway. The fledgling amalgam of lands, however, was not strong enough to withstand the might of bullying neighbours, and it was soon overwhelmed by a series of new masters: the Assyrians, Babylonians and Persians. It would be centuries before Jordan achieved a similar distinct identity within its current borders.

The Middle Men of the Middle East (333 BC–AD 324)

War and invasion were not the utter disaster that they might have been for the people of the region. Located at the centre of the land bridge between Africa and Asia, the cities surrounding the King's Highway were particularly well placed to service the needs of passing foreign armies.

HISTORY OF A HIGHWAY

When pondering the King's Highway, a fair question to ask is, 'Which king?' In fact, the highway was never the personal project of royalty: it gained its name through the sense of major thoroughfare, often referred to in the Arabian Orient as 'royal road'.

The highway runs for 297km between Madaba and Petra; for a thousand years before Christ it linked the kingdoms of Ammon, Moab and Edom. One of the earliest mentions of the highway is in the biblical episode in which Moses was refused passage along the highway by the King of Edom. The Nabataeans used the route to transport frankincense, originating in southern Arabia, and other exotic commodities to the important trading posts of Syria. In later times, the highway received a suitably Roman makeover under Emperor Trajan, who widened and rerouted part of the highway to facilitate the passage of troops.

The highway has great religious significance for both Christians and Muslims. Attracted by the holy sites of Mt Nebo and protected by the Crusader forces, Christians used the route for pilgrimage, building and embellishing many shrines along the way, such as the Church of St Stephen at Umm Ar-Rasas. Muslims used the route on pilgrimage to Mecca until the Ottomans developed the Tariq al-Bint in the 16th century – the approximate path of the Hejaz Railway, built in 1900, and the modern Desert Highway.

Inevitably, the importance of the King's Highway declined and it was only in the 1950s and 1960s that it was upgraded to a tarmac road. Today it's a rural, often pot-holed route, which despite ambling through some of the loveliest and most striking landscape in Jordan betrays little of its former status as a road fit for kings.

AD 26	106	111–14	c 200–300
Jesus Christ is baptised in Bethany-Beyond-the-Jordan by John the Baptist. The first church is built soon after at Rihab, 40km from Amman, protecting Jesus' disciples from persecution in Jerusalem.	Roman emperor Trajan absorbs the Nabataean empire into the province of Arabia Petraea, signalling the end of Petra's heyday.	The Romans build the Via Traiana Nova, following the path of the ancient King's Highway between Bosra and the Red Sea, bringing new life to an ancient thoroughfare.	The golden age for Roman Arabia is marked by grand monuments in the cities of the Decapolis. Emperor Hadrian honours Jerash with a visit en route to Palestine.

They also profited from the caravan routes that crossed the deserts from Arabia to the Euphrates, bringing shipments of African gold and South Arabian frankincense via the Red Sea ports in present-day Aqaba and Eilat. The Greeks, the Nabataeans and the Romans each capitalised on this passing bounty, leaving a legacy of imported culture and learning in return.

The Greeks

By the 4th century BC the growing wealth of Arab lands attracted the attention of a young military genius from the West known as Alexander of Macedon. Better known today as Alexander the Great, the precocious 21 year old stormed through the region in 334 BC, winning territories from Turkey to Palestine.

At his death in 323 BC in Babylon, Alexander ruled a vast empire from the Nile to the Indus, with similarly vast dimensions of commerce. Over the coming centuries, Greek was the lingua franca of Jordan (at least of the written word), giving access to the great intellectual treasures of the classical era. The cities of Philadelphia (Amman), Gadara, Pella and Jerash blossomed under Hellenistic rule, and prospered through growing trade, particularly with Egypt, which fell under the same Greek governance.

The Nabataeans

Trade was the key to Jordan's most vibrant period of history, thanks to the growing importance of a nomadic Arab tribe from the south, known as the Nabataeans. The Nabataeans produced only copper and bitumen (for waterproofing boat hulls) but they knew how to trade in the commodities of neighbouring nations. Consummate middlemen, they used their exclusive knowledge of desert strongholds and water supplies to amass wealth from the caravan trade, first by plundering and then by levying tolls on the merchandise that traversed the areas under their control.

The most lucrative trade involved the transportation, by camel, of frankincense and myrrh along the Incense Route from southern Arabia to outposts further north. The Nabataeans were also sole handlers of spices shipped to Arabia by boat from Somalia, Ethiopia and India. Suburbs at the four corners of their capital, Petra, received the caravans and handled the logistics, processing products and offering banking services and fresh animals before moving the goods west across the Sinai to the ports of Gaza and Alexandria for shipment to Greece and Rome.

The Nabataeans never possessed an 'empire' in the common military and administrative senses of the word; instead, from about 200 BC, they established a 'zone of influence' that stretched from Syria to Rome. As

Key Nabataean Sites

Petra, Jordan

Siq Al-Barid, near Petra, Jordan

Madain Saleh, Saudi Arabia

c 284–305	324	560	614
The Romans build the Strata Diocletiana linking Azraq with Damascus and the Euphrates. A string of forts in the Eastern Desert shores up the rim of the empire.	Emperor Constantine converts to Christianity. Christianity becomes the dominant religion of the Byzantine Empire and many churches are built. Madaba becomes the focus of pilgrim trails to Jerusalem.	The so-called Mosaic Map is crafted in Madaba; found under rubble by church builders in 1884, it remains the oldest map of Palestine found to date.	Emperor Heraclius forces invading Persians to make peace; despite this victory Byzantine Christian rule in the Trans-Jordan soon ends. A storm is brewing in Arabia, bringing Islam in its wake.

GATEWAY TO THE AFTERLIFE: THE NABATAEAN RELIGION

A young family, arriving early for the Petra Night Tour, was waved on alone through the candlelit Siq (gorge). Haunted by the sound of their own footsteps, they soon began to feel there was something amiss. Halfway, the young daughter, overwhelmed by the towering shadows of this sacred way, begged her parents to turn back. A few moments later, all three were hastily beating a retreat. Only those who have been in Petra's Siq alone will understand the power this extraordinary passage has on the soul. It was chosen surely for exactly this reason, for it was no ordinary passage: it was a gateway to the afterlife.

Surprisingly little is known about Nabataean religion, considering that their preoccupation with the afterlife dominates much of their capital at Petra. It is known, however, that the early desert polytheistic religion of the original Arabian tribe absorbed Egyptian, Greek and Roman, and even Edomite and Assyrian beliefs, to create a unique faith.

The main Nabataean god was Dushara, the mountain god, who governed the natural world. Over the years he came to be associated with the Egyptian god Osiris, Greek god Dionysus and the Roman god Zeus.

For fertility, the Nabataeans prayed to the goddess Al-'Uzza (the Very Strong), who became associated with Aphrodite and Isis. Al-Kutba was the god of divination and writing, linked to Hermes and Mercury. Allat (literally 'Goddess') was associated with Athena.

Early representations of the Nabataean gods were non-figurative. Divine stones known as *baetyls* marked important wadis, junctions, canyons and mountaintops, representing the presence of the divine. Religious processions to Petra's spiritual 'High Places' were an important part of the community's religious life, culminating in a sacrifice (perhaps human) and ritual purification.

Though the secrets of Nabataean religious ceremonies are hidden in history, there is a strong sense of what one might call 'spiritual presence' enveloping Petra's high places of sacrifice: the god blocks, carved niches, altars and sacrificial basins all indicate that the hilltops were holy ground, used by the priests for mediating between heaven and earth.

the Nabataean territory expanded under King Aretas III (84–62 BC), they controlled and taxed trade throughout the Hejaz (northern Arabia), the Negev, the Sinai, and the Hauran of southern Syria. Nabataean communities were influential as far away as Rome, and Nabataean tombs still stand at the impressive site of Madain Salah in Saudi Arabia.

The Romans

You only have to visit Jerash for five minutes, trip over a fallen column and notice the legions of other columns nearby, to gain an immediate understanding of the importance of the Romans in Jordan – and the importance of Jordan to the Romans. This magnificent set of ruins is grand

629	c 700	747	1095
Muslim forces lose the Battle of Mu'tah against Christians. After Prophet Mohammed's death (632), they win the decisive Battle of Yarmouk (636) and Islam becomes the region's dominant religion.	The Umayyads from Syria overtake the region and build some extraordinary bathhouses, hunting lodges and fortified meeting places (known today as the desert castles) in the arid desert east of Amman.	An earthquake shatters northern Jordan and Syria, weakening the Umayyads' hold on power. They're replaced by the Abbasids, signalling a period of Persian cultural dominance and less tolerance towards Christianity.	Pope Urban II sparks a 'holy war' in revenge for church destruction by Seljuks and to protect pilgrim routes to the Holy Land. Crusaders soon capture Jerusalem, slaughtering countless inhabitants.

on a scale that is seldom seen in modern building enterprises and indicates the amount of wealth the Romans invested in this outpost of their empire. Jerash was clearly worth its salt and, indeed, it was the lucrative trade associated with the Nabataeans that attracted the Romans in the first place. It's perhaps a fitting legacy of their rule that the Jordanian currency, the dinar, derives its name from the Latin *denarius* (ancient Roman silver coin).

The Romans brought many benefits to the region, constructing two new roads through Jordan – the Via Traiana Nova (AD 111–114) linking Bosra with the Red Sea, and the Strata Diocletiana (AD 284–305) linking Azraq with Damascus and the Euphrates. A string of forts in the Eastern Desert at Qasr al-Hallabat, Azraq and Umm al-Jimal was also built to shore up the eastern rim of the empire.

The 2nd and 3rd centuries were marked by a feverish expansion of trade as the Via Traiana became the main thoroughfare for Arabian caravans, armies and supplies. The wealth benefited the cities of Jerash, Umm Qais and Pella, members of the Decapolis, a league of provincial cities that accepted Roman cultural influence but retained their independence.

With the eventual demise of the Roman Empire and the fracturing of trade routes over the subsequent centuries, Jordan's entrepreneurial leadership of the region never quite regained the same status.

Spirit of the Age (AD 324–1516)

For 1500 years after the birth of Jesus, the history of Jordan was characterised by the expression of organised faith in one form or another. Under the influence of Rome, Christianity replaced the local gods of the Nabataeans, and several hundred years later Islam took its place – but not before a struggle that left a long-term legacy and a string of Crusader forts.

Conversion to Christianity

Think of the history of the Christian religion and most people understandably focus on the 'Holy Land' to the west of the River Jordan. And yet, if recent evidence is to be believed, the Christian church may never have evolved (at least not in the way we know it today) if it hadn't been for the shelter afforded to the early proponents of the faith on the *east* bank of the Jordan.

In 2008, 40km northeast of Amman, archaeologists uncovered what they believe to be the first church in the world. Dating from AD 33 to AD 70, the church, which was buried under St Georgeous Church in Rihab, appears to have sheltered the 70 disciples of Jesus Christ. Described in the mosaic inscriptions on the floor of the old church as the '70 beloved by God and Divine', these first Christians fled persecution in Jerusalem

Jordan's Roman Spectacles

Citadel, Amman

Roman Theatre, Downtown Amman

Forum, Jerash

Decumanus maximus, Umm Qais

Hint of former glories at Pella

HISTORY SPIRIT OF THE AGE (AD 324–1516)

The discovery in 2008 of the world's oldest church was described by senior Orthodox clerics as an 'important milestone for Christians all around the world'. Jordanian authorities are now hoping to develop the site as a tourist attraction.

1115	1142	1187	1193
Crusader King Baldwin I builds Montreal (Mount Real or the Royal Mountain) – the picture-perfect castle in Shobak. It withstood numerous attacks from the armies of Saladin.	The imposing Karak Castle is built to withstand Saladin's armies; in 1148 it is inherited by the sadistic Renauld de Châtillon of France who delights in torturing prisoners.	Despite superb defences at Shobak and Karak, Karak is overrun after an epic siege in 1183; Saladin goes on to beat the Crusader armies in the decisive Battle of Hittin.	Saladin dies and the ensuing family in-fighting enables the Crusaders to recapture much of their former territory.

and lived in secrecy, practising their rituals in the underground church. Pottery dating from the 3rd to the 7th century shows that these disciples and their families lived in the area until late Roman rule.

The conversion by Emperor Constantine to Christianity in AD 324 eventually legitimised the practice of Christianity across the region. East of the Jordan River, churches were constructed (often from the building blocks of former Greek and Roman temples) and embellished with the elaborate mosaics that are still visible today at Madaba, Umm ar-Rasas and Petra. Christian pilgrims began to search for relics of the Holy Land, building churches en route at biblical sites such as Bethany, Mt Nebo and Lot's Cave. It was the archaeological rediscovery of these churches 1400 years later that confirmed the lost location of these biblical sites to a forgetful modern world.

The Rise of Islam

Reminders of Christianity are scattered across Jordan today, for instance in the observance of the faith in towns such as Madaba. But listen to the bells peal on a weekend and moments later they will be replaced by the muezzin's call to prayer from the neighbouring mosque. Islam is present not just in Jordan's mosques but in the law, in social etiquette and at the very heart of the way people live their lives – in Bedouin camps as well as in modern city centres. So how did Islam reach here and how did it replace Christianity as the dominant religion?

From 622 (10 years before the death of the Prophet Mohammed) the armies of Islam travelled northwards, quickly and easily spreading the message of submission (Islam) well beyond the Arabian Peninsula. Although they lost their first battle against the Christian Byzantines at Mu'tah (near Karak) in 629, they returned seven years later to win the Battle of Yarmouk. Jerusalem fell in 638 and Syria was taken in 640. Islam, under the Sunni dynasty of the Umayyads, became the dominant religion of the region, headquartered in the city of Damascus, and Arabic replaced Greek as the lingua franca. Within 100 years Muslim armies controlled a vast empire that spread from Spain to India.

The Umayyads' rich architectural legacy included the Umayyad Mosque in Damascus and the Dome of the Rock in Jerusalem. In eastern Jordan, the Umayyads' close attachment to the desert led to the construction of a string of opulent 'desert castles', including the brooding Qasr Kharana (built in 710) and Qusayr Amra (711).

Despite the blossoming of Islamic scholarship in medicine, biology, philosophy, architecture and agriculture over the next three centuries, the area wedged between Jerusalem and Baghdad remained isolated from the sophisticated Arab mainstream. This is one reason why Jordan possesses relatively few demonstrations of Islamic cultural exuberance.

Prophet Mohammed's son-in-law, the caliph Ali, was assassinated in 660. He was succeeded by Mu'awiyah, who established the Umayyad dynasty (661–750). The bitter dispute over this succession split Islam into two factions, the Sunnis and the Shiites.

Amin Maalouf's lively *The Crusades Through Arab Eyes* recasts the West's image of knights in shining armour as ruthless barbarians who pillaged the Middle East, the horrors of which still reside in the collective Arab consciousness.

1258	1453	c 1516–1916	1798
Mongols storm Baghdad and the armies of Genghis Khan's son reach Ajloun and Salt. They are repelled by Mamluks who rebuild the castles at Karak, Shobak and Ajloun.	Ottoman rule is established in Constantinople (modern-day İstanbul), creating one of the world's largest empires that extends throughout the Middle East.	The Ottomans lavish their attentions on Jerusalem and Damascus while the area east of the Jordan River becomes a cultural and political backwater.	Napoleon Bonaparte invades Egypt, bringing the Middle East within the sphere of Western political rivalry – a rivalry which influences the political landscape of Trans-Jordan over the next 150 years.

The Crusades & Holy War

The armies of Islam and Christianity have clashed many times throughout history and the consequences (and language of religious conflict) resonate to this day both within the Middle East and across the world at large.

The Crusades of the 12th and 13th centuries are among the most famous of the early conflicts between Muslims and Christians. Survey the mighty walls of the great Crusader castles at Karak and Shobak and it's easy to see that both sides meant business: these were holy wars (albeit attracting mercenary elements) in which people willingly sacrificed their comfort and even lives for their faith in the hope of gaining glory in the hereafter – ironically, according to Islam at least, a hereafter shared by Muslims and the 'People of the Book' (Jews, Christians and so-called Sabians).

Built by King Baldwin I in the 12th century, the castles were part of a string of fortifications designed to control the roads from Damascus to Cairo. They seemed inviolable, and they may have remained so but for Nureddin and Saladin, who between them occupied most of the Crusader strongholds in the region, including those of Oultrejordain (meaning 'across the Jordan'). The Damascus-based Ayyubids, members of Saladin's family, squabbled over his empire on his death in 1193, enabling the Crusaders to recapture much of their former territory along the coast.

The Ayyubids were replaced by the Mamluks, who seized control of the area east of the Jordan River and rebuilt the castles at Karak, Shobak and Ajloun. They used these strongholds as lookouts and as a series of staging posts for message-carrying pigeons. Indeed, thanks to the superior communications that this unique strategy afforded, you could argue that the Crusaders were defeated not by the military might of Islam but on the wings of their peace-loving doves.

Western Love Affair with the Middle East (1516–1914)

The Ottoman Turks took Constantinople in 1453 and created one of the world's largest empires. They defeated the Mamluks in present-day Jordan in 1516, but concentrated their efforts on the lucrative cities of the region, such as the holy city of Jerusalem and the commercial centre of Damascus. The area east of the Jordan River once again became a forgotten backwater. Forgotten, that is, by the Ottoman Empire, but not entirely ignored by Western interests. Indeed, the period of gradually weakening Ottoman occupation over the next few centuries also marked an increasingly intense scrutiny by the Europeans – the British and the French in particular.

> The Qala'at ar-Rabad at Ajloun was built by the Ayyubids. In 1250 they were ousted by the Mamluks, a group of foreign, adolescent warriors serving as a soldier-slave caste for the Ayyubids, and the Mamluks ruled for the next 300 years.

> Nureddin (literally 'Light of the Faith') was the son of a Turkish tribal ruler. He united the Arab world and defeated the Crusaders in Egypt. His campaign against the Crusaders was completed by Saladin (Restorer of the Faith), a Kurdish scholar and military leader.

HISTORY WESTERN LOVE AFFAIR WITH THE MIDDLE EAST (1516–1914)

1812	1839	1908	1914–18
Burckhardt rediscovers Petra for the Western world, sparking off an enduring fascination with the fabled Pink City, and the region in general, among Western travellers, archaeologists, writers and artists.	The British artist David Roberts (1796–1864) visits the region and immortalises Petra in lithographic prints that are still popular today.	The Ottoman Empire, now 'the sick man of Europe', builds the Hejaz Railway linking Damascus with the holy city of Medina, via Amman, in an effort to reassert regional influence.	During WWI Jordan sees fierce fighting between Ottoman Turks (allied with the Germans) and the British, based in Egypt. By 1917 British troops occupy Jerusalem, and Syria thereafter.

Jordan has two recognised ethnic minorities, though most have integrated through marriage. Circassians (Muslims from the Caucasus who fled Russian persecution in the late 19th century) live near Amman. Chechens, related to the Circassians historically and ethnically, live near Azraq. Together they comprise around 2% of Jordan's population.

In the preface to *Les Orientales* (1829), Victor Hugo wrote that the whole of the European continent appeared to be 'leaning towards the East'. This was not a new phenomenon. Trade between the West and the East was long established and stories of the 'barbaric pearl and gold' of Arabia soon aroused the interests of a wider public. By the late 18th century Europeans were making pleasure trips to the Syrian desert, adopting articles of Albanian and Turkish dress, carrying pocket editions of Persian tales and penning their own travelogues.

Swiss explorer Jean Louis Burckhardt's monumental rediscovery of Petra in 1812 led to a further explosion of interest in the region. Societies were founded for the purpose of promoting Middle East exploration and scholars began translating Persian, Arabic and Sanskrit texts. Many aspects of the Orient were explored in Western fiction, much of which attracted a wide and enthusiastic readership. Indeed, by the end of the 19th century the fascination with the Arabian East was, to use Edward Said's phrase, no 'airy European fantasy' but a highly complex relationship defined by scientists, scholars, travellers and fiction writers.

This is the cultural backdrop upon which the political manoeuvrings of the 20th century were played out.

Fighting for an Arab Land (1914–46)

Writing of the Arab Revolt that passed through the heart of Jordan in the early 20th century, TE Lawrence described the phenomenon as 'an Arab war waged and led by Arabs for an Arab aim in Arabia'. This is a significant statement as it identifies a growing sense of political identity among Arab people throughout the last half of the 19th century and beginning of the 20th century. This pan-Arab consciousness grew almost in proportion (or at least coincidentally) to the territorial interest of Western powers in Arab lands. Slowly, in place of loose tribal interests Arabs came to define themselves as a single, unified entity – an Islamic 'other' perhaps to the Christian European threat pulsing around the Suez.

Arabs were prepared to fight for this new Arab nationalism, as Lawrence describes in the *Seven Pillars of Wisdom,* his account of the Arab Revolt:

As time went by our need to fight for the ideal increased to an unquestioning possession, riding with spur and rein over our doubts. Willy-nilly it became a faith.

History shows that it was to take more than just 'spur and rein' to create viable Arab states; indeed complex diplomacy, both within Arab countries and in their relationship with the West, characterised the pursuit of nationalism throughout the 20th century.

1916	1917	1923	1930s
The Arab Revolt, led by Faisal and backed by the British with the famous assistance of TE Lawrence, storms Aqaba, disrupts the Hejaz Railway and marches on Damascus.	The Balfour Declaration giving Jews a home in Palestine is not the reward the Arabs are promised. In a reluctant compromise, Faisal's brother, Abdullah, becomes ruler of Trans-Jordan.	Britain recognises Jordan as an independent emirate under its protection. A small defence force, the Arab Legion, is set up under British officers and the nominal control of Emir Abdullah.	The Nazi persecution of Jews accelerates Jewish immigration to Palestine, fuelling more violence between Jews and Arabs. A 1939 proposal to create a bi-national state is rejected by both sides.

The Arab Revolt

Ironically, the new Arab nationalist movement cut its teeth not on a Western Christian enemy but on the Ottomans, the apathetic Muslim rulers who dominated most of the Middle East, including the area on either side of the Jordan River. The revolt was fought by Arab warriors on horseback, loosely formed into armies under Emir Faisal, the ruler of Mecca and guardian of the Muslim holy places, who had taken up the reins of the Arab nationalist movement in 1914. He was joined by his brother Abdullah and the enigmatic British colonel TE Lawrence, known as Lawrence of Arabia. Lawrence helped with coordination and securing supplies from the Allies, as well as attacking the Turkish-controlled Hejaz Railway, in a campaign that swept across the desert from Arabia, wrested Aqaba from the Ottomans and eventually ousted them from Damascus. By 1918 the Arabs controlled modern Saudi Arabia, Jordan and parts of southern Syria. Faisal set up government in Damascus and dreamed of an independent Arab realm.

Glad of the help in weakening the Ottoman Empire (allies of Germany during WW1), the British promised to help Faisal. The promise was severely undermined, however, by the 1917 Balfour Declaration:

> His Majesty's Government view with favour the establishment in Palestine of a National Home for the Jewish people, and will use their best endeavours to facilitate the achievement of this object.

This contradictory acceptance of both a Jewish homeland in Palestine and the preservation of the rights of the original Palestinian community lies at the heart of the seemingly irreconcilable Arab-Israeli conflict.

The Creation of Jordan

The Arab Revolt may not have immediately achieved its goal during peace negotiations, but it did lead directly (albeit after over two decades of wrangling with the British) to the birth of the modern state of Jordan.

Between 1775 and 1825, 87 volumes on aspects of the Near East were published in Britain alone and 46 reviews of the same books appeared in leading journals between 1805 and 1825.

HISTORY FIGHTING FOR AN ARAB LAND (1914–46)

THE HEJAZ RAILWAY

The Hejaz Railway was built between 1900 and 1908 to transport pilgrims from Damascus to the holy city of Medina, reducing the two-month journey by camel and on foot to as little as three days. For Jordan, and Amman in particular, this meant a boom in trade. The 1462km line was completely funded by donations from Muslims – but functioned for less than 10 years. The trains and railway line were partially destroyed in the Arab Revolt of 1917 during WWI. The line was rebuilt as far south as Ma'an, but is now only used for cargo. There is occasional talk of introducing a tourist passenger service between Aqaba and Wadi Rum.

1931	1946	1947	1948
The colourful Desert Camel Corp is set up by a British officer, Major Glubb, as a branch of the Arab Legion; it is comprised mostly of nomadic Bedouins.	Jordan gains full independence from the British; Emir Abdullah, who took a leading role in the Arab Revolt, is crowned the king of Jordan.	The UN votes for the partition of Palestine but the proposal is rejected by the Arab League on the grounds that the whole territory should remain Arab.	The State of Israel is proclaimed, the British withdraw immediately and renewed hostilities break out between Arabs and Jews. Half a million Palestinians flood into the 'West Bank'.

At the 1919 Paris Peace Conference the British came to an agreement with Faisal, who was given Iraq, while his elder brother Abdullah was proclaimed ruler of Trans-Jordan, the land lying between Iraq and the east bank. A young Winston Churchill drew up the borders in 1921. Abdullah made Amman his capital. Britain recognised the territory as an independent state under its protection in 1923, and a small defence force, the Arab Legion, was set up under British officers. A series of treaties after 1928 led to full independence in 1946, when Abdullah was proclaimed king.

The betrayal of the Arab cause by Western allies was underlined by the secret Sykes-Picot Agreement of 1916 in which 'Syria' (modern-day Syria and Lebanon) came under French control, and 'Palestine' (an area including modern Israel, the Palestinian Territories and Jordan) came under British control.

Troubles with Palestine (1946–94)

If there is one element that defines the modern history of Jordan, it's the relationship with the peoples on the other side of the river – not just the Jews but also (and perhaps more especially) the Palestinians, who today make up the majority of the population of Jordan.

Much of the conflict stems from the creation of a Jewish national homeland in Palestine, where Arab Muslims accounted for about 90% of the population. Their resentment was understood by Arabs across the region and informed the dialogue of Arab-Israeli relations for the rest of the 20th century.

New Hashemite Kingdom of Jordan

In 1948 resentment escalated into conflict between Arab and Israeli forces, with the result that Jordan won control of East Jerusalem and the West Bank. King Abdullah, reneging on assurances regarding Palestinian independence, annexed the territory and proclaimed the new Hashemite Kingdom of Jordan (HKJ). The new state won immediate recognition from Britain and the USA, but regional powers disapproved of the annexation, added to which the unprecedented immigration of Palestinian refugees placed a strain on limited domestic resources.

In July 1951 King Abdullah was assassinated outside Al-Aqsa Mosque in Jerusalem. The throne eventually passed to his beloved 17-year-old grandson, Hussein, in May 1953. Hussein offered a form of citizenship to all Palestinian Arab refugees in 1960, but refused to relinquish Palestinian territory. Partly in response, the Palestine Liberation Organisation (PLO) was formed in 1964.

The Six Day War

After a period of relative peace and prosperity, conflict between Arab and Israeli forces broke out again in the 1960s, culminating in the Six Day War, provoked by Palestinian guerrilla raids into Israel from Syria. When the Syrians announced that Israel was amassing troops in preparation for an assault, Egypt responded by asking the UN to withdraw

1950	1951	1953	1958
King Abdullah annexes the West Bank and east Jerusalem, despite paying lip service to Arab declarations backing Palestinian independence and expressly ruling out territorial annexations.	King Abdullah is assassinated at Al-Aqsa Mosque (Jerusalem), ending his dream of a single Arab state encompassing Syria, Lebanon, Jordan, Israel and Palestine – a dream that antagonised Arab neighbours.	Hussein becomes king of Jordan after his father is diagnosed with schizophrenia. Despite his British education, Hussein makes his mark by ousting remaining British troops.	King Hussein's gesture of independence doesn't last long as British troops are invited to return after Hussein's failed attempt at union with Iraq.

its Emergency Force from the Egypt–Israel border. Egyptian president Nasser then closed the Straits of Tiran (the entrance to the Red Sea), effectively sealing the port of Eilat. Five days later Jordan and Egypt signed a mutual defence pact, dragging Jordan into the oncoming hostilities.

On 5 June 1967 the Israelis dispatched a predawn raid that wiped out the Egyptian Air Force on the ground. In the following days they decimated Egyptian troops in Sinai and Jordanian troops on the West Bank, and overran the Golan Heights in Syria.

The outcome for Jordan was disastrous: it lost the whole of the West Bank and its part of Jerusalem, which together had supplied Jordan with its two principal sources of income – agriculture and tourism. It also resulted in yet another huge wave of Palestinian refugees.

Black September

After the 1967 defeat, the frustrated Palestinians within Jordan became increasingly militant, and by 1968 Palestinian *fedayeen* (guerrilla) fighters were effectively acting as a state within a state, openly defying Jordanian soldiers.

In 1970 Palestinian militants fired on King Hussein's motorcade and held 68 foreigners hostage in an Amman hotel, while the rogue Popular Front for the Liberation of Palestine hijacked and destroyed three Western planes in front of horrified TV crews. Martial law and bloody fighting (which claimed 3000 lives) followed. Yasser Arafat was spirited out of Amman disguised as a Kuwaiti sheikh in order to attend an Arab League summit in Cairo. A fragile ceasefire was signed, but it was not until midway through 1971 that the final resistance (around Ajloun) was defeated. The guerrillas were forced to recognise Hussein's authority and the Palestinians had to choose between exile and submission. Most chose exile in Lebanon.

Relinquishing Claims to Palestinian Leadership

In 1974 King Hussein reluctantly relinquished Jordan's claims to the West Bank by recognising the PLO as the sole representative of Palestinians with the right to set up a government in any liberated territory. By 1988 the king had severed all Jordan's administrative and legal ties with the West Bank.

In the meantime profound demographic changes, including a sharp rise in population, particularly of young people, had reshaped Jordan. Economic migration, both from the countryside to the city and from Jordan to the increasingly wealthy Gulf States, together with improved education, changed social and family structures. Most significantly, Palestinians no longer formed an edgy minority of refugees but instead took their place as the majority of Jordan's population.

HISTORY TROUBLES WITH PALESTINE (1946–94)

When it was founded, the PLO had the blessing of the Arab League to represent the Palestinian people and train guerrilla fighters. The Palestine National Council (PNC) became the executive body of the PLO, with a remit to govern Palestine.

Queen Noor is not the mother of the present king. That distinction belongs to King Hussein's second wife, Princess Muna, who was from England. They were married for 10 years (1961–71), having met on the film set of *Lawrence of Arabia*.

1960	1967	1970	1988
Jordan offers partial citizenship to Palestinian Arab refugees but refuses to relinquish Palestinian territory. In response, the Palestine Liberation Organisation (PLO) is formed in 1964, backed by the Arab League.	Israel wins Jerusalem and the West Bank in the Six Day War resulting in another influx of Palestinians. Al-Fatah dominates the PLO under Yasser Arafat, training guerrillas for Israeli raids.	Black September results in thousands being injured in clashes between the Jordanian government and Palestinian guerrillas. Three hijacked aircraft are blown up by the PLO.	King Hussein relinquishes remaining ties with the West Bank. The focus turns to home where women are now allowed to vote (from 1989) and political parties are legalised thereafter.

The complete integration of Palestinian refugees into all aspects of mainstream Jordanian life is due in no small part to the skilful diplomacy of King Hussein. The numerous assassination attempts (there were at least 12) that dogged the early years of his reign were replaced with a growing respect for his genuine, deep-rooted concern for the Palestinians' plight – which is significant in a region where few other countries were willing to shoulder the burden.

Peace with Israel

On 26 October 1994, Jordan and Israel and the Palestinian Territories signed a momentous peace treaty that provided for the removal of all economic barriers between the two countries and closer cooperation on security, water and other issues.

KING HUSSEIN

Since his death, King Hussein has become a legend. On succeeding to the throne on 2 May 1953 at the age of 17, the youthful, British-educated Hussein was known more for his love of pretty women and fast cars. Forty-five years later he was fêted as one of the Middle East's great political survivors, king against the odds and the de facto creator of the modern state of Jordan.

King Hussein's loyalty to his people was notable. In a role emulated by his son decades later, Hussein would disguise himself as a taxi driver and ask passengers what they thought of the king.

Hussein's lasting legacy, however, extends beyond his successful domestic policy. Throughout his reign he maintained close and friendly ties with Britain and courted trade with the West. From his sustained efforts at diplomacy to avert the 1991 Gulf War to his peace agreement with Israel in 1994, the urbane and articulate king of a country in one of the world's toughest neighbourhoods came to be seen as a beacon of moderateness and stability in a region known for neither attribute. This reputation was secured in 1997 when a Jordanian soldier shot and killed seven Israeli schoolgirls in northern Jordan. King Hussein personally attended the funeral in a public display of grief and solidarity with the Israeli families.

Hussein married four times and fathered 11 children. He was a highly popular man with many interests and was an accomplished pilot. After a long battle with cancer, during which time he continued his role as peace negotiator between Israel and Palestine, he died in Jordan in February 1999. He was greatly mourned not just by those who knew him but by Jordan and the region at large.

He is now regarded as a man who firmly steered the nascent country of Jordan through potentially devastating crises, balancing the demands of Arab nationalism against the political expedience of cooperation with Western interests. In so doing, he helped pave the way for Jordan's modern role in the world as a bridge between two ideologies.

1990	1994	1999	2000
Saddam Hussein's invasion of Kuwait, supported by the Palestinians, requires careful diplomacy by King Hussein, who publicly supports Baghdad while suing for peace. Palestinian Gulf workers flood into Jordan.	A historic peace treaty between Israel and Jordan ends 46 years of war and gives Jordan a 'special role' over Muslim holy shrines in Jerusalem – straining relations with Arab neighbours.	King Hussein dies (7 February). His funeral is attended by former and current presidents of Israel and major powers, honouring his role as peace mediator. His son, Abdullah, becomes king.	Jordan accedes to the World Trade Organisation, and the European Free Trade Association (2001). Trade significantly increases under the free-trade accord with the USA and Jordanian Qualifying Industrial Zones (QIZ).

But there is a twist to the final chapter of relations between Jordan and Palestine in the 20th century. There was a clause in the treaty recognising the 'special role of the Hashemite Kingdom of Jordan in the Muslim holy shrines in Jerusalem'. This inclusion aroused the suspicions of some Palestinians regarding the intentions of King Hussein, who at the outset of his long career had enjoyed more than just a 'special role' on the west bank of the Jordan. The treaty made Jordan unpopular within the region at the time, but in the longer term barely cast a shadow over the illustrious reign of one of the Middle East's most beloved rulers.

Relations with Israel & the Palestinian Territories Today

It has been a long time since the historic 1994 peace treaty and the long-term effect of peace with Israel is still being assessed. While the treaty was branded by some Palestinians as a betrayal, the world at large regarded it as a highly significant step towards vital East–West ties. Flare-ups between the two nations continue to occur, not just over the fate of the Palestinian people but also over issues such as water supply, which many predict will replace oil as the issue of conflict of the next few decades.

Relations with Iraq (1990–)

Arab Federation

For the past two decades Jordan has been preoccupied with its neighbours to the east rather the west – a shift in focus necessitated firstly by the Gulf War and subsequently by the US-led invasion of Iraq.

Given that the founding fathers of the modern states of Iraq and Jordan were brothers, it is not surprising that the two countries have enjoyed periods of close collaboration over the years. In 1958 King Hussein tried to capitalise on this dynastic dimension by establishing the Arab Federation, a short-lived alliance between Jordan and Iraq that was intended to counterbalance the formation of the United Arab Republic between Egypt and Syria. Although the alliance did not last long, the connection between the neighbours remained strong, especially in terms of trade.

The Gulf War

When Saddam Hussein invaded Kuwait in 1990, Jordan found itself in a no-win situation. On the one hand, the Palestinian majority in Jordan backed Saddam's invasion, having been given assurances by Saddam that the showdown would result in a solution to the Palestinian question on the West Bank. On the other hand, King Hussein recognised that siding with Iraq would antagonise Western allies and risk Jordan's US trade

---

HISTORY RELATIONS WITH IRAQ (1990–)

Modern History of Jordan

A History of Jordan (Philip Robbins; 2004)

The Modern History of Jordan (Kamal Salibi; 1998)

A PLO-Israeli declaration of principles in September 1993 set in motion the process of establishing an autonomous Palestinian authority in the Occupied Territories. With this declaration, the territorial question was virtually removed as an obstacle to peace between Jordan and Israel.

2001	2005	2007	2008
The US invasion of Iraq is strenuously protested by Arab countries. King Abdullah sides publicly with Baghdad while complying, officially at least, with the UN embargo on trade with Iraq.	Three hotels in Amman are blown up in coordinated suicide attacks, masterminded by Al-Qaeda. Tourism, booming since the 1994 peace treaty, takes an immediate hit.	As one of many steps in the modernisation of the country's political, economic and social structure, 20% of seats in municipal councils are reserved for women.	Iraq contributes to the maintenance of the 500,000 Iraqi refugees in Jordan. The Iraqi arrival is the fourth influx of refugees in the modern history of this geographically small country.

and aid. As a solution, he sided publicly with Baghdad while complying, officially at least, with the UN embargo on trade with Iraq. As a result, although US and Saudi aid were temporarily suspended, loans and help were forthcoming from other quarters, particularly Japan and Europe.

Despite these new streams of income, the Gulf War exacted a heavy financial penalty on the small and relatively poor, oil-less state of Jordan. Ironically, however, Jordan's third wave of refugees in 45 years brought some relief as 500,000 Jordanians and Palestinians returned from the Gulf States. They brought with them a US$500 million windfall that stimulated the economy throughout the 1990s and helped turn Amman, in particular, into a cosmopolitan, modern city.

Growing Tensions with Iraq

Ongoing resentment about the outcome of the Iraqi refugee crisis is one reason for a cooling of relations between Jordan and Iraq; another reason is concern over the weakened state of Iraq, resulting in a general vulnerability of the region to radical terrorism. There is already anxiety, for example, over Iraq's porous borders and incursions from self-styled Islamic State militants. Many in Jordan also fear that a weak Iraq leaves Jordan vulnerable to increased Iranian and Shiite influence.

The heightened tensions between Jordan and Iraq was further exacerbated in 2014 when over 150 Sunni leaders from various groups opposed to the official government in Iraq met for a two-day meeting in Amman, pledging to depose Nouri al-Maliki, the Iraqi prime minister. Although the Jordanian government denied involvement in promoting the opposition alliance, the Iraqi government threatened to revisit agreements regarding fuel prices. At present, Jordan receives Iraqi oil on favourable terms and the Iraqi oil pipeline project, giving Iraq access to the Red Sea from the Jordanian port of Aqaba, is another area of jeopardy if tension between the two countries continues to escalate.

UN assessments put the total cost to Jordan of the Gulf War (mid-1990 to mid-1991) at more than US$8 billion. The UN naval blockade of Aqaba alone, aimed at enforcing UN sanctions against Iraq, cost Jordan US$300 million a year in lost revenue between 1991 and 1994.

2011	2012	2012–13	2014
Protests in Amman mark the 'Arab Spring', a period of uprising against the establishment across the region and expressed in Jordan in a series of mass demonstrations.	Protests continue, largely as a response to rising costs of living, and result in the unsuccessful demand for the end of the monarchy and the abdication of King Abdullah II.	Jordan experiences its fifth major wave of immigration as a result of civil war in Syria. Some 600,000 refugees pour into the north creating the world's second-largest refugee camp.	Pope Francis visits Jordan and celebrates mass at a stadium in Amman. During his visit he praises the country for its generosity in welcoming the refugees from Syria.

Amateur Archaeology

Jordan has been the site of intense archaeological scrutiny for decades, but you don't have to be Indiana Jones to take interest – anyone can gain pleasure in rummaging around Jordan's many ancient sites. If just looking isn't enough, however, and you can't resist the temptation to get physical with the past, then here are a few ideas on how to join an amateur dig, with some of the key archaeological sites to focus on.

Digging Up the Past

Take any path off the beaten track in central Jordan and you will be sure to stumble on something ancient – a fallen column with poppies dancing on the capital, coloured tesserae from a broken mosaic, a coin of indiscriminate currency. Look more carefully, and you'll probably see the remains of a fence enclosing a patch of land fast returning to wilderness – evidence, if any were needed, that human habitation extends back to the very earliest periods of human history.

Two Centuries of Archaeology in Jordan

In many respects, the modern study of Western archaeology was founded in what we now call Jordan, arising out of a fascination with tracing the traditions of the Bible to the unearthed ruins of the Holy Land – on both sides of the River Jordan – and setting them in a historical context.

For decades, this was an occupation that attracted largely foreign interest as the people of the region were more focused on the demands of the present than on digging up remnants of the past.

Today this is no longer the case, as Jordanians have the time and the means to take a greater interest in their heritage, and education helps new generations to come to a better appreciation of the country's position within the cradle of civilisation. Each year more funding is put aside for archaeological exploration, with the result that some of the greatest finds, involving teams from universities in Jordan and abroad, have been

1812
Swiss explorer Jean Louis Burckhardt, aged 27, 'rediscovers' Petra for the West, stimulating a fascination with ancient history in the region that endures for the next two centuries.

1868
The precious Mesha Stele, one of the earliest examples of Hebrew script, is discovered by a missionary at Dhiban – and promptly shattered by bickering locals.

1900s
Jordan and the Levant are explored by British, American, French and German surveyors, including a young archaeology student from Oxford by the name of TE Lawrence (of Arabia).

1920s
Following the British mandate of Jordan, modest excavation projects aimed at consolidating the main standing monuments begin throughout Jordan.

1930s
Remarkable mosaics, regarded today as some of the finest in the Levant, are unearthed in Madaba.

1940s
The Dead Sea Scrolls are discovered by a Bedouin shepherd in Qumran at a time when parts of the western shore of the Dead Sea belong to Jordan.

1950s–60s
The Arab-Israeli wars and the aftermath of WWII leads to a lean period in archaeological study in Jordan.

made within the last 30 years, culminating in 2008 with the world's oldest church – a befitting discovery for a discipline that arose largely out of Christian curiosity.

Volunteering on a Dig

Archaeological fieldwork is a painstaking process but the rewards are great, particularly if you uncover something special like a coral bead worn by an ancient, a piece of copper cast six thousand years ago or a shard of pottery with the design intact. It's not so much the finding of an object as the sense of connection with a bygone age that makes archaeology so compelling. In Jordan, there are numerous sites across the country, from ancient Pre-Pottery Neolithic (PPN) sites to more contemporary excavations in and around the Crusader castles. Archaeologists, not known for consensus on many things, have at least agreed that there remains huge potential for major finds despite the intensive work in the field for the past three decades.

If you fancy being part of an archaeological team and you have the patience and discipline to spend long hours in a dusty hole tickling dirt off a lump of masonry, then it's not too difficult to become a volunteer on one of these digs. Here are some guidelines:

➡ There are usually only a limited number of volunteer positions available on each site, so find out who is conducting which digs and apply early.

➡ Make contact with the project leader and be sure to emphasise any special skills (like photography or drafting) you may have.

➡ Mention any travels in the region or Arabic-speaking skills.

➡ Emphasise your experience on group projects (archaeology is all about teamwork, despite the way it's presented in films).

➡ Ask how much your volunteer placement will cost. This fee helps cover the costs of adding your name to the team.

➡ Allow plenty of time. In order to gain access to sites, project leaders must obtain permits and security clearance, which can take up to six months to complete.

➡ Don't be put off if you don't succeed with your first application; it takes persistence to find a placement – a quality you'll need when you're on your first field trip!

Field Work Opportunities in Jordan

American Center for Oriental Research (ACOR; www.bu.edu/acor) Prepares an extensive annual listing of field-work opportunities in Jordan and the Middle East.

Digs on the Web

Madaba Plains Project (www.madabaplains.org/hisban) Excavation at Tell Hesban.

Great Temple Excavation (www.brown.edu/Departments/Joukowsky_Institute/Petra) Brown University's Petra excavations.

Virtual Karak (www.vkrp.org) Castle archaeology.

ARCHAEOLOGY MUSEUMS IN JORDAN

If you want to see the finds from some of the key archaeological digs in Jordan, then head for the following museums.

Jordan Museum (p45) Ain Ghazal fertility sculptures and examples of the Dead Sea Scrolls.

Museum of Archaeology (⏃5355000; ◷8am-5pm Sun-Thu) At the University of Jordan in Amman; has artefacts from all eras.

Salt Archaeological Museum (p102) Good coverage of domestic history.

Museum of Archaeology & Anthropology (p91) Includes numismatic displays.

American Schools of Oriental Research (www.asor.org) This organisation supports the study of the culture and history of the Near East.

Archaeological Institute of America (AIA; www.archaeological.org) The largest and oldest archaeology organisation in the USA is a valuable resource for information.

Biblical Archaeological Society (www.bib-arch.org) Produces the magazine *Biblical Archaeological Review,* runs archaeological tours and lists volunteer openings.

Council for British Research in the Levant (CBRL; www.cbrl.org.uk) British Academy–sponsored institute with research centres in Amman and Jerusalem.

University of Jordan (☑06-5355000; www.ju.edu.jo) The archaeology department at this Amman-based university is a good contact point.

University of Sydney (www.sydney.edu.au/arts/archaeology) This prestigious Australian university runs a highly reputable field project at Pella.

1970s

Excavations near Amman unearth the oldest statues in the world, the 8500-year-old, life-size Ain Ghazal figures.

1980s

Projects around Jordan unearth the remains of the Temple of Hercules at the Citadel in Amman, a Greek manuscript library at Petra, and ancient temple complexes in the Jordan Valley.

1990s

Early mining sites west of Karak and the baptism site of Jesus Christ at Bethany-Beyond-the-Jordan are just two of many discoveries marking the end of the century.

2008

The world's oldest church, which once sheltered 70 disciples of Jesus Christ, is uncovered under St Georgeous Church in Rihab, near Amman.

AMATEUR ARCHAEOLOGY FIELD WORK OPPORTUNITIES IN JORDAN

Biblical Sites of Jordan

Whatever one's beliefs, visiting sites of biblical significance can still be a moving experience – for many people this is 'hallowed, holy ground'. From Abraham and Moses to John the Baptist and Jesus Christ, the founding fathers of the three great monotheistic traditions are intimately tied to the Jordanian landscape. Little wonder then that Jordan has been a destination of religious pilgrimage for centuries. The following are some of the most significant sites associated with the Good Book.

Locating Bible References

For an illustrated and comprehensive listing of locations, Bible Places (www. bibleplaces.com) offers links to a pictorial library covering many biblical sites in Jordan.

For hundreds of years pilgrims, historians and the culturally curious have been travelling to Jordan in search of the sites of biblical importance. The eastern banks of the Jordan River alone are home to no fewer than 100 such sites. The most famous are listed here, together with the biblical reference.

'Ain Musa or Ayoun Musa

Then Moses raised his arm and struck the rock twice with his staff. Water gushed out, and the community and their livestock drank.
Numbers 20:11

The exact location of where Moses struck the rock is open to debate – it's either 'Ain Musa, which is north of Wadi Musa near Petra, or Ayoun Musa, near Mt Nebo.

Dead Sea

...while the water flowing down to the Sea of Arabah was completely cut off...
Joshua 3:16

The Sea of Arabah (Dead Sea), also known as the Salt Sea, is mentioned several times in the Bible.

Jebel Haroun

Remove Aaron's garments and put them on his son Eleazar, for Aaron will be gathered to his people: he will die there. Moses did as the Lord commanded: they went up to Mount Hor in the sight of the whole community.
Numbers 10:26-27

Mt Hor is believed to be Jebel Haroun in Petra, which is also revered by Muslims as a holy place.

Jebel Umm al-Biyara

He [the Judean king, Amaziah] was the one who defeated ten thousand Edomites in the Valley of the Salt and captured Sela in battle...
2 Kings 14:7

The village on top of Umm al-Biyara mountain in Petra is believed to be the ancient settlement of Sela.

Biblical Sites of Jordan

Lot's Cave

Now Lot went up out of Zo'ar, and dwelt in the hills with his two daughters, for he was afraid to dwell in Zo'ar; so he dwelt in a cave with his two daughters.

Genesis 19:30

The cave where Lot and his daughters lived for years after Lot's wife turned into a pillar of salt is thought to be just off the Dead Sea Highway, not far from Safi.

Machaerus

The King was sad, but because of his oaths and his dinner guests, he gave orders that her request be granted, and had John beheaded in the prison.

Matthew 14:9-12

John the Baptist had claimed that Herod Antipas' marriage to his brother's wife, Herodias, was unlawful. So, at the request of Salome, Herodias' daughter, John was killed.

Mt Nebo

Go up into...Mount Nebo in Moab, across from Jericho, and view Canaan, the land I am giving the Israelites as their own possession. There on the mountain that you have climbed you will die.

Deuteronomy 32:49-50

Mt Nebo is revered as a holy place because it is where Moses is reported to have died, although his tomb has never been found.

Tell al-Kharrar

Then Jesus came from Galilee to the Jordan to be baptised by John.

Matthew 3:13

Tell al-Kharrar is regarded as Bethany-Beyond-the-Jordan where Jesus was baptised by John the Baptist.

Umm Qais

When he [Jesus] arrived at the other side in the region of Gadarenes, two demon-possessed men coming from the tombs met him.

Matthew 8:28-34

Umm Qais is known as Gadara in the Bible, as well as in other ancient scriptures.

Digs on the Web (Biblical)

American Schools of Oriental Research *(p271) Covers the sites of the Hebrew scriptures.*

Franciscan Archaeological Institute *(www.christusrex.org/www1/ofm/fai/FAImain.html) Excavations around Madaba and Mt Nebo.*

People & Society

Many visitors enter Jordan with the sole priority of ticking off the antiquities. Some go in search of past heroes; others are led to Jordan in the spirit of pilgrimage and acquaintance with the 'soul posts' of their faith. Whatever their motivations to root out the past, however, people invariably return home impressed by the Jordan of today and the way it has opened its doors to those in need and embraced a modern outlook towards the world at large.

Jordan's Bedouin Roots

Tradition of Hospitality

Ahlan wa sahlan! It's one of the most common greetings in Arabic and one that defines the way Jordanians relate to the people around them, especially guests. The root words mean 'people' or 'family' *(ahl)* and 'ease' *(sahl)*, so translated loosely the expression means 'be as one of the family and at your ease'. It's a gracious thought, and one that ends up in English simply as 'welcome' or (more commonly to tourists) 'welcome to Jordan'.

Bedouin traditions of hospitality and kindness are deeply ingrained in the Jordanian psyche. Rooted in the harsh realities of life in the desert,

---

SOCIAL GRACES

Standing wedged between the door and a table and with no room to back out politely, my Jordanian companion looked in horror as a foreign man proffered a large hairy hand in her direction and gushed a greeting. 'Can you believe it,' Maryam said, 'and in Ramadan too!' I asked why she didn't simply refuse to shake hands: 'I didn't want to embarrass him,' she said. This common scenario highlights both the desirability of learning a few courtesies as a traveller and also the Jordanian good-natured tolerance of social faux pas.

Here are a few social graces that will help break the ice without breaking a friendship. If all else fails, there's not much harm that can't be undone with a smile, a box of baklava and a compliment about the lovable children.

Handshaking This is an important part of the ritual of greeting in Jordan but usually only between members of the same sex. If you witness an accident, for example, the first few moments will probably be taken up with copious handshaking, greeting and asking after each man's family...before a slanging match erupts about who is to blame.

Public displays of affection Don't think that seeing two men kissing gives you the right to do the same. All signs of affection, except between members of the same sex (and of the strictly platonic kind), is frowned upon in public. Not that you'd guess these days from the relaxed attitudes of trendsetters in the city who openly walk arm in arm with a loved one.

Hands and arms Blundering with these limbs includes using your left hand to give something, forgetting to touch your heart when refusing something and, on that matter, forgetting to refuse something you intend eventually to accept.

Feet These appendages are both a host's and a guest's worst nightmare. For anyone contemplating a visit to a home or a mosque, the advice for feet is to wash them, unsock them and tuck them under you when sitting on the floor.

these traditions have been virtually codified into all social behaviour. Century-old notions of hospitality combine with a wonderful sense of humour to make Jordanians easy to connect with.

Love of the Desert

Over 98% of Jordanians are Arab, descended from various tribes that migrated to the area from all directions of the Middle East over the centuries. Most tribes trace their lineage to the Bedouin, the original desert dwellers of Arabia, perceived by many as the representatives and guardians of the very essence of 'Arabness'. Bedouins form the majority of the indigenous population, although today no more than 40,000 Bedouin can be considered truly nomadic. Living a traditional life of livestock rearing, the nomadic Bedouin who travel from oasis to oasis in quest of water are concentrated mainly in the Badia – the great desert plains of Eastern Jordan.

Despite the settlement of some Bedouin (recent examples include the Bdoul, who once roamed the hillsides of Petra but who now live for the most part in the modern settlement of Umm Sayhoun), many Jordanians retain a deep sentimental attachment to the desert. This isn't always obvious given the littering and general despoliation of public access areas such as at Wadi Rum, but it is evident in the way Jordanians claim kinship with the principle tenets of desert-dwelling – hospitality, loyalty, dignity, pride and courtesy.

Modern Caretakers of the Desert

Whether Zawaedha, Zalabia or Bdoul, whether from Wadi Rum, Wadi Musa or the great Badia beyond, the Bedouin are universally proud of 'their Jordan' and welcome guests who visit them in their ancient tribal lands. It's not surprising, then, that many of the country's Bedouin now make a living from tourism and many feel it is their modern mission to reveal the wonders of their country to new generations of visitors. In some senses, the Bedouin have been doing the same, albeit for slightly different purposes, for centuries, offering bread and salt to those in need on the understanding that the same courtesy will be offered to them in return. The currency today is usually money, but the principle of easing the passage of strangers through traditional tribal territories remains unchanged. Unchanged, too, is the principle of 'word of mouth' in advertising friendly encampments, though today the internet has replaced the camel caravan as the modus operandi.

Not everything about the modern life of the Bedouin has stayed the same, however. It is easy to romanticise the traditional way of life – managing goats and sheep and looking for water – as simple and free, but the reality of life in the desert is uncompromisingly hard, entailing goat-hair beds and scorpions, insufferable heat and freezing nights, not enough to eat and being forever thirsty. Add to that the modern complexities of life (compulsory education, impinging urbanisation, and the tough and fickle demands of working with tourists) and it's easy to see that there's nothing simple or free in a modern Bedouin life.

It's little surprise then that while many regret the passing of the golden age of nomadic life, the majority of Jordan's indigenous population look towards settlement and the convenience that it brings. Today, therefore, as a visitor to Jordan, you are just as likely to run into the Bedouin on a mobile phone at the bus station or in public-assisted housing at the edge of Petra. They are wistful for the stories of their grandparents, but they are not nostalgic about the hardships. Television, internet and 4WD transport have changed their lives forever, but as they are not regretful of this, then neither should a visitor be!

The checked *keffiyah* headdress is an important national symbol – red and white for Bedouin; black and white for Palestinians. It's held in place by the black rope-like *agal*. There are no official dress restrictions for women and few wear a veil. Almost none wear full-body chador.

The Bedouin are known for their sense of humour, which they list – alongside courage, alertness and religious faith – as one of the four secrets of life, encouraging tolerance and humility.

Good Manners

There are many ways in which Jordan's Bedouin roots have influenced the national psyche. For the visitor, perhaps the most easily identifiable aspects of this inheritance is the value placed on good manners. Etiquette in Jordan has been refined over centuries of tribal interaction and is an important expression of national identity. Social mores cover all aspects of life from the length and depth of an introductory 'hello' to how many cups of coffee should be offered and accepted, and who offers what to whom at supper.

For a visitor, learning the subtleties of 'custom and manner' is challenging, but making the effort to fit in is invariably appreciated, particularly if visiting Jordanians at home.

Respect for the Royals

Another noticeable trait of the Bedouin inheritance is an ingrained tribal respect for local elders, or sheikhs. This character trait is extended to the ultimate leaders of the country. Claiming unbroken descent from Prophet Mohammed, Jordan's Hashemite royal family is a nationally beloved and regionally respected institution. All monarchies have their

> While many aspects of Bedouin life have modernised, living arrangements under the *beit ash-sha'ar* (goat-hair tent) remain firmly divided between the private women's harem and the more public men's quarters.

THE ROYAL WOMEN OF JORDAN

Two influential women have helped shaped the modern face of Jordan. Both have used their marriage into royalty to make positive social changes and have set up nationally respected charities.

Queen Noor

Royal Connection Fourth wife of the former king, King Hussein (now deceased); married in 1978

Former Name Lisa Halaby; adopted the name Queen Noor upon conversion to Islam

Former Occupation Architect and urban planner

From Washington DC; studied at Princeton

Background Born into a distinguished Arab-American family (her father served under the administration of John F Kennedy and was head of Pan Am for a while)

Community Service Set up her own charity, the influential Noor Foundation

Public Relations Important role in explaining Jordan's stand against the 1990 Gulf War to American audiences and active campaigner for women's rights, children's welfare and community improvement

Further Information See Queen Noor's website (www.nooralhusseinfoundation.org)

Queen Rania

Royal Connection Wife of the present king, King Abdullah; married in 1993

Former Name Rania Al-Yassin

Former Occupation Business administration

From Kuwait; studied at the American University of Cairo.

Background Born into a notable Jordanian family of Palestinian origin

Community Service Set up her own charity, the influential Jordan River Foundation

Public Relations Not afraid of a public profile; can be seen in activities as diverse as campaigning for the rights of women and advocating MOOCs (online education courses) to running the Dead Sea Marathon

Further Information See Queen Rania's website (www.queenrania.jo)

Crossing Cultures

Into the Wadi (Michele Drouart; 2000)

Married to a Bedouin (Marguerite van Geldermalsen; 2006)

critics from time to time, not least for seeming arcane in their function, but Jordan's modern royal family has helped to redefine the royal image through benign and diplomatic governance (especially with regard to Middle East peace issues), as well as through a history of charitable works. It was evident that after the Arab Spring of 2011, despite protests against the government, there was limited enthusiasm for a republic. Jordanians look to their royalty for leadership and an example of how to live a modern life in the context of their largely Islamic and Arab heritage.

In a region where men are more commonly the public face of royal initiatives, Jordan has been unusual for the high profile of its royal women. Visit many of the small women's cooperatives like Bani Hamida in Mukawir, and you are likely to find some mention of either Queen Noor or Queen Rania in the patronage or even funding of the project.

Daily Life

Importance of Family

Family ties are all-important to both modern and traditional Jordanians and paying respect to parents is where the sense of obeisance to elders is engendered. Socialising generally entails some kind of get-together with the extended family, with lines drawn loosely between the genders. This is reflected in terms of physical divisions within the house, where separate seating areas are reserved for men and women.

Women Writers on Jordan

Nine Parts of Desire (Geraldine Brooks; 1995)

West of the Jordan (Laila Halaby; 2003)

Meals are generally eaten on the floor, with everyone gathered around several trays of food shared by all. More traditional families are often quite hierarchical at meal times. The grandparents and male head of the house may eat in one circle, the latter's wife and the older children and other women in the family in another, and the small children in yet another.

In the evenings, in common with people the world over, locals in the cities window shop, stroll around the streets, enjoy a leisurely meal, go to the cinema or watch TV. With more regional nuance, men may pass the time in a local coffeehouse, playing cards, smoking a nargileh (water pipe) or perhaps watching European football on the TV, while the kids play the real thing on the streets outside or diligently attend to homework.

Marriage

Jordan's Female Firsts

1979: Government minister

1995: Mayor (in Ajloun)

1996: Judge

1997: Taxi driver

2010: Attorney general

2011: Ambassador to Washington

2013: Carpenter

Marriages reflect the sense of family allegiance and are often arranged for the benefit of the families involved, with matches commonly made between cousins. It is fair to say, however, that parents do not often enforce a wedding against their daughter's wish. In 2001 the legal age of marriage was lifted from 15 years old for women and 16 for men to 18 for both, although Islamic judges are still permitted to sanction underage marriages.

The marriage ceremony takes place either at the mosque, church or home of the bride or groom. After the marriage ceremony, the men of the family drive around the streets in a long convoy, sounding their horns, blasting out music and partying until sunrise.

Polygamy (by men) is rare but it is legal. Men who marry more than once (Islam allows four wives if each wife is assured equal treatment) are obliged to inform both their first and their new wives. Amendments to the law in 2002 made it possible for women to file for divorce if they repay the dowry given by their husband. That said, the social stigma regarding divorce remains strong.

A DISHONOURABLE HOAX

In 2004 a book entitled *Forbidden Love,* written by Norma Khouri, arrived on the book-shelves. Within weeks the author (to the delight of her publisher, Random House) found she had a bestseller on her hands. Better and bigger than that, she had overnight become the convenient voice the West wanted to hear: an Arab woman speaking out against the supposed 'tyranny of Islam'. Soon she was fêted on chat shows and courted by newspaper journalists, and her tale assumed the quality of moral crusade taken up with indignation by worthy people around the world.

Her story was a harrowing one that described the death in Jordan of her childhood friend, Dalia: a killing carried out by the girl's Islamic knife-wielding father for a harmless flirtation with a Christian soldier. This event, together with the author's description of it, apparently led to Khouri's flight to the USA from the benighted country of her birth and a *fatwa* being placed on her head. Comparisons with author Salman Rushdie begin to form...except that Rushdie never claimed his works of fiction were fact.

A 2008 documentary, *Forbidden Lies,* charts the exposure of Khouri as a con artist and her book as a pack of lies. The very existence of Dalia is called into question and with it a pall of uncertainty covers the issue of 'honour killings', which is the book's central theme.

And this, of course, is the real tragedy behind one of the biggest literary hoaxes of the 21st century. Honour killings – where a woman is killed by members of the family to pro-tect familial honour – do occur in Jordan, albeit in ever-reducing numbers. Sensationalist accounts that capitalise on the practice, however, undermine the work of various interest groups who try to work quietly and discreetly to change attitudes without compromising the sense of national pride.

The documentary *Crimes of Honour* by Shelley Saywell, filmed in Jordan and the West Bank, gives more information on this sensitive subject.

The Concept of Honour

In Jordan, a woman's 'honour' is still valued in traditional society, and sex before marriage or adultery is often dealt with harshly by other members of the woman's family. In rare cases it can lead to fatalities with women in the family often complicit in the murder.

Jordan's legal code exempts a husband or close male relative for killing a wife caught in an act of adultery and offers leniency for murders committed in a 'fit of rage'. Most perpetrators are given short prison sentences, sending the message that the state in part condones these actions.

Internationally renowned journalist Rana Husseini is one among several high-profile Jordanians who are committed not just to bringing so-called 'honour killings' to the Jordanian public's attention but also to spreading intolerance towards the practice. Even King Abdullah has tried to impose tougher sanctions against honour killings, but little progress has thus far been made. Effecting radical change of deep-rooted cultural values is not something that can be accomplished overnight and only a change of attitude, rather than a change of law, is likely to be effective in driving the practice out.

On average (according to government statistics) 15 women are murdered each year for bringing shame on their families by having sex out of wedlock, refusing an arranged marriage, leaving their husbands or being the victim of rape or sexual assault.

Confronting Modernity

A New Role for Women

Traditional concepts of honour *(ird)* run deep but sit uneasily with the freedoms many affluent Jordanian women have come to expect, largely thanks to universal access to one of the region's best education systems. Women are entitled to vote (Jordanian women got the vote in 1967 but didn't have a chance to use it for the first time until 1989) and a minimum of six women MPs is guaranteed by royal decree.

PALESTINIAN REFUGEES

More than 2 million people in Jordan are registered Palestinian refugees with around one-half of Jordan's population estimated to be of Palestinian descent. The majority comprise Palestinians who fled, mostly from the West Bank, during the wars of 1948 and 1967, and from Kuwait after the Gulf War in 1990–91. Their numbers are likely to have increased by around 20,000 at the end of 2014 as a result of the ongoing civil war in Syria.

Many Palestinians have exercised the right to Jordanian citizenship and they now play an integral part in the political, cultural and economic life of Jordan. Others, however, continue to dream of a return to an independent Palestine. Some commentators suggest that this is partly why so many have resisted integration and continue to live in difficult conditions in refugee camps that dot the landscape.

Around 370,000 refugees (18% of the total refugee population in Jordan) are housed in 10 official camps administered by the UN Relief & Works Agency (UNRWA), which is responsible for health, education and relief programs. The largest camps are centred around the north of Jordan where the original tent shelters have long since been re-placed with more permanent structures and often resemble suburbs more than refugee camps. This is in contrast to the Za'atari camp on the Syrian border and Azraq camp to the east of Amman, set up to manage the crisis inflow of displaced refugees from Syria.

The following agencies give reliable statistics on all refugees in Jordan.

Department of Palestinian Affairs (☎06-5666172; www.unrwa.org)

Minorities at Risk (www.cidcm.umd.edu/mar)

UNHCR (The UN Refugee Agency; www.unhcr.org)

In 1991 only 14% of the labour force was made up of women; today, according to UN data, this figure has risen to around one quarter, mainly in health and education. Many women now work in male-dominated industries and businesses; fewer are in media or legal professions where less than 1% of judges are women.

Women in more traditional societies are also starting to gain some financial independence and a greater say in society. This is partially through the success of a number of Jordanian organisations that encourage small-scale craft production and local tourism projects.

Jordan has a regionally renowned education system; literacy levels are around 98% for Jordanian males and 94% for females. About 98% of children attend primary school, and school is compulsory for children from the ages of five to 14.

Urbanisation

There is an increasing polarisation in Jordanian society between town and country. In Amman, modern Western-leaning middle- and upper-class youths enjoy the fruits of a good education, shop in malls, drink lattes in mixed-sex Starbucks outlets and obsess over the latest fashions or dreams of democracy. In rural areas, meanwhile, unemployment is high and many struggle with making ends meet.

For this reason, economic migration is common in Jordan and many working-class families have at least one male who is temporarily working away from home, whether in Amman, the Gulf States or further abroad. The remittances sent home by these absent workers are increasingly important to family budgets, with each economically active person supporting, on average, four other people. The absence of a senior male role model, however, is changing the pattern of Jordanian family lives and tensions inevitably rise between the expectations of those who are nostalgic for the traditions of home and those of the families left behind who are forced to steer their own course into a rapidly modernising environment.

Islam

Islam is not the only religion in Jordan – around 6% of the population are Christian. This mixed inheritance, together with a long tradition of hosting visitors, has led Jordanians to be tolerant towards those of other beliefs and customs. Islam is, however, the predominant religion. For a visitor, understanding the country's Muslim roots will help make sense of certain customs and manners. In turn, it guides in appropriate conduct and minimises the chance of giving offence.

Faith & Society in Jordan

It's probably fair to say that there is not the same overt dedication to faith as one sees in neighbouring countries such as Saudi Arabia, nor the exuberant outpouring of Islamic culture seen in the mosques and fine arts of Syria. However, this doesn't mean that Islam is any less central to Jordanian life. Islam governs what people wear, how they plan their lives, how they settle their disputes and spend their money. It gives a purpose for being and gives shape to the future. In other words, faith and culture seamlessly combine in Jordan, giving people a shared ethic upon which society is founded.

People of the Book

Founded seven centuries after the birth of Christ, Islam shares a common heritage with the two other great monotheistic faiths, Judaism and Christianity. For Muslims, Islam is the apogee of the monotheistic faiths but they traditionally attribute a place of great respect to Christians and Jews, whom they consider *ahl al-kitab* (the People of the Book).

Founding of Islam

Born into a trading family in Mecca (in present-day Saudi Arabia) in AD 570, Mohammed began receiving revelations in AD 610, and after a time began imparting the content of Allah's message to the inhabitants of Mecca. Mohammed's call to submit to God's will was not universally well received, making more of an impact among the poor than among the wealthy families of Mecca, who feared his interference in the status quo.

The words *al-hamdu lillah* (thanks be to God) frequently lace sentences in which good things are related and the words *in sha' Allah* (God willing) mark all sentences that anticipate the future. These expressions are not just linguistic decoration, they demonstrate a deep connection between society and faith.

THE HOLY QURAN

Muslims believe that the Quran, the holy book of Islam, is the literal word of God, unlike the Bible or Torah, which they believe were inspired by God but were recorded subject to human interpretation. Communicated to the Prophet Mohammed directly in a series of revelations in the early 7th century, the Quran means 'recitation' and is not just the principal source of doctrine in Islam, but also a source of spiritual rapture in its own right. It is recited often with emotional elation, as a blessing to the reciter and the hearer. The use of the 'sacred' language of Arabic, with its unique rhythms, gives the recitation a sacramental quality that eludes translation, and many Muslims around the world still learn large portions of the Quran in its original form to feel closer to God's words.

Websites on Islam

Al-Bab (www.al-bab.com) Comprehensive site with links to information and discussion on Islam.

Islamicity (www.islamicity.com) Good reference for non-Muslims interested in Islam.

By AD 622 Mohammed was forced to flee with his followers to Medina, an oasis town to the north of Mecca, where he continued to preach. This migration (the Hejira) marks the beginning of the Islamic calendar: year 1 AH. By AD 630 his followers returned to take Mecca, winning over many of the local tribes who swore allegiance to the new faith.

After Mohammed's death in AD 632, Arab tribes conquered the Middle East, Egypt and North Africa, Spain and eventually southern France, taking Islam with them. The Arabic language and Islamic faith remained long after the military conquests faded into history, uniting large parts of Europe, Africa and Asia in a shared cultural and religious ideology.

Sunnis & Shiites

Islam split into different sects soon after its foundation. When the Prophet died in AD 632, he left no instructions as to who should be his successor, nor the manner in which the future Islamic leaders (known as caliphs) should be chosen.

In the ensuing power struggle, *shi'a* (partisans) supported the claim of Mohammed's cousin and son-in-law, while others supported the claim of the Umayyads. From that point the Muslim community split into two competing factions: the Shiites, who are loyal to the descendants of Mohammed, and the Sunnis, the orthodox bedrock of Islam.

Within Jordan most Muslims are Sunnis, belonging to the Hanafi school of thought. A minority of around 15,000 Druze in Northeast Jordan (including the town of Azraq) follow a form of Shiite Islam.

Mecca is Islam's holiest city. It's the home of the sacred Kaaba – a cube-shaped building allegedly built by Ibrahim (Abraham) and his son Ismail and housing a black stone of ancient spiritual focus. Muslims are enjoined to this day to face Mecca when praying. Medina is Islam's second-holiest city.

Teachings

Despite modern connotations with fundamentalism and the violent beginnings of the faith, Islam is an inherently peaceful creed. The word 'Islam' means 'submission' or 'self-surrender'. It also means 'peace'. Taken as a whole, Islam is the attainment of peace – with self, society and the environment – through conscious submission to the will of God. To submit to the will of God does not just entail paying lip service to God through ceremony, but through all daily thoughts and deeds.

The principal teaching of Islam is that there is only one true God, creator of the universe. Muslims believe that the God of Islam is the same God of Christians and Jews, but that he has no son and he needs no intermediary (such as priests). Muslims believe that the prophets – including Adam, Abraham and Jesus, and ending with Mohammed – were sent to reveal God's word but that none of them were divine.

HISTORICAL ORIGINS OF ISLAM

AD 570 Prophet Mohammed, founder of Islam, is born in Mecca.

610 Mohammed receives his first revelation considered by Muslims as God's word and captured in the Quran.

622 Mohammed and his followers flee Mecca for Medina, marking the birth of the first Islamic state.

632 Mohammed dies and the Muslim capital moves to Damascus.

656 Ali bin Abi Taleb becomes caliph; his followers are known as Shiites.

661 Ali is assassinated by troops loyal to Mohammed's distant relative, separating the Muslim community into two factions.

680 Ali's son is murdered at Karbala, widening the gap between the two factions, Shiites and Sunnis.

THE FIVE PILLARS OF ISLAM

A good Muslim is expected to carry out the following Five Pillars of Islam.

Haj The pinnacle of a devout Muslim's life is the pilgrimage to the holy sites in and around Mecca. Haj takes place in the last month of the Islamic calendar and Muslims from all over the world travel to Saudi Arabia for the pilgrimage and subsequent feast of Eid al-Adha. Returning pilgrims earn the right to be addressed as *haji*.

Salat This is the obligation of prayer, expressed five times a day when the muezzins call upon the faithful to pray before sunrise, noon, mid-afternoon, sunset and before midnight. Communal prayers are only obligatory on Friday, although the strong sense of community makes joining together in a masjid ('place of prostration', ie mosque) preferable at other times.

Shahada This is the profession of the faith and the basic tenet of Islam: 'There is no God but Allah and Mohammed is his prophet' (*La il-laha illa Allah Mohammed rasul Allah*). This is part of the call to prayer, and is uttered at other events such as births and deaths. People can often be heard muttering the first half of the sentence to themselves for moral support.

Sawm Ramadan, the ninth month of the Islamic calendar, commemorates the revelation of the Quran to Mohammed. As a renewal of faith, Muslims are required to abstain from sex and from letting anything (including cigarettes) pass their lips from dawn to dusk throughout the month.

Zakat Giving alms to the poor is an essential part of Islamic social teaching and, in some parts of the Muslim world, has been developed into various forms of tax as a way of redistributing funds to the needy. The moral obligation towards poorer neighbours continues to be emphasised at a personal and community level, and many Islamic groups run large charitable institutions, including Amman's Islamic Hospital.

Historically, this creed obviously had great appeal to the nomadic peoples of the land we now call Jordan as they were given access to a rich spiritual life without having to submit to incomprehensible rituals administered by hierarchical intermediaries. Believers needed only to observe the transportable Five Pillars of Islam in order to fulfil their religious duty. This is true to this day and is perhaps one of the reasons why Islam is one of the world's fastest-growing religions.

Islamic Customs

Muslims should pray five times a day and follow certain rituals, washing their hands, mouth, ears, arms, feet, head and neck in running water. If no mosque is nearby and there is no water available, scouring with sand suffices; where there is no sand, the motions of washing must still be enacted.

Muslims must face Mecca (all mosques are oriented so that the mihrab, or prayer niche, faces the correct way – south-southeast in Jordan) and follow a set pattern of gestures and genuflections. Muslims do not require a mosque to pray and you'll often see Jordanians praying by the side of the road or at the back of their shop; many keep a small prayer rug handy for such times.

In Jordan, which has a history of welcoming tourists to its world-class sites of largely pagan origin, people may be surprised if you take an interest in Islam but they will also be delighted. Any sympathetic discussion of faith is treated as an olive branch in a region where religion has all too often led to conflict – as the great Crusader castles at Karak and Shobak and the heavily militarised border with Israel illustrates.

Islam, Judaism and Christianity share many of the same prophets: Abraham (Ibrahim), Jesus (Isa), John the Baptist (Yahya), Job (Ayyub), Joshua (Yosha), Lot (Lut), Moses (Musa), and Noah (Nuh). Mohammed is not considered divine, but rather the last of these prophets.

Traditional Crafts

For the visitor who chooses the right outlets, there is a special pleasure in buying something handmade, practical and aesthetically pleasing from Jordan as the craftsperson very often earns money that directly benefits his or her community. Taking an interest in the crafts of Jordan, then, is not a remote aesthetic exercise. It represents sustainable tourism at its very best. Find out how to make your purchases count towards Jordan's regional cottage industries.

Made in Jordan

Traditional handicrafts in Jordan are not designed to be viewed in a museum, but to be bought and bartered over. Jordan's position at the crossroads of numerous caravan routes throughout the ages has made craft, the most practical and portable of all the arts, into a currency of practical benefit.

Walk the streets of Madaba, with bright coloured kilims flapping in the wind, hike to the soap-making villages of Ajloun or watch elderly Bedouin women threading beads at Petra, and the country's strong handicraft tradition is immediately apparent. The authorities have been quick to support this aspect of Jordan's heritage and now craft cooperatives are widespread, resulting in benefits for local communities and ensuring that Jordan's rich legacy of craft endures for future generations.

Weaving

Jordan has a long-established rug-making industry dating back to the country's pre-Islamic, Christian communities. *Mafrash* (rugs) are usually of the flat, woven kind, known as kilims, compared with carpets that have a pile. To this day, especially in Madaba and Mukawir, it's possible to watch kilims being made that are based on early Byzantine designs. Even if you hadn't intended to buy one of these woollen rugs, you'll find it impossible not to get carried away by the enthusiasm of the carpet vendors, who will good-naturedly unfurl all their rugs for you without much prospect of a sale.

Embroidery

Heather Colyer Ross looks into popular art forms in *The Art of Bedouin Jewellery*, a useful asset for those contemplating purchasing some pieces.

Embroidery is an important skill among Jordanian women and most learn the craft at a young age. Teenagers traditionally embroidered the clothes they would need as married women. Embroidery provides an occasion for women to socialise, often with a pot of tea spiced up with a pinch of local gossip. Palestinian embroidery is famed throughout the region and you'll see the characteristic red embroidery cross-stitch on traditional dresses, known as *roza*, in shops across Jordan. Purses featuring intricate flower designs in silk thread make portable mementos.

Mosaics

The craft of mosaic-making has a noble and distinguished lineage in Jordan. Mosaics are made from tiny squares of naturally coloured rock called tesserae. The first part of the process is preparing the stone, which is hewn in blocks from the rock face and then cut into thin cuboid rods. These are then snipped by pincers into the tesserae. The smallest tesserae make the most intricate designs but they are much harder to work with and the mosaics take longer to assemble. It's rather like the knots on a carpet – the more tesserae per centimetre, the finer and more valuable the mosaic. Many workshops in the Madaba area will ship items home.

Copperware

Some of the oldest copper mines in the world are traceable in Jordan (especially near Feinan, now in the Dana Biosphere Reserve). Copper is used in everyday utensils, as well as for heirlooms such as the family serving dish, copper tray or coffee pot. These pieces are mostly replicated for the tourist industry, but you can still find the genuine articles – with a bit of spit-and-polish they'll light up the corner of a room back home. Quality pieces can be found in the antique stores in Amman, many of which are attached to top-end hotels. You won't find an antique older than about 50 years (and it's illegal to export anything older than 100 years), but the items are likely to have been much loved by the families who once used them.

Jewellery

A bride traditionally receives a gift of jewellery on her wedding day as her dowry, and this remains her personal property. The most common designs are protective silver amulets, such as the 'hand of Fatima' (daughter-in-law of the Prophet Mohammed). These are used as protection from evil spirits known as *djinn* (from which we get the word 'genie'). Antique items such as silver headdresses decorated with Ottoman coins and ornately decorated Bedouin daggers (straight, rather than the famously curved Yemeni and Omani versions) are becoming harder to find. Many of the most beautiful antique pieces were crafted by Circassian, Armenian and Yemeni silversmiths in the early 20th century.

Fine examples of Bedouin jewellery, Jordanian crafts and traditional costumes are on display at the Folklore Museum and Museum of Popular Traditions at the Roman Theatre in Amman.

MAKING MOSAICS

Push the door open on a mosaic workshop and it's like entering the Hall of the Mountain King. Clouds of dust plume from the masonry saws and the workspace echoes with the screech of metal against rock and the persistent snapping of the workers' pincers as they cut stone rods into tiny, coloured squares. During our visit, all the workers engaged in this dedicated craft (from the stone-cutters to the assembly teams) were women. One of the ladies dusted her hands against her overcoat and, parking her mobile phone among the tweezers, the paste brush and the glue pot, gave us an ad hoc tour.

Artists, Mayzoon explained, sketch a design freehand or trace the image from books, in the same way as their ancient predecessors would have copied scenes from pattern books. Designs usually feature everyday life, with depictions of plants and animals (look for the chicken – almost every mosaic seems to feature one). Hunting and viniculture, personification of the seasons, and religious or mythological scenes are typical subjects. But it's the detail that captivates – the bell on a gazelle's neck, palm trees at an oasis, a wry human smile.

Once the design is in place, the tesserae are then painstakingly arranged – traditionally on a thick coating of wet lime and ash to form permanent flooring. Today they are more likely to be attached to wet plaster and affixed to wooden boards for use as table tops or wall decorations.

The tour concluded and Mayzoon returned to the assembly table. 'You took our photograph, no?' one of the ladies said. I was about to apologise when she added 'Please, take it again. This time with all of us!' A shaft of brilliant sunshine cut through the dusty air, lighting up the eight faces gathered in intense concentration around the half-built mosaic. The team worked rhythmically together, tapping and snapping, inching and coaxing the stones into a tree of life. With a little definition in malachite and sandstone, the women could have found their own immortalisation in stone.

GETTING A GOOD DEAL

Jordanians are committed shoppers and they make an art form out it, promenading the main street and popping into a shop to vex the owner without any intention of buying. Buying, meanwhile, is a whole separate entertainment, focused on the business of bartering.

Bartering implies that items do not have a value per se: their value is governed by what you are willing to pay balanced against the sum the vendor is happy to sell for. This subtle exchange, often viewed with suspicion by those from a fixed-price culture, is dependent on many factors, such as how many other sales the vendor has made that day, whether the buyer looks like a person who can afford an extra dinar or two, and even whether the vendor is in a good mood or not. Although bargaining when craft buying is essential, note that some cooperatives charge fixed prices.

As with all social interaction, there's an unwritten code of conduct that keeps negotiations sweet. Here are a few tips for making it an enjoyable experience.

➡ View bartering as your chance to decide what you are willing to pay for an item and then use your interpersonal skills to see if you can persuade the vendor to match it.

➡ Understand that haggling is a sociable activity, often conducted over piping-hot mint tea, so avoid causing offence by refusing hospitality too brusquely.

➡ Don't pay the first price quoted: this is often considered arrogant.

➡ Start below the price you wish to buy at so you have room to compromise – but don't quote too low or the vendor may be insulted.

➡ Never lose your temper: if negotiations aren't going to plan, simply smile and say goodbye – you'll be surprised how often the words *ma'a salaama* bring the price down.

➡ Resist comparing prices with other travellers; if they were happy with what they paid, they certainly won't be if you tell them you bought the same thing for less.

➡ Above all, remember that a 'good deal' in Jordan generally means a good deal more than just the exchange of money. It's a highlight of travelling in the country.

Added-Value Craft

Several NGOs, such as the Noor Al-Hussein Foundation and Jordan River Foundation, have spurred a revival of locally produced crafts as part of a national campaign to raise rural living standards, improve the status of rural women, provide income for marginalised families, nurture artists and protect the local environment. Nature shops figure prominently at the Wild Jordan Centre in Amman and RSCN visitor centres in Ajloun, Azraq, Mujib, Dana and Wadi Rum.

If you want to spend your money where it counts, then you may like to buy from the outlets of community-based income-generating programs.

Good Buys

Silver jewellery (Wadi Musa)

Handmade paper (Iraq al-Amir, Aqaba, Jerash)

Ceramics (Salt)

Painted ostrich eggs (Shaumari)

Weavings (Mukawir)

Traditional clothing (Madaba)

Dead Sea soap (nature reserve shops, Amman)

Beit al-Bawadi (p67) Quality ceramics made by local artisans working on site. Pieces cost around JD50 to JD80.

Jordan Handicraft Producers Association (34 Khirfan St, 1st Circle; ⊙8am-4pm Sat-Thu) Encompassing 500 members working from home or from small workshops, it showcases the output in a 120-year-old stone building in a suburb of Amman.

Jordan River Foundation (p66) Handloomed rugs from Bani Hamida and exquisite Palestinian-style embroidery. Also has high-quality cushions, camel bags, embroidery, baskets and Dead Sea products.

Madaba Tourism Development Association (www.visitmadaba.org) A voluntary community-based organisation, developing tourism products that use local skills and resources.

Made in Jordan (p187) Products include olive oil, soap, paper, ceramics, table runners, nature products from Wild Jordan in Amman, jewellery, embroidery, camel hair shawls, and bags, as well as Jordan River Foundation goods.

Noor Al-Hussein Foundation (☑5607460; www.nooralhusseinfoundation.org; Aqaba Fort) Maintains a showroom in Aqaba as well as links to now-independent projects selling NHF-labelled products in Iraq Al-Amir, Salt and Wadi Musa (Nabataean Women's Cooperative).

Souk Jara Street Market (Fawiz al-Malouf St, Jebel Amman; ◷10am-10pm Fri May-Aug) A village initiative within the city of Amman, the Jebel Amman Residents Association spearheaded the now-famous Souk Jara street market.

Wild Jordan Centre (p66) Sells products made in Jordan's nature reserves, including silver jewellery, organic herbs, jams, and candles. Decorated ostrich eggs are another speciality.

The cost of a kilim (anywhere between JD50 and JD500) depends on whether natural vegetable dyes are used, the length, thickness of thread, intricacy of pattern and age of the rug – the older the better.

Shopping for Crafts

If you are after goods of a high quality it pays to visit specialised craft centres as opposed to one-stop shopping in souvenir shops. Unfortunately, some shop owners have jumped on the cooperative bandwagon and claim to be part of charitable foundations when they are not. Check that a shop's sign exactly matches the outlet you are looking for!

Duty Free

Most upmarket shops offer tax rebates. If you spend over JD350, keep your receipts, fill out a tax rebate form and leave the country within 90 days, you can get the 16% tax refunded to your credit card at a booth at the airport, just before check-in.

Export Restrictions

Exporting anything more than 100 years old is illegal, so don't buy any craft or artefact (including 'ancient' coins or oil lamps) described as 'antique' – if only because it probably isn't. If you're unsure about an item's provenance, contact the Customs Office (p68) in Amman.

TRADITIONAL CRAFTS SHOPPING FOR CRAFTS

Flavours of Jordan

Eating in Jordan is primarily a social experience, whether conducted over a chat in Amman's cafes or sitting in cross-legged silence in a Bedouin tent. Anyone venturing beyond the bus-station kebab stands will quickly find that Jordanian food is not a tedious affair of felafel sandwiches but deliciously varied and culturally nuanced. Jordan is also beginning to be noted for its home-grown wines.

Food

The word 'mezze' is derived from the Arabic *t'mazza*, meaning 'to savour in little bites'. Meat mezze usually comprise mutton, goat, chicken or lamb, but never pork – which is *haram* (forbidden) for Muslims. However, Jordan's Christian community is free to buy it – if they can find it.

On the crossroads of Arab caravans, bringing spices from India and rice from Egypt, Jordan's hybrid cuisine has absorbed many traditions from its neighbours, particularly from Turkey and Lebanon. Jordan's home-grown fresh fruit and vegetables are a highlight. There are two distinct cuisines in Jordan, which for argument's sake we'll call Pan-Arab and Bedouin.

Pan-Arab

The day starts for most Jordanians with a breakfast of eggs and locally produced olives, cheese, sour cream and *foul madamas* (a fava-bean dish with olive oil) and, of course, bread. Arabic unleavened bread, *khobz*, is so ubiquitous at mealtimes it is sometimes called *a'aish* (life). A favourite breakfast staple is bread liberally sprinkled with *zaatar* (a thyme blend) or sesame-encrusted rings of bread, which often come with a boiled egg.

Lunch is usually the main meal of the day, which could explain the habit of nap-taking in the afternoons. Invariably, lunch involves rice or potatoes and includes some form of seasonal vegetable, prepared as a slow-cooking stew with a meat bone or chicken. In a restaurant, or for a special occasion, *maqlubbeh* may be on the menu: a pyramid of steaming rice garnished with cardamom and sultanas, and topped with slivers of onion, meat, cauliflower and fresh herbs such as thyme or parsley.

The evening meal is a ragged affair of competing interests – children snacking over schoolwork, mothers preparing dishes for surprise visitors and fathers sneaking out for a kebab with friends. At the weekend, Jordanians go out as a family. In cities that could mean a Thai curry, while in small towns it will be the chef's special. In an Arab-style restaurant, the evening is whiled away over mezze – a variety of exquisite little delicacies such as peppery rucola (rocket) leaves, aromatic chopped livers, spicy aubergine (eggplant) dips or a dish of freshly peeled almonds.

Bedouin

Bedouin food consists of whatever is available at a particular time. Camel's milk and goat's cheese are staple parts of the diet, as are dried dates and water. Water takes on a particularly precious quality when it is rationed, and the Bedouin are renowned for consuming very little, particularly during the day when only small sips are taken, mostly to rinse the mouth.

The Bedouin speciality *mensaf* – consisting of lamb, rice and pine nuts, combined with yoghurt and the liquid fat from the cooked meat –

was once reserved for special occasions. Now visitors can try such dishes in Wadi Rum and Wadi Musa. The dish is cooked in a *zerb* (oven), which consists of a hole in the sand and enough firewood to make glowing coals. The oven is sealed and the meat cooked for hours until succulent.

Seasonal Specialities

Spring Lamb cooked in a *zerb* (ground oven) will ruin your palate for mutton. Fresh, frothy camel's milk is abundant and giant watermelons ripen in fields alongside the Desert Highway.

Summer The fruit harvest brings pomegranates, pistachios, peaches and limes. During Ramadan, fast with the locals (dawn to dusk) and see how hunger enhances the flavours of traditional evening sweetmeats.

Autumn Pluck dangling figs or grapes from the vine and sample corn drizzled with newly pressed olive oil from local groves. In the Jordan Valley bananas and mangoes ripen in subtropical warmth.

Winter Copper-coloured persimmons ripen for Christmas – a good time to try Bethany's 'Baptism Fish'. It's not carnage on the roads – it's tomatoes. Crates of them fill the fields near Safi.

Quick Eats

Local 'fast food' is safe, tasty and available in every town, usually from stands. The most popular dishes are as follows.

Shwarma Lamb or chicken sliced with great flourish from a revolving spit, mixed with onions and tomato and packed into flat bread.

Felafel Deep-fried balls of chickpea paste with spices, served in a piece of rolled-up *khobz* (bread) with varying combinations of pickled vegetables, tomato, salad and yoghurt.

FLAVOURS OF JORDAN FOOD

Water is safe to drink in hotels and restaurants and is available in earthenware ewers along rural roads; bottled water minimises stomach upsets. Fresh pomegranate and rockmelon juices *(aseer)* are a highlight. Discreet imbibing of alcohol, such as wine and arak, is acceptable for non-Muslims.

EATING ETIQUETTE

Travel in Jordan for any length of time and inevitably you'll be invited home for a meal, especially if you are travelling alone, and most especially if you are a woman. Jordanians are very accommodating of other people's habits but you will impress your hosts if you manage a few of the following courtesies.

Eating in Someone's House

➡ Bring a small gift of baklava or, better still, a memento from home.

➡ It's polite to be seen to wash your hands before a meal.

➡ Use only the right hand for eating or accepting food. The left is reserved for ablutions.

➡ Don't put food back on a communal plate: discard in a napkin.

➡ Your host will often pass the tastiest morsels to you; it's polite to accept them.

➡ The best part – such as the meat – is usually saved until last, so don't take it until offered.

➡ If you're sitting on the ground, don't stretch your legs out until after the meal.

Eating in a Restaurant

➡ Picking your teeth after a meal is acceptable and toothpicks are often provided.

➡ It's traditional to lavish food upon a guest. If you're full, try one more mouthful!

➡ Leave a little food on your plate. Traditionally, a clean plate is thought to invite famine.

➡ It's polite to accept a cup of coffee after a meal and impolite to leave before it's served.

➡ Avoid eating and drinking in public during daylight hours in Ramadan. Many rural restaurants close at this time.

Farooj Chicken roasted on spits in large grills in front of the restaurant, served with bread, raw onion and pickles.

Shish tawooq Spicy minced chicken kebabs, grilled over charcoal.

Vegetarian Options

Jordan, like many countries in the region, has a strongly carnivorous bias in the national diet – at least in restaurants. At home, people enjoy their vegetables and dairy products and often consider meat as something to be enjoyed during special occasions.

Delicious vegetable and dairy dishes, especially mezze, can be found in many restaurants in Jordan, but the concept of 'vegetarian' is still an alien one. As such, there may well be meat stock within a soup or animal fats used to prepare pastries. The following 'vegidex' of restaurants is recommended for the variety of vegetarian options, but not for a non-meat pedigree.

Ajloun Ajloun Forest Reserve restaurant (p90)

Amman Wild Jordan Café (p61); Beit Sitti (p54); Hashem Restaurant (p60)

Aqaba Ali Baba Restaurant (p203); Formosa Restaurant (p203); Royal Yacht Club Restaurant (p204)

Azraq Azraq Lodge (p233)

Dana Biosphere Reserve Feynan Ecolodge (p152); Dana Guest House (p151); Rummana Campground (p151)

Jerash Lebanese House (p85)

Karak Kir Heres Restaurant (p145)

Madaba Abu Yousef (p131); Haret Jdoudna (p131)

Mt Nebo Asa Moses Restaurant (Siyagha Restaurant; p135)

Petra Basin Restaurant (p176)

Umm Qais Umm Qais Resthouse (p98)

Wadi Musa Petra Kitchen (p179)

Wadi Rum Bait Ali (p221); Rum Gate Restaurant (p222)

Desserts

Jordanians have an incorrigibly sweet tooth, and there are pastry shops in every town dedicated to the sublime cuisine of baklava. The giant circular trays of filo pastry, tickled with honey, syrup and/or rose water and cut into lozenges, are almost works of art.

The sweetest highlight of travel in Jordan is *kunafa,* a highly addictive dessert of shredded dough and cream cheese, smothered in syrup. Customers generally order desserts by weight: 250g is generally the smallest portion so have some friends (or a toothbrush) at the ready.

Drinks

Tea & Coffee

Tea and coffee are the major social lubricants in Jordan.

Tea *(shai)* is probably the more popular drink, taken without milk and in various degrees of sweetness: with sugar *(sukkar ziyada),* a little sugar *(sukkar qaleel)* or no sugar *(bidoon sukkar).* In most cafes you can ask for refreshing mint tea *(shai ma n'aana).* Za'atar (thyme) and *marrameeya* (sage) herbal teas are especially delicious in Dana.

Coffee *(qahwa)* is served strong, sweet and flavoured with cardamom, and usually contains thick sediment. You can specify a small espresso-sized cup *(finjan)* or large cup *(kassa kabira).* In traditional Bedouin areas coffee is served in small porcelain bowls and the host will always refill a guest's coffee cup. A good guest will accept a minimum of three cups; gently 'dancing' the cup from side to side indicates you've had enough.

During Ramadan Muslims fast during daylight hours. They savour a large pre-dawn breakfast called *suhur* and eagerly await *iftar* (breaking the fast) at dusk. Always something of a celebration, this dish-of-the-day is fun to share with hungry patrons at a busy restaurant.

Jordan is locally famous for its dairy products, especially salty white cheese. A popular soft white cheese is *kashkawan* (or *kishkeh*) while *haloumi* and Lebanese-style *shinklish* have a firmer texture.

COOK YOUR OWN AT PETRA KITCHEN

It was an inauspicious start one cold day in winter: the knives were large, the onions eye-smartingly malevolent and the aubergines too big for their own good. But just as I was thinking this wasn't the activity for me, I caught sight of fellow apprentices. With a smile of collusion across basins of parsley, we placed ourselves in the hands of Mr Tariq, professional Petra chef and our teacher for the evening. Within moments, he had us shaving garlic with prodigious speed and chopping industrial quantities of tomatoes without them collapsing into sauce.

Petra Kitchen (p179) in downtown Wadi Musa is a novel idea. Instead of going out for supper, you pay a little extra to cook your own mezze, soup and a main course. The local experts who teach you how to cook Jordanian food give you valuable tips throughout the evening. If you get hooked on the flavours you learn to create, the dishes on the menu card change each night so within a week you could be returning home with a whole cookbook.

The experience of cooking in the company of strangers makes you realise that cooking in Jordan, just like dining, isn't about the locally grown ingredients or the handed-down recipe: it's about being sociable. As Sharon Stark, my fellow apprentice from New Zealand, said: 'If we'd tasted that meal at a restaurant, without all the fun of creating it, the four of us meeting and talking to each other and our hosts, it would still have been delicious but not as nice as it tasted that night.'

If the concept appeals, you can also put your culinary skills to the test at Beit Sitti (p54) in Amman.

For men, Jordan's coffeehouses are great places to watch the world go by, write a letter, meet the locals and play a hand of cards, accompanied by the incessant clacking of domino and backgammon pieces and the gurgling of fruity nargileh (water pipes). Foreign women, with a bit of courage and modest attire, are usually tolerated. Traditional coffeehouses don't generally serve food.

Sahlab is a delicious traditional winter drink, served hot with milk, nuts and cinnamon. Look for it at hot-drink vendors, recognisable by their silver samovars.

Alcoholic Drinks

In a Muslim country where alcohol is considered haram for most of the population, it may come as some surprise that the country supports not only a small wine industry but also the region's only microbrewery. The latter was set up by a Christian Jordanian engineer who brought the concept of home-brewing from the USA. The resulting Carakele brand is a full-bodied beer much appreciated by aficionados.

Unlike the nascent brewing industry, viticulture has an ancient regional lineage. In contrast to neighbouring countries, however, Jordan's modern tradition of wine production was only revived a generation ago – almost single-handedly by Omar Zumot. A Christian from Amman who studied winemaking at a monastery in France, Zumot's organically produced St George wines give the lighter Mt Nebo wines a run for their money. If you're not convinced, it's easy to try both in top-end restaurants throughout Jordan.

In addition to beer and wine, arak (an aniseed-derived spirit) is drunk with enthusiasm by Christian Jordanians, in Amman and Madaba especially. Dilute with water to avoid the aftereffects!

Cookbooks

Jordanian Cooking Step by Step (Lina Baydoun and Nada Halawani)

The New Book of Middle Eastern Food (Claudia Roden; 2000)

The Natural Environment

With application, you can breakfast in the desert, lunch under a pine and dine on bananas from the subtropical Jordan Valley. Not many countries exhibit such diversity within such a compact area. For the naturalist, this makes Jordan a dream. Thankfully Jordanian authorities have been quick to recognise the country's wild appeal and have actively encouraged ecotourism. Whether you're a raptor enthusiast or a casual fan of flowers, there's sure to be something to please you in Jordan's modest acreage.

The Land

Jordan's endemic plant species are represented in the newly opened Royal Botanic Garden, a 30-minute drive north of Amman. Featuring Jordan's national flower, the black iris, the gardens are the vision of conservation-minded Princess Basma and an impressive addition to Jordan's eco-projects.

At 91,860 sq km, Jordan is slightly smaller than Portugal or the US state of Virginia. Distances are short – it's only 430km from Ramtha, on the Syrian border in the north, to Aqaba in the south. TE Lawrence was pleased that he could cover Azraq to Amman in a hard, three-day camel ride. Today you can travel by car from tip to toe in around six hours. If you want to see anything, though, there's a lot to be said for the camel.

Jordan can be divided into three major regions: the Jordan Valley, the East Bank Plateau and the desert.

Jordan Valley Ecosystem

Jordan edges the Great Rift Valley, stretching from East Africa's lakes to southern Syria. The rift was created as the Arabian plate pulled away from the African plate, a geological event that gave rise to the Red Sea. Jordan's Wadi Araba, the Dead Sea and the Jordan Valley lie on this fault line. Sit under the effervescent springs at Hammamat Ma'in and it's obvious that this process of tectonic separation isn't yet complete.

Trickling through the northern part of the valley is the lowest-lying river on earth, the River Jordan, fed from the Sea of Galilee (Lake Tiberias), the Yarmouk River and hillside streams. The permanent fresh water has given rise to a humid, subtropical valley, highly fertile and intensively farmed.

Walking under the valley's flame and tamarisk trees you may see sunbirds and kingfishers or an endangered otter heading for the reeds. What you won't see is the lion, bear, elephant, rhino and herds of wild ass that Palaeolithic remains prove were once resident here.

Not everything in the region has changed, however. The fish in Madaba's famous mosaic, twisting back from certain death at the mouth of the River Jordan, show that the Dead Sea was as insupportable of life in Byzantine times as it is today.

East Bank Plateau Ecosystem

High above the Jordan Valley – cut by a series of epic gorges carved out in slow motion by the wadis of Zarqa, Mujib and Hasa – is the hilly and temperate East Bank Plateau. It comprises the forested hills of northern Jordan (less than 1% of Jordan is wooded), rich in Aleppo pines, oak and red-barked strawberry trees and home to ill-tempered wild boar, pole-cats, stone martens and porcupines.

Wildflowers, including pink hollyhocks, poppies and yellow daisies, bloom in magnificent abundance in spring. This is the time to spot the black iris (which is actually a deep purple), the national flower of Jordan.

The East Bank Plateau contains the main centres of population (Amman, Irbid, Zarqa and Karak) and has been crossed by caravans for centuries. The plateau landscape of fig and olive groves, occasional vineyards and closely cropped pastureland reflects this human interaction. If you hike near Madaba in the summer you'll see Bedouin grazing their stock on the hillside; they descend to lower ground in winter to escape the bitter winds. Since the time of Moses, their husbandry has shaped the land, etching ancient paths around the closely cropped contours.

Pockets of pristine plateau wilderness remain towards the southern end of the plateau around Dana. This rocky wilderness of outstanding biodiversity is the habitat of elusive caracals (Persian lynx), felines with outrageous tufts of hair on the tips of their outsized ears. It is also home to ibex, endangered goats with enormous horns that cling to the craggy folds of limestone.

From a height of 600m to 900m above sea level, the plateau ends near the Red Sea port of Aqaba.

Jebel is the Arabic word for arid mountain. Jebel Umm Adaani (1832m), the highest peak in Jordan, lives up to that description. Wadi is the word for dry watercourse or flood channel. Wadi Mujib belies that description with its permanently flowing water.

THE NATURAL ENVIRONMENT THE LAND

JORDAN'S BIODIVERSITY

Birds Jordan's location on the edge of the Great Rift Valley makes it an important migration route for birds. More than half a million birds transit between Russia, Central Europe and Africa, breaking their journey in Jordan's dwindling oases and wetlands.

Animals A successful breeding program for the Nubian ibex by the Royal Society for the Conservation of Nature (RSCN) began in Wadi Mujib Nature Reserve in 1989. Some have been reintroduced into the wild and the herds are increasing. An attempt to release oryx bred at Shaumari Wildlife Reserve into Wadi Rum initially met with less success, with some wandering over the border to Saudi Arabia and others resistant to the sandy terrain.

Reptiles Jordan's brightly coloured reptiles are shy but considerably less elusive than the foxes and other fur and feather clad predators that feed on them. The bright turquoise Sinai agama and the changing coloration of the chameleon are two of many striking inhabitants of Jordan's jebel landscape. Around 35 snake species have been recorded in Jordan, some of which are venomous; they are seldom aggressive unless provoked.

Invertebrates In arid areas of Jordan, scorpions are common but shy nocturnal residents. It's worth knocking out boots in the morning to check for stowaways.

Fish The Gulf of Aqaba, part of the Red Sea, sustains 230 species of coral and 1000 types of fish.

Plants Jordan boasts more than 2500 species of wild plants, including 20 species of orchid. *Wildflowers of Jordan & Neighbouring Countries* by Dawud M H Al-Eisawi has useful photographs helpful in identification. A trip to the Royal Botanic Garden outside Amman (p86) is a good way to become familiar with native species.

Jordan's Nature Reserves

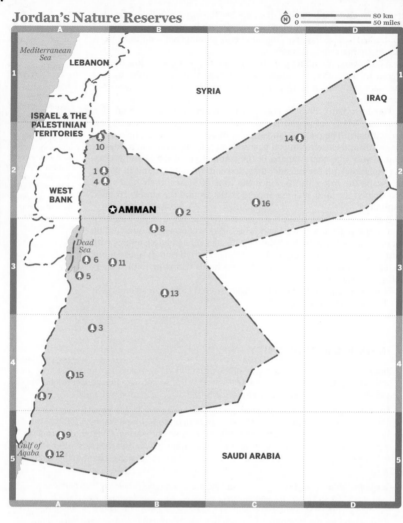

Jordan's Nature Reserves

Desert Ecosystem

On its eastern flank, the East Bank Plateau glides gradually into the desert. More than 90% of Jordan is desert, but it's home to only 5% of the population. The forbidding volcanic basalt rock of the northeast gives way to soft-whittled sandstone and granite in the south and the famous escarpments of Wadi Rum. In between, the stony wasteland known as the Badia slides into 1000km of nothingness, interrupted only by the occasional succulent, a wandering camel or camouflaged lizard.

When you travel along empty Route 10, it's impossible to imagine that anything could survive such desolation. But then, miraculously, you reach Azraq Wetland Reserve, a desert oasis attracting great numbers of migrating birds. Herons and egrets fish patiently among the croaking toads, and predators such as the desert fox, wolf and jackal lurk beyond the fringes of the oasis waiting for a careless desert hare to run out of luck.

Some desert species ran out of luck a long time ago, hunted to extinction before conservation became part of the modern sensibility. In Shaumari Wildlife Reserve (currently closed) there's a chance to see the animals that once roamed these plains before they are reintroduced to the wild.

The Dead Sea might be virtually barren, but the surrounding cliffs are not: small oases of date palm and hanging gardens of fern hide noisy Tristam's grackle (a native starling), and the sandstone bluffs shelter the elusive and endangered Nubian ibex.

Protected Areas

The true servants of the most gracious are those who tread gently on the earth.

Quran (sura 25, verse 63)

Established in 1966, the Royal Society for the Conservation of Nature (RSCN) is an unusual NGO in that it has a national mandate to run biodiversity projects on behalf of the nation. It is now Jordan's main environmental agency.

The RSCN has been successful in its founding remit: to help save animal and plant species from extinction and to reintroduce several locally extinct species, such as the Arabian oryx. Over the past two decades, however, the RSCN has developed a much wider focus, recognising that tourism has an important role to play. The result has been a modern and highly successful program of ecotourism projects, centred on RSCN reserves.

The RSCN conducts public awareness programs among Jordanians, especially children; sponsors environmental clubs; trains guides; combats poaching and hunting; and lobbies against mining, helping the uphill struggle to preserve the country's natural treasures for future generations.

Jordan's Nature Reserves

The **RSCN** (www.rscn.org.jo) maintains nine reserves (not the Wadi Rum protected area) and is hopeful of establishing others in locations of natural interest (for example at Burqu and Jebel Masuda). These reserves should not be confused with Jordan's 'national parks', which are unstructured, recreational areas, such as Zay National Park, near Salt.

Ajloun Forest Reserve (p88; 13 sq km, established 1988) This pretty reserve has easy trails, pistachio and oak forest, spring flowers and cottage industries.

Azraq Wetland Reserve (p236; 12 sq km, 1977) In spring and autumn, hundreds of migratory birds can be seen from a bird hide and boardwalk through this damaged and shrunken marshland.

Dana Biosphere Reserve (p147; 320 sq km, 1989) A spectacular wilderness area with various trails, Dana encompasses rugged mountains and desert with 600 species of plants, 200 species of bird and over 40 species of mammal.

THE NATURAL ENVIRONMENT THE LAND

Nature Guides

Field Guide to Jordan (Jarir Maani; 2008)

The Birds of the Hashemite Kingdom of Jordan (Ian J Andrews; 1995)

Dibeen Forest Reserve (p86; 8 sq km, 2005) One of the last Aleppo pine forests left in Jordan, Dibeen protects endangered species such as the Persian squirrel.

Fifa Reserve (27 sq km, 2011) Rare subtropical vegetation, home to migratory water birds.

Mujib Biosphere Reserve (p117; 212 sq km, 1988) Used for the captive breeding of Nubian ibexes, Mujib has an impressive ecotourism program, with canyon walks and waterfall rappelling.

Qatar Nature Reserve An arid terrain on the edge of the Wadi Araba escarpment.

Shaumari Wildlife Reserve (p236; 22 sq km, 1975) This small reserve was established to reintroduce the locally extinct Arabian oryx, ostrich, gazelle and onager.

Wadi Rum Protected Area (p194; 540 sq km, 1998) This beautiful desert – a Unesco site since 2011 and controlled by the Aqaba government – is the Bedouin heartland, offering camping, camel treks and 4WD excursions.

Yarmouk Nature Reserve (30 sq km, 2011) Undeveloped home to water birds, endangered gazelles and otters.

Green Jordan & Ecotourism

Despite 'green' being something of a nascent concept in the Middle East, Jordan has shown both ingenuity and commitment for more than a decade in embracing an environmentally-friendly approach. This approach extends both to an assortment of environmental challenges and to tourism, which is perhaps the biggest challenge of all. Find out how you can minimise the impact of your visit in a country that at times is too popular for its own good.

Environmental Issues

Water

Swim across one of the infinity pools in Aqaba surrounded by lush gardens and you may not realise that Jordan has a chronic shortage of water. The facts are alarming. Relying mainly on rainwater and subterranean aquifers that are already in many cases overexploited, Jordan has sunk to the fourth-most water-impoverished country in the world. With 90% of Jordan's rivers already being diverted, a population increasing by almost 3.5% annually and persistent droughts, this situation is likely to worsen rather than improve. Currently, about 60% more water is used than replenished from natural sources and, by some estimates, the country is due to run out of water within 20 years.

Jordan is not alone in this problem. Water is a hot political issue across the region, contributing to several skirmishes over the years and continuing to spike relations between Jordan and its neighbours. After the 1994 peace treaty, Israel and the Palestinian Territories permitted Jordan to extract 50 million cu metres per year from the Sea of Galilee, but disputes rumble on over whether Jordan is getting its fair share.

> Jordan has just 140 cu metres of renewable water per capita per year, compared to the UK's 1500, Israel's 340 and the Palestine Territories' 70. Jordan's figure is expected to fall to 90 cu metres by 2025. Anything under 500 cu metres is considered to be a scarcity of water.

Hunting

Visit a nature reserve in Jordan and you'll see lots of information about elusive animals that reside there, but the fact remains that a staggering 20 species of mammal have become extinct in Jordan in the past 100 years. Some were hunted and poached (especially after WWII, when weapons flooded the region), spelling the end for Jordan's lion, cheetah, bear, gazelle and wild ass. The last leopard was killed near Dana in 1986, although there have been unsubstantiated sightings since.

The continuing threats to bird and animal species (24 out of Jordan's remaining 77 species of mammals are globally threatened) include poor land management, such as deforestation; the pumping of water from vital areas such as the Jordan River, Dead Sea and the Azraq Wetlands; urban sprawl; unremitting use of pesticides, especially near water sources in the Jordan Valley; and air and water pollution.

> **Green Info on Jordan**
>
> ....
>
> *Friends of the Earth Middle East (www.foeme.org)*
>
> ....
>
> *Ministry of Environment (www.kinghussein.gov.jo/geo_env.html)*

Overgrazing & Desertification

Survey Moses' promised land from Mt Nebo and you'll find little left of promise in the semi-arid landscape – that's if you can see it through the haze of dust kicked up by livestock. This once fertile land has been devastated by centuries of overgrazing and this, together with erosion and drought, has led to widespread desertification (the seemingly unstoppable spread of the desert to previously fertile, inhabited and environmentally sensitive areas). According to the Royal Society for the Conservation of Nature (RSCN), millions of hectares of fertile land have become infertile and uninhabitable. This means there are now fewer pastures for livestock and crops, and reduced land for native animals and plants. Jordan is home to about three million sheep and goats, but there is no longer enough pasture to feed them, resulting in their encroachment on nature reserves and urban fringes.

Since the 1960s Israel and the Palestinian Territories has drawn one-third of its water from the Jordan River; reduced to a trickle, the river comprises raw sewage and effluent from fish farms.

Overcoming the Challenges

Recognising the threat environmental problems posed to the country, the Jordanian Parliament passed the Protection of the Environment Law in 1995. This included measures banning hunting and restricting grazing.

Environmental strategies have focused on addressing the water issue. Jordan's farmers (comprising around 5% of the population) use 75% of the water (quite often inefficiently), so modernising farming practices and plugging leaks in city pipelines is a priority. More radical approaches include the extraction of non-renewable fossil water from aquifers near Wadi Rum and controversial plans, finalised in 2013, to construct a series of desalination plants, hydroelectric power stations and canals linking the Red Sea with the Dead Sea, thereby raising the level of the Dead Sea and creating a fresh water supply. If the looming water crisis is not resolved swiftly, many commentators predict that 'water wars' will replace oil crises as the major source of conflict in the near future.

Ecotourism

Effects of Tourism

Tourism has caused a rapid increase in pollution from cars and industries, and has exacerbated the demand for precious water. In addition, vandalism and unwitting damage to sites such as Jerash and Petra, the effects of flash photography on fragile rock art, and rubbish left at hot springs have made some people wonder whether tourism is worth the trouble.

In 2013 King Abdullah II inaugurated a new pipeline to extract 120 million cu metres of water annually from the 30,000-year-old aquifer in Diseh near Wadi Rum. The near-billion-dollar project took four years to complete, and involved drilling 64 wells and building a 325km pipeline from Diseh to Amman.

But it is not all doom and gloom. In a region only recently concerned with conservation, it's refreshing to discover that Jordan is ahead of the game. The authorities are keen to promote sustainable tourism while maintaining the country's cultural heritage. This is illustrated through the preservation of Islamic values, promotion for arts and craft initiatives, and support for traditional lifestyles (as with the employment of Bedouin drivers in Wadi Rum).

The RSCN has been at the forefront of attempts to promote a more sustainable form of tourism through its various ecotourism projects. Such projects provide a major means of funding environmental programs.

It's not easy balancing the need for increased tourism against the environmental cost of more visitors. For example, tourism revenue at Wadi Rum is needed for the upkeep of the protected area, but it's hard to minimise the impact of more feet and wheels upon a fragile desert ecosystem. A balance can be achieved, however, with the cooperation of visitors.

TEN TOP ECO-EXPERIENCES

➡ Hike to see soapmakers at work in Ajloun Forest Reserve (p88)

➡ Savour a wild-berry smoothie in Amman's Wild Jordan Centre (p306)

➡ Learn about Azraq's Chechens over a home-cooked feast at Azraq Lodge (p233)

➡ Buy a hand-loomed rug from the Bani Hamida Centre (p138)

➡ Wake up to birdsong at beautiful Rummana campground (p151)

➡ Enjoy a vegetarian supper in candlelit Feynan Ecolodge (p152)

➡ Give your sunglasses an embroidered treat from the craft shop at Dana Biosphere Reserve (p147)

➡ Splash through the permanent pools of Mujib Biosphere Reserve (p117)

➡ Take a camel trip in the company of a Bedouin guide in Wadi Rum (p222)

➡ Stay overnight with the Bedouin at the Ammarin Camp (p191) near Wadi Rum

Impact Neutral Checklist

If you'd like to know how to minimise the negative impact of your visit, then think about using the following checklist to inform the choices you make on the road.

Save water Every drop helps given Jordan's chronic water shortage.

Use local guides and services This is an opportunity to learn about a unique way of life and help preserve local traditions.

Buy wisely Profits are returned to local communities from specialist craft centres.

Dress and behave respectfully The liberalisation of customs and manners is seen by many Jordanians as a bad habit caught from the West and an erosion of their cultural and Islamic heritage.

Pay your dues Entrance fees are the lifeline that helps to maintain Jordan's reserves.

Spend money... This will help make your visit count more positively than surviving on muesli you brought from home.

...but don't give it away Tips should only be given for services rendered (such as buying a souvenir from kids at Petra) to discourage the counter-productive activity of begging.

Leave as found For as long as outsiders have been searching for, and stumbling over, the ancient monuments of Jordan, they have also been chipping bits off, hauling items home or leaving their contributions engraved on the stones. Please don't be one of their number.

Bag it and bin it This is the one time when you shouldn't follow local example; be a trendsetter instead and take your litter home.

Follow the rules As tempting as it may be to reach out for a starfish in the Red Sea, light a fire at an *ad hoc* campground, take a photo without someone's permission or skinny dip in a waterhole, these are acts that erode the natural and cultural heritage of the country.

Jordan's nature reserves represent about 1% of Jordan's total land area – a small percentage compared with land allocated in Saudi Arabia (9%) and the USA (11%). When measured as a ratio of habitable land versus size of population, however, the figure is considerably more generous.

Making Your Stay Count

There are lots of ways in which you can turn your visit from a potential burden into a blessing. By supporting responsible enterprises, you will be contributing positively to local communities. Also don't forget that you can add value to your purchases by shopping at community-friendly outlets.

RSCN: A BYWORD FOR SUSTAINABLE TOURISM

Teamwork is a good way of describing the RSCN policy of environmental management. The RSCN directly employs 330 Jordanian people and has given employment opportunities to 16,000 Jordanians over the years. Its role includes getting corporate business involved to back eco-ventures (such as the chic Wild Jordan Café within the RSCN headquarters building in Amman). Crucially, it also involves local communities, such as those of Ajloun or Dana, through income-generating projects that complement rather than threaten traditional lifestyles.

Thanks to the combined interests of all these 'stakeholders', the RSCN's work is high-profile in Jordan, with Jordanian nationals comprising a significant proportion of the annual 60,000 visitors to the country's nature reserves.

With great accommodation serving wonderful food in beautiful places; walking, hiking and scrambling trails to suit all legs; and a series of shops that make you wish you'd packed a bigger suitcase, the RSCN's flagship reserves are a highlight of a 'sustainable visit' to Jordan.

A successful breeding program of the Nubian ibex by the RSCN began in the Mujib Biosphere Reserve in 1989. Some have now been reintroduced into the wild and the herds are increasing well. The killifish, unique to the Azraq Wetlands, has recently been saved from extinction, and numbers are increasing.

Things to Do

Abraham Path Initiative (www.abrahampath.org) Weaves a path from Ajloun to Pella in Jordan and connects to the bigger route through Israel and the Palestinian Territories. An excellent website aids planning and shows how to make the most of the journey by connecting with the local communities who stand to benefit from the passing trade of hikers.

Jordan Living History Association (JLHA; www.jerashchariots.com) Promotes accurate historical re-enactments at Jerash (where the JLHA supports 65 people, including army veterans) and other parts of the country.

Neighbours Paths (www.foeme.org) Community-based tours along the Jordan River, focusing on cross-border issues such as water and peace-building.

Zikra Initiative (www.zikrainitiative.org) Connects 'urbanites' (Jordanian and international city dwellers) to 'ruralists' – a modest participation fee helps fund microloans for village 'entrepreneurs'.

Places to Stay

RSCN (www.rscn.org.jo) Provides excellent ethical and sustainable accommodation within Jordan's reserves – reservations are necessary and can be made online.

Bedouin Cooperative Campgrounds Camps such as the Ammarin Bedouin (p191) near Little Petra with an on-site museum showcasing the local tribe, and other camps at Wadi Rum and Diseh, help preserve the Bedouin way of life.

Finding Fair Services

Jordan Inbound Tour Operators Association (www.jitoa.org) A voluntary umbrella organisation is a good place to research 'green' tour operators.

Survival Guide

Safe Travel

JORDAN SINCE THE ARAB SPRING

Jordan is very safe to visit and, despite local dissatisfaction with issues such as Iraqi immigration, the Syrian refugee crisis, unemployment and high inflation, you are unlikely to feel any hint of the turmoil of neighbouring countries.

The democratic uprising during the Arab Spring of 2011 was only fleetingly experienced in Jordan. King Abdullah II is a respected leader and has wide public support for his efforts in introducing democratic reforms and curbing public corruption.

TERRORISM

Jordan is in a tough neighbourhood, and has had to deal with civil wars across the border in Syria and Iraq, as well as the aftermath of the Egyptian revolution and the ongoing Palestinian situation. For all this, the country is reassuringly calm and stable. That said, there are occasional demonstrations in support of the Palestinians in Karak, Tafila and Ma'an, and in the university areas of Irbid, Mu'tah and northern Amman, and disturbances in the Zaatari camp for Syrian refugees.

The last major terrorist attack in Jordan was the 2005 suicide bombing of three hotels in Amman, which killed 60 people and injured 115, carried out by Iraqi Al-Qaeda affiliates. A similar plot was foiled in 2012. Jordan strengthened its anti-terrorism laws in 2014 to clamp down on potential trouble from Syrian jihadists, and maintains close links to US and British security forces.

COMMITMENT TO SAFETY

Over the past decade, the Jordanian government has invested significantly in tourism. Now, with so much at stake in terms of revenue, there is a collective desire among Jordanians to maintain Jordan's reputation as a safe destination. Some of the measures taken by the government for this purpose include the following:

➡ A high security presence in many tourist hotels throughout Jordan.

➡ Metal detectors at hotels and some public buildings.

➡ Tourist police are present at all major sites.

➡ Checkpoints monitor all border zones.

KEEPING SAFE & AVOIDING TROUBLE

Some Dos

➡ Be vigilant in the cities, keeping clear of large public gatherings.

➡ Cooperate politely with security checks in hotel foyers and at road checkpoints.

➡ Keep abreast of the news in English-language newspapers published in Amman.

➡ Check the latest travel warnings online through your country's state department or ministry.

➡ Consult your embassy or consulate in Jordan for specific concerns.

➡ Register with your embassy or consulate on arrival if there has been recent public order issues.

➡ Trust the police, military and security services. They are overwhelmingly friendly, honest and hospitable, like their compatriots.

Some Don'ts

➡ Don't be paranoid – the chances of running into trouble are rare.

➡ Don't get involved if you witness political protests or civil unrest.

➡ Don't strike up conversations of a stridently political nature with casual acquaintances.

Government Travel Advice

Many government websites offer travel advisories and info on current hot spots.

Australian Department of Foreign Affairs & Trade (☑1300 555 135; www.smart-traveller.gov.au)

British Foreign & Commonwealth Office (☎0845-850-2829; www.fco.gov.uk)

Canadian Department of Foreign Affairs & International Trade (☎800-267 6788; www.dfait-maeci.gc.ca)

US State Department (☎888-407 4747; http://travel.state.gov)

OTHER DANGERS

Minefields

Jordan is a signatory to the Ottawa International Mine Ban Treaty, and in 2012 became the first Arab country to declare itself free of landmines. Sections of the Jordan–Syria border previously contained large minefields. These have now been cleared, although there are unsubstantiated reports that more mines have been laid on the Syrian side recently due to that country's civil war.

Theft & Crime

Jordan has low levels of crime. Leaving your bag under the watchful eye of a member of staff at a bus station or hotel is generally safe so avoid jumping to conclusions if something goes missing – locals have a lot to lose in a country where stealing from guests is particularly frowned upon.

Punishments are harsh and, in a country where unemployment is high, there is a serious chance of losing a job without much hope of recovering a livelihood in future. Inevitably, however, there are one or two scams to look out for.

Common Scams

Taken for a Ride The taxi fare quoted on the meter is in fils, not in dinars, and visitors often misunderstand this when paying. Perhaps understandably, it is rare for a taxi driver to point out this mistake.

Crafty Business Shop owners often claim something is locally crafted as part of a profit-share scheme, when in fact it is imported from abroad.

Money for Old Rope So-called antiques are often merely last year's stock that's gathered an authentic-looking layer of dust. Similarly, 'ancient' oil lamps and coins are seldom what they seem.

Simple Safety Precautions

➤ Agree on a fare before you get in the taxi (or make sure the driver is using the meter).

➤ Do some research about genuine fair-trade establishments if you want purchases to have added value.

➤ Pay the sum for an item based on how much you like it and want it, not on how much you think it is worth.

➤ Carry wallets or purses in a front pocket and avoid carrying too much cash. Keep small change (for taxis and the like) separate to avoid getting your main stash out in public.

➤ Keep a copy of your passport buried in your luggage, and a digital photo in an email account or on an online server.

➤ Be careful late at night outside nightclubs in Amman: pickpockets and muggers are attracted by the patronage of intoxicated and comparatively wealthy foreigners.

TAKE TIME TO TALK

Taxi driver wouldn't use the meter? Paid more than a friend for the same item? These may sound like routine scams but there's invariably a legitimate reason. Jordanians take pride in their moral compass and tourists on the whole are treated with respect and fairness. Here are some different perspectives given by service providers that may cast so-called scams in a different light.

Taxi fares? The fare is set by the government and hasn't been adjusted for inflation; taxi drivers usually agree on fair fares with locals but it's harder to negotiate with tourists who don't speak Arabic.

Room rates? Small hotels have to respond to fluctuations in tourist numbers or they go bust. For some this means offering unrealistic rates in low season; for others, it means raising prices to cover investments made in anticipation of a good season.

Minibus overcharging? Foreigners don't like waiting until the bus is full – drivers are happy to leave early but it means making up the cost of a full load. As for luggage, that often takes up the place of a passenger.

Double standards? When you're haggling, an item costs whatever a vendor is happy to sell for, balanced against whatever a buyer is happy to pay for during that one transaction. Comparison with other travellers' experiences can be a pointless exercise.

Women Travellers

ADOPTING THE RIGHT MINDSET

Plenty of women each year have travelled through Jordan alone (this author included) and have enjoyed the experience thoroughly. That said, there are bound to be times when you will have male company in Jordan that you would rather do without. This may involve nothing more than irritating banter, proposals of marriage and declarations of love. On rarer occasions it will involve leering and minor physical contact – a grope in a bus for example. Where possible, it's best to ignore such behaviour or pass it off as part of the experience, or a few sad individuals will spoil your whole trip. Needless to say, many women, such as the celebrated author Marguerite van Gledermalsen, have enjoyed male encounters enough to stay a lifetime.

ATTITUDE TOWARDS WOMEN

Being highly gregarious as a nation, Jordanians will be surprised that you want to travel alone. Men, who have little or no contact with women, let alone sex, before marriage, may misinterpret this as an invitation to provide company. Stereotypes of foreign women based on Western films and TV convince some that all foreign women are promiscuous and will jump into bed at the drop of a hat.

AVOIDING TROUBLE

Dressing Appropriately

Nothing gives more offence in Jordan – a country with largely conservative and Islamic sensibilities – than bearing too much flesh. To minimise harassment and to be respectful of local customs, it's imperative to dress appropriately, especially in small towns and rural areas.

In the trendy districts of Amman such as Abdoun and Shmeisani, in large hotels and resorts, or even in the middle of Petra (where tour group parties generally wear whatever they feel like) you can comfortably dress as you would at home. Outside those areas, aim for knee-length dresses or loose trousers, and cover your shoulders and upper arms.

On public beaches at the Dead Sea and in Aqaba, wear a swimsuit (and preferably a T-shirt and shorts) when swimming and save the bikinis for top-end resorts and dive centres. Never go topless – especially in the wadis where skinny dipping in freshwater pools is not as unseen as you might imagine.

Some foreign women go to the extent of covering their head, but this is inappropriate for non-Muslims in Jordan and can be misconstrued – particularly by the women of Jordan's Christian communities who do not wear headscarves.

Advice from Fellow Women Travellers

Some Dos...

➡ Sit next to a woman if possible on public transport.

➡ Be cautious when venturing alone to remote parts of Petra, Jerash and Wadi Rum.

➡ Check for peepholes in rooms and bathrooms (particularly cigarette holes in curtains).

➡ Place a chair against your locked hotel room door in case of 'accidental' intrusions.

➡ Pay for a better hotel, generally associated with less hassle.

➡ Be suspicious of lovelorn guides, especially the handsome ones!

WHAT DOES A GIRL HAVE TO DO TO GET A BEER AROUND HERE?

Author's Diary Entries of 1995, near Jerash

Thankfully times have changed since my first trip to Jordan, and solo women no longer present such an unusual spectacle. Or is it that I've grown older and no-one's interested anymore? Either way, girls are warned: eating on your own may bring more (or less) to your table than you expect. On the upside, travelling solo may well lead to delicious home-cooked meals by locals taking pity on you.

20 April 1995 Despite the neatly laid tables there were no guests to warrant the preparation of food – except me. I braved a seat and sat shivering over the tablecloth in the corner. Eventually a waiter greeted me and brought coffee. Shocked when I drank all the hot milk, he didn't return and there was a limit to the length of time I could sit staring at the fairy lights intermittently beaming over the concrete grotto. Another waiter came: 'Like to buy Roman coin,' he said (I was thinking rather more of a kebab – with chips). 'What about guide for tomorrow?' And finally, grabbing his crotch with gusto, 'Need a man?' I said, 'No thank you, but I wouldn't mind a beer'. That was the last I saw of him – or of anybody else for that matter.

21 April 1995 Went down to breakfast with renewed hope of food and was glad to find it arrived without further negotiation. I could have done without the services of the hotel manager who felt it necessary to put most of the breakfast things on the table in such a way that he had to brush my left breast to rearrange them. After the third 'accident', I gave him the evil eye and he went out grumbling. Gobbled a few olives, tried mixing the strawberry jam with the soured goats' milk and popped a butter pat in whole thinking it was the local cheese. Another meal to remember in Jordan!

➡ Prepare a cover story – Jordanians will be mystified you have no family or friends to travel with.

➡ Chat to men in the company of women – not all men are one-track minded.

➡ Wear a wedding ring – this will add to your respectability in Arab eyes. A photo of husband and kids will clinch it.

➡ Bring tampons and contraceptives – they're hard to find and embarrassing to purchase outside Amman.

Some Don'ts...

➡ Don't go to a local bar unaccompanied.

➡ Don't make eye contact with strangers – dark glasses can help.

➡ Don't sit in the front seat of a chartered private or service taxi.

➡ Don't go outside with wet hair – this apparently implies you've had sex recently!

Public Spaces

It's not easy finding where to eat and drink, or even just sit, in public without becoming the centre of attention. Here are some guidelines.

Coffeehouses & Local Bars Often seen as a male domain; in some places the stares will evict you even if the landlord won't.

Midrange Bars & Cafes Almost always welcoming of women in Amman and Aqaba; less 'comprehending' (of your solo status) in smaller towns.

Public Beaches Magnet for unwanted attention; best to stick to resorts.

Restaurants Most have a 'family section' where women can eat alone and in peace.

Toilets Usually only one in small restaurants and bars; avoid where possible!

Tourist Sites Counter-intuitively, the best places to be 'alone' as a woman.

Persistent Harassment

Some behaviour may warrant a public scene: bystanders will quickly support you if someone has overstepped the mark. Say out loud *imshi* (clear off): this should deter most unwanted advances. Be firm but stay calm. Swearing or losing your temper will lose you public sympathy.

EMERGENCIES

Assault and rape are rare in Jordan, but if you do suffer a serious problem, follow this advice:

➡ Go to a police station or tourist-police booth; the latter can be found at most tourist sites.

➡ Be clear about the facts: the tourist police in Jordan take reports seriously.

➡ Call the nationwide **emergency number** (☏911); this central point has English-speaking staff.

Directory A–Z

Accommodation

Jordan has accommodation to suit most budgets, although away from the main tourist centres there's limited choice. Jordan is so compact, however, that most attractions can easily be visited in day trips from the main towns.

Prices are highest during the two peak seasons, which are from September to October and from March to mid-May. Holiday weekends are also peak times in Aqaba and at the Dead Sea resorts.

High inflation and rises in taxes continue to contribute to escalating prices. Although accurate at the time of writing, expect significant increases in the cost of accommodation.

Camping

For many people, spending a night under the stars – or at least under canvas – is a highlight of a trip to Jordan. One popular option is to sleep in a traditional 'house of hair' at a Bedouin camp in Wadi Rum. Facilities in these goat-wool tents are basic but it's a great experience.

Camping with your own tent is permitted in a few places in southern Jordan, especially in the desert surrounding Wadi Rum. Camping 'off piste' in the north is more problematic, not least because you'll have competition for the best spots from the Bedouin and it's surprisingly hard to find a secluded place to pitch a tent.

Bringing a tent to save money on accommodation isn't cost effective as camping is rarely possible without your own transport. Besides, cheap rooms are plentiful in areas close to the major sites of interest.

STAYING IN JORDAN'S NATURE RESERVES

A variety of accommodation, from camping and cabins to luxury rooms in ecofriendly lodges, is offered within several of Jordan's nature reserves. To see what is on offer in each reserve and to make an online booking, visit the website of the **Royal Society for the Conservation of Nature** (RSCN; www.rscn. org.jo). In some areas, such as the beautiful Dana Biosphere Reserve (open March to November), advance booking is required.

Camping in these reserves is not a cheap option. It is intended for those who are happy to pay extra to wake up in the wild and who want to contribute to the sustainable tourism ethic of the RSCN. Bookings can also be made through the **Wild Jordan Centre** (Map p46; ☑4616523; www.rscn.org. jo; Othman Bin Affan St, downtown) in Amman.

Hotels

From family-run guesthouses to opulent pleasure palaces on the Dead Sea, Jordan offers some interesting hotel accommodation. Reservations are recommended during peak seasons, especially at the Dead Sea Resorts, in Jerash, and for midrange and top-end hotels in Aqaba and Wadi Musa.

Breakfast varies from a humble round of bread with a triangle of processed cheese in budget hotels to a delicious assortment of locally made yoghurt, hummus, *fuul* (fava bean paste) and olives in midrange hotels. The buffet-style breakfasts at top-end hotels can fill up a hungry hiker for a week.

Hotels indicated as offering 'air-con' have both cool-

BOOK YOUR STAY ONLINE

For more accommodation reviews by Lonely Planet authors, check out http://lonelyplanet.com/hotels/. You'll find independent reviews, as well as recommendations on the best places to stay. Best of all, you can book online.

ing and heating appliances available in at least some of their rooms.

BUDGET

Budget rooms are available in most towns and vary from stark and basic to simple and homey. Most are spotlessly clean.

Private rooms in less-frequented towns start from JD15/20 for singles/doubles, with less stark rooms with a private bathroom costing around JD25/35. Prices are negotiable, especially during quieter seasons. A few places in downtown Amman have dorm rooms, but these are otherwise not common; most budget places have 'triples' (rooms with three beds), which you can ask to share with other travellers, cutting the cost of accommodation considerably. In summer you can even sleep on the roof in some places for about JD5 per person. There are no youth hostels in Jordan.

Some things to consider: many budget places are located above shops and cafes that can be noisy at night; avoid windowless rooms that are stifling hot in summer; winter in Jordan is bitterly cold so ensure the heater is working before checking in.

Payment usually needs to be made in cash in Jordanian dinars.

MIDRANGE

Midrange hotels offer travellers the best value for money in Jordan. They are often privately owned by families who take pride in welcoming their guests. The owners can also be a fount of local knowledge and can provide assistance in catching transport or advising on sights of interest. Some even organise their own tours. Most family-run hotels offer some kind of home cooking for breakfast and guests may even be asked to join the family if they have ordered an evening meal.

There is at least one midrange hotel in towns you're likely to visit, with a good selection in Amman, Madaba, Wadi Musa (near Petra) and Aqaba. Rooms in midrange hotels usually have TV (sometimes featuring satellite stations such as CNN), fridge, heater (essential in winter), telephone, reliable hot water and a private bathroom.

Prices are typically around JD40/55 for singles/doubles. Negotiation is sometimes possible, especially if you're staying for several days. Many midrange hotels accept credit cards, but it's best to ask before checking in.

TOP END

There are some excellent top-end hotels in Amman, Wadi Musa (near Petra) and Aqaba, with liveried staff, welcome drinks on arrival, marble foyers and luxurious rooms. Most have a travel agency within their shopping arcades from which you can hire a car and organise hotel bookings for the next part of your trip.

Most of the top-end hotels are owned by international chains, but they invariably reflect the local character of Jordan, with Arabian-style interior design, options for high-quality Middle Eastern dining, shops selling fine Jordanian handicrafts and bookshops with a selection of English-language titles on Jordan.

Independent travellers can often negotiate a walk-in rate. Outside peak seasons and holidays (when booking is essential), you may find a world-class room for a midrange price.

A tax and service charge of 26% is added to the bill in top-end hotels, although it's worth checking to see if this has already been included

SLEEPING PRICE RANGES

The following price ranges indicate the cost of a double room in high season. Rooms generally have private bathrooms unless stated otherwise.

$ less than JD40

$$ JD40-90

$$$ more than JD90

in a discounted rate. Major credit cards are accepted in all top-end hotels.

Rental Accommodation

In Amman, the best places to check for apartments and houses to rent are the accommodation listings in the English-language newspapers, cultural centre noticeboards, and signs up in the cafes around Rainbow Street (including the noticeboard at Books@café). Also see www.expatriates.com/classifieds/amm/housingavailable. There is also a useful noticeboard in the office of the University of Jordan Language Center. For longer stays, wander around the suburbs of Jebel Amman, Weibdeh or Shmeisani, or between the 1st and 5th circles: signs advertising places to rent are often displayed in residence or shop windows.

It generally costs about JD500 to JD1000 per month for a furnished apartment in a reasonable area of Amman (including bills); a little less if it's unfurnished. A furnished apartment or small house in a less salubrious area may cost as little as JD300 to JD500 per month, but for this price don't expect everything to work. Be aware that some landlords may insist on payments of six months' rent in advance.

Resorts

If you have only one night's luxury during your visit to Jordan, plan to stay in one of the Dead Sea resorts. Not only are these state-of-the-art hotels worth a visit in their own right, but they also offer the best access to the Dead Sea – an area where there is next to no alternative accommodation. Residents of one resort can also use the facilities of the neighbouring hotels, which can take care of several nights' worth of entertainment in an area with no local nightlife.

Apart from the Dead Sea, there are also resorts in and around Aqaba – including the flagship resorts of the Mövenpick and Intercontinental chains. With access to the calm waters of the Red Sea, multiple pools, gyms and a selection of top-notch restaurants, they are bringing a touch of class to Jordan's second city.

ACTIVITIES

Jordan offers some of the best outdoor activities in the Middle East. You can hike and climb in stunning landscapes, or painstakingly piece together the past on an archaeological dig. Don't head home without trying at least a couple of these fantastic adventures.

WHAT	WHERE	HOW/HOW MUCH	NOTES
Archaeological Digs	Around Madaba, Mt Nebo, Karak and Petra	Contact an organisation involved in archaeology in Jordan before you arrive.	Even if you don't have much experience, it's sometimes possible to join a dig.
Camel treks	Petra and Wadi Rum	JD30 for two hours	Choose a mounted rather than a walking guide for a more authentic experience.
Cycling	Dana and King's Highway	**Bike Rush** (Map p52; ☑079-9454586; www.facebook.com/bikerush; ☺12pm-9pm Sat-Thu) offers weekly trips from Amman	Bikes can be hired in Amman.
Hiking	Jordan's Nature Reserves	**Royal Society for the Conservation of Nature** (RSCN; www.rscn.org.jo)	Don't expect an organised network of routes, with signposts and watering holes en route: most hiking in Jordan is an ad hoc affair passing through small villages.
Horseback Riding	Petra and Wadi Rum	**Rum Horses** (Map p212; ☑079 5802108, 2033508; www.wadirumhorses.com)	A rare chance to ride an Arabian stallion. Prior knowledge of horseback riding is necessary and don't expect a helmet.
Hot Springs	Dead Sea and King's Highway	Entrance fees vary.	Hot spring water contains potassium, magnesium and calcium, among other minerals with reputed health benefits.
Rock Climbing	Wadi Rum	The following websites detail routes: www.rumguides.com and www.wadirum.net.	Popular climbs all around Jordan are detailed in the excellent books written by Tony Howard and Di Taylor.
Running	Amman, Dead Sea and Wadi Rum	**Hash House Harriers** (http://hashemitehhh.googlepages.com)	Dubbed 'drinkers with a running problem' on its website, the HHH organises local runs each Monday from Amman.
Turkish Baths	Amman, Madaba, Wadi Musa and Aqaba	Around JD25, including massage	A great antidote for aching muscles, the hammam is otherwise known as a Turkish bath. Women should call ahead for a female assistant.

Climate

Amman

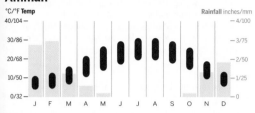

°C/°F **Temp**
Rainfall inches/mm

Aqaba

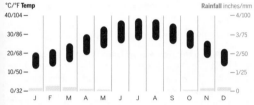

°C/°F **Temp**
Rainfall inches/mm

Customs Regulations

➡ 1L of alcoholic spirits or two bottles of wine

➡ 200 cigarettes or 25 cigars or 200g of tobacco

➡ A 'reasonable amount of perfume for personal use'

➡ Gifts up to the value of JD50 or the equivalent of US$150

➡ Prohibitions include drugs, weapons, and pornographic films and magazines

➡ Exporting anything more than 100 years old is illegal, so don't buy any souvenir (including 'ancient' coins or oil lamps) that is deemed to be 'antique'. If you're unsure about an item's provenance, contact the **Customs Department** (☑06-4623186; www.customs.gov.jo) in Amman.

Electricity

Jordan takes a mix-and-match approach to electrical sockets. European round two- and three- pin plugs along with British square three-pin plugs are all used across the country, with frequency seemingly determined only by what the electrician had to hand during installation.

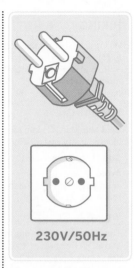

230V/50Hz

230V/50Hz

Embassies & Consulates

Most embassies and consulates are in Amman. Egypt also has a consulate in Aqaba. In general, offices are open 9am to 11am Sunday to Thursday for visa applications and 1pm to 3pm for collecting visas.

Australian Embassy (☑06-5807000; www.jordan.embassy.gov.au; 3 Youssef Abu Shahhout, Deir Ghbar)

Canadian Embassy (Map p59;☑06-5901500; www.canadainternational.gc.ca/jordan-jordanie/; Abdul Hameed Shoman St, Shmeisani)

Dutch Embassy (☑06-5902200; www.netherlandsembassy.com.jo; 22 Ibrahim Ayoub St) Near the 4th circle.

Egyptian Consulate (☑03-2016171; cnr Al-Isteglal & Al-Akhatal Sts, Aqaba; ⊘8am-3pm Sun-Thu)

Egyptian Embassy (☑06-5605175; fax 5604082; 22 Qortubah St, Jebel Amman; ⊘9am-noon Sun-Thu)

French Embassy (Map p52;☑06-4604630; www.ambafrance-jo.org; Al-Mutanabbi St, Jebel Amman)

HIKING

Hiking is an exhilarating activity in Jordan, not least because of the pristine and varied quality of the landscape and the historical allusions that underlie almost every path.

Bear in mind that Global Positioning System (GPS) units and mobile phones may not function between steep canyon walls. Always check local conditions before setting out, as flash floods can occur throughout spring and may make wadis impassable.

When to Go

Best Mid-March to late April when it's not too hot, the rains have finished, the flowers are blooming and wells are full.

Good Late September to mid-October when it's dry but not excessively hot.

Avoid November to March when rains make it dangerous to hike or camp in narrow wadis and flash floods can sweep unheralded out of the hills. Paths are often washed away so routes change frequently. It's also very cold for camping.

Where to Go

The best places for hiking in Jordan are Ajloun Nature Reserve, Dana Biosphere Reserve and Mujib Biosphere Reserve, where most trails require a guide. For more DIY options, there are some exciting hikes in Petra and in Wadi Rum. Bedouin guides also offer accompanied hikes along the old caravan routes that link these two spectacular places.

Several longer routes are possible with a tent. In particular, Dana to Petra is an excellent four-day trek that takes you through Wadi Feinan, Wadi Ghuweir and Little Petra.

What to Bring

Lightweight trousers and long-sleeved shirts are culturally sensitive and best for the terrain. Other essentials include a hat, sunscreen, water bottle, torch (flashlight) and insect repellent. Lightweight walking boots are ideal, and a watertight bag for wet wadi walks.

How to Organise a Hike

The best way to organise a trek is through the RSCN, the visitor centre in Petra or Wadi Rum, or a private tour company that specialises in hiking. If you engage a Bedouin guide

German Embassy (☑06-5930367; www.amman.diplo.de; 31 Bin Ghazi St, Jebel Amman) Between 4th and 5th circles.

Iraqi Embassy (Map p52; ☑06-4623175; www.mofamission.gov.iq/amn; Al-Kulliyah al-Islamiyah St, Jebel Amman) Near the 1st circle.

Irish Consulate (Map p52;☑06-625632; King Hussein St, Jebel Amman)

Israeli Consulate (Map p59;☑06-5503529; http://embassies.gov.il/amman-en; Maysaloon St, Shmeisani)

Lebanese Embassy (Map p52;☑06-5929111; fax 5929113; Al-Neel St, Abdoun) Near the UK embassy.

New Zealand Consulate (Map p46;☑06-4636720; fax 4634349; 99 Al-Malek al-Hussein St, Downtown) On the 4th floor of the Khalaf Building.

Saudi Arabian Consulate (Map p52;☑06-5924154; fax 5921154; 1st Circle, Jebel Amman)

Syrian Embassy (Map p52;☑06-5920684; Abdoun Prince Hashem bin Al-Hussein St, Jebel Amman) Near the 4th circle.

UK Embassy (Map p52; ☑06-5909200; www.gov.uk/government/world/organisations/british-embassy-amman; Dimashq St, Wadi Abdoun, Abdoun)

US Embassy (☑06-5906000; http://jordan.usembassy.gov/; 20 Al-Umawiyeen St, Abdoun)

Yemeni Embassy (☑06-5923771; Al-Ameer Hashem bin al-Hussein St, Abdoun Circle)

Food

See p288 for an idea of Jordanian cuisine and the general eating experience.

The following price ranges indicate the cost of a main dish unless stated otherwise. A main dish is often accompanied by salad and various pickles, dips (such as hummus) and garnishes. These are offered free of charge and invariably served with flat Arabic bread. This means that a main dish often doubles as a meal. Especially at midrange and top-end restaurants, watch out for small print on menus adding independently, make sure you understand exactly what services are on offer to avoid disappointment on either side. Rates vary (and are negotiable) between JD30 to JD100, depending on the skills required.

Royal Society for the Conservation of Nature (RSCN; ☏06-4616523; www.rscn.org.jo) Wide range of guided hikes in Jordan's nature reserves; can arrange long-distance treks if given prior notice.

Terhaal Encounters (☏06-5813061; www.terhaal.com) For individual or group adventure hikes, including abseiling and canyoning, that minimise environmental impact and bring benefits to local communities.

Tropical Desert Trips (☏07-95438708; http://tropicaldeserttrips.com) Hiking, climbing and canyoning trips across Jordan.

Desert Guides Company (☏06-5527230; www.desertguidescompany.com) Specialises in adventure hikes, treks and climbs throughout Jordan.

Yamaan Safady (☏077 7222101; www.adventurejordan.com) Leads weekly hiking trips to places such as Wadi Yabis and Wadi Hasa as part of the Adventure Jordan Hiking Club.

Where to Find out More

It's best to buy both maps and books abroad as their availability in Jordan is sporadic.

Trekking & Canyoning in the Jordanian Dead Sea Rift by Itai Haviv contains numerous trekking and canyoning routes in the wadis of Central Jordan; its cultural and environmental insights alone make it worth the trouble to find.

British climbers Tony Howard and Di Taylor have spent much of their lives exploring and mapping the hiking, trekking and rock-climbing possibilities in Jordan. Their books include the following:

➡ *Treks & Climbs in Wadi Rum*

➡ *Walks & Scrambles in Wadi Rum*

➡ *Jordan: Walks, Treks, Caves, Climbs & Canyons*

---

the 16% sales tax and 10% service charge – increasing your bill by a quarter (where possible, all prices listed in the book include taxes).

$ Less than JD5

$$ JD5-10

$$$ More than JD10

Gay & Lesbian Travellers

Homosexuality is illegal in most Islamic countries in the Middle East, but in Jordan gay sex is legal and the age of consent is 16. Public displays of affection by heterosexuals are frowned upon and the same rules apply to gays and lesbians, although same-sex hand-holding is a common sign of friendship in Jordan.

The legality of homosexuality shouldn't be confused with full societal acceptance, and discrimination and harassment is common. In February 2014, 10 gay and lesbian Jordanians were arrested at a private party to allegedly prevent a disturbance of the peace. There is a subdued underground gay scene in Amman – if you're keen to explore it, keep your enquiries discreet. Gay-friendly venues that attract young, gay and straight crowds include the multipurpose Books@café and the Blue Fig Café in Amman.

Check www.gaymiddleeast.com and the gay and lesbian thread of Lonely Planet's Thorn Tree bulletin board (lonelyplanet.com) for more information.

Insurance

Travel insurance that covers theft, loss and medical problems is essential. The policy should cover ambulance fees and emergency flights home.

Some policies specifically exclude 'dangerous activities', which can include motorcycling and even trekking. You must have insurance if you plan to dive in Aqaba – decompression-chamber treatment is an expensive business!

You may prefer a policy that pays doctors or hospitals directly. Alternatively, if you submit a claim after the event, ensure you keep all documentation. Some policies ask you to call back (reverse charges) to a centre in your home country where an immediate assessment of your problem is made.

Worldwide travel insurance is available at lonelyplanet.com/travel_services. You can buy, extend and claim online anytime – even if you're already on the road.

Internet Access

Almost every town in Jordan has at least one public internet centre, but wi-fi is becoming increasingly standard in hotels of most budgets, as well as many cafes and restaurants.

To keep connected on the move with your laptop, mobile providers Zain and Orange both offer USB modems, allowing you to get online for less than JD20.

Language Courses

Amman is a popular place to come and study Arabic. For more details on courses, see p54.

Legal Matters

The Jordanian legal system has evolved from distinct traditions. Civil and commercial law is largely based on British-style common law, while religious and family matters are generally covered by Islamic Sharia courts, or ecclesiastic equivalents for non-Muslims. In a nutshell:

➡ The legal age for driving and drinking is 18.

➡ The age of consent for men and women is 16.

➡ You can be prosecuted under the law of your home country regarding age of consent, even when abroad.

➡ Travellers are expected to respect the law.

➡ Penalties for drug use of any kind are stiff.

➡ Criticising the king is illegal.

➡ Excessive speeding, drunk driving and seatbelt avoidance are not tolerated.

➡ If you break the law, your embassy can only contact your relatives and recommend local lawyers.

Maps

The Jordan Tourism Board's free *Map of Jordan* is a handy map, with a plan of Amman on the reverse. The Royal Geographic Centre of Jordan also publishes good maps, including a hiking map of Petra.

Several detailed maps are available outside Jordan: ITMB's 1:700,000 map *Jordan* is probably the easiest map to find, *Jordan* by Kümmerly and Frey is the best driving map, and the latest edition of GEO Project's *Jordan* (1:730,000) has an excellent map of Amman.

Money

Known as the 'jay-dee' among hip young locals, the currency in Jordan is the dinar (JD) and it is made up of 1000 fils. You'll often hear the terms *piastre* or *qirsh*: this refers to 10 fils (so one dinar equals 100 piastres). Often when a price is quoted the unit will be omitted, so if you're told that something is 25, it's a matter of working out whether it's 25 fils, 25 piastre or 25 dinars! Although it sounds confusing, it's usually obvious when you're on the ground, and most Jordanians wouldn't dream of ripping off a foreigner, with

---

INFLATION & TRAVEL COSTS

If there is one bone of contention between our readers and those involved with tourism in Jordan, it is the issue of prices. Many travellers expect to find prices unchanged and become suspicious of landlords and taxi drivers who charge more than expected. By the same token, many service providers in Jordan feel frustrated when travellers insist on prices that may be unrealistic even a relatively short time after printing.

In most instances, prices for accommodation, food and transport in Jordan have remained stable for the past three years, but that is largely the result of a deliberate policy to save the effects of inflation impinging on an already weakened tourism trade. This is unlikely to remain the case for the life of this book. Instability among neighbouring countries and continued immigration have all contributed to high inflation. For some, a slump in tourism due to regional tension means there is no option but to put prices up. For others it means being forced to offer unrealistic discounts.

In summary, while every effort is made to ensure that our published prices for entrance fees, tours, accommodation, restaurants, food items and private transport is accurate at the time of writing, treat this only as a *guide* to pricing, not a definitive statement of costs.

There is one piece of good news for those trying to estimate the cost of their trip to Jordan. Public bus prices, which are heavily subsidised by the government, have only minimally increased from the last edition to this edition and there is no suggestion of an imminent price hike in this sector.

the possible exception of the occasional taxi driver.

Coins come in denominations of 1, 5, 10, 25 and 50 piastres (with the latter two marked as being quarter- and half-dinar respectively). Notes come in denominations of JD1, 5, 10, 20 and 50. Try to change larger notes as often as possible – when paying for petrol, for example, or for your hotel bill – as it can be hard to pay with large notes in small establishments.

ATMs

It is possible to travel in Jordan almost entirely on plastic. ATMs giving cash advances abound in all but the smaller towns – just don't forget your PIN!

There are no local charges on credit-card cash advances, but the maximum daily withdrawal amount is around JD500, depending on your particular card. All banks have large signs (in English) indicating which credit cards they accept.

Visa is the most widely accepted card at ATMs, followed by MasterCard. Other cards, such as Cirrus- and Plus-compatible cards, are also accepted by many ATMs (eg Jordan National Bank and HSBC).

Changing Money

It's easy to change money in Jordan. Most major currencies are accepted in cash and travellers cheques. US dollars, UK pounds and euros are easier to change than Australian or New Zealand dollars.

There are no restrictions on bringing dinars into Jordan. It's possible to change dinars back into some foreign currencies in Jordan.

Syrian, Lebanese, Egyptian, Israeli and Iraqi currency can all be changed in Amman. Egyptian and Israeli currency are also easily changed in Aqaba. Banks and moneychangers charge about the same for exchanging cash (a little

more for travellers cheques), but large hotels charge more. There are small branches of major banks at the borders and airports.

Credit Cards

Most major credit cards are accepted at top-end hotels and restaurants, travel agencies, larger souvenir shops and bookshops. Commissions of up to 5% may be added to the bill, so it may be better to get a cash advance and pay with the paper stuff. Make a note of the emergency numbers on the back of your credit cards in case you lose them.

Duty Free

There are duty-free shops at Queen Alia International Airport and next to the Century Park Hotel in Amman, plus small outlets at the border crossings with Israel and the Palestinian Territories.

Most upmarket shops offer tax rebates. If you spend more than JD350, keep your receipts, fill out a tax rebate form and leave the country within 90 days, you can get the 16% tax refunded to your credit card at a booth at the airport, just before check-in.

International Transfers

Some major banks (such as Arab Bank and Jordan National Bank) can arrange international money transfers. Cairo-Amman Bank is part of the international service offered by **Western Union** (www.westernunion.com). **MoneyGram** (www.moneygram.com) has agreements with several banks. Fees are high with both.

Tax

Jordan has a sales tax of 16%, but this is generally only added to the bill in midrange and top-end restaurants. Midrange and top-end restaurants and hotels may also add an additional 10% service charge. The Aqaba special economic zone has a sales tax

IRAQI MONEY

If you are a collector of notes and coins, you may be interested in old Iraqi money, bearing the portrait of Saddam Hussein, for sale on street corners in downtown Amman. Even if they're fake, they're good as a conversational gambit with the Iraqi refugees who are selling them.

of only 5% and many Jordanians head there on shopping sprees to take advantage of the lower consumer prices.

Tipping

Tips of 10% are generally expected in better restaurants (and often included in the bill). Elsewhere, rounding up the bill to the nearest 250 fils or giving back the loose change is appreciated, especially by petrol attendants and taxi drivers.

Travellers Cheques

Most types of travellers cheques are accepted by money changers, with the most recognised being American Express (Amex). Check the commission before changing them.

Opening Hours

Opening times vary widely across the country. Many sights, government departments and banks close earlier in winter and during Ramadan. The following opening hours are therefore a rough guide only. Always remember that the official weekend in Jordan is Friday and Saturday, so always expect curtailed hours on these days.

Banks 8am to 3pm, Sunday to Thursday

Restaurants midday to midnight, daily

Cafes 9am to midnight, daily

Bars and Clubs 9pm to 1am, daily

Shops 9am to 8pm, Saturday to Thursday; some close 2 to 4pm

Souqs 9am to 8pm, daily

Photography

Equipment

Digital accessories and memory cards are widely available; a 1GB memory card costs around JD15. Many camera shops can burn photos onto a CD and print digital pictures.

Photographing People

Some Jordanians, particularly women and the elderly, object to being photographed, so ask first. Persisting in taking a photograph against someone's wishes can lead to ugly scenes, so exercise courtesy and common sense. Children generally line up to be photographed.

Jordanians are very proud of their country and can be offended if you take pictures of anything 'negative' or suggestive of poverty and squalor; this may include the activity of a marketplace.

Restrictions

Photography in military zones and 'strategic areas' like bridges and public buildings is forbidden. Take particular care in the Eastern Desert as there are several sensitive military sites not far from the desert castles. You also need to be careful along the Dead Sea Highway where there are numerous checkpoints protecting the sensitive border with Israel and the Palestinian Territories.

Post

Stamps are available from souvenir shops where postcards are sold and there are postboxes around towns. Letters posted from Jordan take up to two weeks to reach Australia and the USA, but often as little as three or four days to the UK and Europe. Every town has a post office, but parcels are best sent from Amman or Aqaba. For more detailed postal information, **Jordan Post** (www.jordanpost.com.jo) has an informative website.

Reliable courier companies include **FedEx** (www.fedex.com.jo), which has an office in Amman, and **DHL** (www.dhl.com), which has offices in Amman and Aqaba. Half a kilo costs around JD40 to most countries, although the per-kilo rate decreases dramatically the more you send.

TO	LETTER/ CARD	1KG PARCEL
Middle East	600 fils	JD9
UK/ Europe	800 fils	JD18.600
USA/ Canada	JD1	JD15.300
Australia	JD1	JD14.700

Public Holidays

During public holidays, government offices and banks close. Shops, moneychangers and restaurants generally remain open, and public transport functions normally.

During Eid al-Fitr and Eid al-Adha many shops close as shop owners join their families on these important days of celebration.

Archaeological sites and nature reserves tend to be very crowded on Fridays and public holidays.

New Year's Day 1 January

Good Friday March/April

Labour Day 1 May

Independence Day 25 May

Army Day & Anniversary of the Great Arab Revolt 10 June

Christmas Day 25 December

The main Islamic holidays are as follows (see table below for dates).

Islamic New Year First Day of Muharram.

Prophet's Birthday Celebrated on 12 Rabi' al-Awal.

Eid al-Isra Wal Mi'raj Celebrates the nocturnal visit of the Prophet Mohammed to heaven.

Ramadan Ninth month of the Muslim Calendar.

Eid al-Fitr Starts at the beginning of Shawwal to mark the end of fasting in the preceding month of Ramadan.

Eid al-Adha Commemoration of Allah sparing Ibrahim (Abraham in the Bible) from sacrificing his son, Isaac. It also marks the end of the hajj.

Ramadan

During the holy month of Ramadan, Muslims refrain from eating, drinking, having sex and smoking during daylight hours in accordance with the fourth pillar of Islam. Even gum chewing is considered *haram* (forbidden).

ISLAMIC HOLIDAYS

Dates are approximate, as they rely on the sighting of the new moon.

HEJIRA YEAR	NEW YEAR	PROPHET'S BIRTHDAY	RAMADAN BEGINS	EID AL-FITR	EID AL-ADHA
1436	25.10.14	03.01.15	18.06.15	18.07.15	24.11.15
1437	15.10.15	24.12.15	07.06.16	06.07.16	13.09.16
1438	3.10.16	12.12.16	27.05.17	25.06.17	02.09.17
1439	22.09.17	01.12.17	16.05.18	15.06.18	22.08.18

Although many Muslims in Jordan do not follow the injunctions to the letter, most conform to some extent. Foreigners are not expected to follow suit, but it is bad form to eat, drink or smoke in public during this period. Note that for the lifetime of this guide, Ramadan will fall in the long hot days of early summer.

Business hours during Ramadan are erratic and tempers tend to flare towards the end of the month. As the sun starts to dip, many villages turn into ghost towns as people go home to break their fast. Tourist attractions and hotel restaurants remain open and public transport generally functions normally, but the serving of alcohol may be restricted to room service or simply be unavailable.

Telephone

The telephone system in Jordan is privatised, so visitors can make a call from a private telephone agency, call from a hotel or shop, or buy a telephone card from one of the 1000 or more payphones throughout Jordan.

Local calls cost around 150 fils for three minutes. The easiest place to make a call is at your hotel, where local calls are often free. The cost of overseas calls from Jordan varies widely: check with your service provider.

Overseas calls can be made at any card payphone or from hotels, but are substantially more expensive. Reverse-charge telephone calls are not normally possible.

Mobile Phones

Mobile phones in Jordan use the GSM system (900/1800). Two main service providers are **Zain** (www.zain.com) and **Orange** (www.orange.jo), both of which offer a full range of plans and prepaid SIM cards (ID required

PRACTICALITIES

Newspapers & Magazines Available in Jordan

Jordan Times (www.jordantimes.com)
The Economist (www.economist.com)
Time (www.time.com)
Newsweek (www.newsweek.com)

Radio

Radio Jordan (96.3 FM)
BBC World Service (1323 AM)
Popular hits (99.6 FM)

TV

Jordan's Channel 2 (French and English)
Satellite channels (BBC, CNN, MTV, Al-Jazeera) Available in most midrange and top-end hotels.

Discount Cards

International Student Identity Card (ISIC) Can be used for discounts at some tourist sites.
University ID cards Not accepted.

Smoking

There are laws banning smoking in public places, but these are rarely enforced, with the following exceptions:
➡ Top-end hotels in Amman, the Dead Sea and Aqaba reserve a few nonsmoking rooms.
➡ The occasional quality restaurant enforces a non-smoking policy at selected tables.

Weights & Measures

Jordan uses the metric system.

to purchase). 3G is available throughout Jordan.

Phone Codes

➡ 962 Jordan country code
➡ 00 International access code

To make a call from a landline, you must precede the six- or seven-digit number with a two-digit area code.
➡ 02 Northern Jordan
➡ 03 Southern Jordan
➡ 05 Jordan Valley, central and eastern districts
➡ 06 Amman district

➡ 07 Prefix for eight-digit mobile phone numbers
➡ 0800 Prefix for toll-free numbers
➡ 1212 Local directory assistance (Amman)
➡ 131 Local directory assistance (elsewhere)
➡ 132 or 133 International directory assistance

Emergency Numbers

➡ 911 Ambulance
➡ 911 Fire department
➡ 911 Police

Time

Jordan is two hours ahead of GMT/UTC in winter and three hours ahead from April through September, when daylight saving time is in effect. Note that Jordan's daylight saving time is slightly out of sync with summer clock changes in Europe. There are no time differences within Jordan. Jordan is on the same time zone as Israel and the Palestinian Territories, Syria and Egypt.

Toilets

Most hotels and restaurants, except those in the budget category, now have Western-style toilets. In most others you'll be using squat toilets with a hose for ablutions and a water bucket provided for flushing.

Toilet paper (the use of which is considered an unsanitary practice in most Middle Eastern countries) is seldom available, except in the midrange and top-end hotels and restaurants. Local people prefer to use the hose and then deposit any toilet paper (used for drying purposes) in the basket by the side of the toilet bowl; these baskets should be used to avoid blockages as the sewerage system is not designed for paper. For those who can't do without it, toilet paper can be bought in most grocery shops throughout Jordan.

If caught short in the desert or hillsides of Jordan, it is imperative you choose a spot well away from water courses and bury the outcome in as deep a pit as possible.

Tourist Information

Jordan has a good network of tourist offices and visitor centres. The main tourist office in Amman is located on the ground floor of the **Ministry of Tourism & Antiquities** (Map p52; ☎ext 254 4603360; fax 4646264; ground fl, Al-Mutanabbi St, Jebel Amman; ◷8am-9pm) in Jebel Amman.

The comprehensive website of the **Jordan Tourism Board** (JTB; www.visitjordan. com) has regularly updated information. JTB also publishes some excellent brochures in several languages. These are available from its offices in Jordan and abroad. Contact your local office for a brochure and map package.

Visit Jordan France (☎01 55 60 94 46; hala@visitjordan. com; 122 rue de Paris, 92100 Boulogne-Billancourt, France)

Visit Jordan Germany (☎069-9231880; germany@ visitjordan.com; Weser Strasse 4, 60329 Frankfurt)

Visit Jordan UK (☎020 7223 1878; uk@visitjordan.com; 115 Hammersmith Rd, London, W14 0QH)

Visit Jordan USA (☎877-733 5673, 703-243 7404; contactus@visitjordan.com; Suite 102, 6867 Elm St, McLean, VA 22101)

Travellers with Disabilities

In late 2000 Jordan celebrated its first-ever Olympic gold medal, won by the female athlete Maha Barghouthi in the Sydney Paralympics. It was a proud moment for Jordan and it threw a spotlight on people with disabilities – albeit briefly. More than a decade on and Jordan is still not a great place for travellers with disabilities. Although Jordanians are happy to help, cities are crowded and the traffic is chaotic, roadside kerbs can be uncommonly high, and visiting tourist attractions – such as the vast archaeological sites of Petra and Jerash – involves long traverses over uneven ground.

There is some good news, however:

➡ The Jordanian government has legislated that wheelchair access must be added to all new public buildings.

➡ Horse-drawn carriages are provided at Petra for visitors with disabilities to help with access to the main sites.

➡ The Royal Diving Club is a member of the **Access to Marine Conservation for All** (AMCA; www.amca-international.org), an initiative to enable people with disabilities to enjoy diving.

Visas

Visas (JD40 for most nationalities) are required by all foreigners entering Jordan. Visas can be obtained on arrival either at the airport or at most of Jordan's land borders. Tourist visas are valid for three months (that is, you must enter the country within three months of the date of issue) and allow stays of up to one month from the date of entry. Your passport should be valid for at least six months after you arrive in Jordan.

At the Airport

Visas are issued on arrival at the immigration desks in the airport in Amman. There's no form-filling involved. Payment must be made in Jordanian dinars (cash only). There are moneychangers adjacent to the counters, but as these are sometimes closed and ATMs are only available after immigration it pays to bring the correct amount of Jordanian dinars with you.

At Land Borders

Visas for Jordan are issued with a minimum of fuss at any of Jordan's land borders, with the exception of King Hussein Bridge.

Via the Aqaba Economic Zone

If you arrive in Jordan's southern city of Aqaba by air on an international flight, by sea from Nuweiba in Egypt or by land from Eilat, you are entitled to a free visa as part of the free-trade agreement with the Aqaba Special Economic Zone Area (ASEZA). If you stay in Jordan for more than 15 days, you must register at the office of **ASEZA** (☏03-2035757; www.aqaba-zone.com) in Aqaba.

Multiple Entry Visa

Multiple entry visas (around JD60) must be obtained in advance from Jordanian consulates or embassies outside the country. In the Middle East, you can find Jordanian embassies in all the neighbouring states, including Israel and the Palestinian Territories. You may want to avoid getting a Jordanian multiple-entry visa from the latter, however, if you intend to travel elsewhere in the region. This is because many Arab countries refuse entry to those who have Israeli stamps or documentation in their passports.

Visa Extensions

In Amman and Aqaba visas can easily be extended, at no extra charge, for stays of up to three months. The process is simple but involves a little running around, although you're unlikely to spend more than 30 minutes in each office.

➡ Ask staff at your hotel to write a short letter confirming where you are staying.

➡ Ask them to fill out two copies of a small card (or photocopy) that states all the hotel details.

➡ Fill out the application form for an extension on the back of this card (it's in Arabic but staff at your hotel can help you read it and answers can be in English).

➡ Take the form, letter, photocopies of the front pages of your passport and the Jordanian visa page, and your passport to the relevant police station.

➡ Plan to arrive at the police station between 10am and 3pm Saturday to Thursday (best to go early).

➡ Wait for the extension (usually granted on the spot).

After assembling the necessary paperwork, it takes about 30 minutes to complete the registration process at a police station. You may be required to have an HIV test, which usually takes 24 hours to process. The maximum stay allowed on an extended tourist visa is six months. Failure to register results in a fine of JD2 for every day you have overstayed. This is payable when you extend, or on departure from Jordan at a counter just before immigration at Queen Alia International Airport in Amman.

For longer-term residency, or to sort out any problems with your visa, you may be asked to go to the **Directorate of Residency & Borders** (☏06-5505360; Majed al-Idwans St, Shmeisani, Amman; ☺8am-3pm Sun-Thu, to 1pm Sat). Take service taxi 6 or 7 from downtown to Shmeisani; from there it's a 15-minute walk. The office is next to the Shmeisani central police station (*markaz mudiret ash-shurta*).

Al-Madeenah Police Station (Map p46; ☏06-4657788; 1st fl, Al-Malek Faisal St, downtown) Opposite the Arab Bank in downtown Amman. Start the process of lodging your visa extension paperwork here.

Muhajireen Police Station (Markaz Amn Muhajireen; Map p52; Al-Ameerah Basma bin Talal Rd, downtown) West of the downtown area. Police stations are usually open for visa extensions from 10am to 3pm Saturday to Thursday, although it's best to go in the morning. Complete the process at this station.

Visas for Other Middle Eastern Countries

EGYPT

Most nationalities are issued a visa (US$20, payable in dollars) either on the boat from Jordan or on arrival in Egypt.

If you only intend to visit the Sinai Peninsula (check government advice before travelling; much of this area is currently considered dangerous), you can get a free 'Sinai Entry Stamp', valid for 15 days. This is not valid elsewhere in Egypt.

If you wish to travel further than Sharm el-Sheikh, you need to request a full visa for Egypt on arrival (not available at Egypt's Taba border). Single/multiple entry visas (JD20/25) can be obtained in advance from the Egyptian consulate in Aqaba or the Egyptian embassy in Amman.

IRAQ

Travel to Iraq is not advised at present. It takes two to three weeks to get approval for visa applications from the Ministry of Interior in Baghdad.

ISRAEL & THE PALESTINIAN TERRITORIES

Visas are available at the three border crossings currently open to foreigners – Sheikh Hussein Bridge, King Hussein Bridge and Wadi Araba – and many nationalities do not require one.

LEBANON

Lebanese visas are readily available at Lebanese entry points, but not at the Lebanon embassy in Amman. If you are travelling to Lebanon via Syria, it's worth noting that you will need to obtain your Syrian visa *before* you arrive in Jordan.

SAUDI ARABIA

It is not possible to visit Saudi Arabia as a casual traveller.

You must either have a Saudi resident's visa to enter the country or, if you are travelling from Jordan to Kuwait or to Yemen and you can prove there is no other way of getting to your destination (ie you are travelling in your own car), you may be granted a three- or seven-day transit visa. You need to apply well in advance of travel, in your country of residence, and visas are subject to many additional stipulations. Check with the Saudi Arabian embassy in your own country before attempting this process.

SYRIA

Travel to Syria is not recommended at the time of writing. If conditions improve and you intend to travel to Syria, you must obtain a visa either in your home country or in İstanbul, Ankara or Cairo *before* you arrive in Jordan. Only foreign residents in Jordan (ie expatriate workers and diplomats) and residents of a country without Syrian representation can be issued a Syrian visa at the embassy in Amman.

It's important to remember that you cannot enter Syria from Jordan if you have a visa stamp in your passport from Israel and the Palestinian Territories.

Volunteering

For further ideas see www.volunteerabroad.com/jordan.cfm.

New Orthodox School

(Map p124; ☎05-3250636; diodoros@orange.jo) For those who like Madaba well enough to stay, there's an opportunity to teach English at this boys school that makes for an excellent gap-year experience. Run by Father Innocent (Innokentios) and attached to St George's Church, the school promotes 'mutual respect and peaceful coexistence' among youngsters of different religious communities. The school is a nonprofit organisation, supporting needy students.

Volunteers receive free accommodation, pocket money and private Arabic lessons.

RSCN (www.rscn.org.jo) If you are keen to learn more about Jordan's ecological projects, there are limited opportunities to work within some of the country's nature reserves on a three-month voluntary program. Board and lodging are generally offered in return for a variety of services such as working in the visitor centres.

These posts are best filled by local Jordanian people, but if you have a specialist skill in management or conservation, you may strike it lucky.

Royal Botanic Garden

(http://royalbotanicgarden.org; Rumman) The soon-to-be-opened Royal Botanic Garden near Rumman north of the capital welcomes volunteers, particularly those with a horticultural bent.

Work

There's not much in the way of casual work in Jordan as all such jobs are in hot demand from Palestinian and Iraqi refugees. If you are interested in staying longer in the country and have a specific skill or qualification, it's best to apply for work before leaving home. That way, your employer will be responsible for paying for your air ticket and will sponsor your work permit.

Diving

Qualified dive instructors or divemasters may be able to get work at one of the diving centres in Aqaba, particularly during peak season (September to March). Keep in mind, however, that positions are hotly contested by locals.

Language Teaching

English-teaching opportunities are open to those with TOEFL qualifications. The **British Council** (Map p52; ☎06-46033420; www.britishcouncil.org/jordan.htm) recruits teachers from the UK; you need the RSA Preparatory Certificate (the Diploma is preferred) or equivalent and at least two years' work experience. For details contact the British Council **information centre** (☎020 7389 4385; www.britishcouncil.org) before arriving in Jordan. Casual vacancies within Jordan occasionally arise: address your CV to the Teaching Centre Manager.

The **American Language Center** (☎06-5523901; www.alc.edu.jo) runs the other top language school. Like the British Council, teachers are mostly recruited before arrival in Jordan.

Transport

GETTING THERE & AWAY

Ever since Swiss explorer Jean Louis Burckhardt rediscovered Petra for the Western world in the 19th century, tourists have been visiting Jordan, resulting in well-established and efficient inbound and onward travel routes. Most notable of these are the routes to Israel and the Palestinian Territories, and the ferry across the Red Sea from Aqaba to Nuweiba in Egypt, though check travel advisories before taking the latter route as the security situation in Nuweiba (part of South Sinai) is change-able. The once popular Amman-Damascus route is off-limits due to the Syrian crisis, but it's hoped that this will eventually reopen in the event of peace.

Combining a trip to Jordan with visits to neighbouring countries is also possible by flying from Amman to regional capitals; as Amman is well connected with other Arab countries, it's also possible to combine a trip with Dubai in the UAE and other destinations in the Arabian Peninsula.

Flights and tours can be booked online at lonelyplanet.com/bookings.

Entering the Country

Entering Jordan is straight-forward whether by air, land or sea, with visas and money-exchange facilities available at all borders.

Always carry your passport with you when travelling around sensitive areas such as near the border of Israel and the Palestinian Territories, along the Dead Sea Highway and roads linking the Dead Sea Highway to interior towns. Checkpoints and passport checks are common in all these areas.

It is important to remember that you may have difficulty entering some Middle Eastern countries from Jordan if you have a visa stamp in your passport from Israel and the Palestinian Territories.

Air

Airports & Airlines

Queen Alia International Airport (Map p73; ☑06-4010250; www.qaiairport.com), about 35km south of Amman, is the country's main gateway. Recently sub-ject to a highly impressive refurbishment, it has ATMs, foreign-exchange counters, a post office and left-luggage counter. The departure lounge has several cafes and a good range of duty-free gift items, including Arabic sweets and Dead Sea prod-ucts. Car-rental agencies are in the arrivals building.

Amman Airport Ho-tel (☑06-4451000; www.ammanairporthotel.com; r from JD100), the only airport

CLIMATE CHANGE & TRAVEL

Every form of transport that relies on carbon-based fuel generates CO_2, the main cause of human-induced climate change. Modern travel is dependent on aeroplanes, which might use less fuel per kilometre per person than most cars but travel much greater distances. The altitude at which aircraft emit gases (including CO_2) and particles also contributes to their climate change impact. Many websites offer 'carbon calculators' that allow people to estimate the carbon emissions generated by their journey and, for those who wish to do so, to offset the impact of the greenhouse gases emitted with con-tributions to portfolios of climate-friendly initiatives throughout the world. Lonely Planet offsets the carbon footprint of all staff and author travel.

DEPARTURE TAX

Jordan's departure tax for travellers is JD4 by land, JD6 by sea and JD15 by air. If you are leaving by air, the departure tax is generally included in the ticket price.

hotel, is 2km from the airport terminal.

The only other international airport is at Aqaba, where some international carriers stop en route to Amman. Flights to Sharm el-Sheikh in Egypt are handled from here and occasional charter flights from Europe stop here, too.

The national airline, **Royal Jordanian** (☎06-5100000; www.rj.com), is well established with a good safety record. It has direct flights to most major cities in Europe and all Middle Eastern capitals, and runs short flights from Amman to Aqaba (twice daily). **Royal Wings** (www.royalwings.com.jo), a subsidiary of Royal Jordanian, has smaller planes and runs expensive charter flights.

A number of airlines fly to Jordan and have offices in Amman.

Air France (Map p59; ☎06-5100777; www.airfrance.com)

British Airways (☎06-5828801; www.ba.com)

Emirates (Map p52; ☎06-4615222; www.emirates.com)

Fly Dubai (☎06-5004445; www.flydubai.com)

Gulf Air (Map p52; ☎06-653613; www.gulfair.com)

Iraqi Airways (☎06-4638600; www.iq-airways.com)

KLM (Map p46; ☎06-655267; www.klm.com)

Kuwait Airways (Map p59; ☎06-5690144; www.kuwait-airways.com)

Lufthansa Airlines (Map p59; ☎06-5200180; www.lufthansa.com)

Qatar Airways (Map p59; ☎06-5679444; www.qatarairways.com)

Saudi Arabian Airlines (☎06-5777766; www.saudiairlines.com)

Turkish Airlines (Map p52; ☎06-5548100; www.turkishairlines.com)

Land

It's easy to reach Jordan by land from Israel and the Palestinian Territories. Foreign residents of Saudi Arabia (and transit passengers who can show they have no other way of reaching Jordan) are also able to cross Saudi Arabia and enter Jordan by land.

Most overland travellers arrive in Jordan by bus or service taxi, though it's also possible to bring your own vehicle.

Getting to/from Jordan's Borders
EGYPT

Most people travel between Jordan and Egypt by boat. It's quicker and cheaper, however, to travel overland via Israel and the Palestinian Territories using the Wadi Araba border (but be aware of the Israeli border-stamp stigma before making a decision). If you choose this route:

➡ Take a taxi to Wadi Araba and another taxi between Yitzhak Rabin and Taba on the Egyptian border.

➡ Taxis also run from either border to Eilat and there are buses from Eilat to either border.

➡ The whole trip takes about 1½ hours.

ISRAEL & THE PALESTINIAN TERRITORIES

Several cities in Jordan have direct bus links to cities in Israel and the Palestinian Territories. Travelling by bus directly between Amman and Tel Aviv saves the hassle of getting to/from the borders on your own, but it's more expensive than crossing independently and you'll have to wait for all passengers to clear customs and immigration.

From Amman, **Trust International Transport** (☎06-5813427) has buses from its office at 7th Circle to Tel Aviv (six hours), Haifa (seven hours) and Nazareth (seven hours), departing daily except Saturday at 8.30am. Buses cross the border at Sheikh Hussein Bridge. Bus schedules change frequently, so check departure times and book (and collect) tickets in advance from the bus station. There is one **Jordan Express Tourist Transport** (☎06-5664141; www.jett.com.jo; Al-Malek al-Hussein St, Shmeisani, Amman) bus to King Hussein Bridge (JD8.500, one hour, 7am).

If you wish to go it alone, there are three route options: King Hussein Bridge, Sheikh Hussein Bridge and Wadi Araba.

KING HUSSEIN BRIDGE (ALLENBY BRIDGE)

➡ Take a service taxi from Amman's Abdali or South bus station to King Hussein Bridge (JD8, 45 minutes) or there's a single daily JETT bus (JD8.500, one hour, 7am) straight through to the Israeli side of the border. A private taxi to the bridge costs around JD22. Public transport stops at the immigration terminal for locals; make sure you're dropped at the second terminal, for foreigners.

➡ The two border posts are 5km apart. Buses (JD7 plus JD1.500 per piece of lugggage, 10 minutes to one hour – depending on waiting time) shuttle between the two borders (expect long delays). It's not possible to walk, hitch or take a private vehicle across this border. Try to sit at the front of the bus so you can be near the front of the queue at Israeli immigration.

→ Jordanian immigration officials won't stamp your passport here – you're given an exit form instead. If you're coming back to Jordan, you can return at this crossing within 2 weeks without needing a new visa. Longer than this, you'll need to return via the Sheikh Hussein Bridge (or get a new visa at the Jordanian embassy in Tel Aviv). There's an exit fee of JD10.

→ At Israeli immigration, make sure you are given the immigration form with your photo on it – issued nowadays rather than a stamp in the passport.

→ Be prepared for slow progress at the border – plan for a couple of hours, and leave early to make the complete Amman–Jerusalem run in case of security delays. Sunday morning (ie, after the weekend) and around holidays are the busiest – and therefore slowest – times to cross. If you're in a rush, a VIP service at the terminal is available to rush you through both immigration and security on both sides. This typically costs around JD80.

→ To get to Jerusalem from the border, take a sherut (Israeli shared taxi; around 50NIS, 30 minutes) to Jerusalem's Damascus Gate.

→ Travelling in the other direction, there's an Israeli exit tax of 177NIS. If you intend to return to Israel, keep the Jordanian entrance form safe – you will have to present it on exiting the border.

→ The border is open 8am to 10pm Sunday to Thursday and 8am to 1.30pm Friday and Saturday. The border is closed for Yom Kippur and Eid al-Adha.

SHEIKH HUSSEIN BRIDGE (JORDAN BRIDGE)

→ Regular service taxis travel between the West bus station at Irbid and the border (JD1, 45 minutes). A taxi from Amman costs around JD40, or about JD20 from Irbid.

→ You can ask Jordanian immigration not to stamp your passport here.

→ From the bridge it's a 2km walk to the Israeli side. Buses across the bridge (JD1.5) run roughly every 30 minutes.

→ Taxis go to the Beit She'an bus station (10 minutes) for onward connections. To get to Tel Aviv, it's quickest to get from Beit She'an to Afula and change there.

→ Travelling in the other direction, take a bus to Tiberias and change at Beit She'an (6km from the border). From there, take another bus to the Israeli border (arrive early because there are few buses).

→ Israeli exit tax is 102NIS at this border. The transfer bus across the bridge to the Jordanian side costs 7NIS.

TRANSPORT LAND

ISRAELI BORDER-STAMP STIGMA

Given historic tensions between Arab countries and Israel, any evidence of a visit to Israel in your passport (such as an entry or exit stamp from a Jordanian border crossing) can potentially bar you from entering a number of countries in the region in the future, so if you're combining your stay in Jordan with a trip to Israel, there are a few things to bear mind.

→ When you enter or leave Israel, immigration officials issue you with a separate immigration form instead of stamping your passport. Keep this safe, as losing it can cause big problems.

→ If you're crossing into Israel from Jordan via the King Hussein Bridge, you can ask the Jordanian officials to stamp a piece of paper instead of your passport. Alternatively you can fly into and out of Ben-Gurion airport in Tel Aviv (there are direct flights from Amman).

→ Proof of having visited Israel isn't a problem for every Arab or Middle Eastern country. It's fine for Jordan, Egypt, Turkey, Tunisia and Morocco. Officially, Bahrain, Qatar, the UAE and Oman will refuse you entry if you have evidence of a visit to Israel in your passport, but in reality they don't always look for an offending stamp. Lebanon, Iran, Saudi Arabia, Libya, Yemen, Iraq and Syria will all automatically refuse you entry.

Border Bothers

If you're thinking of a day trip to Jerusalem from Amman, think again! Many readers complain of difficulties using the King Hussein Bridge border crossing, particularly on the Israeli side, reporting intrusive security, luggage X-rays, chaotic queues and rude officials. You'll be grilled about why you want to visit Israel – a hard question to answer if you've spent half the day at the border.

➡ The border crossing here is considerably faster than at the King Hussein Bridge. It's also more convenient if you're travelling in a small group and can share transport costs.

➡ The border is open 6.30am to 9pm Sunday to Thursday and 8am to 7pm Friday and Saturday. The border is closed for Yom Kippur and the Islamic New Year (but not for Eid al-Adha).

OVERLAND TRANSPORT IN A HURRY

It is possible to get from Petra to Jerusalem (and vice-versa) in a day, and also to a handful of other popular travel destinations across the Middle East. The following is a summary of routes. For information on visas, see p316.

Petra & Jerusalem via Amman & the West Bank

Taking this route means you may be able to avoid evidence of a visit to Israel in your passport (see box, p321). Beware of long delays at the border. Note that you can't take your own car through this crossing. From Petra, catch a bus to Amman's South bus station (three hours), a service taxi or bus to King Hussein Bridge (Allenby Bridge; one hour), a bus across the border (three-hour delay; border closed by noon Friday and Saturday) and a service taxi or bus to Jerusalem's Damascus Gate (30 minutes). This route also works in reverse, to get from Jerusalem to Petra.

Petra & Jerusalem via Aqaba & Eilat

You can travel with your own vehicle this way. If you're arriving in Jordan at Wadi Araba (Yitzhak Rabin), you'll be exempt from paying for a Jordanian visa as you'll be entering via the Aqaba free-trade zone. There are less border delays involved on this route.

From Petra, catch a bus to the main bus station at Aqaba (2½ hours), then a service taxi or bus to Wadi Araba (Yitzhak Rabin) border (15 minutes). Walk across the border (30 minutes; open every day), then take a service taxi or bus to Eilat (15 minutes) and a bus to Jerusalem's Damascus Gate (five hours). This route also works in reverse.

Petra & Sharm el-Sheikh via Aqaba & Nuweiba

Note that from Sharm el-Sheikh or Nuweiba to Wadi Rum or Petra requires an overnight stop in Aqaba. The security situation in South Sinai, where Nuweiba is located, is changeable; check travel advisories before attempting this route.

From Petra, catch a bus to the main bus station at Aqaba (2½ hours), then a service taxi or bus to the ferry terminal (30 minutes) and catch a boat at 2pm to Nuweiba (one hour). From here, take the bus to Sharm el-Sheikh (2½ hours).

The trip from Sharm el-Sheikh to Petra is not possible in a day by public transport as you will arrive in Aqaba too late. First up, catch a bus from Sharm el-Sheikh to Nuweiba ferry terminal (three hours), then catch the 3pm boat to the passenger terminal south of Aqaba (three hours) followed by a service taxi or bus to Aqaba (30 minutes). Catch a private taxi to Petra or stay overnight in Aqaba and catch a bus to Petra the following day (2½ hours).

Be aware that the Aqaba–Nuweiba ferry can be prone to long delays in both directions.

Petra & St Catherine's Mount via Aqaba

At the Wadi Araba crossing you can only get a visa for the Sinai Peninsula, so if you want to travel further than Sharm el-Sheikh, this trip needs some careful planning: full visas can be obtained in advance from the Egyptian consulate in Aqaba or the Egyptian embassy in Amman. Note that the security situation is changeable in Taba and St Catherine's Mount, part of South Sinai; check travel advisories before attempting this route.

From Petra, catch a bus to the main bus station in Aqaba (2½ hours), then a service taxi to Wadi Araba (Yitzhak Rabin) border (15 minutes) and walk across the border (30 minutes). Catch a service taxi or bus to Taba (15 minutes) and a service taxi to St Catherine's Mount (three hours). While the reverse trip is not possible in a day on public transport, you can avoid a night's stay in Aqaba by taking a private taxi.

WADI ARABA (YITZHAK RABIN)

➡ Taxis run between Aqaba and the border (JD10, 15 minutes). There's an exit fee of JD10.

➡ You can walk the short distance across the border in a matter of minutes.

➡ Buses run to central Eilat, 2km away (five minutes). Taxis cost around 50NIS.

➡ Travelling in the other direction, buses from Jerusalem to Eilat will stop at the turn-off for the border (five minutes), a short walk away.

➡ Israeli exit tax is 102NIS at this border.

➡ If you enter Jordan at this border, visas are free due to the Aqaba Economic Zone. You may travel freely in Jordan on this visa, but the visa lasts only two weeks.

➡ The border is open 6.30am to 8pm Sunday to Thursday and 8am to 10pm Friday and Saturday. The border is closed for Yom Kippur and the Islamic New Year.

SAUDI ARABIA

Getting a visa, even a transit visa, to Saudi Arabia is very difficult. If you are eligible for a visa, the main land route for public transport is at Al-Umari, south of Azraq. The other two crossing points are Ad-Durra, south of Aqaba, and further east at Al-Mudawwara. Several companies run services to and from Jeddah and Riyadh from Amman's Abdali bus station.

The air-conditioned **Jordan Express Tourist Transport** (☑06-5664141; www.jett.com.jo; Al-Malek al-Hussein St, Shmeisani, Amman) bus travels to Jeddah, Riyadh and Dammam.

Elsewhere in the Middle East

For other destinations in the Middle East, travellers need time, patience and, most importantly, the necessary visas. Most trips involve long, hot journeys with frustrating delays so most people end up flying.

JETT (☑06-5664141; www.jett.com.jo; Al-Malek al-Hussein St, Shmeisani, Amman) has a coach service to Cairo (JD32), four times per week departing from the international bus office in Amman. Check with the JETT office ahead of your departure as schedules and prices change frequently.

Sea

Visiting Egypt is both a popular side trip from Aqaba or feasible as part of your onward journey. As Jordan has no land borders with Egypt, the journey involves a short boat ride to either Nuweiba or Taba (check travel advisories before taking these routes). At most times of the year this is a matter of turning up and buying your ticket. During hajj (late August or September for the next few years; dates move with the Islamic calendar), however, when Aqaba is abuzz with thousands of excitable Egyptian pilgrims returning home from Mecca, you may find the journey becomes something more epic. Most nationalities can obtain Egyptian tourist visas on the boat or on arrival at Nuweiba (the Egyptian consulate in Aqaba also issues visas). Note that full visas are not issued in Taba, only the two-week Sinai Visitor Pass.

There are two main boat services to Egypt, which leave from the passenger terminal just south of Aqaba. Departure times are often subject to change so check with **Arab Bridge Maritime** (☑03-2092000; www.abmaritime.com.jo/en), which operates the services, before travelling.

The fast boat to Taba (US$95, 45 minutes) leaves daily at 6pm. Fares for children under eight are US$70. The return ferry leaves Taba at 6.30am.

There is also a slower car-ferry service (1st/economy/3rd class US$95/75/65, three hours) departing twice daily at 12pm and 2pm. It's notorious for being delayed (voyages can take up to 12 hours if the sea is rough) or even cancelled, although the night departure, which carries heavy commercial traffic, is regarded as being more consistent. Fares are reduced for children under eight (1st/economy/3rd class US$70/60/55). Services from Nuweiba leave at 6am and 3pm.

Departure tax (JD6) is not included in the ticket prices. You need to show your passport to buy tickets. Note that fares from Nuweiba must be paid for in US dollars, but there are currency-exchange facilities at the terminals at Aqaba and Nuweiba.

Passports are collected on the boat in both directions and handed back on arrival at immigration. Bear in mind, if you are travelling from Egypt you will arrive in Aqaba too late for public transport to Petra or Wadi Rum, so you'll have to stay in Aqaba or pick up a taxi from the city centre.

GETTING AROUND

Jordan is a relatively small country, making it possible to drive the 430km from the Syrian border in the north to the Saudi border in the south in just over five hours – but of course size isn't everything. Most of Jordan's attractions lie not along the main arteries (such as the Desert Highway) but along the spectacular switchbacked mountain roads of the north or the historical, ambling and rural King's Highway. As such, if you want to make the most of your trip to Jordan, you need to factor in more time for your journey than the distance on the map may indicate.

Public transport is designed primarily for the locals and as it is notoriously difficult to reach many of the sights of interest (especially the Dead Sea, desert castles and King's Highway) consider hiring a car or using tours organised by hotels in Amman and Madaba. Alternatively, hire a yellow private taxi; often the driver adds untold value to the trip by giving you local information and cultural insights.

Air

There is only one domestic air route, between Amman and Aqaba. You can buy tickets at any travel agency or Royal Jordanian office.

Royal Jordanian (⏱06-5100000; www.rj.com) Flights twice daily between Amman and Aqaba (one way around JD40, one hour).

Royal Wings (www.royal-wings.com.jo) A subsidiary of Royal Jordanian, offering expensive charter flights.

Bicycle

Cycling can be fun or sheer folly depending on the time of year. From March to May and September to November are the best times to get on your bike – you won't have to battle with the stifling summer heat or the bitter winter winds. Spare parts aren't always common in Jordan, so carry a spare tyre, extra chain links, spokes, two inner tubes, repair kit and tool kit with spanner set. Also bring a low-gear set for the hills and a couple of water containers; confine your panniers to a maximum of 15kg. If you don't want to bring your bike, the cycling outfit **Bike Rush** (Map p52; ⏱079 9454586; www.facebook.com/bikerush; ⏰noon-9pm Sat-Thu) offers bike hire from its Amman shop (it will deliver to your address too), as well as

weekly vehicle-supported bike trips around the country.

Bus

Local Bus

The two largest cities, Amman and Irbid, have efficient, cheap public bus networks. There are often no timetables available at chaotic local bus stations. Locals are always willing to help though.

Minibus

Public minibuses are the most common form of public transport. They normally only leave when full, so waiting times of an hour or more are inevitable, especially in rural areas. Tickets are normally bought on the bus. Standing is not usually allowed and some seat shuffling often takes place to ensure that unaccompanied foreign men or women do not sit next to members of the opposite sex. Locals signify that they want to get off by rapping a coin on a side window.

Tourist Bus

The larger air-con buses offer a speedy and reliable service, departing according to a fixed schedule. They don't stop en route to pick up passengers. Tickets should ideally be bought a day in advance.

JETT (⏱06-5664141; www.jett.com.jo; Al-Malek al-Hussein St, Shmeisani, Amman) The national bus company JETT operates the most comfortable bus service from Amman to Aqaba. It also has services to King Hussein Bridge border crossing, Petra and Hammamat Ma'in.

Trust International Transport (⏱06-5813427) Has daily buses to Aqaba from Amman (JD7, four hours, four daily) between 7.30am and 7pm. All buses leave from the office conveniently located at 7th Circle, near the Safeway shopping centre. Trust also has a booking office at Abdali bus station. Other services, such as to Irbid, are sometimes on offer.

Check with the office for current timings. To reach the departure office, a taxi from downtown costs JD2.500 to JD3.

Hijazi (⏱02-7240721, 06-638110) To Irbid.

Car & Motorcycle

Jordan is an easy country to drive in (with the exception of Amman) and there are some spectacular routes linking the high ground with the Jordan Valley below sea level. Indeed, there aren't many countries where you can claim to be driving uphill to the sea, but if you're on the Dead Sea Highway heading for the Red Sea, Jordan is one of them!

Strictly speaking you don't need an International Driving Permit (IDP) to drive in Jordan unless you plan on crossing any borders, but it may help if you meet with an accident.

Bringing Your Own Vehicle

If you are travelling with your own vehicle, refer to the following checklist of items to bring with you (contact your local automobile association for details):

➡ The vehicle's registration papers and liability insurance

➡ *Carnet de passage en douane* (passport for the vehicle that acts as a temporary waiver of import duty)

➡ Specifications of any expensive spare parts, such as a gearbox, on board (designed to prevent car-import rackets)

➡ Spare parts and some mechanical knowledge for motorcycles

Royal Automobile Club of Jordan (⏱06-5850626, for carnets 4622467; www.racj.com) Can arrange a *carnet*.

Checkpoints

There are many checkpoints in Jordan, particularly when driving along the Dead Sea

Highway near the sensitive border with Israel and the Palestinian Territories, or on the roads that climb out of the Jordan Valley. Always stop at checkpoints. Foreigners are generally waved through without any fuss, though you may have to show your passport. As such, always keep your passport, driving licence, hire agreement or proof of ownership and registration papers handy.

Fuel & Spare Parts

Petrol stations can mostly be found on the outskirts of major towns and at some junctions. Along the Desert Highway (the only fully dual carriageway) there are plenty of stations. There are fewer along the King's Highway and *very* few along the Dead Sea Highway. Unleaded petrol (*khal min ar-rasas*) is only reliably available in Amman and even then at only a few petrol stations.

Garages with mechanics can be found in the outskirts of most towns. They can handle most repairs. Check with your car-hire company first.

4WDs

Four-wheel drives are only necessary if you're going to remote parts of the desert, such as Burqu. You are highly advised to have prior experience of off-road driving before attempting soft sand: getting stuck in 45°C heat, for example, is a recipe for disaster if you don't know what you're doing.

Four-wheel-drive vehicles can be hired from reputable agencies in Aqaba and Amman; they are far more expensive than normal sedans, costing at least JD150 per day.

Hire

Hiring a car is a great way of getting the most out of Jordan, especially if travelling the King's Highway or Dead Sea area.

There are many car-hire agencies in Amman (King

WHAT TO DO IN AN ACCIDENT

⇒ Don't move the vehicle.

⇒ Find a policeman from the local station to attend the scene immediately.

⇒ Get a police report (essential for insurance – Arabic is OK) and contact the car-hire company.

⇒ If there's a serious injury, call ☑911 for emergency services; you'll be answered by English-speaking staff.

⇒ Contact your travel insurance company at home and your embassy/consulate in Amman.

⇒ If your own car is involved, your driving licence and passport will be held by the police until the case is reviewed in a local court – which may take weeks.

⇒ Beware: drivers are always considered guilty if they hit a pedestrian, regardless of the circumstances.

Abdullah Gardens in Shmeisani is lined with international and local hire offices), a few in Aqaba and one or two irregularly staffed offices at Queen Alia International Airport and the King Hussein border with Israel and the Palestinian Territories. Most car-hire agencies outside these areas usually consist of an office with one guy, one desk, one telephone and one car for hire (usually his!). The best deals are in Amman, where competition among agencies is fierce.

Daily rates run at around JD40. This usually includes unlimited mileage, although many agencies specify a minimum hire of 48 hours. You can normally drop off the rental car in another city (such as Aqaba) for an extra fee. All companies require a deposit of up to JD400 payable upon pick-up (usually by credit card) and refunded upon return of the car.

Road maps are not provided by car-hire agencies, but child-restraining seats are generally available for an extra fee.

Most agencies only hire to drivers over 21 years old; some stipulate that drivers must be at least 26 years. It's not possible to drive a hire car from Jordan into neighbouring countries.

Avis (Map p59; ☑06-5699420, 24hr 777-397405; www.avis.com.jo; King Abdullah Gardens, Amman) Offices at King Hussein Bridge and Aqaba; branches at the airport, Le Royal Hotel and Jordan InterContinental Hotel in Amman. The biggest car-hire company in Jordan.

Budget (Map p59; ☑06-5698131; www.budget.com; 125 Abdul Hameed Sharaf St, Amman)

Europcar (Map p59; ☑06-5655581; www.europcar. middleeast.com; Isam Al-Ajlouni St, Amman) Branches at Radisson SAS, King Abdullah Gardens and in Aqaba.

Hertz (Map p59; ☑06-5920926; www.hertz.com; King Abdullah Gardens, Amman) Offices at the airport, Grand Hyatt Amman, Sheraton and in Aqaba.

Insurance

Most car-hire rates come with basic insurance that involves a deductible of up to JD400 (ie, in case of an accident you pay a maximum of JD400). Most agencies offer additional Collision Damage Waiver (CDW) insurance for an extra JD7 to JD10 per day, which will absolve you of all accident costs (in some cases a maximum of JD100 excess).

Insurance offered by major companies often includes Personal Accident Insurance and Theft Protection, which may be covered by your travel insurance policy from home. Read the conditions of the contract carefully before signing – an English translation should always be provided.

If you're driving into Jordan in a private vehicle, compulsory third-party insurance must be purchased at the border for about JD35 (valid for one month). You also pay a nominal customs fee of JD5 for 'foreign car registration' (obtainable at the borders with Jordan and the ferry terminal in Nuweiba, Egypt).

Road Safety

The condition of roads varies; unsigned speed humps are common, usually at the entrance to a town but also across main highways. It's important to note that the term 'highway' doesn't mean dual carriageway in Jordan – simply a main thoroughfare.

Despite the small population, and relatively well-maintained roads, accidents are alarmingly frequent.

If you're driving around Jordan, read the following carefully:

➡ Signposting is erratic – generally enough to get you on your way but not enough to get you all the way to the destination.

➡ Most road signs are in English, but they are sometimes badly transliterated (eg 'Om Qeis' for Umm Qais).

➡ Brown signs denote tourist attractions, blue signs are for road names and green signs are for anything Islamic, such as a mosque.

➡ Take care when it's raining: water and sand (and sometimes oil) make a lethal combination on the roads.

➡ The Jordanian road system makes more use of U-turns than flyovers.

➡ Beware herds of goats and camels crossing all roads, including highways.

➡ Petrol stations are not that common, so fill up when you see one.

➡ Straddling of two lanes and overtaking using the slow lane are common practices.

Road Rules

Visitors from any country where road rules are rigorously obeyed may be shocked by the traffic in Jordan, especially in Amman. Indicators are seldom used, the ubiquitous horn is preferred over slowing down and pedestrians must take their chances. But anyone who has driven elsewhere in the Middle East may find the traffic comparatively well behaved. Provided that you minimise driving in Amman and take reasonable care, you're unlikely to encounter too many difficulties.

Vehicles drive on the right-hand side of the road in Jordan. The general speed limit inside built-up areas is 50km/h or 70km/h on multilane highways in Amman, and 90km/h to 110km/h on the national highways.

Wearing a seatbelt is now compulsory, though many Jordanians are reluctant to use them. Traffic police are positioned at intervals along the highways.

Hitching

Getting a Ride

Hitching is never entirely safe in any country in the world, and we don't recommend it. Travellers who choose to hitch should understand that they are taking a small but potentially serious risk. That said, hitching is sometimes used as a means of transport in Jordan in areas where public transport is limited or nonexistent, such as parts of the King's Highway and to the desert castles east of Amman. Police stationed at major junctions and checkpoints are often happy to wave down drivers and cajole them into giving you a lift – or even give you a ride themselves.

If you do decide to try hitching, some tips to bear in mind:

➡ Avoid 1pm to 4pm when traffic is reduced.

➡ To flag down a car, raise your index finger in the direction you're heading.

➡ Be prepared to pay, and ask up front how much the driver wants.

➡ If no sum is requested, offer a token amount when you get out – it will often be refused.

➡ Carry a hat and lots of water.

➡ Don't look scruffy or hitch in groups of more than two.

➡ Women shouldn't hitch alone.

➡ Avoid riding in trucks on steep and windy roads (such as between the Wadi Rum turn-off and Aqaba) as they can be painfully slow.

Picking up Hitchers

On remote routes like the Wadi Mujib stretch of the King's Highway, where public transport is limited or even nonexistent, it's common for Jordanians to pick up hitchers. If you're driving and choose to do the same, take the same safety precautions you would anywhere else, and never charge for the lift.

Taxis

Private Taxis

Yellow private taxis work like ordinary taxis and can be chartered for the day. In Amman most drivers use the meter – note that fares are displayed in fils not dinars. Outside Amman negotiate a reasonable fare before you set off. Taking a private taxi in Jordan is generally safe for women but those travelling alone may prefer the anonymity of sitting in the back seat.

Service Taxis

White service taxis (*servees*) run along set routes within and between many towns, as well as between Jordan and neighbouring countries. They are shared by more than one passenger and usually have writing and numbers (in Arabic) indicating their route. They usually only leave when full. They cost up to twice as much as a minibus and about 50% more than a local bus, but are quicker because they stop less often along the way to pick up passengers. To avoid waiting for passengers, or to give yourself extra room, you can always pay for an extra seat. In contrast to private taxis, female travellers are likely to be ushered into the front seat if the back seats are occupied by men: this is an accepted practice for local women as well as visitors.

Tours

An alternative to a group tour organised from abroad is to arrange your own private mini-tour with a Jordanian travel agency. Many of these can arrange hiking or archaeological itineraries and provide a car and driver.

For hiking and activities in Jordan's nature reserves contact the tourism department of the **Royal Society for the Conservation of Nature** (RSCN; ☎06-4616523; www. rscn.org.jo), which can arrange short activity breaks or entire itineraries. For an extended trip to Wadi Rum it's best to contact a local Bedouin agency such as **Wadi Rum Mountain Guides** (www. bedouinroads.com).

If you're travelling independently, and on a tight budget, jumping on a budget-priced organised tour from Amman to a remote place like the desert castles of eastern Jordan is far easier, and often cheaper, than doing it yourself.

Atlas Travel & Tourist Agency (☎06-4642034; www.atlastours.net) Also offers side trips to Israel and the Palestinian Territories and Lebanon.

Desert Guides Company (☎06-5527230; www.desert-guidescompany.com) Trekking, mountain-bike and adventure trips.

Engaging Cultures Travel (http://engagingcultures.com) Highly regarded small group and tailor-made tours from Amman, with strong emphasis on culturally immersive experiences.

Golden Crown Tours (☎06-5511200; www.golden-crowntours.com) Offers archaeological, religious and adventure tours.

Jordan Beauty Tours (☎079-5581644; www.jordan-beauty.com; Petra) Local tour operator offering archaeological and Biblical tours, as well as hiking, camel trips, diving and cross-border tours to Israel.

La Beduina (Map p180; ☎06-5541631; www.labeduinatours.com) Specialist tours including hiking, cooking, horse- and camel-riding, and yoga tours.

Petra Moon Tourism Services (Map p180; ☎079 6170666; www.petramoon.com) Petra Moon is the most professional agency in Wadi Musa for arranging trips inside Petra and around Jordan (including Wadi Rum and Aqaba). The office is on the main road to Petra. It can arrange horses to Jebel Haroun, fully supported treks to Dana (four to five days), hikes from Tayyibeh to Petra and camel treks to Wadi Rum.

This agency runs a popular 14-day tour around Jordan for 10 to 18 people.

Tropical Desert Trips (☎07-95438708; http:// tropicaldeserttrips.com) Active tours, including hiking, climbing, canyoning and desert exploration.

Zaman Tours & Travel (Map p180; ☎2157723; www. zamantours.com; Wadi Musa) Adventure tours, camping, camel treks and hiking.

Health

Prevention and common sense is the key to staying healthy when travelling in Jordan. Infectious diseases occur in Jordan, but these can be avoided with a few simple precautions. If you need vaccinations, remember to visit the doctor around eight weeks before travelling as some require multiple injections; this will also give time to ensure immunity on arrival as some vaccinations take time to come into effect. The most common reason for travellers needing medical help is as a result of traffic accidents, which can be easily avoided if you remember to look the right way when crossing the road, wear a seatbelt even though no one else in Jordan seems to bother and stick to the speed limit on Jordan's less than perfect roads. Medical facilities are generally very good, particularly in Amman where there are some excellent modern hospitals. In case of an emergency, contact your embassy or consulate where you will at least receive sound local advice. Don't forget to take out health insurance before you leave!

BEFORE YOU GO

Insurance

You are strongly advised to have insurance before travelling to Jordan. Check that it covers you for the following:

➡ direct payments to health providers (or reimbursement later) for expenditure while in Jordan

➡ assistance in locating the nearest source of medical help

➡ emergency dental treatment

➡ repatriation home or aeromedical transport to better medical facilities elsewhere

Packing Checklist

Items you should consider packing:

➡ acetaminophen/ paracetamol (Tylenol) or aspirin

➡ antibacterial ointment (eg Bactroban) for cuts and abrasions

➡ antidiarrhoeal drugs (eg loperamide)

➡ antihistamines (for hay fever and allergic reactions)

➡ insect repellent containing DEET (for the body)

➡ insect spray containing Permethrin (for clothing, tents and bed nets)

➡ iodine tablets or other water-purification tablets

➡ oral rehydration salts

➡ sunblock

Vaccinations

Note that some vaccinations should not be given during pregnancy, to people with allergies and to very young children – discuss this with your doctor.

Required & Recommended Vaccinations

The following vaccinations are recommended for most travellers to Jordan:

➡ diphtheria & tetanus – single booster recommended if you've not had one in the previous 10 years

➡ hepatitis A – a single dose at least two to four weeks before departure gives protection for up to a year; a booster 12 months later gives another 10 years or more of protection

➡ hepatitis B – now considered routine for most travellers

➡ measles, mumps and rubella – two doses of MMR recommended unless you have previously had the diseases; young adults may require a booster

➡ polio – generally given in childhood and should be boosted every 10 years

➡ typhoid – recommended if you're travelling for more than a couple of weeks

→ yellow fever – vaccination is required for entry into Jordan for all travellers over one year of age if coming from infected areas such as sub-Saharan Africa and parts of South America

Travelling with Medication

Bring medications in their original clearly labelled containers. A signed and dated letter from your physician describing your medical conditions and medications, including generic names, is also a good idea. If carrying syringes or needles, be sure to have a physician's letter documenting their medical necessity and keep these handy when entering or exiting any of Jordan's borders.

Websites

It's a good idea to consult your government's travel health website before departure.

Australia (www.dfat.gov.au/travel)

Canada (www.travelhealth.gc.ca)

UK (www.doh.gov.uk)

US (www.cdc.gov/travel)

In addition to government health websites, the following provide useful health information:

Centre for Disease Control (www.cdc.gov) Overview of the health issues facing travellers to Jordan and neighbouring countries.

Lonely Planet (www.lonelyplanet.com) General advice.

MD Travel Health (www.mdtravelhealth.com) Complete travel-health recommendations for every country, updated daily, also at no cost.

World Health Organization (www.who.int/ith) Publishes a free, online book, *International Travel and Health*, revised annually.

Further Reading

Healthy Travel – Asia & India (Lonely Planet) Packed with useful information including pre-trip planning, emergency first aid, immunisation and disease

information and what to do if you get sick on the road.

International Travel Health Guide (Stuart R Rose, MD)

The Travellers' Good Health Guide (Ted Lankester) An especially useful health guide for volunteers and long-term expatriates working in the Middle East.

Traveller's Health (Dr Richard Dawood)

Travel with Children (Lonely Planet) Includes advice on travel health for younger children.

IN JORDAN

Availability & Cost of Health Care

Health-care provision is of a high standard in Jordan and any emergency treatment not requiring hospitalisation is free. The availability of health care can be summarised as follows:

→ Modern, well-equipped public and private hospitals in Amman, Irbid, Aqaba and Karak

TRAVEL PROBLEMS & PREVENTION

PROBLEM	SYMPTOMS	PREVENTION/TREATMENT
Deep Vein Thrombosis (DVT) – formation of blood clots in the legs during long plane flights; some may break off and travel through the blood vessels to the lungs, where they may cause life-threatening complications	Swelling or pain of the foot, ankle or calf, usually but not always on just one side; chest pain and difficulty in breathing – immediately seek medical attention.	Walk about the cabin. Perform isometric compressions of the leg muscles (ie contract the leg muscles while sitting). Drink plenty of fluids. Avoid alcohol and tobacco.
Jet Lag – common when crossing more than five time zones	Insomnia, fatigue, malaise, nausea	Drink plenty of fluids (non-alcoholic). Eat light meals. Upon arrival, seek exposure to natural sunlight and readjust your schedule (for meals, sleep etc) as soon as possible.
Motion Sickness	Nausea	Antihistamines such as dimenhydrinate (Dramamine) and meclizine (Antivert, Bonine). A herbal alternative is ginger.

➡ Good regional hospitals in Madaba, Ramtha and Zarqa

➡ Basic health centres (all towns)

➡ Fairly modern and well-equipped dental surgeries in cities

➡ Well-stocked pharmacies (most towns) dispensing advice as well as medicines

➡ All doctors (and most pharmacists) speak English; many have studied abroad

➡ Telephone numbers for pharmacies and hospitals in all cities are listed in the English-language newspapers

➡ Ambulance number in Jordan: ☎911

Food & Water

Water

Tap water in Jordan is generally safe to drink, but for a short trip it's better to stick to bottled water. This is readily available but check the seal has not been broken. Alternatively, you can boil tap water for 10 minutes, use water purification tablets or a filter.

The tap water in southern Jordan, particularly Wadi Rum, comes from natural springs at Diseh and so is extremely pure. Avoid drinking water from wadis in the wild as pools may have been used as waterholes for livestock. In the Jordan Valley, amoebic dysentery can be a problem.

If you get stuck in the desert without water, remember that you are more likely to be seriously ill (and even die) from dehydration than you are from an upset stomach, however unpleasant it may be. In summary, if water is offered and you need it, worry about its provenance later!

Avoiding Diarrhoea

The risk of becoming sick from unhygienic food preparation in Jordan is slim, especially if you follow this advice:

➡ Avoid tap water unless it has been boiled, filtered or chemically disinfected (iodine tablets).

➡ Beware of ice cream that may have melted and then been refrozen (eg a power cut in the last day or two).

➡ Be careful of shellfish such as mussels, oysters and clams, particularly outside of Aqaba, as well as the raw-meat dishes available in Lebanese restaurants.

➡ Eat meals only at busy restaurants and be cautious of buffets that may have been standing for more than a day.

Infectious Diseases

Diphtheria & Tetanus

Diphtheria is spread through close respiratory contact. It causes a high temperature and severe sore throat. Sometimes a membrane forms across the throat requiring a tracheostomy to prevent suffocation. Vaccination is recommended for those likely to be in close contact with the local population in infected areas. The vaccine is given as an injection alone, or with tetanus (you may well have had this combined injection as a child), and lasts 10 years.

Hepatitis A

Hepatitis A is spread through contaminated food (particularly shellfish) and water. It causes jaundice and, although it is rarely fatal, can cause prolonged lethargy and delayed recovery. Symptoms include dark urine, a yellow colour to the whites of the eyes, fever and abdominal pain. Hepatitis A vaccine (Avaxim, VAQTA, Havrix) is given as an injection; hepatitis A and typhoid vaccines can also be given as a single-dose vaccine, hepatyrix or viatim.

Hepatitis B

Infected blood, contaminated needles and sexual intercourse can all transmit hepatitis B. It can cause jaundice and affects the liver, occasionally causing liver failure. All travellers should make this a routine vaccination. Many countries now give hepatitis B vaccination as part of routine childhood vaccination. The vaccine is given singly, or at the same time as the hepatitis A vaccine (hepatyrix). A course will give protection for at least five years. It can be given over four weeks, or six months.

HIV

This is spread via infected blood and blood products, sexual intercourse with an infected partner and from an infected mother to her newborn child. It can be spread through 'blood to blood' contacts such as contaminated instruments during medical and dental procedures, acupuncture, body-piercing and sharing used intravenous needles.

Reliable figures aren't available about the number of people in Jordan with HIV or AIDS (even the lead United Nations agency, UNAIDS, lacks data) but given the strict taboos in Jordanian society about drugs, homosexuality and promiscuity, the disease is relatively rare. Contracting HIV through a blood transfusion is about as unlikely as in most Western countries, and anyone needing serious surgery will probably be sent home anyway.

You may need to supply a negative HIV test in order to get a second visa extension for a stay of longer than three months.

Polio

Generally spread through either contaminated food or water, polio is one of the vaccines given in childhood and should be boosted every 10 years, either orally (a drop

ENVIRONMENTAL HAZARDS

PROBLEM	SYMPTOMS	TREATMENT	PREVENTION
Diarrhoea – occurs usually after eating unhygienically prepared food	Onset of loose stools	Take oral-rehydration solution containing salt and sugar; sip weak black tea with sugar; drink soft drinks allowed to go flat and diluted 50% with clean water.	Drink plenty of fluids; eat in busy restaurants; wash your hands regularly.
	More than four or five loose stools	Antibiotic (usually a quinolone drug); antidiarrhoeal agent (such as loperamide).	As above
	Bloody diarrhoea persistent for more than 72 hours; accompanied by fever, shaking chills or severe abdominal pain	Seek medical attention; in an emergency you can make up a solution of six teaspoons of sugar and half a teaspoon of salt to 1L of boiled or bottled water.	As above
Heat exhaustion – occurs following heavy sweating and excessive fluid loss with inadequate replacement of fluids and salt	Headache, dizziness and tiredness; dehydration; dark yellow urine	Replace fluids with water or fruit juice or both; cool with cold water and fans; take salty fluids through soup or broth; add a little more table salt to foods than usual.	Get fit before planning a long hike; acclimatise to the heat before exercise; wear a hat and cover your neck in the sun; avoid the midday sun in summer; wear sunscreen.
Heat stroke – occurs when the body's heat-regulating mechanism breaks down	Excessive rise in body temperature; cessation of sweating; irrational and hyperactive behaviour; eventually loss of consciousness and death	Give rapid cooling by spraying the body with water and fanning; seek emergency fluid and electrolyte replacement by intravenous drip.	As above
Mosquito bite – can spread dengue fever but not malaria	Irritation; infection	Don't scratch the bites; apply antiseptic.	Use DEET-based insect repellents; sleep under mosquito netting.
Bed bugs	Very itchy, lumpy bites	Apply lotion from pharmacy.	Spray mattress or move hotel!
Scabies	Itchy rash, often between fingers	Apply lotion from pharmacy; treat those you are in contact with.	As above
Snake bite	Pain; swelling	Seek medical attention; see p332.	Wear boots, socks and long trousers when hiking; avoid holes and crevices; careful handling wood piles.
Scorpion bite	Intense pain	Seek medical attention.	Check your shoes in the morning, particularly if you are camping near Little Petra.

IF BITTEN BY A SNAKE...

➡ Don't panic: half of those bitten by venomous snakes are not actually injected with poison (envenomed).

➡ Immobilise the bitten limb with a splint (eg a stick).

➡ Apply a bandage over the site, with firm pressure, similar to bandaging a sprain.

➡ Do not apply a tourniquet, or cut or suck the bite.

➡ Get the victim to medical help as soon as possible so that antivenin can be given if necessary.

on the tongue), or as an injection. Polio may be carried asymptomatically, although it can cause a transient fever and, in rare cases, potentially permanent muscle weakness or paralysis. Polio is not currently present in Jordan but is prevalent in neighbouring countries.

Rabies

Spread through bites or licks on broken skin from an infected animal, rabies is fatal. Animal handlers should be vaccinated, as should those travelling to remote areas where a reliable source of post-bite vaccine is not available within 24 hours. Three injections are needed over a month. If you've come into physical contact with an infected animal and haven't been vaccinated you'll need a course of five injections starting within 24 hours or as soon as possible after the injury. Vaccination does not provide you with immunity, it merely buys you more time to seek appropriate medical help.

Tuberculosis

Tuberculosis (TB) is spread through close respiratory contact and occasionally through infected milk or milk products. BCG vaccine is recommended for those likely to be mixing closely with the local population. It is more important for those visiting family or planning on a long stay, and those employed as teachers and health-care workers. TB can be asymptomatic, although symptoms can include cough, weight loss or fever, months or even years after exposure. An X-ray is the best way to confirm if you have TB. BCG gives a moderate degree of protection against TB. It causes a small permanent scar at the site of injection, and is usually only given in specialised chest clinics. As it's a live vaccine it should not be given to pregnant women or immunocompromised individuals. The BCG vaccine is not available in all countries.

Typhoid

This is spread through food or water that has been contaminated by infected human faeces. The first symptom is usually fever or a pink rash on the abdomen. Septicaemia (blood poisoning) may also occur. Typhoid vaccine (typhim Vi, typherix) will give protection for three years. In some countries, the oral vaccine Vivotif is also available.

Yellow Fever

Yellow-fever vaccination is not required for Jordan, but you *do* need a yellow-fever certificate, from a designated clinic, if arriving from an infected area, or if you've been in an infected area in the two weeks prior to arrival in Jordan.

Environmental Hazards

Jordan is not a dangerous place to visit but it does have a few hazards unique to desert environments (see the table on p331 for more information). Some visitors get themselves into trouble hiking through the desert in the heat of the day, especially around Wadi Rum. While heat-related problems are the most common, don't forget that the desert can be bitterly cold in winter: there is a real risk of hypothermia if camping between December and February without adequate bedding.

Language

Arabic is the official language of Jordan. Note that there are significant differences between MSA (Modern Standard Arabic) – the official lingua franca of the Arab world, used in schools, administration and the media – and the colloquial language, ie the everyday spoken version. The Arabic variety spoken in Jordan (and provided in this chapter) is known as Levantine Arabic.

Read our coloured pronunciation guides as if they were English and you'll be understood. Note that a is pronounced as in 'act', aa as the 'a' in 'father', ae as the 'ai' in 'air', aw as in 'law', ay as in 'say', e as in 'bet', ee as in 'see', i as in 'hit', oo as in 'zoo', u as in 'put', gh is a guttural sound (like the French 'r'), r is rolled, dh is pronounced as the 'th' in 'that', th as in 'thin' and kh as the 'ch' in the Scottish *loch*. The apostrophe (') indicates the glottal stop (like the pause in the middle of 'uh-oh'). The stressed syllables are indicated with italics.

BASICS

Hello.	مرحبا.	mer·*ha*·ba
Goodbye.	خاطرك.	*khae*·trak (m)
	خاطرك.	*khae*·trik (f)
Yes.	ايه.	'eeh
No.	لا.	laa
Please.	اذا بتريد.	'i·za bit·*reed* (m)
	اذا بتريدي.	'i·za bit·ree·dee (f)
Thank you.	شكراً.	*shuk*·ran
Excuse me.	عفواً.	'af·wan
Sorry.	آسف./آسفة.	'aa·sif/'aas·fe (m/f)

How are you?
كيفك؟/كيفِك؟ kay·fak/kay·fik (m/f)

Fine, thanks. And you?
منيح./منيحة. mneeh/mnee·ha (m/f)
وأنتَ/أنتِ؟ oo 'ent/'en·tee (m/f)

What's your name?
شو اسمَك؟ shoo 'es·mak (m)
شو اسمِك؟ shoo 'es·mik (f)

My name is ...
اسمي ... 'es·mee ...

Do you speak English?
بتحكي انجليزي؟ btah·kee 'inj·lee·zee

I don't understand.
ما فهمت. maa fa·he·met

Can I take a photo?
بتسمحني اخذ btsa·*mah*·nee 'aa·khud
صورة؟ soo·re

ACCOMMODATION

Where's a ...?	وين ...؟	wayn ...
campsite	مخيّم	mu·*khay*·yam
guesthouse	بيت الضيوف	bayt id·du·*yoof*
hotel	فندق	*fun*·duk
youth hostel	فندق شباب	*fun*·du·sha·*baeb*

Do you have a ... room?	في عندكن غرفة ...؟	fee 'ind·kun ghur·fe ...
single	بتخت منفرد	bi·*takht* mun·fa·rid
double	بتخت مزدوّج	bi·*takht* muz·*daw*·wej
twin	بتختين	bi·takh·*tayn*
How much is it per ...?	قديش لـ...؟	kad·*deesh* li·...
night	ليلة	*lay*·le
person	شخص	shakhs

Can I get another (blanket)?
اعطني/اعطيني 'a'·ti·nee/'a'·tee·nee
(بطانية) تاني (ba·taa·nee·ye) tae·nee (m/f)

The (air conditioning) doesn't work.
(المكيف) مانه (il·mu·*kay*·yef) mae·nu
شغال. sha·*ghael*

LANGUAGE DIRECTIONS

SIGNS

Entrance	مدخل	
Exit	مخرج	
Open	مفتوح	
Closed	مغلق	
Information	معلومات	
Prohibited	ممنوع	
Toilets	دورات المياه	
Men	الرجال	
Women	النساء	

DIRECTIONS

Where's the ...? وين الـ...؟ wayn il·...

bank	بنك	bank
market	سوق	sook
post office	مكتب البريد	mak·tab il·ba·reed

Can you show me (on the map)?
بتورجني (عالخريطة)؟ btwar·ji·nee ('al·kha·ree·te)

What's the address?
شو العنوان؟ shoo il·'un·waen

Could you please write it down?
اذا بتريد/بتريدي 'i·za bit·reed/bit·ree·dee
اكتبه/اكتبيه؟ 'ik·tu·bu/'ik·tu·beeh (m/f)

How far is it?
قديش هو بعيد kad·deesh hu·wa ba·'eed
من هون؟ min hoon

How do I get there?
كيف بوصل لهناك؟ kayf boo·sal la·hu·naek

It's ... هو/هي ... hu·we/hi·ye ... (m/f)

behind ...	خلف ...	khalf ...
in front of ...	قدام ...	kad·daem ...
near to ...	قريب من ...	ka·reeb min ...
next to ...	جنب ...	jinb ...
on the corner	عند الزاوية	'ind az·zae·wi·ye
opposite ...	مواجه ...	mu·wae·jeh ...
straight ahead	للقدام	lil·kad·daem

Turn left/right.
اتجه 'it·ta·jih
ليسار/لشمال. li·ya·saer/li·shi·mael (m)
اتجهي 'it·taj·hee
ليسار/لشمال. li·ya·saer/li·shi·mael (f)

EATING & DRINKING

Can you recommend a ...?
بتوصي btoo·see
بـ...؟ bi·...

bar	بار	baar

cafe	مقهى	mak·ha
restaurant	مطعم	mat·'em

I'd like a/the ..., please.
بدي ...، bid·dee ...
لو سمحت. law sa·maht

nonsmoking section	قسم غير المدخنين	kism ghayr il·mu·dakh·khi·neen
table for (four)	طاولة لـ(أربع اشخاص)	tae·wi·le li·('ar·ba·'at 'esh·khaes)

What would you recommend?
بشو بتوصي؟ bi·shoo btoo·see

What's the local speciality?
شو الوجبة الخاصة؟ shoo il·waj·be il·khae·se

Do you have vegetarian food?
في عندكن fee 'ind·kun
طعام نباتي؟ ta·'aem na·bae·tee

I'd like (the) ..., please.
بدي ...، bid·dee ...
لو سمحت. law sa·maht

bill	الحساب	il·hi·saeb
drink list	قائمة المشروبات	kae·'i·met il·mash·roo·baet
menu	قائمة الطعام	kae·'i·met it·ta·'aem
that dish	ذالك الوجبة	zae·lik il·waj·be

Could you prepare a meal without ...?
بتقدروا btak·de·roo
تحضروا وجبة tu·had·de·roo waj·be
بدون ...؟ bi·doon ...

butter	زبدة	zeb·de
eggs	بيض	bayd
meat stock	مرق لحم	mirk lahm

I'm allergic to ...
أنا عندي 'a·na 'in·dee
حساسية ha·sae·see·ye
من ... min ...

dairy produce	الألبان	il·'al·baen
gluten	الغلوتين	il·ghloo·teen
nuts	المكسرات	il·mu·kas·si·raet
seafood	الطعام البحري	it·ta·'aem bah·ree

Drinks

beer	بيرا	bee·ra
coffee	قهوى	kah·way
orange juice	عصير برتقال	'a·seer bur·te·kael
mineral water	مياه معدنية	mee·yaah ma'·da·nee·ye
red wine	نبيذ احمر	nbeez 'ah·mer
tea	شاي	shaay
white wine	نبيذ ابيض	nbeez 'ib·yad

EMERGENCIES

Help! ساعد! sae·'id (m)
ساعدي! sae·'i·dee (f)

Go away! روح!/روحي! rooh/roo·hee (m/f)

Call ...! اتصل بـ...! 'it·ta·sil bi·...
 a doctor دكتور duk·toor
 the police الشرطة ish·shur·ta

I'm lost.
أنا ضائع. 'a·na dae·'i (m)
أنا ضائعة. 'a·na dae·'i·e (f)

Where are the toilets?
وين الحمامات؟ wayn il·ham·mae·maet

I'm sick.
أنا مريض. 'a·na ma·reed (m)
أنا مريضة. 'a·na ma·ree·de (f)

I'm allergic to (antibiotics).
أنا حساسي/ 'a·na ha·sae·see/
حساسية من ha·sae·see·ye min
(مضاد حيوي). (mu·daed ha·ya·wee) (m/f)

SHOPPING & SERVICES

Where's a ...? وين ...؟ wayn ...
 department store محل المنوعات ma·hal il·mu·naw·wa·'aet
 grocery store بقالة ba·kae·le
 newsagency وكالة الأنباء wi·kae·let il·'en·baa'
 souvenir shop محل التذكارات ma·hal it·tiz·kae·raet
 supermarket سبر مركت su·ber·markt

I'm looking for ...
بدور عن ... bi·daw·wer 'an ...

Can I look at it?
ورجني ياه؟ war·ji·nee yaah (m)
ورجيني ياه؟ war·jee·nee yaah (f)

Do you have any others?
في عندكن غيره؟ fee 'ind·kun ghay·ru

It's faulty.
هو خربان. hu·we khar·baen

How much is it?
قديش هقه؟ kad·deesh ha ku

Can you write down the price?
اكتب الهق. 'ik·tub il·hak (m)
اكتبي الهق. 'ik·tu·bee il·hak (f)

That's too expensive.
هيدا غالي اكتير. hay·dae ghae·lee 'ik·teer

What's your lowest price?
شو احسن سعر 'shoo 'ih·sen si'r
طبعكن؟ ta·ba'·kun

There's a mistake in the bill.
في خطأ بالحساب. fee kha·ta' bil·hi·saeb

Where's an ATM? وين جهاز الصرافة؟ wayn je·haez is·sa·rae·fe

Where's a foreign exchange office? وين مكتب صرافة؟ wayn mak·teb sa·rae·fe

What's the exchange rate? شو سعر التحويل؟ shoo si'r it·tah·weel

Where's the local internet cafe? وين أقرب مقهى الانترنت؟ wayn 'ak·reb ma'·ha il·'in·ter·net

How much is it per hour? قديش بتكلف لساعة وحدة؟ kad·deesh bit·kal·lef la·sae·'a wah·de

Where's the nearest public phone? وين أقرب تلفون عمومي؟ wayn 'ak·reb te·li·foon 'u·moo·mee

I'd like to buy a phonecard. بدي اشتري بطاقة تلفون. bid·dee 'ish·ta·ree bi·tae·ke te·li·foon

TIME & DATES

What time is it? كم الساعة؟ kam 'is·sae·'e

It's one o'clock. الساعة وحدة. 'is·sae·'e wah·de

NUMBERS

1	١	واحد	waa·hed
2	٢	اثنين	'it·nayn
3	٣	ثلاثة	ta·laa·te
4	٤	اربع	'ar·ba'
5	٥	خمسة	kham·se
6	٦	ستة	sit·te
7	٧	سبعة	sab·'a
8	٨	ثمانية	ta·maa·ne
9	٩	تسعة	tis·'a
10	١٠	عشرة	'ash·re
20	٢٠	عشرين	'ish·reen
30	٣٠	ثلاثين	ta·laa·teen
40	٤٠	اربعين	'ar·be·'een
50	٥٠	خمسين	kham·seen
60	٦٠	ستين	sit·teen
70	٧٠	سبعين	sab·'een
80	٨٠	ثمانين	ta·ma·neen
90	٩٠	تسعين	tis·'een
100	١٠٠	مية	mi·'a
1000	١٠٠٠	الف	'elf

Note that Arabic numerals, unlike letters, are read from left to right.

LANGUAGE

ARABIC ALPHABET

Arabic is written from right to left. The form of each letter changes depending on whether it's at the start, in the middle or at the end of a word or whether it stands alone.

WORD-FINAL	WORD-MEDIAL	WORD-INITIAL	ALONE	LETTER
ـا	ـلـ	اـ	ا	alef'
ـب	ـبـ	بـ	ب	'ba
ـت	ـتـ	تـ	ت	'ta
ـث	ـثـ	ثـ	ث	'tha
ـج	ـجـ	جـ	ج	jeem
ـح	ـحـ	حـ	ح	'ha
ـخ	ـخـ	خـ	خ	'kha
ـد	ـدـ	د ـ	د	daal
ـذ	ـذـ	ذـ	ذ	dhaal
ـر	ـرـ	رـ	ر	'ra
ـز	ـزـ	زـ	ز	'za
ـس	ـسـ	سـ	س	seen
ـش	ـشـ	شـ	ش	sheen
ـص	ـصـ	صـ	ص	saad
ـض	ـضـ	ضـ	ض	daad
ـط	ـطـ	طـ	ط	'ta
ـظ	ـظـ	ظـ	ظ	'dha
ـع	ـعـ	عـ	ع	ain'
ـغ	ـغـ	غـ	غ	ghain
ـف	ـفـ	فـ	ف	'fa
ـق	ـقـ	قـ	ق	kuf
ـك	ـكـ	كـ	ك	kaf
ـل	ـلـ	لـ	ل	lam
ـم	ـمـ	مـ	م	mim
ـن	ـنـ	نـ	ن	nun
ـه	ـهـ	هـ	ه	'ha
ـو	ـوـ	وـ	و	waw
ـي	ـيـ	يـ	ي	'ya
	ء			hamza
ـا	ـذـؤ	أ	أ	a
ـأ	ـثـؤ	أ	أ	u
ـا	ـذـؤ	إ	إ	i
ـا	ـثـؤ	أ	أ	' (glottal stop)
ـا	ـاـ	آ	آ	aa
ـو	ـوْـ	أو	أو	oo
ـيْ	ـيـ	إيْ	إيْ	ee
ـوْ	ـوْـ	أوْ	أوْ	aw
ـَي	ـْيـ	أَيْ	أَيْ	ay

It's (two) o'clock.
هي (تنتين). *hi·ye* (tin·*tayn*)

Half past (two).
(تنتين) ونص. (tin·*tayn*) oo nus

At what time ...?
امتى ...؟ *'em·ta* ...

At ...?
في ... fee ...

yesterday ...	مبارح ...	*mbae·*reh ...
tomorrow ...	بكرة ...	*buk·*ra ...
morning	صبح	*su·*beh
afternoon	بعد ظهر	ba'd zuhr
evening	مسا	ma·*sae*
Monday	يوم الأتنين	yawm il·'it·*nayn*
Tuesday	يوم التلات	yawm il·ta·*laat*
Wednesday	يوم الاربعة	yawm il·'ar·ba·'a
Thursday	يوم الخميس	yawm il·kha·*mees*
Friday	يوم الجمع	yawm il·*jum·*'a
Saturday	يوم السبت	yawm is·*sabt*
Sunday	يوم الاحد	yawm il·'a·had

TRANSPORT

Please take me to (this address).
اوصلني عند *'oo·sal·nee* 'ind
(هيدا العنوان). (*hay·*dae il·'un·*waen*)

Please ...	اذا بتريد ...	*'i·za* bit·*reed* ...
stop here	قف هون	kif hoon
wait here	استنّا هون	*stan·*naa hoon

Public Transport

Is this the ... to (Petra)?	هيدا الـ ... لـ(بيترا)؟	*hay·*dae il· ... la·(*bee·*tra)?
boat	سفينة	*sfee·*ne
bus	باص	baas
plane	طائرة	tae·'i·re
train	قطار	ki·*taar*

What time's the ... bus?	أمتى الباص...؟	*'em·*ta il·*baas*...
first	اول	*'aw·*wel
last	اخر	*'ae·*khir
next	قادم	*kae·*dim

One ... ticket (to Beirut), please.	تذكرة ... (لبيروت) اذا بتريد.	taz·ki·re ... (la·bay·*root*) *'i·za* bit·*reed*.
one-way	ذهاب	za·*haeb*

return	ذهاب واياب	za·*haeb* oo wee·*yaeb*

How long does the trip take?
الرحلة كم ساعة ar·*rih·*le kam sae·'a
بتاخد؟ bi·*tae·*khud

Is it a direct route?
الطريق مباشر؟ it·ta·*reek* mu·bae·*shir*

What station/stop is this?
شو هيدا shoo *hay·*dae
المحطة/الموقف؟ il·*mhat·*te/il·*maw·*kif

Please tell me when we get to ...
اولي/اوليلي لما *'oo·*lee/'oo·*lee·*lee *lam·*ma
منوصل عند ... *mnoo·*sal 'ind ... (m/f)

How much is it to ...?
قديش الاجرة لـ ...؟ kad·*deesh* il·*'uj·*re la ...

Driving and Cycling

I'd like to hire a ...	بدي استأجر ...	*bid·*dee 'is·*ta'·*jir ...
4WD	سيارة ذات الدفع الرباعي	*say·*yae·re zaat id·*daf'* er·ru·bae·'ee
car	سيارة	*say·*yae·re

with a driver
ومعها سائق oo ma·'aa sae·'i'

with air conditioning
بالمكيف bil·mu·*kay·*yef

How much for ... hire?	قديش الاجرة لـ...؟	*'ad·deesh* il·*'uj·*re la·...
daily	يوم	yawm
weekly	أسبوع	*'us·boo'*

Is this the road to (Tyre)?
هيدا الطريق لـ(صور)؟ *hay·*dae it·ta·*ree'* la·(soor)

I need a mechanic.
لازمني lae·*zim·*nee
ميكانيكي. mee·kaa·*nee·*kee

I've run out of petrol.
خلص البنزين *kha·*las il·bi·*trool*
بسيارتي. bi·say·*yae·*re·tee

I have a flat tyre.
اطار السيارة ما *'i·taer* is·say·*yae·*re ma
فيه هواء. *fee·*hu ha·*wae*

QUESTION WORDS		
When?	امتى؟	*'em·*ta
Where?	وين؟	wayn
Who?	مين؟	meen
Why?	ليش؟	leesh

GLOSSARY

This glossary lists terms used in this book that may be unfamiliar to those living outside Jordan. Most are Arabic words commonly used in Jordan but some abbreviations are also included. See p340 for architectural terminology, which may come in handy when visiting ancient sights such as Petra and Jerash.

abeyya – women's floor-length, black over-garment

abu – father of...

agal – black headrope used to hold a keffiyeh in place

ain (ayoun) – spring or well

amir – see *emir*

arak – alcoholic spirit

ASEZA – Aqaba Special Economic Zone Authority

Ayyubid dynasty – the dynasty founded by Saladin (Salah ad-Din) in Egypt in 1169

bab (abwab) – gate

Badia – stony desert

Bedouin (pl Bedu) – nomadic desert dweller

beit – house

beit ash-sha'ar – goat-hair Bedouin tent

bin – son of...; also *ibn*

caliph – Islamic ruler

caravanserai – large inn enclosing a courtyard, providing accommodation and a marketplace for caravans

Circassians – Muslims from the Caucasus who emigrated to Jordan in the 19th century

Decapolis (Latin) – literally '10 cities'; this term refers to a number of ancient cities in the Roman Empire, including Amman and Jerash

deir – monastery

eid – Islamic feast

Eid al-Adha – Feast of Sacrifice marking the pilgrimage to Mecca

Eid al-Fitr – Festival of Breaking the Fast, celebrated throughout the Islamic world at the end of Ramadan

emir – Islamic ruler, leader, military commander or governor; literally 'prince'

haj – the pilgrimage to Mecca

hammam(at) – natural hot springs; also a Turkish steam bath

haram – forbidden area

hejab – woman's headscarf

ibn – son of...; also *bin*

il-balad – downtown; the centre of town

imam – religious leader

jebel – hill or mountain

JETT – Jordan Express Travel & Tourism; the major private bus company in Jordan

JTB – Jordan Tourism Board

keffiyeh – checked scarf worn by Arab men

kilim – flat, woven mat

Koran – see *Quran*

Kufic – a type of highly stylised old Arabic script

mafrash – rugs

maidan – town or city square

malek – king

malekah – queen

Mamluk dynasty – Muslim dynasty named for a former slave and soldier class; mamluk is literally 'slaves'

medina – old walled centre of any Islamic city

mezze – starters, appetisers

mihrab – niche in the wall of a mosque that indicates the direction of Mecca

minaret – tower on top of a mosque

muezzin – mosque official who calls the faithful to prayer, often from the minaret

Nabataean – ancient trading civilisation based around Petra

nargileh – water pipe used to smoke tobacco (used mainly by men)

oud – Arabic lute

PLO – Palestine Liberation Organisation

qala'at – castle or fort

qasr – castle or palace

qibla – direction of Mecca

Quran – holy book of Islam

qusayr – small castle or palace

Ramadan – Muslim month of fasting

RSCN – Royal Society for the Conservation of Nature

Saladin – (Salah ad-Din in Arabic) Kurdish warlord who re-took Jerusalem from the Crusaders; founder of the Ayyubid dynasty

servees – service taxi

sheesha – see *nargileh*

sheikh – venerated religious scholar, dignitary or venerable old man

siq – gorge or canyon (usually created by tectonic forces rather than by wind or water)

souq – market

tell – ancient mound created by centuries of urban rebuilding

Trans-Jordan – Jordan's original name

Umayyad dynasty – first great dynasty of Arab Muslim rulers

umm – mother of...

UNRWA – UN Relief & Works Agency

wadi – valley or river bed formed by watercourse, dry except after heavy rainfall (plural: *widyan*)

zerb – Bedouin oven, buried in the sand

Dining & Drinking Glossary

Note that, because of the imprecise nature of transliterating Arabic into English, spellings will vary. For example, what we give as *kibbeh* may appear variously as *kubbeh*, *kibba*, *kibby* or even *gibeh*.

Mezze

baba ghanouj – (literally 'father's favourite'), dip of mashed eggplant (aubergine) and tahini

balilah – snack of boiled salty legumes

basterma – pastrami, popular from Armenia to Lebanon

buraik – meat or cheese pie

fatayer – triangles of pastry filled with white cheese or spinach; also known as *buraik*

fatteh – garlicky yoghurt and hummus, sometimes with chicken

fattoosh – salad with sumach (a red spice mix), tomatoes and shreds of crouton-like deep-fried bread

fuul medames – squashed fava beans with chillies, onions and olive oil

gallai – sautéed tomato, garlic, onion and peppers topped with cheese and pine nuts on Arabic bread

hummus – cooked chickpeas ground into a paste and mixed with tahini (a sesame-seed paste), garlic and lemon

kibbeh – Lebanese-style kofta made with minced lamb, bulgur/cracked wheat and onion; served raw or deep fried

labneh – cream-cheese dip

makdous – pickled eggplant, walnut and olive-oil dip

manaqeesh – Arabic bread with herbs

manoucha/manaqish – baked breads or pies with thyme (*zaatar*) and cheese

mosabaha – hummus with whole chickpeas in it

mouhamara – walnut, olive oil and cumin dip

muttabal – eggplant dip similar to *baba ghanouj* but creamier

sambousek – meat and pine-nut pastry

shanklish – tangy and salty dried white cheese, sometimes grilled, sometimes in a salad

tabbouleh – salad of cracked (bulgur) wheat, parsley and tomato

treedah – egg, yoghurt and meat

yalenjeh – stuffed vine leaves

Main Dishes

fareekeh – similar to *maqlubbeh* but with cracked wheat

fasoolyeh – bean stew

gallayah – traditional Bedouin meal of chicken with tomatoes, other vegetables, garlic and Arabic spices

kofta – meatballs, often in a stew

maqlubbeh – steamed rice topped with grilled slices of eggplant or meat, grilled tomato, cauliflower and pine nuts

mulukiyyeh – spinach stew with chicken or meat pieces

musakhan – baked chicken served on bread with onions, olive oil and pine nuts

sawani – meat or vegetables cooked on trays in a wood-burning oven

sawda dajaj – chicken livers with grenadine syrup and lemon

shish tawouq – grilled boneless chicken served with bread and onions

shwarma – chicken or lamb sliced off a spit and stuffed in a pocket of pita-type bread with chopped tomatoes and garnish

Dessert

ftir jibneh – large pastries

haliwat al-jibneh – a soft doughy pastry filled with cream cheese

halva – soft sesame paste, like nougat

kunafa – shredded dough on top of cream cheese smothered in syrup

ma'amoul – biscuits stuffed with dates and pistachio nuts and dipped in rose water

m'shekel – a form of baklava

muhalabiyya – rice pudding, made with rose water

wharbat – triangular pastries with custard inside

Staples

beid – egg
ejja – omelette
jibna – cheese
khobz – bread

labneh – yoghurt
makarone – all varieties of pasta
ruz – rice
shurba – soup
sukkar – sugar

Meat & Fish

farooj – chicken
hamour – a grouper-like fish from the Red Sea
kibda – liver
samak – fish

Vegetables

adas – lentils
banadura – tomato
batata – potato
khadrawat – vegetables
khiyar – cucumber

Fruit

battikh – watermelon
burtuqal – orange
inab – grape
mish-mish – apricot
moz – banana
rumman – pomegranate
tamr – date
tin – fig
tufah – apple

Other Dishes & Condiments

fil fil – chillies
sumach – red-spice mix
tahini – sesame-seed paste
torshi – pink pickled vegetables
tum – garlic
zaatar – thyme blend
zayt – olive oil
zaytun – olives

Drinks

asir – juice
karkade – sweetened hibiscus tea
maya at-ta'abiyya – mineral water
qahwa – coffee
sefeeha – lemon and mint drink
shai – tea

Architecture Glossary

Reading a guidebook to some of Jordan's most famous sights can seem like an exercise in linguistics encompassing Latin, Nabataean, Greek, Arabic and the languages of geography and classical architecture. Listen to any tour guide, especially at Petra and at Jerash, and you'll assume they're expert in all of them. But you don't have to be a polyglot to make the most of Jordan's wonders. Have a quick *shoof-ti* – Arabic word meaning 'you (female) looked' – at the glossary of architectural terms following and you'll soon know your pediments from your porticos.

agora – open meeting space for commerce

baetyls – divine stones

capitals – carved tops of columns

cardo maximus – Roman main street, running north–south

colonnade – row of columns

Corinthian – look for fluted columns with leafy capitals

decumanus – Roman main street, from east to west

Doric – look for unfluted columns with plain 'book-shaped' capitals

forum – open public space for meetings

high place – sacred site on mountaintop

hippodrome – stadium, usually for horseracing and chariot racing

Ionic – look for fluted columns with ram-horn (two curls in opposite directions) capitals

loculi – grave

macellum – indoor market building

necropolis – cemetery

nymphaeum – literally 'temple of the Nymphs'; public baths, fountains and pools

pediment – triangular crowning feature on front of building

portico – structure supported by columns

propylaeum – gateway or grand entrance

stele – commemorative stone or column with inscriptions

temenos – sacred courtyard

tetrapylon – an archway with four entrances

triclinium – Roman dining room

Behind the Scenes

SEND US YOUR FEEDBACK

We love to hear from travellers – your comments keep us on our toes and help make our books better. Our well-travelled team reads every word on what you loved or loathed about this book. Although we cannot reply individually to your submissions, we always guarantee that your feedback goes straight to the appropriate authors, in time for the next edition. Each person who sends us information is thanked in the next edition – the most useful submissions are rewarded with a selection of digital PDF chapters.

Visit **lonelyplanet.com/contact** to submit your updates and suggestions or to ask for help. Our award-winning website also features inspirational travel stories, news and discussions.

Note: We may edit, reproduce and incorporate your comments in Lonely Planet products such as guidebooks, websites and digital products, so let us know if you don't want your comments reproduced or your name acknowledged. For a copy of our privacy policy visit lonelyplanet.com/privacy.

OUR READERS

Many thanks to the travellers who used the last edition and wrote to us with helpful hints, useful advice and interesting anecdotes:

Anders Pilgaard, Andrea Pape-Christiansen, Anette Nybom, Arlo Werkhoven, Bastien Poirier, Chris Banoub, Elli & Wilfried Koerbl, Frédérique Hélion, Isabel Jordan, Jobin Laurie, Jonathan Skinner, Joseph Stanik, Judy Gage, Kathryn Ward, Lukas Pavek, Maarten Oskam, Melanie Cannon, Nick Thorne, Nilesh Korgaokar, Sabine Gerull, Sara Atkinson, Schmitt Klaus, Seth Almekinder, Tim Laslavic, Tony Smith, Torben Retboll, Velko Miloev, Vera Chiodi, Wancy Lam, William Fitzhugh

AUTHOR THANKS

Jenny Walker

Re-engaging with the people of Jordan is always a great pleasure. Guidebooks are a team effort: big thanks to Paul Clammer, fellow author on this project. Thanks are also due to my beloved husband, Sam Owen, for his unlimited patience during research and write up. As usual, I couldn't have completed this edition without him. Each of our trips to Jordan has felt like a treasured homecoming: heartfelt thanks to all those who helped us.

Paul Clammer

In Amman, big thanks to Susan Andrew and Soda (the occasionally borrowed, mad, one-eyed kitty), Steve Catling and Sandra Tahir Wells. Thanks also to Luma Qadoumi of BeAmman, and Daniel Robards of Engaging Culture Travel. For the sneak preview of the Royal Botanic Gardens, thanks to Habiba Dingwall and Ryan Guillou. Finally, thanks and love to Robyn, whose idea it was to go to Jordan in the first place.

ACKNOWLEDGMENTS

Climate map data adopted from Peel MC, Finlayson BL & McMahon TA (2007) 'Updated World Map of the Köppen-Geiger Climate Classification', *Hydrology and Earth System Sciences*, 11, 1633-44.

Illustration pp162-3 by Michael Weldon

Cover photograph: The Treasury (Al-Khazneh), Petra, Jordan; Danita Delimont Stock/AWL

THIS BOOK

This 9th edition of Lonely Planet's *Jordan* guidebook was researched and written by Jenny Walker and Paul Clammer. The previous edition was also written by Jenny Walker. This guidebook was produced by the following:

Destination Editor
Helen Elfer

Coordinating Editor
Lorna Parkes

Product Editor
Kate Mathews

Senior Cartographer
David Kemp

Book Designer
Clara Monitto

Assisting Editors Bruce Evans, Kate Evans, Kate James, Christopher Pitts, Ross Taylor, Simon Williamson

Cover Researcher
Naomi Parker

Thanks to Shahara Ahmed, Samantha Forge, Andi Jones, Karyn Noble, Katie O'Connell, Martine Power, Ellie Simpson

Index

INDEX N-S

Map Legend

Sights

- Beach
- Bird Sanctuary
- Buddhist
- Castle/Palace
- Christian
- Confucian
- Hindu
- Islamic
- Jain
- Jewish
- Monument
- Museum/Gallery/Historic Building
- Ruin
- Shinto
- Sikh
- Taoist
- Winery/Vineyard
- Zoo/Wildlife Sanctuary
- Other Sight

Activities, Courses & Tours

- Bodysurfing
- Diving
- Canoeing/Kayaking
- Course/Tour
- Sento Hot Baths/Onsen
- Skiing
- Snorkelling
- Surfing
- Swimming/Pool
- Walking
- Windsurfing
- Other Activity

Sleeping

- Sleeping
- Camping

Eating

- Eating

Drinking & Nightlife

- Drinking & Nightlife
- Cafe

Entertainment

- Entertainment

Shopping

- Shopping

Information

- Bank
- Embassy/Consulate
- Hospital/Medical
- Internet
- Police
- Post Office
- Telephone
- Toilet
- Tourist Information
- Other Information

Geographic

- Beach
- Hut/Shelter
- Lighthouse
- Lookout
- Mountain/Volcano
- Oasis
- Park
- Pass
- Picnic Area
- Waterfall

Population

- Capital (National)
- Capital (State/Province)
- City/Large Town
- Town/Village

Transport

- Airport
- Border crossing
- Bus
- Cable car/Funicular
- Cycling
- Ferry
- Metro station
- Monorail
- Parking
- Petrol station
- Subway station
- Taxi
- Train station/Railway
- Tram
- Underground station
- Other Transport

Note: Not all symbols displayed above appear on the maps in this book

Routes

- Tollway
- Freeway
- Primary
- Secondary
- Tertiary
- Lane
- Unsealed road
- Road under construction
- Plaza/Mall
- Steps
- Tunnel
- Pedestrian overpass
- Walking Tour
- Walking Tour detour
- Path/Walking Trail

Boundaries

- International
- State/Province
- Disputed
- Regional/Suburb
- Marine Park
- Cliff
- Wall

Hydrography

- River, Creek
- Intermittent River
- Canal
- Water
- Dry/Salt/Intermittent Lake
- Reef

Areas

- Airport/Runway
- Beach/Desert
- Cemetery (Christian)
- Cemetery (Other)
- Glacier
- Mudflat
- Park/Forest
- Sight (Building)
- Sportsground
- Swamp/Mangrove

OUR STORY

A beat-up old car, a few dollars in the pocket and a sense of adventure. In 1972 that's all Tony and Maureen Wheeler needed for the trip of a lifetime – across Europe and Asia overland to Australia. It took several months, and at the end – broke but inspired – they sat at their kitchen table writing and stapling together their first travel guide, *Across Asia on the Cheap*. Within a week they'd sold 1500 copies. Lonely Planet was born.

Today, Lonely Planet has offices in Franklin, London, Melbourne, Oakland, Beijing and Delhi, with more than 600 staff and writers. We share Tony's belief that 'a great guidebook should do three things: inform, educate and amuse'.

OUR WRITERS

Jenny Walker

Coordinating Author; Madaba & the Kings Highway; Petra; Aqaba, Wadi Rum & the Desert Highway; Azraq & the Eastern Desert Highway Jenny's first involvement with Arabia was as a student, collecting butterflies for her father's book in Saudi Arabia. She went on to write a dissertation on Doughty and Lawrence (Stirling University) and an MPhil thesis on the Arabic Orient in British literature (Oxford University). Current PhD studies (Nottingham Trent University) focus on Arabian deserts in contemporary literature. A member of the British Guild of Travel Writers and the Outdoor Writers and Photographers Guild, she has written extensively on the Middle East. With her husband, Wing Commander (retired) Sam Owen, she authored *Off-Road in the Sultanate of Oman* – home for the past 16 years. Jenny has travelled in over 110 countries and is Associate Dean of an engineering college in Muscat. Jenny also wrote the Women Travellers chapter for this guide.

Paul Clammer

Amman; Jerish, Irbid & the Jordan Valley; Dead Sea Highway Paul has contributed to over 25 Lonely Planet guidebooks and worked as a tour guide in countries from Turkey to Morocco. In a previous life he may even have been a molecular biologist. He's travelled extensively in the Middle East and wider Islamic world, and prior to researching this guide he spent nearly a year living in Amman, which allowed him plenty of time to track down the finest felafel, hummus and shwarma the city has to offer. Paul also wrote the Safe Travel, Directory, Transport and Health chapters for this guide.

GRAYSLAKE AREA PUBLIC LIBRARY
100 Library Lane
Grayslake, IL 60030

Published by Lonely Planet Publications Pty Ltd
ABN 36 005 607 983
9th edition – July 2015
ISBN 978 1 74220 801 5
© Lonely Planet 2015   Photographs © as indicated 2015
10 9 8 7 6 5 4 3 2 1
Printed in China

Although the authors and Lonely Planet have taken all reasonable care in preparing this book, we make no warranty about the accuracy or completeness of its content and, to the maximum extent permitted, disclaim all liability arising from its use.

All rights reserved. No part of this publication may be copied, stored in a retrieval system, or transmitted in any form by any means, electronic, mechanical, recording or otherwise, except brief extracts for the purpose of review, and no part of this publication may be sold or hired, without the written permission of the publisher. Lonely Planet and the Lonely Planet logo are trademarks of Lonely Planet and are registered in the US Patent and Trademark Office and in other countries. Lonely Planet does not allow its name or logo to be appropriated by commercial establishments, such as retailers, restaurants or hotels. Please let us know of any misuses: lonelyplanet.com/ip.